The Challenge
of Hidden Profits

The Challenge of Hidden Profits

Reducing Corporate Bureaucracy and Waste

by *MARK GREEN*
and *JOHN F. BERRY*

105140

William Morrow and Company, Inc.
New York

Library of Congress Cataloging in Publication Data

Green, Mark J.
  The challenge of hidden profits.

  Bibliography: p.
  Includes index.
  1.Industrial productivity—United States.
2. Efficiency, Industrial—United States. 3. Waste
(Economics)—United States. I. Berry, John F. (John
Francis), 1935–   . II. Title.
HD56.G73 1985   658.1'55   85-11554
ISBN 0-688-03986-3

Printed in the United States of America

First Edition

1 2 3 4 5 6 7 8 9 10

BOOK DESIGN BY PATTY LOWY

To Steve Green and Jay Frand,
my business guidance counselors
—and the memory of Howard Samuels

—MG

To Nancy Davison Berry

—JB

Acknowledgments

Books may be written by authors, but they are produced by a small army of indispensable friends, colleagues, and sources.

We'd like to especially thank six people whose time, research, and insights proved essential: Michael Calabrese, Eileen Daspin, John Siegel, Stephen Solow, Bonnie Tenneriello, and Michael Waldman. Others who assisted us in various stages of the book include Jack Albertine, George and Mary Lee Berridge, Pat Burke, Gina Calabrezze, Alec Foege, Tony Kaye, Hayes and Tina Kavanagh, Wendy and Doug Kreeger, the librarians at the Larchmont (New York) Public Library, Thomas J. Murray, Joel Olesky, Andrew Schepard, Rachele Silverberg, John and Barbara Slattery, Myra Smith, Kerwin Tesdell, Dody Tsiantar, Eric Rasmussen, and Joyce Wadler.

We also wish to thank those who took the time to read all or part of the manuscript: Alice Priest, Sheldon Weinig, Abraham Krasnoff, Warren Buffett, Richard Hackman, Sidney Harman, Corey Rosen, Michael VerMeulen, and Francis T. Vincent. Also, copy editor David Falk and assistant editor Elizabeth Terhune were invaluably thorough as the book progressed. Of course, any errors or omissions belong to us, not to any of them, however tempting that thought might be.

Author Mark Green appreciates the intellectual and financial support provided his organization, The Democracy Project, by the ARCA Foundation; Stuart Beck and the Pro Bono Publico Foundation; Steve Haft and the Bydale Foundation; David Hunter; Mary and Tom Morgan; Richard Parker and the Sunflower Foundation; Stanley Sheinbaum, Jan Pierce, and Philip Stern.

Author John Berry would like to acknowledge all the help and support provided by his former colleagues at *The Washington Post,* including Peter Behr, Merrill Brown, Joel Garreau, Caroline Mayer, Morton Mintz, James Rowe, Dan Morgan, T. R. Reid, Peter Silberman, and Tom Zito. He especially thanks executive editor Benjamin Bradlee and assistant managing editor Frank Swoboda for allowing him a leave of absence. He also appreciates the patience of his new colleagues at ESPN's *Business Times*—Chris Graves, Jonathon Meath, and Alice Priest—during the final days of this book, as well as the generosity of Mrs. Annette Davison through the whole project.

We are indebted to the hundreds of people we interviewed around the country who gave so generously of their time and intelligence. We couldn't cite everyone in our footnotes, including those who understandably requested anonymity given their business positions, but all contributed to our understanding and analysis.

Of course, without the encouragement of our agents, Carl Brandt and John Ware, and our editor, Bruce Lee, *Hidden Profits* would quite simply have stayed hidden from view.

Finally, we'd like to convey our love and thanks to the real *sine qua non*s of this effort, our families—Deni, Jenya, and Jonah . . . Nancy, Annette, and Sean—for putting up with the long hours and missed dinners that invariably accompany a book. And they did it with much humor. When Mark Green said to his wife, Deni, that he wanted to thank her and asked if she would like a dedication, she replied with a smile, "No, I want an apology." Because of their encouragement and support, this book is theirs too.

—Mark Green
—John F. Berry
March 1985

Contents

Acknowledgments 7

Introduction: An Inquiry into "Avoidable Waste" 11

1 Corpocracy: The Rise of the Corporate Bureaucracy 23

 The Layered Look 23

 Ten Telltale Traits 27

 Managers in the Middle: How a Corpocracy Grows 44

 Why CEOs, Boards, and Shareholders Don't Tame
  the Corpocracy 55

 Profiles and Paradigms: How to Trim Corporate
  Waste-Lines 80

2 Wasteful Workplace: The Participation Solution 102

3 Innovation: Corporate Luddites or Pioneers? 150

4 Mergers: The Production Ethic Versus the Predator
 Ethic 189

5 From Pay to Perks to Parachutes: Why Not "Merit
 Pay"? 218

6 The Waste of Fraud and Abuse: When Laissez *Isn't*
 Fair 254

7 Consumer Value: The Pass-Along Economy 296

8 The Gross Legal Product: The High Cost of Lawyers'
Featherbedding 326

9 Corporate Welfare: America's Implicit Industrial
Policy 344

Epilogue: The $862-Billion Annual Weight—Fault-Lines
and Trend-Lines 385

Notes 393

Index 437

Introduction: An Inquiry into "Avoidable Waste"

In recent years wasteful government spending has attracted much critical attention. In 1982, for example, President Ronald Reagan created the Grace Commission—160 business executives under the leadership of J. Peter Grace, head of W. R. Grace and Company—to investigate and expose excesses in the federal sector, which annually spends a trillion dollars. Their report and J. Peter Grace's subsequent campaign, Citizens Against Waste, attracted widespread coverage and comment.

But there's another arena of extravagance that receives scant attention. What about "waste, fraud, and abuse" in the three-trillion dollar corporate sector that can squander billions in the form of higher costs, higher prices, lower dividends, and lost jobs?

The Challenge of Hidden Profits is the first book to report on waste in the *corporate* bureaucracy—a phenomenon we call "corpocracy" to distinguish it from its governmental cousin. In a literal sense, this book urges these 160 executives of the Grace Commission also to mind their own businesses, because they are vulnerable to the same charges they have so vigorously leveled against the government.

Looking at American enterprise through the lenses of waste and bureaucracy, *The Challenge of Hidden Profits* investigates how corporate bloat erodes efficiency, reduces profits, and weakens our ability to compete internationally—and suggests ideas that would instead spur economic growth. These changes are hardly reaching for the impossible, for we discuss many pioneering firms that are installing productive new management and labor methods. Such innovative enterprises are models of how to reduce waste-lines in order to boost bottom lines.

This book has had a long gestation period. Through the 1970s and 1980s, each of the authors has been writing articles that describe the gap between business's performance and its potential—covering such areas as business secrecy, the lack of market competition, law firms that overcharge and over-lawyer, the diminishing role of shareholders, insular corporate governance, excessive executive compensation, business fraud, and unnecessary government subsidies. Discussing such topics, we began to see that these were, in reality, threads that formed a larger pattern of systematic business waste and mismanagement that clashed with the theory of free-market efficiency. This pattern was initially described by coauthor Mark Green in a 1981 article in *The Washington Post,* which was titled "The Trouble with Business, Says Business, Is Business."

From that point, we spent most of 1982–84 researching existing literature and crisscrossing America to interview more than four hundred business executives, management consultants, labor officials, public officials, government regulators, workers, and scholars. Our questions were three: (1) How extensive and expensive is business waste? (2) Why does it occur? (3) Which companies best avoid it?

Of course, a threshold problem is how to define *waste,* which unfortunately has much in common with Justice Potter Stewart's whimsical and much quoted definition of pornography, "I know it when I see it." One possible definition is this: Waste occurs whenever a company fails to maximize the return on an asset. But that overinclusive standard view fails to distinguish between *necessary waste* and *avoidable waste.*

Necessary waste is built into our economy. No matter how many market surveys and focus groups review a new product, a company cannot know with absolute confidence what will happen until millions of consumers spend their dollars in a vote of confidence—or rejection. This healthy uncertainty creates an economic system in which competing companies duplicate teams of managers, engineers, and workers to make comparable products—because the necessary waste produced by competition is less than the inevitable waste caused by monopoly (higher prices, less innovation). Ted Turner's Cable News Network (CNN), Universal Pictures' *Animal House,* and Ford's Mustang all succeeded; but Time Inc.'s *TV Cable Week* magazine, United Artists' *Heaven's Gate,* and Ford's Edsel were expensive and spectacular failures. We only knew that they were spectacular failures, however, after the fact. They were the cost of progress in a system of trial and error—a system that the great Austrian economist Joseph Schumpeter approvingly and appropriately referred to as "the perennial gale of creative destruction."

The real enemy of quality, innovation, productivity, and profits is avoidable waste—when managers make decisions that they know, or should know, will cost more than they yield. In our investigation, we concentrate on three varieties of avoidable waste: *waste internal to the corporation,* such as extravagance or inefficiency that raises costs (redundant staff, excessive compensation); *waste to the economy,* such as a practice that might benefit the firm but still impoverishes the larger economic system (pollution, payoffs); *waste to the consumer,* such as the passing along of needless costs to unaware purchasers (poor quality, price-fixing).

Many executives and economists contend that such wasteful behavior cannot be extensive. They assume that in a competitive market driven by self-interest and profit seeking, rational decision-makers will shun waste in order to avoid losing markets to competitors—that is, Adam Smith's "invisible hand" guides companies to maximize profits by minimizing waste. But this assumed wisdom is often wrong. For while Smith's "perfect competition" is a desirable goal, too often his "invisible hand" is quite literally invisible.*

Despite laissez-faire theory, corporations are run by real peo-

---

*There are several imperfections in the real market, as compared to the theory of the market: Managers may be more interested in maximizing their short-term compensation than in the company's long-run market share; labor is not very mobile because of the financial and psychological costs of uprooting families; the "free rider effect" means that often consumers lack adequate information to educate their choices; oligopolies, large firms that dominate markets, frustrate competition; external effects like pollution transfer costs from company to community; and many firms are content to make adequate profits ("profit-satisfice"), rather than to profit-maximize.

ple with real flaws and real discretion. "Corporations are organizations of human beings," wrote Adolf Augustus Berle in his 1954 work, *The 20th Century Capitalist Revolution.* "The corporate management can determine what markets it will supply—no American law yet exists requiring any corporation to go into or develop a market it does not choose to serve." This thesis was ably elaborated on by Professor John Kenneth Galbraith in his 1967 book, *The New Industrial State,* one of the first books to explore how planners in the corporate bureaucracy attempt to shape the marketplace, rather than be shaped by it.

Economists who try to define away waste, bureaucracy, and inefficiency are like scientists who can prove that a bee cannot fly. These defenders of the faith should speak to the scores of business executives who, when asked if there was substantial waste in corporate bureaucracies, replied with a version of "Are you kidding?"—and went on to volunteer chapter and verse. Our book explores their examples of avoidable waste.

By itself, each example may seem trivial in a massive corporation that has hundreds of thousands of employees and billions of dollars in annual revenues. But just as John Galsworthy once referred to some weighty subjects in a small volume of his as "significant trifles," so too can these significant trifles, when added together, weigh down even the biggest corporation—and, inevitably, the entire economy. We are here reminded of Senator Everett Dirksen's classic comment about small tax loopholes: "A billion here, a billion there, and pretty soon you're talking about real money."

For example, avoidable waste is a chief executive officer (CEO) who, motivated more by ego than efficiency, erects a huge conglomerate empire—a phenomenon so extensive that corporations in 1979–83 spent more on M and A (mergers and acquisitions) than on R and D (research and development). Avoidable waste is an executive who persuades his handpicked board of directors to approve a lush compensation structure that rewards market failure and dilutes shareholders' value. Avoidable waste is a swelling bureaucracy that produces risk-adverse executives who say, "But we've always done it that way!"

Avoidable waste is treating "human capital" as having all muscle and no mind, forfeiting the inventory of ideas possessed by labor. Avoidable waste is the toleration of long-standing "work rules" that keep employees from reaching their productive potential. Avoidable waste is sitting on your market dominance and allowing foreigners to pioneer with such novel products as radial tires, small fuel-efficient cars, and continuously cast steel. Avoidable waste is illegally dumping toxic waste or not hiring qualified minority job applicants. Avoidable waste is paying outside law firms twice as much as it would cost inhouse lawyers for the same job . . . costing automakers $500 per car for employees' health benefits because firms fail to act like smart consumers toward medical-insurance providers . . . increasing the ratio of supervisors to employees by more than 50 percent in the past three decades . . . pursuing short-term capital gains instead of investing in state-of-the-art machines, as foreign competitors are doing.

One consequence of avoidable waste can be seen in the saga of Carborundum, which coauthor John F. Berry examined both in its heyday and after its decline.

Back in 1966, as a business journalist, he wrote a corporate profile of Carborundum, which was then a prospering and innovative abrasives manufacturer. In reporting for this book, he returned to Niagara Falls to discover that the once-vibrant company had virtually self-destructed. What had happened was that in the late 1970s, Carborundum had begun neglecting its abrasives business, treating it as a "cash cow" to support trendy unproductive new businesses. Management had grown lax, favoring benefits and accounting gimmickry over long-term gains. Then, in 1977, Carborundum became a takeover target, and was finally acquired for over $571 million by Kennecott Corporation. The mining company knew nothing about abrasives— and cared less. The acquisition proved a disaster for both firms. Four years later, Kennecott was acquired by Standard Oil Company of Ohio (Sohio), which was far more interested in mining than in manufacturing; in 1983, the Cleveland-based Sohio closed down most of Carborundum. More than twelve hundred jobs were lost as Niagara Falls's leading corporate citizen and taxpayer virtually disappeared. (See Chapter 4, "Mergers.")

High up in an office building that once was Carborundum's world headquarters, Berry found William Wendel, the former Carborundum chief executive who had so impressed him nearly two decades before. Now in his seventies, Wendel had become very rich from selling his stock, but he also had regrets: "It was an economic waste, no question in my mind about that," sighed the executive. "I just wish it hadn't happened."

* * *

Change is constant, but the rate of change isn't. And while there is no convenient measuring stick, the pace of economic development has accelerated from first to fourth gears in the postwar era.

The decade immediately after World War II was called "the Golden Age" by British economist Angus Maddison, a time when "economic growth in the advanced capitalist countries surpassed virtually all historical records." This was especially true for the United States: Our markets were isolated by high transportation costs, and our industrial facilities, unlike much of Western Europe's and Japan's, were entirely intact. We held captive the richest marketplace in the world, enjoying what was commonly referred to in international commerce as "effortless superiority."

But success bred sloth. "We had this huge, homogeneous market in the United States for so long that American industry got spoiled," said Reginald Jones, soon after he retired as chairman of General Electric. So when the pace of change quickened in the 1970s and 1980s—hurried along by computerization, miniaturization, and extensive technology exchange among nations— much of American business adapted slowly, if at all.

This period has seen some stunning shifts and new problems in our economy. The United States suffered four recessions, each one leaving us with a higher level of unemployment. The OPEC oil shocks of 1973 and 1979 essentially transferred $100 billion annually in wealth from America to the oil-producing members of the cartel. Pretax profit rates, which averaged 15 percent in the 1960s and 10–11 percent in the 1970s, fell to below 10 percent in the 1980s. Our productivity growth of more than 3 percent annually between 1948 and 1965 led the world, yet we slumped badly in the decade 1970–1980. (Over this ten-year period, productivity growth in the United States was 20 percent; Germany, 75 percent; France, 77 percent; Japan, 145 percent.)

During the seventies, America's share of world exports to non-Communist countries fell. And while imports accounted for just 9 percent of American consumption in 1970, this figure had risen to 19 percent by 1983. Even some services are exposed to cheap foreign labor. An American insurance company has announced that, by using satellite microwave communication, it can have secretarial dictation typed by English-language students in China for one-seventh the cost in the United States, and then have the dictation returned in printed form to its New York City office in under fifteen minutes.

All these dislocations are extremely destabilizing to business executives. They are understandably defensive about the conclusion that America is "managing our way to economic decline," as it was expressed in the title of a seminal 1980 *Harvard Business Review* article by Robert Hayes and the late William Abernathy. When pollster Louis Harris asked Americans in 1966 whether, for example, they had "a great deal of confidence" in the people running major companies, 55 percent answered yes; by 1983, this number had plunged to 18 percent.

When it comes to acknowledging the role that mismanagement and bureaucracy might play in our roller-coaster economy, the reaction of many CEOs brings to mind a scene from Mel Brooks's film *Young Frankenstein:* When Frankenstein expresses sympathy to his assistant Igor for the huge hump on his back, Igor replies, "What hump?" Denying their own unpleasant growth (i.e., bureaucracy), business boosters point instead to the usual suspects: Federal spending saps the private economy; the costs of complying with federal regulations is staggering; trading partners unfairly subsidize their home industries; labor is overpaid.

These "culprits" are more convenient than convincing. Other industrial nations spend more of their gross national product (GNP) on social services (for example, West Germany spends 30.6 percent; Japan, 17 percent; while the United States spends only 14.2 percent). And federal spending for roads, airports, education, and social security are investments in the physical and human infrastructure on which a modern economy is built. The United States ranks next to last among Western economies in the amount business is taxed; only Great Britain, not usually our economic ideal, taxes capital less. And regulatory expenditures save money in the long run, in reduced product defects, less consumer fraud, and less illness and dangers in the workplace. The Environmental Protection Agency and the *Annual McGraw-Hill Survey of Pollution Control Expenditures* separately concluded that less than 1 percent of plant capacity shutdowns could possibly be attributed to environmental expenditures.

As discussed in Chapter 9, "Corporate Welfare," the billions of dollars put into federal R and D, loan guarantees, overseas insurance programs, the Export-Import Bank, and direct subsidies—as well as "voluntary" import quotas—indicate how the U.S. government has subsidized domestic industries at least as much as Japan's more visible MITI (Ministry of International Trade and Industry). As for the final scapegoat, American workers on average do earn more than the workers of most of our trading partners. But these nations still have to pay extensive shipping costs to reach our markets, and labor costs alone can't explain our competitive slippage. For example, James Harbour, in his definitive study of the nearly two-thousand-dollars-per-car advantage Japanese cars have over American cars in the U.S. market, concludes that most of the differential is due not to labor costs but management costs.

The Harbour study documents a major premise of this book: The trouble with business is not in Washington, Japan, union halls, or in the stars; it's in the executives' suites themselves. When it comes to waste and bureaucracy, American managers are often their own worst enemy. That's the view of Commerce Secretary Malcolm Baldridge, who was a CEO before his stint with the Reagan administration. When we asked him during a 1983 taping of *Firing Line* whether our trade problems were due more to unfair Japanese competition or American mismanagement, Baldridge replied:

> U.S. management, I think, should take at least 75 percent . . . of the blame involved in this. We had the best managers in the world in the 50s, coming out of World War II. There's no question about that. In the 60s and 70s other countries around the world, from Mexico to England to Japan and Germany had their backs to the wall. . . . They had to learn how to be efficient to compete with this giant U.S., and they did it gradually.
>
> In the meantime, the U.S. managers were sitting on their past laurels. In the 60s and 70s, we saw people fiddling around trying to have each quarter's earnings go up one increment over the last quarter. Our staffs got too big. We didn't put enough into research and development. We didn't get down to manage on the factory floor. Our quality stayed about the same, and everybody else's quality was coming up. We don't have good enough quality now . . . and that is a management problem.

A growing chorus of business experts concur. The late businessman Howard Samuels commented, "My own experience is that inefficient management may be the fact economists have underestimated in attempting to analyze our productivity failure." Management consultant Arnold Judson, writing in the *Harvard Business Review,* concludes that, based on his study of 236 top-level executives, "management ineffectiveness is by far the single greatest cause of declining productivity in the U.S." Charles Rourke, a top executive with Harbridge House, said in our 1983 interview that "there isn't a CEO I know who can't tell you there are pockets of waste in his company. And you start asking him why he doesn't do something about it, and he'll say 'That's not a high priority now because it's only several thousand dollars.' They give you all kinds of rationales. . . . And if the economy turns around in the next year or two, these problems will not be talked about until the next recession."

On the other hand, one prominent economist was sanguine about the prevalence and cost of company waste. "[O]wing to the very high productive efficiency of the modern mechanical industry," he said, "the margin available for wasteful occupations and wasteful expenditures is very great." But that economist was Thorstein Veblen. And the year was 1904. By 1984, the "margin" was gone.

Can American business meet the challenge of reducing waste and bureaucracy? If Japan can convert the "Made in Japan" label from a joke to a credential, America can escape bureaucratic capitalism and evolve toward enterprise capitalism—but only if executives are willing to look self-critically at their own managerial failings. Many are. In our travels and interviews we have seen the slow emergence in recent years of a more adaptive, creative brand of business, one that finds and frees the hidden profits in a corporation.

We saw it in the kind of innovative spirit instilled at MCI Communications Corporation by its crusty CEO, William G. McGowan, who told us that "significant progress doesn't come from the formal planning process of an American corporation. It comes from a couple of guys doing something that hasn't been set down on a list." Putting his theory into action, McGowan split off a small group of innovators, setting them up in offices several blocks from MCI's Washington corporate headquarters and assigning them the task of developing a new mail system. "I told them, 'I don't just want you to come up with another in-house mail system. But if you come up with an electronic replacement for the whole part of a system, then we'll have something.'" The result was MCI Mail, an electronic way of sending letters. Concludes McGowan, "I put a bunch of guys over there, said they could buy forty million dollars' worth of capital equipment, and they come up with this son of a bitch. Now you say, 'That came out of MCI.' Bullshit! It came out of a bunch of hungry bastards with high energy levels."

At the Nucor Corporation in Charlotte, North Carolina, CEO Ken Iverson, an engineer with an M.S. in metallurgy from Purdue, runs what one analyst has called "the closest thing to a perfect company in the steel industry." While most integrated steel firms have seven to nine layers of staff, Nucor has just four; a corporate headquarters staff of only fifteen runs this mini-mill steel company of thirty-six hundred employees. The firm's incentive plans and no-frills philosophy—its offices are in a nondescript building in a ho-hum shopping center, as opposed to the palatial suites of competing Pittsburgh giants—help keep its cost per ton at half that of most steel plants. This leads to higher profits, higher pay, and a no-layoff policy. "We haven't laid off an hourly worker in fifteen years," says Iverson in what he calls his "executive dining room," a deli in the shopping mall. "That's important. But I don't want to give the impression that we're overly paternalistic. We have some very difficult requirements. If you're late for any reason, you lose your bonus for the day. And if you're late more than thirty minutes, you lose your bonus for the week."

We saw it at the H. J. Heintz Company, which refuses to allow "golden parachutes" and directly links executives' compensation to shareholders' gain. Because of its "pay for performance" plan, managers can earn as much as 30–50 percent over their annual salaries in a year if net profits exceed specific annual targets, which usually aim for a 12–13-percent growth rate. Heintz and other firms believe in merit pay for managers.

We saw it in a "pay for productivity" program at the Parker Pen Company of Janesville, Wisconsin, which pays hourly employee bonuses, under a so-called Scanlon Plan, if they reach productivity targets—an incentive system that spurs productivity, wages, and profits. The plan has averaged monthly bonuses of 12 percent, except during the 1983 economic slump. "Workers are disappointed when the bonuses aren't there," says a company executive, "but because of the Scanlon Plan, they know *why* they aren't there."

We saw it at the Materials Research Corporation (MRC), a high-tech manufacturer of ceramics and etching systems for computers in Orangeburg, New York. Its founder, ebullient former professor Sheldon Weinig, attempts to expose what he calls padding. "We each pad a little, whether its a schedule or a delivery date," says Weinig. "It wastes money, it wastes time. Employees have to be honest with me and I have to be honest with them." When a vice-president sent him a copy of a letter outlining a complex $100,000 license deal, for example, Weinig told his secretary, "Tear it up and tell his secretary it's his job. Be sure to use the word 'faith.' Tell her I have total faith in him." Weinig obviously also has enough faith in his own ideas that he is willing to risk his $25 million stake in MRC. "Boy, I'm telling you this is a balls game we're playing. That's what I told my executives. I said that I could sell the company. Instead, I'm betting that they can earn trust."

Over at the Ford Motor Company, an extensive employment involvement program, also based on trust, has tapped workers' ideas, improved efficiency—and helped soften decades of labor-management antipathy. Peter Pestillo, a Ford VP, proudly tells how "one day Ford took all the supervisors out of a plant in Richmond, California, for the day for training. Left the place unsupervised. This was more a demonstration of faith than any great business principle. But it worked. The place ran perfectly. It contributed to the pride of the people who worked there, who thought, by God, they do trust us. We have to respond."

Another way to increase employee satisfaction and performance is to provide people with stock. At Eakers, a chain of twenty-five clothing stores in Colorado, an employee stock ownership plan (ESOP) was set up in 1976. Management credits the ESOP with a beneficial impact on productivity, morale, turnover, and work quality. Sales per employee grew 40 percent in the six years since the plan was inaugurated—and while 60 percent of nonparticipating employees turn over annually, only 5 percent of ESOP employees exit with them.

And we saw it at Atlantic Richfield and Johnson and Johnson, which showed how fighting government regulation every inch of the way is neither inevitable nor profitable. While OSHA (Occupational Safety and Health Administration) is a four-letter word to many companies, management at Atlantic Richfield realized that an injured worker is not an efficient worker; so it sent letters to its 50,700 employees urging them to report instances of corporate conduct that could endanger employee safety. And when the Tylenol scare erupted in 1982, J&J could have denied blame and refused to cooperate with federal authorities. Instead, as is discussed more extensively in Chapter 6, its quick cooperation and recall helped save lives—and probably its reputation as well.

These and other firms demonstrate the truth of that lyric from "The Gambler"—the song made popular by Kenny Rogers—that "every hand's a winner, and every hand's a loser." No federal policy can save a mismanaged and top-heavy firm, but a management determined to cut the fat, can cut the mustard. The message of the success of Nucor, Materials Research Corporation, Johnson and Johnson, Ford, Eakers, and others is that management can make a loser a winner—or a winner a loser—depending on how it plays the hand it is dealt.

These firms are living examples of what the new corporation in the next economy can look like. Strong and empathetic managers, answerable to independent-minded directors, pay attention to the ideas and needs of line workers. Such companies obey the laws, pursue competition rather than protection, and prefer innovation to acquisition. Hierarchies are flattened, as workers take stock in their workplace in a form of "employee entrepreneurialism." In the corporation of the future, managers, workers, and shareholders will be economic partners, contributing direction, work and capital, respectively, toward their common goal of market success. Competition *among* firms and cooperation *within* firms will help maximize both profits and satisfaction for their economic partners.

As we approach our twenty-first century, the biggest economic issue for businessmen, then, is not so much the size of the federal bureaucracy as the size of their own corpocracies. For regardless of the current phase of the business cycle, regardless of macroeconomic policies set in our federal city, economic production can be yet greater if efficient companies expose and eliminate their own avoidable waste. The unresolved question, still, is whether wasteful mismanagement is a tapeworm embedded in our body economic—or whether the resilient competitive market system will in the long run penalize bureaucratic capitalism and help produce the Partnership Economy. And the answer should interest not only readers of *Forbes* and *Fortune*. Since U.S. chief executive officers are effectively the stewards of our national economy and wealth, their performance affects the quality of life of all our citizens.

1

Corpocracy: The Rise of the Corporate Bureaucracy

The principle of hierarchical office authority is found in all bureaucratic structures: in state and ecclesiastical structures as well as in large party organizations and private enterprises. It does not matter for the character of bureaucracy whether its authority is called "private" or "public."

—Max Weber, *Essays in Sociology*

The Layered Look

"The government is doing a whole lot of things that our Founding Fathers never meant it to do," says J. Peter Grace in one of his spirited attacks on government waste and bureaucracy. What about corporate waste? we asked the feisty executive. "I'll tell you, I'm tougher on the government than I would be on a company."

Donald B. Marron could not afford the luxury of Grace's single-minded focus on waste in Washington. He had problems closer to home. A few years ago, Marron, the chief executive officer of Paine Webber, found himself heading a firm strangling on paper work and struggling under layers of bureaucracy. Faced with a Hobson's choice—either attack the brokerage's bureaucracy or go out of business—Marron went on the attack to save his company. But as he tried to change the company and its people, he kept hearing the same phrase repeated over and over. "But Mr. Marron, we've always done it that way." Finally, enraged and frustrated at listening to "the most debilitating phrase that exists in American business," he called a meeting and announced, "I will not accept that answer!"

Is Marron's tale of corpocracy an aberration or an illustration as compelling as anything Peter Grace found in Washington? Are our largest corporations becoming economic dinosaurs, their large lumbering bodies connected to a small remote brain, an entity too slow and clumsy to contend with sleeker competitors? As Jewell Westerman and Jeremy Main separately observed in *Fortune* in the early 1980s, many businessmen wear blinders when it comes to viewing bureaucracy. "The [cost of] bureaucracy of business management itself," concluded Westerman, a consultant who earns his living telling CEOs how to save money, is "far larger" than the cost of government bureaucracy. In the corroborating view of journalist Main: "Ask a businessman if bureaucracy is getting him down and he becomes a fountain of indignation about the vexations of dealing with government red tape. Ask him about the bureaucracy in his own company, and you'll likely find he hasn't given it much thought."

But he should. For the corporate community has its own case of organizational arteriolsclerosis, although the public hears little about it. There's no Freedom of Information Act, for instance, compelling companies to disclose embarrassing deeds as there is for government. But though less visible, the corpocracy obeys the same laws of growth, girth, and waste.

The great German sociologist Max Weber was the first to study and define the phenomenon of bureaucracy. In his turn-of-the-century essay on the subject, Weber described a "perfect bureaucracy" as a system in which everything is decided by inflexible written rules of operation. Important decisions are made at the top, then orders flow down a chain of command. Members of the command are chosen for their technical competence. All along the chain there is rigid adherence to the most minute details of the orders. To Weber, then, bureaucracy was not a producer of red tape but a means of avoiding it—a management tool that provided a structure for getting productive work from large numbers of people.

On paper at least, Weber created a perfect organizational model. But like other large notions such as democracy and Marxism, something happens when the model is put into practice. Instead of Weber's chain of command, there are "too many folks between the chief executive and the guy who does the useful work," says Henry Gunders—who retired in 1984 as co-chairman of Price Waterhouse Company—in what is a pretty fair definition of what bureaucracy has come to mean. Business firms often resemble less chains of command than layer cakes, with up to fifteen levels between the chief executive and the production line, each stratum bulging with interlocking and redundant committees and task forces.

Why? Partly it's the inevitable consequence of sheer size. As with its federal analogue, which grows regardless of the party in power, bureaucracy in corporations comes with numbers of people: the more people in an organization, the more paperwork, committees, discussions, clearances. But corpocracy has at least three other inspirations that are both wasteful and avoidable, as some of the best corporations discussed throughout this book demonstrate.

First, lax or no competition allows a growing bureaucracy to become indolent instead of innovative. "When at peace, these firms get to be goddamned bureaucratic," observes Burton Klein, author of numerous books on corporate economics. "Managers don't take risks, and it becomes the internal culture to protect themselves. No one wants to get blamed."

Second, the insecurity of middle management provokes them to find safety in numbers and surround themselves with supportive staffers. "What happens is that middle managers are put in jobs having only a very narrow span of control," explains Westerman. "Having only a fraction of a job to perform, they struggle and strive to create a whole job and ask for more accountants or more systems analysts, and pretty soon they have added so many more staff positions that they now need to add another level of supervision. The span of the new managers is also narrow, so the process starts all over again."

Third, top executives often act on the belief that, in American business, bigger is better. Not without reason do they think that the CEOs of sprawling, splashy $5 billion conglomerates are more likely to appear on the covers of *Business Week* and *Forbes* than the heads of no-name, single-line $500 million firms. The CEOs of INA and Connecticut General Life Insurance Company so feared they might lose their posts in a hostile takeover in 1982 that they got their boards to agree to a merger of the two insurance bureaucracies to form CIGNA Corporation, a vast, inefficient insurance conglomerate manned by an army of forty-five thousand. Wall Street gave its opinion of the merger by sending CIGNA's stock to the basement. Comments one former CIGNA executive, "Why did they merge if there were no savings from the consolidation? They did it to protect their own asses, that's why."

As a result, bureaucratic growth often supplants economic growth, which in turn produces the much publicized periodic difficulties at Chrysler, Eastman Kodak, Ford, Procter and Gamble, General Motors, Alcoa, among so many others. Anthony Downs, the noted scholar of bureaucracy, describes what he calls the "law of diminishing control," which postulates that "the larger any organization becomes, the weaker is the control of its actions exercised by those at the top." The American Business Conference, a membership group of 199 fast-growing medium-sized firms, commissioned a study that concluded: "One of the great problems associated with success and the achievement of great size is the risk that executives will behave as bureaucrats, not as creative thinkers." The costs of this bureaucratic inefficiency can go undetected, if not increase, for decades—until jolted by such external shocks as foreign competition, domestic deregulation, competing technologies, or an energy crisis. For in these days of the global marketplace, the race goes to the swift and innovative.

Such commentary jars many top executives, who still regard bureaucracy as something in the government or in somebody else's company. Some executives in our interviews dismissed it as simply a necessary evil. Others did try to define it, though usually with a series of vague "too" phrases—too many people or too many memos or too many committees or too little productivity.

From the belly of the bureaucracy comes quite a different view. Middle managers spoke of mind-numbing work, furious politicking, corporate mazes, needless secrecy, and hostility to criticism from the lower echelons. They described a trickle-down style of management, where orders issued from above slowly pass down, losing direction and authority along the way. In bureaucratese it's known as "line loss." Recall the story about the boss who orders a swing designed, envisioning something made from two ropes and a board. But after his order passes down through and back up the organization chart, what emerges looks more like an elaborate gondola.

So, while many executives view the business bureaucracy as a cross between the emperor's clothes and the purloined letter— obvious yet unrecognized—those below the pinnacle of the corporate pyramid see it and live it. For them bureaucracy's existence and cost are not a matter of conjecture. In fact, there hasn't been much scientific study of the costs of bureaucratic waste in business, but what evidence there is suggests the numbers are monumental.

While blue-collar employment increased by 2 percent between 1977 and 1981, white-collar employment soared by 12 percent. By 1980, "administrative and managerial personnel" constituted 10.8 percent of total nonagrarian employment in the United States; in West Germany it was 3 percent; Sweden, 2.4 percent; and Japan, 4.4 percent. Federal statistics document a more than 50 percent increase in the number of nonproduction workers as a percentage of total employment between 1947 and 1981.

Economist F. M. Scherer concludes (based on eighty-six interviews with business executives) that unit costs tend to rise with an organization's size. "My own belief is that padding as high as ten percent of costs is not at all uncommon," Scherer told us in an interview. According to Jude Rich, a management adviser with Sibson and Company, his firm does "administrative value analysis" and "overhead analysis" for corporate clients trying to control bureaucratic costs. "We normally find thirty percent to forty percent waste," said Rich.

Statistics may mirror the story, but they don't tell it. To appreciate the problem of avoidable waste in large corporate bureaucracies, corpocracy must first be defined and detected. Are CEOs, boards of directors, and middle managers the problem *and* the solution? What companies are struggling to escape bureaucracy's very visible hand? By attempting to answer these questions, this chapter will diagnose whether the American corpocracy is terminal or curable.

Ten Telltale Traits

What follows is an illustrated guide to the Ten Telltale Traits of Corporate Bureaucracy. Most firms have some of these wasteful traits; the most bureaucratic have all of them. And while small companies can have these characteristics as well, it is in the larger business organizations that wasteful bureaucracy normally gets out of control. As an Opinion Research Corporation survey reported, "Employee feelings are more positive in fast growth companies; these firms are more democratic; slow growth companies [are] hierarchical." This message is reflected in the Ten

Telltale Traits and will reverberate throughout the rest of the book.

1. Corpocracy is insensitive to employees. "Our employees are our most important asset" is a corporate cliché as often ignored in practice as it is intoned at annual meetings. Abraham J. Briloff, professor of accounting at Bernard M. Baruch College in New York and author of numerous books on accounting practices, asserts that corporations frequently factor in people as if they were equipment. "Everything gets crammed into the computer, and the human gets forgotten. It all gets reduced to accounting, and it's dehumanizing."

A leading example of bureaucratic insensitivity is what could be called managing by layoffs. "Think about the impact of treating thousands as just numbers; the first time business turns down, they know they'll be laid off," observes Jude Rich. Sitting in his firm's purposely sparse Manhattan office, the consultant continues, "That's why we have an adversarial relationship between management and labor in this country." Like a general far distant from the deadly consequences of his military actions, top managers often have little difficulty shutting down profitable but not-profitable-enough plants of subsidiaries in communities they've never visited. Invariably, Rich and others compare corporate human relations in this country and Japan. Says John Schnepp, a member of the Lexington, Massachusetts, consulting firm Temple, Barker and Sloan, "One of my Japanese friends says he doesn't understand American companies. In bad times, they lay off the workers and keep the dividend. In Japan, it's just the other way around."

Even when bureaucracies aren't laying off workers in still-profitable divisions, their silly status symbols, like executive lunchrooms, parking spaces, elevators, and washrooms, set up needless barriers between people. The late Professor William J. Abernathy of the Harvard Graduate School of Business Administration called these symbols of power "pernicious" because they "create a subclass of people who feel like second-class citizens." During lunch breaks at Exxon's corporate headquarters in New York City, for example, senior executives go upstairs, where their lunch is paid for by the company, while middle managers and below go to the basement, where they pay for their own food. "I take the staff upstairs with me when I can," one executive told us, "but it's noticed and frowned upon."

In such an elitist and aloof hierarchy, a near-gravitational force separates top managers from those below. It's a natural state of affairs which the best managers struggle to overcome. As New York City's top cop from 1895 to 1897, Theodore Roosevelt would routinely and unannounced prowl city streets to see how his men in blue were doing. By choosing street work instead of desk work, and "workers" over subordinates, TR showed that he cared and kept everyone on their toes.

Nearly a century later, Tanemichi Sohma, a vice-president of Sanyo Manufacturing Corporation, tells what happened when he was sent from Japan to run the company's plant in Forrest City, Arkansas, which has an American work force:

> I walk around the factory every day so that I get to know people and people get to know me. In the beginning they thought I was checking on them, that I thought American work force may be slower than the Japanese. Actually, I was not checking on them. I was looking around to see that they were working comfortably. If I saw something wrong, then I responded immediately and sent the maintenance man to cure the problem. Finally, they realized why I was so inquisitive. . . . I often go out of town for business. When I come back, I go to the factory immediately. People say, "Where have you been? What did you do?" That reflects a very warm feeling and I enjoy it. Because people are now with me. And we are with them.

2. Corpocracy encourages politics instead of productivity. At MCI Communications Corporation, chief executive William G. McGowan, the driving force behind the once-tiny company that challenged the big daddy of bureaucracy, AT&T, sees office politics as a constant threat to a company. "The more I think about it, the more I realize that politics and bureaucracy are the same thing, and that many companies are being run by politicians rather than business executives," said McGowan in an interview at MCI's Washington headquarters. "How do we control that? One way is not to be people-intensive. At MCI, every department is measured every month on revenue per employee, and they're compared with each other. And they'd better improve. They have to increase revenue per employee, which means we grow in size, we don't grow in the number of people."

In a runaway corpocracy, though, managers typically emphasize politics over production—office politics. Advancement comes from know-who, not know-how. Well-placed flattery, the right school, sex, religion, and sports all help. To be sure, the skilled manager, like the smart politician, can use politics to motivate and mobilize people behind an idea. More commonly, however, top management in a corpocracy chooses to ignore or allow political intrigue and backbiting to obstruct the flow of ideas, products, or services.

When political fighting takes place on the highest level of a firm, it can demoralize and distract everyone below. At Lehman Brothers Kuhn Loeb, for example, the struggles between the two top executives, the street-tough trader Harold Glucksman and the patrician Peter G. Peterson, disrupted the powerful Wall Street firm during the early 1980s. And in the end, the firm turned out to be the loser. For while Glucksman used his Machiavellian political skills to oust Peterson, the firm never recovered from the struggle. In 1984, with profits sagging and the firm seemingly adrift under Glucksman's inept management, he was forced to resign his hard-fought place at the top.

Consider the politics at big financial institutions like insurance companies and banks: Since all their products are colored green, excelling at office politics becomes one way to distinguish yourself. "The way you got ahead," recalls a former Chemical Bank officer in New York City, "was getting more people under you than your rival had, which created more bureaucracy, of course." Over at Citibank, its combative, recently retired CEO, Walter Wriston, tried to alter the bank's staid image by injecting giant doses of high anxiety into the ranks of management. The trouble was, the competition inside the bank sometimes got so heated that the bank's business competitors were forgotten. Such was the case in the formative days of FOCUS, a cash management scheme to attract the investment accounts of well-heeled bank customers.

Known at Citibank as "Wriston's baby," FOCUS specifically aimed to compete with the immensely successful cash management account at Merrill Lynch, Pierce, Fenner and Smith. But instead of hiring people with experience in the brokerage business, Citibank used FOCUS as a political plum to reward loyalists who didn't know anything about investment management. Three vice-presidents, an assistant vice-president, and a few managers were layered atop a sales force, the people who were supposed to bring in the new business. Not surprisingly, FOCUS was an overnight disaster. Citibank's answer? Add another vice-president, who got the job because she was assistant to then vice-chairman John Reed, who subsequently was named successor to Wriston. Complicating matters, the new vice-president was a political rival of the other VPs, who, in turn, were rivals of each other. Observed a frustrated FOCUS officer, "It's clear that they were more interested in bringing in politically connected, high-powered VPs than in getting qualified people who could make FOCUS work."

3. *Corpocracy fosters secrecy and stifles communications.* *I've Got a Secret* was a popular TV show whose theme was that one person had secret information and everybody else tried to figure out what it was. The same game is played in wasteful corpocracies: Secrets mean power, and if I know something you don't, that puts me one step ahead of you. As Max Weber said more than sixty years ago, "Every bureaucracy seeks to increase the superiority of the professionally informed by keeping their knowledge and intentions secret." But if the right hand doesn't know what the left is doing, they can hardly be expected to clap together.

Bureaucratic secrecy often serves to hide a sloppy job. The government's mechanism for covering up incompetence, if not corruption, was amply demonstrated by the Watergate and Pentagon Papers exposés. But it isn't only government that hides its sins under a "Confidential" stamp. Joseph Bensman, author and sociology professor at City College in New York, believes that management's need to cover up errors is one reason why employees are not asked for their opinions. They see firsthand the poor quality of products that a company manufactures. Ask workers and they will tell what they know. Don't ask them, and the secret of poor quality is safe. This omission puts them in the role of keepers of corporate secrets—and allows management to ignore its responsibility.

Experts, in comparing American management techniques with those in Japan, invariably cite the openness of communications there. For example, in April 1982, JETRO (Japan External Trade Organization) sponsored a seminar on the subject along with the Conference Board, the nonprofit management research institution in New York City. It was a curious affair: Here were some 250 high-level American executives listening to other high-level American executives, who happened to work for Japanese-owned companies, telling them that their management techniques were all wrong. Managers from Sanyo, Sharp Electronics Corporation, and Auburn Steel, among others, extolled the Japanese credo of information-sharing among all employees. One worried guest asked, "Is the effectiveness of middle management undermined by top management's direct contact with workers?" Exclaimed an American who is vice-president at NEC Electronics U.S.A., "This confidentiality excuse is one I've been fighting in every corporation I've ever worked for, for the last twenty years. Everybody hides behind it; every corporation I've ever been affiliated with hides behind it."

Audrey Freedman, an economist with the Conference Board, analyzed secrecy by American executives in a report on the conference published in the *Journal of Japanese Trade and Industry:*

> Each American hierarchical position may be rationalized, in a fundamental way, by the possession of *more information* (or broader information) than the people working one level below. If the underpinning of hierarchy is knowledge about the enterprise, then each level has an "investment" in the relative ignorance of those beneath. Now come the Japanese managers and advocate *sharing* information—on production costs, on quality, on future plans. That means, for some traditional American managers, giving away the source and reason for their "power."

But even if corporate bureaucrats don't want to be secretive, the nature of corpocracy frustrates information flow. A decision that passes from person to person down the chain of command, making frequent stops at staff levels to be reviewed by dozens of second-guessing staffers, becomes altered along the way. One thinks of the party game of whispering a secret at one end of a group of people to see how mangled it becomes by the time it reaches the last person. And "transactional loss" increases geometrically with bureaucracy: that is, a bureaucracy of two people have one conversation; of four people, six conversations; of eight people, twenty-seven conversations; ad infinitum. Columbia law professor John C. Coffee, Jr., writing in the *Virginia Law Review,* discussed how the "serial relay of information" results in significant information loss: "Information theorists have formulated the rule that each additional relay of the communications system halves the message while doubling 'noise.'" To help the corporate bureaucracy adapt to the communications explosion, FMC Corporation in Chicago has appointed a "director of information resources" to separate "noise" from substance.

When executives are asked to desribe a bureaucratic trait, they invariably mention long memorandums. The president of Apple Computer, in fact, won't accept a memo longer than one page. That curbs verbosity, but it also stifles communications.

For a different approach, consider the Pall Corporation, a Long Island manufacturer of highly sophisticated filters with sales of about $250 million and an impressive 20 percent compounded annual growth for the past decade. Pall's president, Abraham Krasnoff, is a courtly, brilliant communicator who spices business conversations with literary and political allusions. Krasnoff says that because his product line is narrowly focused, exchanging information about competition and innovation is the key to survival. "Everybody who's out in the field or makes a trip writes a report. We don't spare paper. It goes to technical people, sales and marketing people, management, financial, R and D. From all that flow of information, we decide what we are going to do. We also promote very assiduous listening and reading habits. We work on communications all the time by nagging. With open communications, a young person in the company is certain to hear from me or some other executive about a report he wrote. You need to work on that to establish a company ethic."

4. Corpocracy produces paralysis by paper work. Contrast the reports demanded by Abe Krasnoff with the paper work generated by wasteful bureaucracies: One is purposeful, elevating and controlled; the other purposeless, burdensome, and totally out of control. One computer scientist argues that top management is crippled less from the lack of adequate information than from an "overabundance of irrelevant information." This paper proliferation results in sensory overload, lost time, and delayed decision-making, which prevent a company from moving rapidly into new opportunities. At one company described in *In Search of Excellence,* 221 committees had to pore over reports—and then write their own reports—before a new product could be marketed; and, not surprisingly, few were. Unless checked, this paper maze mimics Hamlet's description of his mother's love for his late father, the king, "as if increase of appetite had grown by what it fed on."

Procter and Gamble Company elevated memo writing to a fine art, but in recent years corporate communicators have complained that the $12 billion consumer packaged-goods company has become a paper-bound tiger. The intricate memo-system, they say, flows only upward so that all decisions are made by a few men in the Cincinnati headquarters, far removed from the marketplace. As reported in *Business Week,* it took two years of memo writing for P&G to decide whether to sell Folger's instant coffee in two-, six-, and ten-ounce jars or in two-, four-, and eight-ounce jars.

A vice-president at CIGNA, the insurance company, traces the paper chase he went on just to get his secretary a five-hundred-dollar raise: "I called personnel and they told me to write a description of what my secretary does. Do you know what it's like writing a job description for a secretary? It takes a lot of time, and of course I exaggerated to make sure she got the money. Next, they sent me a long form to rate her performance. That had to be approved by my supervisor, then approved by personnel. A personnel officer then came to interview me and the secretary. After a few more telephone exchanges, they told me that the head of the investment division where I worked had to approve the application. Finally, two months later, I got a phone call telling me that the raise had been approved—but that I couldn't tell the secretary *until I got it in writing.*" The frustrated executive speculates that, in a paper-producing corpocracy like CIGNA, one administrator per half dozen employees is needed just to process all the paper work.

5. *Corpocracy forgets markets.* Just as Washington bureaucrats often become snugly insulated in their world "inside the beltway," rarely meeting the citizens they supposedly serve, corporate bureaucrats can forget the marketplace that is their *raison d'état*. Theodore Levitt, the respected Harvard professor, argues that the corporation's function is "to create and keep a customer," because if a company concentrates on satisfying customers, "the rest, given reasonable good sense, [will] take care of itself." But bureaucracy creates so many layers between management and markets that top executives forget where their paychecks come from.

"I don't meet very many CEOs who are concerned about their customers; in fact, I don't run across many who ever see any customers," says Lewis H. Young, the past editor in chief of *Business Week.* "The customer has become a bloody nuisance whose unpredictable behavior damages carefully-made strategic plans, whose activities mess up the computer operations, and who stubbornly insists purchased products work." Case in point: Atari.

Steven J. Ross is the show-biz CEO of Warner Communications who parlayed a family funeral parlor into a grasping conglomerate. To the financial community, however, Warner's diverse businesses—parking lots, movies, car rental agencies.

record companies—had long smacked of financial flakiness. Undaunted, Ross kept acquiring new companies because, he explained, "It's like a car going up a hill. The first time you go into neutral, you're going backward." Then, in 1976, Ross paid a paltry $28 million for Atari. In a single leap, Warner entered the wonderworld of high tech. By 1981, Atari's sales grew to $1 billion as it controlled about 75 percent of the fast-growing video game market. The dizzying climb continued into 1982, with Pac-Man alone bringing in over $200 million. Atari accounted for half of Warner's $4 billion revenues and over 60 percent of its operating net. Ross, on whose office couch sits a pillow embroidered with LIVING WELL IS THE BEST REVENGE, gave himself a $22 million salary package, the largest of any American executive that year.

But at the end of 1982, one day after predicting to the now-satisfied analysts a 50-percent rise in earnings for the year, Warner disclosed that—whoops!—profits would rise by only about 15 percent after all. After that, Atari's dive deepened. By mid-1983, the market value of the company's shares had plunged 60 percent from the 1982 high.

What went wrong? It's apparent that Steve Ross and his executive team were so busy counting their Pac-Man profits that they didn't even feel the market being pulled out from under them. Ross admits in retrospect that Atari hired "droves of people" as "the mentality changed from earnings to sales." Didn't somebody look at the market? Maybe even talk to a salesman? Ross allowed that the conglomerate's four-man office of the president "didn't have time to meet frequently with me and think about longer-term concerns."

Ross reacted to adversity in time-honored fashion: He fired dozens of executives and hired somebody from outside to put the Atari mess together again, a marketing expert from a cigarette company who didn't know Donkey Kong from King Kong. Showing himself the true bureaucratic leader, Ross then *added* a new layer of vice-presidents to act as a liaison between the four top executives and the heads of the four Warner divisions. As a result, Ross ended up even more bureaucratically distant from the marketplace than he was before the fall of Atari. Predictably, Atari never got any better, and in 1984 Ross sold it to Jack Tramiel for $240 million in hopes that a new owner might save the company.

Like Warner, Xerox Corporation totally ignored the messages

from the marketplace. Thanks to the incredible success of its 914 copier, Xerox in 1970 controlled 80 percent of the domestic copier market. By 1983, however, its share had plunged to 47.7 percent. IBM had grabbed off chunks of the expensive copier market, while Japanese manufacturers won 21 percent of the low-priced market, nearly doubling their share between 1976 and 1983. "Xerox management became estranged from the marketplace. They lost touch with reality," a securities analyst told *Dun's Business Month*. Why?

- They manufactured sophisticated, expensive machines that didn't please customers. "The customer really wasn't interested in our high standards. He wanted a machine that didn't have to be repaired repeatedly," says Xerox vice-president Dwight F. Ryan.

- They ignored cost control. Personnel ranks swelled as design and manufacturing costs soared. When Xerox belatedly realized what was happening in the early 1980s, it eliminated some 12,500 employees, 10.6 percent of the work force.

- They ignored quality. The 3300 line of copiers, introduced in 1979, was so plagued by glitches that it had to be called off the market. This recall indelibly stained Xerox's reputation for quality engineering.

- In the 1960s, then chief executive C. Peter McColough hired Ford executive Archie McCardell to handle day-to-day operations as president. McCardell and a management team from Ford brought with them the Detroit disdain for the Japanese. And like Ford, Xerox came to suffer from that arrogance. (McCardell went from Xerox in 1977 to International Harvester Company, where as CEO he took that famous company to the brink of bankruptcy.)

For all these reasons, the once-mighty Xerox saw its market share slip away, never to be regained.

6. Corpocracy diffuses responsibility. Shunning responsibility often characterizes American corporate hierarchies, especially the larger ones. Projects are scrutinized endlessly by committees, study groups, outside experts, and consultants ostensibly to limit the chance of error, but which in fact serve to diffuse responsibility. "Avoid making any decisions if at all possible," is what one middle manager told sociologist Robert Jackall, "and if a decision has to be made, involve as many people as you can so that, if things go south you're able to point in as many directions as possible."

A favorite method of avoiding executive responsibility is to hire consultants. In 1982, U.S. businesses spent as much as $3 billion on them. *Forbes* observed that dependence on consultants "can lead to a clear abdication of [top managers'] responsibility," and in a survey, the magazine found that some of the best-managed companies used consultants only sparingly, if at all. Consultants, for their part, complain that top executives often are reluctant to follow their advice, especially if it involves something unpleasant.

Doomed projects often live on because no one will take responsibility for ending them. For example, Jennifer Horn, a certified public accountant in her early thirties with Cities Service in Tulsa (now merged with Occidental Petroleum), discovered in 1982 that two separate departments at Cities were spending lavishly on projects that she recalls were "eighty percent identical." One was a business model, a forecasting tool done by corporate planning that took two years and $200,000 to design. At the same time, the finance department was creating its own look-alike forecasting model at $500,000.

"I tried for two months to get one of the two projects killed," Horn says in an interview. "You know what happened to them? Zero. We spent nearly one million dollars and they died a natural death because of lack of follow-through. You have to have the top people involved, but because the two projects were *only* a million dollars, none of the top executives bothered with them." She adds that there were other similarly wasteful projects. Horn, who once worked for Peat, Marwick, Mitchell and Company, the biggest of the Big Eight accounting firms, finds such management indifference offensive to her educated sense of accountability. "Under the old cost accounting, cost variance analysis, you set a budget and when you went ten percent over, you had to write a long variance report explaining why you were off," she says. "I don't think budgets are being monitored the way they used to be."

Sociologist Robert Jackall sees such laxity as flowing from the top. "One might ask why top management does not institute codes or systems for tracking responsibility," observes Jackall, who answers: "An explicit system of accountability for subordinates would probably have to apply to top executives as well and would restrict their freedom. Bureaucracy expands the freedom of those on top by giving them the power to restrict the freedom of those beneath."

J. Richard Hackman, a professor of organizational behavior at the Yale School of Organization and Management, sees another problem in bureaucratic diffusion of responsibility: "A major issue is how an organization chops up work in tiny, separate segments—and then ties people to those tiny sub-tasks in ways that keep them from seeing, let alone having real responsibility for, the larger picture. Nobody, in such circumstances, has responsibility for the overall work outcome. This problem, widely discussed as it applies to rank-and-file jobs, is increasingly a problem for management jobs as well."

7. Corpocracy produces short-term thinkers. "Forecasts are dangerous," Sam Goldwyn allegedly once remarked, "especially about the future." That famous Goldwyn witticism pretty well captures the attitude of many corporate bureaucracies. For example, what could be more shortsighted than for a company to give away its capital. Yet when the Financial Accounting Standards Board, an accounting industry group, surveyed the accounting practices of 568 companies in 1981, it found that, restated for inflation, dividends far exceeded profits. The Japanese have a phrase for paying dividends out of capital: *tako hai,* which means an octopus (*tako*) eating its own tentacles to survive.

In their pursuit of quick gains at the sake of long-run prosperity, shortsighted managements sometimes resort to hiding debts from investors. One way is to sell receivables due the company. Although accountants see this as actually creating a debt, the transaction is hidden as a footnote and doesn't show on the balance sheet. Another gimmick, used by Avis in 1980, is to create a trust in which to stash debt. The result: Avis kept $400 million in borrowings to pay for cars off the balance sheet that year. Avis wasn't kidding about trying harder! Investors in Avis's parent, Norton Simon, might not appreciate such efforts—in the unlikely event they ever figure it out. (For more on Norton Simon, see page 84.)

Banks, under pressure from brokerage firms and the other competing businesses that now offer services once only offered by banks, have shaken off their traditional bankerly ways and become lenders to the world. They are seeking short-term profits and running counter to the caution developed over the centuries—a radical change in the banking bureaucracy that has bought predictable results: loans gone bad, major banks in trouble, and public confidence in financial institutions shaken. Continental Illinois National Bank, for instance, declared in 1976 that it would pursue an aggressive lending policy, and by 1981 it had become one of the three biggest lenders to U.S. business. But $1 billion of the loans, processed through tiny Penn Square National Bank in Oklahoma City, were made to oil and gas speculators on the dicey premise that energy prices would continue to rise. They fell, and in 1982 Penn Square went belly up.

But even more troubling than the domestic dealings by banks are massive foreign loans—totaling about $357 billion in 1984—to countries and businesses, many of them guaranteed by economically and politically unstable governments. The loan process here was, to say the least, sloppy, as the experience of S. C. Gwynne indicates. At twenty-five and with one and a half years of banking experience, Gwynne was tapped because of his fluency in French by a $5 billion midwestern bank to wander the world seeking lending opportunities. He found himself in a fraternity of "aggressive, bright, but hopelessly inexperienced lenders in their mid-20's [who] travel the world like itinerant brushmen, filling loan quotas, peddling financial wares, and living high on the hog." Gwynne continues, "In international lending, American banks frequently violate the oldest precepts of lending against security." No matter. In the new, short-term-perspective world of international banking, most of the young hustlers lining up those loans will have moved to other jobs by the time they go sour. (Similarly, a senior executive at Citibank told us angrily that many of the young executives responsible for the bank's rocky Latin American loans had moved to bigger jobs and were never held responsible for what they did.)

Why would a bank want such chancy loans on the books? Because in the all-important short run, they dress up the bank's profit and loss statement. Concludes Gwynne, "Even though the banks may allow a country such as Poland to 'reschedule' its debt—allowing it twenty years instead of ten to repay, for example—the *interest* payments keep coming. And it is interest that hits the bottom line of a bank's profit-and-loss statement. This means that Citibank can have a very good year even though many of its loans may be in serious trouble."

8. Corpocracy is habit-forming. It is much safer for the bureaucrat to stick with last year's winner, avoid taking risks, and save capital. Again, autos, tires, and steel—when those industries enjoyed unchallenged oligopoly status—learned bad habits that lasted for decades.

For example, there is the ritualistic worship of cows—cash cows, that is. These are aging plants and equipment that would be costly to replace and lines of business that have no future but still generate profits. They enrich corporate balance sheets because they allow a company to produce short-term profit without much risk or thought.

The habit of milking cash cows for too long is what got rubber and asbestos, among other industries, into such economic trouble. Oil companies still cling to theirs. Economist Burton Klein tells how breaking up with the cash cow convulsed one oil company: "I got to know the people well over at ARCO, and they got me over one afternoon to talk to them. They said they knew they were not going to be able to make lots of money forever in oil. But they didn't know how to break the company's dependence on it. So I suggested that they change incentives—give big bonuses for discovering new things. The vice-president for engineering said he'd been planning to do that for ten years, but whenever he made a move in that direction, members of the internal bureaucracy found it threatening. So the president of ARCO, who endorsed this idea, was forced to back down."

Consider what happened at Bethlehem Steel's Sparrows Point, Maryland, shipyard. For years, Sparrows Point had blindly bought steel from its parent corporation, and paid top price for doing it. Nobody raised any questions. Then, a short time ago, a young female clerk at the Sparrows Point plant discovered that her company was paying $460 a ton to Bethlehem for the same steel for which competitor Newport News Shipbuilding and Dry Dock Company paid Bethlehem $310 a ton. Surprise! Sparrows Point had been paying for steel out of habit while the rest of the industry was off shopping for bargains.

Companies once in regulated businesses—airlines, banking, trucking, communications—especially fell into such lax bureaucratic habits. Remember comedienne Lily Tomlin's imitation of a Ma Bell phone operator of years ago: "We don't have to care. We're the phone company"? Then came the shock of deregulation and the necessity to adapt.

For many firms this adjustment was wrenching. ITT World Communications was one of three major companies that divvied up international communications, under the benign oversight of the Federal Communications Commission. A middle-level manager, who requested anonymity, describes what happened: "We had been leasing lines where the terms and conditions were tightly controlled. Prices were high enough so almost anybody could make money. As a result, reducing costs and adding efficiencies were not important because you knew that year after year you would make a profit. There was no incentive to adopt new technology or search for new markets." After deregulation, says the manager, the old habits are proving tough to break. "Dealing with unpredictability is something the industry is not used to. The top managers are good men, smart men, but they wish the world was once again predictable and stable."

Bad habits, like indifference to markets, can be contagious, as when the auto industry infected the tire industry. In the 1950s and 1960s, the Detroit "original equipment" market accounted for about one quarter of the total sales for U.S. tire makers; Akron, consequently, took its orders from Detroit. And Detroit wanted cheap tires that produced the biggest profit margins. In France, meanwhile, the superior radial tire had been in production since the 1920s, when it was invented by the Michelin brothers. But Detroit stuck with the cheaper, soft-riding bias-belted. Not until the shock of the 1973 OPEC oil embargo did Detroit abruptly drop the bias-belted. But the tire industry, so accustomed to feeding off Detroit, could not answer the sudden clarion for quality. It took years for most tire companies to recover.

Against the promise of easy profits, it takes an extraordinary company not to follow the herd. Cabot Corporation, which manufactures a reinforcing agent called carbon black used in tires, chose not to ape Akron's bad habits. Instead, Cabot poured vast sums into research and development, figuring it would pay in the long run. "The rubber companies just didn't want to pay us for our technology or our quality," explains Robert Charpie, the publicity-shy but convivial nuclear physicist who has been Cabot's chief executive for nearly two decades. "It didn't take us long to figure there were only two or three tire companies that were really spending on the future—Michelin, Goodyear, and Bridgestone. So we made up our mind we would spend our discretionary funds in support of their quality and innovative improvements. And look what happened. Those companies are on the way to taking over the rubber industry all over the world." As for Cabot, it remains the world's lowest cost producer of carbon black with the biggest share of the market. The company's concern for technology and quality spills over to its other businesses, energy and specialty alloy manufacturing.

These two business lines now represent a near equal share with carbon black of Cabot's profit picture.

9. *Corpocracy hates boat rockers.* To get along, go along, Speaker of the House Sam Rayburn would say to younger congressional colleagues. It's no different in a corpocracy. Boat rockers simply aren't welcome because they threaten to unravel comfortable assumptions.

Such was the case with William F. Buehler, a manager at the granddaddy of all corporate bureaucracies, American Telephone and Telegraph Company. In January 1983, AT&T made Buehler a vice-president in charge of marketing phone systems to small businesses all across the country. The ambitious forty-one-year-old executive ran General Business Systems (GBS) with its three thousand people as if it weren't part of Ma Bell. Salesmen were told to produce or leave, results were posted to spur competition, Buehler made quick decisions that took Bell years. He became the first vice-president to visit branches, eating lunch with low-level employees. "That was radical by AT&T standards," said one branch manager. Staffers caught "Buehler fever" and sales took off—until the bureaucracy asserted itself. *The Wall Street Journal* described how Archie McGill, the president of AT&T Information Systems who had hired Buehler, was eased out because higher-ups reportedly found him tough to control. (He says he quit.) Then, a few months later as GBS's sales surged ahead, McGill's successor suddenly transferred Buehler to an obscure planning position. The official explanation was revealingly opaque: "to integrate two discrete sales staffs . . ." In fact, the Buehler affair demonstrates how corpocracy demands conformity.

Young bureaucrats, such as one junior executive at Exxon Enterprises, quickly find out the risks of disturbing the status quo. According to another former Exxon manager, the young executive fretted about a relationship between a superior and a consultant. The consultant, he learned, received pay for phony projects. Mindful that every year Exxon employees sign statements showing they understand the company's code of ethics, the young executive felt morally bound to turn in the supervisor. He went directly to the top of Exxon Enterprises and reported the questionable behavior. "But there's an old boy network that says, 'I'll protect you, you protect me,'" observes the former manager relating the incident. The whistleblower ended up "in bad grace"—a person who could not be trusted with a secret— while the offender got off with a slight wrist slap.

An even worse fate befell another whistle blower at Michigan Consolidated Gas Company. Arthur Suchodolski, an internal auditor at the utility, reported what he viewed as fraud in the credit division of the company. Suchodolski found that the state might have been paying the utility twice for unpaid heating bills of welfare cases. "My report was ignored by top company officials," said Suchodolski. There followed the typical treatment of a boat rocker. Shuffled to a new job, he suddenly started getting "poor" ratings in job performance reports, which called his work "hit or miss." Not long after, he was fired because, said his boss, "You disturb the operations of this office."

10. Corpocracy spawns isolation. From the Kremlin to the Pentagon to a giant American corporation, any huge organization can become isolated from its constituency or clientele. It takes a novel like *Gorky Park* or a tragedy like the 1983 Soviet shooting down of the Korean Air Lines Boeing 747 to spotlight the frightening bureaucratic isolation of the Kremlin. Revelations about military contractors charging a thousand dollars for a hammer show how the Pentagon, with its gorged budget, has lost touch with reality. Similarly, the economic decline of many of our elephantine firms in the past decade testifies how they too fell out of step and out of touch with the world outside their skyscrapers.

John Z. De Lorean may not be the most credible executive around, following his near-peripeteia in 1983–84, but he did earlier give the world its first unexpurgated peek at the auto industry in the best-selling book *On a Clear Day You Can See General Motors.* De Lorean described the splendid isolation of the fourteenth-floor executive row at GM headquarters. Increasingly, production decisions emanated from this lofty height, even though the men there "lost sight of the corporation's management goals of keeping a keen eye on the marketplace and a firm hand on the corporate tiller." High up on the fourteenth floor, "You were too harassed and oppressed by committee meetings and paperwork. It [GM] has gotten to be a total insulation from the realities of the world." Recall also that these men, who design the cars we drive, don't own any, since they are chauffeured wherever they go.

The solution: Visit the real world. Two men did just that and related their experiences to Ralph Nader: A steel company chairman once decided to descend into a coal mine owned by his firm. After spending thirty minutes chatting with the miners in their cramped and cold conditions, he emerged saying that he would not again be so quick to say that coal miners were over-paid. Paul Austin, when he was the CEO of Coca-Cola, said that his visit to observe the conditions of migrant workers in the company's Florida orange groves made him resolve to improve their plight.

At the hourly rather than managerial level, the computer age imposes its own kind of isolation. In the Blue Cross office in the Boston area, clerks sit glued to computers all day, typing information about subscribers. The computers automatically monitor their productivity, so most workers only take a fifteen-minute lunch break in order to keep pace with the computer's productivity demands. That leaves little time for human exchanges, as is made dramatically clear in this story told to author Bob Kuttner by a Blue Cross source in 1983: "Last Christmas they organized a little office party. They had a 'Christmas grab,' where everybody picks a name out of a hat. You bring in a little gift for somebody and they bring in one for you. We realized that nobody knew anybody else's name."

Managers in the Middle: How a Corpocracy Grows

> In the office in which I work there are five people of whom I am afraid. Each of these people is afraid of four people (excluding overlaps), for a total of twenty, and each of these twenty people is afraid of six people, making a total of one hundred and twenty people who are feared by at least one person. Each of these one hundred and twenty people is afraid of the other one hundred and nineteen, and all of these one hundred and forty-five people are afraid of the twelve men at the top who helped found and build the company and now own and direct it. . . . In my department, there are six people who are afraid of me, and one small secretary who is afraid of all of us. I have one other person working for me who is not afraid of anyone, not even me, and I would fire him quickly, but I'm afraid of him.
>
> —Joseph Heller, *Something Happened,* 1974

A Legacy of Angst and Antagonism
You are vice-president for marketing at Altoona Creations Corporation, a $250 million soap powder manufacturer in Houston, Texas. At thirty-nine years old, you earn a respectable $68,500 a year; you are married and have two teenage children, live in an

affluent suburb, drive a two-year-old BMW, and belong to a prestigious country club. In short, you have all the trappings of success and security.

Then why are you so worried? Like Bob Slocum, the hero of *Something Happened,* you are scared. You worry that you never get to talk with any of the company's top six executives, and that all your memos about product innovations go unanswered. You worry about Altoona's profit slide. Nobody talks openly about it, but there are rumors that the CEO and his closest sidekicks have arranged golden parachutes for themselves. Does this mean that Altoona is a takeover prospect? What will happen to you? You scrutinize all the business publications, finding stories about corporations shucking managers in staff jobs just like yours. One night you go home and your wife tells of seeing Lee Iacocca on the Phil Donahue show boasting about how he rid Chrysler's payroll of middle managers. "Those twenty thousand white-collar workers are gone forever," she quotes Iacocca as saying.

The fate of middle managers has long fascinated sociologists, psychologists, and scholars. C. Wright Mills, in his book *White Collar: The American Middle Class;* Erich Fromm, in *The Sane Society;* and William H. Whyte, Jr., in *The Organization Man,* all wrote about how the corporate bureaucratic system forced conformity. In *Life in the Crystal Palace,* Alan Harrington described a neutral corporate world where nobody failed, but nobody excelled either. Michael Maccoby, in *The Gamesman,* concluded, "Bureaucracies tend to type people to fit the requirements of their hierarchies." Author and advertising executive Earl Shorris, in his book *The Oppressed Middle,* borrowed from Hannah Arendt to describe middle managers as victims of corporate totalitarianism. But other commentators also see some of them as empire builders who leech the company strength to feed their own egos. Regardless of varying interpretations, however, middle managers are the body and soul of the corporate bureaucracy.

On an organization chart, middle management falls between the half dozen or fewer senior executives at the top, and the foremen, salespeople, and production personnel below. In the more top-heavy bureaucracies, middle managers account for as many as one third of the employees. They are supervisors who are supervised, and they generally earn between $25,000 and $85,000 a year for their efforts. "Managers are the quintessential bureaucratic work group," writes sociologist Robert Jackall in the *Harvard Business Review*. "They not only fashion bureaucratic rules, but they are also bound by them. Typically, they are not just in the organization, they are *of* the organization."

It is widely reported that middle managers lost jobs in record numbers during the economic recessions of the early 1980s. Tens of thousands of them hit the street as companies searched for greater productivity and lower break-even points. But aside from the considerable anecdotal evidence in magazines and newspapers chronicling the gutting of middle management, what statistical proof is there of this widespread cutback of middle managers? The answer is, there isn't any.

In fact, management ranks actually *increased* during the early 1980s. According to the Bureau of Labor Statistics (BLS), these increases stretch across all segments of the economy, including even the hard-pressed manufacturing sector where most of the anecdotal evidence suggests huge cuts. There were 9 percent *more* managers and administrators in the American economy by December 1982 than there were in January 1980. And this apparent case of management featherbedding happened in the face of a 1-percent decline in overall employment and a 12-percent drop in blue-collar jobs. Service industries were up 15.7 percent; construction, 11.9 percent; finance and insurance, 11.3 percent; transportation and utilities 9.4 percent; manufacturing of nondurables, 6.7 percent; retailers and wholesalers, 5.1 percent; public administration, 2.7 percent; and manufacturing of durables, 2.4 percent. According to Michael Pilot of the BLS Division of Outlook and Trends, "You can say that between 1972 and 1982, the number of managers has grown steadily. And even during the recent recession, employment of managers did not drop off."

But while top management may have impressed Wall Street by exaggerating the actual bloodletting, it had a devastating effect on middle management morale. Sar Levitan, an economist, worries about the "destabilizing effect" of the bluff. "After all, middle managers hold things together," he observes. Indeed, the relationship between middle and top management, tentative in the best of times, turned downright hostile, as two management surveys published in 1983 demonstrate. Hay Associates, a Philadelphia-based human resources consulting firm, found that 65.9 percent of top management rated the performances of their middle managers as unsatisfactory. The percentage of middle managers expressing confidence in corporate leaders fell from 50 percent in 1974–75 to a troubling 39 percent by 1981; only 44 percent of middle managers viewed their bosses favorably, down from 70 percent in the 1970–74 period. Similarly, Opinion Research Corporation in Princeton, New Jersey, reported that fully 50 percent of managers believed top management "had lost touch" with employees. Concluded the ORC survey, "What the work force really wants is management leadership whose competence and concern they can trust."

In tracing the ascendancy of the middle manager, commentators invariably begin with the end of the Protestant ethic. Business historian Alfred D. Chandler, in *The Visible Hand,* writes that "as late as 1840 there were no middle managers in the United States—that is, there were no managers who supervised the work of other managers and in turn reported to senior executives who themselves were salaried managers. At that time nearly all top managers were owners; they were either partners or major stockholders in the enterprise they managed. It was a no-nonsense time of hard work and disdain for material goods. This prudence and perseverance—plus this country's staggeringly rich resources—produced a unique strain of innovators and entrepreneurs: Henry Ford I, James Buchanan Duke, Cyrus Eaton, J. P. Morgan, Cyrus McCormick, John D. Rockefeller, and Thomas Edison, among others.

Soon, the big organizations created by these individualists came to dominate the economy. With the innovators gone, professional managers emerged to run their creations. Graduate business schools appeared at the Universities of Chicago and California (1899), Dartmouth and New York University (1900), and Harvard (1908), giving the title of manager a professional patina. "The great transformation," observes Jackall, "produced the decline of the old middle class of entrepreneurs, free professionals, independent farms and small independent businessmen—the traditional carriers of the old Protestant ethic—and the ascendency of a new middle class of salaried employees whose chief common characteristic was and is their dependence on the big organization."

Companies begun back then flourished for decades: Quaker Oats, Procter and Gamble, Eastman Kodak, International Harvester, Ford, and General Motors. "Bigger is better" became a slogan of American industry. An expanding staff became another way to crow, "Look at us, we're growing!" Then, too, corporate America has an enduring love affair with external size, as conglomerate mergers ballooned many firms in the late 1960s and 1970s. These strung-out structures presented massive communications problems, so more and more staff was added—which, of course, only worsened the communications problems. At the same time, staff functions, such as accounting, personnel, and legal, grew to meet increased demands by federal regulators for information about securities transactions, occupational safety, pensions, and taxes.

Beyond these external pressures to proliferate staff, high anxiety in the ranks of middle management is also a motor that drives bureaucrats to expand their bureaus. Each bureau within an organization grows and expands to ensure security and opportunity for its members. Indeed, to hear middle managers tell it, this type of unproductive phenomenon is all too common in big corporations. Just mention the words *bureaucracy* or *waste* to a middle manager, and he or she immediately pours out personal experiences. But ask if they ever do anything to change it, and they become defensive, seeking assurances that they not be quoted. There aren't many whistle-blowing middle managers—for obvious reasons. "Everybody covers up, because if they expose the waste they may be jeopardizing their own jobs," says a middle manager at Colgate-Palmolive Company. With jobs, income, and living standards at stake, most bureaucrats will swallow hard and shuffle papers rather than make waves.

Top managers rule this swelling yet remote bureaucracy by setting objectives for the tens or hundreds or thousands of middle managers beneath them. This process can become a game of numbers, where product quality, consumers, and even outside competition are abstractions; reality is only within the headquarter's walls. Top management religiously reviews the numbers, so hitting them becomes an obsession for the ambitious middle manager. Too often, say middle managers, the consequent waste and turmoil are never known to the people at the top. Honeywell vice-president James J. Reiner, for instance, says that when the recession in the early 1980s forced his company to cut expenses, top management was shocked to learn how many staffers had "Planner" attached to their titles.

The result of these overlapping and interacting trends, concludes Peter Drucker, has been an "inflation in management titles . . . more severe in these last thirty years than the inflation of money." Drucker adds, "Middle managements today tend to be overstaffed to the point of obesity. This slows the decision process to a crawl and makes the organization increasingly incapable of adapting to change. Far too few people, even in high positions with imposing titles, are exposed to the challenge of producing results. And it isn't only in the armed services that 'support' has grown to the point where it overshadows the combat troops and employs many more people. A good many businesses, large and small, became equally bureaucratic and equally suffer from gross overweight around the midriff."

John F. Welch, Jr., CEO of General Electric, recalls how in the 1970s GE adopted the strategic planning ideas suggested by consultants. A staff was formed to implement planning and to educate some five thousand managers on anything from turbines to toasters. Each department, division, group, and sector of GE's hierarchy churned out voluminous annual reports each year like clockwork, regardless of whether or not there had been a change in strategy over the months since the last report was written. "We found ourselves in a position where we were hiring people to read reports of people who had been hired to write reports," Welch says. GE has since scrapped strategic planning as a separate staff function, instead making it one of a manager's responsibilities. As for GE's report writing, it now depends on the business: A fast-moving, rapidly changing business like audio requires yearly planning projections, whereas longer-range projects such as locomotive and jet engine manufacturing don't.

The Real Bottom Line of Bureaucracy
Beyond the forgotten markets, soaring overhead, higher prices, lost sales, and shrunken profit margins mentioned earlier, a turgid corpocracy produces even more serious costs that are less easily defined. "The biggest waste is the untapped potential of people in a corporation," asserts Jude Rich. "We haven't found the way to tap their motivation." But how do you motivate people to be productive if they are, like the Colgate-Palmolive middle manager, afraid?

Harvard professor Chris Argyris surveyed the attitudes of top and middle management in one major corporation. Senior managers rated relations with subordinates "relatively good to excellent," adding that "we talk to each other frequently and openly." But here's what middle managers told Argyris: 71

percent didn't know where they stood or how they were being evaluated; 65 percent didn't know the qualities that led to success in the organization; 65 percent rated the most important unsolved problem as top management's inability to overcome intergroup rivalries, lack of cooperation, and poor communications; 53 percent said if they could alter one aspect of their superior's behavior, it would be to help him or her see the "dog eat dog" communications problems that existed in middle management. And if it sounds like these two groups work for different corporations, the reason may be that whenever the president of the corporation asked the managers to reveal any problems they considered important, none of those problems they discussed with Argyris were mentioned.

This conspiracy of silence suggests more complex deceptions by nervous middle managers. Scholars who study this dynamic find that the more hierarchical the organization, the more complex and arcane the methods of the bureaucrats—and the more wasteful the results. Like everyone else, middle managers' chief concern is survival, and when that is challenged by an unpredictable or dictatorial top management, managers form a fifth column within the organization. Not only do they resist corporate policies they find potentially harmful, they actually alter those policies to guarantee their own well-being.

Anthony Downs, a scholar of bureaucracy, finds that top management in huge organizations often uses various devices to control middle management, the most common being to demand an endless stream of reports. Reports have three purposes: (1) to inform remote top management of what's going on; (2) to remind middle managers that certain standards must be met; and (3) to instill fear of punishment if he or she fails to complete a job successfully—or at least to report having done so. "These compliance-inducing functions explain why bureaus normally require so many more reports than high level officials can possibly read," observes Downs. But such policing tactics, so common in corporate hierarchies, lead to manager resistance, which Downs describes in his Law of Counter Control: "The greater the effort by a sovereign or top level official to control the behavior of subordinate officials, the greater the efforts made by those subordinates to evade or counteract such controls."

And the taller the corpocracy, the more vulnerable it is to middle management sabotage. The reason, explains Chester Bernard, the former president of New Jersey Telephone Company who turned business theoretician, in *The Functions of an Executive,* is that policies in all organizations are defined at all levels, not just on top. As information passes down through the layers, each manager has certain discretion to alter and interpret the information. Middle managers will predictably embellish data that reflects favorably on themselves and minimize information that exposes their shortcomings. There is at least a 10-percent distortion of information on each level, observes Gordon Tullock. So if a piece of information travels down five levels, "almost one-half of the activity carried out by the entire organization is wasted motion." The usual solution by top management: Create a parallel source of information to check on the accuracy of regular middle management sources. This adds further expense and distrust to the whole process.

Middle management manipulates information to resist anything that might be threatening to them—including changes that could help the corporation be more efficient and productive. "To the organization members, who will be affected by the change, the costs to them are likely to be directly and immediately felt; the benefits are something that will accrue remotely to 'the organization,'" observes Harvard professor James Q. Wilson. Middle managers are also upset at both internal and external threats to their traditional status. "Quality circles" and similar efforts at blue-collar involvement, observes D. L. Landen, retired director of organizational research and development at General Motors, "are pushing decision-making down to the shop floor, by-passing middle managers. A lot of managers fear that if the trend toward quality circles continues to grow, before long there won't be a need for a boss."

Politics, as described earlier in "Ten Telltale Traits," thrive in a middle management bureaucracy, where members are far removed from the sources of executive power and the satisfactions of line productivity. The result is a corporate subculture characterized by intrigues and personal loyalties—not to the organization but to powerful individuals within the organization. For the leader, such loyal subjects provide support, intelligence, and affirmation of his chosen role as a leader. The loyalist, on the other hand, hopes his mentor will provide him with promotions, protection, and job security. According to one former middle manager at New York's Chemical Bank, Robert I. Lipp, who has long wanted to be chairman and chief executive officer of the bank, sprinkled all levels of management with graduates of his alma mater, Harvard Business School. The ambitious executive's maneuver triggered a morale problem in many bank departments where middle managers bridled at having Harvard M.B.A.'s put over them. But it helped Lipp, who in two decades moved up in the hierarchy until he became president in 1983—just a step below his goal.

"Personal merit is difficult to measure, because decisions are made collectively," observes sociologist Joseph Bensman about the plight of the ambitious middle manager caught in a large bureaucracy. In his comfortable, art-decorated Central Park West apartment, Bensman chain-smokes cigarettes and talks with the intensity of a man obsessed by a subject; indeed, he spent ten years in the 1950s and 1960s as a middle manager in a big Madison Avenue advertising agency, "a level below the top." Bensman describes one popular political route to the top, which he calls the "paternalism among executives" but which sounds more like a corporate variation on *The Godfather*. It develops this way: In his mid-thirties, the ambitious middle manager in a big corporation becomes one of perhaps one hundred struggling to break out of the herd. Competition is brutal, so the young manager latches onto a higher-up executive, perhaps five or ten years older, who has an even better shot at the top. "If he goes up, you go up. At that point, all considerations, other than paternalistic loyalty, tend to be sacrificed—that includes considerations of efficiency and waste. Financial and personal considerations take precedence. You have to support your patron, cover up for him, and sometimes even take the blame for him. You create a set of personal credits, which he will redeem when he gets promoted."

Bensman worries about the ethical and moral dilemmas that grow out of these relationships. "While personal loyalties and networks evolve out of the best of reasons, there is within the network of friends special elements of secrecy and lawlessness." To support Bensman's concerns, one need only review the business scandals of a decade ago. ITT, Occidental Petroleum, Gulf, Northrop, and Lockheed among others became tainted by questionable or illegal political activities at home and abroad. And in many cases, an ambition-blinded middle manager got caught doing the dirty work for someone higher up.

Squash the Hierarchy

It seems inevitable that middle managers, in their limited bureaucratic roles, will always be restless and uncertain. But their redundancy, angst, and suppressed hostility to management is hardly inevitable. The first step is to squash the corporate hierarchy.

"Inequalities of power, income, and prestige," writes Downs in *Inside Bureaucracy*, "are greater in tall hierarchies than in flat ones, since the former have more ranks, and the latter have greater delegation of authority." Flatten out the hierarchy, advise reformers of bureaucracy, and this will provide managers with new challenges. As a result, the number of middle managers in an organization decreases, while the number of people they manage increases. Charles K. Rourke, a leading authority on "management spans," puts it this way: "The biggest waste in corporations is management talent. Theoretically, we pay our managers to manage, but actually we don't want them to. We know from what we call 'span of utilization' that if a manager is capable of managing ten people, he's normally managing only four point eight on average—that is, a forty-eight percent span of utilization. So here is the most expensive item in the company that I'm using half-time. I'm talking about millions and millions of dollars in salaries, not to mention inefficiencies and morale problems. American corporations feel that more managers give them more management, but all you really get is more confusion. Fewer managers mean more management."

Squashing the hierarchy means that companies must stop paying managers based on the number of people they manage. An abiding frustration of Patrick McFadden, who was chief executive of the First Bank Corporation in New Haven (Connecticut) before it merged out of existence in 1984, was getting branch managers to think of managing assets, not people. "The number of people working for a manager should be stricken from his job description and replaced with the amount of assets he manages," says McFadden, now vice-chairman of Connecticut National Bank. But old, wasteful habits die hard. McFadden notes, for example, that a system devised by Hay Associates, the compensation consultants, relies on head counts—and many banks and other financial institutions rely heavily on the Hay system. This means that adding bodies to the bureaucracy is literally built into the system.

Staff jobs, those hierarchical inflaters, must be diligently policed. As J. Stanford Smith, the retired CEO of International Paper Co., warns: "There are just two basic kinds of valid staff work—work that is clearly corporate, such as the treasury function, and consulting to line managers in specialized areas such as robotics. You need clearly spelled-out corporate policies indicating that actual business decisions are to be made by line managers and that no one [in a corporate staff slot] will second-guess them." IBM, 3M, and Digital Equipment Corporation have only a few permanent staffers. Otherwise, line executives move in and out of staff jobs. Realizing they will soon be back on the line, they avoid creating burdensome bureaucracies. Observes Jack F. Reichert, president, Brunswick Corporation: "We've been rewarding bookkeepers as if they created wealth. U.S. business has to make more beans rather than count them several times."

Title inflation must be fought. For decades, job evaluation systems have rewarded the title "manager" with status symbols and increased earnings potential, observes Richard E. Wintermantel, the director of Organization and Human Resources at Motorola. "This has increased layers of management and converted thousands of excellent professionals into lousy managers. Industry has been rewarding the wrong behavior." Peter Drucker agrees, and warns that with the "baby bust" coming by the end of this decade, titles that proliferated to accommodate the fading baby boom should be eliminated. "Twenty years ago, we built into the performance review of managerial people the question: 'Are they ready for promotion?' Now we need to rephrase the question: 'Are they ready for a bigger, more demanding challenge and for the addition of new responsibilities to their existing jobs.'"

Finally, a symbolic though significant relic of bureaucratic hierarchy is the silly status symbol. These should be squashed along with the hierarchy. Executive lunchrooms and parking lots that make middle managers feel like second-class citizens should be done away with. The Opinion Research Corporation, in suggesting ways to redress its findings of broad management discontent, mentioned earlier, counseled that "top management ensure that privilege, both social and psychological, of being a manager, be eliminated. Management functions should be treated as a regular workplace job, no different from that of a secretary, lathe operator or sales person . . . get rid of second class job citizenship."

In Silicon Valley, south of San Francisco, such corporate egalitarianism has become a way of life. For a visitor from the East, where corporate hierarchies are as normal as cherry blossoms in a Washington spring, the experience can be disarming.

One meets Robert N. Noyce, an inventor of the microchip and a founder and vice-chairman of Intel, in his small, corner office with shoulder-high partitions, a setting that invites visitors to drop in. "We started out with the usual mahogany row, but about seven or eight years ago we decided that it was almost antisocial, that people didn't see any of the officers around the place, and that it would be better to disperse them. So now the president's office is downstairs, the chairman's office is in another building. We've got vice-presidents out where they can be seen. It's been an important source of spirit in the company."

Why CEOs, Boards, and Shareholders Don't Tame the Corpocracy

The Chief Executive Officer

Charlie Rourke is angry, even livid. For more than two decades, he has counseled top corporate managers on running their businesses, first at Harbridge House, then as president of SMC Hendrick, and now as chief executive officer of the Organizational Analysis Group, a Harbridge House subsidiary. "I love business. I love running a company, everything about it," asserts the contagiously enthusiastic executive who describes himself as "a really conservative guy. I came out of the B-School [Harvard]." But Rourke has some very unconservative remarks to make about a powerful group of businessmen, whom he thinks have abused their trust: the chief executive officers at the top of the corporate bureaucracy.

In the late 1970s, Rourke began noticing things about some of these American managers that troubled him; for example, too many wanted big remuneration and little responsibility. "What I saw was CEOs getting two hundred thousand to six hundred thousand dollars a year while the company's going downhill. He keeps getting pay increases while he closes down plants and lays off blue-collar workers. And all the time, he's blaming the government and the unions. . . . The reason is that the CEO wants to make as few changes as possible, because the more changes, the more antagonism and internal conflict he must face."

Rourke recalls the following exchange with the CEO of a major company.

CEO: "Charlie, I'm shocked to hear you say that I have

twenty-five percent too many managers. But you have to understand that we're a very paternalistic company."

Rourke: "You may get angry at me for saying this, but that's nonsense!"

CEO: "What do you mean?"

Rourke: "You just closed a plant in Ohio and two thousand people are out of work. Don't tell me you're paternalistic. You're paternalistic to the people you have to face on the elevator every day, not the people you don't see."

Short-term thinking by the CEO has become endemic, Rourke says. "I've stopped asking CEOs—and I'm talking about billion-dollar companies—for strategic plans. I say, 'Just tell me your thoughts for the next couple of years.' And I almost always end up with nothing." Once he proudly showed the CEO of a big timber company how the firm could reap extraordinary profits over the next twenty years. Rourke's enthusiasm was quickly cooled, however, by the CEO's indifference. What was wrong, he asked. Replied the executive, "The only thing you missed is one major factor—I won't be here in twenty years."

"They surround themselves with people who have the same tie, same striped suit, come from the same school. Now, there's nothing wrong with not wanting a pain in the ass reporting to you—life's too short for that. But there *is* something wrong with just getting one side of the story." Absorbing information carefully filtered by devoted aides, the CEO begins to think of himself as godlike. This attitude is reinforced, says Rourke, by his involvement in outside activities, where he is accorded great deference, hobnobs with politicians, and makes speeches.

What do the chief executives say when you tell them your findings, the consultant is asked. "They all say, almost without exception, 'I didn't know it was happening.'" Then, as if startled by his own answer, Rourke muses, "Was it Mellon who said, 'Take away all my factories, take away everything else, but I will be back in business in a year because I can organize'? Well, we've lost that. We've lost sight of the reason we're in business. And when companies go downhill, you'll find that not many decisions were made to ensure success in the future, but a lot were made to ensure the bureaucracy continued."

Charlie Rourke's *cri de coeur* reflects a growing concern among thoughtful consultants, academics, and businessmen about the quality of leadership in American corporations. A single CEO in a major corporation wields extraordinary power to an extent unknown in business history until recent times. He can, by his actions, change the course of a multibillion-dollar corporation and, in some cases, a whole industry. The wealth, health, and existence of thousands of lives hang on his decisions.

"Organizations bear the imprint of men who lead them and work in them and do not evolve simply as depersonalized structures," writes Abraham Zaleznik in *Human Dilemmas of Leadership*. If this is true—and our research bears out Zaleznik's observations—then many American corporations tolerate sprawling bureaucracies because the executives who run them want them that way. Max Weber explored one reason why: A "bureaucratic organization is technically the most highly developed means of power in the hands of the man who controls it." The problem comes when the CEO loses control, either because of inability, disinterest, or the sheer size of the organization—or a combination of all three. Evidence shows that this is precisely what has happened with some of America's biggest corporations. Lacking leadership, a corporate bureaucracy slips into sloth, and becomes wasteful. With strong, caring leadership, corpocracies can be tamed and motivated.

That's the lesson to be learned from the experiences of Sidney Harman and Warren Duffett.

Harman International Industries produced some of the finest stereo equipment in the world under the names Harmon-Kardon and JBL. Sales and profits grew at a compounded rate of 30 percent and Harman International's stock became a darling of the New York Stock Exchange. CEO Harman proudly recalls the Rolls-Royce director who told him, "We consider ourselves the JBL of the auto industry." Then, in 1977, Sidney Harman decided to join the Carter administration as number-two person in the Commerce Department, so he arranged the sale of Harman International to Beatrice Foods, the conglomerate now called Beatrice Companies.

By 1980, however, Beatrice had grown disenchanted with the business. Under the Beatrice system, says the precise and softspoken Harman, "There's no conceit they know how to fix a company. They just get rid of a failing company." With his government stint over, Harman bought back much of the original company he had sold to Beatrice. But three years in the conglomerate had exacted a toll; the company's flagship subsidiary, JBL, was in deep trouble and quality had slipped. A long-time employee in the JBL plant in Los Angeles warned, "Sidney, I wouldn't buy the product I'm making." Alarmed, Harman reacted unlike traditional corporate bureaucrats do—he temporarily moved from his home and family in Washington to Los Angeles for five months in late 1983 to try to personally nurse his once-valued asset back to health.

He found a company suffering from what he describes as "corporate colonization." That's when a division or subsidiary of a huge bureaucracy is left to drift without leadership from the headquarters. "The feeling of people working there," he said in an interview, "is that 'We're lost in the stars and nobody knows we're here.'" To recover, Harman, who has a doctorate in psychology, took several swift steps. First, he dismissed the president; then he called the score of managers together to let them know he would be supportive and receptive. He found that the suppliers had gotten an upper hand and inventories were out of control. Bills hadn't been paid, so suppliers were pressuring defenseless JBL buyers. At Harman's urging, the JBL staff finally confronted vendors, telling them, "We need cooperation not bullying."

The staff carted every piece of paper produced by the company—memos, reports, letters—to the boardroom and Harman demanded justification for its continuance. "It was remarkable how much paper and paper-work we were able to get rid of," he recalls. And he told his managers, "I want you to contemplate this business as if you were just starting. I want you to ignore the bureaucracy that exists, forget the legend 'This is how we've always done it.' Then go to the blackboard and sketch on the left side all the services we must provide and on the right, all our resources. Then I want you to reorganize the company. Come at it as if you were spending your own money."

Soon, JBL changed from losing a substantial amount each month to making a substantial percent on sales again. While he won't call this effort a total success, Harman does believe that "we were able to cut out literally layers of personnel and activity that had been built over the years by some self-aggrandizement."

Another CEO who keenly understands how the undertow of corpocracy can quietly pull down American business—his own and others—is Warren Buffett, chief executive of Berkshire Hathaway, an insurer with major holdings in publishing, textiles, steel, and retailing. A brilliant money manager who invests

his own and his company's capital only in companies he understands, Buffett raised the book value of Berkshire Hathaway
from $19 a share in 1965 to $737 by 1983. His and his wife's
shares of Berkshire Hathaway recently were pegged at $460 mil-
lion. (Buffett, who values the anonymity of his base in Omaha,
Nebraska, broke into the news in 1985 when Capital Cities Communications, a company in which he was a major stockholder
with holdings of $517 million, bought the American Broadcast-
ing Company.)

What separates Warren Buffett from Rourke's visionless
CEOs are his strong and thoughtful opinions. And he expresses
them in his company's colorless, pictureless annual report,
whose simplicity contrasts with the multicolored comic books of
other corporations, which are long on smiling executive faces
but short on unvarnished facts. Most chairman's letters in annual reports read like they are crafted by legal, PR, and accounting departments, which in fact they are. But Buffett sees
the chairman's letter as an important communication device that
allows him, as the corporate leader, to inform his employees and
his stockholders of his thinking. He talks to shareholders, says
Buffett, as if they were partners. Respectfully.

For example, here's what he had to say in Berkshire Hathaway's 1983 annual report about American business's recent
merger and acquisition binge:

> In many of these acquisitions managerial intellect wilted in
> competition with managerial adrenaline. The thrill of the
> chase blinded pursuers to the consequences of the catch. Pas-
> cal's observation seems apt: "It has struck me that all men's
> misfortunes spring from the single cause that they are unable
> to stay quietly in one room." (Your chairman left the room
> once too often last year and almost starred in the Acquisition
> Follies of 1982. . . . Had it come off, this transaction would
> have consumed extraordinary amounts of time and energy, all
> for a most uncertain payoff. If we were to introduce graphics
> to this report, illustrating favorable business development of
> the past year, two blank pages depicting this blown deal
> would be the appropriate centerfold.)

About Berkshire Hathaway's insurance business, Buffett
wrote:

> The insurance industry operates under the competitive
> sword of substantial overcapacity . . . the industry sells a rela-

tively undifferentiated commodity-type product. Future profitability of the [insurance] industry will be determined by
current competitive characteristics, not past ones. Many managers have been slow to recognize this. It's not only generals
that prefer to fight the last war. Most business and investment
analysis also come from the rear-view mirror.

Puncturing corporate conceits delights Buffett. One of his fa-
vorites is the way CEOs unilaterally contribute stockholders'
money to charities of the company's choice. Berkshire Hathaway each year tells stockholders how much the company will
contribute to charity and asks them to designate a cause of their
choice. In 1981, Buffett told them that the board had decided to
contribute $2 million, or $2 a share. A shareholder with three
hundred shares gives $600, and the charity is advised that al-
though the money comes from the company, the contribution is
made by the stockholder. Noting that 95.8 percent of eligible
shares participated, Buffett commented.

> The "father-knows-best" school of corporate governance
> will be surprised to find that none of our shareholders sent in
> a designation sheet with instructions that the officers of
> Berkshire—in their superior wisdom, of course—make the
> decision on charitable funds applicable to his shares. Nor did
> anyone suggest that his share of our charitable funds be used
> to match contributions made by our corporate directors to
> charities of the directors' choice (a popular, proliferating and
> non-publicized policy at many large corporations).

In 1982, Buffett admitted, "In a characteristically rash move,
we have expanded . . . by 252 square feet (17%)" to give more
room to the six people who work in the "World Headquarters."
Concluded the Omaha executive, "A compact organization lets
all of us spend our time managing the business rather than managing each other."

If all CEOs were like Harman and Buffett, then Rourke
would have little to complain about. But what sets his teeth on
edge are companies that are pages out of the "Ten Telltale
Traits of Bureaucracy." Typically, these are run by accountants,
financiers, and attorneys who have risen from their staff positions to the top of bureaucracy's greasy pole. They entered the
corporate world from Harvard or Wharton or Stanford or Tuck
or Columbia in a staff job, and remained in one all their careers,
so how could they understand how a corporation runs? They are

what Robert B. Reich called "the paper entrepreneurs." Mergers, acquisitions, litigation, tax avoidance, leveraged buyouts, floats, and currency trades are specialties of these paper-hangers. Product quality, employee morale, and customer satisfaction are someone else's problem. And when markets sour in that world, they roll out the handy scapegoats to cover up their wasteful management practices: regulations, labor, imports, the press, unproductive workers, high wages, and that hardy perennial, the "cost-price squeeze."

One would think that the economic afflictions in the past decade of the steel, auto, chemicals, rubber, utilities, and textiles industries would have driven home the need for corporate leadership instead of stewardship. But GE's Jack Welch wonders. In a recent speech, he expressed his concerns: "Today, as business starts to feel better, the questions for each of us mount: Will our offices again fill up with staff? Will we revert to the memos that need to be signed off by ten layers of authority, that make a mockery of entrepreneurship, that make big go bust? Will we forget so quickly our drive to be competitive?"

Because history does indeed repeat itself—and because many companies still seem to operate in the past—it is useful to explore the personal characteristics of those CEOs who have given that good title a bad name. From our interviews and observations, it's clear that three types of antileaders have risen to the top of too many American corporations. They are *the autocrat, the egoist,* and *the isolationist.* All corporate chieftains have some of the characteristics of each group; obviously, any person who rises to the top of a big organization comes equipped with a sense of command and an outsize ego. The types described below, however, err in their excesses.

The autocrat. "Federal judges and CEOs are the two groups with the least checks and balances in this country. They are accountable to no one," observes Francis T. Vincent, a former Securities and Exchange Commission official who was appointed president of Columbia Pictures Industries in the wake of the 1977 scandal when studio chief David Begelman was caught embezzling. Vincent's soft voice and quiet manner masks the strong opinions formed in government, law, and business. Federal judges, he says, have their jobs for life and many of their day-to-day decisions are not appealed. But CEOs have even fewer restraints. Once they are in office, it is almost impossible to eject them; they are beholden only to stockholders and board members—two traditionally ineffectual monitors. Who can effectively challenge a CEO who chooses to run his company as a feudal barony?

Typically, the autocrat sets rigid rules for the rest of the organization and quite different ones for himself. "They don't want to be subject to the same restraints that true bureaucracy entails," says sociologist Joe Bensman. "They want to be free from rules, which they insist others follow."

The autocrat leads from brute strength. "Jungle fighter" and "empire builder" are macho phrases used by author Michael Maccoby to describe tough, demanding managers. But a fine line separates the hard-driver from the autocrat. And while nobody expects the CEO to be a pussycat, the driven-leader-turned-tyrant can produce disastrous waste. He can instill such fear of failure in his managers that right and wrong become blurred as the means come to be justified by the ends—even palpably illegal means. As John Coffee, Jr., observes, "It seems more than coincidental" that the chief executive officers of three corporations caught paying bribes to foreign officials in the 1970s (Northrop, United Brands, and Gulf) were "strong-willed imperious men who totally dominated and seldom confided in or relied on their boards of directors." Then there's the example of Dr. Armand Hammer, who for decades ran Occidental as if he personally owned it. The M.D.-turned-businessman drove his executives with his philosophy of success at any cost. As a result, the company and Hammer repeatedly were sued by the SEC for accounting gimmickery, among other things. And in 1976, Hammer pleaded guilty to ordering his top aides in Washington to make illegal political contributions to Richard Nixon's 1972 reelection campaign.

Like Hammer, most autocrats believe they are irreplaceable and squander the talents of underutilized top managers, to the frustration of their potential successors. For example, Edward G. Uhl of Fairchild Industries often complained about the quality of management, yet some executives who have worked at the Hagerstown, Maryland, headquarters see him as wanting to run the fast-growing military-contracting firm almost single-handedly. In the early 1980s, Fairchild's executive suite acquired a revolving door as the executives turned over regularly under the autocratic CEO. The problem is trust, explains John Dealy, a onetime heir apparent who left Fairchild after learning he wasn't going to succeed Uhl after all. "Too much direction is given. At some point you have to let some of the players on the team hit the ball."

Similarly, corporate chieftains who practice nepotism also frustrate ambitious and talented managers by throwing family members into their paths. In a private company, family management is understandable. But in too many public companies, top executives feel free to waste corporate resources by doing business with children, brothers, sisters, and uncles. An indication of how widespread such relationships are came in 1982, when the Securities and Exchange Commission sought to broaden its disclosure rules on nepotism. The SEC scaled back its proposals after getting a torrent of protesting letters from such blue-chip companies as BankAmerica Corporation, Phillips Petroleum, Du Pont, and Texas Instruments.

But most top executives who practice nepotism don't like to discuss it, let alone read about it. In 1979, William Tavoulareas, then president of Mobil Corporation, brought suit against *The Washington Post* for libel for reporting that his son was "set up" in a shipping business which then obtained many of its contacts from Mobil. And in 1984, Mobil boycotted reporters from *The Wall Street Journal* after the newspaper described how Mobil planned to build an office tower in Chicago using a real estate firm that employed the son-in-law of Mobil's chairman, Rawleigh Warner, Jr. Victor Posner, the Miami financier and corporate raider, puts his relatives in top jobs of companies he takes over. When Sharon Steel Corporation, a company he controls, acquired 43 percent of Evans Products Company in 1984, his son Steven was made a vice-president, his brother, Bernard, a director, and his daughter, twenty-one-year-old Tracy, a recent college graduate, was appointed to the newly created post of vice-president, assistant secretary, and assistant treasurer. The next year, Evans Products had to declare bankruptcy. Then there are the Kays of Kaypro Computer Corporation, whose sales soared between 1982 and 1984. Even with success and growth, founder Andrew F. Kay and his two sons treat the company like a mom-and-pop operation, which some analysts worry will be its undoing.

Probably the most celebrated corporate autocrat of his time was the slight, humorless accountant who presided over International Telephone and Telegraph for two decades, Harold Geneen. Geneen was admired and imitated as a management genius for acquiring more than 275 companies and converting what was an overseas telecommunications company into a multinational conglomerate, covering the earth with everything from Sheraton hotels and Avis rental cars to Hostess Twinkies and Scotts grass seed. But inside ITT, many executives had a far less flattering view of the man and his methods.

Here is the untold story of a palace revolt at ITT in which Geneen's closest lieutenant became a government informant in an abortive attempt to topple the CEO. Found in documents from the special prosecutor's office now gathering dust at the National Archives in Washington and fleshed out in interviews, the story grows out of ITT's unrelenting pressure on the Nixon administration for approval of its merger with the asset-rich Hartford Fire Insurance Company, then the biggest merger in history. The Hartford was to be the crowning deal of Geneen's extraordinary acquisitive career.

Geneen got the idea of acquiring the Hartford with its rich securities portfolio from Charles ("Chick") T. Ireland, Jr., a brilliant executive who Geneen in 1967 had lured away from the presidency of Allegheny Corporation by promising him the presidency of ITT. Ireland became a senior vice-president charged with delivering the Hartford. Apply "inexorable pressure," ordered Geneen, and for a while Ireland did what he was told. Then Ireland changed. "Chick found the memo writing demeaning, and he grew tired of being humiliated by Geneen at meetings," recalls a source who was close to Ireland and who requested anonymity. Nor was he alone in his frustration. On weekends, says this source, Ireland and other executives gathered at dinner parties and talked bitterly about Geneen, blaming "Attila the Hun" for their drinking, broken homes, and bleeding ulcers. Ireland also realized that Geneen wasn't going to deliver on his promise, that he wanted to keep all the titles to himself: president, chairman, *and* chief executive officer.

So Ireland began hatching his "conspiracy." At night in his rambling suburban home in Chappaqua, New York, he carefully listed his grievances on sheets of paper, signing them with his code name, "XYZ," then neatly filing them in a folder marked simply "X."

On a spring night in 1971, Ireland hatched his plot with a phone call to Joseph Borkin, a Washington antitrust attorney whom Ireland knew from Allegheny. Borkin was an extraordinary man—a highly regarded attorney, an art collector, and a best-selling author who wrote on subjects ranging from Nazi arms manufacturers to corrupt judges. But most important to Ireland at this moment, Borkin was well connected at the Justice Department. Borkin agreed to help Ireland "establish an untraceable chain to communicate information from inside ITT to the antitrust division lawyers" who were probing the ITT-Hartford merger. The link established, Ireland fed Justice attorneys a series of questions for them to ask Geneen in an upcoming interview in the ITT-Hartford antitrust investigation. The queries were crafted by Ireland to force Geneen either to admit to questionable legal tactics in arranging the merger or to perjure himself. But to the dismay of Borkin and Ireland, Geneen or his attorney apparently so cowed the Justice attorney that he never asked the questions. Ireland continued to feed information to Justice, but the department was determined to approve the troublesome merger, which it eventually did after gaining certain concessions from ITT.

In September 1971, Ireland finally escaped his personal hell at ITT and became president of CBS; nine months later he was dead of a heart attack. Borkin also died, in July 1979, as he was preparing to write a book about ITT.

As for Geneen, after masterminding his succession in 1976, he retired to become a venture capitalist and board member in a number of corporations. Time apparently altered his perspective or dulled his memory, for in 1984 Geneen published *Managing,* in which he impeached many of his own autocratic tactics. For example, he complained that 95 percent of the corporate boards "are not fully doing what they are legally, morally and ethically supposed to do. They are not doing their jobs. And they couldn't, even if they wanted to." Geneen forgets that as CEO of ITT, he was a notorious loner whose board, like his executives, did his bidding. And when he proudly recalls buying companies "after only a 10- or 20-minute inspection of their books, without ever seeing the company itself," he forgets that in recent years ITT, like other conglomerates, has been selling off just such wasteful and poorly planned acquisitions. In early 1985, Geneen's successor announced he would unload a staggering $1.7 billion in assets accumulated by Geneen.

The egoist. A pervasive conceit among many American managers says, I can run anything. For them, products simply are objects to be sold; only numbers count. That's the style of supreme egoist, Jimmy Ling, who once controlled the LTV conglomerate made up of an aerospace company, a meat packer, an airline, and a steel company. He boasted that he knew nothing about any of the companies, and once for a hearing before the House Ways and Means Committee, he displayed a chart that contained the question, "How many people in LTV know the steel business?" Then he proudly flashed the answer: a big red zero.

Typically, egoists don't stick around to take blame for their own wasteful actions; employees, taxpayers, stockholders, and banks are left to suffer the consequences. On Long Island, for example, electrical users and taxpayers had to pay for the egoistic decision by top management of the Long Island Lighting Company (LILCO) to construct a huge, unnecessary nuclear power plant. Meanwhile, the top executives of LILCO responsible for the mess had long since gone into a comfortable retirement.

Usually there is only room for one big ego in the executive suite; William Agee and his egoistical equal, Edward L. Hennesy, Jr., CEO of Allied Corporation, didn't last long under the same roof when Bendix was taken over by Allied in 1982 after Bendix's abortive bid for Martin Marietta. Another example of a clash of corporate egos occurred in 1983 when Thomas Vanderslice, president of GTE Corporation, was forced out by the man whom he was supposed to succeed, chief executive Thomas Brophy. The lesson in this case was, in a bureaucracy, all credit goes to the top.

Brophy, a conservative lawyer and card-carrying member of the Business Roundtable, had presided over the utility since becoming its chairman in 1976. In 1979, Brophy hired Vanderslice, a star at General Electric who had been passed over for president, to challenge GTE's massive bureaucracy. From all reports, Vanderslice did a first-class job. Analyst Edward Greenberg of the brokerage house Sanford C. Bernstein and Company credited Vanderslice with redeploying GTE's assets and energizing the staff while "moving what was a fat, lazy utility into areas of high growth."

But like Brophy, Vanderslice boasted a big ego; he insisted, for instance, that he be called Doctor in deference to his Ph.D. in chemistry and physics. But compared to Brophy's image as senior overseer of GTE, Vanderslice came on as a corporate populist, abolishing silly executive perks like the special dining room. Saying he was "an agent of change" in an interview before he was fired, Vanderslice added, "I honestly believe in all humility that the board decided that they needed someone in there to change the company." Perhaps, but he still had to contend with Brophy, who refused to reward Vanderslice by sharing the additional authority that the ambitious subordinate yearned for. That forced a showdown, ending in Vanderslice's exit.

The cost to a company of a CEO with runaway ambition can be seen by studying the case of Toro Company, the Minneapolis snowthrower manufacturer. In the 1970s, Toro was riding a growth curve. Its charismatic CEO, David McLaughlin, became a darling of Wall Street as Toro's sales from 1974 through 1979 grew, on average, 27 percent annually and earnings per share, 45 percent. McLaughlin dreamed aloud about Toro becoming a billion-dollar company, and even though sales by 1979 had reached only $360 million, he began acting like it had happened: Toro commissioned a new headquarters in the poshest section of town, acquired a corporate jet and increased white-collar employees by 15 percent. Expenses rose from 23 percent of sales in 1978 to 26 percent in 1980. Looking back, one Minneapolis securities analyst describes Toro as "confusing the strength of one's own efforts with the strength of the markets. In the top of a bull market, everyone thinks they're geniuses."

Spurred on by his king-size dreams, McLaughlin pressed his executives to achieve the 20-percent annual growth that his admirers on Wall Street expected. "He had a fascination with size and success and the big time. It kind of consumed him," observed one Toro board member. Indeed, McLaughlin's ambition blinded him to everything—including the fickleness of the weather.

In 1980, Toro built $160-million worth of snowthrowers, but no snow fell. Dealers sold less than half of the machines. In 1981, Toro turned out another $100-million worth of throwers, but the snow again failed to fall. That year, dealers sold only $25-million worth. McLaughlin's fast-growth policy also called for introduction of a line of new products, such as garden supplies. Staffed by managers with scant manufacturing experience, the new division sidestepped Toro's quality control system in the headlong rush to production. The result: a black eye to Toro's quality image, as new garden hoses clogged, cultivators shocked users, and batteries in trimmers wore out prematurely.

In 1981, McLaughlin departed Toro to become president of Dartmouth College, leaving his successor to pick up the pieces.

A postmortem of the McLaughlin period at Toro, written by journalist Linda McDonnell, sums up the threat to any company that gets an egoist at its helm. Why, she asked, didn't anyone understand the risks in McLaughlin's plan for explosive growth that seem so obvious in retrospect? "The answer involves some fundamental criticisms leveled at American managers in recent years: the way chief executives can be driven by their own ambition and fail to listen to subordinates and customers and then become captives of those predictions . . . the way American firms often embrace opportunities for rapid growth without realizing the risks."

The isolationist. "CEOs have the same problem that Richard Nixon had," observed Lewis Young during an interview at *Business Week*'s editorial offices before he resigned in 1984 to become president of John Diebold and Associates, consultants. "They let themselves get isolated and listen only to the people inside. It's fascinating how many CEOs never see a customer or important business contacts. For example, we had lunch one day with David Lewis when he became CEO of General Dynamics. It looked like the company was going down the tubes, so I asked him who he dealt with at Chase Manhattan, the company's lead bank. 'Oh,' he said, 'I met with a regional vice-president once.' I asked if he had ever met Butcher [Willard C. Butcher, chairman of Chase], and he said he saw him at a party once. 'No,' he said, 'I never met David Rockefeller.'"

GenCorp, the $2.2 billion Akron conglomerate that produces everything from Penn tennis balls and MX missile parts to RKO General movies and disposable diaper linings, is a company that has suffered from being run by an isolationist CEO, M. Gerald O'Neil. For decades, while GenCorp grew by acquisitions, O'Neil, who is in his mid-sixties, spent more time on outside interests than in running the huge company. One pet project, for example, was building Sharon Country Club, a male-only preserve he helped finance because he got tired of playing golf behind women at other Akron clubs. In fact, some executives have complained that only those among them who played golf got to discuss business with the CEO, who spent lots of time on the links. By 1984, the price of such neglect included a broad array of litigation: a $44-million court-ordered payment for breach of contract in Algeria, a brace of suits in California and Michigan over toxic waste dumping, and Federal Communications Commission proceedings challenging the licenses of all but one of the company's fifteen broadcast stations because of a 1977 consent decree involving alleged illegal political payments.

The bigger the company, the more susceptible to the evils of isolation is the CEO. "In a huge corporation, the CEO runs things by reading reports," says sociologist Bensman. "But how is he to know whether reports are accurate or merely rosy presentations to please him created by ambitious middle managers?" Economist Kenneth Boulding goes one step further: "There is a great deal of evidence that almost all organizational structures tend to produce false images in the decision-maker, and that the larger and more authoritarian the organization, the better the chance that its top decision-makers will be operating in purely imaginary worlds. This perhaps is the most fundamental reason for supposing that there are ultimately diminishing returns to scale."

Autocracy, egoism, and isolation generate avoidable waste— excessive staffs, excessive perks, lack of vision for the future, lack of respect for subordinates. "Like stewards of a rich man, they are apt to consider attention to small matters as not for their master's honour, and very easily give themselves a dispensation from having it," wrote Adam Smith about the arrogance that besets the manager of other people's assets. This failing leads inevitably to the doorstep of the board of directors. They formalistically chose the CEO; can they not oversee his performance and direct him to change his ways for the good of the corporation and its stockholders?

The Board of Directors
In most of the fifty states, the laws of incorporation provide that the affairs of a publicly owned firm shall be "managed" by the board of directors or "managed under the direction of" the board. States have no easy way of enforcing such laws on billion-dollar multinational corporations far larger than they, but just their existence on the books disturbs many corporations. Consequently, many big firms gravitate to tiny Delaware—more than half of the New York Stock Exchange members are incorporated there—because Delaware's laws reinforce the power of CEOs by limiting the authority of board members and the rights of aggrieved stockholders. So while by law they are supposed to police unproductive or dishonest actions by top management, in fact, board members too often become silent accomplices to wasteful practices by shucking their statutory responsibility.

In many—if not most—public corporations, the CEO picks the members of the board of directors who are to "oversee" him. Commentators have long seized on this irony. "Directors do not direct," asserted the late Supreme Court Justice William O. Douglas in the 1930s. Harvard professor of business administration, Myles L. Mace, in his 1971 study, *Directors: Myth and Reality,* concluded that "boards of directors in most companies do not do an effective job in evaluating, appraising and measuring the company president until the financial and other results are so dismal that some remedial action is forced upon the board." A decade later, Edward S. Herman in his seminal study, *Corporate Control, Corporate Power,* found that the CEO typically controls "his" board by dictating who will serve on it. "Gaining directorships through the processes of corporate democracy, as now constituted, is close to impossible."

Often, young companies with first generation, entrepreneurial managements have a heavy percentage of financial backers and consultants on their boards. That's understandable, because backers want both to closely watch their investment and to lend support to the young management. What is troubling is when such inside boards become institutionalized in the second generation and beyond.

Why does this matter? Because if a CEO, for reasons of isolation or ego, makes an uninformed or illegal decision or even "bets the company" on a high-risk product, who other than a watchful board can restrain him?

John Cross, the sixty-seven-year-old chairman of Elphinstone Inc., of Baltimore, credits the advice of four outside directors with causing him to phase out of a still-profitable yet dying part of his business—selling highway construction material. "Without the board asking why, we probably wouldn't have reached that decision because we had been in the business for so long." So impressed is Cross with his outside directors that they can outvote management members on the board. Isaac Fogel, chief executive of Classic Corporation in Jessup, Maryland, found that the three outside executives on his board helped him from making "classic mistakes" such as overexpanding his business. "The decisions seemed correct based on my limited knowledge, but their broader experience made me realize otherwise."

Another example of a vigilant board occurred back when foreign payoffs were flourishing in 1976. Eberhard Faber, who headed the famous pencil company, found out that officials of a foreign company, with which he planned to make his company a partner in a joint venture, were routinely making payoffs to government officials in their country. Faber shrugged this off, concluding it was none of his business because "it is a common and accepted practice there." But his board disagreed, arguing that the Eberhard Faber Company would itself be unethical by virtue of owning stock in an unethical company. Faber and the board, which included his own mother, fought bitterly over the issue, and in the end he lost. Concluded Faber: "I have to admit, though, that while I think they made the wrong decision in this case, I'm kind of proud of these directors of mine for their concern about avoiding unethical practices. It couldn't have been any more fun for them to fight me on the issue than it was for me to fight them. And when even your mother votes against you, you know you have an independent board."

But boards ordinarily don't challenge a CEO for several reasons. Most directors are underpaid and meet only once a month, if that. Dependent on management for information—and often getting too much or too little—how can board members be expected to raise intelligent questions, whether about the CEO's paycheck or an obscure balance sheet entry? If an executive whose salary is $200,000 to $500,000 a year goes on a board and is paid $10,000 to $20,000, will he give his best effort? On the other hand, are $20,000-a-year watchdogs, who meet six times a year or less, capable of overseeing a multibillion-dollar corporation? As one board member commented to Mace, "I don't have time to get the facts, and I prefer not to look stupid. Silence is a marvelous cover." William Niskanen, who was chief economist at Ford before joining the Council of Economic Advisers, observed, "I never in five years heard any probing questions asked or answered" at Ford's board of directors meetings.

The board's effectiveness is also limited both by the size of the corporation and of the board itself. Experts agree that boards bigger than fifteen become bureaucratic and ineffective, and being on the board of a conglomerate is like overseeing several companies simultaneously. Also, in many companies, decisions are made without consultation with the board; management simply goes to the board for affirmation. The CEO proposes and the board disposes. In those companies, members are treated as graybeards, expected to speak sagely—but only when spoken to.

Perhaps the most enduring trait of many corporate boards is their lack of independence. In the worst cases, the majority of the board is linked financially to the parent corporation, as an employee, former employee, supplier, banker, consultant, attorney, or customer. Such conflicts of interest can lead to a blatant waste of corporate assets. An attorney retained by a company who also serves on the board, for instance, cannot easily make independent judgments as a board member over the CEO who controls his legal business. Employees and former employees are almost totally dependent on the CEO; putting them on the board is tantamount to converting an ostensibly independent body into a corporate executive committee. As for bankers, Columbia Business School dean Courtney Brown, in his book, *Putting the Corporate Board to Work,* notes, "Too often the company's business is limited to the bank or investment house represented on its board."

A former CEO of a *Fortune* 500 company who shared his experiences with us on the basis that his name would not be used, understands this problem firsthand. Needing capital, he shopped for a good rate in the capital markets and easily found a firm willing to offer a discount to get the business. Sitting on the CEO's board was the firm's normal investment banker, however, who grew angry when told that his firm had to compete for the business. Claiming he'd lose his job if he lost the company's business, the banker even threatened to become a hostile board member. The outcome of this corporate blackmail was that the investment banker kept the business, and still has it now a decade later.

Powerful companies are also tied together in more subtle ways through boardroom interlocks. Direct interlocks occur when two companies have a common director and thus are readily able to communicate; indirect interlocks are when two companies each has a director on a third. A long history of federal probes disclosing the inefficiencies and irregularities of interlocks began in 1913 with the Pujo committee investigation of J. P. Morgan and the "money trust," leading to passage of the Clayton Antitrust Act. "The practice of interlocking directorates is the root of many evils," wrote Justice Louis D. Brandeis, citing "suppression of competition . . . violation of the law that one man can't serve two masters . . . [and] inefficiency for it removes incentives and destroys soundness of judgement." Section 8 of the Clayton Act does prohibit a person from being a director of two or more competing companies, but vertical linkages are not discouraged (between, say, a manufacturer and a supplier), and indirect interlocks (two competitors on the board of a third company) are not specifically addressed. Moreover, there's no penalty under the act if interlocks are dissolved after a warning.

In January 1978, then Securities and Exchange Commission chairman Harold M. Williams called for a radical change in the makeup of the board of directors. He said that the board of directors should be purged of all members of management except the CEO—and, "ideally," the CEO should not also be chairman of the board. Also banned from Williams's dream board were a corporation's outside counsel, suppliers, accountants, bankers, retired officers of the company, and anyone else who is dependent on the corporation.

Williams wasn't the first to urge that boards be wholly "independent" of management's sway, but his important position as SEC chairman gave his words special significance. His recommendations certainly drew the attention of interested groups, such as lawyers, bankers, and chief executives, almost all of whom vigorously disagreed. Today, himself a CEO of the $2.2 billion J. Paul Getty Trust, Williams says, "I still feel the same way." At the trust's Century City offices overlooking Beverly Hills and Bel Air, the executive observes, "The key to what I was talking about is how one really makes a board function effectively. There's not any specific prescription; it's a matter of sociology. A board can still fall on its ass if people are selected who are content to fall asleep. But the probability of that happening is substantially reduced."

Williams's proposal triggered a national debate over how a board should be composed: The variations included insiders (management board members) versus outsiders (nonmanagement)—and outsiders versus independents (no ties to the corporation). For the CEO, a friendly board (with interlocks to bankers and suppliers, and sprinkled with corporate insiders) reduces naysaying, angst and uncertainty. But how can such board ever fulfill its legal obligation to stockholders? If board members are lapdogs and sleeping dogs rather than watchdogs, they can't be expected to be alert to managerial waste. It is perhaps understandable that chief executives would want boards to leave them basically alone. Many of us may also wish there were no speed limits or stop signs when we're in a rush, but should we each be allowed to unilaterally abolish traffic rules?

"Williams was right," says Henry Gunders, the former co-chairman of Price Waterhouse. "If you're going to be working for old Charlie for the rest of your life—and you talk to him every day anyway—and you have a [board] meeting, what are you going to tell him? But if you've had lots of experience elsewhere, and you do independent research, you [can] say, 'Charlie, I don't like what's happening in our inventory area. We don't seem to run our inventory; why is that, Charlie?'"

The history of RCA illustrates the costs and consequences of an unassertive board of directors. RCA's troubles began with an autocratic CEO—"General" David Sarnoff, a true genius but one who treated most employees as gofers and board members as window dressing. His boards typically were dominated by insiders, and the half dozen outsiders had close ties to Sarnoff. So it wasn't surprising that when Sarnoff retired in 1970 after forty-five years of building RCA into a billion-dollar company, the board members stood by while the General passed the publicly owned company to his son, Robert. It was nepotism at its wasteful worst.

No sooner did he succeed his father than Robert caught conglomerate fever. He acquired Random House, Banquet Foods and Oriel Foods, Hertz, Coronet furniture and carpets, among others. In a clear example of a board member's doing business with the company he is supposed to oversee, director André Meyer of Lazard Frères and Company, powerful investment banker, did a lot of business with young Sarnoff. Meyer, for example, actually sold Random House, Banquet, and Hertz to RCA, giving his firm a large commission. Meyer even tried to persuade Sarnoff to sell about 20 percent of RCA to his friend the shah of Iran, but other board members finally drew the line on that. But Meyer wasn't the only board member involved in such a conflict. In 1983, Lehman Brothers Kuhn Loeb, whose chairman, Peter Peterson, was on the board, collected $200,000 for helping RCA sell Gibson greeting cards, having already arranged the sale of Banquet Foods and parts of CIT Financial Corporation.

Board members watched—and in the case of the investment bankers, profited—as Sarnoff squandered RCA's consumer electronics birthright. Instead of challenging the Japanese imports, RCA reaped quick gains by licensing technology to Japan. In 1970, RCA stock was viewed by Wall Street as "blue chip" and Sony as "speculative," but a decade later Merrill Lynch ranked Sony as "blue chip" and RCA "speculative." The company spent vast sums in a fruitless challenge to IBM's computer dominance. In 1971, RCA's debt—already swollen from acquisitions—rose further when it ended its foolhardy challenge to IBM by taking a pretax $490-million write-off. While in the mid-1970s, the board included a couple of impressive outsiders, Lawrence Fouraker, then dean of Harvard Business School, and ARCO president Thornton Bradshaw among them, it nevertheless seemed doomed to live in the late General's powerful shadow. Finally, in 1976, six years after he succeeded his father, Robert Sarnoff was forced to resign by the board, which replaced him with an apparently level-headed executive whom it hoped would return RCA to normalcy, Anthony Conrad. But within months, Conrad resigned after becoming the target of a federal tax fraud investigation.

The Conrad fiasco panicked the board, according to one insider, and in a midnight meeting they hurriedly tapped Edgar Griffiths, an accountant and longtime RCA employee whom nobody—except the board—had ever previously considered CEO timber. Griffiths, however, fit all three descriptions presented earlier of what is wrong with many CEOs: An isolated and autocratic egoist, he was a loner who ran the company from the printouts he pored over during his long daily commute between Manhattan's Rockefeller Center and Philadelphia, where he insisted on living. Griffiths was a numbers juggler who hyped the bottom line by selling off Sarnoff's acquisitions, then acted as if he had created the profits by management savvy. But aside from the resurrection of the famous dog Nipper as the corporate symbol, about the only significant development under Griffiths—indeed the only major new consumer product development by RCA since television—was the videodisk player. Unfortunately, it turned out to be an inflexible alternative to the VCR since it didn't permit the recording of television programs. By 1984, after losing more than $105 million on the videodisk player over several successive years, RCA took a $175 million pretax write-off on the product.

The hot-tempered Griffiths bullied the board of directors, according to one director, into spending millions for executives, many of whom he subsequently fired with costly severance arrangements. For RCA's subsidiary, NBC, he hired Fred Silverman, for example, whose genius at producing lowbrow programs made fortunes for ABC. But by the time Silverman was fired in 1981 after six years, NBC's ratings had gone through the floor and costs through the roof. One example of the Silverman touch: He ordered up scripts, hired producers, and scheduled a show called *Pink Lady and Jeff*, a series about two Japanese singers, before learning that neither of its stars could speak English.

In January 1981, with earnings per share off 10.6 percent, just pennies above the $3.11 reported in 1977, Griffiths's first year as CEO, the board finally fired him. But nobody leaves RCA without being richly compensated, and Griffiths walked away with a "consulting" contract worth $1.5 million.

After Robert Sarnoff, Conrad, and Griffiths, the board this time took pains to find the right person for the job. It paid fellow board member Ronald Smiley, the retired CEO of Macy's, a handsome fee of $250,000 to negotiate Griffiths's retirement deal and to search the globe to find a CEO who could rescue RCA from its disastrous past. And for his regal fee, Smiley chose the person everyone figured he would—fellow board member Thornton F. Bradshaw, who resigned as president of ARCO to take a job paying him a minimum of $938,500 annually for five years. Ironically, Bradshaw, a respected executive and former Harvard Business School professor who had been on the RCA board since 1974, would have been chosen originally over Griffiths, according to an insider; but on that September night in 1976 when the nervous directors hastily tapped Griffiths, Bradshaw was on a Greek island with his new wife and was unreachable. The board felt it couldn't wait, a rash and costly mistake as it turned out.

Pressure from the SEC, consumer groups, shareholders, and congressional critics, combined with the publicity over derelict boards like RCA, has significantly improved the performance and structure of the corporate board. Also, a 1985 decision of the influential Delaware Supreme Court, which concluded that the board of the Trans Union Corporation had hurriedly and negligently approved of a sell-out and hence was liable for damages to shareholders, has the potential, unless reversed, of reducing directorial genuflection to management.

"We are in that midst of a board revolution that will have as profound and positive an impact on business as did the Industrial Revolution and computerization," exclaims Lester Korn.

Cynics might say that Korn has a stake in such a revolution; his Korn/Ferry International, the world's biggest executive search firm, has prospered from encouraging restiveness among board members and executives. But between sips of coffee from a porcelain cup in his elegantly furnished Los Angeles office, Korn rolls out statistics to show that there has been a change, if not a "revolution," in the boardroom.

Korn/Ferry's 1983 annual survey of the one thousand largest corporations shows a sharp reduction in the number of companies with such management-dependent directors as outside counsels (52 percent in 1973 to 28 percent) and bankers (commercial from 55 percent to 34 percent; investment, 37 percent to 24 percent). At the same time, the boardroom mix broadened with increases in the number of companies among the one thousand that have at least one board member who is an academician (35 percent to 50 percent), ethnic minority (9 percent to 23 percent), and women (11 percent to 41 percent).

Another advance was the inclusion in 1980 of Douglas Fraser, then president of the United Auto Workers, on the Chrysler board of directors. Invited on because of the financial sacrifices made by labor in the automaker's struggle for survival, Fraser's performance quickly won high praise from other board members. "He's terrific on the board," Gerald Greenwald, vice-chairman of Chrysler, said enthusiastically. "He's been in the car business for almost forty years and he knows more about it than most people. And having him helps break down the adversarial relationship between management and labor." (See Chapter 2 for a longer discussion of labor representation on boards.)

The Shareholders

Few stand to lose more from inefficient and wasteful corpocracy than the owners of the corporation—the stockholders. Yet in big corporations, they are the most benign of bosses. Stockholders, by law, elect board members who are their representatives to direct the corporations and vote on fundamental corporate actions, such as buying other firms, hiring new accountants, and amending the bylaws. But most individual stockholders don't have the time, ability, or inclination to force change on corporate management—a reality that hasn't stopped managers from claiming they are accountable to their stockholders. And while such claims may apply to small companies with few substantial stockholders, in large companies it's a widely recognized myth—

but a useful one. It permits managers to attribute their power to the democratic process. "It is the system that is worrisome because it engenders illusions of shareholder power while discouraging alternative restraints," asserts Georgetown University law professor Donald Schwartz.

To be sure, beginning with the 1970 challenge to GM by the Project on Corporate Responsibility, public interest groups have tried to use proxies to force management to justify or drop certain kinds of businesses. But given management's control of the proxy machinery, these protest proxy fights never get more than a handful of votes. And big institutional investors such as banks, pension funds, and insurance companies seldom challenge management or explain why they buy one company's stock rather than another's. When opposed to management policies, institutional investors traditionally follow the so-called "Wall Street rule" of selling out their stock rather than trying to throw out management—an effect discussed in Chapter 4 on mergers.

Occasionally, however, these institutions have turned against the management of companies in which they own securities, sending chills through top executives. The reason: Institutions own more than 60 percent of the stock sold on the New York Stock Exchange, and private pension fund assets alone exceed $750 billion and are expected to grow to $3 trillion by 1995. True, there are the challenges by "raiders" like Carl Icahn, the New York investor. But Icahn typically doesn't attempt to force change; his whole approach is to threaten management until, in fear or frustration, they buy him out at a profit.

Portfolio managers, with their incredibly deep pockets, could be a far more potent threat to management. In the early 1980s, a few institutions did impressively flex their muscles. For example:

- In 1981, Fidelity Management and Research Company, owners of a big block of Penn Central Corporation stock, scuttled Penn Central's acquisition of Colt Industries. "It just didn't make any sense from an investment point of view," explained a Fidelity executive.

- Citibank's trust department in 1983 voted against an antitakeover proposal by the management of Superior Oil—even though the corporation is a customer of the bank. Peter Vermilye, Citibank chief investment officer, says that such measures are bad for trust clients and "undemocratic."

- International Paper Company in 1982 needed a two-thirds majority to get an antitakeover provision passed, but fell short with about 57 percent of the vote. Institutions, as major shareholders, were the deciding votes.

- In 1982, Citibank was managing a fund for salaried employees that controlled 23 percent of Bendix stock. These shares became pivotal in the company's takeover battle with Martin Marietta. When Martin Marietta made a tender offer for Bendix, Citibank urged management to permit employees to participate. But Bendix refused, claiming that the trust agreement (which could be amended by Bendix at will) gave management discretion over the funds of its employees. Citibank, ignoring management, tendered all its Bendix shares to Martin Marietta.

  Vermilye, the able manager of Citibank's vast holdings, has diversified the big bank's portfolio away from the "nifty fifty" biggest stocks where most of its funds went until the late 1970s. He is clearly impatient with inept, bureaucratic corporate management. After leading the defeat of the Superior Oil management proposal, Vermilye declared in *The New York Times,* "When a trust department can vote against the bank's depositors and clients, it's cause for celebration." That slight indiscretion drew an angry reaction from a major depositor and a reprimand to Vermilye, according to one bank insider. In fact, Vermilye says, "We're not in the business of overturning managements. But we do assume fiduciary responsibility."

- In 1983, Odyssey Partners attempted to force management to split up Trans World Corporation into five independent units. The dissidents—a group of well-known New York investors— argued that shareholders would benefit because the whole conglomerate was less valuable than the individual parts. The dissidents got 30 percent of the vote—indicating strong institutional backing. But TWC, for its part, was able to put pressure on suppliers, bankers, and other business friends to win support. Boeing and Lockheed alone have combined pension assets of $6 billion handled by thirty-four different management firms, many of which held TWC stock. It's notable that soon after its victory, TWC managers did almost precisely what Odyssey had proposed—but they did it their way.

While institutional shareholders have some leverage—even if it is rarely applied—individual shareholders in large corporations do not. Most, in fact, are interested only in investing, not in governance. And those who are and who raise their concerns at annual meetings are often lampooned as loudmouths—sometimes for good reason. Is it any wonder that the annual meeting now is generally seen as a management indulgence? The management view of annual meetings was once captured in a classic *New Yorker* cartoon, which showed an irate stockholder screaming into a microphone while up on the stage the chief executive whispers to another executive, "This is the part of capitalism I hate."

Annual meetings may be generally ineffective, but like democracy, the alternative is even worse. Moreover, most corporations are relatively small, with a modest number of stockholders who are better able to make their voices heard, which is another reason why small to mid-size companies are better able to control waste and inefficiency. Even in the biggest companies, a modest vote on a shareholder initiative may not change corporate policy, but it often affects it. As professor Donald Schwartz notes, "Often management has chosen 'voluntarily' to do that which only five percent of the shareholders voted for, illustrating the political potential of opening the decision-making process to a larger forum."

But like virtually everything else in the corporate governance process, the impact of stockholders depends on the willingness of one man, the CEO, to react. The corporation is a sensitive mechanism that operates most efficiently when all its parts are in balance—when the corpocracy is headed by a strong, thoughtful leader whose actions are supported and reviewed by an independent board and who shows a healthy respect for the rights of the owners of the business.

Profiles and Paradigms: How to Trim Corporate Waste-Lines

Considering all the telltale traits previously discussed, it should not be surprising that America's prolonged productivity swoon has paralleled the growth of the corporate bureaucracy. Corpocracy has been a contributing cause, inefficiency and waste the result.

When a company does become bureaucratic, what can a concerned management do about it? Richard Hackman, the Yale professor of organizational behavior, says there are two opportune periods when corporate bureaucracy can be most effectively attacked: "One, when you are in a start-up or rapid growth situation. And two, when you are in a crisis, when your world is crumbling around you."

The remainder of this chapter deals with several diverse examples of companies and CEOs that have changed, challenged, and reformed their corpocracies. By trimming their bureaucratic waste-lines to get in shape for the competitive 1980s and 1990s, these companies have proved that the growth of corpocracy is not irreversible—and provide models for emulation.

Plane Sense at People Express

"I feel they're on the leading edge of a wave that is going to change the way we run companies," exclaims Richard Hackman about People Express, the innovative airline that grew out of the 1978 deregulation of the airline industry. Although he is a consultant to the airline, Hackman's proclaimed management revolution has nothing to do with People's cut-rate fares. Instead, Hackman talks about People's militantly antibureaucratic attitude, a philosophical keystone of the airline since its incorporation in 1980.

People was the creation of Donald C. Burr, a Harvard Business School graduate (1965) whose love for planes goes back to his college days at Stanford University when he got his pilot's license. He started out on Wall Street as a venture capitalist investing in airlines, eventually joining troubled Texas International Airline as chairman of the executive committee. By 1979, Texas International was flying high with Burr as its president, but six months later the restless executive quit to start People Express; other Texas International executives followed the charismatic Burr, then thirty-nine years old. His reason for launching the venture: "I guess the predominant reason that I cared about starting a new company was to try and develop a better way for people to work together. It's where the name of People Express came from. It drives everything else we do."

The air carrier became an overnight success by offering no-frills, low-cost travel. In 1982, its first full year of operation, People made a net profit of $1 million, and by the end of 1984 that figure had climbed to $1.6 million on revenues of $587 million. From the beginning, the airline has kept fares down by flying secondhand planes, by charging customers for food and even luggage storage, by keeping a tight reign on labor costs, and by setting up its headquarters at low-rent and functional Newark International Airport, whose offbeat status changed right along with People's success. By the end of 1984, after only four years in business, People was landing at twenty-nine domestic airports (plus London) and it had acquired sixty-four planes. During 1984, 70 percent of the seats on all its flights were filled, compared with an average of 56 percent for the eleven major carriers.

The passengers flying People are not the expense-account travelers that are the staple of most airlines. Rather, it's a bargain-hunting crowd that jams Newark terminal on most days: students lugging knapsacks, blue-collar families, pensioners, and people with small businesses and modest travel budgets. They are the kinds of travelers who used to go by bus or rail, but People has undercut trains, buses, and even private cars on many routes. An advertisement for People's Newark–Rochester $29 fare exclaims, "The cost of driving to Rochester is $69.70. We didn't come up with that figure, the federal government did."

Guiding the company are "six precepts" that were set to paper by Burr and his fellow executives back in December 1981. (1) Offer service and a commitment to personal growth in employees. (2) Be the best provider of air transportation. (3) Have the highest quality of management. (4) Be a role model for other airlines and other businesses. (5) Keep everything simple. (6) Maximize profits. "When we discuss new ideas at People," observes Hackman, "executives always ask, 'How does that figure into the precepts?'"

But what makes the airline truly unique is that from the beginning, management has focused on employees as the key to success. Reversing the conventional wisdom, Burr likes to refer to people as hard assets and planes as soft. "The people dimension is the value added to the commodity," he says. "Many investors still don't fully appreciate this point, but high commitment and participation, and maximum flexibility and massive creative productivity are the most important strategies at People Express."

The airline keeps its hierarchy to a minimum, even in the face of soaring employment rolls which grew to about 4,000 by 1984. At the top is Burr, who is president, chairman, and chief executive officer. Under him are a team of 15 managing officers and general managers who oversee both line and staff functions, such as human resources and maintenance, legal affairs and flight operations, planning and finance, and reservations. Reporting to them are some 140 team managers, who oversee the fourth and final layer—custom service managers, flight managers, and maintenance managers. There are no executive assistants, no support staff, no secretaries—not even Burr has one. That work is done by an administration pool. Public relations, advertising, accounting, legal, and other staff jobs that usually expand a corpocracy are not on the People payroll, either. Those services are hired when needed. As Burr puts it, "We're here to run an airline."

People carefully screens job applicants to see if they will fit the company's unorthodox "self-management" approach. Guidelines to self-management state, "Within the context of our precepts and corporate objectives, and with leadership direction but no supervision, individuals and/or teams have the opportunity (and the obligation) to self-manage . . . setting specific, challenging, but realistic objectives . . . monitoring and assessing the quantity/quality/timeliness of one's own performance." Instead of large groups of workers under a supervisor, People divides its workers into self-managing problem-solving teams of three or four persons. Layers of supervisors are thus avoided.

Pilots, who are usually paid far more than other airline personnel and for fewer hours, have had to forgo their cushy workstyles at People. Like everyone else hired by the airline, pilots are "cross-utilized" as needed; that is, they're expected to do more than just fly planes. It's not unusual, for example, to see off-duty pilots working in the accounting department or helping out on PR. Burr calls it a process of continuing education, which gives workers a broader view of the company and the opportunities for advancement.

Sharing in the gains is at the heart of People's human resources program—as the company profits, so do all its workers. Basic pay scales range from some $17,000 for customer service managers to about $56,000 for Burr—a fraction of what CEOs earn in bigger but less profitable airlines. But three profit-sharing incentive plans augment the low pay at People. One plan is paid based on quarterly profits, a second on annual profits, and a third on stock—that is, everybody who works for People is a stockholder. A person starting out at the bottom in customer service is expected to buy one hundred shares. The stock price is discounted and the employee can purchase it through payroll deduction. As a result of this plan, employees have a large stake in the success of the company. In early 1985, the average market value of stock investments by pilots was about $125,000, while the average for all employees was about $40,000.

People Express manages to run counter to just about every one of the telltale traits of corpocracy. But the lingering question is, will the success, and the bigness that has inevitably accompanied it, spoil this important experiment? Nobody can answer that yet, but to Professor Hackman, People Express remains a lesson in how companies should be run. Pointing to the hundreds of books on management that line his comfortable office at Yale, Hackman says he's hard pressed to suggest one that tells as much about how to run a company as does the People Express experience. "We management schools are terrific at teaching technical skills, but how do you provide the vision for people to hook onto, to empower them so they feel, 'I make a difference'?"

Two CEOs

The following are two classic American success stories. One concerns a man from a working-class Irish family in the Bronx, whose father ran a construction crane and mother was a telephone operator; the other, a man who was raised in Brooklyn by Jewish parents of modest means. Both are World War II veterans who went on to acquire an education by force of their own personal drive, and with the help of the GI Bill. Both are populist Democrats who move easily between the two political parties in Washington, fascinated more by the power of politics than any ideology. Both can afford such fascinations: Each is worth more than $25 million.

But this is where the similarity between David Mahoney and Sheldon Weinig ends. For their contrasting styles of management tell a lot about what is right and what is wrong with corporate leadership in America.

David Mahoney's rapid rise from a lowly advertising grunt to chairman of Norton Simon, (NSI), at just forty-six years of age, properly earned the handsome, smooth-talking executive the title of "golden boy." And for many of his close and important friends, such as National Football League Commissioner Pete Rozelle, Congressman Jack Kemp, Henry Kissinger, and former

Urban League head Vernon Jordan, he remains someone special, a businessman who dared speak out about such issues as civil rights and women's rights. "He's one of the most charming persons in this country, in this world," says Bob Woodrum, his former public relations adviser. "There is a tremendous aura around him."

But despite his rise to prominence, Mahoney's corporate performance is regarded as less than magical by many others in the business community and on Wall Street. Many of the executives interviewed for this book, when asked for examples of what's wrong with American managers, pointed to Mahoney—an executive whose skill at self-promotion appears to exceed his managerial competence. A café society figure, he regularly appears in columns and profiles: *People* gushed he's "sooooo urbane"; *Success* fawned over his "star quality." And his decision to become the sole spokesman on TV for one of his companies, Avis (acquired from ITT), was seen on Madison Avenue as more a function of ego than of efficiency.

Mahoney became the undisputed boss of NSI in 1969, when he won a three-man race for the top job arranged by financier and founder Norton Simon, who was retiring to pursue interests in art and politics. "I felt possessed rather than possessing," observed the creator of the conglomerate, which included Hunt-Wesson Foods, Canada Dry, Johnnie Walker, and Max Factor. Simon added, "I was looking for a way out for thirteen years. The bureaucracy had me." If the company was bureaucratic then, Mahoney made it even more so by buying and selling more than two dozen businesses over the next fourteen years.

He had long boasted that he would turn NSI into a marketing powerhouse like Procter and Gamble. But in 1983, when *Fortune* compared the two, the magazine found that while P&G was nearly four times bigger in sales and seven times in profits, it had less than twice the number of employees of NSI (35,000 against 64,500). That is, even compared with P&G's well-known bureaucracy, NSI was suffocating from flab. This helps explain why Norton Simon, Inc.'s return on sales was only 3.5 percent (versus 6.5 percent for P&G) and its return on equity, 14.4 percent (versus 18.7 percent).

Mahoney also promised Wall Street and shareholders a 15 percent annual growth rate. In an effort to accomplish this, he followed a well-worn path of American CEOs: He chose quick, short-term results instead of the slow, steady growth that could be achieved only by producing quality products for carefully cultivated markets. And when various high-paid division chiefs failed to "make the numbers" demanded by Mahoney, he lopped off their heads: Seventy-seven officers, including company presidents, quit or were fired. Each year four or five pictures of executives would disappear from the annual report until finally, in 1981, Mahoney decided to run only a picture of himself. "I burn out people," he said.

But to what end? *Forbes* reported in 1983 that, during the previous five years, NSI ranked only nineteenth of twenty-five diversified food companies in return on equity and twentieth in return on total capital. NSI's earnings between 1974 and 1980 failed to keep pace with inflation.

Finally, not even Mahoney's demonstrated charm could deter stockholders from wondering what had happened to the glittering promises. Mahoney's answer, in his 1982 letter to shareholders, was to blame the government for the 33-percent profit decline: "Stagnation, uncertain governmental fiscal and monetary policies, and high interest rates" were the culprits. Not mentioned, of course, was that Mahoney's own total earnings had soared almost in direct proportion to the conglomerate's swoon. In 1982, his compensation package was $1.85 million, making him among the highest-paid executives in the country.

Something else Mahoney didn't explain to the stockholders was why, for the past three years, he had been causing NSI quietly to repurchase its shares. Indeed, during those three fiscal years ending in 1983, NSI spent $460 million to repurchase stock (with much of the money borrowed) versus only $313 million on capital expenditures for new plants and equipment. In short, Mahoney was acting as if he owned the company, and the NSI board of directors, controlled by insiders, shirked their responsibility to stockholders by not demanding a public explanation from the CEO. Not incidentally, Mahoney personally had accumulated 3.3 percent of the shares outstanding through a variety of stock option awards presented him by his board.

His motive became clear, in June 1983, when the sixty-year-old executive announced that he and a group of associates wanted to buy the company for $29 a share. Outraged stockholders, calling the price an insult, filed suit. Mahoney quickly abandoned his scheme, and began entertaining outside bids. In a meeting with one bidder, Mahoney listened impassively to a thorough explanation of the package, and then asked, "What's in it for me?" When he persisted in asking the astonished bidder what *he* personally would make if the offer were accepted, the bidder walked out. That July, Esmark acquired NSI for $35.50 a share. What was in it for Mahoney was a $12-million settlement on his employment in addition to $23.5 million from selling stock and options.

No one should be surprised at his success in bending the bureaucracy to his advantage, because Mahoney himself predicted it back in 1972. When the restless executive was asked by *Forbes* how long he planned to remain at Norton Simon, Inc., he replied, "Eight to ten years, I think. By then I'll either have made my pile or flopped." In the end, he did both.

His name may not be familiar, but that's not Sheldon Weinig's fault. In his outspoken way, fifty-seven-year-old Weinig strives hard to spread his ideas, expressing them graphically in words more suited to a loading dock than a boardroom. He speaks passionately about the future of American business, and sees himself popularizing his philosophy as secretary of commerce or even ambassador to Japan.

In 1957, Weinig was teaching metallurgy at New York University when he concluded that production of high-purity metals was an industry of the future. He founded Materials Research Corporation upstairs from a yo-yo manufacturer, and with government funding came up with some extraordinary metals, including the kind eventually used in Gillette Platinum Plus blades. Over the years, the Orangeburg, New York, high-tech company has gained worldwide recognition as a leading designer and manufacturer of ceramics and of thin film coating and etching systems used for integrated circuits. MRC supplies the semiconductor industries in Europe as well as the United States, and in 1983 became the first foreign-owned company to obtain a direct loan from the Japan Development Bank. MRC used the yen to build a plant there.

Building a company from scratch and sustaining its growth has made Weinig personally prosperous and secure. He has a 13-percent interest in his successful mid-size company (1984 sales were $97 million; earnings, about $4 million) which pays him as its chairman and chief executive $250,000 annually (including bonuses). But with prosperity, Sheldon Weinig, the industrialist, has reverted to Dr. Weinig, the professor. He worries about the troubled state of American free enterprise in the United States and compares it to that in Japan, where he has shuttled to and from for some twenty years. "Nothing is stopping them," he says of the Japanese. "In Japan, there is no social contribution above making business work. We won't win if we're fundamentally unwilling to work at it." Putting his thoughts into action, Weinig is betting his company and his personal fortune that he can change things by challenging old rules about employee-employer relations.

His first gamble came in 1981 when he formalized a no-layoff policy at MRC. A few giant companies, like Digital Equipment Corporation and Hewlett-Packard, have similar policies, but they are not formalized. "MRC will not lay off an employee who is a contributor to MRC's goals," Weinig declared to the company's one thousand employees. This policy, as Weinig views it, is not some offbeat charitable act, but a long-term investment in building employee morale to raise productivity. "Whether you hire Charlie as an engineer or as a technician, he requires training. Even a Ph.D. spends six months learning where the bathroom is. A year from now Charlie is a very expensive asset." He hopes to keep trained and talented staffers, on whose training he has spent a great deal of money. Weinig delights in comparing MRC to those high-tech firms south of San Francisco, which allegedly have enlightened attitudes toward workers: "Silicon Valley companies use layoffs as an ongoing way of balancing their work load with their labor. Then the bosses start pissing and moaning because someone quits to join XYZ Company. Why not? What loyalty can you have to a company that come Friday lays off two thousand people?"

Some Wall Street analysts fret that a policy of no layoffs, while nice for employees, is unfair to investors because income is used to carry workers during bad times instead of to boost profits. Weinig shrugs off such criticism, suggesting that if stockholders don't like it, they can invest somewhere else. "I tell analysts, 'Hey, before you even consider making an investment in this company you'd better know my philosophy, because if you don't like it, keep your money in your pocket.'" In his 1982 letter to MRC shareholders, Weinig declared that the company "remains faithful" to its no-layoff policy, explaining that "trained and experienced personnel are our most important resource, and we must take all prudent steps to retain them."

In the early 1980s, Weinig's policy was severely tested, as sales plunged some 15 percent from a high in 1981 of $72 million, and by 1983 the company had registered a loss. But no one was laid off. Employees worked at other jobs more menial than their usual ones, but they kept their same pay. When business picked up, they showed appreciation by offering to work without pay for a series of Saturdays. But state law prohibited it.

Don Marron's Meritocracy

What happened to Paine Webber, the investment house, is a classic case of a service company becoming so entangled in its own bureaucracy that customers are forgotten. The brokerage business lives or dies on sales, but behind the brokers and researchers are the back-office staffers who handle the administrative duties once stock is bought or sold for a customer. At Paine Webber's back office, customers' accounts were in chaos, stock certificates disappeared, and transactions regularly went unrecorded. By 1980, back-office problems had escalated to the point that the New York Stock Exchange censured Paine Webber and fined it $300,000, the largest fine ever levied against a member firm.

A major event on Wall Street some years earlier presaged the decline of Paine Webber and other inefficient firms. In 1975, the NYSE gave in to pressure from the SEC, the Justice Department, Congress, and a slew of investor groups and dropped the practice of fixing commissions on the purchase and sale of stocks listed on the Big Board. The end of that 183-year-old monopolistic practice, described by author Chris Welles as *The Last Days of the Club*, meant that big institutional customers could now negotiate with individual brokerage houses the amount of commission they would pay on each transaction. Without fixed rates to prop them up, inefficient, marginal firms like Paine Webber couldn't compete with aggressive, service-minded competitors.

The arrival of Donald Marron at Paine Webber was also tied to the 1975 NYSE decision. A self-made multimillionaire, Marron in the 1950s dropped out of Baruch College to help support his family. In 1958, he founded D. B. Marron and Company, an investment banking firm, merging it in 1965 with the Street's leading institutional research firm, Mitchell Hutchins and Company, where he became president in 1969. Along the way, Marron became cofounder, with economist Otto Eckstein, of Data Resources, a leading economic data firm sold to McGraw-Hill in

1970 for $103 million. His wealth financed a stunning personal collection of modern and abstract art that now decorates Paine Webber's offices.

Once fixed fees fell in 1975, research firms like Mitchell Hutchins lost business, as major brokerage houses began building up their own research operations as a way to attract new investment banking clients. Mitchell Hutchins thus found itself in need of an investment banking partner; at the same time, Paine Webber was looking to build a research department. So in 1977, the two firms merged, but it wasn't a marriage made in heaven. Marron, who had known nothing but success during his days on Wall Street, suddenly found himself in a big, troubled company. In 1979, Marron and others tried to save Paine Webber by merging it with the respected investment banking firm, Blyth Eastman Dillon and Company. It was a move akin to dousing a fire with kerosene; the weight of the additional administrative load just about scuttled the already sagging firm. Operating costs quadrupled by 1980 as 720 temporaries wrestled with paper work. News reports of impending doom at Paine Webber appeared almost daily. That helped, thinks the trim, athletic Marron. "I don't think the institutionalized bureaucracy is crackable except during a period of crisis or extreme difficulty," he says. With a crisis at hand, Marron and a group of aides took very specific steps toward reforming the bureaucracy at Paine Webber, which included (1) defining the business and the problem areas; (2) setting out precise measurements of expected performance; (3) explaining to employees what they were doing; (4) creating a strong example for the whole firm to follow; (5) rewarding those who perform.

At first, the team "applied basic management," in Marron words, to understand how the business ran, what the key issues were, and how to measure performance. Because the most serious problem at Paine Webber was errors, the team began measuring and analyzing them. They counted each and every error. If a completed transaction came back and had to be put through again, that counted as an error. In one extreme case, an order had to be reprocessed 124 times. "That happens in big companies all the time but you don't hear about it," says Marron. "The very act of putting in place the measurement trigger in the minds of the people—somebody will know—that's the accountability."

Employees resisted the change at first. Just finding out the number of people who worked at the firm took the Marron team two weeks. Some managers told to cut people instead shifted them to remote sections of the firm. To show his determination to make cuts, Marron held meetings to review figures, daily at first, then weekly as the cuts were made. In the end, twelve hundred people were cut from the staff of sixty-eight hundred, about two thirds of them by attrition. The seven hundred temporary workers, called to support the harried back-office staff, were reduced to two persons. Next, the team went around and described to each employee what was going to happen. Recalls Marron, "I told them, 'We're going to find the good people and reward them with honor, responsibility, and money. And we're going to find the bad people and shoot them.' But it was the next sentence that was crucial. I said, 'We will tell you what to expect, we will show you how we're going to measure it, and we will jointly look at the results.'" Marron would sit with individual workers for as long as it took to agree on a fair measurement of their job performance. "It's important that this is done at the beginning, because if it's not done, then at the end of the year when I say to an employee, 'You didn't do a very good job this year,' and he says, 'Oh, yes I did,' it ends up in a debate."

Bold statements of change need to be followed with equally strong examples, says Marron, so when he kept hearing variations of the statement, "But we've always done it that way," the CEO called a meeting and said, "I will not accept that answer." The reformers picked a particularly flagrant example of waste, and then Marron himself learned how to do the job and do it efficiently. "The point is, if you can focus the whole organization on something they know needs improvement, then improve it by some objective means, your credibility for correcting other areas goes up dramatically. There's no way of getting somebody's attention by just talking about cutting waste. That's an abstract term; it's what the other guy is doing."

In the past, Paine Webber paid people relatively equally, so that the good performer often was not earning much more than the slouch sitting at the next desk. Marron introduced an incentive system, which he touted far and wide in corporate literature. "I'm for meritocracy," asserts Marron. "But the only way this will work is if you identify the good people." Paine Webber started a program, called Excel, which had the goal of trumpeting the heroes and rewarding them for their efforts.

Marron's meritocracy produced dramatic results in a very

short time. Profits in 1982 were up 345 percent over the previous year, ranking it tenth among *Business Week*'s "Corporate Leaders" that year. And *Financial World,* in its August 31, 1983, edition, rated Paine Webber among the top growth companies. Commented an analyst report of Jesup and Lamont Securities Company in recommending the "new" Paine Webber to investors: "[Marron] sets high standards of expectation, establishes a fair and objective reporting and control system for evaluation, and rewards performance well. Internal competition and politicking are strongly discouraged, and underachievers find themselves unwelcome."

Marron, who collected a $2-million pay package in 1983 to celebrate his success, worried about keeping it alive. People in control should feel insecure enough that they don't get smug, he says. "I think American businessmen have been scared to death. I think that's absolutely terrific. I think you should scare them one more time."

Marron, inadvertently, got his wish in 1984–1985. Paine Webber, along with other major brokerage firms, suddenly saw profits plunge. Small investors, bobbing helplessly in the wake of enormous stock price changes brought on by institutional trading, began seeking more predictable investments. At the same time, all brokerage firms have found overhead creeping up as the supports behind individual brokers become more costly. Merrill Lynch, for one, warned salesmen that if they didn't meet quotas to pack up their desks. Meanwhile, the smaller, regional brokerages, where salesmen were closer to the customer, were enjoying record profits.

It was the old bugaboo of bigness. For no sooner had Marron conquered his back-of-office headaches than things went sour in the front office. It was, Marron commented, more complex a problem than the back-office woes of the early eighties. Indeed, this one seemed beyond even Marron's meritocracy. "We've had Booz•Allen in here for a year," sighed the frustrated but determined executive.

Autos: Ford Finally Has "A Better Idea"

If a single industry deserves to be crowned the All-American Bureaucratic Wastrel, it has been the automobile industry— which is not just any industry. Not long ago, it provided one in nine manufacturing jobs and used more than one fifth of the nation's steel and machine tools. All these resources and people involved in building cars meant that automakers, more than any other group of businessmen, were in a position to set national standards for high quality and reliability. They set standards all right, but of a different sort.

"I was arrogant, but GM made a science of goddamn arrogance," asserts Chrysler's irrepressible chairman, Lee Iacocca. "I think the Townsends [Lynn Townsend, chairman of Chrysler from 1967 to 1975] of this world, the Henry [Ford] God IIs and some of the GM chairmen wrecked this industry. That arrogance should be gone by now. We got our comeuppance." Henry Ford II himself in 1982 told an industry group, "We let our quality go bad. We got careless, we got sloppy, we built lousy quality cars."

Because American car companies built lousy cars, American car buyers revolted. Back in 1950, 79.4 percent of the world's cars were manufactured in the United States; by 1981, the U.S. share of the market had plunged by more than half to below 30 percent—and Detroit became just another car-manufacturing city like Suzuka or Turin. In 1982, foreign automakers, most particularly the Japanese, captured a record 28 percent of the U.S. market; in California, it was more than 50 percent. And in Marin County, across the bay from San Francisco, 67 percent of the cars sold were imports. Import quotas, imposed in 1981, kept Japanese car sales at a steady level into 1985.

There are differing views among industry experts about when U.S. auto executives began ignoring quality, innovation, and the marketplace, and instead began fixating on promotional hoopla, style changes, and pumped-up balance sheets. The first impulse in that direction may have been as early as 1910, wrote William Abernathy and his two coauthors in *Industrial Renaissance.* Ford then decentralized assembly operations to meet soaring demand, and began a process that "efficiently produced the all-purpose roadcruiser, which controlled the market for thirty years." The industry figured it had solved the mysteries of manufacturing, so "the next several decades were to see a redirection of managerial effort and attention away from production and toward marketing and finance."

If the managers in Detroit acted as if they were running a perpetual money-making machine, it was because they had been taught to think that way. They were the descendants of Alfred P. Sloan, Jr., who built GM into a corporate colossus over four decades beginning in the 1920s and whose management philosophy spread across all industry. It was Sloan who in the 1930s elevated the American automobile from basic transportation to a chromium status symbol with obsolesence built in. General Motors was not in the business of making automobiles, he declared; it was in the business of making money. Quality was a word notably missing from that aphorism.

This shortsightedness of making money not cars caught up with Detroit in the 1970s. The first OPEC oil shock of 1973 sent gasoline prices skyward, but the chief concern of Detroit remained "getting the metal out the door." Bigger cars returned bigger profits. Because nobody in Detroit wanted to build small cars, a growing segment of the market was ceded to the importers.

Part of the problem has been the executives who run the car corpocracy—and who all seem cut from the same mold. To get to a top executive job, a junior executive has to follow a carefully groomed path—a "name" graduate school of business, long service with the company, increasingly more impressive homes ending up in suburban Bloomfield Hills, friendships with other up-and-coming executives. The result, says Brock Yates, a columnist for *Car and Driver* magazine, is "the Detroit mind," which he describes as "an internalized set of attitudes, thought patterns and work habits that have brought him to where he is today [and are] also responsible for the precarious position of the American automobile industry."

A former GM executive from the 1970s offers a view that complements Yates's: "They had good people and a good training system. But they suffered from being number one for too long. GM never fired a white-collar worker except if he was caught stealing. Blue-collar workers would be laid off. But that was never blamed on the company's performance. It was always the economy that was at fault. GM had a management system based on good times." It followed that the auto industry—without effective competition for so many years, enjoying exclusive access to the world's richest customer base, and governed by an executive elite—would grow insular and bureaucratic.

One who saw the difference between Detroit's cocoon and Japan's competitiveness was James Bowling, senior vice-president and assistant to the chairman of Philip Morris, a company long known for its marketing savvy in peddling Lite beer and cigarettes. Bowling, dragging deeply on a Player's cigarette, told the following story, incredulity occasionally ruffling his otherwise soothing Kentucky accent: "Back in 1968, the former chairman of Philip Morris, Joe Cullman, was on Ford's board of directors. Joe came back from a meeting and said the board had been shown a fantastic marketing presentation at Ford. He arranged for us to see it, and a bunch of us flew out. It was a dazzling, multimedia view of the automotive market. After it was over, I asked the first question. 'I noticed in the section on foreign competition you didn't include Japanese cars,' I said. The answer came back, 'They'll never be a factor in the U.S. market.' But I continued, 'I read that they have thirty percent of the California market. Didn't Ford think that was significant?' No, they said, Californians are nut cases. Now in our business we watch California very carefully for trends. So when I came back to New York I said, 'Forget the auto industry,' and I sold all my stock in auto companies."

Just as these firms remained aloof to the dramatic changes taking place in their markets, so, too, were they oblivious to the quality of work being done by their suppliers. At Ford, nearly 50 percent of the parts in its cars came from outside suppliers. Many of these, such as Budd, Bendix, and Goodrich, industrial giants in their own rights, were actually auto industry satellites. Their profits depended on selling tires and seat covers, light bulbs, and brake liners. So suppliers would have snapped to attention if executives at GM or Ford or Chrysler had made demands. But none did. It was a wasteful, undemanding relationship between America's industrial giants—a relationship, said *Fortune,* that produced an "era of stunning complacency."

Gus W. Rylander, a twenty-seven-year sales veteran at Armco recalls how it was when, at the beginning of each year, steel suppliers were awarded fixed percentages of the business. "We did the same thing the same way every year," he says. "We'd go up there [to Detroit] and get our share of the pie." Auto companies that requested certain specifications often had to accept tolerances dictated by the American Iron and Steel Institute. Quality control problems were obvious from the rejected steel that piled up outside auto plants. But steel companies produced the stuff on almost a take-it-or-leave-it basis. As Merrill Lynch's steel analyst Charles Bradford put it, "The steel companies' attitude was, 'We make steel. If you want it, you buy it.'" Not only did the automakers take what they were given, GM even paid sellers' list prices for the steel instead of using its huge buying power as leverage to demand discounts.

Those old comfortable relationships ended abruptly not long ago, done in by foreign automakers who studied and understood the American consumers, whom the American carmakers had long since ignored. The U.S. Department of Transportation has estimated that by 1983, the Japanese had about a $1,500- to $2,000-per car cost advantage over American manufacturers. While much of that comes from labor costs and currency differences, the bulk of it is a result of managerial inefficiency, according to numerous experts. James E. Harbour, a management consultant in Berkley, Michigan, declares, "The Japanese don't have better technology. They're stomping us into the ground because they're better managers." To survive, American automakers had to change their once-sacred authoritarian management techniques and adopt the golden rule of Japanese industry: Eliminate waste, and efficient operations and high quality will follow naturally.

July 24, 1980. The outlook for Phil Caldwell seemed decidedly bleak. A year earlier, when he succeeded Henry Ford II, Caldwell became the first chief executive officer of Ford Motor Company who was not a member of the family. A historic event, to be sure, but now some observers wondered if the mannered, meticulous financial man might be Ford's last CEO—family or otherwise. The company's balance sheet had turned bloody red as Ford lost $1.5 billion that year, and would lose another $1.1 billion the next. The dividend was cut, soon to be eliminated altogether. Short-term debt mounted, bill-paying dates came and went. Worse, its share of car sales in the U.S. market had slipped badly, from a respectable 24 percent in 1978 to less than 17 percent in 1982. But even with the company foundering badly, Caldwell had no choice but to spend some $3 billion annually for five years to update Ford's uncompetitive operation.

So on that summer day in 1980, Caldwell could be forgiven if he wasn't in a buoyant mood for the opening of a new transmission plant in Batavia, Ohio. The Ford executive managed to give the workers a standard speech exhorting quality work. More noteworthy, however, was the presence on the dais of two other men who would influence Caldwell and Ford in the crisis-filled months ahead. One was Peter J. Pestillo, a forty-two-year-old attorney who had joined Ford six months earlier as vice-president for labor relations; the other, Donald Ephlin, fifty-four, a United Auto Workers vice-president who had been assigned to Ford only a month before.

What Pestillo and Ephlin did—with enabling support from Caldwell—was to bridge the chasm between labor and corporate management. In a revolutionary development, workers for the first time were to be asked for their help in building a better product.

Sitting in his large office atop the Ford world headquarters in Dearborn, dressed in a loud checked suit, red tie, and designer shirt with a "P" monogrammed on the pocket, Pestillo looks more like an old-time labor organizer than the vice-president in charge of labor relations for the sixth largest corporation in the United States. A glance at his curriculum vitae, however, shows that Pestillo touched all the Establishment bases: Georgetown Law School, Harvard Business School's Advanced Management Program, labor-management committee of the Business Roundtable and the U.S. Chamber of Commerce, and executive jobs with General Electric and B. F. Goodrich. But if his credentials look traditional, his performance at Ford certainly has not been. "We want our executives to spend time out in the plants, because we don't want to run a holding company. My old company, Goodrich, has what I call 'balance sheet management.' It's when you say, 'Show me the performance sheets and I'll tell you how you're doing.' At Ford, I guess we have gone from a more nearly authoritarian managerial operation to one that is more participative. We're not social reformers. We're trying to run a business, and asking people to help solve your problems is a pretty useful way to do it."

At Solidarity House in Detroit, meanwhile, Ephlin was more committed to the controversial issue of worker participation than were others in the UAW hierarchy. Though they never admitted it, many leaders viewed employee involvement as undermining their own power bases, an antipathy that some insiders say may have cost Ephlin the presidency of the UAW when he ran for it in 1983.

Several important factors helped this duo in their effort to change the face of Ford. First, they had the support of the chief executive officer, which is of paramount importance in altering anything in a major corporation. Second, both Ford and the UAW realized they were destined for disaster unless the corporation made a dramatic change of direction. Still, union officials watched unhappily as Ford shrank and jobs disappeared. Some forty-seven thousand workers were laid off indefinitely when Ford closed thirteen district offices and nine of fourteen assembly plants. Ford began contracting out work once done at Ford by UAW members to foreign and domestic manufacturers. A survey conducted at the Louisville truck plant in 1979 reflected the labor-management strain throughout the company. It found "deep distrust, anger, and alienation," "feelings of helplessness and resignation" among hourly workers, and a "top-down, blame-oriented hierarchy."

In 1981, Pestillo and Ephlin arranged for a novel, two-week visit to Japan by a union-management team. The trip, both men agreed, taught the group that the Japanese system demanded trust and goodwill between workers and managements—attitudes notably absent at Ford, and at most other American companies, for that matter. Then, in 1982, UAW president Douglas Fraser agreed to reopen the 1979 contract settlement. One participant characterized the unique talks as "Here's our mutual problem, now how do we solve it?" The union eventually agreed to a ceiling on cost-of-living increases and eliminated certain paid holidays; the company, for its part, established a retraining program for laid-off employees, and a guaranteed income for those employees out of work after fifteen years with the company. Everyone would share in any future profit, and for 1983, the plan's first year, each employee collected about $400. In March 1985, employees collected 6 percent of their total 1984 paychecks—an average of $2,000 per employee.

Ford also cut its white-collar staff, swollen by decades of undisciplined growth. Donald E. Petersen, then president of Ford, who in 1985 succeeded Caldwell as CEO, attributes the company's massive corporate bureaucracy to the distrust of subordinates by top executives, who add layers of staff to keep tabs on line operators. Staff salaries in North America alone were approaching $4 billion annually, twice that of its much larger rival, General Motors. In the end, Ford let go twenty-one thousand salaried employees, or 28 percent of the staff.

Communications became a religion. Engineers began discussing car designs with the manufacturing division, instead of simply presenting them with a drawing, as in the past. The manufacturing staff talked to suppliers about "just in time" inventory, the cost-saving Japanese innovation by which suppliers deliver parts to plants as needed so that inventory doesn't tie up capital and space.

Suppliers suddenly were told to meet quality standards or else. At an annual dinner in 1981 with sixty or so top suppliers, the normally convivial, informal affair suddenly turned deadly serious when Caldwell in a speech spelled out Ford's demands for quality. If that meant fewer suppliers getting bigger orders, so be it. Ford would no longer slap its logo on products that didn't live up to new standards, he declared. Ford established five-day seminars on quality control for suppliers, which were so popular the company built a two-story Ford Supplier Institute at Detroit Metropolitan Airport.

The results were quick and impressive. For example, Essex Corporation, a United Technologies subsidiary that makes engine switches for Ford, reduced its rejection rate from 40 percent to less than 1 percent within eight months; ITT Hancock, maker of auto seat tracks, cut its rate from 20 percent to 0. Ford boasted that if its twelve hundred suppliers continued that way, it could mean a cut of about $500 from the nearly $2,000 differential between its manufacturing costs and those of the Japanese.

Probably the most significant change at Ford was the institution of EI, for employment involvement. In the fall of 1980, Caldwell met eighty top managers in the Ford boardroom and, according to Pestillo, said, "Ladies and gentlemen. We're going to do employee involvement. Spend money, but do it and do it right." Some union officials in the early days tried to use cooperation in EI as leverage, Pestillo recalled. "Ephlin would stand up and say, 'No hostages. We're going to do it because the people want it and it's going to stand on its own.'" At a plant in Wixom, Michigan, workers returning to work after a two-year layoff found themselves in five days of EI training before they entered the facility. At the once-troubled Louisville plant, where EI was introduced in 1980, workers during the next three years made 749 proposals to improve the Ranger and Bronco II trucks. The company adopted 542 of them, and by 1983, industry experts were calling the Louisville-built trucks equal in quality to their Japanese competitors.

At the Wayne, Michigan, assembly plant, for example, employees were shown films by a psychologist on why people act the way they do, and at least half the participants found the messages so compelling they asked to see the films again with their families. Workers were divided into groups and played the Aggressive Corporation, a strategy game that shows how to work as teams for a single goal. Hourly workers and low-level salaried employees, who for years simply came to the plant each day, did their jobs and went home, were shown for the first time precisely what overall part they played in the plant and in Ford's worldwide operations. Marty Kennedy, a Ford human relations expert at Wayne, explained the program this way: "We're trying to bring the individual back to the plant. The philosophy of EI is that we hired the whole body, including the mind. Up until a few years ago, we told workers, 'I'll make it simple for you—come in here, do what you're told, and we'll have no problems.' But that wasn't the real world."

Out on the assembly line, workers on lunch breaks were cautious in interviews in assessing the program. Some mentioned the problem that low-level supervisors sometimes resisted change. Others passively accepted EI as simply another management directive. Although 90 percent of the Ford work force was not actively involved in EI, all workers were directly affected by the program. Worker complaints, which once festered as union grievances, now were dated and posted on blackboards in the middle of their departments. There they remained, in full view, until redressed.

Indeed, Caldwell himself became a member of an EI team. The CEO escorted Pestillo and Ephlin on a demonstration of an EI project at the Chicago stamping plant, once notorious for poor productivity. The three were shown how racks used to ship parts came back battered and had to be repaired. An EI group at the plant made a videotape about how to care for the racks, which were sent out to other EI groups in the offending plants. As a result, $600,000 was saved in avoided rack repairs. Caldwell was made a member of the Chicago Stampers EI team—and given a jacket that said so on the back. Months later he got a letter from team members asking his advice about how to deal with a supervisor who was being particularly inattentive to the goals of EI. Stamper Caldwell got in touch with the unfortunate supervisor.

While no one can deny that American automakers made tremendous progress in a very few years, they also enjoyed the benefits of a protected market during their recovery period. For four years the Japanese had voluntarily agreed to limit car exports to this country—1.65 million for three years and 1.85 million for the last year. Naturally, Japanese automakers sent over the larger, more expensive models loaded with options. American consumers snapped up these cars—showing their lingering respect for Japanese quality by paying car dealers a premium of $1,300-plus over the sticker price for the imports. The higher-priced cars produced higher profits for the Japanese, so the quota system was a boon to both the Japanese and the American carmakers. Detroit even got a leg up in subcompact sales, an area dominated by the Japanese in normal times. But it was the consumer who lost out from the controlled competition, not only in choice but in price as well. According to a study by Wharton Economotrics Forecasting Associates, the average price of a new car has gone up nearly $2,000 since quotas were first established, an unusually high boost for that short a period. In March 1985, President Reagan announced an end to voluntary restraints.

Out at Dearborn, management remained convinced that the new Ford would thrive even without quotas, and that the company's old, wasteful ways were gone forever. "This management is determined not to let the overhead creep back in," declared David McCammon, vice-president for planning. Ephlin was optimistic, though guarded: "I don't think it will ever be the same as it was. But it's always been one of my great worries that the progress we made was so very fragile."

2

Wasteful Workplace: The Participation Solution

Don't assume that the interests of employer and employee are necessarily hostile—that what is good for one is necessarily bad for the other. The opposite is more apt to be the case. While they have different interests, they are likely to prosper or suffer together.

—Louis Brandeis

The most valuable of all capital is that invested in human beings.

—Alfred Marshall

Introduction: The Quiet Revolution

Annoyed at a scheduling snafu, the customer was taking out his anger, that May 1984 morning, at two women behind the airline counter. As he became more voluble, the line behind him grew and eyes rolled. Finally, he snapped, "Okay, who are your superiors?" And the two Eastern Airlines ticketing agents replied briskly and simultaneously, "We are!"

There is no dramatic strike or song to commemorate the change—no violence at Homestead Steel or "Ode to Joe Hill"— but a quiet revolution is now under way in many American workplaces. The Eastern employees were referring to their new contract guaranteeing employees ownership of 25 percent of all stock and four seats on the firm's nineteen-member board of directors. Eastern is one of thousands of firms that, buffeted by cheaper competition, swelling labor costs and lagging productivity, are betting that more employee participation (EP) can spur profits and save jobs. The rationale was expressed well in national magazine advertisements in 1984 for United Technologies Corporation, a large defense contractor employing two hundred thousand people: "Employers have a vast intellectual resource in employees. . . . People on the job have ideas—good ideas, productive ideas—about their work and how it could be done better. Who is better equipped to do this than the person who actually does the job? People want to be involved and to participate."

As the subsequent scan of labor relations indicates, the traditional "adult-child relationship" between management and labor, in the phrase of consultant Walter Cupples of the Core Group, has left a legacy of strikes, sabotage, absenteeism, and indifference that wastes America's productive potential. For like a broken machine, mistreated or unmotivated workers can also lead to higher overhead, lost production, and economic failure. The recent trend toward democracy at work, however, has the potential to inaugurate profound changes, if not a new era, in the economics of the workplace.

The first stage of the movement for workplace democracy, of course, was the struggle of employees to organize into unions in order to collectively bargain for pay and benefits, a struggle that culminated with the Wagner Act of 1935. Stage two, a half century later, involves employees fighting management not merely for more pay but also for more say. Since they "prosper or suffer" together, in Brandeis's words, workers want to be treated with respect in the boardrooms as well as the bargaining table.

This movement could combine the two great American principles of capitalism and democracy—expressed as competition *between* firms and participation *within* firms. Consider several helpful analogies. Top managers understand how the profit motive inspires them, just as political conservatives stress how freedom allows individuals to flourish. Similarly, workers can be motivated by more profits from their firms as well as by greater freedom within them. We also know, for example, that morale is both unmeasurable and essential to armies: witness Israel's success against larger forces. So too can an adult-adult relationship between executives and employees—by making employees shareholders and stakeholders in the places where they work—boost morale, and hence effort.

Like many CEOs, Philip Caldwell at the Ford Motor Company was slow but willing to appreciate the psychology of employee morale. In early 1982, he toured a Chicago stamping plant with Donald Ephlin, then the UAW's chief negotiator with Ford. After chatting with many of the line workers, Caldwell told Ephlin, "The workers in there have a great contribution to make in helping to improve the operation of the plant, and they've got a lot of good ideas. They're as concerned about the problems we face at Ford as I am." To which the blunt Ephlin responded, "I don't know what the hell's so surprising about that. They've got more invested in the company than you have."

What they have invested is their sole source of wealth—their job. And if EP programs can make the difference between failing firms and profitable ones, they can save jobs that would otherwise be lost to workplace waste or foreign competition. Indeed, according to a report of the Senate's Select Committee on Small Businesses, some fifty thousand to one hundred thousand jobs were saved in the 1970s because of workers buying their businesses.

Unemployment, of course, is one of the clearest examples of waste to the economy, an insight eloquently stated and first observed by the great economist John Maynard Keynes in 1930: "In the enforced idleness of millions, enough potential wealth is running to waste to work wonders. Many millions of pounds' worth of goods could be produced each day by the workers and the plants which stand idle—and the workers would be the happier and the better for it. We ought to sit down to mend matters, in the mood of grave determination and the spirit of action at all costs, which we would have in a war. . . ." Today, not only is there the lost portion of the gross national product ($75 billion for every 1 percent of unemployment), lost taxes ($25 billion per 1 percent), and added public expenditures ($25 billion per 1 percent), but there is also the untallied emotional cost to the 25 percent of Americans who at some point during the year are without work. "I'm not proud of myself to have to come down here," one unemployed steelworker getting free food told a commentator on a recent news broadcast. "I just wish I could get back to work and take care of my family. I'm a go-getter; I'm not one to sit back. And I look for anything I can get my hands on to help my family."

Enhancing employees' stock and participation can also affect public policies for economic growth. Although the U.S. Congress often appears to think that economic revival depends only on increasing incentives for capital, this overfocus on one factor of production ignores the fact that there are three ways to increase productivity: (1) better use of intellectual resources (increasing know-how by research and development), (2) better use of physical capital (modernizing plant and equipment), and

(3) better use of human capital ("working smarter" to increase output per person-hour). And the evidence, from studies and case histories, indicates that this third category of employee relations—of "human" capital formation—may yield more productive gains than the other two. So the way to continuing economic growth may be not so much providing incentives to capital via tax breaks (trickle-*down* economics) as providing incentives to labor via stock holdings and participative management (trickle-*up* economics).

Employee participation has broad appeal. In recent years, the pope, Ronald Reagan, Margaret Thatcher, and Gary Hart,* among many others, have touted its virtues. Yet for all its appeal and supporters, it has not overcome the tradition of a managerial class who regard labor as just another cost of production. EP is still a movement, not yet a habit.

A History of Management-Labor Hostility: Taylor-Made to Fail

Around the turn of the century and through at least the 1930s, laissez-faire theory predominated economic thinking. Because the economy was supposedly guided by the "unseen hand" of the laws of supply and demand, *by definition* management could do no wrong. So huge mergers, low wages, long hours, union busting, and pollution of the environment were conveniently regarded as the inevitable consequences of survival of the econom-

---

*Pope John Paul's 1981 encyclical, "Laborem Exercens" ("On Human Work"), suggests that each person, on the basis of his or her work, should be "fully entitled to consider himself as a part owner of the great workbench at which he is working with everyone else. A way toward that goal could be found by associating labor with the ownership of capital, as far as possible."

In a February 1983 speech to the American Legion, President Reagan said, "There is no more damaging misconception than the notion that capitalism is an economic system benefiting only the rich. . . . Developing countries need to be encouraged to experiment with the growing variety of arrangements for profit-sharing and expanded capital ownership."

In mid-1984, Prime Minister Margaret Thatcher circulated a draft document within her Conservative party urging that it seek to promote employee shareholding plans and campaign in the next election on a platform using the slogan, "Every man a property owner, every man a capitalist."

During his unsuccessful 1984 presidential campaign, Senator Hart said more "workplace democracy" would be one of the five policy areas he would emphasize if he were elected.

ically fittest. At the same time, classical economists and business managers contended that management-labor relations were fair: Management could fire workers just as workers were free to quit.

While this situation obviously pleased owners and managers, workers regarded it as a masquerade to cover up abuse. In the real world, there was no parity between a ruling management and a solo worker "free" to be unemployed. Again, it was labor lawyer Louis Brandeis who framed the issue best. When an industrialist opposing a strike said, "We can't run the risk of our property being destroyed by these six thousand men," Brandeis is said to have replied, "Well, how can the six thousand men run the risk of their lives being destroyed by you?"

These conflicting views produced the great clashes now familiar to students of labor relations: from the railroad strike of 1877 in Cumberland, Maryland (leaving twelve dead and the station set ablaze), through the so-called Memorial Day Massacre of 1937 in Chicago (ten dead, fifty-eight injured). When Claire Booth Luce asked about the guards with machine guns on a tour of a mine in the 1930s, a company official matter-of-factly replied, "You can't run a coal mine without machine guns."

But if classical economists provided the philosophy for management's authoritarian treatment of labor, Frederick Taylor provided the rationale: Benevolent despotism, he argued, worked.

Taylor, an industrial engineer who had invented carbon steel machine tools, worked in several metals firms in the late 1890s. When he rose from a common laborer to a "gang boss" at one company, he found himself at odds with employees who limited their effort to a third of their machines' potential. So he decided to measure objectively what constituted a fair day's work in order that managers and employees could agree to the discipline of numbers. The result was Taylor's "time and motion" studies.

In his most famous test, Taylor calculated that a really good handler could carry 47 tons a day instead of the average 12½ tons. He said that a good pig-iron handler should be strong and "so stupid and phlegmatic that he more nearly resembles in his mental make-up the ox than any other type." He promised a 60 percent increase in wages to those workers who met the standard, but gave them these instructions: "If you are a high-priced man, you will do exactly as this man tells you, from morning till night. When he tells you to pick up a pig and walk, you pick it up and you walk, and when he tells you to sit down and rest, you sit down. You do that right straight through the day. And what's more, no back talk."

What came to be called "scientific management" had several components: division of jobs into numerous narrow functions; separation of manual from mental work; total control by management in assigning workers to perform these functions; standardized tools and equipment; and bonuses for better efficiency. Taylor worked diligently to popularize his ideas, especially in three important lectures in 1909 at the Harvard Business School, and in his enormously popular book published in 1911, *The Secret of Saving Lost Motion.*

Although his name is not a household word, Taylor has probably had as large an impact on economic production as Keynes or Marx—but it has not been the impact this well-intentioned reformer expected. "Within a few short years," wrote author Robert Reich of Taylor's influence, "America's factories were governed by rigid job classifications and work rules. Toolmakers did not clean their own tools. Light-machine operators and miscellaneous-machine operators worked on different machines. Millrights, not electricians, unscrewed the covers of electrical contacts."

For an era with numerous uneducated immigrant workers, Taylorism made some sense as a way of organizing and spurring production. But as employees grew more educated, sophisticated, and independent—the number of American workers with high school diplomas has doubled in the last thirty years—they chafed under the authoritarianism of the "scientific method." At the same time, unions adjusted to Taylorism by negotiating work rules and job classification systems to prevent management from arbitrarily assigning jobs, all of which keep many firms from adapting to changing economic circumstances. So when auto and steel executives today try to reduce more than fifteen skilled craft classifications to four or five broad categories, they're pulled back by the long arm of Frederick Winslow Taylor. "The typical American manager today," writes Charles G. Burck in *Fortune,* "holds forth in a rigid and stratified system that is the organizational equivalent of a multi-story 19th century factory building . . . no area of management has been more neglected than improving the way people work together."

As a former UAW vice-president Irving Bluestone put it, "Scientific management is neither science nor management."

The accumulated costs of Taylorism gathered force and broke through into public consciousness at the Lordstown strike in 1972. General Motors was proud of its new assembly plant in Lordstown, Pennsylvania, which was state-of-the-art in engineering design. Unfortunately, GM also had so thoroughly absorbed the Taylor ethic that the young, educated work force felt bored, frustrated, and impotent. They responded to a high-speed assembly line—where 101 Vegas per hour zipped past, allowing each worker thirty-six seconds to complete his or her task—by absenteeism, by sabotage, and finally by a bitter twenty-two-day strike. GM tried to explain away the strike as a natural spasm after a major reorganization. Instead, it was the spasm of a system that assumed the worker to be a "stupid ox," but who was in fact a smart American.

Labor-management dealings have improved dramatically from the warring relations of decades ago. Especially in the flush period following World War II, a growing American economy enabled management to buy labor peace with annual wage increases and extensive fringe benefits. In return, labor didn't challenge management's control over the organization of work and over investment decisions. But the oil shocks of the 1970s, and the recessions and waves of imports of the past decade have made both sides of the workplace dig in their heels—and occasionally revert to turn-of-the-century attitudes and practices. "We are the only country in the free world where the labor union is fighting for its life,"* says UAW vice-president Donald Ephlin.

The following are some examples of the continuing harshly adversarial relations between unions and management.

—Some companies that want to repudiate their union contracts are simply declaring bankruptcy and reorganizing without a contract. C. Raymond Grebey, the former chief labor nego-

---

*Since some business people believe that labor unions are per se wasteful, they regard the decline of union strength as a boon to productivity. But recent evidence indicates otherwise. In their massive analysis, *What Do Unions Do?*, economists Richard Freeman and James Medoff estimate that the monopoly efficiency losses due to unions (in restricted output and higher wages) is more than offset by the value of collective voice (reduced training expenses, lower turnover). On balance, they conclude that organized labor is an important force for both increased productivity and equity.

tiator for GE and major league baseball, calls it "the most dramatic new ingredient to collective bargaining that we have seen in more than a decade."

—Journalist Ron Chernow in *Working Papers* magazine describes the growth of what he calls "Grey Flannel Goons" and "the New Pinkertons." These consultants advise managers how to use the labor laws to break unions; no violence is involved, if you don't count the violence to the spirit and letter of the law that guarantees workers the right to organize free from harassment. For example, despite a law against intimidations and threats (e.g., "We'll shut down the plant if workers vote for a union"), these antiunion advisers show how to threaten lawfully. Here is an excerpt from a film shown to hospital workers:

WOMAN 1: Everyone has their pet peeves and gripes about the hospital. These pushers will try to blow these gripes up into major issues.
WOMAN 2: Pushers?
WOMAN 1: Oh, not drug pushers, no, union pushers.

And here's how the Oster Corporation of Tennessee implicitly intimidated employees, according to a local organizer: "One weekend, shortly before the election, the entire supervisory staff came into the plant and completely removed two assembly lines, moving them to another plant several miles away. When the employees came in on Monday they found only empty space in that part of the plant. The maneuver was apparently designed to demonstrate to the employees that the plant could and would shut down, and its operations would be moved, if the union prevailed."

—Twenty-seven employees at a computer warehouse in Detroit were shocked when they showed up for work on September 10, 1984, only to discover that their firm had moved its operation to Indiana over the weekend, throwing them out of work. "We regret we could not give the employees prior notice but it was due to the practicality of operating the business that we couldn't," said Carl Patterson, president of Slater-Standard Wallcovering.

—Some companies corroborate the criticisms of General Robert E. Wood, for years chairman of the board of Sears, Roebuck and Company. Wood said that "we complain about government . . . but we have created more or less of a totalitarian system in industry, particularly in large industry."

For example, most subsidiaries of Ma Bell, before its break-up, required operators to get permission to go to the bathroom. Steve Williamson, who was an assistant service manager at Vulcan Fuel Corporation in New York City, asked for information about chemicals in waste oil after he broke out in a rash and had trouble breathing; he was demoted and eventually fired, said management, "for asking questions he shouldn't have asked." At Coors, the beer company, interviewers have asked applicants the following questions: "Are you having sexual relations? Have you ever been involved with a homosexual? Have you ever done anything with your wife that could be considered immoral?" Twenty-five percent of the *Fortune* 500 companies, according to the American Polygraph Association, routinely resort to lie detector tests on suspect employees—a procedure that, according to one AFL-CIO official, "achieves just what employers really desire: an intimidated scared worker, rather than a certified, blemish free background."

—In their book *Corporate Cultures,* authors Terrence Deal and Allan Kennedy demonstrate the continuing appeal of the discipline of Taylorism. Managers should not try to be "warm and humane," they write, but rather "bastardly and . . . heroic. The point is this: modern managers who try to be humane may at the same time undermine the values upon which the 'culture' of the institution rests. Modern heros may need to be hard and 'insensitive' to keep a company consistent with its goals and visions—the very elements that made it strong in the first place."

—"In today's harmonious *Search for Excellence* atmosphere," wrote Myron Magnet in *Fortune,* "it's easy to forget that the class struggle is still raging unabated in some parts of the labor movement." Of the bitter strike by a twelve-union coalition in 1983 against Phelps Dodge, for example, the unions' chief negotiator said that there prevailed "a warlike atmosphere. Everytime the company does something, we suspect there must be a dark and devious reason for it. The same with them: they think we're trying to whittle away at management rights." The Litton Industries' campaign to avoid unionization showed a similar pattern of strife. By mid-1984, according to author Robert Kuttner, Litton's efforts included "cutting benefits to punish workers who have voted for a union, firing pro-union workers, organizing company unions, threatening plant closings and in several cases simply mov[ing] entire plants. Over a twenty year period, the NLRB has lodged forty-four unfair labor practice complaints

against Litton Industries; it was found guilty in twenty-one cases
. . . and [there were] settlements in thirteen more."

From Bell's bathrooms to Litton's illegality, the price of workplace waste is staggering. For disrespect, contempt, strife, and
autocracy produce abused workers who are not productive
workers. Labor grievances in the United States are seventeen
times the number in West Germany—and however necessary for
fairness to workers, the process of resolving grievances steals
time from a production schedule. The average number of days
annually lost to strikes in the United States is double that in
Great Britain, six times that in Japan, and twenty times that in
West Germany. In 1957, the National Labor Relations Board
reinstated 922 workers who had been fired for union activity; by
1981 this number jumped to 10,000. Of course, if 10,000 such
cases have been proved, the number of unproved illegal firings is
likely to be a multiple of that. According to an article by Paul
Weiler in the *Harvard Law Review,* about one employee in
twenty who belongs to a union is fired "for exercising rights supposedly guaranteed by federal law a half century ago."

All these numbers have consequences. As one top manager
quoted in John Kotter's book *The General Managers* indicated,
"I spend a fair amount of my time trying to reduce contempt in
the organization. It's absolutely deadly. Not conflict, but contempt. It's the ultimate in desecrating people's self-images."
Workplace authority Michael Maccoby reports that one large
company calculated that at least 50 percent of labor costs could
be attributed to distrust. Sixty years after Herbert Hoover's extended monograph *Waste in Industry,* it appears that his goal
number eleven has still not been accomplished. That goal was
"reduction of the waste arising from industrial strife between
employers and employees."

Is there any way out of this history of hostility?

The Rise of Employee Participation: Obstacles and Opportunities

The origins of employee stock ownership and workplace participation can be traced back to New England factories of the
1840s, where such ownership was widespread, and to John
Stuart Mill's *Principles of Political Economy,* published in 1848,
which advocated employee ownership. There were some em-

ployee-owned producer co-ops existing in the 1880s that for a time were quite successful. Around the turn of the century, several companies established suggestion boxes, which permitted employees at least to some extent to contribute not only their labor but their thoughts. But there was no "dialogue between floor superior and employees," says one steel executive, because "the box can't reply."

It wasn't until a group of psychologists in the 1920s and 1930s began to challenge the theoretical and empirical bases of Taylorism that the concept of employee participation took root. In his famous experiment at Western Electric in Hawthorne, Illinois, Dr. Elton Mayo of the Harvard Graduate School of Business Administration investigated why morale and production were so poor despite the best efforts of Taylor's time-and-motion experts. John Simmons and William Mares describe what happened in their book *Working Together:*

> Mayo began his studies with the conventional Taylor premise that if various adjustments in working conditions were made, management could determine the one best way for doing each particular job, which would result in higher production. The first part of the experiment isolated a number of women in a separate room, where their production of radio relay equipment was continually monitored. Following an initial period of work under existing conditions, the women were put on a group piece rate. After eight weeks, the group was allowed to take two rest periods of five minutes apiece. Subsequent changes included rearrangement of seating and changes in lighting.
>
> The astonishing result was that with each variation production increased. Out of curiosity, the researchers then reversed the variables; turned the lights back down, changed seating positions again, and reduced the break time; still production increased.

Mayo thus discovered the "Hawthorne effect": Production can be boosted not so much by mechanical changes in working conditions but by paying more attention to workers, especially by consulting the workers about proposed changes. "The group unquestionably develops a sense of participation in the critical determinations and becomes something of a social unit," he concluded, thereby giving rise to the "human relations" school of management—the reverse of Taylorism. Treat people well and they'll work well.

But business and union leaders treated Mayo's conclusions like an unwanted child on the doorstep. Business was so enthralled with Taylor's time-and-motion methods that they barely noticed a competing school of thought. Labor feared that direct employee participation with management would weaken attachment to the union and advance allegiance to the company. So instead of employee participation, "management rights" clauses proliferated: Management alone had the right "to determine the means, methods, and processes of production," while labor could organize to further the well-being of its members. "You manage, we grieve" became the prevailing ethic.

Further studies in the 1950s, though, demonstrated how cooperation rather than conflict promoted employee efficiency. Douglas McGregor, who would write *The Human Side of Enterprise,* developed his now widely known "Theory X" and "Theory Y" approaches: X was Taylorism, which assumed that employees need to be directed and coerced; Y assumed that respected, involved, and satisfied workers worked better. The difference between Theory X and Theory Y was the difference between authoritarian and participatory managements.

By the early 1970s, this growing body of literature began to reach a critical mass, provoking reaction. The first International Conference on Improving the Quality of Work Life drew fifty people to Harriman, New York, in 1972 (a decade later the second international conference would attract fifteen hundred). Then, in 1974, Senator Russell Long (D., La.)—who enjoys calling employee ownership "Populism without Robin Hood"—steered legislation through Congress that enabled employees to own their firms via a tax-exempt employee benefit device called an employee stock ownership plan (ESOP), originally developed by San Francisco attorney Lewis Kelso.

That same year, Senator Edward Kennedy (D., Mass.) held a hearing on "blue-collar blues" at which two industrial pioneers met for the first time: Irving Bluestone, then the director of the UAW's GM department, and Sidney Harman, the president of Harman International Industries. After testifying how unions and management should cooperate more, Bluestone was "astonished" at Harman's testimony, "because I'd never heard a business executive express himself with such concern . . . about satisfying the workers and treating them as adult human beings." In the hallway after the hearing, Bluestone approached Harman: "I said to him, 'Are you for real?' and he said, 'Certainly I am.' Well, I knew that the UAW had one or two Harman International Industries plants organized, and I suggested to him that we ought to try to put into practice what both of us had been saying. He readily agreed." And so was born one of the first quality-of-life programs, at the Harman auto mirror factory in Bolivar, Tennessee.

During the past decade, there have been scattered attempts to institute employee participation at various firms, but no massive move by management or labor to embrace the concept. As when strong men pull on a rope in a tug-of-war, there are powerful forces pulling workplace democracy back and nearly equally powerful forces trying to drag it forward. The resistance is formidable: executives who don't like to share power; middle managers fearful of being squeezed out; union leaders apprehensive at being regarded as irrelevant.

The habit of top-down authority is deeply embedded throughout American business. Today's top executives have got where they are by issuing directives and expecting employees to obey them. A New York Stock Exchange report describes "a tacit 'conspiracy of dependence,'" in which superiors find it hard to relinquish some of their control and subordinates are reluctant to assume greater responsibility for their behavior." Since routine is comforting and change frightening to CEOs who value stability, it will take an upheaval in managerial thinking to embrace more employee participation.

Middle managers, especially, see increasing employee participation as a threat to their position and prerogatives. They too are used to telling workers what to do, not the reverse. And since the job of supervisor is to supervise, if employees assume more responsibility for managing themselves, where does that leave supervisors? Since his firm is further along in EP than most American companies, Pehr G. Gyllenhammar, chairman of Volvo, understands this problem well. "For decades we told [foremen] in essence that they had two main functions. The first was to supervise the pace of the work, to keep the line moving. The second was to give technical advice and assistance whenever necessary. Thus, most of the people promoted to foremen's positions had been skilled employees who could solve technical problems. To keep people working, they became disciplinarians, experts at saying, 'Thou shalt not.' Suddenly we asked foremen to develop a rather different set of skills. We wanted them to be good 'managers of people' . . . and this created problems."

Also, when CEOs decide to try a quality-of-work-life program, often they just order insecure middle managers to cooperate, which is grossly inconsistent with the philosophy behind the program. When National Steel Corporation's Midwest Steel division decided on a more cooperative relationship with labor, they merged separate dining facilities for foremen and workers into one dining room open to all. Company official Thomas McKenna reports the move "upset a lot of people" because a private dining room "was part of the status of being a manager."

Many union leaders are similarly underwhelmed at the prospect of more workplace democracy, for several reasons. Feeling under siege from an unsympathetic President, a hostile NLRB, wage givebacks, and declining membership (where one worker in three was a union member in 1945, today it's under one in five), labor has long regarded EP as a sideshow—or worse. Whenever labor leaders hear how EP can boost "productivity," they interpret the word as a euphemism for a speedup or a reduction in personnel. Some more militant labor voices consider it a "Trojan horse . . . to undermine unions," a collaborationist exercise where workers surrender their class consciousness for "enterprise consciousness," with little in return. Or, as labor pioneer Samuel Gompers himself once reportedly described the situation at the turn of the century: "As soon as the union becomes part of management, that's when you need another union."

There is also the fear that managers may, as a result, try to avoid or bypass unions, says William Roehl of the AFL-CIO, by "giving workers the impression that all their problems will be solved by quality circles, which implies that there's no need for unions." William Winpisinger, the tough-talking president of the International Association of Machinists, explained his opposition to EP. Seated in his huge office adorned with a large American flag, a bust of Lincoln, and the latest in word-processing equipment, Winpisinger said, "Their version of cooperation is—cooperate for eight hours a day by busting your ass—and the other sixteen hours a day they reserve the right to destroy your job by pushing for right-to-work laws. So I say, forget it. If they want to cooperate, cooperate all day."

Writing in the *California Management Review*, management professors William E. Halal and Bob S. Brown summarize the consequence of such strong, institutional opposition. "Although the virtues of participative management have been preached for at least two decades now in management textbooks, training programs and by managers themselves, actual organizational practices have not moved very far from the traditional authoritarian approach." Adds professor Mason Haire of MIT, "Almost all managers talk in Theory Y terms [participation], but act in Theory X terms [authoritarian]."

Like cable TV and the "China market," the success of widespread employee participation has been long promised and long delayed. Yet despite the formidable obstacles, the forces opposed to EP are not winning the tug-of-war. The advocates of EP are holding their own, thus preserving the hope that waste in the workplace is not an inevitable consequence of modern, large-scale production. For we may yet see the fulfillment of the axiom of Henry Sée, the French historian, who emphasized that a social movement operates like ocean waves lapping against the bottom of a cliff: for decades nothing seems to be going on, until one day the side of the cliff falls in.

There are several new waves lapping away at the cliffs of workplace traditions.

First, American business is in the midst of an era of nearly unparalleled change and challenge. The back-to-back recessions of 1980 and 1981–82 and the legislated deregulation of the air, truck, bus, energy, banking, and telecommunications markets has helped restore competition—and thereby threaten previously secure firms. Simultaneously, a tidal wave of high-quality, low-cost imports has persuaded many managers—especially in import-sensitive industries such as the automobile, steel, and machine tool industries—to realize that business-as-usual may mean no business at all.

Second, to keep up with international competition, CEOs who don't like to share authority may no longer be able to ignore the profitability of participation. The benefits are palpable, both in terms of employee morale and company efficiency. A seminal 1982 study by the normally staid New York Stock Exchange concludes that productivity would increase an unheard-of 20 percent in one year (20 percent in one decade wouldn't be bad) if employee ownership and involvement efforts were widespread. The Government Accounting Office investigated twenty similarly situated coal mines in the same area of Wyoming—all of which produced the same kind of coal, used similar equipment, and functioned under the same regulations. Yet production ranged from 58 to 242 tons per workday. The difference, concluded the GAO, was that the most productive firms provided their employees with more individual responsibility and involvement in decision making. In another study of ninety-eight employee-owned firms in the United States and Canada, the authors found that "the more equity the workers own, the more profitable the company, other things being equal"—and the more equity, the higher the employee morale.

Third, middle managers and supervisors are coming to realize that their jobs may be saved, not threatened, by an employee participation program that makes their firms more profitable. And these programs can make clear that the *delegation* of authority to workers doesn't mean the *abdication* of authority. There's still a role for supervisors to review employee participation programs, or to be the "facilitators" of quality-of-work-life circles. (See next section.)

Fourth, the explosion of labor concessions and givebacks in the past half decade has made union leaders more willing to consider versions of workplace democracy. They appreciate that any concessionary bargaining should be reciprocal—and that if managements often can't give employees more pay and benefits, they can at least give them more equity and authority.

Consequently, Tom Donahue, the secretary-treasurer of the AFL-CIO and a longtime critic of EP said in a 1984 interview that unions could favor it *if* it grew out of a collective bargaining agreement and was not regarded as a substitute for wages and benefits. Victor Gotbaum, a visionary labor leader who heads District Council 37 of AFSCME (Association of Federal, State, and County Municipal Employees), provided the rationale for a new labor sentiment: "The traditional union stance has been against worker participation. I don't believe we can afford this luxury anymore . . . How in good conscience can you deprive teachers of the right to participate in the curriculum? A hospital worker who's part of a life-saving team in an admissions center should certainly be able to contribute suggestions stemming from day-to-day experience. . . . Unions that traditionally chose to stay out of management's prerogatives now realize that the quality of management's prerogatives is labor's business too."

Last, an increasingly educated and rights-conscious rank-and-file will not easily submit to a traditional "management knows best" ethic. And as baby-boomers and "Doonesbury" graduates enter and mature in the work force, they will likely carry with them the spirit of individual rights and justice their generation has come to expect.

Not unexpectedly, surveys in the early 1980s indicated that worker job satisfaction was at a twenty-five-year low; Jerome Rosow, president of the Work in America Institute, says the reason is younger workers of "the 'me generation' and the self-fulfillment ethic." An Opinion Research Corporation poll in 1982 of 250,000 employees in 200 representative firms concludes that "employees' image of their companies has worsened . . . fewer employees like their companies as places to work, and fewer say they would choose their companies again. . . ." When a 1980 Gallup poll asked workers who would benefit from improvements in their productivity, only 9 percent said they would; most assumed the beneficiaries would be management, stockholders, or consumers. . . . The University of Michigan had a sample of workers keep a diary of activities on the job, which revealed that between 1965 and 1975 the amount of time employees actually worked declined by more than 10 percent. . . . A 1984 survey by the Public Agenda Foundation found a similar pattern of underachievement: Fewer than one in four said they were performing up to their full capacity and 44 percent acknowledged that they didn't put much effort into their jobs beyond what was required.

Why are employees often discontented underachievers? Part of the answer may be a "participation gap," in the phrase of EP expert John Simmons, which describes the distance between how much workers want to be involved in decision making and how much they actually are. While 84 percent of the work force wants to participate more, and 66 percent would prefer to work in an employee-owned firm, in fact only some 10 percent of the work force actually participate in quality-of-work-life programs or employee stock ownership plans.

The 74-percent gap between employees' goals and their accomplishment is one measure of the lost potential of the workplace—one legacy of Frederick Winslow Taylor.

Taking Stock—And Other EP Success Stories

If the participation gap is the bad news, the good news is that those 10 percent of employees whose firms have encouraged EP are now showcases of how the participation model outperforms the authoritarian model. For Theory X is an economic dinosaur in a high-tech age. If the market model works—that is, if efficiency outcompetes inefficiency, as ink gave way to typewriter ribbons which in turn gave way to word processing—then the following case studies should be harbingers of the American economy by the year 2000. All six categories of employee involvement described in these studies pivot on managerial appreciation of three fundamental principles.

First, *management should treat employees more as partners and less as costs,* more as colleagues than as cogs; this can take the form of something as small as eliminating separate cafeterias for hourly and salaried workers or of simply speaking to line workers, for example, in the tradition of General Paul X. Kelley, commandant of the Marine Corps in 1983, who said, "I make it a habit of talking to at least one junior enlisted person a day. If you rely on the chain of command, you'd never know anything."

Second, *management should realize that positive rewards can motivate employees better than negative threats.* In other words, Taylor was on the right track but the wrong train: Environmental incentives *can* affect employee motivation and effort, but the carrot excels the stick. Or as behavioral psychologist B. F. Skinner put it, "The person who has been punished is not thereby simply less inclined to behave in a given way; at best, he learns how to avoid punishment." Finally, *management must believe in the value of investment in human talent.* Charles Sporck, an engineer and the unsentimental, bottom-line-oriented CEO at the National Semiconductor Corporation, expressed well the importance of an intelligent, motivated work force: "Today, our ability to succeed is entirely wrapped up in our labor. Take the alignment operator in our 'wafer-lab.' Her decision making determines the profit-ability of the company. If her decisions are not right, our yields go down the tubes and our profits go down the tubes. She has to be motivated to the company's best interests. We cannot be in our environment where somebody checks in at seven o'clock, turns off the mind, puts in eight hours, punches out. The company would go bankrupt. We are not hiring people because of their arms and legs, we are hiring them because of their heads."

1. Quality-of-Work-Life Programs
UAW president Owen Beiber recalls that, as a young die-setter in 1948 at McInerney Spring and Wire, in Grand Rapids, Michigan, "nobody asked me what I thought of my job and how I might do it better. It was a crazy way to do things."

A better way originated in America but spread most rapidly in Japan, a country of such limited resources it had to extract the most value possible from its work force. Put simply, quality-of-work-life (QWL) circles assume that managers should not only employ labor, but learn from labor, who, after all, are the people who know the most about daily production. The circles are small groups of supervisors and employees that meet regularly to spot and solve workplace problems, from production flaws to personnel failings. A sense of teamwork and impact replace the feeling of individual helplessness that previously characterized workers' attitudes about the process of change. Offshoots of the QWL circle concept go by different names—job enrichment, work redesign, sociotechnical systems—but all involve enlisting employees more in workplace decisions. Instead of companies taping a "productivity department" onto the existing hierarchy when production problems arise, every employee is assumed to be a productivity department. Management becomes more a network than an office, more a set of concepts than a specific set of people. Management spawns self-management.

More than 14 percent of American firms with over 100 employees have some form of QWL, with 750 companies having an average of ten apiece. According to preliminary data, they work. A study of 23 GM assembly plants with the most groups engaged in QWL showed that these plants had higher product quality, higher customer satisfaction ratings, lower absenteeism, fewer grievances, and lower labor costs than other GM facilities. It may be significant that in 1973, only 6 auto locals settled before the national UAW agreement; while in 1979, 54 settled early, 40 of which had QWL programs. And in two separate surveys of companies with this version of EP, 57 percent to 86 percent regarded their efforts as "very" or "moderately" successful.

Successful QWL circles meet most or all of the following criteria:

—They must be voluntary. So when GM wanted to start one at its Chevrolet gear and axle facility, it didn't go forward until 80 percent of employees signed on; the other 20 percent were neither required nor pressured into joining.

—No one can be laid off as a consequence of QWL savings. It is inconceivable that employees will donate their time and ideas to management if as a possible result they lose their job.

—The program cannot pursue productivity as its only goal, or else employees may regard it as a speedup in democratic garb. Its goal should be greater employee satisfaction, out of which will inevitably come gains in productivity.

—If management does not adopt a quality circle suggestion, it should say why. An unexplained veto collides with the participatory philosophy of QWL—and deters future suggestions, which can fight waste. (Toyota Motor Corporation, for example, gets five hundred thousand proposals annually from its quality circles program, which saves an average of $230 million.)

—Each circle should have few employees (ten to twelve), all from a common area; it should meet on company time; it should be lead by "facilitators" (usually supervisors) who are trained in group dynamics.

—Circles must be part of the entire corporate structure. If a few managers impose the idea on grudging colleagues or uninvolved supervisors, this betrays the spirit of cooperation on which quality circles are based. Also, after the initiating manager leaves, the program may collapse, as happened at Lockheed and General Foods in the 1970s. So management practices toward bonuses, status symbols, and division of labor should be internally consistent with the spirit of employee participation.

—Bankers understand the term *patient capital,* that is, loans that pay off in the long run. Managers should also appreciate the need for "patient human capital" when it comes to QWL. It takes time to produce results. Successful quality circles at such companies as Solar Turbines International, Northrop Corporation, RCA Corporation, Reynolds Metals Company, Control Data Corporation, and others have proceeded at a deliberately slow pace. Rene McPherson, the former president of Dana Corporation, describes how his firm patiently established its program: "[O]ne of the reasons it has worked so well is that it took us five years to get it installed. It involved everyone in an operation, from the sweeper to the plant manager. It made you stop once a month and talk to everyone about how you were doing . . . To get somebody's philosophy moved around takes two, five, ten years. If you jam it down their throats . . . then it won't work."

—If there is a union at the company, the QWL program should be a joint management-union effort, ideally based on contract provisions. Rudy Oswald, research director of the AFL-CIO, believes that QWL "can't work without a union because these programs talk about how production *should* take place but *not* about how the fruits are to be shared." There's also the political reality that a union shouldn't be expected to watch management meet with their members without their involvement. So when a Ford plant in Great Britain tried to introduce quality circles without clearing it with its unions, the unions rejected the idea.

Even when these standards are met, QWL still faces opposition. Many managers fear that it means running the company by committee, although management retains final authority over the firm's policies. And while in Japan a premium is placed on respect for authority and teamwork, the greater stress on individualism in the United States conflicts with the group ethic of QWL circles. But such hurdles apparently have not tripped up GM, the Central Bank of Denver, Solar Turbines International, Jones and Laughlin Steel, and Bethlehem Steel.

At GM's Chevrolet gear and axle plant in Detroit, top company executives had just about given up the old assembly line for dead, another victim of labor-management tension and poor communications. Then in 1981, the plant tried a QWL program, and the result has been something of an economic Lazarus. A management-union committee concentrated on making the job satisfying and producing quality products. In the old days, recalls a QWL coordinator, Richard Danjin, line employees "used to get together on Thursday and say, 'Let's all work Saturday and get some overtime.' So we would purposely scrap five hundred axles that would have to be rebuilt on the weekend. You do that now, and you work yourself out of a job, pal. That axle's going to cost twice as much and the Japanese will move in."

So while the plant used to be a typical assembly line with workers doing unvarying, small tasks, today it has some sixty-five teams of hourly workers, according to writer Charles Burck, where each worker "is now responsible with other team members for the production and quality of an entire brake system. All the workers are capable of doing one another's jobs, and as Dough Latkowski, a quality-assurance inspector, observes, 'all of us are inspectors.'"

At the Central Bank and Trust of Denver, an employee who each night pushed a car loaded with $7 million in cash into the vault had long wondered why the money wasn't put to some use instead of sitting in stir all that time. But because he was an isolated and lowly employee, no one ever asked his opinion. When the bank created a quality circle, however, he shared his view with colleagues. The group investigated and, sure enough, the bank only needed to keep about $1.5 million on hand. From then on, the $5.5 million was shipped over to the nearby Denver Federal Reserve Bank where it earned interest overnight for the bank.

Solar Turbines International is the leading manufacturer of 1,200- to 4,000-horsepower gas-turbine-driven compressor pump and generator packages. After a costly four-month strike in 1975, the firm began experimenting with various QWL programs to improve low management credibility and poor rapport between salaried supervisors and hourly workers. Two years later, Solar began a formal quality circle program.

The QWL circles are led by volunteering supervisors who take training in brainstorming, data gathering, cause-and-effect analysis, how to make oral presentations to managers, and how to run meetings so they don't turn into gripe sessions. Most circles are comprised of ten employees, who meet once a week during regular working hours. The supervisor lists all employees' problems on a blackboard at the start of a meeting, arranges them in an agreed-upon order of priority, and then begins discussion of solutions. Solar thinks the groups are improving the quality of work, employee understanding of the firm, and profitability. At Solar's Kearny Mesa plant, for example, a quality circle discovered that the electrical assembly department did not have a sufficient number of company-supplied tools. After spending forty-four employee hours analyzing the amount of worker delay caused by this lack of tools, and making a $2,200 investment in new tools, the annual savings have amounted to $31,700.

After the United Steelworkers of America established the concept of labor-management participation teams (LMPTs) in their 1980 steel contracts, some critics predicted these quality circles would descend to the trivial. They haven't. According to Sam Camens of the United Steelworkers, LMPTs concentrated on forty-two problems at Jones and Laughlin's Hennepin, Illinois, plant: "Only one ('Food Machines') deals exclusively with employee convenience; three with employee relations; two with employee scheduling. Expressed another way, about 16 percent of their problems have concerned employee working conditions and relations; 84 percent have dealt with production, maintenance and quality. This is typical of all plants."

At other steel facilities, LMPTs of supervisors and employees developed a tool availability program at a blast furnace, which cost $16,000 and saved $330,000 annually by minimizing furnace delay, and established a standard operating procedure to stop excess rolling for each order on a cold-mill, which was costing $713,043 a year. By the end of 1983, there were some three hundred LMPTs of ten to fifteen hourly and salaried employees each operating at Jones and Laughlin Steel Company, Bethlehem, Republic, Armco, and National Steel.

QWL programs don't only help boost employee self-worth and company net worth; they also enable employees to understand better the profit-making function of companies of which they're a part. At a large manufacturing plant in the South, one member of a quality circle asked why the firm had allowed inventories to fall so low. A fellow circle member, rather than the supervisor, responded, "Do you know what the cost of interest is these days? For every piece that we have in inventory, we have to pay a finance charge, man! That comes straight out of profits. We have to keep inventories low if our business is going to make a profit!"

2. Employee Stock Ownership

The argument for stock ownership by employees has at least four rationales. First, necessity. In hard times, firms may have to compensate employees with more stock rather than more salary, which is essentially the substitution of future profits for current profits. As part of its bailout package, for example, Chrysler provided its employees with $162.5 million in stock, distributed over four years. In the most extreme instance of necessity, employees may be forced to choose between their firm's bankruptcy and their buyout of stock.

Second, equity. Giving employees stock is one way to provide capital ownership to people who can't save their way to significant holdings. And in a society where some 6 percent of stockholders control 70 percent of all individually held stock, even conservatives such as Ronald Reagan have urged more widespread stock ownership.

Third, antibureaucracy. Einar Thorsrud, a Swedish social scientist and leader in Europe of efforts at workplace democracy, has said, "Our basic mission is how to bring meaning back to the job. Since the start of the Industrial Revolution, we have moved in only one direction—toward increased bureaucracy." By motivating rather than merely monitoring employees, firms can strip away many layers of supervisory personnel.

Fourth, efficiency. If workers have an ownership interest in their jobs, they will probably try harder since they are, in a sense, working for themselves. "Any man worth his salt would fight to defend his home," Mark Twain once said, "but only a fool would fight to defend his boarding house."*

Some businessmen regard the unusual approach of employee ownership as radical, if not socialistic. But since socialism means state ownership while employee stock ownership involves privately held corporations that operate in a competitive market economy, these firms are examples not of state socialism but worker capitalism. If it's fine to own stock in companies where one doesn't work, why should it be heretical to own stock where one does?

Like QWL, employee stock ownership is not without its risks and problems. If the acquired company is undercapitalized, ineptly managed, or in a declining industry, employees may be placing their savings and pensions on a bad bet. So workers desperate to save their jobs should still only buy into their facilities if the terms and prospects are reasonable, and not engage in what could be regarded as "lemon capitalism."

When Ford workers refused to take a 50-percent wage and benefits cut for the privilege of buying their faltering aluminum-casting plant in Sheffield, Alabama, Ford shut it down. In very successful companies, on the other hand, employee-owners may be tempted to sell their appreciated stock to nonemployees in the stock market, which could dilute the degree and purpose of employee ownership. Indeed, this degenerative process undermined one of the best-known employee-owned corporations, the Vermont Asbestos Group.

In an act that brings to mind T. S. Eliot's description of be-

---

*Indeed, several independent studies indicate that firms with employee stock ownership are more profitable and have higher productivity. For example, a University of Michigan study of ninety-eight firms found that firms with employee stock ownership plans (ESOPs), described subsequently, averaged 50 percent higher profits than similar non-ESOP firms—and the greater the equity, the greater the profits. A survey of 229 firms with ESOPs for the *Journal of Corporation Law* concluded that employee stock firms had an annual average increase in productivity of .78 percent while other comparable firms had a decline of .74 percent. The National Center for Employee Ownership found that firms with employee stock plans added employees at roughly three times the rate of conventional firms. And the Conference Board concluded in a 1983 analysis that of sixty employee buyouts designed to avoid plant closings, only two ended in financial failure.

trayal—"the greatest treason [is] to do the right deed for the wrong reason"—some firms may adopt an ESOP *only* because it helps them lower taxes, raise capital, or ward off hostile takeover attempts (because employee-owners wouldn't sell if they might lose their jobs under new owners). If these reasons induced companies to try employee ownership, which in turn produced greater job satisfaction and production, fine. But such reasons could also induce a company to create an employee ownership program that is mere tokenism—in which employees participate on paper, but not in practice. For example, if employee owners have neither a majority nor significant influence on the board of directors, they may feel like coerced investors and lose the motivational boost that should accompany ownership. So, although the South Bend Lathe was 100 percent employee-*owned*, the CEO ran the firm in a traditionally autocratic manner because it was not employee-*controlled*. These frustrations led to a strike by the employee-owners. William Foote Whyte of Cornell University accurately summarizes the two stages that many employee buyouts go through. The first is a period of euphoria because "we saved the plant," which lasts from several months to a couple of years. Stage two can occur when employees realize that, despite their status of "owner," managers haven't altered old attitudes and habits.

One failure was the Rath Packing Company. After Rath had lost $23 million in eight years, its workers made large wage concessions and bought the firm in a last-ditch effort to save their jobs. Lyle Taylor, the union president at the Waterloo, Iowa, firm, became the company president. Under employee ownership, productivity rose 20 percent; but since production costs were only some 20 percent of total costs, there was only a 4 percent reduction in total costs, which proved not enough to overcome a deteriorating situation. New and efficient firms paying one third union scale took business away. Also, said Taylor in 1984, "The banks let this company down. You get along with banks pretty good until you mention employee ownership. Then they say, 'we'll think it over. And that's that.'" Large losses led to great distrust between employee-managers and employee-workers, to the point that Rath's eighteen hundred employees even picketed the firm—in effect, themselves. By the end of 1984, Rath had entered bankruptcy proceedings.

But for every Rath, there are dozens of instances of employee ownership in firms that generate more workplace satisfaction, productivity, and profitability for the psychological reason Twain alluded to—if you give people a stake in their job, they're more likely to put out than to slack off.

The most common form of stock ownership today is the employee stock ownership plan (ESOP). According to Corey Rosen of the National Center for Employee Ownership, these have grown from 843 plans covering 520,000 workers in 1976 to 7,500 plans covering 9.6 million workers by 1985.* In only some five hundred companies, however, do the employees own a majority of stock.

Because of various tax preferences, under an ESOP workers can form a company, issue stock to a trust, and borrow money using the stock as collateral—paying no tax on either interest or principal.† Most commonly, ESOPs take stock in successful firms, small and large, such as Eakers, for example, the company noted in the Introduction. Founded in 1923, it is a chain of twenty-five clothing stores having outlets throughout Colorado. The consistently profitable company set up an ESOP in 1976, primarily as a motivational tool but partly to derive tax benefits. Half of Eakers 250 full-time employees participate in the plan, which owns 25 percent of all shares. Stock is allocated according to salary and it vests 100 percent only after someone works for the firm three years. Management credits the ESOP with a beneficial impact on productivity, morale, turnover, work quality and competition. Sales per employee grew 40 percent in the first six years after the plan was inaugurated—and after the three-year vesting period concludes, on average only 5 percent of the

---

*These numbers do not reflect employee pension funds, which hold nearly $600 billion in stock or a quarter of all privately held wealth. Despite Peter Drucker's provocatively titled book, *Pension Fund Socialism,* workers may technically own, but actually have no control over, "their" stock. There are so many layers of trustees, lawyers, money managers, and banks between them and their assets that employees whose pension funds buy stock don't feel or think like owners—and don't connect their personal productivity with a bigger paycheck down the road.

†The ESOP gets a bank loan guaranteed by the corporation. The ESOP then buys the firm's stock, which collateralizes the loan and which becomes vested in the employees, who "own" the stock when they terminate their employment or retire. The company's periodic cash contributions to the ESOP pay off the bank loan—contributions that are tax deductible because they are considered deferred labor compensation. The employees get stock paid for, in effect, by the dilution of existing shares and forgone taxes.

ESOP employees leave the firm annually, as compared to 60 percent of the non-ESOP employees.

Although they are far fewer in number, more newsworthy ESOPs are those that dramatically rescue jobs by buying out 100 percent of the stock of faltering firms, such as Hyatt Clark Industries and Weirton Steel.

In 1981, GM decided to sell its Hyatt Roller Bearing plant—an aging red-brick factory in Clark, New Jersey—because the auto company thought that labor costs were too high and that bearings could be supplied more cheaply by outside firms. But when many potential buyers shied away because of the reported militancy of the UAW Local 736, local workers and managers began to consider an employee buyout. Most employees put up $100 apiece to finance an Arthur D. Little management study that prescribed harsh measures: For the plant to survive as a profitable, independent company, wages would have to be cut by 25 percent and benefits by 50 percent.

GM supported the buyout idea, as several executives remarked they wanted to avoid "another Mahwah"—a reference to the Ford plant in Mahwah, New Jersey, that closed in 1980, costing thirty-three hundred assembly workers their jobs. Despite obstacles (the UAW national office refused a loan to a plan that specified benefits below those in the national contract), the plant's joint Job Preservation Committee pulled it off in October 1982: GM and a consortium of banks came up with the $53-million purchase price; GM also agreed to purchase bearings from the plant for at least three years; numerous inefficient work rules were eliminated; and employees swallowed the recommended wage-benefit concessions and the lenders' insistence that the ESOP own but not initially control the firm.

The newly christened Hyatt Clark Industries within six months hired a new CEO, Howard Kurt, who repeatedly stressed the value of "psychological ownership." He began holding regular meetings with small groups of employees and promised that all future pay increases would be based on merit. Reserved parking and exclusive dining rooms were eliminated. Hyatt introduced a statistical quality-control program based on the Japanese technique of machine operators recording quality and productivity data. In the first six months, productivity rose by 80 percent and the percentage of defective products fell from 10 percent to 7 percent. For example, although many employees knew they could run three machines, they had only run one each before the purchase. "There has been a huge increase in worker effort," concludes James Zarello, head of the union bargaining team, because a lot of people who were only putting in a few hours a day were now pulling their weight.

At the time of the takeover in 1981, Hyatt Clark employed 800 workers. By 1984, it employed 1,550 workers. And while the firm lost money in the first fiscal year of the ESOP, it went into the black in each of the next two years.

The largest ESOP purchase by far began on a cold day in March 1981, when National Steel Corporation CEO Howard Love announced that he would begin phasing out the company's Weirton Steel Division in Weirton, West Virginia, a hardscrabble town of twenty-six thousand inhabitants bracketed by the high hills on the east and the Ohio River on the west. But since the sprawling 389 acres of furnaces, smokestacks, and coils comprising the *company* of Weirton was also the *town* of Weirton's largest employer—with ten thousand full- and part-time employees—the announcement was received as an economic neutron bomb in this blue-collar town.

Love's threat, as Dr. Johnson remarked of a prospective hanging, concentrated the minds of the company's workers and community's residents—an immigrant enclave of Poles, Greeks, Italians, and Yugoslavs where the hometown scenes of the movie *The Deer Hunter* were shot. A series of bake sales, raffles, and telethons, as well as worker contributions based on seniority, funded a million-dollar feasibility study by McKinsey and Company, which concluded that Weirton could be nursed back to health with a prescription like the one Arthur D. Little provided Hyatt Clark: a one-third cut in pay and benefits to generate $100 million annually to finance capital expenditures, and then a buyout via an ESOP. National, for its part, promised to assume all pension costs if the new company failed in its first five years.

In September 1983, 92 percent of voting employees approved the plan, since, as one shop steward put it, "It's a two-horse race. One of 'em's dead and one of 'em's not." According to the final agreement, the new employee-owned company paid $386 million for the facilities and liabilities; pay increases, strikes, and lockouts were prohibited for six years; employee-owners will receive one third of profits when Weirton reaches $100 million in equity and one half of profits once equity exceeds $250 million; and the facility would be controlled not by employees but by a ten-member board dominated by investment advisers. As a condition of the loan, banking sources insisted that the ESOP couldn't distribute its shares to employees until 1989. For a while, in effect, employees would be workers by day and owners by night.

The investors and the workers signed the deal because while Weirton Steel was not profitable enough for National Steel, it was profitable enough to cover costs and make a little money. "It's not a dying operation," says the union's lawyer David Robertson. "You can talk all you want about 'worker participation,' but you don't have anything unless you have a decent business." Joshua Gotbaum of Lazard Freres, the plan's investment adviser, sees it similarly: "This is worker capitalism, not worker management. If this thing is going to work, no matter who owns it, it's going to have to be run like a business."

So the company town became a town company, with favorable initial results. Dick Heilman, a thirty-six-year veteran at Weirton, recalls, "The minute it was announced that we were going to buy the plant, I noticed people in my section working longer and taking shorter breaks. There's a lot we can do without." The new CEO, fifty-five-year-old Robert Loughhead, who says he accepted the challenge because "a large employee-owned company was the perfect environment to prove that employee participation could work," began installing "employee participation teams" where workers can make suggestions and objections. And each week Loughhead himself fields questions from small groups of workers on the shop floor.

In the year after the sale, Weirton began picking up customers and earning higher profits per ton ($41) than any of the largest six steel firms. Although most steel firms lost money in 1984, Weirton earned $48 million in profits in the first nine months of the year. And where seventy-two hundred employees were working when the ESOP went through, there were eighty-two hundred employees at Weirton a year later. Considers a pleased Loughhead, "Employee participation has got to be the wave of the future in manufacturing."

Worker cooperatives are a second form of employee ownership. Like ESOPs, cooperatives seek to provide employees with more voice and profits. But unlike ESOPs, there is a policy of one vote per employee (not one vote per share); all net income accrues to labor; labor theoretically hires capital (paying salaries, interest) rather than capital hiring labor; and because membership rights are personal rights, not property rights, they can't be sold to nonemployees—just as citizens have the right to vote but can't sell that right. So cooperative employee-owners can't trade their stock. After a defined number of years or when they leave, employees receive the balance of their individual capital accounts.

There are some two hundred cooperative companies in America. One small though representative example is the Workers Owned Sewing Company, a racially mixed "cut and sew" factory in Bertie County, North Carolina. It cuts finished cloth to patterns, and sews the cloth into garments. Confronted by the pending bankruptcy of the predecessor company, the firm's manager sought the assistance of the Massachusetts-based Industrial Cooperative Association to create a new company owned and managed by its workers as a cooperative. In August 1979, the Workers Owned Sewing Company (WOSC) began when the prior and new manager, Tim Bazemore, purchased the first share of stock. Each worker at WOSC, after a six-month trial period, is required to buy one and only one share of the stock under the one-vote-per-share principle. The worker-owners elect all of the firm's board, which oversees management much as a traditional board does.

Rising like some phoenix from its near-bankrupt predecessor, WOSC made its first profit only eight months after opening. From twenty-five employees, the firm grew to one hundred within two years. Turnover is low and productivity high, which is the only way to survive in such a highly competitive industry with so many fixed costs. "Everybody here's trying to make money for the company," says one employee-owner. "I find myself more interested in the quality since I'm working in a workers' co-op." Board member Louise White agrees: "I feel like I'm doing it for myself."

Among the most enduring and successful of employee-owned cooperatives are sixteen separate plywood companies in the Pacific Northwest. Founded in the 1920s and 1930s by their employees, these cooperatives give back to the employees a share in the company and a say in directing the firm's business. According to a study done in the 1970s by scholar Paul Bernstein, these firms range in size from 60 to 450 shareholder-employees each, and from $3 million to $15 million in sales. In two or three general meetings a year, owner-employees elect from their own ranks a board and a general manager—who hold down their regular jobs as well—and vote on large capital expenditures. The owner-employees are informed monthly of the firm's financial position—and between these times have direct access to company officers, who work right next to them.

These firms are 25 to 60 percent more productive than the industry average, according to a tax court ruling allowing higher-than-average wages. There are several dividends to this enhanced productivity. CEO Leamon Bennett of Puget Sound Plywood observes that bureaucracy is reduced since managers have to discipline and police employees less. Bernstein writes that one benefit "has been the uncommon ability of these firms to change output and wage rates when necessary for all members to survive in the face of highly variable markets. Instead of laying off workers when orders or prices decline, these firms call a meeting of all employees and decide how to cut costs, including reducing wages if necessary . . . knowing they can raise them back up again whenever the company can afford it, which, unlike in other companies, they are in a position really to know." Management consultant James O'Toole, author of *Making America Work,* adds that "the psychic benefits of ownership are the most remarkable. Independent observers all comment on the pride and 'rugged individualism' of the millers. These people take guff from no master, and this is apparently worth a great deal to the millers, many of whom could earn more working for someone else."

3. Gain Sharing
Sharing the spoils has been advocated by people from the UAW's Walter Reuther in 1958 ("profit-sharing . . . would help to democratize the ownership of America's vast corporate wealth") to GM's Roger Smith in 1984 (who sought the day when "the autoworker will turn to the stock pages before he turns to the sports pages"). Here again, the goal has been to motivate employees by returning to them some of the profits of their increased productivity; the form, however, is not actual ownership of stock but the right to added income in prosperous times. Of course, when Reuther first proposed profit sharing, the auto industry denounced the idea as "socialistic" and "radical." By the red ink year of 1982, however, Detroit couldn't provide their workers with long-expected annual salary increases. So they instead provided Reuther's long-shunned "radical" plan.

"Management is saying to the unions," explained Bert Metzger, president of the Profit Sharing Research Foundation, "if you are willing to share losses with us on the way down, we're willing to share profits and ownership or job security with you on the way up." Reuther's spiritual and institutional legatee, Douglas Fraser, agreed that profit sharing made sense in uncertain times: "Until this year [1982], basically, we've tried to divide up the economic pie before it's baked. That's not really a logical way to go about it—we can't accurately predict what's going to happen to a company for the next three months, let alone the next three years."

Today some 17 million workers in 435,000 companies are covered by profit sharing—and the number of new plans has grown by half from 1979 to 1984. The concessionary bargaining that swept industry in 1982 added this approach not only in the UAW contract but also at Pan Am, Uniroyal, Wheeling-Pittsburgh Steel Corporation, International Harvester, and the New York *Daily News*, among many others. Of corporations of over 500 employees with profit sharing, 77 percent report a beneficial impact; and those with the longest-running profit-sharing plans report the best performance.

While most profit-sharing programs are strictly deferred plans, about 20 percent do offer some immediate cash returns, which would appear to be the preferred way to persuade employees that their extra effort will yield an extra return to them. Cummins Engine Company, in Columbus, Indiana, for instance, began its plan in February 1984 after several quarters of losses or low profits. Earnings then rose because of an improved economy and the cash profit-sharing plan that paid an average $2,100 per employee in the first ten months. Also, the plan covers all its thirteen thousand workers and not just, as before, top executives.

Despite these favorable results and a pedigree tracing back to Reuther, much of American labor is antagonistic to profit sharing. Chrysler workers in 1982 rejected by a ratio of two to one continuing a three-year-old profit-sharing plan that had produced no bonuses; they held out for and got a raise. "People want something in their hand," says Joe D'Amico of UAW Local 420. "If it's in the bush, you don't know if you're going to get it." And Ray Majerus, the beefy secretary-treasurer who narrowly missed succeeding Fraser in 1982, worries that "profits are manipulable—there's lots of ways you can make money, lose money, hide money. . . . And what happens when they go through that cycle again, when they make the wrong guess and build the wrong car?"

Such concerns have helped spur a variation of profit sharing—what is being called productivity sharing, or pay for productivity. Instead of receiving a share of any profits over a certain threshold, employees earn additional pay or benefits if they exceed an agreed-upon productivity measure. Only an estimated one thousand corporations utilize pay-for-productivity plans for hourly employees.

One example of productivity sharing is the Scanlon Plan, named after union leader Joseph Scanlon who pioneered the idea at a failing steel mill during the Depression: Plant management determines an "allowable" labor cost and then monthly compares it to the actual labor cost. Unlike profit-sharing plans, whose benefits are usually deferred until retirement, Scanlon plans promise a monthly or annual "paycheck enrichment"—a form of positive reinforcement consistent with the gain-sharing goal of encouraging workers to work smarter.

Motorola Incorporated began a "participative-management program" in the early 1970s based on Scanlon principles. Team bonuses have averaged 11 percent of base pay monthly—and Motorola has experienced a 40-percent reduction in monthly scrap, a 50-percent reduction of work-in-progress inventory, and a 50-percent reduction in employee turnover. TRW has had a Scanlon plan since 1975, and every May since then has given bonuses averaging 5–15 percent of base pay. "We're not just looking at whether we're paying competitive wages in a community in which we have a plant," says TRW vice-president for human relations, Howard Knicely, "but our real priority now is to focus on individual competitors and make certain that our total labor costs are lower."

"Improshare" is another gain-sharing approach that also establishes benchmarks to measure variations in a plant's labor productivity, with gains (not losses) split fifty-fifty between the firm and its employees. Because this program indexes the group's rather than the individual's productivity, employees learn to cooperate with colleagues and to understand the entire production process better. Columbus Auto Parts, a manufacturer with over eight hundred employees in Ohio making auto and truck front-end parts, was suffering in the late 1970s from management's Theory X approach and from a series of strikes and an avalanche of grievances. So in 1979, Columbus eliminated the individual-incentive plan it had used since World War II and replaced it with an Improshare program combined with quality circles and a suggestion plan. (All suggestions are assigned a number and sent to the industrial engineering department, where they are investigated from an economic standpoint. Management responds initially to all suggestions within one week.) Productivity rose 10.4 percent the first month, then leveled off with the recession. According to Kenneth Maguire, the company's manager of industrial engineering, "We would have gone under during this recession without employee involvement and gain-sharing."

Finally, a far more ambitious version of profit/gain sharing would make an employee's "bonus" a significant part of his or her compensation. "Under a fixed wage rate system," argues economist Lester Thurow, "workers have little incentive to cooperate with management or to take the initiative in suggesting new ideas for raising productivity." Thurow goes on to urge that up to a third of employees' income be based on a bonus tied not to profits, which an accountant can juggle, but to "value added per hour of work." Similarly, Martin Weitzman advocates an expanded bonus system in his book, *The Share Economy*. Weitzman points out that because a fourth of all pay is linked to corporate performance in Japan, that nation can weather price and demand shocks better: in bad times, instead of massive layoffs, there are bonus declines; the bonus system spreads the pain of a turndown so that all suffer slightly, rather than some suffering greatly, by being laid off, and others not at all.

Indeed, the GM-UAW pact of 1984 took a step in this direction when it established future pay increases as bonuses tied to a firm's performance, rather than automatic wage increases. In effect, the union opted for preserving jobs rather than routinely higher pay, though if management and union improve productivity, employees can have both.

4. Workplace Due Process

Ten weeks before being vested into the E. J. Korvette pension plan, Morton Savodnik—a fourteen-year veteran of the New York retail chain who had always received glowing recommendations—was fired. "It was done very ungraciously," said Savodnik, now sixty-one years old. "I was called to the home office at 2 p.m. and told that was it. I was to leave at 4 p.m. Six months prior to that I had gotten an increase in pay." Displaying the kind of determination that had made him a model employee, Savodnik sued Korvettes and won the right to his $85.50-a-month pension. A federal judge ruled that the 1977 firing was an unconscionable attempt to avoid paying his retirement benefits.

From the dawn of the industrial age, the law governing employee dismissals was based on the "employment-at-will" doctrine—that is, companies could fire people at will "for good cause," "for no cause," or even "for cause morally wrong," according to standard judicial terminology. The doctrine was grounded in the appealing fiction that a corporation had the same right to terminate the employment relationship as the employee did. Hence, Korvettes' summary dismissal of Savodnik.

In recent decades, however, collective bargaining, judicial decisions, and protective legislation have taken a lot of the arbitrariness out of the at-will doctrine. A trend toward more workplace due process rights has allowed employees to, in effect, participate more in the terms of their employment status. And lower turnover and greater employee security can motivate workers to work more effectively.

One fifth of all working Americans belong to labor unions and are thus protected from arbitrary firing by contracts specifying that an employee can be discharged only with "just cause." So these twenty million employees today feel the security of knowing that only their personal incompetence or economic disaster can deprive them of their livelihood, not the caprice of an antagonistic supervisor unchecked by any reviewing authority.

Judicial decisions began chipping away at the at-will formula's invincibility in 1959 in *Petermann* v. *International Brotherhood of Teamsters,* a case involving a worker who was fired because he refused to perjure himself before an investigative legislative body. "It would be obnoxious to the interests of the state and contrary to public policy and sound morality," said the California appeals court, "to allow an employer to discharge any employee . . . on the ground that the employee declined to commit perjury."

Subsequently, in cases similar to Morton Savodnik's, courts have ruled in favor of fired employees because, among other reasons, the employee wouldn't go on a date with a supervisor, had needed to take time off for jury duty, had refused to participate in an illegal price-fixing scheme, or had rejected an order to lobby a state legislature against a no-fault insurance bill. Such decisions have helped produce common-law precedents in twenty-two states that establish some limitations on the ability of corporations to fire employees. Management attorney Frederick Brown, after studying the results of forty jury verdicts in unjust-dismissal cases, now advises his corporate clients that they will "be held to the [fairness] standard of the average person on the street." Basically, this means the corporation is required to provide a notice and a warning rather than an abrupt "You're fired!"

Legislation too now protects certain classes of employees—including those with specified physical traits and those called whistleblowers. Title VII of the Civil Rights Act of 1964 prohibits termination because of race, gender, religion, or nationality—and subsequent statutes did the same for employees aged forty to seventy and for the handicapped. As of 1984, five states (Michigan, Connecticut, Maine, New York, and California) have enacted specific "whistleblower protection laws" covering workers in the private sector.

"Whistleblowers" are employees who report what they regard as harmful or unlawful company activity to management or the appropriate authorities. This occasional practice infuriates many businessmen who, according to former GM chairman James Roche, regard it as nothing less than "industrial espionage . . . another tactic for spreading disunity and creating conflict." Going even further, the usually penetrating Peter Drucker ransacked history to claim that "it is not quite irrelevant that the only societies in Western history that encouraged informers were bloody and infamous tyrannies—Tiberius and Nero in Rome, the Inquisition in Spain of Phillip II, the French Terror and Stalin."

Legislators, however, appear to regard whistleblowing as more Jeffersonian than Stalinistic—as free speech that can deter illegal and costly conduct. They agree less with Roche and Drucker and more with Harold McGraw, Jr., chairman of McGraw-Hill, who asserts that "American society needs people ready to blow the whistle on wrongdoing, and corporate top management needs them too." So in the Truth-in-Lending Law, the Environmental Protection Act, the Occupational Safety and Health Act, the Fair Campaign Practices Act, the Fair Credit Reporting Act, and the Foreign Corrupt Practices Act, Congress has included provisions that define circumstances when an employee can refuse a company order, or even report it, without fear of reprisal.

And the Civil Service Reform Act of 1978 created a Merit Protection Board to protect *federal* employees who disclose alleged governmental abuse.

In sum, twenty million union members have protection against unjust firings—as do some private whistleblowers, most federal whistleblowers, and minorities, women and the handicapped because of their physical status per se. What about the seventy-five million or so other American employees? For them, the employment-at-will doctrine is as controlling in 1984 as 1884. Jack Steiber of Michigan State University's School of Labor and Industrial Relations estimates that since half of employer firings of union members are reversed by grievance procedures, perhaps half of the three million nonunion people fired a year are fired unfairly.

Businessmen are understandably wary of having to endure a judicial proceeding every time they want to get rid of an incompetent employee. In West Germany, for example, a law against unjust dismissal led the manager of a major chemical company to tell an American peer that he envied the freedom of American corporations to fire people. "You wouldn't believe the deadwood we support," he said. When asked whether it was impossible to fire incompetents, he replied, "If you spit directly into the eye of the director general, he might fire you; or, he might just say that it was raining!"

Despite this fear, several American companies have established arbitration panels that successfully hear employee complaints about allegedly unfair firings or treatment generally. According to David Ewing, writing in *The Wall Street Journal,* the Bank of America's employee assistance office handles five hundred employee complaints a month. Control Data has introduced at two of its facilities "complaint review boards" where an aggrieved employee presents his or her complaint to a panel of peers, an executive selected at random, and a personnel officer. At Pitney Bowes, Incorporated, employee representatives meet monthly with managers to review complaints. In addition, GE has installed at several plants a five-member grievance panel and three specially trained hourly employees. Citibank employees who feel mistreated can discuss their concerns with a five-member management review board. On receiving a complaint from a disgruntled worker, IBM quickly sends out special investigators to gather evidence—investigators who operate on the assumption that the complaint is justified. And going even further,

Lockheed, TWA, and Northrop submit unresolved employee grievances to *outside* arbitrators.

Perhaps as many as half of the *Fortune* 500 companies now allow employees access to their personnel records to resolve disputed promotions or firings, according to Alan Westin, an expert on corporate privacy. This level of access assures employees that their documentable performance, and not the whim of a hostile supervisor, controls their livelihood. Firms like Aetna Life and Casualty, AT&T, Atlantic Richfield, Cummins Engine, Du Pont, IBM, Prudential Insurance Company of America, and Standard Oil Company of Indiana report that their open-files policy helps sharpen the judgment of supervisors and gives employees a better definition of merit.

In the area of speech, some companies again try to be solicitous of employees rather than censorial. Dow Chemical and American Airlines, for example, distribute publications to employees where they can criticize management policies, and where managers have a chance to respond. This process has two virtues: It provides a safety valve by which critics can blow off steam, so they will likely be more sympathetic to management's position once they have aired their case; and an employee's criticism might provoke managers to take corrective action.

These examples of a willingness to talk to, rather than down to, employees can help reduce the waste that results when workers consider their supervisors the enemy. If these companies believe that their programs are affordable and efficient—and if unionized work forces are more productive even with "just cause" clauses in their contracts—it is hard to argue that workplace due process is wasteful. What's wasteful is workers who work poorly because they feel ignored, abused, and frustrated.

5. Owning Your Job?

When United Technologies, in December 1982, announced it would shut down its Otis Elevator facility in Yonkers, New York, putting three hundred employees out of work, the Republican mayor of Yonkers responded in an unusual way—he picketed the firm. While the mayor got national headlines and vented his frustration, he didn't stop UT from leaving Yonkers.

The United Technologies incident is merely one publicized example of how communities nourish large companies with tax breaks, rely on these firms for local employment, and then are economically devastated when they pull up stakes and leave. Is this process, however dismaying in particular cases, simply the cost of a market economy governed by private investment decisions?

To be sure, no one has an enforceable right to work or to a particular job, the aspirational language of the 1946 Full Employment Act and the 1978 Humphrey-Hawkins Act notwithstanding. If such an absolute right existed, we might actually risk long-term high unemployment of the type that afflicts Western Europe. There, many firms choose new machinery over new employees because of the legal obstacles to letting people go during economic downturns.

At the same time, for most Americans, their job is by far their most valuable asset. And according to a major study done in 1984 by the Work in America Institute, "Companies are beginning to realize that a stable, highly trained work force will help them attain higher productivity and product quality." So a company with a hire-and-fire reputation will neither attract good workers nor keep costs down, which can lead to what the Introduction referred to as "waste to the company."

The Institute's study goes on to demonstrate how companies benefit from fewer layoffs or firings: The firms avoid future costs of replacing and retraining employees; escape community opprobrium, which could affect sales; pay less in unemployment insurance; attract better employees eager for long-term security; gain support for new technologies by employees, whose jobs aren't at stake; and develop in their employees a sense of loyalty that helps assure a long-term concern for increasing profitability.

There is also "waste to the economy" when employees are dumped onto unemployment rolls without any transition period to allow for retraining or relocation. Of course, the sudden loss of a job can also be personally calamitous to the unemployed worker. A U.S. Labor Department study showed that two years after a shutdown, an average of 40 percent of the workers laid off are still unemployed and many of the rest are working at less than their prior wage. Reviewing plant closings over a thirteen-year period, researchers at the University of Michigan found a suicide rate among dismissed workers that was thirty times higher than the U.S. norm; also, only 70 percent of these previously employed people had health insurance, showing that many of those who might need it the most could not afford it.

Can the conflicting concerns of the company's need to keep investment mobile, and the workers' need for security, ever be reconciled? Beyond the suggestion, made in the prior section, of internal review or arbitration to reduce arbitrary firings, there are two additional ideas that could further assure insecure employees: notice of plant closings, and a voluntary "no layoff" program.

If markets shift or disappear, or a company manufactures slide rules in an age of hand calculators, plants will inevitably close. Still, was it necessary for Slater-Standard Wallcovering to leave town over a weekend without first telling its employees? Or for Atlantic Richfield in September 1980 to announce over the radio the immediate closing of the seventy-five-year-old Anaconda copper smelter, where a quarter of the town worked? Usually companies know months beforehand that they plan to close a factory or facility. Providing notice to the community and employees can enable them to cushion the blow by making plans on how to retrain or relocate. Or in situations where a plant is still potentially profitable—for example, a Hyatt Clark or Weirton Steel situation—notice allows the company, community, and workers the opportunity to see if an employee buyout is feasible.

Some companies and states provide for notification. The Big Three auto companies pledge to provide the UAW with at least six months' notice before closing a facility. When Brown and Williamson Tobacco Company had to shut down its fifty-one-year-old plant in Louisville, Kentucky, the company gave the twenty-seven hundred affected employees three years' notice even though the labor contract called for only eighteen months. Three hundred fifty workers were able to relocate to a new B&W plant in Georgia; the others all got six months' separation pay and health care coverage, as well as financial counseling and vocational training for new jobs. "There's no such thing as a good plant closing," said the head of the Tobacco Workers Union, "but they gave us a fair deal."

A law passed in Maine in 1977, after several companies left abruptly without giving any severance pay to employees, requires firms with one hundred or more employees to pay a minimum of one week's severance for each year worked. And a 1985 Massachusetts statute supported by both management and labor blends voluntary cooperation with state aid: A "social compact" encourages firms to provide three months' notice before a shutdown, and three months of health insurance coverage and thirteen weeks' severance pay after a shutdown. The state also established an office to monitor the Massachusetts economy and assist troubled companies and displaced workers.

Then there are at least forty American companies that maintain a "no layoff policy," a modified version of the "lifetime employment" in Japan, which covers some quarter of the work force there. In bad times, Japanese workers are retrained or reassigned, but not dismissed. The plant manager of one electronics components factory explained what happens with subpar workers: "We give a chance to improve even if there has been a big mistake. For example, the quality control manager didn't fit, so we transferred him to sales engineering and now he is doing fine." A study of thirteen Japanese and thirteen comparable U.S. firms during the recession of 1974–75, for instance, found that the Japanese firms laid off 2.8 percent of their work force versus 11.8 percent for the Americans. And compare Chrysler, which in its recent years of crisis dismissed tens of thousands of employees to cut costs despite UAW concessions, with the example of Toyo Kogyo. When this Japanese car company had a similar brush with bankruptcy, the union allowed management to send factory workers out as car salesmen. After sales improved, the employees shifted back to their old jobs.

Led by pioneers like IBM and the Hewlett-Packard Company, American firms trying out the Toyo Kogyo model include, among others, Motorola, Du Pont, Procter and Gamble, 3M, Upjohn, Control Data, Lincoln Electric, and R. J. Reynolds Tobacco. Experiments vary. Kimberly-Clark, the huge paper corporation, faced with laying off one hundred production workers, persuaded eighty of them to become marketers of company products. The new unit produced millions in new sales. In its 1980 contract, Ford promised lifetime employment at three plants, no shutdowns as a result of "out-sourcing" (making parts abroad), and a "guaranteed income stream" for those who might be laid off (for example, a fifteen-year veteran would get half pay for life unless he gets another job). In 1984, GM's Packard Division and the International Union of Electrical Workers agreed on lifetime jobs (six-month layoffs during downturns being the one exception), although the union had to agree to allow paying newly hired employees at half the current assembly-line rate. The agreement succeeded only because of improved relations resulting from Packard's worker participation program, involving thousands of employees in self-managed work teams.

In a form of "work sharing," Hewlett-Packard during the 1970 recession rejected massive layoffs and instead ordered everyone in the company to take a 20-percent pay cut and to work 20 percent fewer hours. When Allied Tube and Conduit saw its business slow drastically in the early 1980s, the firm and its union, the United Steelworkers, chose to adopt a four-day week rather than accept layoffs. And twenty workers who were not needed for production took training in QWL at full pay.

These novel approaches help balance the need to minimize cost in the short term *and* provide employees with the security that minimizes costs in the long term. What these firms have in common is their willingness to challenge old workplace habits, in the tradition inspired by Henry Ford in January 1914. That's when Ford, in a move considered crazy at the time, doubled the minimum he paid workers to five dollars a day, saying the increase, "was one of the finest cost-cutting moves we ever made." Ford reasoned that he could sell more cars if his employees could afford to buy them and could make more cars if his employees rewarded generosity with effort. His employees returned the favor.

6. A Labor Seat on the Board

The UAW's vice-president in charge of Chrysler in 1976 tried to persuade the country's third largest auto firm to accept two union representatives on its board of directors. Especially since the union had been urging Chrysler to build smaller, fuel-efficient cars since 1949, the union vice-president believed that having an institutional voice on the board might help avoid "the kind of blunders" that nearly sank the firm in 1974–75.

Chrysler said no. But with its corporate life hanging in the balance just four years later, the new Chrysler CEO, Lee Iacocca, asked UAW president Douglas Fraser to join the firm's board. Since Fraser had been the UAW vice-president rebuffed by Chrysler in 1976, he relished the irony of the mountain going to Muhammad. He accepted, and made history by becoming the first American union leader to sit on the board of a major corporation.

At the time, labor on boards was nothing new in Western Europe. In West Germany, for example, *Mitbestimmung,* or "co-determination," has been required by law since 1951. Labor comprises one third of the supervisory board (comparable to the American board of directors), which in turn appoints a management board to conduct the firm's day-to-day business. Also, "works councils," a cross between union locals and quality circles, contribute their say in workplace decisions concerning hours, breaks, assignments, dismissals, safety, training, and so on. These laws, according to *Business Week,* "work reasonably well in that much smaller country with a hierarchical social structure and a long tradition of labor-management cooperation."

But in the absence of such a tradition in the United States, Fraser's selection managed to raise the hackles of *both* the management and labor communities. Representatives of each side worried about the potential conflict of interest between a board member's fiduciary obligation to represent *all* the company's shareholders and Fraser's special obligation to represent his *particular* corporate constituency. Business leaders fretted about surrendering any of their managerial powers, and labor militants feared what their French brothers called a "trap of class collaboration."

Fraser, who had once referred to Chrysler's board as a group of "well-meaning, honorable, but incompetent men," brushed aside the objections. "I can't represent my members if I'm always reacting to management decisions," he said. "We have to be there when the decisions are made. And we can bring an important resource to the board. People in the plants will tell me things they can't tell management." As for the conflict-of-interest charge, it never previously came up against bankers or lawyers who provided services to the company and also sat on its board. And Fraser announced that if a board began to discuss negotiating strategy, he would simply walk out of the room and, as judges do in similar circumstances, "recuse" himself.

By the time he retired from the UAW and the board in 1983, most observers judged the experiment a success, as did Fraser and Iacocca. Fraser, who was succeeded on the Chrysler board by his UAW successor, Owen Beiber, recalled how he persuaded the seventeen-member board to study the impact of plant closings on workers and communities; in one instance, this approach managed to keep a glass plant open by bringing more work into the plant. "The weakness of traditional boards is that the outside directors hesitate to challenge decisions of the inside members because they don't know the business," Fraser added. "I brought to the Chrysler board a different life's experience, a different perspective than the business members have."

By 1985, the presence of labor leaders on boards was still not typical, but, thanks to Fraser's precedent, it was no longer considered revolutionary, either. At least fourteen corporations had labor representatives on boards, all as a result of concessionary bargaining by managements insisting on givebacks and unions demanding something in return. Such firms include not only Hyatt Clark and Weirton Steel, discussed earlier, but three airlines struggling to adjust to the turbulence caused by rate deregulation.

One of these airlines, Eastern, provides the most prominent example of board cooperation between labor and management—and one of the most surprising in light of the company's history of antagonistic labor relations. Since 1975, Eastern has been run by former astronaut Frank Borman, a charismatic loner. Borman, unfortunately, made a major miscalculation: He bought too many planes too fast. As a result, Eastern lost a quarter of a billion dollars in 1981–83, and Borman lost the confidence of the unions that he had to persuade to swallow concessions.

Union members report that things deteriorated to the point that management used binoculars to "spy" on workers, and workers retaliated by smashing some equipment. Worse, Borman had so frequently cried wolf by threatening bankruptcy unless demands were met that employees stopped believing him. "We were getting a snow job about Eastern's finances," recalls Charles Byran, the president of the International Association of Machinists local union. "They stayed on the brink of disaster by design, to justify wrenching concessions from the employees." For example, in September, 1983 Borman attempted to pressure his unions by calling a press conference to announce that Eastern might have to file for bankruptcy. Unfortunately, since his remarks stampeded customers holding Thanksgiving and Christmas tickets into switching to other carriers, his ploy almost became a self-fulfilling prophesy.

With a December 31, 1983, possible bankruptcy pending, a desperate Borman chose two outsiders—former Labor Secretary W. J. Usery, Jr., and former B. F. Goodrich Company executive Jack W. Johnson—to persuade Eastern's employees of the firm's genuine peril. The two got the unions to abide by an agreed-upon outside audit, which demonstrated that the company would indeed lose another $380 million unless something dramatic was done. And it was. In return for $370 million in wage concessions and anticipated productivity gains that year, Borman agreed to what Byran calls "the legitimate sharing of decision making" with the unions—four labor seats on the board, 25 percent of the common stock, unlimited access to the books, and the right to appeal business plans that the unions considered unwise. The company also pledged to lower the ratio of supervisors to workers and to implement an effective QWL program.

According to the headline of a *Wall Street Journal* investigative report a year later, "Labor's Big New Role Inside Eastern Airlines Seems to Be Succeeding." Although he had frequently denounced Borman in the past, Byran voted as a board member to extend the CEO's contract five more years. Unions have access to profit and loss figures, and in turn are easing strict work rules to allow ground crews to do more than one job.* The number of formal grievances filed by the machinists union fell by two thirds from 1983 to 1984. The new agreement didn't remove wages as a continuing source of contention between management and labor, but still labor director Robert Callahan tells a small but illustrative story of how relations have improved. Several directors wanted to change flight attendants' uniforms because they looked "too military"; Callahan countered that inflight assaults were significantly discouraged precisely because potentially threatening passengers viewed the military style as more than just appearance—and Callahan prevailed. As a result of this relative harmony, the firm ended 1984 with a loss of only $38 million, far less than the projected $380 million and one fourth of the 1983 total. The first quarter of 1985 was Eastern's most profitable ever. And though he initially opposed it, Borman now calls participatory management "the only way to manage."

There are still too few firms with labor representatives on boards to be able to predict whether this form of employee participation will spread or wither. Again, there is a conflict between management's desire to be in total control and management's desire to turn a good profit. At a minimum, the examples of Chrysler and Eastern make it less likely that a CEO will say, as one did to scholar Myles Mace, that the impressive names of

---

*For example, supervisors are no longer needed to turn planes around when they arrive at the Atlanta hub. Not only is this now done by self-managed ramp crews, but they are doing it faster, with 15 percent fewer lost bags and the elimination of six supervisor positions. (The supervisors are relocated to new jobs elsewhere as they open up through attrition.)

board members are "nothing more or less than ornaments on the corporate Christmas tree." For if employee representatives can successfully challenge clubby and misguided board decisions, then Doug Fraser and Charles Byran will be less ornaments than harbingers.

The New Economic Partnership

For decades, management and labor have often acted as if they were occupants of the same lifeboat, each drilling holes in the bottom to teach the other side a lesson. As a result, American companies have been sinking in the rough waters of international competition.

There now exists, however, the opportunity to inaugurate a new era in labor relations, if only companies will understand the new workplace paradigm. The paradigm is that if managers treat employees more as economic partners than as external costs, the return to both will increase. For cooperation is both economically and ethically preferable to conflict.

This model is possible, not inevitable, since it requires changes that managers and unions will find wrenching. Employee participation requires a closer collaboration between management and labor, which can be the kiss of death for elected union officials. Will these leaders have the courage to be statesmen, if the cost could be that they'll become *former* leaders? And will managers have the courage to surrender the habit of authority? Already, there have been tense disputes at both Eastern and Hyatt-Clark about how willing executives really are to share power. And of course, as ESOP expert Joseph Blasi has said, "Worker ownership doesn't magically eliminate the complexities of a poor market, poor management and a poor economy."

To succeed, any EP program requires the perception of community, as explained by economist Lester Thurow:

> Adversarial relations can only be eliminated when there is a genuine community of interests. If no such community exists, then there is nothing to agree on. Labor and capital, according to the prevailing American theory, are genuine adversaries and the firm is the battleground upon which their economic warfare takes place. The capitalists arrange a temporary truce, they may fight each other into exhaustion, but there is no basis for cooperation.

> To build the motivation, cooperation and teamwork neces-
> sary to construct a successful economy . . . the firm is going
> to have to become not a battleground but a partnership of
> labor, management, and shareholders collectively trying to
> maximize the firm's value added. Each partner is an owner
> with an interest in maximizing the value added of the firm. As
> a partial owner, each partner has a long-run interest in the
> survival of the firm.

Companies such as People Express (discussed in Chapter 1),
Eakers, Weirton Steel, Hyatt-Clark, Ford, GM, GMW, Motorola, Control Data, Hewlett-Packard, and many others demonstrate the validity of the participation/partnership paradigm.
True, these companies have innovated more as the result of crisis than by design, but they are models of how negotiated quid
pro quos can greatly boost workers' output and satisfaction. Or
as Nobel laureate economist Wassily Leontif told a New York
audience of union and public officials in November 1983, his
thick eyebrows raising to punctuate each point, "Labor would
be prepared to accept hardship for a while *if* they knew why—
and toward what end. The givebacks should be part of a broader
renegotiated social contract."

Given the avalanche of supporting data and examples, it is
now possible to describe what Thurow's new economic partnership—or Leontif's renegotiated social contract—would look
like for the corporation of the future. Employees would periodi-
cally meet during working hours in quality circles to contribute
their ideas on production. They would elect some share of all
board seats and their representatives would have confidential access to company performance data. Employees would receive a
base salary, supplemented by an agreed-upon "bonus" tied to
their firm's or their plant's economic performance, plus dividends from their ESOP. Management would establish a joint
arbitration committee to review challenged dismissals. And in
return for this greater pay and say, workers and unions would
shun those inefficient work rules that were designed in an earlier
era to protect against untrustworthy managers.

The government can play an important catalytic role in this
new partnership, helping overcome the inertia of decades of adversarial habits. Its involvement would be more in the facili-
tative tradition of an Agriculture Extension Service and a
National Labor Relation Board than the regulatory tradition of
a Federal Trade Commission. For example, a joint office of the

Commerce and Labor departments could provide technical assistance and information to interested but unsophisticated firms. What are the ten best steps to an effective QWL program? How can an ESOP be quickly established in a buyout situation? Government can distribute material on models that work, ensuring that companies don't constantly have to reinvent the wheel.

Going further, legislation introduced by Representative Stanley Lundine (D., N.Y.) in 1983 would authorize the Economic Development Administration to economically assist local communities in buying faltering firms. In those few cases where the EDA or Small Business Administration has already made such loans or grants, *none* of these communities have lost any money. Or, a U.S. president who believed that more employee participation would produce more economic growth could issue an executive order declaring it to be a national policy. He could direct each relevant federal agency to report annually on what it had done to carry out this policy. A Bureau of Labor Statistics might pursue research in this area; the SEC could review its regulations to make sure they do not unintentionally raise barriers; agencies like the EDA and SBA that make loans or loan guarantees could target them to companies adopting versions of workplace participation.

Ultimately, though, replacing the authoritarian model with the participation model is a decision that executives and unions will have to adopt. No law can make a manager devoted to Frederick Taylor's principles or a union leader attracted to the ideas of Ned Ludd work out a new partnership agreement. Either because of crisis or insight, management and labor will have to accept as their economic credo what Benjamin Franklin suggested in a political context for our fledgling republic: "We must all hang together, or assuredly we shall all hang separately."

3

Innovation: Corporate Luddites or Pioneers?

Why, I could make anything a body wanted—anything in the world, it didn't make any difference what; and if there wasn't any new-fangled way to make a thing, I could invent one—and do it easy as rolling off a log.

—Plant Superintendent in *A Connecticut Yankee in King Arthur's Court*

Some Research/Little Development

The creative individualism that produced the kind of spunky, boastful pride voiced by Mark Twain's Connecticut Yankee survives to this day. No country can match this one in scientific and technological breakthroughs—not even Japan. Indeed, if the greatest form of flattery is imitation, then the Japanese have elevated American ingenuity to godlike status.

Consider this representative story told of Adam Priest, a young talented student at Merrit College in Berkeley, California. Whenever he entered the computer lab to write a new computer program, the Japanese students would hover around him, waiting to see what he wrote before trying their own program. It was an efficient way for them to learn, but it wasn't innovation. So desperate are the Japanese to pick our creative brains, in fact, that executives from one of the major companies, Hitachi, felt compelled to steal trade secrets from IBM—and got caught. How many times have American executives been caught stealing from Japanese companies?

The United States continues to lap the world in scientific and technological breakthroughs. We developed the first computer-controlled robots, the transistor, the integrated circuit, the videocassette recorder, the communications laser, fiber-optic cable, gene splicing, and the software that enables computers to design, test, and manufacture products. We have won 144 of the 355 Nobel Prizes awarded for all three categories of science. "By almost every measure," asserts the National Science Foundation (NSF) in its 1983 biennial assessment of American science and technology, "the United States continues to lead the world in scientific and engineering achievement."

But innovation is more than scientific breakthroughs—and that's our problem. For while we have made spectacular technological and scientific advances, the United States lags behind in finding commercial applications of those breakthroughs. The Japanese are far ahead in businesses that emerged out of many of these inventions. The transistor was invented in Bell Laboratories in 1947 by Nobel laureates William Shockley, John Bardeen, and Walter H. Brattain, yet Sony began selling the first transistor radios in this country in 1956. Ampex, a U.S. company, may have introduced the first videotape recorder in 1956, but Sony greatly improved on the design with its Betamax in 1975. Now none of those machines are made in the United States. American firms did much of the initial research of optical character readers, but when the U.S. Postal Service requested bids for $500 million in the devices, all six proposals came from overseas.

Now the NSF warns there may be widespread slippage: "The United States is losing some of the overwhelming pre-eminence in the sciences, engineering and technology that it enjoyed during the past several decades." NSF cites, as straws in the wind, a decline in America's share of world trade in research-intensive products (while the Japanese share has increased), and a decline in the number of patents granted to Americans. From 1971 to 1982, U.S. domestic patenting dropped by almost 40 percent, while 40 percent of all U.S. patents granted in 1982 went to foreigners.

All this has perplexed the admiring Japanese, who wonder how it could happen to a vigorous America that only four decades ago conquered Japan and then helped rebuild her. Observes Akio Morita, the chief executive of Sony, "America has a strong pioneer spirit. You paved roads, you put gas stations and telephone lines all over the streets, and you fought many diseases and Indians and all kinds of troubles. I want to ask, 'Where is such an America?' You have such a spirit in your heart but now you have forgotten it, just like the Japanese after the war when they lost their confidence."

What indeed has happened to the Connecticut Yankee spirit of innovation? The answer is—nothing. It's still there in individuals and in many of our restlessly innovative corporations. But what did happen is that in too many American companies, management has failed to inspire, direct, reinforce, and support America's raw and ample innovative talent. It wasn't until these wasteful management practices caused American business to slip dangerously in world competition that executives began to seek answers. And where do they now go? Japan.

So while the Japanese beg, borrow, and steal from our innovative bounty, American business executives—in a tacit admission of failure—trek to Japan for its management skills as if searching for some mysterious curative waters. And one after another they return to announce in amazement that there's nothing magical about Japanese management. It's just common sense, they say. But it is precisely the lack of commonsense management that has caused American business to waste its priceless innovative legacy. True, we still get the prizes—but, increasingly, others are getting the sales.

The Importance of Innovating

The word *innovation* and all its connotations—invention, research, development, and so on—mean different things to different people. Bergen and Cornelia Evans got so upset by loose-lipped use of the term *research* that they wrote in their *Dictionary of Contemporary Usage,* "Research is frequently used to describe reading by those to whom reading, apparently, is a *recherche* activity. . . . The word needs a rest or at least less promiscuous handling." Similarly, many American businessmen toss around the word *innovative* with the same abandon as advertising executives use *creative*—and often with the same justification. Ask a corporate executive for proof that his company is "innovative" and he points to the annual report showing funds budgeted for research and development. But R and D can be a tax dodge (those funds are taxed at a lower rate) or a way of impressing Wall Street analysts and investors that the firm is alive and well.

There are, in fact, two kinds of research: basic and applied. *Basic research,* or the pursuit of knowledge for its own sake, is undertaken by all the major drug companies and only a few other unique corporations such as IBM, Xerox, and AT&T (Bell

Labs); more typically, universities engage in this type of research. Devoted exclusively to creating new knowledge, basic research generally is long-term in scope and yields an uncertain payoff. When successful, it can produce such impressive and financially rewarding results as computers, new energy sources, and biotechnology. *Applied research,* by contrast, pursues specific, practical, and commercial aims. It is less chancy than basic research, although the payoff may not be as big. Then there is *development,* which is what most companies mean when they speak of "R and D." Most corporations acquire or modify an inventor's creation or another firm's product, then market it as their own. Most outsiders, however, think that what's being done in Silicon Valley, the high-tech haven south of San Francisco, is invention. But while firms like Apple, Fairchild, National Semiconductor, and Tandem Computer may do some applied research, mostly what they do is development. They use their considerable financial resources to manufacture and market semiconductors, computers, disk drives, programs, and other high-tech equipment and paraphernalia. The inventing—basic research—may have been done in a garage somewhere, according to high-tech lore, or more likely in a university lab.

But innovation doesn't end with the invention and marketing of a new product. Innovation continues through the whole process, specifically in the manufacture of the new product. According to Professor Edwin Mansfield, some 40 percent of the cost to companies of innovating goes not for acquiring a new piece of technology or for inventing or selling it but for construction of new plant and equipment used to manufacture it: the bricks and mortar of the innovative process.

Why is innovation so important? Economist Joseph Schumpeter answered that question more than four decades ago: "The fundamental impulse that sets and keeps the capitalist engine in motion comes from the new consumer goods, the new methods of production or transportation, the new markets, the new forms of industrial organization that capitalist enterprise creates." And what happens when the new turns old? Without innovative breakthroughs, industry creates fewer jobs, factories become obsolete, productivity growth declines. Inflation also worsens, because if goods and services are not turned out more efficiently, then rising costs must be covered by hiking prices. Inevitably, with sagging growth comes a restriction on the standard of living and on the ability of people to achieve social and personal goals.

In non–high-tech firms in the United States, R and D expenditures have been declining. The lackluster performances since the mid-1960s by many of these firms illustrate the cause-effect relationship between innovation and productivity. For as R and D spending has remained constant or declined, productivity has slumped. Mansfield is the first researcher systematically to amass evidence that the composition and size of an industry's R and D expenditures affects its rate of productivity. Studying the R and D patterns of 119 companies over an eighteen-year period, he and his colleagues found that "an industry's rate of productivity increase . . . seems to be directly and significantly related to the extent to which its R and D was long term."

Supporting this thesis are figures on R and D spending and productivity: Civilian R and D spending by the United States has remained low since the mid-1960s, at about 1.7 percent of the gross national product, while West Germany and Japan have spent above 2.3 percent of their GNPs. Productivity per hour by American workers in nonfarm businesses, meanwhile, declined from 2.6 percent during the 1948–65 period to 1 percent in 1979–83, according to the Bureau of Labor Statistics. Moreover, a report by the Organization for Economic Cooperation and Development (OECD) predicts only a 2.2 percent U.S. growth in productivity to the year 2000—compared with 6.2 percent for Japan, 5.5 percent for Italy, 4.2 percent for Germany. "The United States has ceased to be exceptional," the OECD concluded glumly.

How Bad Management Has Squandered the United States' Innovative Legacy

A review of the recent history of innovation in this country suggests five significant interacting trends. Taken together, they lead to the conclusion that while Americans are as impatiently innovative as ever, that creative spirit has been misdirected by the wasteful policies of top managements:

1. The dis-economies of scale. Ever since American managers first heard of economies of scale, they have preached bigness. According to this sermon, only the biggest companies have the resources, wealth, and imagination to be innovative. Lewis

Mumford, in his 1934 book, *Technics and Civilization,* saw the trend toward giantism with the advent of steam power, which was more efficient in large units: "The industrial leaders not only accepted concentration and magnitude as a fact of operation, conditioned by the steam engine; they came to believe in it by itself, as a mark of progress. With the big steam engine, the big factory, the big bonanza farm, the big blast furnace, efficiency was supposed to exist in direct ratio to size. Bigger was another way of saying better."

In 1942, bigness was given a boost by the highly respected economist Schumpeter, who wrote that technological progress requires masses of long-term capital to finance R and D. Any government action that decreases the size of firms or the volume of resources they control could destroy their ability to carry out innovation. Longer and longer production runs in bigger and bigger factories would cut per-unit costs. This view predominated for decades. John Kenneth Galbraith, in his 1952 book, *American Capitalism: The Concept of Countervailing Power,* picked up the theme: "A benign Providence . . . has made the modern industry of a few large firms an almost perfect instrument of inducing technical change." David Lilienthal wrote that same year, "Bigness and research activity are largely synonymous whether in big business or in government."

However, as experience and evidence accumulated to contradict this economic theory, Galbraith and others reassessed Schumpeter's thesis. Now, not only is bigness seen as an impediment to innovation by many economists, but the industry concentration that often accompanies it further dampens creative impulses. The famous Jewkes study of inventions showed that of sixty-one basic inventions examined, only sixteen resulted from organizational research by large companies. For example, the ball-point pen was invented by a sculptor and the dial telephone by an undertaker. Consider also the elapsed time between invention and development by large, dominant firms. The safety razor took nine years for Gillette to manufacture; television, twenty-two years; radio, eight years; the cotton picker, fifty-three years; nylon, eleven years; the zipper, twenty-seven years. Xerography, invented by patent attorney and amateur physicist Chester Carlson in his New York City kitchen, was patented in 1937, but IBM, RCA, Remington Rand, and General Electric rejected it. Finally, in 1944, Carlson got financing from the Battelle Memorial Institute in Columbus, Ohio, in exchange for sixty percent of the proceeds—and Xerox was born.

The record is full of examples of hesitation toward innovation by big, often oligopolistic companies. For one thing, there is simply the bureaucratic inertia that retards most big firms. New ideas have to hurdle so many internal obstacles that often exhaustion preempts implementation. What's more, these firms have so much invested in existing plant and equipment and so dominate their markets already that they have little incentive to attempt to build a better mousetrap—an effort that, if successful, will render their existing investment obsolete. So they pursue the path of least resistance—which means inertia rather than innovation.

Would Xerox today again turn away Chester Carlson? Its Palo Alto Research Center boasts some of the best people in the world in computer sciences, yet it has failed repeatedly to exploit the technologies created there. "Most large corporations tend not to be entrepreneurial," laments Jack E. Goldman, former vice-president and chief scientist for Xerox who created its Palo Alto Research Center. "It is probably one of the greatest frustrations of my life that it was Apple that used some of those great new technologies the Palo Alto Center developed, or that little Symbolics near Boston is putting out a laser printer that we invented and had working in the laboratory—and even had it in distribution in a couple of spots around the country in 1972. But we [at Xerox] delayed for years introduction of this product because of the standards, the service requirements, the sales rollouts, and so forth, that the large company demands before it incorporates a new technology in a product. By the way, it is today a very successful product in the marketplace."

In the 1970s, international competition made it clear that the old economies of scale were, in fact, dis-economies. Rapid technological change has shortened product life cycles in industries such as consumer electronics, rendering obsolete big, inflexible plants and even whole corporations. Allan Kennedy, former McKinsey and Company consultant who coauthored the book, *Corporate Cultures,* predicts serious consequences for big companies that don't shrink to gain the innovative edge. "If I had to go way out on a limb I would say that large corporations as we know them will not exist in thirty years' time. They won't be able to sustain their positions. They won't be able to hold their people. . . . The evidence seems to point to between fifty and 100 people as the most efficient work unit."

2. *The costs of technological chauvinism.* So blessed is this country in human and natural resources that, over the decades, many of our industries have come to operate like a self-sufficient island, free from troublesome foreign competition. And if America dominated world trade, it was not always so much from skillful business practices as from this natural bounty.

We always have felt kinship with Europe, of course. Valuing these historic ties, we renew them by visiting the countries of our forebears and perhaps sending our children to vacation there. Economically, our ties have been there, too; when an American businessman announced he was "going abroad," his destination was assumed to be London or Zurich or Frankfurt or Paris.

But this smug satisfaction with the domestic market and Americans' European bent has for generations caused this country habitually to ignore the Pacific Basin. This has been a costly chauvinism—first came the surprise attack on Pearl Harbor, then the attack on our once-insular markets.

Now the world is entering the "century of the Pacific," predicts U.S. ambassador to Japan Mike Mansfield, with the economies of Taiwan, South Korea, Hong Kong, and Singapore growing even faster than Japan's and three times as fast as the U.S. economy. "Some trade specialists," reported Steve Lohr, Tokyo correspondent of *The New York Times,* "say that as these countries export more sophisticated manufactured products, the United States is in danger of becoming an 'economic colony' of East Asia, supplying raw materials and providing a market for profitable finished products." Asserts Akio Mikuni, a financial consultant to many Japanese companies: "Japan is now the global price-setter in autos, electronics, and some semi-conductor products; this is an epoch-making change that reflects the shift of competitive advantage toward Japan."

In the decades after World War II, U.S. companies became the primary source of technological innovation to the world, particularly to Japan. Between 1950 and 1980, Japanese companies acquired almost all of the world's available advanced technology by signing at least thirty thousand licensing or technical agreements with Western companies, mainly American. The Japanese paid about $10 billion in royalties and fees, less than one fifth of what is spent in the United States for research and development in one year. Observed Michael Boretsky, senior operations research analyst at the Commerce Department,

"The worldwide dissemination of these U.S. innovations in a naked form . . . has been, by historical standards, almost instantaneous, and the U.S. trade balance in these products not only failed to grow, but gradually turned into the red."

"The biggest fire sale in history," is how James Abegglen, the retired director of Boston Consulting Group's Tokyo office, describes the wholesale technology transfer. "From the seller's side, surely most of us in U.S. business would agree that this sale of technology represents a disastrous decision by many U.S. companies who put Japanese firms into business in a range of product sectors, at a high level of technology, at low cost, enabling those firms to compete better in world trade." He calls it a "fire sale" because U.S. corporate executives went for a quick profit instead of seeking longer-term agreements that would give them direct entry to the Japanese market. (Only a few firms, like IBM, Texas Instruments, and little Materials Research Corporation of Orangeburg, New York, which opened a small plant there in 1983, used their technology as levers to gain entry to the Japanese market. They now all have extremely successful operations in Japan.)

The Japanese companies, for their part, gained a technological springboard; by applying innovative engineering and quality control to American inventions, they leaped ahead into the marketplace in a number of areas. To take one instance, Japan used U.S.-designed computer graphics systems and electron-beam etching devices to produce 64,000-bit computer memory chips, ahead of American chip makers. Also, scientists at Bell Labs in 1970 successfully tested a tiny laser that promised a new era of "optical" communications. Turned on and off tens of millions of times a second, tiny lasers can transmit telephone conversations, messages, and other information in the form of light waves pulsing through extremely pure glass fiber cable. Yet in 1980, when Bell Telephone shopped for a company to supply lasers to go with the first light-wave cable under the Atlantic Ocean later in this century, it didn't choose Hewlett-Packard, RCA, Exxon, Xerox, or even its own manufacturing subsidiary, Western Electric. It tapped Hitachi of Japan because the company had "the most reliable laser in the world." As Dan Morgan of *The Washington Post* commented, the fact that all the American companies had access to Bell's patents and were working on lasers in the 1970s "raises questions about U.S. industry's ability to take advantage of technologies being developed in its own back yard."

The American response was ineffectual. Hewlett-Packard—one of the premier R and D companies—developed a laser program, then gave up, according to a former H-P scientist, "because they couldn't generate cash flow within a year." Exxon Enterprises, meanwhile, tried to buy into laser research by acquiring a company; Exxon, only twenty-four months later, unloaded the firm after a costly and frustrating experience. And guess who bought it—a U.S. subsidiary of Mitsubishi Chemical Corporation.

Consumer electronics provides an even more striking example of how we literally gave the Japanese our markets. In 1955, the annual output of U.S. consumer electronics makers stood at $1.5 billion; Japan's, a mere $70 million; by 1980, Japanese companies produced more than twice as much as U.S. electronics firms. The Japanese accomplished this role reversal by acquiring the manufacturing rights to video recorders, color television, and transistor technology from their American developers, especially RCA, which saw licensing as a financial windfall.

William Abernathy and Richard Rosenbloom of Harvard Business School, who studied the industry in the late 1950s and 1960s, quote one technical manager as saying, "The standing orders from the television division were to offer them [the Japanese] 'any new technology available, as long as it gets cost out of the product.'" However, the Japanese believed American consumers would buy televisions and other electronics of high quality and technology. "While the Japanese electronics firms were developing video technology," write Abernathy and Rosenbloom, "they were also investing in their manufacturing systems, nurturing employee relations, effectively engaging the skills of employees at all levels, introducing innovative manufacturing processes, and emphasizing quality and productivity throughout. They did so with a view not only to current requirements, but to constant improvement for the future."

American management was so supremely self-confident that they sold America's innovative birthright to the Japanese—and sold it cheap at that. The following are three informed opinions why such short-term thinking prevailed:

- "It was done through a combination of generosity and arrogance, or perhaps generosity and self-confidence," says William Baker, former president of Bell Labs who was head of research from 1955 to 1973, a period when, in his words, "we really set them [the Japanese] up in the whole computer electronics area. Sure, we got money for it, but it wasn't very much." Bell invented the transistor in 1947, which led to development of the semiconductor and to the integrated circuit, the very heart and soul of today's computer technology. Not only did Bell license this technology to the Japanese and others, but Bell Labs, as a matter of policy, opened its doors to foreign visitors and Bell scientists willingly discussed published material with them. Of course, Japanese scientists visited the labs as often as Bell would permit. Bell even established links to major Japanese microelectronics research laboratories. "This linkage may have constituted the single most important source of technical know-how for the Japanese electronics companies," said one knowledgeable scientist.

- "I think it was done in innocence, and I never detected any moves to pump the bottom line," says Dr. Thomas Vanderslice, the former president of General Telephone and Electronic Corporation (GTE) who has a Ph.D. in chemistry and physics and is the holder of more than a dozen patents. "The theory was that you sell off technology today, but by the time they implement it, you're way beyond it. And all of a sudden, we're not way beyond it. In sum, I'd say it was more arrogance than generosity."

- "It was a waste of resources from the point of the view of the nation," asserts Michael Boretsky, the Commerce Department research analyst. "I hold the unique view that technology is a natural resource. If you sell an oil well, you won't be able to sell oil. If you sell technology, you won't sell products unless the market is limitless. In due time you have built up competition. . . . When you lose competitiveness, it's a long-term effect. It doesn't change day to day, quarter to quarter, year to year. It deteriorates over time. And it can't be corrected over the short term, either."

Now that the Japanese and others have acquired our technology cheap, should American businessmen seek repayment in kind? We're not and, in fact, we may be unable to, according to many experts on the two economies. Increasingly, Japan is becoming an exporter of technology, but Dr. James Abegglen of the Boston Consulting Group's Tokyo office, for one, doesn't believe U.S. business can put that technology to profitable use. Abegglen thinks we're unprepared to assimilate and apply substantial technology flows because of our poor labor relations, our undereducated work force (compared to Japan's), and the relatively low level of ongoing capital investment by industry.

Many American managers remain adamantly aloof to the accomplishments of foreign competitors. A survey by the Boston Consulting Group of twelve major companies found that only four actively followed Japanese technology. Another survey, done in 1984, concluded that "almost without exception, American technology experts stationed [in Japan] say their colleagues in America underestimate the Japanese accomplishments."

3. Shunning human initiative. Management's indifference to human initiative has long concerned Robert Noyce, a founder of Intel and an inventor of the integrated circuit, the successor of the transistor and one of the most significant innovations in history. Until recently, economists calculating the theory of comparative advantage typically ignored the work force, says Noyce. Not the Japanese, however. "They couldn't feed the population. They had no iron ore, they didn't have energy. According to the old theories of comparative advantage, all they could do was starve. They rejected that. They said, 'We do have a resource, we have people, and we will make our people superb.' And they have done it." As for this country, Noyce adds, "I think we still are under the misapprehension that having the Mesabi Range and the coal mines is a comparative advantage. It isn't. The advantage comes from the technology and the people who create it and operate it."

Nor is talent a boundless commodity to be squandered. Too many American businesses, especially those stressing marketing, use up innovative talent to produce slight variations on the same product theme. "There is only a limited amount of talent around, and if you waste it, innovation will not happen," says William O. Baker, the retired head of Bell Labs. "There is a basic fallacy in heavily devoting talent to product differentiation—using this talent to show that the sweetener made by General Foods is slightly different than that made by GD Searle, that a soap has slightly different detergent values. . . . I understand the competitive system demands some of this, but we overdo it. It's so futile. The Japanese method of xerography copying, for example, didn't depend on slightly bruised electrostatic deposition of solid particles, as Xerox Corporation did. But it depended on an entirely different concept of liquid elements rather than solid particles. We're going to find that over and over. The function will be done by something dramatically different, rather than some minor, trivial modification of the same product."

While technological innovation can boost firms and industries, it also can boost the morale of individuals who labor within the system. An innovative corporation excites and drives the employees. To understand the sensitive relationship between innovator and organization, consider these conflicting tales involving Hewlett-Packard:

- In 1966, when calculators were largely mechanized, a young man had an idea for an electronic model; rejected by his own calculator firm, he came to H-P. Despite unfavorable market research forecasts, William Hewlett personally championed the project and, in the early 1970s, hand-held calculators powered H-P's phenomenal growth.

- In 1980, at a much bigger H-P, a lab manager tried to convince that company to enter the new field of biotechnology. He later reported that he was "laughed out of the room." A venture capitalist convinced the manager to quit and staked him with $5.2 million to form a company to manufacture gene machines, which produce DNA, the basic material of the genetic code and the essential raw material in the business of genetic engineering. Not long ago, H-P had second thoughts and entered into a joint venture with Genentech. One product under consideration: gene machines.

At least H-P batted .500, considerably better than business's average. What matters is how companies can create an atmosphere that nurtures innovation. That's what James McManus is trying to do. McManus was the youngest brand manager in Procter and Gamble's history, but when bureaucracy frustrated his innovative notions, he quit and in 1971 formed his own company, Marketing Corporation of America. Located in a renovated factory along the Saugatuck River in picturesque Westport, Connecticut, MCA has enjoyed a 61 percent compound annual growth rate in recent years by encouraging individual thinking and rewarding innovation. McManus, whose polo shirts and sneakers set the casual, informal tone at MCA, says he borrowed his formula for success from Walt Disney. He describes it this way: "Stay in a learning environment, hire smart people who can teach each other, make people as rich as you can, and have fun."

In a few rare big organizations, the spirit of innovation can come from a top executive whom everyone below respects because of his sheer knowledge of the business. At Champion International Corporation, for instance, CEO Andrew C. Sigler can rightly boast that he enjoys an edge because he hasn't strayed far from the company's basic business of wood-related products. Sigler says he gets a kick out of listening to the conglomerate kings boast they can run anything. "They say, 'All you do is put a good man in and let it run.' Bullshit! If you just put a body in and let it run, you're going to have a tar race." Instead, Sigler says he's constantly struggling against the natural tendency of high executives to be remote, indifferent to products and markets. "Go to the mills, listen to those people. And if I go to the mills and some guy gives me a great line about how his operation runs and how he gets along with people, give me ten minutes out there walking through that mill with him and I know whether he's bullshitting me or not. You know, that's my world."

4. *The expensive quick-fix.* In many industries, managers who reach the top are not equipped to think beyond today. They are selected for their managerial skills and may have little appreciation for the technical base of the company. Therefore, they are less likely to appreciate the need for long-range research and development.

Ironically, this part of the legacy of waste, like most of the others, grows out of America's success. In this country's unchallenged growth after the war, industries enjoyed a captive market with only limited competition. Because oligopolies flourished, competition didn't force corporations to produce innovative products of high quality, Either competition didn't exist or the "competitors" tacitly agreed not to disrupt the marketplace. Economic concentration allowed double-digit increases in earnings to become the norm. Wall Street analysts and brokers came to expect these lush returns on investment, and they, in turn, educated investors to it.

When competition came, both from foreign imports and from the deregulation of domestic industries such as transportation and communications, much of American business couldn't shake off its sloppy habits. Accustomed to high returns and pressed by Wall Street to keep them coming, many managers have responded in every which way—except by innovation. They have squeezed every last bit of productivity from aging plants, practiced accounting legerdemain to cover over flagging profits by paper shuffling, and launched desperate acquisition campaigns. Ironically, in most cases it was the stockholders who suffered most from this kind of short-term management.

Buying innovation as a quick fix almost always ends badly, especially for a big, bureaucratic company that acquires a firm in an unrelated field; often the object of its affection gets suffocated. Raytheon tried to go high-tech in a hurry by snapping up Lexitron Corporation, a small but leading word-processing firm, for $14.7 million. Over the next few years, it spent huge amounts but it never seemed to understand the business and, by 1984—seven years after the acquisition—Raytheon sold its data system division, which included Lexitron, taking a $95-million write-off. Burroughs and 3M each acquired tiny word-processing firms and watched them founder. Worse, AM International's high-tech acquisitions drove it into bankruptcy in 1982.

A classic example of how an innovation quick-fix can be wasteful is Exxon's abortive foray into office systems market. When Exxon became nervous about the future of the oil industry in the 1970s, it sought to develop trendy businesses. It invested in Zilog (micropressors), Vydec (graphic terminals), Qyx (electronic typewriters), Magnex (storage technology), Kylex (telephoning switching), APD (scanners), and many more similarly high-tech–sounding deals. Stoutly projecting sales of $1 billion by 1985, Exxon management said the Office Systems Company would soon be in a league with IBM, DEC, Xerox, and Wang Laboratories. (Exxon made similar predictions when it acquired Reliance Electric and ended up with a $650 million loss.)

But by late 1984, Exxon's dreams had been shattered: many of the creative geniuses of the various systems had fled and those who remained complained of being stifled by the corpocracy. No major commercial customers had been signed up, not even Exxon itself, which turned its back on its own creations and chose IBM equipment instead. Exxon Office Systems was put up for sale, but because the loss was embedded deep in Exxon's complex balance sheet, it was hard to calculate the loss. A former top executive in the company estimated, in an interview, that the whole disaster may have totaled about $1 billion.

Exxon management's attempt to invest in innovation failed so miserably, according to the former executive, because the oil company crushed the spirit of the office systems company. "It was a cultural clash," he recalls. "We valued innovation and marketing, while the oil industry heroes were all chemical engineers. Every time a key executive slot opened up, Exxon would fill it with an oil executive who knew nothing about the business."

5. *Management's rich and wasteful uncle.* "Until 1930, the United States was in effect a scientific backwater," asserts Ian M. Ross, president of Bell Laboratories. "Before then, if you were an American physicist, you would have gone to Europe to get your Ph.D." What triggered the new order of things, of course, was Adolf Hitler. Both before the war, to flee oppression, and after, to escape the devastation as well as the Communists who took control of Eastern Europe, scientific talent crossed the ocean in droves. The migration inspired a period of intense innovation in America that lasted into the 1960s. Ross offers one measure of the scientific surge: "Only 17 American scientists received Nobel prizes during the first forty years that these prizes were awarded; by contrast, there were 117 Nobel laureates in science from the United States in the second forty years—more than from all the rest of the world combined."

On a more practical level, the war resulted in the "GI Bill," providing government-financed education to returning war veterans, many of whom studied science and engineering. American corporations benefited immensely from this pool of talent. According to George E. Pake, group vice-president for corporate research at Xerox, "Much of the postwar technical ascendancy depended upon this cadre of professionally trained people."

During World War II, 40 percent of everything manufactured in the United States went to the war effort. After the war, spending for military, and then for space, has been the greatest single continuing influence on innovation in American industry. In 1952, 11.6 percent of the gross national product was spent for defense, and that figure never fell below 6 percent for the next two decades. In the 1950s, the Korean War spurred military contracting, and the government generously funded university research and graduate training, resulting in a major expansion of basic research. This government-provided largesse, recalls Pake, helped provoke the second migration from Europe. Labeled the "brain drain" by disgruntled officials there, premier European talent flocked to American universities and the Bell Labs, among other emerging research meccas. Next came the Sputnik, and the maddening beep-beep from that Russian space satellite

incited President John F. Kennedy to launch NASA and the ex-
penses-be-damned effort to beat the Soviets to the moon. In the
early 1980s, with a new chill in Soviet relations, President
Ronald Reagan and Defense Secretary Caspar Weinberger reaf-
firmed Kennedy's commitment to spending for space, but this
time for the expensive "Star Wars" program.

Government contracting has indeed produced a fair volume of
useful technological innovation, not to mention Nobel laureates.
Innovations that have found civilian applications include cheaper
semiconductors, integrated circuits, more efficient and powerful
jet engines, hard plastics, lasers, nuclear power, and optical and
scientific equipment.

But government research can also be a Faustian bargain. It is
often tied up in secrecy, according to Eric Alterman, a research
associate with Business Executives for National Security, a trade
association that monitors defense issues. "It's like going to
Boston by way of Biloxi," is how Alterman, in an article he
wrote for *The Washington Monthly,* describes the process of getting civilian technology from military R and D. "The Department of Commerce has found that it takes ten man-years of
civilian R and D to produce a commercial patent, while it takes
1,000 man-years of defense R and D to produce the same results. Moreover, the secrecy required of defense R and D often
precludes such spin-offs since the Pentagon isn't about to let a
vital new technology find its way into a radio that a Russian
diplomat might buy."

Military contracting also saps American industry's ability to
compete. In the United States, about one half of the total R and
D funds used by industry come from NASA and the Pentagon
for military and space projects. The Japanese government, by
contrast, provides less than 25 percent of research money to industry, and very little of it goes for military work. So, for example, while the Japanese government announces a seven-year,
$140 million research effort involving ten private companies to
develop "intelligent" robots capable of assembling dozens of different products, the U.S. government's main robotics research
program, at Wright-Patterson Air Force Base in Dayton, Ohio,
is geared primarily to making defense contractors more efficient.
Observes author Chalmers Johnson: "Over time, as the United
States draws off its limited engineering resources into the defense sector, while Japan keeps its big engineering establishment
working on the civilian-commercial front, the industrial ca-

pabilities of the two nations *must* diverge, regardless of how many Nobel Prizes in basic science Americans win. Thus the United States is in danger of ending the twentieth century as the leading producer of ICBMs and soybeans, while the Japanese monopolize the production of everything in between."

If ever there was any doubt that the government has played a dominant role since World War II in setting industrial standards, witness America's troubled machine tool industry, a key industry for national defense and, indeed, for any manufacturing process. Seymour Melman, a professor of industrial engineering at Columbia University, found that the sharp decline of this industry was due, at least in part, to bad habits acquired by management as a result of contracting from the government. The industry's recent woes trace back to the 1950s and 1960s, when it got fat "cost-plus" contracts for supplying the government's defense and space programs. This program, writes Melman, "gave the contracting firms a strong incentive to run up costs, and the cost of overruns were actually encouraged by the Pentagon's managers and the federal government's economists on the grounds of 'bolstering the economy' and 'getting America moving again.'"

The Air Force in the 1950s did push the industry to greater technological innovation, such as the computer-controlled machine tools that are being installed today in factories. But on the other side, observes Melman, the industry found itself catering to a state management for whom capability and performance were the dominant requirements, while cost was a matter of less significance. The result: In 1939–47, the average hourly earnings of industrial workers rose 95 percent, while the prices of machine tools increased only 39 percent; in 1971–78, hourly earnings were up 72 percent, machine tools 85 percent. It was a classic inversion of cost-minimizing pattern. In Japan, by contrast, machine tool prices in 1971–78 rose only 51 percent, while wages increased 177 percent. "These data," observes Melman, "mark the end of a way of industrial life in the United States."

Consequently, American manufacturers increasingly bought tools from the Japanese, who, incidentally, were engineering to near-perfection the technological innovations created for the Air Force some three decades earlier. The U.S. machine tool industry, meanwhile, returned to the government, this time to get protection from low-cost imports. Ironically, the chief argument put forward by management was the industry's importance to national defense.

Stymied Innovation in High Tech and Low

The Tortoise and the Hare—in Computers

One of the world's most beautiful highways runs south from San Francisco. Route 280 cuts across hills and through passes, winding its way past Palo Alto, Mountain View, Sunnyvale, and Cupertino to San Jose. Back in 1937, two of the best and the brightest engineering students at Stanford University in Palo Alto, William Hewlett and David Packard, set up a business in a garage near the university. So was born Hewlett-Packard, today the world's largest producer of electronic measuring devices and equipment, among other products.

The next significant date for the area was 1955, when William Shockley, who had won a Nobel Prize at Bell Labs for co-inventing the transistor, moved back West near Stanford and started Shockley Transistor Corporation, gathering around him some brilliant, innovative minds. But Shockley's men, led by Robert Noyce, mutinied against the founder (who later became famous for his racial theories that blacks are intellectually inferior to whites because of genetic differences). With a wad of venture capital, the rebels set up Fairchild Semiconductor. Next, in 1968, Noyce and his friend Gordon Moore split with Fairchild and founded Intel. This mitotic process, encouraged by rich San Francisco venture capitalists, would be repeated hundreds of times: new high-tech companies begot new high-tech companies, which begot new high-tech companies. . . . And so was born Silicon Valley* in Santa Clara County, south of San Francisco.

---

*Silicon, extracted from rocks and common beach sand, is a semiconductor, having a composition between that of copper (a conductor) and of glass (an insulator). Melted and "grown" into crystal ingots, the purified silicon is sliced into ultrathin wafers that are divided into hundreds of chips, each the size of a newborn's thumbnail. Each chip is crammed with tiny transistors and switches connected by "wires." Electricity passing across the silver-gray silicon chip can be channeled through the integrated circuitry, activating its logic and memory. The quarter-inch square microprocessor—"a computer on a chip"—can contain a million electronic components, ten times more than the thirty-ton ENIAC, the world's first electronic digital computer dedicated in 1946. But ENIAC cost thirty thousand times more than the microprocessor and it operated on the power of a lighthouse instead of a night-light.

(Today, there is also a "Silicon Valley" ninety miles from Moscow, and in Canada, Poland, Brazil, and Scotland; Kyushu is Japan's "Silicon Island.")

What has made Silicon Valley world-renowned is its so-called innovative culture, a phenomenon that directly relates to the style of management there. Participatory and democratic, the companies of Silicon Valley proudly boast of their rebellion against the hierarchical structure typical of most American corporations. Outwardly, it's a "hot tub culture" famous for employee beer busts, corporate gymnasiums, and casual dress styles. But along with the swimming pools and lax work rules, there's also a palpable creative tension in the valley whose inhabitants typically are extremely ambitious, single-minded, and success-motivated.

Despite this unique style of management, which many view as the hope of American business, some companies in Silicon Valley recently fell victim to something akin to writer's block caused by the same management lapses that have come to plague more mature American industries. For having brought the world the microprocessor and its attendant wonders, many Silicon Valley companies suddenly found themselves unable to satisfy customer quality demands. It is a story of how the brilliant innovators of Silicon Valley very nearly lost the "chip war."

In the 1970s, the Japanese launched a drive to capture a single segment of the computer market: the computer memories, which are the chips that store digital data. Success came quickly for the Japanese, and by the end of 1979, they had captured 42 percent of the market for 16K random access memory (RAM) chips. These chips can store sixteen thousand bits of information, at that time the largest storage capacity available. Then, in 1980, the Japanese beat the United States to market with 64K RAM chips, and by 1982 controlled 70 percent of the world market for them. By the mid-1980s, the question was, would the Japanese do the same with the 256K RAM, a market expected to be worth at least $2 billion a year by the late 1980s? And what about the so-called supercomputer that's so vital to national defense?

Alarmed, the Semiconductor Industry Association (SIA) several years ago followed the well-trodden path to Washington for help. It alleged predatory trade and pricing practices, and "targeting" of the semiconductor industry by the Japanese government. The Japanese freely entered this market, the American organization argued, while its members' access to the Japanese market was limited. The SIA failed, however, to mention that American manufacturers of chips were having serious quality problems. Motorola and Texas Instruments, the biggest U.S. merchant producers, couldn't match the quality of chips produced by Nippon Electric, Hitachi, and Fujitsu. So concerned about quality problems were IBM and Western Electric, the two biggest American consumers of chips, that they decided to make their own in order to control the quality. And when IBM needs more chips than it can produce, it buys from the Japanese because other American manufacturers can't meet the company's high-quality standards.

These quality problems first came to light at a March 1980 meeting of electronics industry executives in Washington. Richard Anderson of Hewlett-Packard told how in 1977, when U.S. manufacturers couldn't produce enough 16K RAM chips to meet his company's needs, H-P turned to the Japanese. The company soon discovered that its computers, using Japanese chips, performed longer without memory failure. So H-P reluctantly began buying its chips from Japan, Anderson explained apologetically, adding that American quality had improved since then.

But according to an internal memorandum written by an official in the U.S. embassy in Tokyo, American chips still lagged in quality three years after the Anderson revelation. The memo's author, Jack Osborn, then economic attaché for high technology and now an executive in Tokyo for TRW, wrote, "Generally, Japanese success in the 64K RAM merchant market has been attributed to government support and heavy capital investment that was not matched by U.S. firms. . . . [But] there is evidence that the Japanese lead in 64K RAM chips might be due primarily to better technical decisions at the engineering/planning/production stages." Osborn dismissed the SIA's charge of "targeting" by the Japanese government. The Japanese succeeded, he contended, because management chose "the most cost-effective (though not necessarily the most technologically advanced) production equipment. American companies may have selected what eventually became a more costly, less efficient, and much more technologically complicated route."

Finally, Osborn cited an elementary strength of the Japanese chip-manufacturing process over the American—cleanliness. Japanese managers demand that the sensitive silicon chips be manufactured under operating room conditions: makeup by employees is forbidden, body hair is carefully covered, the air is purified, and robots are used extensively. As a result, Osborn found that the quality of their chips is consistently 20-plus percent above those chips manufactured in apparently less antiseptic conditions in American firms with less demanding managements.

The message of this memo is that innovative management should affect every part of the business, from the lab table to the store shelf. Silicon Valley may be the most creative and stimulating business environment in the world, as its reputation suggests. But it's a waste when a firm like Intel pioneers an extraordinary sliver of silicon that can remember, and then the Japanese end up capturing the market for the product. Will the same thing happen in chips that happened in color television, digital watches, microwave ovens, and video recorders? Most observers believe not, for the managers in Silicon Valley, unlike the others, have spotted their errors and are determined to correct them. Nevertheless, there is an important lesson in all this, which is that too many American executives have forgotten the fable learned in their childhood about the tortoise and the hare.

Old Businesses, Old Tricks—in Steel, Etc.

While the high-tech wizards in Silicon Valley, despite their problems with quality, never tire of finding new uses for the semiconductor, managers of more mature, less dynamic industries have a different kind of challenge. They must decide when to innovate new life into an aging yet profitable product, and when to let it die. If management merely continues to milk aging "cash cow" businesses, chances are a new, hungry competitor will revolutionize the production process, improve the quality of products, and steal the markets. Resting on the status quo is a sure way to disaster. "If we focus on a small slice of time, we mainly see gradual change," observes Richard Foster, a director of McKinsey and Company. "If we focus on a little larger slice of time, we find that revolutionary change is more the order of the day."

Foster cites four examples of companies that lost major markets and millions of dollars because they failed to manage technology. National Cash Register wrote off $140 million worth of inventory in the early 1970s that had been rendered obsolete by new electronics products. Goodrich struggled to control the bias-ply tire market in 1976 and succeeded, but three years later nobody wanted the bias-plies; new cars rolling off the Detroit assembly lines came equipped with French-made Michelin radial tires. RCA, in 1955, set the standard among ten manufacturers of vacuum tubes. So when the standard setter failed to get into high technology, the others followed suit. As a result, says Foster, "between 1955 and 1980, all of the leading electronics manufacturers in the United States ceased to be significant competitors in solid-state electronics." Du Pont's nylon was the favored cord used to strengthen tires, until Celanese came out with polyester tire cords, which were cheaper to produce and had inherently better qualities than nylon cords. Fighting back, Du Pont spent five to ten times as much as Celanese to make an equivalent amount of technological progress with nylon. Ultimately, of course, the big Delaware company lost the battle to the smaller competitor.

In an appropriate analogy, Foster compares companies that resist change and continue to invest in old technology to the sailing ship manufacturers in the last century. When steamships appeared, sailing ship builders derided the new technology while adding more sails to make their ships go faster to meet the new competition. "By the 1890s, they were up to seven masts with as many as fifty-five sails. These sailing ships were really marvelous things to see. Unfortunately, not much ocean transport is carried by sail these days."

Surely no industry better illustrates the costs and consequences of management falling out of step with the times than big steel. For more than seventy years, steel was the all-American metaphor. Created by titans like J. P. Morgan and Andrew Carnegie, steel built rails and locomotives, bridges and skyscrapers, and the hammers and drills used by American workers. So important was steel that President Harry S. Truman seized the mills to end a crippling strike and President Kennedy lashed out against the industry's arrogance. And who was the "man of steel"? Superman, of course, who was so strong he could "bend steel with his bare hands."

But looking back now, it seems the big steel companies have been so enduringly inefficient and wasteful that only an economy as rich as this one could have tolerated it. Steel's complacent attitude dates to the turn of the century, when Carnegie, Federal, and National Steel merged in 1901 to form $1.4 billion United States Steel, the dominant firm in an oligopolistic industry. From the beginning, innovation was viewed as unnecessary in the captive market, causing *Fortune,* in a 1936 article, to comment bitingly, "The chief energies of the men who guided [U.S. Steel] were directed to preventing deterioration of the investment value of the enormous properties confided in their care. To achieve this, they consistently tried to freeze the steel industry at present, or better yet, past levels." A description of U.S. Steel by a management consulting firm, prepared in the 1930s, called it "a big sprawling inert giant . . . with inadequate knowledge of its domestic markets and no clear appreciation of its opportunities in foreign markets . . . slow in introducing new processes and new products."

The industry did undertake a massive expansion and modernization program during the Korean War, and by 1959 the increased production alone exceeded the combined output of Germany and Japan. But amazingly, the industry in modernizing ignored much of the innovative technology that had been developed overseas. Companies filled their aging, inefficient structures with dated technology. "Most of the melt shops were already obsolescent the moment they were installed; the blast furnaces were energy-inefficient; and worst of all, little effort was made to eliminate plants that were poorly located with respect to raw materials and market growth," wrote the economists Hans J. Mueller and Walter Adams.

Worse, the American companies were expanding capacity at the very time that steel production was expanding almost everywhere else in the world. Developing and advanced countries alike had access to the same technology and all viewed steel exports as a way to improve their balance of payments. And they saw the rich American market as their primary target.

One wonders how the industry could have been so blind to these developments in other parts of the world. Father William T. Hogan, S.J., of Fordham University, author of a five-volume history of the steel industry, concludes that the industry "has never been export-minded. We export two or three million tons of ninety to one hundred million produced in a good year." Another critical view can be found in a recent book, *Steel: Upheaval in a Basic Industry,* one of whose authors, Donald F. Barnett, is former chief economist of the industry's own trade association, the American Iron and Steel Institute. The industry's lethargy, the authors assert, "stems from deeply entrenched oligopolistic traditions. Faced with new competition—either from other suppliers of steel or from competing materials—the industry has groped in vain for a strategy that could reverse the erosion of its position." However, it "has been mesmerized by nostalgia for its former dominance."

Thus steel executives, insular and indifferent, overlooked the effects of the wave of innovation that began in the mills of Europe after the war and later swept through the Far East. And when, inevitably, cheaper imports threatened their once-captive market, the industry executives petitioned Washington to restrict imports. They got support in this political ploy from officials of the United Steelworkers, who in exchange gained the highest wages of any industry for their members. All these costs were added to the price of American steel, making it even more noncompetitive in world markets.

Clearly, the managers of American steel companies should have begun innovating decades ago. Instead of adding more steel-making capacity, however, they should have begun a thoughtful diversification program. They didn't, of course, which explains why U.S. Steel would go into debt to buy an oil company and why the industry seems to spend nearly as much time in Washington seeking protection as in Pittsburgh making steel. This is also why one expert source told us, "What the steel industry needs now is not modernizing but plowing under."

This source, an important venture capitalist, confided in us on the basis that we would not disclose his name. In 1982, he headed a group of investors invited by Kaiser Steel in Fontana, California, in the hope that they would take over the plant there. There, they found an ark of a plant that was poorly located seventy miles inland from the coast (built during World War II to avoid the threat of shelling from Japanese ships) and hundreds of miles from coal and ore supplies. Kaiser had spent hundreds of millions modernizing the plant, but its finished slab was still more expensive than that imported from British plants, which, in turn, probably had imported the unfinished steel from Brazil.

"After spending all that money to modernize it," he says, "they were offering us the whole plant for *nothing*. Just to get it off their hands. But spending money on it had been like paying for a Ph.D. for a retarded child; it was hopeless. I didn't want any part of it."

Mismanaged Manufacturing

Executives of other major American industries have mismanaged innovation for at least two reasons: First, top management is often dominated by executives with financial or legal backgrounds; second, many managers don't understand the manufacturing process, and don't really care about it.

That's the conclusion of a recent Booz•Allen and Hamilton survey, which also found that, in 75 percent of the companies surveyed, technical people are not even a part of the planning process. This worries former GTE president Vanderslice: "I think it's a very real criticism of American industry that the directorates, the top management, have never been involved in running anything themselves. They've never really been in productivity or the manufacturing end. Many of them probably have never been on the manufacturing floor."

Echoing that sentiment, T. Vincent Learson, the former chairman of IBM, considered production technology so important that he established a mandatory retirement age of sixty for all officers (including himself) because keeping IBM's technology up-to-date demanded younger minds. "When I was made president, in January 1966, I took off my hat to no one in the business on my personal ability to choose products, which is, after all, the game," Learson said during an interview. "Technically, I was with all the engineers and I knew what the market needed. I'm not an engineer by training, but I'd spent most of my life in that area. That's where I made my reputation at IBM and that's why I was chosen to be president. I started in sales, but technology never bothered me. I liked it, and I mixed in it all the time. But two or three years after I became president, I was away from the labs and I just wasn't with it. I had to trust others, I had to delegate. And by the time I became chairman, I would no more pick the product than fly, because I wasn't with it anymore."

Not enough executives, however, share Learson's interest in or concern for product technology. Managers need not be technological geniuses—most scientists and technologists are notoriously poor managers—but they must at least understand and appreciate the innovative mind in order to direct it.

Many American manufacturers, who have stood by while foreigners stole their innovative thunder, must now either catch up or give up. Consider, for example, flexible manufacturing systems (FMS) that integrate computer-aided design and computer-aided manufacturing (CAD/CAM) robots, and remotely guided carts to deliver materials, all linked by electronic controls. American management has been slow to adopt these crucial processes. The systems are difficult to understand—especially for top managers with financial and legal training—time-consuming to install, and extremely costly, with a payoff several years in the future. It cost Deere and Company $1.8 billion for its Waterloo, Iowa, tractor plant, probably the country's most automated manufacturing facility; GE spent $300 million on its automated Erie, Pennsylvania, factory that produces a locomotive frame a day, untouched by human hands (it used to take seventy skilled machinists sixteen days to do the same thing); GM's Delco high-speed radio-manufacturing plant in Kokomo, Indiana (which brought back twelve hundred jobs from Singapore where the radios were being made) cost $500 million.

Unfortunately, these are exceptional examples of American companies that have spent the time and money it takes to modernize. It is more common to hear such stories about the wondrously automated plants in Japan, like the sprawling Fujitsu Fanuc robot-manufacturing plant near Mount Fuji that operates around the clock with one hundred people during the day and only whirring machines at night. With American manufacturers making pilgrimages to these Oriental meccas of modern manufacturing, the casual observer must conclude that the Japanese invented FMS. But as usual, it was the Americans who pioneered FMS—the Japanese simply put it to work. Developed in the early 1970s by Cincinnati Milicron, Kearney and Trecker, and White Consolidated, "FMS was greeted with a yawn by U.S. manufacturers," writes Gene Bylinsky, *Fortune* magazine's specialist in manufacturing. The Japanese, in typical contrast, "have become the implementers par excellence of this new type of factory automation not because they are great technical innovators, which they admit they are not, but because they have moved fast in putting the new systems into their factories. Once again, the path to success in new manufacturing leads through Japanese factories."

The story of one element of FMS, the robot,* is illustrative. Back in the 1950s, a couple of Americans named Joseph Engelberger and George Devol (the inventor who designed and

---

Robot is derived from the Czechoslovak word *robota,* meaning servitude, drudgery. It came to English in Karel Capek's play *Rossum's Universal Robots* and was popularized by science fiction writer Isaac Asimov.

patented the "programmed article handling device") got together and manufactured Devol's devices—in a garage, of
course. Thus was born Unimation, a company boasting a unique
product that its founders fervently believed would revolutionize
American business. But American business didn't share their
enthusiasm for the robot, and in 1968 Unimation licensed Kawasaki Heavy Industries to build Kawasaki Unimates. Finally,
in 1982, Unimation was acquired by Westinghouse. (Unfortunately, the Westinghouse bureaucracy took its toll: By 1984,
after many of the robot maker's managers and scientists had fled
the heavy-handed Westinghouse bureaucracy, Unimation's sales
dropped by two thirds.)

An Innovative Comeback?

If this picture of innovation in many of America's most important industries seems unrelentingly bleak, have faith. So says an
early critic of our manufacturing processes, Wickham Skinner, a
professor of management and manufacturing at Harvard Business School and consultant to numerous corporations and governments. Back in 1969, Skinner published a scathing critique of
U.S. manufacturing. It said, "The fact is that manufacturing is
seen by most top managers as requiring involved technical skills
and a morass of petty daily decisions and details. It is seen by
many young managers as the gateway to grubby routine, where
days are filled with high pressure, packed with details and limited to low-level decision making—all of which is out of sight
and minds of top level executives." Concluded Skinner, "In my
opinion, manufacturing is generally perceived in the wrong way
at the top, managed in the wrong way at the plant level, and
taught in the wrong way in the business schools." In a 1984 interview, we asked the professor whether things had changed
any. "On a scale of one to ten," Professor Skinner replied,
"we've gone from one to about six. I'm not on the finish line
cheering, but I am more optimistic."

Not only in manufacturing but in all phases of the innovative
process, there are heartening individual stories of progress.
Here are some of them:

In Charlotte, North Carolina, we visited Nucor, a mini-mill
specialty steel company (as opposed to the integrated operations
like U.S. Steel), which is pioneering in approaches to productivity and personnel.

It should be noted in analyzing Nucor's phenomenal success that it is nonunion, so it doesn't have the work rules and payroll that weigh down integrated companies. Nevertheless, chief executive Ken Iverson—an engineer with an M.S. in metallurgy from Purdue—has structured pay so that his workers make as much as those in big steel (averaging between $28,000 and $30,000 in recent years). But they earn this in exchange for productivity levels comparable to those in Japanese mills. The employment cost of Nucor's steel, on average, is $65 a ton (versus about $160 in big unionized plants), the same as Japanese plants. Nucor's no-frills operating philosophy—in sharp contrast to the palatial, overstaffed offices of the Pittsburgh giants—means higher pay for the workers and for Iverson, and higher profits, too; earnings have grown about 40 percent yearly for the past decade. Iverson, who built Nucor using only the most advanced foreign-made equipment, recalls that "the rolling equipment we bought in 1968 was not even available from mill builders in the United States."

Many of the recent innovations at Nucor come from the so-called incentive groups, which are paid according to their productivity. "We haven't laid off an hourly worker in fifteen years," says Iverson. "That's important. We could go down tomorrow and put in robots, which we are, in fact, considering for some sections of the mills, and the workers would accept them gladly. They know they aren't going to lose their jobs because of the robots. That's why they really are more innovative than workers in most companies; they want to find ideas that make things go faster, because they know they're going to share in it, and they're not going to be out of jobs."

At Johnson Controls, president Fred Brengel bucked obsolescence by fomenting a technological revolution in the century-old thermostat manufacturer. As a result, in the 1970s, Johnson became the first company to market with a computer-run system for managing a building's energy use. Similarly, Monsanto saw in the 1970s that oil companies were invading its big money-makers, bulk chemicals and plastics. Instead of clinging to its cash cow, as so many others might have done, Monsanto drastically reduced its traditional businesses and spent $1 billion to move in two new directions: biotechnology and fabricated manufactured products.

But Monsanto didn't plunge into the new business. Instead, it moved cautiously by investing in start-up biotechnology firms

Biogen, Genentech, Cetus, and Genex. Initially, Monsanto invited scientists from those firms to train Monsanto employees. Next, the big company began biotechnology projects within the organization, tripling its basic research budget and constructing its own research park near St. Louis.

The management of Monsanto and some other big companies worry that they will smother innovative smaller outfits. They have decided to buy only a piece of the action, playing the role of venture capitalists. For example, McKesson Corporation put $2 million into ByVideo, a Silicon Valley firm, and Ramtek Corporation, itself a big R and D firm, invested $2 million in a smaller firm that was working on an advanced graphics machine it needed. Also, RCA invested in Odetics' mobile robots, Johnson and Johnson owns a piece of Enzo Biochem's DNA research, and Becton Dickinson underwrote Oncogene Science's work on a cancer diagnostic kit.

Perhaps the most heartening trend is the appearance of managements that appreciate and understand innovative marketing and technology. Though financial and legal types continue to predominate in most major companies, exceptions are appearing. John Welch, the much discussed and admired CEO of General Electric, has a Ph.D. in chemical engineering. One of three executive vice-presidents at Deere is an engineer. General Motors, long dominated by financial men, now has a vice-chairman who specializes in advanced technology, and its president concentrates on production. Donald E. Petersen, Ford's new CEO, is an engineer by training, as is Lee Iacocca, chairman of Chrysler; and Cessna Aircraft in 1983 hired a former Deere executive as president specifically to improve its manufacturing operations.

Still, just as American managements should not be comprised solely of deal makers and number crunchers, neither should we deify the technocrat. Engineers and scientists are not saviors of American industry. Too many small firms die because the brilliant inventor, who created a company from a product he invented, insists on running the show even though he hasn't got the managerial instinct and training to capitalize on his or anyone else's innovative genius. Richard Hackman of the Yale School of Organization and Management observes that in a number of corporations he studied, engineers and technologists were sources of resistance to change. In one microelectronics manufacturer, engineers treated rank-and-file operators as mere executors of their ideas and plans. "Real innovation occurred,' recalls Hackman, "when a new organization design got the operators and the engineers working together to improve productivity and quality. Now the engineers come voluntarily to operation-team meetings and production is way up. The engineers do not view themselves as the priesthood as they did before. But in giving up that elevated status they have become a happier, more productive, and more innovative group."

Success in innovation comes down to understanding people—praising not punishing them and instilling in them a sense of mission. That seems to demand an intimacy that comes with smallness, with the efficient working units of fifty to one hundred people mentioned earlier by management expert Allan Kennedy. "If the economy is moving in that direction," says Kennedy, "then if you are running IBM the biggest 10-year challenge you face is how to break IBM into the 10,000 little units of 100 people, each with an entrepreneurial stake."

In fact, that process already has begun at Big Blue—and experience shows, where IBM goes, other companies follow. A few years ago, IBM began chartering independent business units (IBUs) and special business units (SBUs) to explore areas beyond the company's main business. The idea was to break them away from the parent and encourage innovation. One of those IBUs spearheaded IBM's belated but spirited entry into the personal computer (PC) market.

Operating from a single-story, leaky-roofed converted warehouse in Boca Raton, Florida—far from the Armonk, New York, headquarters bureaucracy—the unit moved smartly to challenge Apple's lead. "We were allowed to develop like a startup company," says Philip D. Estridge, the project leader. "IBM acted as a venture capitalist. It gave us management guidance, money and allowed us to operate on our own." While IBM usually grinds through all stages of the innovative process for a new product, this time it operated as a developer, acquiring much of the technology from others. So instead of using proprietary electronic circuitry, as IBM usually does, it used a microprocessor designed by Intel for the guts of the PC. "To get it done quickly, we relied on our management to run interference with the rest of the IBM's management," says one participant. IBM thinks the PC experience has stimulated the company, which had become defensively bureaucratic in the 1970s and saw its share of the expanding world computer market fall from 60 percent in 1967 to roughly 40 percent in 1980.

Illustrating the PC project's invigorating effect, Lewis M. Branscomb, vice-president and chief scientist at IBM, recalls what happened when the new computer needed lots of software and the company wasn't sure that programs ordered from outside vendors would be enough. "So we provided a generous purchase discount for employees and told those who bought our machine and used it at home that we would buy software from them and pay them a royalty just as we would pay an outside vendor. This put between 15,000 and 20,000 programmers to work innovating for us." Interestingly, Apple *gives* each employee a computer as a way of gathering consumer information. Explains Steve Jobs, Apple's founder, "One time a bunch of people came back after opening a box and said, 'There are six manuals! It's totally intimidating and we don't know which one to read first!' That comment was worth more than $100,000 of market research."

As IBM's experience shows, big companies must continually fight the creeping corpocracy. Only two years following the dazzling debut of the PC, IBM introduced its progeny, PCjr. Surprisingly, the home computer landed on the market with a costly thud. It seemed that IBM had ignored the creative policy so successful with PC; the huge corporation turned inward, seeking little outside advice on design even though the small computer was the company's first true consumer product. For example, IBM closely guarded PCjr's keyboard from outsiders, and when it finally hit the market, critics found its Chicletlike keys unfit for typing.

Meanwhile, Boca Raton, the former IBU hideaway from IBM bureaucracy, had been drawn under the corporate cape by the time PCjr was being developed. Christened with the bureaucratic-sounding title, IBM Entry Systems Division, by 1984 it boasted ten thousand employees and $5 billion in sales—10 percent of IBM's business worldwide. Thus, PC's overnight success led to PCjr's overnight disappointment. And this, in turn, opened the door to Apple which, instead of folding under the threat of IBM, had been spurred to greater innovation. "This is the year Apple fights back," declared president John Scully. "We are betting the entire company." With IBM staggered by the failure of PCjr, Apple in 1984 threw three quick jabs at Big Blue: Macintosh, Lisa II, and the portable Apple IIe, which shined when compared to PCjr. It was a heartening example of the effect of competition on innovation.

Education: Where Innovation Is Born

In seeking the origins of industrial innovation of any society, the search inevitably leads back to its educational system. A strong primary and secondary school system eventually will produce the scientists who invent, the engineers who develop, and the managers who direct and spur innovation. It's no coincidence that in the United States, education and innovation have been on the skids in tandem.

The decline of elementary and secondary education was well documented by the National Commission on Excellence in Education in its 1983 report, which warned, "The educational foundations of our society are presently being eroded by a rising tide of mediocrity that threatens our very future as a nation and a people. What was unimaginable a generation ago has begun to occur—others are matching and surpassing our educational attainments." Similarly, the National Science Foundation found the United States "certainly lagging" in science and math instruction in secondary schools.

Therefore, it's not surprising that corporations complain that fewer engineers, chemists, and physicists come out of the nation's graduate schools, and that those who do often are badly trained. John Opel of IBM sees proof of the deterioration in mathematics and science education, and the worsening apptitude and achievement scores of high school graduates. "The United States is slipping in the race to strengthen the capabilities of its people: talented, educated, and trained human beings— the ultimate source of any nation."

A litany of worries spills from thoughtful executives whose businesses depend on employees educated in the sciences. "When a company like this one works out what we'll need in engineering talent in five to ten years, it's absolutely not going to be there," said Thomas Vanderslice when he was still president of GTE. The executive's point was underscored by a long list of statistics he had recently cited in a speech.

- Only 6 percent of college undergraduates are studying engineering versus 21 percent in Japan and 37 percent in West Germany. (About one half of all the engineers graduating from American universities are nonresident aliens.)
- From 1970 to 1979, Japan expanded its pool of scientific and engineering talent by almost 60 percent, West Germany by 50 percent, the United States by less than 20 percent.

- On average, there isn't one qualified math or science teacher per school district.
- The school year in the United States runs about 180 days a year compared with 240 days in West Germany and Japan.
- Only twenty-five hundred doctoral degrees in engineering were awarded in 1980, and almost half of them were to foreigners. (An unintentionally ironic example of this situation occurred in 1984 when an advertisement for Korea's $3.35-billion Daewoo International America Corporation appeared in a major U.S. publication, showing three company executives wearing sweatshirts from their alma maters: all were Korean and all attended U.S. universities.)

At the same time, universities hooked on rich federal contracts have geared their scientific programs more to missiles and rocketry than industrial innovation. The esoteric replaces the practical, and a kind of hierarchy develops within the universities. Eugene Ferguson, who taught engineering for twenty years at Iowa State University describes it this way: "The totem pole of status has the physicists at the top, the electronic engineers next, and so on down to the industrial engineers at the bottom." Naturally, science students drift to these more lucrative areas of specialization, and corporations, which in recent years have stressed finance over production, hasten this process. So when talented students hear tales of big money and excitement in the world of high finance, they often switch from engineering to business administration—or seek to combine the two.

"This marvelous-sounding combination of business school and engineering, which should produce some very special human beings, in reality produces a peculiarly useless individual," observes Sheldon Weinig, the chief executive of Materials Research Corporation. Weinig becomes nearly apoplectic on the subject of engineers. "We have wasted a critical profession in this society. I'm not going to say engineers are all things to all men, but without them I don't know what we are going to do. We just don't have enough of them, and we waste them like crazy in sales and these M.B.A. functions." No wonder nobody wants to study engineering. "Engineers are badly paid and corporations treat them like slave labor," continues Weinig. "Boeing gets a contract and hires ten thousand of them; they lose a contract and fire ten thousand. They've never really become part of the inner management structure. So we end up with a disenfranchised professional. And then we suddenly wake up and say, 'Good God, we need engineers.'"

The new elitism that has chased many away from industrial engineering has caused those who remain to embellish their jobs with titles and status. Hasashi Shinto, president of Nippon Telegraph and Telephone, the $17-billion Japanese telephone monopoly, chronicled the wasteful effects of this new status-consciousness by American engineers: "In 1953 to about 1963, when I was working in the shipyards, the United States had higher productivity even though your wages then were five times higher than they were in Japan. Your side was extremely competitive in turbines and main generators—and they were of such high quality!" To find out why, Shinto visited the United States, studying American business and assiduously writing down what he learned. "Your young engineers who graduated from the university were working in the workshops, along with the [production] workers. The engineers knew the production program and they knew how to use machine tools. Because they knew the production process in detail, they were able to get greater productivity and high quality."

Returning to Tokyo, he installed that process at the shipyard where he was then president; every graduate engineer was put to work in the shop before doing anything else. Then, in 1980, Shinto returned to the United States and found that today's engineers spent lots of time in front of computers but next to none in the workshop. "I didn't find the same kind of intelligence [as before] in the workshop. It has disappeared, and I am quite astonished."

And what of the graduate schools of business, those American educational creations that for so long were credited for our successes? Commentators seeking causes these days for the lack of innovation by American business invariably zero in on the business schools. "Fortunately for us," snaps investment banker Felix Rohatyn caustically, "Japan is opening its first business school in the near future. This is likely to produce a measurable drop in Japanese productivity."

Significantly, some of the sharpest criticism of business schools and their graduates comes from business school professors. In the harsh judgment of Professor James J. O'Toole of the University of Southern California, "In private (and after a few drinks) most of us who teach MBAs will admit that the letters should stand for Master of Business Arrogance. Compared with the more broad-based European and Asian managers. American MBAs often don't know how to listen, don't know how to ask questions, don't feel the need to read, and don't feel there is anything they can learn from other disciplines or other countries." Even Harvard Business School dean John H. McArthur acknowledges that too little attention has been given to production management and international business, and too much to statistics. "Too often analysis has meant being able to shove a problem quantitatively through the computer nine different ways and come out with a printout the size of the Manhattan phone book."

However, business schools are merely convenient targets. For the fact is, the business school is not a cause of current mismanagement; the business school is a *result* of it. When the schools concentrate on finance and downplay the importance of production, they simply fulfill the wishes of corporations, which are, after all, their ultimate clients. Corporations furnish jobs to graduates, consulting posts to professors, and rich endowments to the schools. With their clients more interested in juggling books than production schedules, business schools design their curriculums accordingly. As that attitude in corporations changes—and foreign competition, among other influences, is forcing that change—it is being reflected in the courses taught at graduate schools of business.

Washington Is Not the Innovation Capital

Back in the early nineteenth century, a raging band of British workers, called Luddites, after their leader Ned Ludd, destroyed new textile equipment because they feared that innovation threatened their jobs. The protest was crushed and the Luddites disappeared, but today their legacy is alive and well. Contemporary Luddites include balky workers and union leaders who resist innovation in hopes of saving jobs, as well as white-collar managers who ignore the need to innovate. Such executives are Luddites by omission, for these paper shufflers threaten their companies' survival just as surely as the raging printer who sabotages a high-speed press or the uncompromising union leader who clings to outmoded work rules.

Corporate Luddites typically expend more resources and energy searching for ways to avoid competition than to meet it. They journey to Washington because, for them, innovation means special tax legislation, regulatory breaks, and trade protection. Curb imports, they tell congressmen and regulators, and it will give us time to modernize to meet competition. Producers of copper, steel, machine tools, autos, textiles, and shoes all have argued this line. Few companies, though, spend increased profits resulting from curbed imports on new plants and equipment. Instead, what they want from Washington are laws that block imports, force up prices, and cause customers to subsidize incompetent management, as Chapter 9, "Corporate Welfare," examines in detail.

Victories won by business in Washington rarely translate into gains in productivity. At the end of the 1970s, for example, pressure from business persuaded Congress to slash capital gains taxes. This action did increase available capital, but businessmen remained reluctant to spend those funds on much-needed plants and equipment. "Is it any wonder that we are viewed as incapable of competing in world markets?" asks M. Kathryn Eickhoff, an economist with Townsend-Greenspan and Company in New York. "For a decade many of our major industries have been engaged in investment that is little more than maintenance and repair, while other parts of the world have been building modern facilities."

Business has also received hefty tax breaks to encourage spending for research and development, but the effect of such special legislation on innovation is not readily apparent. For instance, a 1954 revision of the Internal Revenue Code permitted special handling of funds used for research. Economist John Blair found, however, that the real result was to induce "companies to classify as 'research and experimental' many activities formerly carried on under other accounts." More recently, Edwin Mansfield studied the effect of the R and D tax credit adopted in the 1981 Economic Recovery Act. He found that the credit "had only a modest effect on firms' R and D spending." But the loss to the Treasury in revenues in the first two years of the act ranged from $600 million to about $1 billion. Thus, the well-intentioned legislation simply hyped the bottom line of a few corporations, at the expense of taxpayers.

A more current crusade, led by business groups and members of the Reagan administration, seeks to scuttle the antitrust laws that they contend operate to inhibit American corporations from competing against foreign competition. Although few if any examples of such inhibition are ever provided, Congress acceded to business lobbying and relaxed the antitrust laws to allow more pooling of research by competing companies. One effort, the Microelectronics and Computer Technology Corporation (MCC) in Austin, includes such companies as Control Data, Motorola, Sperry, Honeywell, and RCA. MCC, asserts one participant, will be "a significant national technology resource."

Such sidestepping of America's traditional procompetition ethic is a curious and troubling development for several reasons. First, basic research is one area where American companies already excel, yet the MCC effort is limited to just such research. Second, some of the mature companies involved in these pools have problems precisely because their short-term horizons limit their commitment to innovation. Third, joint research among companies effectively undercuts one factor that always has spurred innovation: competition.

Proponents of MCC argue that such combinations make more efficient use of intellectual resources and avoid wasteful duplication of research. They also see joint efforts as a way for individual firms to escape bearing the burden of costly R and D by themselves. "We are not talking here about price-fixing or sinister conspiracies," asserted Congressman Ron Wyden (D., Ore.). "We are instead talking about economic survival in an increasingly technical and increasingly competitive world."

This kind of plea for joint research among competitors is not a new one. In the 1960s, for example, the auto firms got together to develop an antipolluting exhaust device. But the result, according to a Justice Department lawsuit settled by a consent decree, was "product fixing"—a conspiracy to *suppress* the installation of such a device because the largest firms didn't want the smaller firms marketing the breakthrough.

There is, of course, an alternative to the Luddite legacy. Some of the companies we have profiled—which include GE, Johnson Controls, MCI, MCA, Nucor, IBM, and Monsanto—have found it. It's called innovation, and it isn't found in the hearing rooms on Capitol Hill or in joint ventures with chummy competitors. And it's not located in the federal bureaucracy, to which too many businessmen have developed a love-hate relationship. It comes from hard work, inspired management, and real risk-taking in the rough-and-tumble global marketplace. For when it comes to innovating, Washington is neither scapegoat nor savior. If business can't recapture the pioneer spirit of Polaroid founder Edwin Land, who once told colleagues "We're not here to make profits; we're here to make innovation," they surely won't find it at either end of Pennsylvania Avenue.

4

Mergers: The Production Ethic Versus the Predator Ethic

I'm reminded of the old story about the two guys on the American Stock Exchange who are trading sardines back and forth until finally one of them opened up a can and started to eat it. "Hey," he said, "these sardines are no good." "You don't understand," said his friend. "Those are trading sardines, not eating sardines." People are tossing around companies like they were sardines, but we're talking about dislocation of employees, communities, production and hundreds of thousands of jobs.

—An anonymous arbitrager

Tender Offers That Aren't Very

Probably no person is more closely associated with the surge in mergers and acquisitions during the past decade than New York attorney Martin Lipton. Along with the brilliant lawyer Joseph Flom, he has been the mastermind behind many of the multi-billion-dollar war games that have recontoured the corporate landscape. Mergers have made him rich and are chiefly responsible for the phenomenal success of his law firm, Wachtell, Lipton, Rosen and Katz; he teaches graduate school students the subject and wrote a book about it. So it is somewhat surprising that when Lipton is asked for examples of successful, productive takeovers, he can't come up with one. "Mostly," he sighs, "takeovers are destructive." But how could he build such a brilliant career on something "destructive"? "There's a difference between what you do for a living and what you believe," he candidly admits. Then he adds, "Sure we've represented clients doing takeovers, but ninety percent of our work is defending companies from being taken over."

M and A lawyers, as they're called, haven't lacked work in the past decade. The annual dollar volume of mergers soared from $12.5 billion in 1974 to approximately $124 billion in 1984.

At the same time, mergers triggered by hostile tender offers*
grew in size and number: In 1975, United Technologies, in a
hostile attack, won Otis Elevator for $398 million; in 1977, J.
Ray McDermott beat out United Technologies by paying $748
million for Babcock and Wilcox; in 1979, United Technologies
paid $1 billion for Carrier; in 1981, Elf Aquitaine Development
bought Texas Gulf for $2.3 billion and Du Pont spent $7.8 billion to save Conoco from Seagram; in 1984, Texaco paid $10.1
billion for Getty and Socal spent $13.4 billion for Gulf. "I don't
know what the answer is," admits Lipton. "It's a phenomenon
no one envisaged when they drew up the federal securities laws
back in the thirties."

The results of takeovers often have not justified the time, expense, and human costs. Large mergers often distract top executives from their management responsibilities, produce huge
debt burdens, divert capital from more productive uses, dimin-
ish competition, and dislocate masses of employees. "I think
most of these things are just an absolute waste of energy, waste
of money, and don't add anything to the economy," asserts
Harold Williams, the former chairman of the Securities and Exchange Commission.

Many mergers and acquisitions, certainly, can serve valid economic purposes. Such combinations normally are not hostile,
are carefully planned, and integrate the acquired company into
the organization of the acquirer. James River Corporation, for
example, has grown strictly by acquisition from a tiny maker of
specialty paper goods in 1969 to the fifth largest company in that
field by 1984. It was put together from mills cast off by bigger
companies, which James then shaped in its own image. Ex-
haustive research preceded each acquisition. The twelve acquisitions made by Emerson Electric Company between 1975 and
1983 strengthened the company's hand in its existing prosaic-
sounding but highly successful businesses: bench tools, industrial
drives, and electric utilities.

Consolidation on Wall Street has resulted in some effective
mergers. Before Shearson merged with American Express—a
good synergistic combination—it made a series of very smart

---

*A "tender" offer is a public bid for any or all of a corporation's shares.
Payment can be in securities of the bidder, but these days it is usually in cash.
A tender becomes "hostile" when the target resists and the bidder persists.
The terms *merger* and *acquisition*, while technically different, have come to be
used synonymously to describe the merging of two companies.

acquisitions of other Wall Street houses, including Hayden, Stone; Faulkner, Dawkins and Sullivan; and Loeb, Rhoades, and Company. The acquisition of Dean Witter Reynolds, the brokerage house, by Sears, Roebuck, and Company is admired by Peter Drucker because it was well planned in advance. "Sears . . . thought it through and decided to split along market lines and that there's going to be a distinct and separate consumer-finance business." When Drucker was asked what it took to do a merger properly, he recalled the advice he was given as a young man working in an investment banking house in Europe.

> My senior partner was in his 70s, from an old banking family—300 years old—where marriages were dynastic affairs. The old man always said to me: "Mr. Drucker, you are starting out with the financial figures. That's wrong: one ends with them. You are talking of a marriage. One doesn't marry a girl without a dowry. But one first investigates her . . . ancestry. Then comes the girl. Finally, the dowry. The only thing that's negotiable is the dowry. Neither the ancestry nor the girl is negotiable. They have to be right." And that is the way one looks at an acquisition. If you look at the people who know how to make acquisitions, they follow that rule.

What separates productive mergers from what can be called the "new wave mergers" is the difference between the "production ethic" and the "predatory ethic." In the latter, companies tangle in furious and costly combat. Treasuries are depleted and debts pile high as one side attacks and the other throws up legal barriers. Bewildered employees, the displaced persons of the merger wars, wonder whether they will be left jobless when the smoke clears. This "negative sum game," as columnist Robert J. Samuelson calls it, is consuming more and more of America's talent. Lawyers, consultants, brokers, lobbyists, speculators, are "devoted, usually quite profitably, to maintaining the traffic." Worries Samuelson, "If the predator ethic begins to overwhelm the productive ethic, the country is in deep, enduring trouble."

The circumstances surrounding the acquisition of Carborundum Corporation by Kennecott, mentioned previously, are instructive. In 1977, Niagara Falls-based Carborundum, the country's second largest manufacturer of grinding wheels, sandpaper, and other abrasives, was the subject of a hostile tender offer by Eaton Corporation, the Cleveland-based maker of automotive parts. To defend against Eaton—and, not incidentally, to boost the offering price—Carborundum's investment banker,

Morgan Stanley, circulated the company's vital statistics; Kennecott took the bait. Flush from selling Peabody Mines for nearly $1 billion, Kennecott itself feared falling victim to a cash-hungry predator. At the same time, Kennecott felt pressure from the Continental Group, which also was bidding for Carborundum. So, after only one month of frenzied research with its investment banker, First Boston, the copper company paid a substantial $66 a share for Carborundum, or $19 a share more than Eaton had offered. The $560-million purchase—twice book value—was viewed generally as excessive, but Kennecott's managers told skeptical stockholders they had got a real buy: Carborundum's well-respected management team and highly competitive abrasives business.

But an interview with T. Vincent Learson, the retired chief executive of IBM who served on the Carborundum and then Kennecott boards, shows that Kennecott, in fact, didn't know what it was buying and raises questions about how much research is done prior to any of these huge, high-pressure mergers. For Learson says that Kennecott bought Carborundum on the basis of an unrealistically optimistic forecast created by staffers and not questioned by top management. "Carborundum had come up with a five-year plan, and like all first versions of such plans, it was optimistic. Normally management of any company refines this kind of plan, but it didn't happen that year because management had been preoccupied fighting Eaton. Whatever they came up with on their first go-round was submitted to Kennecott, which was the 'White Knight.' So Kennecott bought [on the basis of] a plan that was not intentionally inaccurate or anything but was blue-sky. Later, [Kennecott] said, 'What about that plan?' Well, they were told that they got the five-year plan that came out of the machine the first time around, not the third or fifth version, which most plans go through."

For the next four years, things soured as a result of the merger. First, the ink no sooner dried on the Kennecott-Carborundum deal than T. Roland Berner, CEO of Curtiss-Wright Corporation, tried to seize control of the copper company, which tangled it up for years. Then, Carborundum's vaunted management, accustomed to fast-paced manufacturing, couldn't adjust to the copper business where it can take a decade just to decide whether to dig a hole in the ground. Almost all the Carborundum managers quit. "The only reason Kennecott paid as much as they did was the diversification Carborundum offered and for the management. They used neither one," recalls Frederick J. Ross, former president of Carborundum and one of the first to jump ship. "Based on what they did with the acquisition, you have to conclude that they tremendously overpaid. It was a waste."

Kennecott then sought salvation by hiring former Exxon executive Thomas D. Barrow to be CEO. Barrow demanded and got a huge salary and abundant perks, including a king-size $5-million executive jet to wrap around his large frame because, says one Kennecott source, he found Carborundum's two existing jets too cramped. What happened next was no surprise. Barrow, whose whole career was spent in the oil industry and who had no expertise in either the copper or abrasives businesses, turned around and sold Kennecott to an oil company. That company, Sohio, didn't know anything about the businesses either, so it decided that Carborundum's abrasives business—which Kennecott had trumpeted to justify the merger—wasn't worth saving.

Clearly, the Eaton-Carborundum-Kennecott-Sohio affair qualifies as a merger fiasco on several levels. It caused incalculable human suffering to the workers—now twice-removed from management—and the economy of already hard-pressed Niagara Falls. But it also undermined the competitive marketplace. With Carborundum gone, the abrasives industry was left with only two major American companies, Norton Company and 3M. If ever there was a rebuttal to the "efficiency argument" of the merger advocates, this was it. Jesse Werner, the former chief executive of GAF who was put on the Kennecott board by his friend and business ally, Berner of Curtiss-Wright, offered a biting postmortem during an interview: "Boy, did Kennecott get conned. One of the things they didn't do was to study the past of Carborundum. Another thing I couldn't understand is why Sohio paid so much for Kennecott."

Merging Through the Decades

Historically, mergers have come in waves stimulated or accompanied by dramatic changes in the economy, according to economist Jesse Markham. During the first wave, lasting from 1890 to 1904, railroads were spreading, use of electricity was expanding, and coal was gaining popularity. Economist George

Stigler describes this period as "merging for monopoly" because industrywide combinations created major corporate powers. Many are still giants to this day: U.S. Steel, General Electric, Westinghouse, U.S. Rubber, American Can, American Tobacco, and International Harvester, among others.

The next merger wave, from 1920 to 1928, coincided with development of the automobile and the radio. Some twelve thousand firms disappeared. Giant utility holding companies formed, which would collapse just as quickly in the coming Depression. And where the first merger period produced monopolies, this time two or more powerful companies formed, causing Stigler to coin the phrase "merging for oligopoly." Mergers raged in such fragmented industries as mining, chemicals, and food processing, resulting in the formation of Kennecott, Anaconda, Allied Chemical, General Mills, Kraft, General Foods, among others.

In reaction to the excesses of these two periods, Congress in 1950 enacted the Celler-Kefauver Amendment to the Clayton Act which, among other things, made it abundantly clear that the act applied to all mergers that "may . . . substantially . . . lessen competition or to tend to create a monopoly."

Blocked from making big vertical mergers (with suppliers) and horizontal mergers (with competitors), the deal makers now came up with a new acquisition strategy that skirted antitrust laws: conglomerate mergers. This became the third wave. Between 1960 and 1971, over twenty-five thousand independent companies disappeared; it was a time of enormous change especially in the transportation and communications industries. Conglomerates such as Textron, Litton, and ITT set a torrid takeover pace, paying for acquisitions with securities inflated by the soaring market of the mid-1960s and dubbed "Chinese paper" by skeptics. This merger wave slowed in 1969 when conglomerate stock fell from favor.

A new era of mergers and acquisitions began in the mid-1970s. Characterized by cash tender offers that often degenerate into hostile corporate battles, the era started slowly in 1974 when International Nickel Company of Canada (now Inco) wanted to buy ESB Corporation, manufacturer of Ray-O-Vac dry cells and Exide car batteries. But so did United Technologies, so Inco initiated a hostile takeover, and a nasty battle ensued. Such goings-on today are considered business-as-usual, but back in 1974, big respectable companies like Inco simply didn't engage in publicity-generating, acrimonious struggles;

that was left to the likes of Victor Posner, Meshulam Riklis, Norton Simon, and other "raiders."

The historic difference in the Inco-ESB battle was the presence on Inco's side of the venerable investment banking firm, Morgan Stanley. Robert Greenhill, Morgan Stanley's high-voltage merger expert, joined by attorney Joe Flom, got Morgan Stanley involved up to its tie clasp in the once-forbidden hostile takeover game. Inco won and from that moment on, hostile takeovers gained respectability; soon everyone from Exxon and Du Pont to Mobil and Allied began prowling for targets. In light of what followed, it's significant that the Inco-ESB combination turned out to be a disaster: Inco ended up selling off, piece by piece, most of the ESB properties it had fought so costly a battle to obtain.

Most mergers have been conglomerate combinations or those involving very large industries that are going through consolidation because of outside economic forces, notably the oil industry. Antitrust laws have played little or no role in limiting these mergers. The only serious attempt to test the legality of conglomerate mergers occurred in 1969 when Richard Nixon's antitrust chief, Richard McLaren, sued to block ITT from acquiring Hartford Fire Insurance, Canteen Corporation, and Grinnell Corporation. But that effort was derailed by Nixon himself, who told Attorney General Richard Kleindienst, "I do not want McLaren to run around prosecuting people, raising hell about conglomerates, stirring things up at this point. . . . My order is to drop the God damn thing." The government did get certain concessions from ITT in exchange for approving the merger, but the antitrust issue was shelved.

Then, in 1974, the Supreme Court set the stage for today's megamergers when it let the General Dynamics Corporation acquire United Electric Coal Companies, even though both were big coal producers that together would control nearly 50 percent of the market in some areas. The court reasoned that because United's coal was committed under long-term contracts, its disappearance into General Dynamics would have little effect on competition. The attitude underlining this decision—that mergers producing bigness are not necessarily undesirable even if they involve major corporations in the same industry—reached full flower under President Reagan's antitrust chief, William Baxter, who returned to academia in 1983 after asserting that economic efficiency is the only legitimate objective of antitrust law; for this reason, he dropped the Justice Department's costly and poorly conceived suit against IBM and pressed to completion the breakup of AT&T. If President Franklin Roosevelt's antitrust chief, Thurman Arnold, is remembered as a great enforcer because he directed the law to check excessive concentration of economic power, then Baxter's legacy is that the marketplace should be the only true test of whether mergers are anticompetitive. Speeches by him and Reagan's FTC chairman, James Miller III, claiming most large mergers to be efficient, flashed a green light to many merger managers. Such an encouraging attitude toward bigness moved columnist "TRB" in *The New Republic* to write that the administration operates "on the theory that the bigger government gets the more wasteful it gets, while the bigger business gets the more efficient it gets."

This attitude led the FTC in 1983 to permit a joint venture between General Motors, the number one carmaker in the world, and number three, Toyota, to build small cars in California. GM, in arguing for FTC approval, said it was seeking to learn Japanese management techniques from Toyota. More to the point, however, is that GM, like other American auto firms, is unable to produce small cars profitably. Under its arrangement with Toyota, it could enjoy all the profits of selling small cars without having to bear the costs of manufacturing them. According to FTC commissioner Michael Pertschuk, a disciple of Thurman Arnold's views and one of two in the minority who voted against the GM-Toyota arrangement, "Cooperation between the two price leaders, with a combined share of 50 percent of the new car market, represents a serious antitrust risk by any standards but this administration's."

Approval of a deal between archrivals GM and Toyota put pressure on other domestic and foreign auto firms to follow suit. And in April 1985 even Lee Iacocca, who had vigorously opposed GM-Toyota, announced that Chrysler would enter into a 50-50 joint venture with Mitsubishi Motors to produce 180,000 cars in the United States. While announcements of megacombinations—whether mergers or joint ventures—have now become almost a daily occurrence as legal barriers tumble, unanswered questions persist: How are consumers better served by more corporate concentration? Does international competition really demand that American companies become bigger, even though they already surpass in size most foreign competitors? What effect does this merger free-for-all have on corporate efficiency? On workers? On the economy?

These and other questions plague Edmund Kelly, who as a senior partner with the New York law firm of White and Case planned and carried out numerous major mergers: B. F. Goodrich's defense against Northwest Industries, financier Kirk Kerkorian's acquisition of Western Airlines, McDermott's defeat of United Technologies to get Babcock and Wilcox. Now vicechairman of the investment banking firm, Dominick and Dominick, Kelly ponders the broader questions raised by hostile mergers: "I think the real question we must consider is, what do we want an American corporation to be? Why is it that in Japan it's considered barbaric to buy and sell companies? How can there be such a distinction between what we consider capitalism and they consider barbarism? If someone were to read a roll of companies merged out of existence, Babcock and Wilcox, Carrier, Mallory, Liggett Group, Kraus Hynes, Gulf, Marathon, Bendix . . . One point of view could be that there were units of American society that involve cultures, traditions, families. Should they be up for sale just because some investment banker whispers in someone's ear?"

Why This Urge to Merge?

There are at least two reasons for the recent spate of corporate mergers—the economic and the egocentric.

The economic incentives to merge include low-priced corporate stock, undervalued corporate assets, and skewed tax laws. A common explanation for one company's acquiring another is that it's easier to buy than to build. It's cheaper and faster to acquire a company with valuable existing assets—unique consumer products, advanced industrial technology, rich natural resources—than it is to develop them from scratch. The stock market's valuation of companies has been relatively low in recent years, while the costs of labor and materials have been rising. As a result, the merger makers find that it's cheaper to "drill for oil on Wall Street" by acquiring a company than it is to sink a well in Prudhoe Bay, Alaska.

What adds kindling to the merger fires is that many companies are suddenly cash rich: some because of economic upturns, others because of selling off unproductive assets, and still others because they have been hoarding profits instead of investing in new equipment and in research and development. The cash-rich company, fearful that someone will try to acquire it for its cash hoard, gets rid of the cash by using it to buy another company.

The Internal Revenue Service has been an important partner to the merger makers. By permitting corporations to deduct all expenses incurred in a takeover battle, the IRS actually encourages corporations to grow by acquisitions instead of by innovative internal expenditures. When T. Boone Pickens spent a month in New York in 1982 fighting for control of Cities Service, he laid out $12 million for investment bankers, lawyers, and living costs for his band of raiders, one half his profit on the deal. "We gave a party, and it was expensive," commented Pickens, who probably wouldn't have been so cavalier if he hadn't been able to write off a big part of it on his taxes. Then, too, if cash-rich Company A acquires debt-heavy Company B, B's debts can be used to reduce A's taxes. And when fully depreciated or otherwise undervalued assets are acquired, tax write-offs can begin again at a new, higher value.

Hungry bankers have done their part to spur mergers. Flush with billions of deposits from IRAs and money market accounts and eager to lend, banks in recent years actually have been pressing loans on companies for mergers and other big deals. While a bank is limited by federal law on the amount it can lend to a single customer, the sky's the limit for a consortium of banks making a loan. For instance, when Socal sought to acquire Gulf in 1984, it obtained a record $14 billion from several banks headed by Bank of America, while would-be suitor Atlantic Richfield waited in the wings with a $12-billion package put together by Chase Manhattan et al. Reflecting on these stratospheric sums, *Fortune* speculated that even Exxon, with a stock-market value of $32.5 billion, is vulnerable. "I think if the right people wanted to do it, they could get anybody," a senior lender at a major bank told the magazine.

In 1984 a new, almost revolutionary financial incentive to corporate raiders appeared called junk financing. Created by the New York investment banking firm Drexel Burnham Lambert Inc., junk financing—so called because it involves the use of unsecured, high-interest securities—permits a raider to borrow 100 percent of the money needed before even beginning a raid. Not surprisingly, Drexel's clients include such famous raiders as Saul P. Steinberg, T. Boone Pickens, Sir James Goldsmith, and Victor Posner. In junk financing, the would-be buyer creates a paper company ("MM" for Mickey Mouse was the name of the paper company that raided Walt Disney Productions Corporation); then Drexel goes to several hundred corporate and individual investors to get letters of commitment to buy the new junk securities to help finance the takeover. The raider, for his part, plans to use the assets of the acquired company to pay off the junk financing.

The bottom line is that junk securities are financing corporate raids that wouldn't be possible otherwise. These low-grade securities are being picked up by institutions and individuals eager to get a piece of the merger-mania action. Trouble is, junk financing means just that—i.e., the quality of that debt is questionable and the possible debt burden on the surviving firm onerous.

Finally, there are the Wall Street money managers who put tremendous pressure on corporate managers for short-term profits. And what easier way to produce quick profits than by a merger? The reason that money managers have so much power is that they manage the investment of pension funds, mutual funds, and the like which control about 60 percent of the stock of Big Board corporations. Their clients pay them for results, so the money managers, in turn, demand results from the corporations. Often money managers control large blocks of stock in a single company, and they show unhappiness in a management's profit performance by selling those shares. These short-term demands—often precipitating unwarranted mergers—caused *Business Week* to ask in a recent headline, "Will Money Managers Wreck the Economy?"

Despite all these economic incentives—depressed stock prices, abundant cash, IRS cooperation, helpful bankers, high-pressure money managers—the best evidence indicates that hostile tender offers and most large mergers are a costly waste of managerial time and talent that generally produce not one new job, not one more barrel of oil, not one more bolt of steel. And they leave the surviving company saddled with massive debt. If this is so, then why do mergers continue at such a breakneck pace?

In many instances, businessmen seem almost compelled to acquire or be acquired. Company A fears if it doesn't swallow Company B, then Company C will swallow it. Personal concerns overcome management responsibilities as incumbent managers fear they will lose their pay and perks, which moves CEOs and boards of directors to constantly worry that their company is targeted or should be targeting another. Those interviewed also cited the unspoken belief of many chief executives that status positively correlates with size. "A great deal of it is ego. It's a major factor," says Martin Lipton, who certainly qualifies as an expert witness. (The wasteful effects of the executive ego are discussed in detail in Chapter 1.)

Kenneth M. Davidson, an FTC attorney, agrees. In describing the results of an FTC study in which fourteen prominent merger experts were asked why companies merged, Davidson said, "A number of participants cited examples of executives meeting at management training programs or country clubs, introducing themselves in terms of their titles and the sales volumes of their companies or units. . . . Social status, not management power, may be the realm where size counts most." The participants believed "that the market consequences of mergers are often unclear and that the decision to merge is ultimately made by the CEO on unquantifiable factors." They added that the decision could result simply from a friendly investment banker reaching the CEO by phone. More than three decades ago, Henry Simons, founding father of what has come to be called the conservative Chicago school of economics, described the role of ego in building a corporate giant: "Few of our gigantic corporations can be defended on the ground that their present size is necessary. Their existence is to be explained in terms of opportunities for promoter profits, personal ambitions of industrial and financial 'Napoleons,' and advantages of monopoly power."

"They're destructive" is how Harold Williams describes most mergers, and Williams clearly ranks as an expert on the subject. He is a former SEC chairman, former president of Hunt-Wesson Foods (later Norton Simon, Inc.), and dean of the UCLA Graduate School of Management. Most recently, as chief executive of the J. Paul Getty Trust, Williams played a key role in the sale of Getty Oil to Texaco. So when he speaks passionately about mergers, it comes from experience. "Short term, they're distracting. Managers that are subject to a takeover spend too much time defending themselves. It enhances their willingness to distort earnings, to phony them to keep the price of their stock up [so they're not so vulnerable to takeover]. Some companies even dissipate assets, getting rid of cash and buying credit—which is like shooting yourself in the foot to avoid being drafted. On the other side, the acquiring company has decided to grow more by financial manipulation than by building the quality of their business."

The merger wave has its eloquent defenders, ranging from conservative economist Yale Brozen to liberal economist Lester Thurow, who argue that mergers force efficiency. "The sharpest blade for the improvement of corporate management" is how federal judge Henry J. Friendly once referred to mergers. To William Baxter, they are a "very socially beneficial mechanism . . . a mechanism that enables corporate assets to be shifted from lower to higher value uses." Brozen, of the University of Chicago, warns, "The crusade against the growth of the top 100 or 200 industrial firms and against conglomerate acquisition is bottomed on specious fears and a mythical trend in aggregate concentration." MIT's Thurow asserts, "The antitrust approach has been a failure. The costs it imposes far exceed any benefits it brings."

These advocates appear to assume a priori that the free exchange of corporate assets promotes efficiency—that well-managed companies almost invariably take over poorly managed ones. But the testimony of businessmen, plus scholarly and empirical studies, directly contradict this assumption. Harry J. Gray, CEO of United Technologies Corporation and preeminent acquisitor, describes his target of choice: "We want it to be a market leader and profitable, number one, two, maybe three in the market. . . . We'd like [it] to have competent management." Senior vice-president James Q. Riordan says Mobil looks for companies that are "well managed. . . . The purpose for acquiring Marcor . . . was not because we thought we could make Montgomery Ward dramatically more efficient."

Columbia law professor Louis Lowenstein, who was president of Supermarkets General Corporation in the 1970s, views attempts to justify mergers on the basis of efficiency as a smokescreen. "The efficient market hypothesis has enabled us to avoid the question of whether takeovers are good or bad for the world because the clear answer [to advocates] is that they are good." His study of several 1981 hostile takeover bids failed to substantiate the theory that superior managements were buying and reviving faltering firms. "The target companies' average return on equity (ROE) compares favorably with that of American industry as a whole during that period," he found. "Of the ten targets that failed to survive, five had a higher ROE [for the 1977–80 period] than their acquirers. . . . No one suggested that the natural resource companies, such as Conoco, Marathon and St. Joe Minerals, were undermanaged. Indeed, acquiring companies like U.S. Steel and Du Pont went to great lengths, even after the transactions were consummated, to reassure their more experienced target managements."

MIT professor David Birch examined 6,400 independent firms that were acquired by conglomerates, comparing their growth rates before and after acquisition with those of 1.3 million independent firms that were not acquired. His findings support Lowenstein: Conglomerates tend to acquire the faster-growing independents, whose growth rates subsequently slow compared to firms that remain independent. In 1982, *Fortune* looked back at the ten biggest conglomerate mergers of 1971 by companies on its list of 500 largest industrial firms to see how they fared during the intervening decade. Its study, said the magazine, "strongly supports the notion that investing in unfamiliar businesses is unduly perilous—just as the critics maintain. Most of the acquirers evidently were lured into buying unstable companies, or into committing foolish mistakes that harmed stable ones."

A 1982 study of 206 corporations by the Hay Associates in conjunction with the Wharton School similarly questions the value of diversification by acquisition. "After corporations take the first step in diversifying their products, the maximum level of performance attained decreases with every further move forward in diversification." T. F. Hogary, writing in *St. John's Law Review,* asked rhetorically, "What can fifty years of research tell us about the profitability of mergers?" and answered, "Undoubtedly the most significant result of this research has been that no one who has undertaken a major empirical study of mergers has concluded that mergers are profitable, i.e., profitable in the sense of being 'more profitable' than alternative forms of investment." University of Maryland professor Dennis C. Mueller joined fourteen economists at the International Institute of Management in Berlin, West Germany, studying 765 mergers that occurred between 1962 and 1972 in Europe and the United States. The mergers generally didn't increase profits or sales, says Mueller, and in the United States "we saw a significant decline in growth rates of companies that had merged."

All these studies make clear that, contrary to the "efficiency hypothesis," billions of dollars have been spent joining companies whose managements had no clear vision of what would happen after the acquisition. Instead of efficiency, such seat-of-the-pants mergers squander resources, lives, time, and capital.

"To describe a takeover bid as therapeutic is one of the great red herrings of all time," observes Edmund Kelly. "And saying the threat of a hostile takeover makes a company's management do better is like saying a surgeon will operate more efficiently if he's threatened with a gun."

When, say, a Boone Pickens makes a hostile tender offer, it could conceivably help make a slumbering corpocracy more efficient. More typically, an overture from this descendant of Daniel Boone, who retains his ancestor's frontier flair, simply provokes scared managers to save their jobs by going deep into corporate debt to buy off raiders. In 1982, when Pickens bid for Cities Service Company, he drove management into the arms of "white knight" Occidental Petroleum (earning Pickens more than $40 million from his stock holdings). Next, in 1983, he moved on General American Oil Company, which fled to Phillips Petroleum, allowing Pickens to pocket a quick $44.9 million. Along the way he picked up about $31.8 million from selling a 3-percent stake in Superior Oil Company. Pickens's most rewarding play came when he led a raiding team on Gulf Oil Company in 1983, acquiring 21.7 million shares and threatening to reorganize the company if he won control. But there was no reorganization. Instead, Socal saved Gulf from the Texan in March 1984 by making the biggest acquisition in history ($13.4 billion). Pickens and his associates collected $781 million in higher stock prices for their efforts.

The High Cost of Big Mergers

Hit-or-Miss Mergers

When corpocracies try to diversify by acquisition, the acquired company is often smothered by the acquirer. Nowhere is this more evident than in the oil industry, where for decades rich oil reserves made the management of oil companies look brilliant. But when oil companies tried to diversify, they produced a series of wasteful hit-or-miss mergers—mergers that are appealing in theory but little more than very costly crapshoots in reality. Mobil's foray into retailing flopped after it acquired Marcor. Sohio took big losses from Kennecott, as did Standard Oil of Indiana from its acquired unit, Cyprus Mines, and ARCO from Anaconda. Indeed, virtually all the oil companies that tried to manage something other than oil failed.

Perhaps the biggest horror story was Exxon's 1979 purchase of Reliance Electric Company for $1.2 billion. Exxon bought the company to acquire its electric motor, called an alternate current synthesizer. Ebullient Exxon executives predicted that the energy-efficient motor would save as much as a million barrels of oil a day, a staggering figure approaching the 1978 oil output at Prudhoe Bay, Alaska. But just two years later, Exxon abandoned Reliance's design because it was too costly to manufacture. Commented *Fortune,* "The wildcatter mentality of playing your hunches may still be a good way to make money in oil— but all the world isn't oil."

Such blundering is not limited to the oil industry. Many new-wave mergers have an easy-come, easy-go way about them. AMF, for example, has spent years of buying and selling companies, in pursuit of trends. Trouble is, by the time AMF got there, the trend had usually peaked. Formerly known as American Machine and Foundry, the old company changed its name along with its image in the 1960s when it became the big name in bowling. Next a whole line of leisure products, ranging from skis and motorcycles to tennis rackets and clothes. But no sooner had it bought its way into the leisure boom than the energy crises of the 1970s put a crimp in that business. So AMF plunged into energy products to meet the energy crunch of the 1980s. To get there, AMF sold off leisure-products businesses and incurred huge debt. But then, the energy crisis disappeared and the leisure market blossomed again. As a result of its hit-or-miss merging, AMF entered 1984 with many of the wrong products, a top-heavy debt-to-equity ratio, and a depressed Standard and Poor's rating.

"Trial and error" may be an acceptable method of testing products, but it is not a reliable way of testing whole companies. The consequences can now be seen in the growing number of companies selling off once-vital subsidiaries in a kind of corporate triage. In 1978, there were 620 divestitures; in 1981, there were 830; in 1984, there were 900. Merger specialists estimate that in recent years 40 percent of the mergers are later dissolved for one reason or another.

Many giant conglomerates trade their large corporate holdings with the apparent ease of a poker player discarding. Charles Bludhorn of Gulf and Western acquired $12-billion worth of companies over twenty-six years, but no sooner had he died in 1983 than his successor, Martin Davis, began unloading many of those assets. Beatrice announced in 1983 that it would get rid of fifty companies with sales totaling $900 million. NL Industries in New York shed about sixty companies. Esmark, a heterogeneous holding company whose entities produce everything from phosphate and cosmetics to girdles and bacon, unloaded Vickers Energy in 1980 for $1.1 billion and most of Swift and Company for $37.5 million. Then it turned around and acquired Norton Simon, Inc., another sprawling conglomerate. Esmark really wanted Hunt-Wesson from the acquisition; most of the rest it would cast off in the casual fashion common to such deals. Then, in 1984, Esmark itself was acquired by Beatrice. . . . And so it goes.

Investment Bankers at $126,582 an Hour

According to the late William Carey, a former SEC chairman and Columbia law professor, "Takeovers are wonderful for lawyers and bankers, stock jobbers, arbitrageurs and finders. They are keeping some of the best minds on Wall Street busy (and affluent) in a nonproduction pursuit. But they are just shuffling pieces of paper. Organizing and financing new industrial productivity has taken a secondary role." The merger makers are "pie-slicers," in Robert Reich's apt phrase, financially committed to encouraging restlessness and ambition among malleable CEOs.

Indeed, all four merger waves, dating back to the first one that began in 1890, have had one thing in common: investment bankers. Willard Thorp, writing in 1931 in the *American Economic Review* supplement, observed that in the wave of the 1920s, "one businessman regarded it as a loss of standing if he was not approached once a week with a merger proposition. . . . A group of businessmen and financiers in discussing this matter in the summer of 1928 agreed that nine out of ten mergers had the investment banker at its core." Then, like now, big money was the lure; J. P. Morgan reportedly earned $60 million for putting together U.S. Steel, which is a kingly sum even by today's lavish standards. In fact, the enormity of the fees even moved Felix Rohatyn of Lazard Freres to complain, "The level of these fees is beyond what is reasonable and decent. They are going to cause a lot of trouble for all of us. We are all going to suffer from this in due course. We are being held in lower and lower esteem by our clients."

But the fees themselves are not the problem. What is worrisome is how these fees provoke investment bankers to generate unrest among corporations in order to keep the fees flowing. Their relationship with corporations is usually brief: do the deal, collect the commission, then move on to another deal. Their computers operate like those of lonely-hearts dating services, constantly whirring out new matches. Then the bankers try to persuade one of the companies to tender for the shares of another. And if the target turns down their client's offer, they may urge their client to get hostile—with the size of their commission pegged to their success. That's why investment banking firms stand accused of shopping around for companies in order to sustain the profitable business.*

- In 1983, the seventy people in Morgan Stanley's bulging department felt strain because the big deals were going to competitors. Its leader, the high-strung, boyishly pugnacious Robert Greenhill, who started it all with his Inco deal back in 1974, was especially under pressure. Between the summer of 1981, when it represented Conoco in its $7.3-billion merger with Du Pont, and 1984, Morgan Stanley hadn't participated in any of the bigger deals. Then, in March 1984, Morgan Stanley put its client Socal together with Gulf, and this ten-day, $13.2-billion deal—the biggest price ever paid in a corporate acquisition—enriched its coffers by $20 million.

- Goldman, Sachs assiduously cultivates its reputation of the good guy of the merger and acquisition game, allegedly spurning involvement in hostile tender fights. For this classy image, the firm has received lots of good press. In fact, Goldman does quietly set strategies for hostile takeovers on many occasions and picks up seven-figure commissions for its efforts. However, when the offer is made, Goldman often fades into the background and another investment banker gets the headlines.

- A decade ago, when First Boston hired George L. Shinn, then number two at Merrill Lynch, to be its chairman, one business

---

*For their role in putting together *Fortune*'s fifty biggest "Deals of the Year" in 1984, a handful of investment bankers collected at least $367 million, up from $260 million a year earlier. Goldman, Sachs led with more than $63 million. No sooner had 1984 dawned than Texaco paid $10 billion for Getty, earning three investment bankers a total of $44.8 million. But that was soon topped by the Chevron-Gulf deal, which generated $64 million for three financial intermediaries, Morgan Stanley, Salomon Brothers, and Merrill Lynch. In the Texaco deal, First Boston was called in at the last moment and got $10 million for seventy-nine hours of work, or $126,582 an hour.

magazine hailed him as savior of the flagging firm. But just three years later, in 1978, with First Boston's earnings shriveled to $1.8 million, the lowest since the Depression, the magazine, in an article titled "Boos for First Boston's Chief," bemoaned Shinn's failure to "restore luster to one of the greatest names in U.S. finance." Yet by 1981, fees alone were $75 million for handling $32 billion in announced or completed deals. In 1982, the house as a whole earned $93 million, the year its M and A group got $17 million for U.S. Steel/*Marathon,* $6 million for Occidental/*Cities Service,* $6 million for Allied/*Bendix*/Martin Marietta, and $5.5 million for *American General*/NLT (clients in italics). Thanks to the ingenious efforts of Bruce Wasserstein and Joseph Perella, codirectors of the department that now numbers fifty officers, Shinn again is a hero with a heroic salary of well over $1 million a year. And the recently foundering firm now is housed in a opulent glass and steel Manhattan tower that is identified on the firm's stationery simply as PARK AVENUE PLAZA; these days, anyone who matters presumably knows how to find First Boston.

The Price of Defense

As the laws of physics would predict, for every merger action there's a reaction—and it's expensive. Hostile tenders provoke predictable responses from besieged management. If the aggressor retains Flom, the defender hires Martin Lipton. If the aggressor is represented by First Boston, the defender gets Merrill Lynch or Goldman, Sachs or Morgan Stanley.

Since hostile tenders gained legitimacy in 1974, defensive strategies by targeted companies have gone through three overlapping periods. Initially, threatened managements tried to fend off a raider with their own acts of hostility. Then, as the number of hostile mergers increased and no corporation seemed immune, management began devising elaborate defenses *in anticipation* of a hostile attack some day. Finally, some managements are taking the radical step of buying out their stockholders and converting the public company into a private one, thus effectively removing it from the merger battlefield.

The most common riposte to an unwanted takeover attempt is to find a "white knight" to outbid the aggressor. Conoco chose Du Pont against hostile bidders Mobil and Seagram; Allegheny International rescued Sunbeam Corporation from IC Industries; R. J. Reynolds rescued Heublein from the clutches of General

Cinema; Socal was Gulf's white knight against Pickens. But white knights often make the decision to buy on the spur of the moment, with little time for research (see the discussion of the Kennecott-Carborundum merger earlier in this chapter). Observes Robert Pitofsky, dean of Georgetown Law School and counsel to Arnold and Porter, of how Du Pont and Conoco merged quickly to ward off unfriendly bidders: "In the few days between the time Conoco made known that it was available and the time the Du Pont board decided to attempt the acquisition, it hardly seems likely that the companies found through careful analysis that there were true efficiencies in the combination."

The wasteful action-reaction syndrome of the new-wave mergers is vividly displayed in the 1982 Bendix-Martin Marietta debacle. It began with a hostile offensive by Bendix, which Martin Marietta answered by an aggressive "Pac-Man" counteroffensive; in the cannibalistic lingo of the hostile takeover, this means that Martin Marietta turned on omnivorous Bendix and tried to devour it. As expenses mounted, Martin Marietta moved to a "Pac-Man-plus" offense by getting financial backing from United Technologies. As the struggle turned against Bendix, in desperation it offered its "crown jewels" to white knight Allied. In the end, Allied took over Bendix, saddling itself with $2 billion in debt. Martin Marietta borrowed $900 million, in effect, to repurchase its own shares from Bendix, putting its debt-to-total-capital ratio at a threatening 80 percent.

In the new predatory environment, management sometimes uses tactics that in the noncorporate world would be regarded as unethical or even illegal. For example, there is the practice of "greenmail." When the Bass family of Texas picked up 9.9 percent of Texaco's stock, John McKinley, the oil company's chairman, didn't blink at paying the Texans $5 a share above the market just to get rid of them, bringing them an estimated profit from their investment of $280 million in just forty-nine days. Warner Communications, to shake off the acquisitive Australian Rupert K. Murdoch, paid his news syndicate $172 million for its stock in Warner, at a profit to Murdoch of $40 million, plus $8 million for legal fees, for a one-hundred-day investment. Investor Saul Steinberg got Walt Disney Productions to pay him about $14 a share premium for his 12.1-percent block of stock, and Quaker State Oil paid him about $5.25 over the market price. His estimated profit on the two deals: $70.5 million. In these cases and many more like them, management presumes not only to raid the corporate treasury in order to preserve its hold on the company, but also to use that corporate money to pay off the raiders at a premium over what the nonthreatening stockholders can get for their shares.

Even when all stockholders get the same amount, the effects of a raid can stagger a corporation's debt structure—as in the raid on Phillips Petroleum Company. In this highly publicized case, Phillips's management secured its position in March 1985, by paying off everyone, including its own stockholders, who got the same amount as the raiders for their shares. Carl Icahn collected an estimated $50-million profit and Phillips agreed to pay expenses of $25 million while Boone Pickens made a profit of about $89 million and up to $25 million in expenses. To finance this payoff, Phillips went $4.5 billion into debt.

The increasing threat by such outsiders has produced a predictable reaction: Companies are constructing monumental defenses in anticipation of unfriendly tender offers. Typically, management justifies throwing up these legal walls around their companies by claiming they actually are for the protection of shareholders. "You owe your shareholders the best defense," announced First Boston in a full-page 1984 newspaper ad for its "Defense Team." "Few public companies are immune to the threat of unsolicited takeovers. This is the proxy season." It's ironic that First Boston, Pickens and others, when on the offensive, also claim that takeovers are for the stockholders to help them realize the true value of their stock. Indeed, Pickens got his company, Mesa Petroleum, to install a whole raft of so-called "shark repellents"—antitakeover measures—to discourage other would-be predators.

Unfortunately, incumbent managers use the threat of "raiders" as an excuse to secure their jobs from *any* challenge, legitimate or otherwise. For example, instead of boards of directors standing for election each year, companies now are staggering the election, voting for only one third of the board members each year. While this tactic discourages hostile tender offers because raiders are forced to wait three years to control the board, it also blocks stockholders from holding the board accountable through yearly elections. When SEI Corporation asked its stockholders to approve this measure along with another new rule requiring mergers to be approved by three quarters of the shareholders (up from one half), the company acknowledged that the new rules make it difficult, if not impossible, to oust current management. United Technologies got shareholders to approve an amendment requiring that 80 percent of the stockholders must approve mergers. Other companies, fleeing California, have incorporated in Delaware, in order to avoid the former state's requirement that shareholders be allowed to vote cumulatively. Cumulative voting gives minority shareholders a better chance to get representation on the board and has long been opposed by management. Now the hostile takeover threat is being used by management as an excuse to rid itself finally of the nuisance.

But the ultimate defense against the unwanted takeover is for managment to get the corporation's stock out of public hands by converting a publicly owned company into a private one. Called a leveraged buyout (LBO), this occurs when a group of investors—usually the management—borrows large amounts of money to buy out the stockholders, then uses income from the company's operations to pay off the debt. Amstar Corporation made an LBO to ward off Simplicity Pattern Corporation; Natomas, to resist Diamond Shamrock Corporation; and the Continental Group, to stop Diamond Lands. In 1983, some 36 companies went private through LBOs in deals totaling $7.1 billion, while in 1979 there were only 16 such buyouts, valued at just $600 million. In 1984, some 241 companies went private using LBOs—only 117 of them public companies that had to disclose the value of the deals.

When first conceived years ago, LBOs had the worthy purpose of putting new management life into a flagging organization. If an aging division was no longer profitable enough to satisfy the parent corporation, its managers might use an LBO to acquire the division from the company in hopes that they, as owner-managers, could revive the business. Recently, however, many LBOs have been used by top management as a way to ward off the threat of takeover, since the company's stock is no longer on the market, and to give themselves an opportunity of making a lot of money at very little personal risk, since it is the company's assets that are pledged as collateral.* In a typical

---

*Like mergers, LBOs are encouraged by the tax code. After a company goes from public to private, the management writes up its assets and takes depreciation based on the new, higher book value. Income once used to pay taxes is now used to service the huge debt. And the interest on that debt is deductible, so chances are the company will operate tax-free for several years. Moreover, if the company has an employee stock ownership plan (ESOP), employees can also participate in the buyout; the law permits them to deduct some principal from taxes, too (see Chapter 2).

LBO involving the soft-drink company Dr Pepper, CEO W. W. Clements realized $3.5 million profit from his old publicly held shares and options but sank only $1 million of that in the new LBO company. Banks staked him to another $1 million. When the textile firm Reeves Brothers did an LBO, the management team received $15.1 million and invested only $3 million in the new entity. The managers also gave themselves a $410.000 bonus "to compensate for the tax effects of the anticipated disposition of their shares acquired upon exercise of qualified stock options." The Signode Industries LBO was rigged so top management paid no interest on their stock-purchase loans.

"They're converting *Fortune* 500 companies into honeypots for managers and their cohorts," asserts New York attorney William Klein, who often represents stockholders suing management over LBOs. Klein and other critics of LBOs say that while stockholders sometimes get a fair price for their shares, the cards are normally stacked to favor management. So when a group led by William B. Stokely II sought to buy Stokely-Van Camp for $55 a share, they told shareholders it was a "fair and attractive price." Four weeks later, Pillsbury offered $62, and three weeks after that, Quaker Oats weighed in with a bid of $77 that ultimately proved successful. "What does fairness mean," wonders former SEC commissioner Bevis Longstreth, "when management's idea of a 'fair and attractive' price is increased forty percent by the marketplace?"

Competition and Consumers
Conglomerate mergers, while essentially untested by antitrust laws, massively affect markets and consumers. For one thing, there is almost no limit to the size and the variety of conglomerate mergers. "The issue today concerns the maldistribution of . . . power, just as it did in 1890, 1914 and 1950 when the . . . major anti-trust laws were passed," write former FTC chairman Michael Pertschuk and FTC attorney Kenneth Davidson. "That the growth of corporate power through conglomeration is incremental does not make it innocuous."

When a few firms control a particular industry—for example, GM, Toyota, Ford, and Chrysler in autos, or Westinghouse, GE, and GTE in electrical machinery—that's *market concentration*. A conglomerate, by contrast, controls the assets of various industries, and that is *aggregate concentration*. The result largely of the conglomerate merger wave, aggregate concentration has significantly increased. In 1947, the largest two hundred man-

ufacturing corporations accounted for 47.2 percent of total manufacturing assets. By 1968, the last time the phenomenon was
measured, the FTC found that this figure had jumped to 60.4
percent—or an increase of almost one third in two decades.

Merger advocates argue that this "rationalizes" aging industries that suffer overcapacity and inefficiency. "Concentration
persists only where it brings efficiencies or is the consequence of
superior management," asserts Yale Brozen, reflecting the popular advocacy position.

But the economic costs of market concentration are significant. When a few companies dominate a market, they can
charge prices above competitive levels. Economist Leonard
Weiss of Wisconsin collected and analyzed most econometric
studies of concentration and profits: Of forty-five studies, thirty-
eight showed a significant positive correlation—that is, higher
concentration means higher prices and higher profits.

That monopoly has unequal distribution effects was demonstrated in a 1973 study done at the Stanford University School of
Business by economists William Comanor (later to be chief
economist of the Federal Trade Commission) and Robert
Smiley. Calculating that monopoly power overcharges consumers 2 to 3 percent of the GNP annual and that the degree of
monopoly has been fairly constant between 1890 and 1962, they
concluded that monopoly and oligopoly have skewed the distribution of household wealth. For example, they specifically
found that in the absence of monopoly power, (a) 2.4 percent of
American families would control not 40 percent of total wealth
but only 16.6 percent to 27.5 percent, and (b) 95.3 percent of
American families would be better off and only the wealthier 6.7
percent worse off. Without historic monopoly/oligopoly, they estimate that our maldistribution would be as much as 50 percent
less.

The Human Cost

In the high-finance world of mergers and acquisitions, big deals
are consummated in Manhattan high rises but the cost often is
borne by anxious employees in distant communities. "Absentee
control changed the corporation's view of the surrounding community," says Cornell University sociologist Robert Stern.
"Communities [are] viewed as locations for plants . . . appropriate only so long as the location provides economic advantages.
When such a location [is] no longer economically rational, the

plant [is] closed and facilities built elsewhere. This economic calculation creates a fundamental conflict between the calculus of
corporate welfare and local communities welfare."

Far removed from the effects of their actions, the new-wave
merger managers typically ignore the human factor in their
merger equation. For too many of them, figures count, not people. Besides, many deals are done in such a rush that there is
precious little time to do more than scan computer printouts. In
the face of so little forethought, justification turns on the cliché
that new management will make the acquired company more
efficient . . . and that the stockholders demand growth. But
focus on this sole standard has left the American corporation-
scape littered with abandoned people and communities.

There is the case of Draper looms, founded in the nineteenth
century and, until recently, the principal employer in Hopedale,
Massachusetts (population 2,400). It owned 45 percent of the
town's real estate, was the biggest taxpayer, and provided the
town with a hall, high school, country club, airport, sewage
plant, power facility, even the local cemetery. In short, Draper
was Hopedale's leading citizen. Then, in 1967, Rockwell International acquired Draper and took its executives to Pittsburgh. "We began dealing with lawyers from Pittsburgh and top
executives from Pittsburgh. The company-town relationship was
gone," recalls town administrator Bernard Stock. Next, Draper's
research and development staff was reduced and the maintenance staff eliminated. After a century of resident managers,
Rockwell International rotated managers through Draper for
brief periods. Gradually, Rockwell International lost interest in
Draper and in Hopedale, and by the 1980s the town was on the
brink of bankruptcy.

As *Fortune* noted, mergers have a human side, although "no
statistics show how many employees get relocated, lose jobs,
status, benefits or opportunities, are drained of commitment or
self-esteem or develop health or family problems." The magazine estimated that one quarter to one half the employees of the
combined organization are directly affected, and that the ten
largest of 1983's fifteen hundred mergers changed the lives of up
to 220,000 employees.

Creating this much human discomfort is not inevitable, even
in the rough-and-tumble of a profit-oriented market economy.
James C. Abegglen, the experienced Tokyo-based consultant,
explains why there are so few acquisitions, and no hostile take-

overs, in Japan. Like Americans, Japanese investors enjoy earning capital gains, businessmen are just as interested in rapid,
low-risk diversification, and companies have businesses they
would like to divest. The answer, says Abegglen, "lies mainly in
the areas of personnel and human relations."

First, the company is seen as "integrally including the people
who compose it. Therefore, the purchase or sale of a business or
company in Japan has the flavor of the purchase or sale of people." While American management says the company belongs to
shareholders, the Japanese manager believes only that the
shareholder is entitled to a return for providing capital and that
"ultimately the Japanese company exists for the employees, to
ensure their well-being and their future. Thus, sale of the company is not a decision only for the shareholders but is rather a
decision for the entire workforce of the company. (Similarly,
unusual profits in Japan are seldom paid out in the form of a
higher or extra dividend, but rather in extra wages and
bonuses.)"

Removing the Predator's Advantage

In 1985, legislation was pending to outlaw some of the worst
excesses of takeover threats, but the root causes of merger ma-
nia would remain unchanged. Few legislators want to propose
stiff antimerger legislation or new regulations that might limit
business's flexibility. This hands-off attitude has been bolstered
by the growing influence in the Reagan administration of conservative economists and regulators, who view the marketplace
as a kind of corporate survival course where, inevitably, strong
companies overcome weak ones.

But this pure free-market attitude ignores that mergers affect
more than the corporate bottom line. Too many of the new-
wave mergers, especially those resulting from hostile tenders,
have been poorly conceived, hurriedly executed—and hence ultimately wasteful. For mergers present broader questions than
the short-term financial satisfaction enjoyed by one firm from
acquiring another. Three changes in the current system could
help remove the unfair advantage currently enjoyed by takeover
experts and help shift American business back toward the production ethic.

1. Remove a corporate veil. The bottom line to the new-wave mergers is that there is no bottom line; there is no decisive statistical data available to show whether this wave, and the previous waves, have been good, bad, or indifferent for the economy, for society, for workers. To be sure, there is plenty of empirical and anecdotal information to show that many mergers—especially the hostile variety—have a negative impact. Still, there is a significant level of economic concentration under way in the United States, and nobody knows with any certainty the extent to which it is harming the economy, corporations, employees, or investors.

The reason is that corporate secrecy shrouds any accurate analysis of the impact of mergers. Mobil buys Marcor, Du Pont takes over Conoco, United States Steel acquires Marathon, and those once-independent, powerful, and vibrant entities disappear into the survivor's bottom line.

Instead, legislation could require corporations at least to disclose the long-term effects of mergers. The law could provide that if a merger results in a company with assets of, say, $500 million or larger, the books of the two companies will remain separate for five years. That way, the performance of the postmerger company will be visible to investors, board members, and the press. An acquisitive CEO presumably would think twice before gambling a corporation's wealth on a merger if he knew his actions would be subject to market and public scrutiny.

Because the strength of more disclosure is that it helps the marketplace decide whether a merger is productive or wasteful, even the most conservative economists should be willing to support this idea. For disclosure forces managers, who tend to have short-term vision, to think carefully of the long-term implications of their actions.

2. Ban "greenmail." By early 1985, sentiment in Congress was growing to make illegal one of the new-wave mergers' most outrageous by-products, the payment of greenmail. Indeed, the antigreenmail sentiment was shared even by many of the most aggressive players in the mergers game. Martin A. Siegel, who heads Kidder Peabody and Company's merger operation, asserted that "greenmail has no redeeming virtue," adding that a corporation should not pay a premium over the market to buy its own shares without the approval of a majority of the disinterested shareholders.

3. *Remove tax incentives*. Tax incentives to mergers and LBOs should be removed. Edgar M. Bronfman, the chief executive of Seagram Company and himself bloodied in the merger wars when his company made a hostile bid for Conoco, was so disturbed by the experience that he wrote, "If the interest on corporate takeover money borrowed specifically to buy the common stock of another corporation were not tax deductible . . . such activity would be sharply curtailed. . . . Federal tax revenues would be increased and the average taxpayers would thus not be, as they are now, indirectly footing the bill for part of these corporate-takeover games."

Other changes in the tax laws that would discourage mergers include the following:

- Double taxation of dividends should end. It is as an excuse by management to retain cash that can then be used for more acquisitions. This point is analyzed more fully in Chapter 9, "Corporate Welfare."

- Tax deductions should be disallowed on loans of more than a modest amount, say $10 million, to finance leveraged buyouts (LBOs). As discussed earlier, huge tax breaks have drawn deal makers to LBOs. At the same time, corporate employees who want to acquire a division or company from top management should not be discouraged.

These changes would make hostile tender offers more open and fair, without flatly prohibiting them as some entrenched managements would prefer. For there is surely some validity to the claim of raiders such as T. Boone Pickens, Carl Ichan, and Jimmy Goldsmith that they can expose the inefficiencies of otherwise invulnerable corpocracies, as the managements at Gulf Oil and Phillips Petroleum discovered to their displeasure. Raiders may do it for the money, but the message to slothful managers is a useful one. Says Goldsmith: "My countries [France and Britain] are dying because the bureaucracies and the old companies have been protected."

Ultimately, however, corpocracies can only become more efficient over time by painstaking changes from within, not sudden attacks from without—the kind of changes described throughout this and other books. Like many things that sound good only if you don't have the occasion to count the costs, as Louis Brandeis said of large mergers decades ago, the costs of hostile tender offers, or worse yet successful hostile tender offers, are considerable. Perhaps it's true that our elephantine corporations beg to be pushed around, but does that mean that vast quantities of limited credit must be absorbed, companies distracted from their chartered purpose, and production, jobs, and communities become pawns on a business chessboard? And what is the result of actually merging two bloated and inefficient companies, except to produce one very bloated company?

5

From Pay to Perks to Parachutes: Why Not "Merit Pay"?

I can resist everything except temptation.

—Oscar Wilde

When it is a question of money, everybody is of the same religion.

—Voltaire

Jesse Werner's board was an understanding one. Although GAF's stock declined 80 percent (after inflation) during the eighteen years of his tenure and suffered an operating loss of more than $22 million during his last year, the board chose to spare the rod with a vengeance: Werner was given a five-year multimillion-dollar employment contract and compensation for 1981 and 1982 totaling over $1.5 million. He and other GAF executives also received $635,000 in bonus payments in 1982. The generosity of the board was not the only reason that dissident investor Samuel Heyman won his proxy contest for control of the company the next year, but it surely played a role. Heyman said that Werner wasted corporate assets with lavish compensation while the firm was losing millions. Consequently, while Werner's final salary was $969,000 in 1983, his successor Heyman's the next year was $250,000.

If waste is defined as something for nothing, the current system of executive compensation is a quintessential example of the waste of corporate assets. Consider the following: Back in 1975, Meshulam Riklis was chairman of Rapid-American Corporation. Yet while the firm was in the red, Riklis was in the pink, somehow persuading his faltering company to make him the highest-paid executive in the United States. ITT in 1981 realized far lower rates of return than Raytheon on stockholders' equity, growth in earnings per share, and growth in stock price—yet ITT paid its CEO $1.15 million in salary and bonus while Raytheon gave $635,000 to its top officer. In 1982, the CEOs of Ford and American Motors got salary increases, even though their firms lost $658 million and $153 million, respectively. Although sixty of the *Fortune* 500 had losses in 1983—which is the largest number since the survey began three decades before— the chief executives of the top one hundred firms enjoyed a compensation increase of 13.7 percent, compared with an increase of only 5.9 percent for employees' hourly wages.

The question of "merit-less" pay, when raised in our interviews, produced a crescendo of worried business voices lamenting the phenomenon of executive overreaching and self-dealing. Says George H. Foote, the director of McKinsey and Company, who is in charge of its executive compensation policy, "Unfortunately, we've got an advancing juggernaut here. I find much more executive self-interest today than I did a number of years ago. There's a changing value system. The younger executives coming along are much more concerned with money." Archie E. Albright, a director of the Grumman Corporation and chairman of its compensation committee, thinks that "the enormous salaries and bonuses some of these guys are taking" are unwarranted. "No individual is worth that kind of money. You know, it amazes me that Moses Malone can command a million dollars a year. But at least Malone has to bargain for what he gets, and he has a really outstanding talent." In an article provocatively entitled "The Madness of Executive Compensation," *Fortune* magazine found that "so many examples of near-unarguable excess exist that a lot of directors must be thought guilty of falling down on the job."

This growing self-criticism tracks the recent spurt in executive compensation. While only five executives earned over a million dollars in 1977, by 1983 forty-six executives in large publicly held companies were earning over a million annually in direct compensation alone, with at least twenty-five topping the two-million-dollar mark. The average total pay increase for senior executives in 1984 was four times that of blue-collar employees (12.6 percent to 3 percent). Indeed, if one includes smaller firms, private companies, and brokerage houses, and counts realized long-term compensation (stock options), it is likely that several hundreds of executives have crossed the million-dollar threshold. According to a study released by compensation consultants Towers, Perrin, Forster & Crosby, the median direct compensation (salary, bonus, and annualized long-term incentives) for CEOs in a sampling of ninety-nine of the nation's largest corporations was $919,659 in 1984.

Clearly, some American executives are giving new meaning to Harry Truman's expression, "The buck stops here."

A Rich History

During the turn-of-the-century era, if someone earned a fortune there was a presumption that he must deserve it. Also, corporate noblesse oblige was then a fashionable concept that sought to cushion the unpopular excesses of private wealth—John D. Rockefeller's publicized giveaways of dimes comes to mind. One commentator of the time described this period of industrial leadership as having a "body of broad, permanent and socially beneficent principles of action, to which superior minds, forming an aristocracy in industrial affairs, will swear allegiance."

The modern era of high managerial compensation (as opposed to large owner returns) began in 1902 when Bethlehem Steel instituted its first bonus plan for managers. By the late 1920s, 64 percent of all manufacturing companies had them, and Alfred Sloan, the founding father of General Motors, attributed his company's phenomenal success to them. This decade also saw the rise of the stock option—by which an executive was given the opportunity to buy stock in the future at a fixed price. As later explained by John J. Raskob of GM, "We made eighty millionaires in four years in General Motors. We induced [them] to go into debt to buy General Motors stock. Stock they paid $33,000,000 for is today worth $250,000,000 or so."

This well-paid "aristocracy in industrial affairs," however, began to draw some critical comment, especially during the Great Depression. The general manager of one large corporation told a reporter, "The reason why we all work so hard here and give up everything for our jobs is that every one of us knows that he is getting more money than he is worth. I should be well paid at about a third of what I am getting, but I hope no one finds out." A 1930 headline in *Literary Digest* magazine dryly described Eugene Grace's income from Bethlehem Steel: "Salary $12,000, Bonus $1,623,753." Shareholders of the American Tobacco

Company legally challenged a stock option plan under which "president George W. Hill not only gets a cash compensation of a round million dollars yearly, but is enabled to make an additional $1,275,000 in profits on stock issued at a special low price to officers and employees." Remember, this was in 1931 dollars.

With the emergence of the New Deal, regal managerial paychecks were subjected to more government scrutiny. In 1934, the Federal Trade Commission released a controversial study of the pay of some one thousand top executives. As a result, the infant Securities and Exchange Commission began requiring the disclosure of the compensation of high corporate officials. Chairman Joseph Kennedy explained that "a corporation having securities listed for public trading on the stock exchange should not be permitted to keep under cover the payment of salaries, fees, bonuses and the like which may very well have an important bearing upon net earnings."

In this and following decades, the form of executive compensation varied with external events. With stock prices plummeting during the Depression, there was a shift away from stock options and toward higher fixed salaries. Extraordinary tax rates on earned income in the 1940s and 1950s, which reached 91 percent, encouraged deferred and "unearned" compensation (stocks and bonds). A bull market beginning in late 1962 induced managers to buy their own stock. But a dipping stock market and cuts in the maximum personal income tax in 1964 and 1969 prompted companies to again emphasize salary and perquisites, leading one commentator to summarize the trend with a line from the *Rubáiyát of Omar Khayyám;* "Ah, take the cash and let the credit go."

In 1973, as inflation became a public concern, top management paychecks were subjected to renewed attention. President Richard Nixon's Cost of Living Council imposed a 5.5-percent cap on raises for management officials in all but the smallest firms. Yet that momentary constraint did not stop executive pay hikes from reaching 12.4 percent by 1977. The Carter administration then picked up the battle cry, although in a quieter tone of voice. With inflation again rising, Treasury Secretary Michael Blumenthal wrote to two hundred companies in 1978 to request that they voluntarily keep raises to 5 percent; most never even responded, and only five complied (Uniroyal, General Motors, Allied Chemical, Merck, and AT&T).

Interest in the subject grew, though, in 1978–82 because of

the oddity of a leap in executive compensation simultaneous with two severe recessions. This pattern of higher personal compensation for executives and lower profits for firms—combined with the advent of the Reagan administration, whose economic program assured top executives substantially more after-tax income—raises several important questions. Why are top managers being paid so much more just when foreign competition exposes their deficiencies? Are they being rewarded not only for successes but failures too? Do boards have enough information and decision-making power concerning executive compensation? What more can be done to link pay and performance?

The Pay-Setting Process: Who Decides Who Gets What?

Jesse Werner's captive board at GAF allowed him virtually to write his own paycheck. One board member was the company's banker, another the company's contractor, and others were, in Samuel Heyman's words, "old cronies of Werner's." According to a prominent executive at one of the largest U.S. firms, who spoke on the condition that his name not be used, "Jesse Werner is a longtime personal friend of mine, but he has done a *lousy* job at GAF. And not only has he done a lousy job, but he has continued to pay himself an incredible amount of money, and he would keep increasing his bonuses, his stock options, and everything else in years in which corporate profits were continuing to go down." He went on to say that "Jesse's board was the old buddy system and there wasn't *anybody* who was on the board that was going to do anything about Jesse—it took a stockholder and a proxy fight, which is very tough to do." Indeed, GAF's compensation committee appears to have been about as consequential as a perfumed wig on a British barrister: The group, for example, did not even meet in 1981, although a GAF spokesman says it met twice in 1982.

While few boards are quite as lax as GAF's, all face a dilemma when fixing pay for top management—for they are awarding other people's money to executives who may be friends and peers. Most large corporations now have only "outside directors"—that is, directors who are not related to and are not employees of management—setting compensation. That helps reduce the worst kind of dependency of boards upon management, but still leaves unresolved problems involving back scratching, inadequate time, financial entanglements, and information dependency.

Let's consider each in turn—first, outside directors who are themselves executives at other companies. Of the boards surveyed by Korn/Ferry International in 1983, 88.2 percent contained senior executives from other companies; 66 percent had retired executives from other companies; and 46.8 percent included retired officers of their own corporation. Here friendship, loyalty, and empathy can understandably play an influential if not a decisive role in decision making. Who better understands the difficulties of meeting a tough performance target, or the motivating value of large stock options, than a fellow CEO?

Outside directors, too, have a financial incentive not to be too tough on management pay. One 1983 survey found that the largest U.S. companies pay directors $12,000 to $32,000 a year. And some directors charge special fees for additional services, like the three Ralston Purina directors who were paid $100,000 each for working on a special committee searching for a new CEO. These are not insignificant sums, and one assumes that rational directors would not want to offend management seeking large compensation packages if it could jeopardize their own directorial compensation. This back scratching between boards and executives naturally results, says Grumman Corporation director Archie E. Albright, from the fact that "in many publicly held corporations, most of the outside members of the board have been picked by the chief executive officer."

Then there's the problem of inadequate time, mentioned in Chapter 1, "Corpocracy." According to Virgil Conway, who sits on four boards when he's not running the Seaman's Bank for Savings in New York, "It makes it easier, when you're on several boards, because then you can see what your competitors for executive talent are doing." Perhaps so, but it is doubtful that a director with a company of his own to run will have the time to adequately gauge the appropriate pay package for various management groups.

Even if diligent directors took seriously their fidelity to owner-shareholders rather than to hired managers, and wanted to object to, say, a CEO's undeserved bonus, they would still have to know what was going on to make a critical appraisal. Instead, boards are often kept in the dark—or "they choose to be in the dark" in Sheldon Weinig's view—about the reasons for managerial compensation. Says Graef Crystal, a vice-president at the consulting firm of Towers, Perrin, Forster and Crosby, "You've got a bunch of people who are for the most part well-meaning, intelligent people but they're here an hour a month, or whatever, they don't have too much time to do much homework, a lot of them are not mathematically inclined—this is a very technical field—so they're at the mercy of what you want to tell them."

Our interviews of consultants, board members, and CEOs found that management control—not board control—of the compensation-setting process is remarkably uniform throughout business. Compensation plans "will more often than not come to us from management" says Richard Laster, who has sat on the compensation committees of Firestone Tire and Rubber Company and General Foods Corporation. According to an Exxon public relations representative, the "[internal] compensation and executive development committees [is] where it's all done, actually. . . . The compensation committee only meets infrequently, a couple of times a year, that kind of thing." Explains Robert H. Haines, a director of, and general counsel to, Western Pacific Industries, "The level of compensation for the operating companies is essentially fixed by the senior management, by the chairman of the board, and the president, and the board is always informed about that, and to that extent reviews it."

In two extraordinary examples of corporate chutzpah, senior officers at Western Pacific and at Pacific Telesis actually sit on their own company's compensation committees. With management on the compensation committee, it's not surprising that Western Pacific CEO Howard E. Newman got $466,000 in cash and $83,300 in contingent remuneration in 1982—not to mention stock options outstanding worth $2,287,648—despite what the annual report described as "a year of great difficulty" due to a 25 percent sales decline.

One large cosmetic company has streamlined the process even further. As a vice-president for personnel described it (requesting anonymity for himself and his firm), "We don't have a compensation committee. Compensation philosophy comes out of management." The company dissolved its compensation committee several years ago, feeling that even though such committees are "good PR" for the stockholders, "they just don't have much experience in it. My job is to make proposals to the board. Before I go to the board, it has to go to the executive committee (the three top executives who sit on the board). . . . They have to be sold on it." He then laughed, adding, "and there's one quarter of the board right there."

Beyond compensation committees, it is usually management that hires a compensation consultant and that makes use of the consultant's report as it sees fit. But like board members who might lose their fees by offending the management that effectively selects them, a consultant hired by management may lose his job if he does his job. Should we be surprised that compensation consultants "generally recommend rather high salaries and other perks for top corporate officers," asks businessman Michael Whitney, "when they are in fact, hired to produce exactly that result? In fact, if these compensation specialists were to come in with low figures, the likelihood is very great that they would not be invited back."

Compensation consultants, such as Crystal and Foote, emphasize that the key is access to the board. Without it, they can become pawns of management. One manager who shares their concern is Samuel J. Silberman. When he became head of Gulf and Western's compensation committee, he immediately hired an independent consultant for the committee. "I felt that in a company as complex as Gulf and Western, there was no way I could discharge my responsibility without having a professional expert available. . . . Every other committee has their experts. The audit committee has their accountants. In other committees they have bankers or lawyers. And the compensation committee is sitting there all by itself in the most difficult task, because you're dealing with the people that you're relying on for the effective running of the company."

The result of a board environment where directors lack the independence, time, motivation, and information to critically examine executive compensation packages is that top managers largely write their own ticket. Clarence B. Randall, the late chief executive of Inland Steel, explained the dilemma this presents a CEO:

> The number one man confronts a very special moral equation . . . when it comes to fixing salaries for himself and the other executives. True, his board of directors must give *pro forma* approval to his recommendations, but it almost never challenges them. In actual fact, therefore, he himself is the one who decides what compensation he shall receive. This is a very tough spot for a man to be in.

In this context, accusations of executive greed miss the point. Some surely have overreached—but they should not have had the opportunity to do so in the first place. Too many companies lack board controls and uniform standards to resist wasteful compensation plans. We would expect a store without security guards to be especially subjected to shoplifting. Even without security guards or watchful boards, obviously not all consumers will shoplift and not all executives will insist on undeserved compensation. But neither should we perpetuate a system that allows unguarded managers to write their own paychecks, because they will likely demonstrate, in Oscar Wilde's phrase, their ability to resist everything except temptation.

The Package: "Richer Than All Their Tribe"

Short-Term Incentives—Bonus Babies

Charles Lazarus was paid a salary of $315,000 in 1982, yet his total earnings—counting short- and long-term incentive pay—added up to $43.7 million, making him the second-highest-paid executive in the U.S. (to Frederick Smith of Federal Express). Clearly, salary alone is just the most visible tip of the proverbial iceberg.

Annual bonuses and other short-term "incentive plans" can be the better part of cash remuneration for many executives. Nine tenths of companies have bonus incentive plans for top management. Among *Fortune* 500 CEOs who received bonuses in 1984, the average reward was 52 percent of base pay. And while most of us assume that bonuses are granted for above-average performance, a 1983 Conference Board study found that at least 75 percent of companies with bonus plans paid bonuses.

A glaring example of this phenomenon gained unwanted notoriety for GM and Ford when, in 1984, they announced that chairmen Roger Smith and Philip Caldwell received annual bonuses of $1.5 million and $1.4 million, respectively. In all, GM paid 5,807 executives an average bonus beyond their salaries of $31,289, or about $2,000 more than the average annual *income* of autoworkers; and five officials took home at least $1 million each. True, the industry had dramatically rebounded from the 1981–82 slowdown. But because the gains were due in large measure to government "voluntary import quotas" stemming the flow of Japanese imports, and because the bonuses came after UAW pay concessions, the bonuses attracted an unusual array of criticism. William Brock, President Reagan's trade representative, called them "unbelievable." UAW president Owen Beiber weighed in with "obscene." Chrysler president Lee Iacocca said they were "a shocker" and promised that his firm's bonuses would be only half as much. "You reach a point of asking how high is up. How high is tolerable in a publicly held company?," said the popular executive. "We as an industry had better start acting responsibly."

"Bonus babies" is a term of art that should apply not only to the Ralph Sampsons and Doug Fluties of professional sports, but to businessmen such as Richard Bressler, Marshall F. Smith, and James Morgan as well. For promised bonuses helped attract them to their "franchises." Burlington Northern offered its CEO Richard Bressler a no-strings-attached "signing bonus" of stock worth $1 million when tempting him away from Atlantic Richfield in 1980. Commodore International promised Marshall Smith an $877,500 immediate bonus, plus stock options on three hundred thousand shares. James Morgan was hired away from Philip Morris to Warner Communications' Atari division for a multiyear contract estimated at $8 million (though he lost his job when Atari was sold by Warner in 1984).

These awards were made before the executives had performed at all—let alone performed well. Other bonuses have been paid after years of an executive's service—but without any apparent exceptional performance, such as the onetime bonanza awarded to Archie R. McCardell at International Harvester.

McCardell received substantial bonuses before, during, and after his tenure at Harvester. On his way in, in 1977, he picked up an up-front payment of $1.5 million in addition to a $1.8-million loan, which was granted at 6-percent interest in order for him to buy company stock. By October 1980, that company had suffered a devastating six-month strike and an estimated $400-million loss in the past year. Its net worth had dropped by 20 percent. Despite all this adversity, the board granted McCardell complete forgiveness of the $1.8-million loan based on a "spectacular performance" clause in his contract. And when he was fired in late 1982, he received a $600,000 token of the company's esteem. McCardell admitted that his package had been "an absolute disaster from a public relations point of view," yet of his performance he said, "I think I rate myself superb."

In other cases, too, bonuses appear to be a reward not only

for success, but also failure. By what logic, for example, did ACF Industries award chairman of the board John F. Burditt an $80,000 bonus (on top of a $300,000 salary) for 1982, a year when profits fell from $47.5 million to $33 million and, according to the company's annual report, "conditions in the marketplace [led to] deep reductions in employment levels"? And perhaps there was a reason for the $100,000 bonus A&P gave to each of its top two officers in 1978, but given the firm's lackluster performance, the average A&P stockholder would have been hard put to figure it out.

It is understandable that companies would want to offer handsome rewards to attract and keep competent top-level managers—but should such rewards be unconditional? A company takes a gamble when hiring a CEO, who in large measure has the power to sink or save the firm. It seems reasonable to ask the CEO to share in the gamble, and increase his earnings only when the company does. Few would begrudge Tinkham Veale II his $129,000 bonus from Alco Standard Corporation for 1982, when profits were up by 31 percent for that company. And Charles A. Lynch earned his $175,000 bonus from Saga Corporation by boosting profits 45 percent.

How do bonus plans pay for average or below-average results? A "formula plan" requires that the company achieve a minimum return on investment before it establishes an incentive pool. After that, a certain percentage of earnings is set aside and divided up among plan participants according to salary or other criteria at the end of the performance period. But inflation can make the targets they set meaningless. A bonus pool based on achieving at least a 6-percent return on stockholders' equity made sense in the 1950s, when the median return on equity (ROE) was about 9 percent and long-term corporate bonds were selling at 4 percent. But with the median ROE now about 13 percent and long-term corporate bonds around 10 percent, a 6-percent target is hardly a target. For this reason, Rexham Corporation, a manufacturer of specialized packaging and machinery, has switched its measure of performance from a fixed percentage of growth in earnings (which can be met by inflation) to a percentage of growth in earnings compared with others in the industry (which is inflation-proof).

The "look around" bonus plan, like the Rexham approach, is based on a company's position relative to others in the industry. While these plans do avoid ballooning bonuses during periods when everybody's profit figures are up, in bad times they can allow low performers to take high bonuses—so long as everybody else performs just as badly.

Proxy statements, however, rarely detail the criteria for short-term incentive awards. So shareholders and the public are often left seeing only the results—annual awards handed out like lollipops when, in theory, they should be dangled like carrots. There are, of course, laudable exceptions, which show how bonuses can be considered rewards rather than sinecures. Emmett Pace is the owner and president of Oceana Corporation, a $10-million steel distributor in South Carolina. He has not only turned down expectant executives for bonuses several times because they were "slackening off totally," but Pace also denied himself one. "I didn't think I did a good enough job last year," he candidly told *Inc.* magazine. "We were not as profitable as we should have been."

Long-Term Incentives—Stocking Up

Preferential deals on company stock can top even the biggest salaries or bonuses. A look at the figures for the highest-paid twenty-five executives in *Business Week*'s 1983 annual compensation survey shows the lion's share to be in the column labeled "Long-Term Income." Frederick Smith's stunning $51.5 million for services rendered to Federal Express and the four Toys "R" Us executives who received $7.5 million to $43.7 million all reported such lucrative earnings in 1982 because they cashed in long-term stock options that year.

There are numerous plans that provide for compensation in stock. The most basic is the unqualified stock option, which permits the businessman to purchase shares at a fixed price over a certain period of time. As the market price of a stock soars above the original option price, the fortunate executive can cash in on the difference. In perhaps the best example of capitalism-without-risk, so-called stock-appreciation rights (SARs) allow an executive simply to receive the difference between option price and market price without even putting up money for stock. Going one step further, Martin Marietta announced in its 1983 annual report the following: "During 1982, options previously granted under the 1979 plan for 852,075 shares were canceled and subsequently reissued at lower prices." This is akin to the house allowing a poker player to change his bet after seeing his opponent's hand.

Data on the top one hundred U.S. corporations show the growing popularity of stock incentives. While 87 percent of these firms offered stock options in 1981, a year later the figure rose to 95 percent. SARs went from 56 percent of top firms in 1978 to 77 percent in 1982. Little wonder, if one looks at the benefits. David Glass, vice-chairman of Wal-Mart, had options in mid-1983 valued at $8 million; Richard Gelb's options from Bristol-Myers were worth $4.5 million; Pan Am's C. Edward Acker had options on one million shares at $2.77 when those shares were trading at $6.13 in June of 1983 for a paper gain of over $3.36 million.

The bottom-line defense of stock incentives is that however huge the resulting bounty, stockholders receive a bounty of their own when the market price rises. "Any executive who reaps a reward because of the price of stock is justly compensated, because executives have only one objective, and that is to increase shareholder value," says Louis J. Brindisi, Jr., senior vice-president of Booz•Allen and Hamilton. Few would deny that entrepreneurs like Frederick W. Smith of Federal Express, Charles P. Lazarus of Toys "R" Us, or Edwin H. Land of Polaroid Corporation were responsible for their own stock windfalls. But these founding fathers are more exception than rule. A bull market sweeps many stocks upward in an indiscriminate way. And it doesn't take a mathematical genius to figure out that if a business person is given enough options at low enough prices, he can make a fortune even with mediocre stock performance.

A more democratic incentive plan is being attempted by the Riegel Textile Corporation of North Carolina. In what is widely called a management incentive plan (MIP), the firm provides stock options even to middle managers for achieving goals they can handle—anything from a low labor turnover rate (for a division personnel director) to gains in productivity, sales, or return on investment. The key to Riegel's success is that every target is carefully and individually planned, all the way through middle management. And the targets are tough. "I've had six [incentive plans] and hit three of them," says R. Lane Smith, vice-president for Georgia operations. He knows others that have never hit theirs. Partial awards are rarely given for partial achievement, and goals are never lowered mid-course, ensuring that all stock awards are fully merited.

If the goals are set high, so too are the rewards. A sampling of the Riegel agreements showed a payoff of from 750 to 1,000

shares of stock. So it's no wonder that managers are clamoring
for them. "I think it's the greatest thing in the world," said
Smith. "How many people at my level and my age have a
chance at something like this?" Another benefit of Riegel's plan
is that different levels of management often share the same contract. "The best thing was the chain of command was linked together," says corporate vice-president William S. Rogers, and
this produced "the camaraderie of meeting the same objective."
Other companies that appreciate how middle managers deserve
stock incentives are Beneficial Corporation, with performance-
based plans reaching down as far as the assistant vice-president
level, and GE, which installed a new incentive system that applies to five thousand managers earning $50,000 or more.

Golden Parachutes—Happy Landings

On retiring from Esmark after its acquisition by Beatrice
Company, outgoing chairman Donald Kelly showed company
officials a slide show of his plans. When a picture of a European
castle flashed on the screen, the ebullient executive remarked,
"That's my new home. I call it, 'On Golden Parachute.'"

All laughed at the good-natured remark, but there were fewer
smiles after the triangular battle when the Allied Corporation
beat out Martin Marietta to acquire Bendix. For though Bendix
CEO William Agee lost the war, he won a $4.1-million "golden
parachute" to cushion his fall.

Golden parachutes are agreements by which the firm promises
to pay an executive a specified amount if he should leave after a
hostile takeover. They vary in bulk, ranging up to the estimated
$7.8 million American Family Corporation would give to John
Amos. The accessibility of the rip cord also varies, but a 20-
percent change in control is a common trigger. Usually an executive can take on a new job and salary and yet retain all of the
value of his ex-employer's golden parachute.

About a quarter of the *Fortune* 500 companies have golden
parachute provisions, according to Ward Howell International,
representing an increase from just 14.5 percent in 1982. Some of
the larger companies to adopt them are Phillips Petroleum, Ashland Oil, International Paper, Firestone Tire and Rubber, and
Conoco; although smaller, more vulnerable companies are more
likely to have them. Parachutes range from the 1-person mini-
chute (usually covering the CEO) to Beneficial Corporation's
234-person special.

Why would managers need to be rewarded if they lose a take-over battle? Edwin M. Halkyard, a senior vice-president of Allied, points out the parachute's usefulness in keeping people on board—and loyal—during the fight.

> Your management people obviously become rather anxious because they sit and say "My God, if this hostile takeover is successful I'm going to be out of a job." So what they do is they start looking elsewhere. Even if that hostile takeover attempt is not successful, you may wind up with a management which is decimated, totally contrary to the interests of the organization and the shareholders. Secondly, management may begin to think, "Well it looks like this hostile takeover bid is going to work, therefore I better start playing the other side of the fence a little bit. You know, I may be looking straight into the eyes of new bosses here," and that may begin to erode the underpinnings of what you would want an independent manager to do.

So, for example, Conoco provided for nine parachutes—including a $5-million one for chairman Ralph Bailey—"to encourage the executives to remain in the employ of the company by providing them with greater security." Phillips Petroleum found that $9 million of takeover insurance for top management was necessary "to encourage management to remain with the company and to eliminate management distraction in spite of potentially disturbing circumstances arising from the possibility of a change in control of the company."

This rationale isn't terribly persuasive—and reveals why these devices are an extravagant example of avoidable corporate waste. Is it remotely likely that an executive would bail out during a takeover fight, incurring peer opprobrium—or would he be more likely to quietly surrender in the hope that the new team would want a patsy from the old management? And the idea of paying executives a special fee for paying attention to their job offends even many business partisans. As Senator John Chafee (R., R.I.) says, "What nonsense! Why should executives be offered lucrative parachutes to do what they are generously paid to be doing anyway? Directors had best look for new executives if they have to be bribed to stiffen their spine and do their duty."

Also, why should only top officers be provided extraordinary security when so many may lose their jobs following an acquisition? A lot of middle managers, too, are eventually replaced by a merged company. "Golden parachutes affect the morale of the middle management people who make our corporations run," writes Louis C. Kaufman, associate professor of marketing. "The district sales manager who has lost market share may find himself looking for a job. The top executive whose corporation never hits the target gets as much as two years' protection . . . when a takeover takes place. No wonder so many people are so cynical."

On the whole, golden parachutes would seem to encourage rather than deter takeovers, since they provide the target company's management with larger incentives to lose than to keep their jobs.* Shortly after Seagram's initial overtures for Conoco, in May 1981, Conoco called a special board meeting. *Fortune* reports that "the first item on the agenda, according to one person who saw it, was not what the stock activity meant for the shareholders, but how to put in parachutes." Securities law expert Arthur Matthews, a partner with the law firm Wilmer, Cutler and Pickering, is especially outraged by these kinds of maneuverings during the heat of battle, calling them "outright theft. . . . To me it's no different than stealing the stockholders' money. Because I think under those unusual circumstances you can't have disinterested judgment." Dissident Conoco shareholders did indeed sue, arguing that the agreements constituted fraud and a waste of corporate assets. But the Delaware State Court ruled that they had no "standing" since Conoco had ceased to exist as a legal corporation after the merger. Catch 22.

Perhaps the simplest and most compelling case against the golden parachute is that it simply does not represent compensation for services. Arguing that parachutes buy nothing of value and hence are a waste of corporate assets, shareholders at the Gulf Resources and Chemical Corporation sued when departing executives tried to collect $13 million in parachute money after dissident shareholder Alan Clore waged and won a proxy fight for control of the company. Eventually, the firm settled the dispute by agreeing to pay the former executives $8.5 million.

---

*There is at least one case where golden parachutes *have* prevented a takeover—although not for the expected reasons. "We had an acquisition at Gulf and Western that would have fit very nicely, and it was scrubbed because these people had golden parachutes," says Gulf and Western director Samuel J. Silberman. Was the cost of the parachutes great? "No. It was that distasteful that we would have no part of it. It gives you a cut of people. Anytime a guy asks you for this, it says something about him."

Such legal challenges, however, will run up against the "business judgment rule," which calls for deference to managerial and board judgment, unless there is proof, as courts put it, of "fraud, bad faith, gross overreaching, or abuse of discretion." But if providing a huge bonus on the condition that an executive abandon his company is not considered a waste of corporate assets, then "business discretion" is equivalent to "anything goes"—and courts abdicate their authority to assure that managers do not squander shareholders' assets.

The obvious wastefulness of awarding golden parachutes to undeserving executives has triggered a hostile reaction from public officials and some boards of directors. Senator Slade Gorton, a Republican from Washington State, for example, called them "executive incompetence insurance." Apparently, his colleagues agreed, for the 1984 Tax Act rips some sizable holes in those golden parachutes that are shown to be three times larger than the executives' average annual salary for the previous five years: First, he'll have to pay a 20-percent excise tax—almost like a windfall profits tax—on the total amount received (in addition to normal income tax); second, the amount of the parachute beyond his average annual salary is nondeductible to the corporation. With these changes in the tax laws, it is not likely that the number of large industrial firms with golden parachutes will again double in a year, as happened from 1982 to 1983.

As for boards, some have abstained from awarding parachutes, and others—like Allied Corporation after the Agee-Bendix experience—have withdrawn them. The H. J. Heinz Company, among others, has an alternative that provides a degree of security to company executives—without providing an incentive for them to lose their jobs. If certain events relating to a change of control in the company occur, Heinz executive officers could exercise their stock options and stock-appreciation rights for cash over a sixty-day period. True, this means they need not leave the company to collect their bounty. And this reward may not be based on performance, since options and SARs not exercisable before the threatened change of control presumably were not yet fully earned. Still, the Heinz plan is far more reasonable than parachutes for two reasons: The executive's reward is directly linked to shareholders' gain; and the manager receives no bonus for losing his job.

Severance Pay

But even if the new law rips golden parachutes off the backs of overprotected managers, companies would still be handing out far more than a gold watch to executive retirees. For severance pay is a corporate fact of life, though its levels raise questions.

Why, for example, did Avco Corporation in 1982 pay its president, forty-nine-year-old (and presumably able-bodied) Ross M. Hett, $900,000 a year for the five-year period after his 1981 resignation when its net profits had plunged 39 percent in the previous year and Hett had no employment contract? Then there was Charles Knapp, forced out as chairman of the struggling Financial Corporation of America in 1984 when federal regulators loaned FCA several million dollars to offset withdrawals by depositors jittery over his high-flying finance. Yet, as he exited, he arranged for a $2-million severance payment to be deposited in a private Swiss bank account where it was beyond the reach of company shareholders or federal regulators.

Some departing corporate officials do not get severance pay but lucrative consulting contracts, which serve a similar purpose. After he retired as president of Mobil Corporation in 1984, William Tavoulareas raised eyebrows and money by an arrangement where he would work half time at an annual compensation of $800,000—whereas he had earned $1.1 million working full time previously. Mobil also agreed to pay two thirds of the $36,000 annual maintenance cost of his New York City apartment, which the oil company said was consistent with a practice of making "New York accommodations available to its directors for business-related use." (In his farewell speech to the firm's prior annual meeting, Tavoulareas had complained that press attacks on big corporate paychecks was "wrong.")

Far worse are large settlements to businessmen who leave under legal clouds. Ford, for example, paid executive vice-president Paul Lorenz a bonus possibly as high as $100,000 after holding him responsible for a plan to pay a bribe in Indonesia in 1975 and firing him. Similarly, after firing executive David Begelman because he forged a check, Columbia Pictures Industries settled his claims for severance payment by giving him $732,000 and a car. And what about Boeing's payment of $400,000 to three executives who left to join the Defense Department? At least here a cynic might argue that the payment bought something of value.

Like golden parachutes, severance agreements can often bear

no relationship to the past performance of the departing executive. Even in the case of a highly successful manager, existing incentive and pension plans should be payment enough for years of service. When George S. Deutsch left the not-so-successful Amerace Corporation in December 1982, he took with him $74,000 for the rest of that year, the promise of $300,000 over the following three years, life insurance coverage of not less than $690,000, and 750 shares of stock as deferred awards under the company's compensation plan. In exchange for this, he agreed to secrecy and noncompetition covenants and to provide consulting services to the corporation for three years. One has to wonder, however, about the value of Deutsch's secrets and services, given Amerace's declining sales, the loss of over $10 million in 1982, and the decline of its net earnings per share from $3.41 in 1979 to $.89 in 1982.

Perquisites—Executive Sweets

The monetary value of the company car or expense account may not approach that of other forms of payment, but payment it often is. Perquisites are not even nominally tied to performance (who ever heard of a lunch club membership being withdrawn because corporate profits were down?), yet they often add up to substantial sums. A Hay Associates survey found that the average $100,000-a-year executive gets $30,000 in fringe benefits. At a cosmetics firm where noncash incentives amount to 35 percent of the pay package, one executive explained, "We do provide things like the use of personal cars, medical coverage. . . . We tend to call them 'satisfiers.' It's a satisfier. It's not really a motivator. Cash compensation—that's where you get your motivation." And what motivates managers to award perks, in the view of consultant George H. Foote is that "most of them tend to be hidden ways to provide extra compensation; they just cloud the compensation picture—and the board's ability to oversee compensation."

To be sure, directors or stockholders should not object to providing executives with a routine medical examination. Executives' health is essential to their companies' health. Yet about thirty-five hundred businessmen a year receive a physical checkup *and* the personal pleasure of fishing, skiing, golf, tennis, trap and skeet shooting, mineral baths, luxury hotel accommodations, and other frills at the sixty-five-hundred-acre Greenbrier resort, courtesy of their companies. The line between business and pleasure is certainly fuzzy at this country retreat "where the vacation season never ends."

The line disappeared altogether at the advertising firm Needham, Harper and Steers, which gave one executive a Mercedes-Benz, free parking, and membership in two Manhattan health clubs. Another took some of her vacations at company expense and was treated to Broadway shows by the company—with or without a client. When asked what kind of business value such gifts contained and whether they were reported as taxable income, a spokesman for the company said only, "We do design compensation packages that are competitive within the industry. But we don't talk about them. We don't have to." (The company is privately held.)

The American Management Association reports that 80 percent of 731 companies it surveyed provide their top officers with a company car—though only 10 percent of these stipulated that the car must be primarily for business use. Free tickets to shows and athletic events, bodyguards, and security devices were also common perks, and free financial counseling had leaped in popularity. Says Louis Brindisi, "I saw a report by consulting firm Hay Associates the other day that made me sick, because they were talking about exotic perquisites. I threw the report away, it was so repulsive. . . . They had perks listed there I couldn't believe. Swimming pool maintenance, things like that. Crazy stuff."

Officials may use company funds to make their surroundings regal without shareholder approval or even knowledge. Occidental Petroleum's CEO Armand Hammer, for example, reportedly spent $1.5 million of his company's money installing four private dining rooms (two with fireplaces), a kitchen, a boardroom, a formal reception area, and an art gallery, and offices in sixteen thousand square feet of space—all for himself and his six top assistants. ITT gave chairman Rand Araskog $95,211 to cover some of the expenses of buying and renovating a New York City apartment because, said the company, it wanted him to live closer to work. Lee Iacocca reports that he once had to fly a fireplace from Europe to Detroit on a company plane for Henry Ford. And the candid executive acknowledged a typical weakness for life at the top with other people's money. "I was . . . greedy. I enjoyed being president. I liked having the president's perks, the special parking place, the private bath-room, the white-coated waiters."

An extreme instance of such indulgence was Frigitemp Corpo-ration, which paid for the remodeling of chairman Jerry Lee's three homes, on Park Avenue and Shelter Island in New York, and in Palm Springs, California. The Park Avenue apartment had marble bathrooms, a vestibule in black onyx, $20,000 Tiffany lamps and a Rodin sculpture. When a Frigitemp em-ployee complained that "this is a public company on the Amer-ican Stock Exchange," chairman Lee—who later went to jail for fraud on other matters—said, "It's my company—I'll do what I want."

Perks, like hemlines, change with the times. When the salmon stream in Iceland that Pepsico and Owen-Illinois leased for their top staff became a public embarrassment in the late 1970s after the SEC demanded increased disclosure, it was dropped. The latest perks in vogue are more practical items like the low- or no-interest loan, free legal and financial counseling, luxurious apartments, and "relocation expenses" for executives forced to move by their job. "If you are being moved, don't hesitate to ask for what might seem outrageous," advises *Forbes*. "One ex-ecutive, for example, talked his company into buying the house he wanted to occupy, then selling it to him for 80% of what it paid. When the house is ultimately sold, he will get 80% of the appreciation, and the company, the remaining 20%."

Arguably, a hardworking executive may be able to work even more as he shuttles between appointments in his limousine. But why free financial counseling? It is not enough to say that it allows the officer to concentrate on company matters because (1) he should be doing that anyway and (2) it would justify hir-ing a cook to make his breakfast. And it is hard to imagine that business could not be done without hunting lodges, luncheon clubs, health clubs, or theater tickets—or that it was indispens-able to business for Mary Cunningham, when she was William Agee's assistant at Bendix, to fill out his daughter's application to Princeton. "You know, it's that old case of RHIP—rank has its privileges," says Archie Albright. "I think there's clearly a limit. . . . The IRS and the SEC have closed down a lot of the excesses, and I think rightly so. This is stockholder money, and in some cases it was clearly being used to make life a lot more comfortable for a few top executives, and did not have a lot to do with any real corporate purpose."

The problem is that just about every extravagance could be an aid to business, so how should a firm draw the line between business use and personal benefit? Few try. Most companies state, like Playboy Enterprises, "The Company cannot determine without unreasonable expense the extent or value of such personal use . . . and has concluded that such use does not involve any significant cost to the company." At the same time, large expense accounts make the distinction between company service and self-service virtually meaningless. According to James R. Baehler, a former executive with IBM and Xerox, who now leads seminars for the American Management Associations, "All you need is a few friends on expense accounts and you need never pay for your own lunch again." In his "seven basic principles of expense accounting," numbers 3 and 5 are, respectively, "add everything possible" and "intermingle personal and business expenses." One friend of Baehler's acquired the wardrobe to become a vice-president at the age of thirty-five by charging items of clothing on a company credit card as business lunches.

Some, like Baehler, believe that "an effective CEO aura is created by distance, both physical and psychological. Creating that distance and enhancing the aura of top managers is a primary rationale for the perks of status." But in an era where top-down management is being critically reassessed (see Chapter 2, "Wasteful Workplace"), this model of the worker-manager relationship no longer appears to stimulate productivity, or even to be self-evident. "Distance" between top officers and average workers works *against* productivity, for it is more likely to inspire alienation than emulation in those on the lower rungs of the ladder.

For this reason, at the Nucor Corporation in North Carolina, the "executive dining room," as we've seen, is a Deli-Town luncheonette. Nucor's CEO Ken Iverson explains, "We have no company cars, we have no hunting lodges, no executive dining rooms, no assigned parking places, no executive washroom. Everyone in the company, including the chairman of the board, travels economy-class. Our philosophy is to make as little differentiation as we possibly can between the hourly worker and everyone else. We all have the same insurance program, we all have the same hospitalization, we all have the same vacation program."

Other firms are making cuts in their levels of perquisites for reasons of economy. When profits slumped at CBS, formerly pampered executives began squeezing themselves into economy-class seats. H. Ross Perot is one of the country's wealthiest businessmen. But in 1980, his company, Electronic Data Systems (which merged with GM in 1984), owned no airplanes. "If I wanted one, I'd buy it myself," Perot told a reporter. "I wouldn't force my stockholders to subsidize it." He also noted that a Dallas–Philadelphia round-trip airplane ticket cost around $300 in 1981 but, "if I'd flown a private jet, the cost would have been $5,000." Ford, despite recent record profits, refuses to allow top executives to fly first class on domestic flights. And Eastern's CEO Frank Borman eliminated company jets along with limousines for top officials in 1978. He personally chauffeured Eastern's lenders to a meeting to discuss the company's precarious financial situation in his own '69 Camaro.

Other corporations may now similarly have to tighten up their perks not so much because they see the light but because they feel the heat of the Deficit Reduction Act of 1984. Inspired in part by an indiscreet Rolls-Royce dealer who touted in brochures how the purchase of a $109,000 Rolls would produce $65,913 in tax savings over three years, Congress tried to make the personal use of corporate assets less likely. Under the act, luxury cars will have to be used more than half of the time on company business to qualify for investment tax credits, and only the first $16,000 of a car's price will be eligible for accelerated depreciation over three years. Perks such as medical and life insurance and long-term disability plans can continue to be tax-free so long as firms don't discriminate among employees: A CEO can't get a better deal than his assistant or secretary. Similarly, an employer's product discounts will still be tax-free if made available to all employees and if not provided below cost.

If the IRS enforces these new rules vigorously, it could persuade companies to compensate top executives less in opulent perks and more in bonuses and stock options.

Paying for Performance

When Babe Ruth was asked in 1932 why he was earning $5,000 more than President Hoover, he remarked, "I had a better year than him."

But today, many business leaders with a track record no better than Hoover's earn sums more regal than presidential, via the kinds of bonuses, options, perks, and parachutes just discussed. The available literature indicates that pay often has more to do with *position* than *performance:*

- In 1982, *Fortune* studied the compensation of executives from 140 companies in ten large industries. The magazine concluded, "They show some examples of consistency in which pay and performance match. They show many more examples of irrationality and contradiction." One example cited was Norton Simon, which gave David J. Mahoney $1.5 million for achieving a return on equity of under 12 percent (one of the lowest ROEs of all food companies in the survey), while Kellogg's gave William E. LaMothe less than half as much, $600,000, for achieving a ROE of 26 percent (the highest in the industry).

- The American Management Associations' *Compensation Review* published a similar study in 1981. Looking at salary alone for a five-year period, the author found "the CEO of the best performing company received only a 25 percent increase in salary, while the CEO of the worst performer received a 48 percent increase. The correlation coefficient between salary increase percentage and five-year performance index rank was .16, obviously not very indicative of a pay-for-performance relationship."

- Professor William Steve Albrecht of Brigham Young University and Philip Jhin, a consultant with the Boston Consulting Group, studied pay and performance in 148 companies in 1978. Using shareholder value (stock price plus dividends) to measure performance, they found "absolutely no relationship (either positive or negative) between stockholder return and executive pay." Turning to earnings per share as a performance index, they again found "very little relationship between executive pay and executive performance." A Booz•Allen and Hamilton study found a widening gap between executive pay and shareholder value (defined as the sum of common stock appreciation and dividends paid). Throughout the 1970s and early 1980s, the inflation-adjusted compensation of chief executives ballooned while shareholder value shrank.

- Compensation consultants Sibson and Company developed a "pay-performance index" for *Business Week*'s 1984 annual survey, which compared "the executive's three-year total pay as a

percent of the industry standard and his shareholders' total return as a percent of the industry standard. . . . If his relative
total pay exceeds his shareholders' relative returns, the ratio is
greater than 100%." Out of 412 executives listed, more than
half—or 231 CEOs and presidents—had ratios exceeding 100
percent.

- In their study at the University of Oregon of "Motivation and
  Politics in Executive Compensation," scholars Gerardo R.
  Ungson and Richard M. Steers sought to explain "the poor
  linkage between CEO rewards and performance that has characterized previous research efforts." Among their conclusions:
  "CEO rewards may be more a function of political rather than
  economic variables," by which they mean to include the ability
  of top managers to charm the press, legislators, and board
  members.

Spurred by this divergence between pay and performance,
some farsighted companies are struggling to get their money's
worth with what are called "performance-based long-term incentives." One specific version is the "strategic management" approach, which attempts to link compensation to the corporate
goal-setting process—and tailor incentives to the company's specific needs. Among its leading proponents is Louis Brindisi of
Booz•Allen and Hamilton whose study *Creating Shareholder
Value: A New Mission for Executive Compensation* argues that
"a large number of today's executive pay packages insulate
CEOs from the consequences of weak performance." He goes
on to explain that compensation design is "a critical area of
management because through the executive compensation program, you send powerful messages to executives regarding the
strategic direction of the firm, regarding what's important in
terms of performance, and the kind of culture you're trying to
develop, to maintain, or to change."

To see how "strategic management" works in practice, consider the Sears, Roebuck and Company incentive plan. Sears
pays out for the achievement of objectives that vary according to
an executive's position and responsibility. For corporate officers,
75 percent of the annual bonus is based on the level of return on
average equity and 25 percent on growth in revenues. In addition, a long-term incentive plan runs in four-year cycles and pays
cash awards of no more than 60 percent of an executive's salary
during the cycle. These awards are paid only if the company

ranks above the median of the bottom third of its corporate peers in return on equity and growth, and the rewards increase until the company reaches the median of the top third of the peer group. Division heads receive awards based on ROE and revenue growth relative to their industry peers.

What makes this a "strategically managed" plan? And does it punish poor performers as well as reward excellence? Laudably, the plan responds to outside conditions, since incentive targets are pegged to the performance of others in the industry and not to fixed numbers (which can be rendered meaningless by inflation or other variables). Sears's performance objectives also vary according to the position and responsibilities of each executive. On the other hand, even if Sears were to rank in the middle of the bottom third of its competitors, long-term awards would still be paid out; this would be a true incentive only if the company started out beneath the median of the bottom third. And the short-term plan allows for a "discretionary bonus" to be paid even if minimum targets are not met.

Clevepak Corporation, a $243-million-a-year manufacturer of industrial machinery and construction materials, adopted a long-term incentive plan in 1984 for its top thirteen officers. They will receive bonuses only if Clevepak's own stock outperforms Standard and Poor's index of four hundred industrial companies after three years. If the stock does at least 10 percent better each year than the index, officers receive the maximum rewards, up to 300 percent of their annual base salaries.

Emhart Corporation, too, has tied bonuses to a long-term stock plan, and had some immediate results. In 1984, it had to decide whether or not to update and expand a profitable industrial hardware plant. Under an older incentive plan based on profit growth, managers were unlikely to have directed funds to the facility because it would have reduced short-term earnings, on which their bonuses were based. But at least in part because of the new compensation plan, Emhart's officers gave the green light to the expenditure. "The plan lets us manage with a long-term view of the business," says Sherman B. Carpenter, a company vice-president.

The Case for More: Executives Answer Back

There are few subjects that animate or annoy businessmen more than their own remuneration. Predictably, the most widely read and roundly criticized issue of *Business Week,* report its editors, is the one containing the "Annual Compensation Survey," published every spring.

When criticized, corporate executives and partisans are not lacking explanations for their level of pay and perks. As early as the turn of the century, *The Boston Globe* wrote, "When the salaries paid to great singers and movie stars . . . are borne in mind, the possibility of a million for a business genius does not seem so startling." This early defense of high pay for executives has reverberated ever since—if Larry Bird, Dan Rather, and Robert Redford each earn over a million dollars annually, why, the reasoning goes, shouldn't big businessmen who similarly have limited years at the top?

The competitive market, however, does not function for executives as it does for the stars; as discussed above, many business officials don't have to prove their case to skeptical board members. While athletes and celebrities have batting averages and Nielsen ratings to document their worth, executives have compliant boards who ratify their suggested pay. And fans fill Yankee Stadium to see Dave Winfield, but they don't buy Fords because Donald Petersen runs the company.

Executives also argue that they deserve their big paychecks because of the hardships of the job. Many CEOs are workaholics, no doubt, whose dedication to the company takes its toll, however mitigated by the creature comforts that come with the job. "He sees his children almost never," wrote Professor Malcolm S. Salter of the Harvard Business School. "He is always traveling. He would like to eat breakfast at home, but he can't." Indeed, some chiefs buckle under the severe stress. There have been suicides like Eli Black of United Brands in 1975 and Alvin Feldman of Continental Air Lines in 1981.

Of course, by the criteria of stress and effort, textile workers who lose their lungs and welders who spend their best hours staring at sparks in a noisy inferno would be earning CEO-level salaries. Instead, many CEOs earn more in three or four days than the workers on their shop floors earn in one year.

Along with their claims of stress and hardship, many executives argue that their big pay is justified by big responsibilities. But this reasoning fails to recognize that, as conservative commentator Irving Kristol has pointed out, the executive "is an employee of the company, not an owner of it, and his compensation is to be judged by managerial rather than entrepreneurial standards." As Thomas Mann's *Buddenbrooks* so ably depicted, often the brilliant original generation of a family or firm is succeeded by generations of bureaucrats who lack the founders' ingenuity but still desire their income. So while many fortunes are justifiably earned by businessmen who founded their firms—the Watsons, Disneys, Lands—many more are earned by caretakers and administrators. "They head organizations that were already in being when they reached the top," says Arch Patton, a retired director of McKinsey and Company. "They are selling products or services developed by others and usually remain in the top job for a very short time. Yet directors frequently pay them as though they were entrepreneurs."

Another defense of high compensation says in effect, you won't even know it's missing. Since the cost of high pay is spread among all the thousands of a firm's stockholders, it is argued, nobody should mind, or even notice, footing their small share of the bill. As William F. Buckley, Jr. explained at a 1981 business conference, Lee Iacocca's $400,000 salary at the Ford Motor Company in the early 1970s was "only sixteen cents per car sold." Once you get the hang of this "free lunch" reasoning, everything seems to cost nothing. The top executive at Exxon earns "only" .00039 cent per gallon of gasoline sold. Tobacco subsidies cost only about a buck per taxpayer per year, or better yet, .33 cent per day.

The dilution of stockholders' equity resulting from over-generous stock plans, however, can outstrip salary in terms of cost to the shareholder. Not long ago, General Dynamics had 15 percent of its equity outstanding under option. Harvard's Salter concludes that "extensive use of options can seriously dilute a stockholder's equity in a company and eventually increase its cost of capital."

Perhaps the most common justification for high pay for executives is its incentive value—that is, the lure of $1 million a year is indispensable to obtaining maximum dedication and productivity. Even egalitarian John Rawls, in his 1971 *Theory of Justice,* justified inequality when the results benefit us all, as an efficient and profitable corporation does. The question is, how much is enough to achieve maximum output—and how much is a waste of company assets? One answer is, what the market will bear. But we've seen how there is no genuine market for executive pay since top executives in many companies effectively set their own pay. And is it really credible that Robert K. Jensen of GK Technologies will only perform at his peak if he's paid

$3.7 million but not $1.7 million? Most people would have trouble figuring out how to spend as much as $1.7 million in a year.

Foreign firms have apparently figured out how to pay top executives far less than their American counterparts do, yet keep them highly motivated. In the early 1980s, the chairman of Nissan Motors made $140,000 annually, and the top ten officers at Renault, the French auto firm, earned $100,000 a year on average, yet the chairmen of GM and Ford at the same time earned about a million dollars annually. American auto executives receive thirty-six times the pay of their blue-collar workers, while the equivalent Japanese executive pulls down only seven times as much as his blue-collar workers. After a 1985 meeting between Japanese industrialists and U.S. labor leaders, recalls attendee Jerome Rosow, the Japanese asked the amused union officials "how our economic and social system could support such disproportionate shares of labor income going to such a small handful of people."

"So why do some of these executives keep increasing their salaries and bonuses to such astronomical levels?" asks Archie Albright. "Often because they simply want to be the highest paid guy in their industry. They don't really *need* the money." But they *want* the money, for reasons Adam Smith and Mark Twain long ago spotted. Smith wrote, "With the greater part of rich people, the chief enjoyment of riches consists in the parade of riches." Some executives appear to regard compensation as Mark Twain did bourbon—too much is never enough.

It is proving increasingly difficult for top managers simultaneously to defend their own growing paychecks while cutting those of their employees.

GM found out what can happen when executives at an ailing company neglect to take even a halfhearted vow of moderation. In April 1982, the United Auto Workers signed a two-year contract with GM that included about $2.5-billion worth of wage and benefit concessions. Unhappy UAW workers narrowly approved the pact by 52–48 percent—and then became *very* unhappy when a few hours later GM released its proxy statement. It included a new, sweetened bonus plan for managers that would lower the earnings threshold at which bonus money would be paid. Then UAW president Douglas Fraser said, "I've never seen a situation where workers were more upset." GM chairman Roger Smith lamented, "I'd rather it hadn't happened," shortly before backing out of the new bonus plan.

GM was not the first company, and won't be the last, to offer the stick to workers and a carrot to management. In late 1983, Greyhound forced 12,700 of its line workers to take a 7- to 8-percent pay cut, yet Greyhound managers earned 7 to 10 percent more in 1983 than 1982. In April 1983, Western Airlines encouraged the wrath of the International Brotherhood of Teamsters by splitting a $130,000 bonus pot among ten Western executives. Small as the bonus was, it led the union to cancel a 10-percent wage cut agreed to earlier, making Western's workers "the first airline labor group to rescind a concession to a weak carrier." Two years earlier, Braniff International had increased the salaries of 864 management-level employees by 11.4 percent, just when 11,500 employees covered by union contracts had accepted a 10-percent salary cut to keep the airline flying.

The managements of GM, Greyhound, Western Airlines, and Braniff may not have been politically astute, but in relation to the business world there was a certain logic to their actions. GM's Roger Smith described the situation as "two trains coming down the track," one being the need to pay bonuses big enough to attract and retain good managers and the other being the need to reduce total labor costs. But such corporations, when devising compensation and bonus plans, should also, to be intelligent, calculate the cost of labor resentment. One large defense contractor lost twenty senior engineers and engineering managers, some with twenty-five years' service, because, as one explained, "While our salary increases last year were held to 3% with the argument that any more would be inflationary, the nine people in the top management group voted themselves bonuses and additional stock options amounting to a 25% to 30% increase in their compensation—and that's simply dishonest."

Companies, of course, must take into account the realities of competition when setting top pay. And a firm in dire financial shape may have to offer the biggest rewards to attract managers capable of salvaging their enterprise. But such a firm should then pay high rewards only for successful results and not move goals into easier reach. Moreover, the idea of religiously keeping up with the Joneses' paychecks assumes that no matter how high a CEO's salary, he must be paid as much as—or more than—his peers in the industry or he will lose interest in the job. This obviously leads to leapfrogging ad infinitum and assumes that the CEO has little intrinsic interest in his duties to the company. One wonders why executives allow their character to be so maligned. Or as John Maynard Keynes observed in his

General Theory of Employment, Interest, and Money, executives "are certainly so fond of their craft that their labor can be obtained for much cheaper than at present."

Also, it is not at all obvious why firms assume that endlessly raising executives' pay will improve performance, but that non-executives need no such incentive. In fact, some companies are starting to realize that higher productivity and greater cooperation between management and labor cannot come about if each group rides separately on one of Smith's "two trains." That is, contrary to the philosophy of James Baehler that steep income inequality is essential to motivate executives, less inequality would be not only fair but more efficient. Labor leaders can't be blamed for feeling, as the head of the UAW's GM division, Don Ephlin does, that executives "should not get bonuses unless hourly workers get bonuses. . . . It's ludicrous to say that a man earning five hundred thousand dollars a year needs an incentive to do a good job and a man who earns fifteen thousand doesn't."

One company that does try to provide financial incentives to those who earn in the range of $15,000 annually is the Nucor Steel Corporation. CEO Ken Iverson says that Nucor has applied the pay-for-performance principle to its hourly workers with encouraging results. "The first time we had bonuses that went to one hundred percent . . . I thought, well, maybe we've raised a monster here. But it really works. Now I don't care; I'd like them to earn two hundred, three hundred percent of what their pay is. Because the idea is that we're passing on to them the savings that come from the labor that they put into the product. . . . We believe if we treat our workers the way they like to be treated, it's going to benefit us." And the savings have been considerable. According to Iverson, Nucor's success provides a challenge to companies that still think only executives need a stake in economic gain.

A Menu of Alternatives

Because widely published compensation surveys publicize what the average CEO or executive earns in an industry, and because no one wants to be regarded as merely average, top managers have come to expect ever higher compensation year after year. Pay and perks become more like "entitlements" than earnings.

And the weaknesses of the various rationales for extraordinarily high executive compensation—as compared to compensation abroad, to blue-collar compensation, to the amount needed to motivate managers—confirms the conclusion that there is extensive waste in corporate compensation.

This excess worries friends and scholars of business. As Professor Malcolm Salter wrote several years ago:

> The egalitarian themes running through much of American political economics (such as progressive taxation and a commitment to equal opportunity and modest income redistribution) challenge business to articulate norms of equality and fairness that meet with public approval. . . . If the corporation is perceived to be distributing income inequitably between managers and other employees, skeptics will question more and more the corporate role in society.

At the same time, when people like William Brock, Lee Iacocca, Peter Drucker, and Irving Kristol criticize executive compensation—and when the public by a margin of 74 to 14 percent thinks top executives are overpaid, according to Louis Harris—business leaders begin to get the message that it's time for a change.

Consequently, some top managers and companies are starting to pursue the kind of "merit pay" in American boardrooms that is so often advocated for teachers in American classrooms. Recall the more than a dozen companies mentioned in this chapter that are attempting to improve their compensation systems— Sears, Roebuck (which has a "strategically managed" plan); Allied Corporation (which abandoned golden parachutes); Clevepak Corporation, Emhart Corporation, Riegel Textile, Rexham, and Nucor Steel Corporation (which have instituted pay-for-performance across the board); Beneficial Corporation and GE (which provide for modest incentive plans for middle managers too); GAF (which reduced CEO pay under Samuel Heyman); Eastern Airlines, CBS, and Electronic Data Systems (which cut back on perks); and Oceana Corporation (which has a bonus plan that doesn't always pay bonuses). These companies' actions indicate an appreciation for that ethic once expressed by Robert Townsend, a past and irreverent head of Avis, who observed, "True leadership must be for the benefit of the followers, not the enrichment of the leaders. In combat, officers eat last."

These enlightened firms, however, are the exceptions, and for a predictable reason: When executives have to decide their own levels of compensation, one can hope for, but not expect, voluntary virtue. Which raises the question, beyond *individual* self-restraint by firms, what *institutional* reforms can make for more merit pay in executive suites?

One significant and plausible change would be to strengthen the compensation committee. The committee should be comprised entirely of outside directors, have its own budget, and retain its own consultants, lawyers, accountants, and other professionals independent of management. Then it could analyze, rather than merely rubber-stamp, compensation programs for managers through a reporting and questioning session at the annual meeting. While an independent director may or may not be more conscientious or capable than any inside director, an independent director is more likely to be able to stand up to management's lobbying for an excessive compensation package.

Shareholders are the next level of authority that might act as a brake on pay. The most elementary change would be a more complete disclosure of management pay on the proxy statement. "You can't come close to telling what a person's making from the SEC filings," says Columbia Pictures Industries CEO Francis T. Vincent, who himself helped draft disclosure requirements when he was the SEC's associate director of corporate finance. "It doesn't work. I think most people know that. They're happy with it not working. We made an effort to straighten it out, and it got very complicated and we lost."

SEC rule changes in 1983 further weakened reporting requirements. Only the pay of executive officers and directors, rather than all officers and directors, must be reported; cash remuneration (salary plus bonus) amounting to less than $60,000—instead of $50,000—need not be reported; perquisites valued at less than $25,000 or 10 percent of cash remuneration (whichever is greater) can be ignored, whereas before they at least had to be described; and contingent remuneration can also be excluded from company reports.

By exempting everyone except a few top executive officers and directors from reporting, the SEC claims to be keeping the spotlight focused on "policy makers." But this standard keeps some of the highest pay in the dark. A chief financial officer may be affecting policy as well as pulling in high pay—yet he is not required to disclose his earnings. "The highest-paid officers may not be the highest paid people in the company," says Vincent.

"If you use dollars, you'll get the people who are the highest paid, wherever they are. But the commission does not use dollars, it uses titles."

Perquisites will also be easier to hide from shareholders. It is unclear how the SEC intends to verify a company's judgment that perks amount to no more than $25,000 or 10 percent of an individual's cash pay. But even assuming honest figures, an executive with cash remuneration of $500,000 a year (not unusual for a CEO) could earn perks valued up to $50,000 with nobody the wiser, and a $100,000-a-year executive could earn up to 25 percent of his pay (or $25,000) in perks with impunity.

The SEC argues that "the burdens imposed on registrants under the existing requirements to keep track of non-cash remuneration are sometimes substantial" and that such burdens "may outweigh the importance of such information to investment and voting decisions." Of course, as *The Washington Post* was quick to point out, any "piddling savings" that corporations enjoy from not having to wear out their adding machines tallying perquisites will be "more than offset" by the new perks companies will be free to offer without embarrassment. In addition, it would be irresponsible for management *not* to know how many fringe benefits it enjoys, given that these fringes represent compensation for services as much as any other form of remuneration. As Senator John Chafee (R., R.I.) told the SEC in 1977, "I personally feel there is no reason in the world why stockholders should pay for the lunch, the car, the plane, or the apartment of a highly paid corporate executive. But, if the stockholder is having his money used in such a fashion, he at least has a right to know about it."

Ignorant shareholders cannot possibly help restrain executive overreaching for high pay and perks. But is information enough? What exactly are offended shareholders to do? They can vote with their feet. As one stockbroker wrote to the SEC, "More extensive disclosure will not keep a crook honest but will allow stockholders and prospective stockholders to judge if they are being 'ripped off' by the executive officers." But the investor who buys and sells solely on the basis of management pay is about as common as a doctor who makes house calls. Harvard's John Baker points out that since stockholders in most listed corporations "are numerous, own individually only a few shares in relation to the total outstanding, are widely scattered, and are ignorant of nuances in complicated compensation plans," they lack the means to effectively curb management pay.

So Peter F. Drucker suggested that "the most radical, but also the most necessary innovation would be a published corporate policy that fixes the maximum compensation of all executives, after all taxes but including all fringes, as a multiple of the after-tax and pre-fringe income of the lowest paid regular full-time employee." Drucker offered a 15-to-1 ratio for small businesses and perhaps 25-to-1 for large ones. "A ratio of 25 to 1 is not 'equality.' But it is well within the range most people in this country, including the great majority of rank-and-file workers, consider proper and indeed desirable." Exceptions would be allowed for a "star" or "anyone . . . who makes a truly extraordinary contribution."

How drastic is a 25-to-1 ratio? In 1984, a million-dollar manager earned 34 times as much as a steelworker, 36 times as much as an auto worker, and 50 times as much as a machinist—all of whom were among the highest-paid blue-collar workers in the country. A multiple of 25 would allow the CEO of a large steel company to earn about $726,000 a year—still a comfortable living. Stock options presumably would be included in Drucker's maximum—although he did not specify this—for if they are not, the fixed multiple would do little to curb compensation excess. And while he did not say whether his scheme was to be voluntarily adopted or legally imposed, it is likely that voluntary adoption would only occur in the companies that weren't a problem in the first place.

A nation raised on Horatio Alger and *Dallas* will consider the idea of a fixed ceiling contrary to the entrepreneurial American ethic. A 1981 survey of five hundred Connecticut residents found 75 percent disapproving of a $100,000-a-year limit for incomes. But as the public witnesses a never-ending stream of undeserved pay and corporate waste, a variation of Drucker's ratio-plan might gain broader acceptance: Instead of simply banning compensation plans that exceed a predetermined ratio, why not require such plans to obtain a supermajority shareholder approval? Then very high compensation would require approval by a very high majority, say 70 percent. True, managements routinely win proxy contests with 97–99 percent of the vote. However, when the issue was their own pay, and their proposed remuneration exceeded a standard executive-to-worker ratio, business people would surely have to think twice before seeking

the publicized approval of one- and two-million-dollar remuneration, unless justified by profits and performance.

There is some indirect precedent for this novel approach. A
few managers already seek approval from those who theoretically own the property they distribute. Charles Lazarus, at
Toys "R" Us, sought and won shareholder approval in June
1984 for extending his contract through 1994. (He receives a
base salary of $315,000 annually and one percent of pretax profit
over $18 million, which amounted to $1.9 million in 1983.) And
officers wary of takeovers have no compunction about requiring the approval of two thirds to four fifths of all shareholders
before a merger can occur. In 1984 alone, forty-three managements established the precedent of such supermajority
thresholds for takeovers—a precedent that can be easily extended to extraordinary executive compensation packages.

One other, more simple reform that Congress could enact
would be a ban on golden parachutes, which are giving American business a black eye. The 1984 Tax Act has already reduced
their value, but it is not clear why a handful of executives should
be able to enrich themselves at all in the event of a hostile takeover beyond their normal array of severance pay, stock options,
pensions, and so on. Writing in the *California Management Review,* business scholars Philip Cochran and Steven Wartich reflect the view of many in their field when they conclude that "the
existence of GPs [golden parachutes] today is similar to the existence of insider trading prior to 1933; insider trading amounted
to theft, even before it was made illegal."

Some combination of these and other approaches could help
throw a spotlight on the avoidable waste of paying too much for
managerial talent. The example of companies from Sears to
Riegel prove that companies need not tolerate self-enriching executives who elevate their gains over shareholder returns—and
who treat company assets as personal funds. These firms can
counter the cynicism illustrated by Andrew Undershaft, the industrialist in George Bernard Shaw's *Major Barbara,* who when
asked his religion replied, "Why, I'm a millionaire."

6

The Waste of Fraud and Abuse: When Laissez *Isn't* Fair

In the race for wealth . . . he may run as hard as he can and strain every nerve and muscle, in order to outstrip all his competitors. But if he should jostle, or throw down any of them, the indulgence of the spectators is at an end. It is a violation of fair play, which they cannot admit of.

—Adam Smith, *Wealth of Nations*

History: It Didn't Start with J. R. Ewing

What do W. Michael Blumenthal, Najeeb E. Halaby, and Peter T. Jones have in common?

True, all are prominent in the business world. But more significantly, they stand out because they stood up to business illegality. Blumenthal, as the CEO of the Bendix Corporation in the 1970s, forbid anyone in his firm from offering payoffs abroad in order to win foreign sales. This stance "was unusual enough that it led to a lot of publicity," said Blumenthal, adding with a smile, "and it probably helped bring me to the attention of Jimmy Carter when he made me Treasury Secretary." Najeeb Halaby, the head of Pan American World Airways during this period, specifically rebuffed bagmen from both foreign governments and Nixon's reelection campaign committee. He said, "The top guy has to set the ethical standards." And when he was an officer at Montgomery Ward, Peter Jones figured out a way to stop forty company personnel officers from ignoring equal-pay compliance laws: he put $5,000 to $10,000 of their expected bonuses in escrow until they complied. All did.

These and other business leaders have proved that in economic life, doing well and doing good need not be mutually exclusive. Unfortunately, there is a different tradition in the business world, which existed long before such unflattering fictional renditions as the film *Cash McCall* and TV's *Dallas* began portraying ambitious executives who confuse brand loyalty with blind loyalty. In the real-world "race for wealth," they engage in the "violation of fair play" that Adam Smith warned against. For today's business fraud and abuse, as this chapter will demonstrate, is not only a wasteful tax on innocent consumers, but also as old as business itself.

How old? Merchants in 600 B.C. tried to corner the Grecian olive market. Ancient tablets found in the Middle East refer to business fraud. The Bible mentions merchants who short-weighted their customers. There were prohibitions against monopoly in fifteenth- and sixteenth-century England.

In the early seventeenth century, the first "modern corporation," the British East India Company, negotiated duty-free treatment for its exports by thoughtfully providing Far Eastern Mogai rulers with paintings, carvings, and copper and brass objects.

The end of the nineteenth century saw a group of businessmen so bluntly contemptuous of law and ethics that they projected an enduring image on our memory screen—the robber barons. Among their number was Daniel Drew, who described their new attitude about the marketplace: "A new generation of men came in—a more pushful set. We did things. We didn't split hairs about trifles . . . a prickly conscience would be like a white silk apron for a blacksmith. Sometimes you've got to get your hands dirty. But that doesn't mean that the money you make is also dirty."

Perhaps the exemplar of this breed was John D. Rockefeller, whose 95 percent control of American oil-refining represented the "most gigantic and daring conspiracy a free country had ever seen," according to a congressional committee. Standard Oil's tactics included violence, rebates, and political payoffs. ("He did everything to the Pennsylvania Legislature except refine it," wrote Henry Demarest Lloyd in *Wealth Against Common-wealth*.)

Widespread stock fraud in the 1920s and 1930s led to the 1933 and 1934 securities acts. A congressional committee concluded that of $50 billion in new stock issues in the 1920s, "fully half have proved to be worthless . . . fraudulent." And in 1938, Richard Whitney, the former president of the New York Stock

Exchange who had said, "The exchange is a perfect institution," went to jail for stealing securities from the Exchange's trust funds—a theft known about, but not reported by, partners at J. P. Morgan.

In the 1960s, forty-five individuals and twenty-nine companies, including General Electric, Westinghouse, and Allis Chalmers, were caught in the electrical-machinery bid-rigging conspiracy that sent seven executives to jail. Also, Distillers Ltd. manufactured thalidomide and Richardson-Merrill marketed MER-29, though both possessed studies about their products' severe dangers. In the past decade, employment discrimination cases, toxic chemical dumps, serious product defects, and illegal political gifts regularly landed on the front pages and significantly wasted consumers' dollars.

Despite this historical evidence, many businessmen today belittle the importance of "suite crime" as compared to "street crime." Indeed, the risk of physical injury does make our pulses race far more than the most expensive price-fixing conspiracy. James Q. Wilson, in the introduction to his influential book, *Thinking About Crime,* concludes that public fears about violent crime rather than economic crime are eminently sensible because "these economic violations don't make difficult or impossible the maintenance of basic human communities." And *The Wall Street Journal,* for example, editorializes that "it isn't very helpful to suggest that white collar crime is a more serious threat to the social order than predatory street crime, which inspires fear right across the board."*

---

*Journal editorial writers would do well to read their own newspaper. Here, for instance, is a summary of the news stories of one day, February 27, 1984:

- The Federal Trade Commission concluded that a lumber products corporation had accepted unlawful discounts from furniture manufacturers as part of its office supply business.
- The Securities and Exchange Commission accused a New York securities firm of buying stock for customers' accounts without their permission and with failing to tell other customers that a company they were underwriting was having cash-flow problems.
- A major farm equipment company paid a $109,000 fine for cooperating with the Arab countries' boycott of Israel.
- An Iowa banker pleaded guilty to embezzling at least $440,778 and conspiring to receive tens of thousands of dollars from kickbacks on loans.
- A Chicago bank board met to talk about an investigation of oil venture investments by three farmer bank officials that appear to create a conflict of interest with the bank's loan portfolio.
- A leading citizen of San Diego went to jail for not cooperating with a grand jury investigation of a $125-million foreign-currency speculation pool that the businessman allegedly gathered from gullible investors.

This comparison brings to mind those debates among New Yorkers of the 1950s over who was the best center fielder— Willie Mays, Mickey Mantle, or Duke Snider. Of course, all three were great, though each had his special attributes. Similarly, both street and suite crime impose their special price. And perhaps no one has seen the issue more clearly than Jonathan Swift, when he wrote, "The Lilliputians look upon fraud as a greater crime than theft . . . for they allege that care and vigilance . . . may preserve a man's goods from theft, but honesty has no defense against superior cunning."

Business Illegality: How Come and How Often?

Business fraud appears to result more from *institutional* pressures than from *individual* pathology—pressures such as top-down stress and managerial isolation.

Organization theory explains how a complex bureaucracy can take on a life of its own—and how the individuals who work there will do nearly anything to defend and promote it. Since the marketplace is an uncertain place, the only way to assure stability may be to control market forces, which can mean conspiring with competitors or juggling the books. So when managers come under pressure from superiors to meet certain goals, they may choose illegality over failure. "When we didn't meet our growth targets," complained a former marketing official at the H. J. Heinz Company in 1979, "the top brass really came down on us. And everybody knew that if you missed the targets often enough, you were out on your ear." In this instance, documentation shows that Heinz employees "cooked" their books to make themselves look better, and were caught.

The isolation of top managers in large corporations from both the marketplace and employees (discussed in Chapter 1, "Corpocracy") also contributes to the potential for illegal behavior. In his *Theory of Business Enterprise* (1904), Thorstein Veblen wrote that "honesty is the best policy" in a system of handicrafts and neighborhoods, where one personally and frequently sees his customers. But when industry is carried out on a large scale, Veblen observed, "the discretionary head of an industrial enterprise is commonly removed from all personal contact with the body of customers for whom the industrial process under his control purveys goods or services."

Such pressures and attitudes can produce an ethos of illegality that insinuates itself into a company's culture. Edwin Sutherland, the pioneer in the field of white-collar crime in the 1930s and 1940s, called this phenomenon "differential association," whereby people who associate with those who violate the law are themselves more likely to be violators. There are well-known studies in the literature of criminology that show that ten new boys entering a community with a high delinquency rate are more likely to have a high rate than ten other new boys entering a low delinquency community. So if a few top executives regard the law as just another market problem to be circumvented, the virus of fraud can spread through a company's circulatory system.

How often does unlawful behavior occur in business? If judged by the outbreak of admitted violations just as this book went to press, very often—E. F. Hutton's kiting of millions in checks . . . the First National Bank of Boston's laundering of millions in drug money . . . GE's contractor fraud . . . Paul Thayer's four-year jail sentence for lying about insider trading.

But even beyond such blaring headlines, numerous surveys document that business fraud appears disturbingly frequent. Four fifths of the respondents to a 1961 survey of the *Harvard Business Review* thought some accepted practices in their industries were unethical. After the electrical machinery bid-rigging case that same year, one convicted executive remarked, "No one attending the gathering [of conspirators] was so stupid he didn't know the meetings were in violation of the law. But it is the only way a business can be run. It is free enterprise." To test that hypothesis, one of the authors in 1970 sent a questionnaire to the presidents of *Fortune*'s top 1,000 firms, asking, among other things, whether "many companies price-fix": 60 percent of the 110 respondents agreed.

During the proliferation of admissions of "questionable or illegal payments" in the mid-1970s, implicated businessmen gave the troubling defense that "everybody does it"—and the numbers offered some support for their cynicism. More than a third of the *Fortune* 500 admitted to such payments; 92 percent of an Opinion Research Corporation survey of 531 corporate managers said that such bribery would continue even *if* Congress enacted legislation prohibiting it (which Congress did). In a 1983 Gallup survey, four in ten business people said that a superior had asked them to do something unethical; one in ten said he or she had been asked to do something illegal.

Two other studies have corroborated the findings of these surveys. In the first, Marshall Clinard and Peter Yeager analyzed civil and criminal actions begun or completed by twenty-five federal agencies against 582 of the largest U.S. companies in 1975–76. If anything, this monumental study understated the prevalence of unlawful conduct since it didn't include continuing investigations, state and local investigations, and undetected violations. Its conclusions: 60 percent of the companies had had at least one action brought against them in those two years; 42 percent had multiple charges, while thirty companies had an average of twenty charges brought against each. In the second study, in 1982, *U.S. News and World Report* concluded, "Of America's 500 largest corporations, 115 have been convicted in the last decade of at least one major crime or have paid civil penalties for serious misbehavior. Among the 25 biggest firms—with annual sales that range from $15 billion to $108 billion—the rate of documented misbehavior has been even higher."

Corporate Illegality Is a Wasteful Consumer Tax

One cost of corporate illegality is immense, even if unmeasurable—that is the sabotaging of the trust that binds business and consumer together in a competitive market economy. Instead of "skill, foresight and industry" determining market success, in the words of Judge Learned Hand in the famous 1946 *Alcoa* case, swindling, fraud, and illegality do. Criminologist Herbert Edelhertz describes this pattern. "The pharmaceutical company which markets a new drug based on fraudulent test results undercuts its competitors who are still marketing the properly tested drugs, and may cause them to accept similar methods." It is this kind of Gresham's Law whereby bad companies best good ones that led former Treasury Secretary William Simon to assail bribery abroad as "contrary to every principle under the free market system"—and provoked President Gerald Ford to conclude that "white-collar crime can destroy confidence in and support for the nation's economic, legal and political institutions."

Then there are those costs that are measurable drains on the economy, for business illegality boosts prices, increases injuries, lowers productivity, depresses innovation, and misallocates resources. In the remainder of this section, eight areas of business illegality are discussed, including their taxing costs to the consuming public.

1. The price of price-fixing. As commentators from Adam Smith to Paul McGrath have observed, businessmen have paid lip service to free markets while trying to abolish them. In an oft-cited remark from his 1776 classic, *The Wealth of Nations,* Smith observed that "people of the same trade seldom meet together but the conversation ends in a conspiracy against the public, or in some contrivance to raise prices." McGrath, when he became the head of the Justice Department's Antitrust Division in 1984, announced that "there is a lot of price fixing out there that doesn't get detected."

One recent example of what appeared to be a solicitation of a price-fixing arrangement was detected only because it was taped by Howard Putnam, president of Braniff Airlines. The following is a conversation he had on February 1, 1982, with Robert Crandall, then president of American Airlines, a conversation that led to a Justice Department lawsuit against Crandall.

PUTNAM: Do you have a suggestion for me?
CRANDALL: Yes, I have a suggestion for you. Raise your goddamn fares twenty percent. I'll raise mine the next morning.
PUTNAM: Robert, we . . .
CRANDALL: You'll make more money and I will, too.
PUTNAM: We can't talk about pricing.
CRANDALL: Oh, bullshit, Howard. We can talk about any goddamn thing we want to talk about.

[Two years later, and while the case against him was pending, American elevated Crandall to the CEO post.]

Price-fixing is a criminal offense that raises the price of goods and services to business and consumer purchasers. Federal antitrust authorities have successfully prosecuted companies in several industries with measurable benefits, as the following examples show.

• Between 1953 and 1961, one hundred tablets of the antibiotic tetracycline retailed for about $51, a price that had been set by an illegal conspiracy among some of the nation's largest drug houses. Ten years later, after the exposure of congressional hearings and indictment, the price for the same quantity fell to $5, a 90-percent reduction.

• The twenty-nine companies in the electrical-machinery bid-rigging case mentioned above effectively had stolen some $2 billion by the time of their convictions in 1961. A later presidential commission on crime concluded that this amount alone probably "cost utilities, and therefore the public, more money than is reported stolen in a year."

- After the Federal Trade Commission won a vertical price-fixing case against Levi Strauss in 1978, consumers saved some $225 million in lower prices for Levi-Strauss jeans—about two dollars less per pair—and for the jeans of competitors as well.
- Between 1979 and 1983, federal prosecutors in twenty states obtained 400 convictions leading to 141 jail sentences and $50 million in fines against a highway contractors' bid-rigging conspiracy. After the 1979 indictments, road-building costs in Georgia fell about 20 percent. And with the breaking up of this bidder's cartel, the average number of bidders for federal highway construction jobs grew from 3.4 to 5.3.
- In late 1984, journalists obtained documents from a long-running federal court case in California showing that major oil companies secretly arranged a complex barter system to swap crude oil among themselves beginning in the 1960s. District court judge William P. Gray, the sitting judge in the city of Long Beach's lawsuit charging six oil firms with price-fixing, has said that there is "substantial indication" that the allegations are true.

What is the price of price-fixing? One antitrust commentator analyzed various empirical studies and concluded that, on average, price-fixing "inflates prices by some 25 percent or more above the non-collusive or competitive level."

2. The price of pollution. Based on pure profit-loss considerations, companies have a built-in incentive to pollute the surrounding environment: free waste disposal, to be sure, cuts production costs to the firm . . . but only because residents, workers and other companies involuntarily pick up the tab in the form of more disease, higher health care premiums, increased mortality rates, decreased property values, higher repair costs, and stunted economic growth. These "externalities," as economists call them, are really a kind of transfer payment imposed by private managers on innocent bystanders.

Take air pollution, for example. According to an Environmental Protection Agency study made in 1979, a 60-percent reduction in sulfates and particulates would produce health benefits in the range of $33.5 billion to $74 billion a year.

As for the water pollution "bill," acid rain produced by sulfur dioxide emissions from midwestern coal-burning power plants has destroyed fish life in thousands of lakes and streams in New York, Maine, and Canada, at an estimated annual cost of $5 billion in the eastern United States alone. In 1983, 82 percent of companies failed to comply with EPA regulations before dumping wastes into waterways. One group of researchers estimated that water pollution imposes $12.3 billion in damages annually—most of which is related to lowered property values and loss of recreational activities.

The price of hazardous chemical waste—radioactive materials, asbestos, acids and bases, heavy metals, and synthetic organic chemicals—is perhaps highest of all. Almost two tons of hazardous waste are generated annually for every person in the United States—and 80 percent of the firms disposing of this waste dump it illegally into the environment. According to the EPA, there are thirty-two thousand toxic waste dumps around the United States leaching chemicals into neighboring communities; the cost of cleaning up these dump sites will be between $22 billion (EPA estimate) and $100 billion (Office of Technology Assessment estimate).

The long-term legacy of air and water pollution and toxic waste is an increased incidence of cancer, though experts disagree about the extent of the correlation. There is a consensus, however, that at least 7 to 10 percent of the annual 450,000 cancer deaths in the United States are caused by artificial chemicals—or some 45,000 premature deaths a year. But since fifteen to forty years can elapse between the exposure and the cancer—and since most of the fifty-three thousand commercial chemicals now in existence haven't been tested—scientists and health officials worry that cancer rates may soon climb.

This blizzard of data and correlations reflect the real-life situation—that is, many companies yield to the short-run temptation to save money by subjecting their surrounding communities to a game of toxic roulette.

Most Americans know about the contamination of Love Canal and Times Beach, although less publicized incidents also mar the landscape. Life Sciences, an Allied Chemical subsidiary in Virginia in the 1970s, manufactured Kepone, a highly toxic insecticide that Allied's own tests in the 1960s had showed induced "DDT-like tremors," liver abnormalities, kidney lesions, and atrophy of testes in laboratory animals. Contaminated workers and others suffered severe tremors, weight loss, liver enlargement, brain damage, chest pains, personality changes, and a re-duced ability to walk or stand. To remove the thousands of pounds of Kepone from the James River today, a decade later, would cost from $100 million to $500 million.

Cleaning up dioxin will be more expensive. A by-product of 2-, 4-, and 5-T herbicides (such as Agent Orange), dioxin was called "one of the most perplexing and potentially dangerous chemicals ever to pollute the environment" by President Reagan's EPA. Dioxin was also one of the major toxic chemicals found at both Love Canal and Times Beach. Yet, according to documents produced at a trial involving Agent Orange, the Dow Chemical Company knew as far back as 1965 about dioxin's dangers. One memorandum from Dow's toxicology director warned then that the chemical could be "exceptionally toxic"; the company's medical director said that dioxin-related "fatalities have been reported in the literature." Dow's response was to discuss these problems with its competitors at a March meeting, but *not* to inform the government or public because the situation might "explode" and spur more federal regulation of the chemical industry.

If Dow's cover-up was callous and inexplicable, that of the International Bio-Test Laboratories was literally criminal—"the most massive scientific scandal in the history of the country" in the words of *The Amicus Journal,* an environmental publication. A federal court in April 1984 sentenced three former officials of IBT to jail for terms of six months to one year for fabricating tests for two pesticides and two drugs in order to help them gain government approval. In the 1970s, IBT was the nation's largest independent testing lab, performing over two thousand key safety tests approved by federal scientists to market 212 agricultural pesticides. An EPA review of its files determined that less than 10 percent of IBT's studies were scientifically valid, raising fundamental questions about how many pesticides previously approved as safe really are.

3. *The price of discrimination.* "A mind is a terrible thing to waste," say the advertisements for the United Negro College Fund. So is the talent of an employee. And too often the skills of employees are wasted for the same reason alluded to in the ad—racial discrimination. This discrimination is not merely inequitable but is also inefficient: wasting employees' talents means that they never reach their personal potential and the economy never reaches its productive potential.

At the blue-collar level, blacks on the average earn 63 percent of what whites do—that is, when they get work. Black unemployment is generally double that of whites. Among the reasons, according to documents uncovered in a 1983 civil suit in Alabama, has been the way some businesses refuse to consider new manufacturing facilities in counties with high black populations because blacks are supposedly easier to organize and less job-skilled than whites. A study by the Congressional Research Service found that nonwhites lost $37.6 billion in income in 1978 compared to their white counterparts.

In the white-collar world, the number of blacks holding jobs classified as "managers and officials" grew from 2.4 percent in 1972 to 4.3 percent in 1982—or still only a third of their 12 percent of the general population. And as the past president of the Black M.B.A. Association, Charles Grant, observes, "You would be lucky to find two dozen black senior executives who are heads of divisions or subsidiaries in all the *Fortune* 1,000 companies."

Women fare little better in business. A full-time working woman typically earns 64 percent of a male with the equivalent position, a differential that has endured for a half century despite equal-pay laws. "[A] substantial chunk of the wage gap is simply due to discrimination," concluded demographer Nancy Rytina of the Bureau of Labor Statistics after a study of full-time pay scales in ninety-one occupations—a conclusion concurred in by the women who came to be called the Willimar 8. These women staged a nearly two-year picket of a Minnesota bank that resulted in shaking up American banking and its hiring practices. "How would you feel if you'd been working someplace for nine years making five hundred sixty-five dollars a month," asks Ter Wisscha, then twenty-five, and one of the eight, "and they hired a man for a job you could do but never even got a chance to apply for? Then on top of it they paid him $700 a month, and you had to train him! . . . When the boss says outright you're less than him because you're female, the anger can give you energy you never dreamed you had."

Women's talents are frustrated not only at tellers' windows but also in executive suites, according to Kay Carlson of Catalyst, a nonprofit group in New York City funded by corporations to promote more upward mobility of female executives. "Corporations invest so much looking for the best and brightest—and retraining and developing new leaders. But even when this group includes women, they often see themselves stuck in middle management," she says. "After two or three years in middle management, a thirty-five-year-old woman performing brilliantly begins to get discouraged. And then just when there could be the greatest payoff to the company, she leaves, after a decade of investment." So when companies complain, in the words of the Association of Executive Search Consultants, that "the problem of recruiting women [for executive positions] is we don't have enough women directors," the companies themselves have contributed to the shortage they lament. In 1984, for example, only 2 percent of upper management and boards were female, a fact that cheats both women and management.

4. The price of payoffs—abroad and at home. He had been a descendant of rabbis, a one-time seminarian, a political liberal, and a business leader who lectured workers about their social responsibilities. So when Honduran officials told Eli M. Black, the United Brands CEO, that they would impose a $20-million export tax on his boxes of bananas unless he paid a $1.25-million bribe, he was in anguish. Balancing institutional imperatives and personal ethics, Black eventually authorized the payoff, but apparently at an untenable cost to his conscience. At 8:30 A.M. on February 3, 1975, Black threw his briefcase through a glass window of his office on the forty-fourth floor of New York City's Pan Am Building, then followed it to his death.

Black's suicide began a series of investigations that resulted in what former SEC chairman Ray Garrett, Jr., came to call the "Corporate Watergate . . . bribery, influence-peddling, and corruption on a scale I never dreamed existed." Under pressure from the SEC, some five hundred U.S. firms admitted to at least $1 billion in foreign payoffs, domestic commercial bribery, and illegal political contributions. According to an inquiry conducted by the commission, top management knew of or directed the payments in at least half of all disclosed cases.

The consequences of the disclosures of such payments was catastrophic—and then therapeutic. Payoffs by Lockheed, Gulf, and United Brands played an important role in the resignation of the Tanaka government in Japan, General Rene Barriento's junta in Bolivia, Prince Bernhard in the Netherlands, and President Arellano's regime in Honduras. "When our enterprises stoop to bribery and kickbacks," said George Ball, the former State Department official and international investment adviser, "they give substance to the Communist myth that capitalism is fundamentally corrupt."

The therapy came later. Shareholders sued many of the firms, and in several cases, most prominently Northrop and Phillips Petroleum, boards agreed to accept plaintiff-approved "independent directors" to settle the litigation. And the U.S. Congress in 1977 enacted the Foreign Corrupt Practices Act (FCPA), making it a crime for companies to keep inaccurate books and to pass money to agents abroad when there is "reason to know" it will be used corruptly.

The FCPA proved to be good news to William Odom of the Hudson and Odom Tire Company. His Kansas City, Kansas, company repairs extra-large tires used on earthmovers and other off-the-road vehicles. Because it refused to make questionable payments, however, it lost business to one of its major competitors, Brad Ragan, Inc., which did. "Now," says Odom, "we can get in the door and show that our retread process is better." New orders contributed to a 35 percent increase in firm revenues in the past three years.

Clearly, the incidence of foreign bribery since the 1977 Foreign Corrupt Practices Act has fallen, though not disappeared. The Justice Department in 1984, for example, was conducting an investigation of the Bechtel Group for bid-rigging and illegal payments in South Korea. A Korean chauffeur reportedly told the U.S. Internal Revenue Service that he had several times delivered thousands of dollars in cash from Bechtel consultants to a South Korean utility that was awarding contracts for nuclear plant construction.

What of *domestic* bribes, political and commercial? It turns out that an ethic of corruption abroad can infect decisions at home as well. After all, one management makes both judgments.

Recall how Gulf, Northrop, 3M, American Airlines, Braniff Airlines, Ashland Oil, and dozens of others made unlawful *political* gifts in the 1970s. For one example, 3M gave President Nixon $30,000 illegally out of a slush fund of money laundered through Switzerland. Said its chairman, William L. McKnight, "I don't know that 3M did anything different than a great many other corporations." The Watergate disclosures and the Federal Campaign Act of 1974, which effectively allowed corporations to contribute to politicians legally through political action committees (PACs), have probably shut down these domestic political payoffs.

Domestic *commercial* bribery has been around for centuries—and still is. It seeks to sway the purchasing decisions of government officials or private procurement agents by means of prior payments rather than product quality and price. With millions of dollars riding on a procurement officer's decision, some companies regard payments in the thousands of dollars as a sound, even if unlawful, investment. A director of sales promotion for American Airlines, for example, took some $200,000 in kickbacks in the early seventies in exchange for referring promotion business, largely advertising, worth $2.3 million a year to contributing suppliers. In December 1983, the former CEO and chairman at Frigitemp pleaded guilty in federal court for conspiring to pay $2.7 million in bribes to former General Dynamics executives in order to win subcontracts for liquefied natural gas tankers. Until the indictment, their kickbacks had won $44 million in subcontracts even though the purchasing department had recommended a lower bidder for Quincy Yard in Massachusetts, where General Dynamics was building the ships. The investigator who broke open the squalid Frigitemp story, bankruptcy trustee Lawson Bernstein, found that payoffs in the shipyards were "accepted as a norm."

Commercial bribery appears to be extensive, according to Jules Kroll, the president of a management consulting firm specializing in procurement: "Graft by purchasing officials is considered a way of life in industries as unrelated as entertainment, car and equipment rentals, apparel, printing, construction, retailing and many manufacturing industries. In the New York area's second largest industry, printing, one of every eight dollars is tainted by bribery. And one out of every five purchasing agents involved with printing may be involved in some form of illegal kickback or gratuity." According to Billy Jon Jeter, convicted of kickbacks in the Texas oil industry, "Any little oil service business who tells you he isn't paying kickbacks is lying. You got to buy your business to stay alive." An investigative report by *The Wall Street Journal* confirms that "from the wellhead to the executive suite . . . fraud flourishes in the oil patch. Nurtured by traditions of clubbiness, lax controls and acceptance of petty crime, kickbacks today involve sports cars, boats, cocaine, prostitutes and, increasingly, money."

Based on a 1977 estimate from the American Management Association, commercial bribery and kickbacks ranges from $3.5 to $10 billion a year.

5. *The price of occupational hazards.* There is a long history of industrial workers often having to trade off health for wealth— injury for income.

The good news is that since the creation of the Occupational Safety and Health Administration (OSHA) in 1970, workplace injuries are down 15 percent and deaths 10 percent. The bad news is that occupational injury and disease still waste a huge number of lives and dollars.

Each year some 6,000 workers are killed in workplace accidents (largely construction workers, steelworkers, electricians, loggers and ditch diggers)—and 5 million are injured, with hospital treatment required for 3.3 million. OSHA's research arm, the National Institute for Occupational Safety and Health (NIOSH), has estimated that exposure to deadly chemicals and other toxic materials in the workplace leads to 100,000 deaths annually and 390,000 new cases of occupational disease. The economic toll of this human suffering? For occupational *injuries,* there were $23 billion in lost wages, medical expenses, insurance claims, and productivity delays when last measured in 1978.

Managements cannot be blamed for all of this total, only most of it. One study showed that workers could be faulted a third of the time for industrial accidents; on the other hand, unsafe working conditions contributed to 60 percent of workplace accidents. An OSHA task force estimated that a quarter of all industrial accidents could be prevented through regulatory enforcement of existing standards.

For occupational *disease,* the cost is even higher. A Department of Labor study indicates that the tab for treating all occupational illness would be between $30 billion and $50 billion a year. An examination of asbestos explains why. According to a 1981 NIOSH risk assessment, 25 percent of all those working with asbestos—or 508,000 workers—will die prematurely of asbestosis under current OSHA rules permitting two fibers per cubic centimeter in an eight-hour period. These deaths are in addition to the 200,000 cancer deaths that will likely occur over the next twenty years as a legacy of asbestos exposure from World War II to 1972.

Court documents indicate that such companies as Johns-Manville, Raybestos Manhattan, and Owens-Illinois knew as early as the 1930s of the hazards of asbestos but kept it secret from exposed workers. In one case involving several asbestos firms, South Carolina circuit court judge James Price said that industry correspondence "shows a pattern of denial and disease and attempts at suppression of information. . . . [It] reflects a conscious effort by the industry in the 1930s to downplay, or arguably suppress, the dissemination of information to employees and the public for fear of promotion of lawsuits." This behavior endangered not only workers' health but also the companies' bottom line as well. Manville filed for bankruptcy in 1982. although it was far from broke, after an internal study concluded that a potential fifty-two thousand asbestos health lawsuits could cost it $2 billion in damages.

Some local prosecutors are becoming more aggressive against companies that, in their view, knowingly subject employees to serious danger. They call it manslaughter. One Illinois grand jury, for example, indicted a local company for the death of a worker from cyanide poisoning on the basis of evidence that the firm was aware of the life-threatening risks of its process of recovering silver from film but failed to train or equip exposed workers. "We're trying to establish the same ground rules for safety in the workplace as in any other public area," says the Illinois state's attorney, Jay C. Magnuson. In recent years, California, New York, Pennsylvania, and Kentucky have for the first time specified that corporations can indeed be indicted for manslaughter in certain cases involving deaths from workplace or product dangers.

6. *The price of product hazards.* In the 1920s, the president of General Motors confronted a classic dilemma between ethics and profits: Should he put newly developed safety glass in Chevrolets? Eventually, Alfred Sloan, Jr., rejected the safety glass because it might increase costs and thereby inhibit sales. "Accidents or no accidents," wrote Sloan to a Du Pont executive, whose firm made the glass, "my concern in this problem is a matter of profit and loss." A half century later in 1983, a federal grand jury indicted the Metropolitan Edison Company, the former operator of the Three Mile Island nuclear power plant, on charges of falsifying and concealing records about leaks at the plant before the accident that shut it down. Federal officials reported that if such false reports were filed, they could have contributed to the severity of the accident—one reactor's radioactive core partly melted when the plant's cooling system lost water.

As the General Motors and Metropolitan Edison cases indicate, the technology of harm has grown exponentially. It was

one thing when a century ago the local blacksmith sold a customer a bum horseshoe: The buyer could eventually spot the
defect himself and the likely consequence was an unhappy
horse. Today, even the most sophisticated consumers can't spot
a hidden defect in machinery as complex as cars or reactors—
and the potential for injury is not slight to one horse but severe
to tens of thousands of people.

The drug industry makes this point vividly. For example, in
1951–52 and 1979, Wyeth Laboratories and Syntex Corporation's Diamond Laboratories manufactured batches of infant
formula lacking essential nutrients, one of which was vitamin
B_6. Because formula can be the sole source of nutrition for
babies, many taking these defective batches were left with cere-
bral palsy or severe retardation. In response, Congress gave the
Food and Drug Administration power in 1982 to regulate the
nutritional content of infant formula and to recall defective
products. Yet delay in implementing the Infant Formula Act's
regulations allowed two more defective batches of formula to be
sold in 1982. Incredibly, the manufacturer was again Wyeth and
again vitamin B_6 was deficient.

At a congressional hearing, an outraged Albert Gore, Jr.,
then a Tennessee representative before moving over to the Senate, asked Charles Hagan, a company witness, whether Wyeth
had an obligation to spend some of its $20-million annual adver-
tising budget to alert purchasers of the defective batches. "I
can't say I thought about it, Mr. Chairman," Hagan replied.
Gore then pressed Hagan to explain why the three million cans
of bad formula weren't immediately and voluntarily recalled.
The nervous witness explained that while some cans were defective, others were not. "Would you ask us to recall those?" he
asked. "Yes, yes!" Gore shouted, recalling the adult women he
had recently met who were still brain damaged from Wyeth's
1952 mistake.

Businessmen don't set out deliberately to inflict harm. But occasionally their institutions can so overfocus on the sanctity of
profit, the stupidity of "government overregulation," and the
importance of being a "team player" that decent people make
decisions at work that they would never make at home. Author
Patrick Wright quotes John Z. De Lorean about this syndrome
when he was senior vice-president at GM:

There wasn't a man in top GM management who had anything to do with the Corvair who would purposely build a car that he knew would hurt or kill people.

But, as part of a management team pushing for increased sales or profits, each gave his individual approval in a group to decisions which produced the car in the face of serious doubts that were raised about its safety, and then later sought to squelch information which might prove the car's deficiencies.

In the past decade courts, agencies, public health groups, and the press have exposed a series of product defects in cases where it appeared that the manufacturer knew about the danger. For example, because of design defects in Ford Pintos made from 1971 to 1976, some would burst into flames when their gas tanks ruptured in low-speed, rear-end collisions; as a result, according to one investigative report, five hundred to nine hundred people lost their lives. Yet internal memorandums from the Ford Motor Company showed that the firm both knew of this danger and refused to install an eleven-dollar shield around the gas tank because the total cost would exceed the probable costs of wrongful death claims.

Although the Firestone Tire and Rubber Company knew its radial 500s were exploding on the road at a rate far above that of other tire models, and although its director of development in 1972 wrote in an internal memorandum that "we are making an inferior quality radial subject . . . to belt-edge separation at high mileage," Firestone produced twenty-four million of the tires in the next five years. In all, blowouts of the 500 have been linked to twenty-seven deaths—and *Fortune* magazine said that as a result of its intransigence, the firm "has often been its own worst enemy." In October 1983, the National Highway Traffic Safety Administration released thousands of internal company documents indicating that General Motors had produced 1.1 million X-cars with defective brakes *after* its test drivers had warned the firm about the problem.

Such waste of lives and dollars led to the creation of the Consumer Product Safety Commission (CPSC) in 1973. The agency helped slow down the rate of certain accidents, but, under-funded and statutorily weak, it was not equal to the task of tracking down all hazardous products. According to a report in *The National Journal,* dangerous or misused products still result in 28,000 deaths and 130,000 serious injuries annually.

7. *The price of employee theft.* Though payoffs abroad or toxic dump sites at home garner the headlines, the problem of crime not *by* business but *against* business is very much on business's mind. Based on the variety and cost of this "enemy within"— the theft of merchandise, supplies, cash, or information—it should be. At a California computer company, employees from a vice-president to a porter illegally removed and resold $14-million worth of machines over a period of twenty months. In 1981, an employee at the Wells Fargo Bank embezzled $21.3 million through the bank's computer system. That same year, two former employees of Central Fidelity Bank in Lynchburg, Virginia, were convicted of obtaining a computer printout of securities customers and giving it to their new employer, the First National Exchange Bank in Roanoke.

What all these incidents have in common is computers. To be sure, there are still enormous losses from the more traditional practice of employees misappropiating for personal use company inventory or materials. But it is the growth of computer crime— nearly half the businesses surveyed in 1984 by the American Bar Association reported being victimized by computer crime—that leverages employee theft into even larger numbers.

Altogether, employee theft adds up to a huge bill that is paid for either by lower shareholder dividends or higher consumer prices. A study by the American Management Association (AMA) in 1977 concluded that nonviolent crimes against business cost $30 billion to $40 billion annually. The U.S. Chamber of Commerce cites one insurance company report that says that "at least 30 percent of all business failures each year are the result of employee dishonesty." A Price Waterhouse analysis in 1984 attributes half of all retailing inventory shrinkage to employee theft (and the rest to shoplifting and poor control of paper work).

Security experts fret that one of the reasons for this volume of internal loss is the cavalier attitude of companies themselves. "It is just astounding the number of the top 500 corporations in America that have woefully inadequate security systems," says lawyer and consultant August Bequai. "I should know, because many of them are my clients." Indeed, industrial psychologist Lawrence Zeitlin proposes that firms tolerate a little employee larceny as a way of buying peace. He cites favorably a food manufacturing supervisor who allowed employees to take home small amounts of food because, "This way I know how much is being taken; it keeps them happy and it's a small price to pay for worker cooperation."

8. *The price of financial fraud.* There is a broad range of creative financial frauds where business firms profit by means of deception or the violation of regulatory standards. For example:

- When *The Wall Street Journal* blew the whistle in April 1984 on one of its own writers for allegedly leaking items from upcoming columns to investors, it was the most publicized example of a swelling number of insider-trading cases. In all, forty-four people had been formally charged with illegal insider trading in the two years prior to the *Journal*'s revelations—which accounts for one third of all the cases in the SEC's thirty-five-year history. Other prominent cases included that of Paul Thayer, former deputy secretary of defense and LTV Corporation chairman, who admitted his guilt in 1985, and Reagan national security aide Thomas Reed, whom the SEC charged with using inside information to convert a $3,000 stock option into a $427,000 gain in forty-eight hours.

  Ever since the 1966 *Texas Gulf Sulphur* case, it has been a crime to use nonpublic information to profit from buying and selling securities. The reason is clear: If insider trading were permitted, millions of outsiders would lose confidence in the securities marketplace and opt out of investing in America's future. Unfortunately, sharing privileged information appears to be an irresistible temptation for insiders who want to make huge profits at no risk—a phenomenon especially true as the number of hostile tender offers has ballooned in the mid-1980s. According to a report in the *Journal of Finance,* "approximately half of the market reaction [to impending takeovers] occurs before the public announcement date."

- In 1978, the Department of Energy set out to recover what it said was $10 billion in overcharges and pricing violations by U.S. oil firms, such as firms falsely labeling "old" oil as "new" to charge higher prices. The Reagan administration in 1983 lowered the estimated overcharge to $4 billion and drastically reduced the resources available for pursuing these cases. Still, in that year a federal judge ordered Exxon to refund customers $1.5 billion in overcharges and the Supreme Court refused to overturn a lower court ruling that Texaco had overcharged consumers $1 billion.

- The Amway Corporation is a $1.2-billion firm that claims an army of one million distributors in twenty-five countries going door to door offering two thousand brand-name items. Canada claims that Amway engaged in one of the largest criminal frauds ever prosecuted there. The Ontario Supreme Court in 1983 fined Amway $25 million as punishment for violating Canadian customs laws from 1965 to 1980. According to court documents, Amway created "a web of deception" when it submitted hundreds of false invoices and fictitious sales lists to prove that the prices charged Amway's Canadian subsidiary were the same charged its U.S. distributors, when in fact they were far lower.

• In late 1984, the House Government Operations Committee released a study showing that illegal financial transactions (embezzlement, excessive lending to insiders, and so on) figured in three fifths of the seventy-five federal bank failures between 1980 and 1983. The report concludes that federal bank regulators have been too lax in investigating self-dealing by insiders. And in 1985, the First National Bank of Boston admitted to failing to report $1.22 billion in cash transactions with foreign banks. About half this total, according to an assistant treasury secretary, "was the laundering of drug money. Why else would the money be $20 bills?"

The Business Response: Stonewallers and Crime Stoppers

There seem to be two basic reactions to documented "waste, fraud, and abuse" in business: the *stonewallers* who deny its existence or significance and the *crime stoppers* who strive to keep their companies and competitors honest.

The stonewallers deploy an array of defenses. Among them, it is said that the problem is not the crime but the law. Economist Murray Weidenbaum has written that "the fundamental cause of the lawbreaking can be seen to be the tremendous and often arbitrary power that the society has given the Federal government over the private sector." Irving Shapiro in 1981 approvingly quoted one of his predecessors as Du Pont CEO, who said that, "In the United States we indict a businessman under the antitrust laws for doing the kind of things that in Great Britain he would be knighted for." However, such arguments are like blaming the traffic light for a driver's reckless speeding. Further, with elected officials so reliant on companies that produce jobs and control PACs—a condition ably analyzed by Charles Lindblom in his book, *Politics and Markets*—it is improbable that there would be many laws unfairly criminalizing business conduct. Predictably, Weidenbaum doesn't offer many examples.

A corollary to blaming legislators not violators is blaming the prosecutors of the law. A Chicago corporate lawyer, Albert Jenner, Jr., complains that "the big corporation has become an easy target for demagogues to direct public attention away from more serious crime." Stanley S. Arkin, who defends white-collar defendants for Arkin and Arisohn, agrees. "When the government charges a businessman with a crime, he starts behind the eight ball," Arkin claims, adding that cases are launched by U.S. attorneys with a lot of "ego" invested in conviction. "For a young prosecutor, it's pretty sexy having a big businessman at the end of your tether."

But witch-hunts against business seem about as common as flying fish. Prosecutors often come from and return to commercial practice where they represent business firms, so it is doubtful they'd have a bias against their past and future client community. And it is hardly a cakewalk to obtain convictions against well-represented defendants who belong to the same social milieu as the judges. It is implausible that prosecutors would frivolously risk losing major cases against powerful people.

For decades before the Weidenbaums and Jenners, many corporate defenders instinctively opposed *any* government law enforcement against business abuse. In the 1950s, it was called "creeping socialism." In the 1980s, it is called "big government." A more balanced view was expressed by an unnamed big businessman in Leonard Silk and David Vogel's book, *Ethics and Profits:* "Government without business is tyranny, and business without government is piracy."

Stonewallers also try to invoke shareholders to exonerate illegality—either because these "owners" condone such conduct *or* because they don't. It is true that shareholders usually seem indifferent to their firm's wrongful conduct. When shareholders at the annual meeting in May of 1976 warmly applauded Northrop CEO Thomas V. Jones for his "leadership," outsiders would not have suspected he had just pleaded guilty to the felonies of an illegal campaign contribution to President Nixon and

$450,000 in bribes to Saudi Arabian middlemen. Two statistical studies of stock trading of seventy-four and seventy-five companies, respectively, indicated only a slight negative market reaction after public disclosure of illegal activities. But it hardly excuses wrongful conduct when the community that passively profits from it doesn't object. The views of casino owners on the subject of gambling or of plantation owners on the subject of slavery should not greatly influence our view of gambling and slaveholding.

Even as they argue that shareholders have somehow *ratified* wrongdoing, stonewallers simultaneously contend that shareholders were *unaware* of wrongdoing—and that punishing culpable firms would be to punish innocent owners. Judge Robert Zampano, for example, pulled back from heavily fining Olin for illegally shipping arms to South Africa because he'd be hurting "a corporation composed of 42,000 shareholders and thousands of employees who had nothing to do with these acts." But investment is a matter of risk; and if shareholders share in unexpected or even unlawful windfalls, should they not also assume responsibility for the punishment and penalties associated with prosecuted crime?

Finally, some corporate stonewallers attack the messenger, not the message, when they try to dismiss those who criticize business illegality as "antibusiness." But is defending tens of billions of dollars in annual economic losses really "probusiness"? Business crime no less than street crime is not a right-left ideological issue. No conservative wants to pay 900 percent more for a price-fixed drug, and no liberal enjoys being mugged.

Business fraud need not inspire reflexive defensiveness in business. For there are also the "crime fighters" who publicly challenge the kind of conduct that injures the reputation of all business people—people like those men mentioned earlier: Michael Blumenthal, Najeeb Halaby, Peter Jones. That is, even scholars Marshall Clinard and Peter Yeager found a happy flip side to their disturbing prevalency study. "The fact that 40 percent of the major corporations examined in our research were found to have had no legal action taken against them by 25 Federal agencies during 1975 and 1976 attests that illegal behavior is not essential for successful corporate operations and that many firms do maintain laudable ethical standards."

Back during the 1970s, two executives gained attention because they spoke out. Because Fred Allen of Pitney Bowes was stunned at the procession of admitted payoffs, he commissioned a poll of the ethics at his firm and others. The results enraged him: Most managers, it seemed, would go along with unethical acts to please superiors. So Allen set out his thinking in a series of speeches and articles. "This is an appalling situation. We, who have devoted our lives to the growth of profitability of large corporations, are thought of, collectively, as little more than mini-manicured hoodlums. . . . As businessmen, we must learn to weigh short-term interests against long-term possibilities. We must learn to sacrifice what is immediate, what is expedient, if the moral price is too high. What we stand to gain [by immorality] is precious little compared to what we can ultimately lose."

Blumenthal, then the CEO of Bendix, wrote an article in *The New York Times* in which he called for a professional organization to promote ethics in business. "Business executives are professional people," wrote Blumenthal, "but there is nothing in business life that corresponds to the bar association, the American Medical Association, or the American Society of Architects. Why, then, should business people not set up an association dedicated to defining and maintaining the standards of their profession?"

No such association has ever been created, much less even seriously discussed. But several individual firms have proven that being a "crime stopper" does not preclude business success. These firms are at least as profitable as their average competitors—and by at least one calculation, *more* profitable. In a 1983 speech to the Advertising Council, Johnson and Johnson CEO James Burke asserted his belief that "the most successful corporations in this country . . . were driven by a simple moral imperative—serving the public in the broadest possible sense better than their competition." Burke's staff and the Business Roundtable examined twenty-six companies with long-enforced, "codified sets of principles," finding that these companies' average net income grew 22.8 times in thirty years compared with 4.6 times for the rest of the *Fortune* 500.

Johnson and Johnson's own reaction to the Tylenol poisonings in 1982 is a sharp example of how a company can benefit when it takes ethics seriously.

The company's commitment to ethics was not new. As Johnson and Johnson began a rapid expansion in 1946, founder Robert Wood Johnson drafted a credo to serve as a philosophical guide. Brimming with 1940s earnestness, it pledged responsibility to "the doctors, nurses and patients, to mothers and all others . . . to 'our employees . . . to the communities in which we live and work. . . ." As the company grew into a conglomerate of over one hundred separate firms and divisions, however, the pronouncement hung passively on countless office walls.

Ultimately, top executives worried that the document was regarded by field personnel as a quaint piety. So they staged a series of "creed challenges" with managers and employees, to reaffirm and revivify the code for themselves. (One, in New York's toney Waldorf Astoria hotel, was later described by Burke as "a turn-on, a real happening.") The process lasted eighteen months and involved hundreds of executives.

Coincidentally, shortly thereafter, the first phone calls began to flood Johnson and Johnson's New Jersey headquarters: Chicago police were reporting that people had died after ingesting Tylenol, the company's $1 billion-a-year analgesic that held 35 percent of the market. Autopsies indicated cyanide poisoning. In these first hours, no one knew whether the poison was a by-product of the manufacturing process; whether it had been inserted by an employee somewhere in the distribution chain; or whether, as it turned out, the poisoner was not within the company.

Given these facts, how strong was the credo's hold? The most common corporate instinct in such a situation might be to "stonewall," in the argot of Watergate. At Johnson and Johnson, the opposite reaction was equally swift. Lawrence G. Foster, a vice-president, later wrote, "Within the hour, the decision to be completely open with the press was made simultaneously—without benefit of a telephone call or conference—at Johnson and Johnson's corporate headquarters and at McNeill [the subsidiary that manufactured Tylenol]. And . . . [top executives] were already supplying information to the FDA and other authorities."

A week later, company officials decided to pull all Tylenol products from the shelves; the decision could have permanently interred the product line. For "Tylenol" was now synonymous with "poison," since, the Associated Press later gauged, the Tylenol story was the most-covered domestic news event of 1982. Many observers felt the company would never recover.

But Tylenol and Johnson and Johnson did recover. When the

product was reintroduced in December 1983, four months later, it quickly seized 32 percent of the analgesic market. Johnson and Johnson's ethical standard, recently spread throughout the company by the series of "creed challenges," had proved, not a luxury for good-hearted executives, but the moral guidebook that may have saved a product.

Monday morning CEOs could note that Johnson and Johnson had done little more than act prudently: Unlike Wyeth Labs with its infant formula, the company had nothing to hide and thus hid nothing. Nonetheless, recall that the policy of candor began when no one knew *who* was at fault. More fundamentally, ethical actions easily appear obvious in retrospect. Yet if Wyeth had acted ethically, that, too, would have seemed "natural" and "obvious." The simple fact is that Johnson and Johnson and Wyeth were faced with an initially similar set of facts: One responded with an aggressively ethical policy and recalled a dangerous product; the other didn't.

Unlawful discrimination against minorities, women, and the handicapped is another practice that leeches the economy and corporations of talent. Here, too, conscientious companies are making a special effort to overcome bias.

One company that has fought illegal and wasteful discrimination is the Cummins Engine Company of Columbus, Indiana. Combatting race discrimination has been the personal crusade of the company's leader, J. Irwin Miller, whose zeal was so pronounced that a 1968 *Esquire* magazine profile urged that he be elected President of the United States. Between 1965 and 1973, Cummins recruited approximately one hundred black managers and executive trainees. Two of these managers were tapped by Jimmy Carter for government posts. And while some corporations when making charitable gifts stick to noncontroversial art shows and university chairs, Cummins has steered its gifts toward black economic development (such as the company's Delta Foundation in Mississippi). In the words of Milton Moskowitz and colleagues in their guide, *Everybody's Business,* "Cummins is regarded as a company with a conscience."

Another company whose commitment to combat discrimination is more than a paper pledge is Montgomery Ward. Peter T. Jones, now general counsel to Levi Strauss and Company and a former executive at Ward, recalled that when the retailer's equal-pay compliance program was implemented in the 1970s, a tenth of the chain's store managers did not comply. So Jones, as mentioned previously, notified the managers that their bonus had been docked from $5,000 to $10,000. In the face of predictable protests from the managers, Jones placed the docked salaries in escrow until the managers came around. Not surprisingly, all forty of them did. Explains Jones, "They responded to effective counter-pressures of sanctions of a lost bonus, and incentives to get it back—negative and positive." Jones believes that the way to improve management behavior "is to employ the four S's: stiff, sure, swift sanctions."

A third conscientious company when it comes to discrimination is Du Pont, which has mounted a campaign to make it possible for handicapped people to work at the company. In 1981, Du Pont employed 2,745 handicapped workers, 2.4 percent of its work force—an 89-percent increase from 1973. Aggregate statistics drain the life from individual examples of what Du Pont's policy has meant for its handicapped workers—such as James Prettyman, a blind spin pump mechanic for the company in Seaford, Delaware. Or Bill and Barbara Monaghan, a mentally retarded couple who work as messengers at company headquarters. Or Brian Hennessey, an engineering draftsman who has been deaf from birth. Or, perhaps most impressively, Stewart Wiggins, a computer programmer at the company who became blind in 1972 when a tumor was removed from his optic nerve. Today he reads on the job by using an Optacon, an electronic scanner that vibrates as it "reads" printed lines.

By giving these people a break, the company benefits from grateful employees' superior performance. Du Pont supervisors rated 92 percent of handicapped workers as average or above, compared with 91 percent for nonimpaired employees. And in safety matters, 96 percent of the handicapped were average or above—4 percentage points higher than their peers. Said Mark Suwya, Du Pont's vice-president for employee relations, "The bottom line is we've got a job to be done. And we need to find people who are 150 percent enthusiastic and have the ability to do the job. And we find that there are a lot of handicapped people who can do that."

Cummins, Montgomery Ward, and Du Pont stand out, but they are not alone. Avon, for example, began a minority purchasing program in 1972, when it bought $172,000 in goods and services from thirty minority-owned companies. By 1981, their program had grown to $12.5 million and three hundred firms. And AT&T has reversed its long-standing image as a corporate bureaucracy where Jews "need not apply." William Ellinghaus, then president of AT&T, chaired the New York Regional Task Force on Executive Suite Discrimination, which worked to eliminate religious discrimination and anti-Semitism from competition for executive jobs.

Kickbacks and corporate bribery are other business practices that some executives maintain they must employ to compete internationally—but that some firms manage to do without. Beatrice is one company that backed away from baksheesh. After he left the company, former Beatrice president Wallace Rasmussen told an audience at Hebrew Union College that Beatrice had ditched some of its Middle East businesses because kickbacks and bribery were so prevalent. Rasmussen told the audience, "It was so difficult in some instances to secure compliance with our standards of business conduct," he said, "that we completely disposed of our interests."

Similarly, when Congress passed a law prohibiting companies from complying with the Arab boycott of Israel, a sorry 15,000 companies continued to blacklist Israel and Jewish employees— but at least 152 firms followed the law. In 1966, the Western Union Company received a letter from the Central Office for the Boycott of Israel in Damascus. The letter noted that L. M. Broomall, a Western Union vice-president, had recently been elected a member of the National Board of the American-Israel Chamber of Commerce and Industry. This, the letter pointed out, was a violation of the Arab boycott of Israel. In order for Western Union to maintain good relations with Arab states, the company should furnish, within three months, Broomall's letter of resignation from the American-Israel Chamber of Commerce plus a letter from the organization accepting his resignation. Otherwise, Western Union would face a total ban on trade with Arab states.

The letter cautioned Western Union not to consider the request "according to misleading Zionist propaganda, as an attempt to exert pressure on you or interference in the afffairs of your company." Western Union informed the boycott office that it would not comply with this request—and still managed to retain the Arab states' "goodwill."

The Zenith Corporation, however, which lacked the near-monopoly power of Western Union, was not so fortunate. Zenith refused a boycott request in 1965, saying that it would comply with U.S. policy. The company was promptly blacklisted and remains so to this day. "We took a big beating," said a company spokesman. "We had a watch company that was hurt very badly by the blacklist. . . . We no longer have that company."

Levi Strauss's Jones identified a common characteristic of these corporate crime fighters. "I really am a believer in the key man theory of corporate responsibility," he said, referring to Ralph Waldo Emerson's view that a successful institution is usually the lengthened shadow of one person.

This thesis was corroborated by Donald V. Seibert, the long-time CEO of J. C. Penney. Quiet and self-effacing, Seibert began at the company as a shoe salesman and rose steadily through corporate ranks. Penney—before, during, and since Seibert's tenure—stood out as a proconsumer corporation, which is not surprising when you consider the name of the company's very first store in 1902 in Kemmerer, Wyoming: The Golden Rule. In his 1984 book, *The Ethical Executive,* Seibert advises rising executives that personal integrity can be a ticket to the top. "Every time [your superiors] promote you," he writes, "they are in effect saying to your peers and subordinates, 'This person possesses the qualities we'd like to see in more of our workers.'" Conversely, Seibert adds, "greater power and responsibility in your business necessarily carry greater responsibilities to the people you work with and also to the community at large. . . . The more successful we become, the greater the responsibility we have to share our relative abundance—in both material and experiential terms—with the society that has made our success possible."

Crime and Punishment: Is Justice Collar-Blind?

Does less punishment mean more crime?

Clearly, few among us would begin knocking over banks upon hearing that penalties for armed robbery had been halved or that budget cuts had reduced the number of police detectives. The reason is that bank robbery is *wrong,* regardless of the consequences of getting caught. But according to the "bad man" theory of criminal law, a phrase and concept originated by Justice Oliver Wendell Holmes, Jr., criminal penalties exist to deter that small percentage of citizens tempted by unlawful gain.

This theory has special application to potential white-collar offenders. For they are sophisticated people who can make bottom-line calculations about the profitability of illegality. So some businessmen may cross the line between lawful and illicit profits not merely because of organizational pressure from superiors but also because they think that they can get away with it—that, in Woody Guthrie's words, it's easier to rob at the point of a pen than the point of a gun.

Based on the existing level of law enforcement and punishment, they're right. Historically, the fraud and abuse chronicled in the prior section have enjoyed relative immunity from prosecution, and have been treated leniently after prosecution. For example, imagine a prosecutor having to scale seven different, high walls surrounding a fortress in order to apprehend and convict a suspect sheltered inside.

Wall number one is the difficulty of getting prohibitory laws enacted in the first place. Corporations enjoy special influence in the legislative process because of their fleets of lobbyists, their armies of PAC-men, and their control over job creation. These formidable political assets can dissuade attentive legislators from criminalizing or punishing economic abuses. The 1966 Auto Safety Act, for instance, provides no criminal penalties for willfully manufacturing a dangerous car. Punishment is greater for violating the Bird Migratory Act than for producing a defective car that can cause thousands of injuries or deaths. Even recent increases to $1 million in fines for corporate price-fixing can be dwarfed by the hundreds of millions in possible illegal gain.

Wall number two is the inadequate resources provided to enforce the law. In 1979, the Criminal Laws Subcommittee of the House Judiciary Committee calculated that the Carter Justice Department was spending only 5.5 percent of its total budget on white-collar crime—and this was in the administration whose President that year told the Los Angeles Bar Association that "powerful white collar criminals cheat consumers of millions of dollars. . . . But too often these big shot crooks escape the consequences of their act."

Since then, the Reagan administration has further reduced the resources devoted to prosecuting white-collar crime. It cut the number of people assigned by the FBI to economic crimes, for example, by 15 percent. *Business Week* in 1983 reported that "by cutting the staff and driving for deregulation—at a time when financial markets are increasingly speculative and complex—[chairman John] Shad is also arousing anxieties about whether the SEC is losing its ability to shield investors against fraud." By 1984, OSHA had only four hundred inspectors for four million workplaces, and the average business could statistically expect a visit once every eighty years. And, despite the evidence of prolific "chemical crimes," the number of EPA criminal investigators was just twenty-four in 1984; John Dingell, the chairman of the House Energy and Commerce Committee, says the agency "could probably use four to ten times that number."

Wall number three is the modest number of civil and criminal prosecutions brought against business, especially big business. To take one of several regulatory law enforcement examples, SEC lawsuits against the largest industrial or service companies fell from thirteen a year under chairman Harold Williams (1978–81) to eight a year under chairman John Shad (1982–85). After its staff recommended an action against Citibank for allegedly improper foreign bank transactions—in one internal memorandum, the bank admitted, "There is no doubt in anybody's mind that if all the facts were to emerge, we would not have a case"—the SEC refused to bring the case, offering reasons that revealed more about it than Citibank. John Fedders, Enforcement Division chief from 1981 to 1985, said in internal agency memorandums that he did not believe a corporation that violated tax and exchange laws "is a bad corporation" and that, even if illegal, the transactions constituted a "standard business judgment" to try to maximize profits. Also, Fedders actually argued that since Citibank management had never claimed its top officers possessed "honesty and integrity," they had no obligation to disclose the transactions.

Beyond the reason for his sudden departure in 1985 (because of publicity over wife beating), Fedders revealed why some prosecutors can be prone to pull punches when he told colleagues that he considered his SEC position a sure ticket to financial security once he left government. With this motivation, it is not surprising that, as one critic put it, he "found cases that didn't offend anyone," especially potential employers.

Wall number four is judges who won't sentence felons. A model of this genre, district court judge John Lord, when sentencing convicted school suppliers in a 1960s antitrust case, said, "All are God-fearing men, highly civic-minded, who have spent lifetimes of sincere and honest dedication and service to their families, their churches, their country and their communities. . . . I could never send Mr. Kurtz to jail."

In the first eighty-year history of the Sherman Antitrust Act, only three cases prosecuted under that act resulted in defendants going to prison. It wasn't until 1978 that the first convicted offender was sent to jail for violating the 1972 Clean Water Act, which makes it a crime to dump hazardous wastes into a river without a permit (the violator in that case had logged one hundred state pollution violations over thirteen years). Robert S. Trippet, for example, who masterminded the spectacular $75-million Home-Stake oil fraud, faced up to fifty years in prison in 1976; instead, the judge sent him to jail for one night, put him on three years' probation, and fined him $19,000. David Begelman, convicted of check forgeries as the president of Columbia Pictures, was sentenced in 1978 to three years' probation, fined $5,000, and ordered to make a public service film about the dangers of PCP (angel dust).

That same year the appeals ran out for William Grace and Robert Rowan, chairman and president, respectively, of the Fruehauf Corporation, who were convicted of a conspiracy to defraud the federal government of $12 million in their firm's excise taxes. Rowan was unrepentant: "As a crook you have to steal," he said, "and I don't think anyone accused Grace and I of stealing anything. The worst that can be said is that we worked too hard for Fruehauf and its stockholders." Actually, the worst that can be said is that the government *did* accuse them of stealing and a jury did convict them of stealing. There may be a difference of stealing *from* a corporation or *for* it—but steal they did. Yet federal district court judge Thomas Thornton sentenced them not to jail but to work forty hours a week for a half year in two Detroit social agencies.

Wall number five is judges and agencies who allow one free bite of the apple. Regulatory agencies usually settle their civil lawsuits with consent decrees and cease-and-desist orders—where the defendant, in effect, says he didn't do it, but promises not to do it again. Some 80 percent of all SEC and antitrust civil cases end with such settlements. As for the criminal cases, over 70 percent of antitrust and stock fraud indictments end with defendants "nolo contendere" pleas, which are theoretically tantamount to admissions of guilt but usually result in less punishment than guilty pleas and convictions and which cannot be used in later private damage actions. But when calculating potential violators realize that even if detected they will at worst suffer one unpunished illegality, the law promotes not deterrence but violations.

Wall number six is fines that are tantamount to traffic tickets. Even should companies be caught, convicted, and fined, the deterrent value is minimal because the fines are slight. When Ralston Purina released explosive liquid into Louisville's sewers in 1981, the subsequent explosion caused $10 million in damages; yet the company was fined only $62,500 for violating federal clean water laws. The average fine for an OSHA violation in 1983 was about $240. With fines like this, criminal penalties become just another cost of doing business.

Wall number seven is that even when a company is punished, responsible executives aren't, as in the E. F. Hutton case. Juries engage in a logical impossibility: They convict the company yet exonerate the only executives capable of having committed the prohibited acts. Apparently, socking it to incorporeal Mogul Corporation is more acceptable than punishing a real person, who may evoke sympathy for two reasons: They are invariably described as community leaders who would be ruined if convicted, and they appear to be only a link in a corporate chain of misconduct, hence scapegoats. Such appeals apparently dampen jurors' ardor for retributive justice.

If a court does impose an individual fine, there may still be neither punishment nor deterrence. Unless state law is explicitly to the contrary, most corporations indemnify their executives for fines, court costs, and attorneys' fees. (A U.S. Senate investigation found that government collection techniques are so ineffective that only fifty-five cents out of every dollar of white-collar fines are ever actually paid.) Writes law professor Christopher Stone, "The arrow of whatever law [the executive] has broken is obligingly deflected to the corporation itself, and passed through it to the shareholders, and perhaps the consumers and creditors. . . . The people who call the shots do not have to bear the full risks."

Indeed, the people who call the shots often continue to call them after their own trials. The Fruehauf Corporation analyzed what happened to twenty-eight executives implicated in or indicted for corporate illegality between 1971 and 1978: In fifteen instances, the executive stayed with the firm. So after Rowan and Grace completed their "sentences," the Fruehauf Board reinstated Rowan as CEO and made Grace chairman of the executive committee. Or as Eugene O'Neill put it in *The Emperor*

Jones, "For de little stealin'—dey gits you in jail soon or late. For de big stealin'—dey makes you emperor and puts you in de Hall o' Fame when you croaks."

Just as Troy fell and the Maginot Line was breached, so too can law enforcers occasionally surmount these seven barricades to find and punish suspects within the protective fortress. Ford Motor Company in 1973 paid $7 million in criminal and civil fines for tampering with its cars before they were tested by the EPA. The EPA fined the Union Carbide Corporation $3.9 million for illegally withholding for more than four years that one of its products produced skin cancer in laboratory animals. The mastermind behind the Equity Funding scandal went to jail. The former head of the Drysdale Securities Corporation brokerage firm, whom a court found had "looted and ultimately ruined" the company, was sentenced to eight years in prison for stealing $10 million. And in the classic case of *Park* v. *United States,* the FDA and Justice Department persuaded the Supreme Court to uphold the conviction of John R. Park, the CEO of Acme Markets, for violating the Food, Drug and Cosmetic Act prohibition of "causing" acts that lead to shipping adulterated food. Although Park didn't personally supervise or ship the food himself, he had previously received an FDA warning letter and failed to assure sanitary conditions in his warehouses.

But more often than not, justice is so obviously *not* collar-blind that it becomes the stuff of satire: A *New Yorker* cartoon shows a judge sternly instructing a calm business defendant, "Now come forward for the ritual slap of the wrist"; and Art Buchwald titled a column on white-collar crime, ". . . And 48 Lashes with a Wet Noodle." Of course, the majority of businessmen who think violating the law is ethically wrong, comply. But the minority who cannot resist calculating the possibility of gain without pain, don't. For them, crime pays, only because consumers end up paying the bill.

Deterrence Without Draco: Ten Steps

To deter business fraud and its consequent economic waste, the criminal law has to pursue two goals. First, it must deter without *over*deterring, because society doesn't want to inhibit legitimate business risk-taking and creativity. Remember Draco, the seventh-century Athenian statesman famous for the harshness of his code of punishment? For business illegality in America, Draconian punishment is neither economically sound nor, of course, politically plausible.

Second, centuries after it was established, the criminal law as applied to *individuals* has not much relevance when applied to wrongdoing by *bureaucracies*. Putting a horse thief in jail was one thing; but how do you put a "corporation" in jail? How do you find and punish the responsible corporate official when many hands yanked the rope that produced the wrongful conduct? How can the law pinpoint individual blame within a collective enterprise?

The beginning of an answer is to emphasize that the purpose of punishment should not be vengeance but deterrence. In his classic argument in support of retribution, Immanuel Kant wrote that on the last day of society's existence, a murderer not only may be executed but should be executed. A far preferable guide was articulated three centuries ago by Lord Halifax, who said, "Men are not hanged for stealing horses, but that horses not be stolen." The criminal law, too, should adequately punish business fraud so that consumer dollars "not be stolen."

Nor should it be culturally inconceivable for partisans to advocate more effective law enforcement against their own economic community. Lane Kirkland, the president of the AFL-CIO, supported legislation in 1984 (the Labor-Management Racketeering Act) that provided for stiffer penalties against union corruption—because union corruption undermines unions. In the same vein, business fraud undermines business, argued Admiral Hyman Rickover, the father of the U.S. nuclear navy, who dealt with military contractors for decades. "Businessmen should vigorously advocate respect for law, because law is the foundation of our entire society, including business," he said in 1982 in the final congressional testimony of his sixty-two-year public career. "When businessmen break the law, ignore or destroy its spirit, they undermine business itself as well as their own welfare."

Because of this premise that business fraud is antibusiness, here are ten steps that could help deter and reduce such fraud— steps that companies can adopt voluntarily or that government can enact legislatively.

1. Establish "corporate codes of conduct." A half century ago, the influential management author Chester Bernard wrote that the principal responsibility of the business leader was the "creation of moral codes for others" as well as the "process of inculcating points of view, fundamental attitudes, loyalties, to the organization." Because the ethic of law-abiding behavior starts at the top, managements should create voluntary codes of conduct that define what constitutes improper conduct for employees, backed up by sanctions for violations.

Codes date back to the 1920s and 1930s. In 1932, Henry Dennison's *Ethics and Modern Business* praised corporate codes of conduct as "the first attempts of a great and powerful social group to gain its own self-respect and the respect of other members of society." After the Watergate and foreign payoffs scandals, many companies scrambled to create them as some evidence of a "good faith compliance" with the 1978 Federal Corrupt Practices Act. So while 32 percent of all companies had codes in the 1960s, 75 percent did by 1980.

To be sure, codes invite some skepticism. GE, for example, had "Directive 20.5" banning antitrust conspiracies . . . before its bid-rigging conviction in 1961. Corporate lawyer John J. McCloy doubts their "practicability." *Business Week* worries that existing codes "possess no comparable guidelines on what to do when the codes are violated . . . companies deal with each problem on an individual, catch-as-catch-can basis."

Codes of conduct can help reduce illegal conduct if they have three components: They should try to define for unsophisticated employees what is and is not permissible in controversial areas (e.g., conflicts of interest, antitrust, insider trading, misuse of corporate assets); they should establish what will be the process and penalties if employees violate the code; and they should establish a tone generally throughout the firm that making money and acting morally are not inconsistent values.

Codes vary. Here's some language from Borg-Warner's policy manual that seeks to set a certain tone:

> At Borg-Warner, we traditionally seek to hire only people of high moral standards and, believing we have done so, we trust you to maintain those standards in your service with us. Should there be any doubt about the morality of any action you are considering on Borg-Warner's behalf, ask yourself these questions:
>
> Would I be willing to tell my family about the actions I am contemplating? Would I be willing to go before a community meeting, a Congressional hearing, or any public forum, to describe the action?
>
> In any case, if you would not be willing to do so, Borg-

Warner would not want you to go ahead with the action on the assumption it would help the company.

2. *Gather and distribute better data on business abuse and social performance.* It's still true, as an American Bar Association committee concluded in 1977, that "the federal government does not possess the mechanisms to measure accurately its own efforts against corporate crime, nor the mechanisms to assess the impact of economic crime on the country as a whole."

There are several ways the public and private sectors can better collect and distribute information in this area. The Justice Department, FBI, and local authorities should routinely specify how much they spend on white-collar law enforcement and the number of investigations and convictions per white-collar crime categories (e.g., price-fixing, employee theft, auto repair overcharges, pyramid schemes); when federal agencies refer cases for prosecution to the Justice Department, they should attempt to estimate formally the amount of loss and the number of victims per violation; in their areas of jurisdiction, agencies should publish "compliance reports" estimating the level and cost of violations, the resources needed to prosecute these violations, the conviction rate, and what new legal remedies are necessary. These data should be integrated at one agency and published as an annual "Report on White-Collar Crime in America."

As for corporations, they can voluntarily include in annual reports "corporate social surveys" along with their financial audit. Either in numbers if quantifiable or by narrative if otherwise, these surveys could measure the company's efforts in such areas as equal employment, pollution control, occupational safety, and health. If good companies begin publicly bragging about their efforts both to comply with the law and to exceed its minimal demands, they can create a competitive market pressure on less responsible firms to clean up their performance.

France, Norway, and West Germany require versions of such social reports. But when Commerce Secretary Juanita Kreps suggested a voluntary version in 1978, she encountered severe business opposition and dropped the idea. Business people accustomed to quantifying results in financial audits felt uneasy with less quantifiable performance categories. But many *are* quantifiable, such as the number of outstanding pollution lawsuits, number of workplace injuries, and the percentage of minority employees per job category.

3. Establish a "law compliance committee." Engineers at B. F. Goodrich in the 1960s who knew that their firm's Air Force brake repeatedly failed in tests should not have faced the choice of being mute or canned. A law compliance committee of the board, comprised entirely of "independent" directors, could provide a "safe harbor" where inside employees or retained counsel could confidentially disclose possible violations of law. It is far more likely that employees and lawyers would report to an entity created for this express purpose than to those supervisors or executives for whom they work, and who in fact may be the culpable parties. A law compliance committee could also enforce the company's code of conduct, as well as compile the "corporate social survey" mentioned above. Such a new entity could either be established voluntarily or by law.*

4. Provide notice to victims. When sentencing a company for some fraudulent practice, a court should be permitted to ask the defendant to provide notice through the media or mails to the class of people possibly injured by its action. This notice approach promotes the twin benefits of deterrence and compensation: companies anxious about their goodwill and good name are loath to have to publicize their misdeeds; and potential plaintiffs learn of their victimization and remedies.

5. Provide restitution to victims. Courts should also be able to "sentence" convicted companies to pay back their victims, in cash or kind. The SEC, as part of the consent decree process, has occasionally required firms to pay restitution to defrauded stockholders, but no agency or court can now require it as part of the imposed punishment. The notice and restitution sections can take the profit out of economic crime and compensate its victims.

6. Impose swift, sure, short jail terms on the most serious offenders. When should business felons be imprisoned?

One prominent opponent of incarceration has been Judge Charles Renfrew, who imposed the following "sentence" on five businessmen convicted of conspiring to fix prices in the paper

---

*Legislation requiring a certain corporate internal structure is not unprecedented: the FCPA requires firms to institute adequate auditing procedures; a 1981 drug regulation requires drug firms to establish a process so "the responsible officials of the firm . . . are notified in writing" of FDA investigations; the federal water pollution laws require that a company's permit to discharge a pollutant be signed by "a principal executive officer of at least the level of vice-president."

label industry: suspended jail sentences; $5,000 to $15,000 fines; and a condition of probation that they give twelve speeches to business or civic groups about their crime. Renfrew wrote that "the emotional and financial burden of the prosecution, the fines imposed, and the defendants' embarrassment in appearing before groups of their peers as convicted criminals would apply the deterrent sting." Indeed, looking at the publicly humiliated defendants, it did seem unlikely they'd ever again engage in economic crime or that jail could have any conceivable rehabilitative effect.

Critics, however, point out the difference between specific deterrence (will this offender do it again?) and general deterrence (will other potential offenders do it?). Mark Richards, a seventeen-year Justice Department veteran with twenty-one commendation plaques on his office wall from five presidents, said in an interview, "I'm concerned about dual justice. Why should a ghetto kid who steals a car be put away but a businessman who steals six million dollars get to work in a soup kitchen on weekends?" Richards, the head of the fraud unit in the Criminal Division of President Reagan's Justice Department, adds, "I'm not suggesting long sentences. Three months in the county jail will do."

Among others, FBI director William Webster and Professor S. Prakashi Sethi agree. "If the white-collar criminal faces only a fine, that's a business risk," says Webster. "If he's looking at time in jail, he tends to think twice about what he's about to engage in." Sethi explains how "thinking twice" works: "The assumption in such jail sentences is that the threat of punishment will lead the top-ranking executive of a corporation to exert pressure on his aides who will in turn exert pressure on their aides—a kind of trickle-down theory of . . . ethics."

Balancing the cost of illegality and pain of incarceration, one possible approach would contain the following elements (described in more detail subsequently): Incarcerate those guilty of serious economic offenses for short sentences, since deterrence works adequately if jail terms are brief but certain; attempt to punish responsible individuals as well as guilty companies; impose creative "behavioral" sanctions for those guilty of more technical and less serious offenses; prohibit felons convicted of offenses that threatened widespread injury from holding high positions in business; and make fines fit crimes, which means increasing financial penalties.

7. Impose "behavioral sanctions" on lesser offenders. Some white-collar offenses are what lawyers call *malum in se* (inherently bad in all societies, like rape) while others are *malum prohibitum* (bad because the law says so, like violations of oil-price ceilings). For the latter category, prosecutors and judges should develop purposeful alternatives to imprisonment for first-time, nonviolent business offenders. This approach is beginning to work for those convicted of street crimes: In Batavia, New York, 330 nonviolent lawbreakers spent a total of thirty thousand hours engaged in tasks from bookkeeping to street paving instead of sitting in jail.

Flexible behavioral sentences could work for some business lawbreakers, too: For example, milk adulterers could be sentenced to one year of giving away approved milk in soup kitchens; executives of firms with a certain number of mine safety violations could have to function as safety inspectors in their own mines; the owner of auto repair firms that repeatedly charge for service not performed should have to provide free (and accurate) diagnostic testing to "repay" the community.

8. Punish supervisors who recklessly fail to supervise or 9. who fail to disclose hazardous production. When U.S. authorities tried Japanese general Yamashita for war crimes after World War II, he answered that he should not be responsible for atrocities his soldiers committed in the Pacific Islands so far from headquarters. But the presiding military tribunal thought that someone should be responsible, decided that person was Yamashita—and convicted and executed him.

According to a widely cited article on corporate crime in the 1979 *Harvard Law Review,* American businessmen attempt their version of the Yamashita defense: "Superiors can preserve their ignorance by conveying to employees the understanding they do not wish to be told of information which may subject the corporation to liability." The McCloy Report on Gulf Oil in 1977 referred to this practice as the "shut-eyed sentry" after the line in a Kipling poem, "But I'd shut my eyes in the sentry box/so I didn't see nothin' wrong."

Since the knowing production of hazardous products can inflict such widespread and immediate harm—such as the Pinto and Firestone 500 examples—the law should impose high standards of care on appropriate supervisors. Otherwise, corpocracies will continue to suffocate the individual responsibility so essential for compliance with the law. For example, a supervisor or executive who willfully or recklessly fails to perform his duty to supervise production, which failure leads to the serious endangerment of human life, should be criminally culpable. So should any "appropriate manager" be liable who fails to report a serious hazard to the relevant authority within or outside the firm. Punishment for violations should vary from fines to debarment to jail, depending on the degree of recklessness and risk of harm.

The "reckless supervision" standard assumes that managers need not be omniscient, only prudent: so if he knows sales managers are meeting with competitors or that the reject rate for a batch of chemicals is high, he should inquire into the possibility of price-fixing or a defective chemical process. As for the "affirmative disclosure" provision, a spokesman for the National Association of Manufacturers thought it would be "almost un-American" to oppose such a bill's intent and the late Representative John Ashbrook (R., Ohio), former chairman of the American Conservative Union, said, "I think it's a question of law and order."

Together, these provisions begin to answer economist Robert Heilbroner's question in his concluding essay in *In the Name of Profit*: "When a corporation president or a member of its board of directors says that he is 'shocked' at the absence of safety devices in his plant or at some gross instance of pollution in a distant mill, the chances are that he *is* shocked, just as the high command was shocked at My Lai; the question is: Is being shocked good enough?"

10. Make the fine fit the crime—fix financial penalties as a percentage of the gain derived or the loss created. Because companies can't be imprisoned and executives rarely pay fines, businessmen may cross the line into crime since there is the prospect of organizational profit without personal loss. But if there's one thing that both firms and executives understand, it's uninsured, nondeductible financial loss.

The criminal code should (a) peg fines to the financial volume of the illegal conduct, (b) bar firms guilty of serious, repeat offenses from bidding for government business, (c) prohibit indemnification of or insurance for convicted executives, and (d) forbid the tax deductibility of any fines (now permitted by some states). Then larger firms engaged in larger violations would pay a fine befitting the size of its fraud, and individual officers would realize that they can no longer hide behind the company's legal skirts. "Since corporations are primarily profit seeking institutions, they choose to violate the law only if it appears profitable," concluded the *Harvard Law Review*. "Making these costs sufficiently high should eliminate the potential benefit of illegal corporate activity and hence any incentive to undertake such activity."

These ten steps all lead to the same destination—avoiding "violation [s] of fair play," as Adam Smith put it back in 1776. By altering the mix of reward and punishment for unfair play, the law can help persuade potential offenders that business fraud is a fundamentally antibusiness proposition—hurting profits, competitors, consumers . . . and ultimately themselves. And with economywide laws and regulations, they can no longer plead that acting morally means competitive disadvantage, as Alfred Sloan did. In the new enterprise economy, business leaders should reject the corrupting example of ancient Carthage, where according to the Greek historian Polybius, "Nothing which results in profits is regarded as disgraceful."

7

Consumer Value: The Pass-Along Economy

Once in my life I would like to own something outright before it's broken. I'm always in a race with the junkyard!
—Willy Loman in *Death of a Salesman*

Avoidable waste by corporations affects and afflicts consumers in innumerable ways. This chapter will discuss four illustrative areas that have a profound impact both on consumers and on business in America: (1) poor-quality goods that drive consumers to better-made foreign products: (2) high energy costs that victimize all consumers, both business and private: (3) soaring employee health care costs: and (4) advertising that turns consumers into cynics when products fail to match the hype.

Too often business executives have ignored these swelling and unproductive costs, believing they could be buried in the overall price of a product and be quietly passed along to unaware end users. But these "trifles," to refer to Galsworthy's analogy of the Introduction, are now adding up to such a huge measurable waste that some previously lax managers are finally donning their green eyeshades when the budget line says "defects," "energy," "health" or "advertising."

Product Defect/Product Quality

To appreciate why the phrase "Made in America" has become more a warning than a boast, consider the impact on the American psyche of a series of extraordinary and highly publicized events during two recent periods: 1979, when there was a three-month epidemic of disasters; and 1984, when the government charged that manufacturing incompetence by private industries threatened national defense:

1979
* March 28. Three-Mile Island nuclear power plant near Harrisburg, Pennsylvania, overheats and threatens a "meltdown" as above-normal amounts of radiation spew into the atmosphere. Subsequent investigations produce a massive record of incompetence in the construction and operation of the plant.
* May 3. Conrail tank cars containing toxic and flammable vinyl chloride derail at Sunset Bay, New Jersey, forcing evacuation of five hundred residents. Aging railbeds and equipment, along with poorly trained or supervised crews, have resulted in numerous such rail disasters in recent years.
* May 11. A Gulf oil rig off Galveston collapses in stormy seas, killing eight.
* May 25. An American Airlines DC-10 drops an engine after takeoff from O'Hare Airport and crashes, killing 275 people in the worst aviation disaster in U.S. history. Maintenance of the plane is blamed, but subsequent inspections of all DC-10's in service reveals that one half of them have pylon cracks (like the one that crashed) and are improperly maintained.
* June 4. In Kansas City, Missouri, the roof collapses at Kemper Arena, which happens to be empty at the time. It is the worst structural failure in a major building since the roof of the Hartford Civic Center collapsed seventeen months earlier.

1984
* April 26. General James P. Mullins, commander of the Air Force Logistic Command, tells a gathering of military contractors that like Americans with their cars, the Air Force "somehow accept[s] the lack of reliability as an inherent given of high-technology weapons systems." Mullins estimates that the Air Force, by demanding quality, could save taxpayers more than a trillion dollars over the thirty-year life of a weapons system.
* July 22. Citing "shoddy workmanship," the Navy rejects a batch of Phoenix air-to-air missiles manufactured by Hughes Aircraft. Also the Navy finds flaws in the tail of the F-18 fighter, manufactured by Hughes Aircraft.

- August 15. A congressional report discloses that the Navy recalls twelve Trident I nuclear missiles and raises questions about the reliability of 370 other Tridents deployed on U.S. nuclear submarines.
- August 22. The Army, Navy, and Air Force suspend payments to Hughes Missile Systems Group for three missile systems, detailing sixty-eight findings of "poor workmanship" and "failure of management to ensure the flow-down of contractual requirements to operating levels."
- August 31. The Navy rejects fourteen General Electric engines for F-18 fighters because they contain defective parts.
- September 10. Some forty-seven hundred different kinds of microchips manufactured by Texas Instruments are declared suspect by the Defense Department because of inadequate testing before being installed in major weapons systems. Among the weapons using TI microchips: the bombing and navigation systems of the B-52 and B1-B bombers and the F-15 fighters. These same chips allegedly short-circuited and caused a delay in launching the space shuttle *Discovery* in June, 1984.

Beyond this series of disasters and complaints from government agencies, the consumer public, too, suffers daily inconvenience and frustration. Buyers of dishwashers or ranges find that service is at the seller's convenience. Weeks go by as customers wait for Macy's to locate lost merchandise. Correcting errors on credit card bills feels like almost a full-time occupation. Cavalier auto dealers seem to forget that cars now cost the average person a king's ransom.

Take, for example, the experience of *Washington Post* editor Joel Garreau. Determined to buy an American car to support both American business and labor, Garreau soon changed his mind after trudging from one Washington-area dealer to the next, getting the same indifferent treatment at each. They expected Garreau to buy a $12,000 car without so much as getting a spin around the block. His patriotic resolve shaken, Garreau dropped by a Honda dealership and was looking at a Prelude when a salesman tossed him the keys—and he was hooked. Concluded Garreau, "There is at least one American in the Washington area who knew how to actively sell me a car. He may have learned his attitude from Japanese management. But he learned it. There may be hope for us yet."

How does the poor quality of goods and services demonstrate avoidable waste? For one thing, defects can lead to costly injury, even death (discussed in Chapter 6). Moreover, breakdowns cripple productivity and invariably lead to expensive repairs and service. Money is squandered, jobs lost. In addition, an indifference about quality in products and services turns the public cynical about this country's business and financial institutions, a very expensive development for our consumer-fired economy.

Despite the common-law caution, "let the buyer beware" (*caveat emptor*), business succeeds or fails based on its ability to create consumer trust. Many American companies have lost that trust, as demonstrated by the popularity of imported products and by the raft of consumer lawsuits and complaints.

Once stung, consumers don't quickly forget. "A consumer punch in the eye doesn't go away for maybe a decade," observes John F. Welch, Jr., chief executive officer of General Electric. Illustrative of Welch's point, another GE executive, vice-chairman Edward E. Hood, Jr., tells about the time he was trying to sell jet engines to a mainframe manufacturer. Completing his pitch, Hood asked if he could be of any further assistance. "Well, now that you've brought it up," Hood quotes the would-be customer as saying, "I've got a problem with my GE TV set, and my washing machine doesn't work too well either." Hood arranged for a quick service call to the man's home, and a few months later he asked the mainframe executive if he had any further problems. "No," he told Hood, "I got rid of all my GE appliances."

What is quality and why are so many American companies unable to attain it?

To read glittery ad copy and watch upscale television commercials extolling performance and style, the word *quality* seems to belong only to the very rich. But to most Americans it means sturdiness and reliable service—or your money back. "I don't ask for much, but what I get should be of very good quality," prays the man at his bedside in the *New Yorker* cartoon. Consumers want today's equivalent of "home cooking" and "handmade." For them, the archetypes are not Mercedes, Christian Dior, and Carr's biscuits but Sears's flannel shirts and Ritz crackers.

Not long ago, historian Barbara W. Tuchman, bemoaning the

deterioration of craftsmanship and the arts in America, offered a very practical definition of quality: "Quality, as I understand it, means investment of the best skill and effort possible to produce the finest and most admirable result possible. Its presence or absence in some degree characterizes every man-made object, service, skilled or unskilled labor—laying bricks, painting a picture, ironing shirts, practicing medicine, shoemaking, scholarship, writing a book. You do it well or you do it half well."

The best corporations are known by the quality they keep. When *Fortune,* in 1983, asked six thousand businessmen to rate companies by the quality of their products and services, no one could have been surprised at the companies topping the list: Boeing, Caterpillar Tractor, and Hewlett-Packard, all of whom have well-earned reputations for quality. When the Maytag repairman in that familiar television commercial complains he has no work because the company's washing machines don't break down, customers can attest that it's not just Madison Avenue hype at work. Back in 1960, Vance Packard wrote in his book, *The Waste Makers,* "When I asked my local repairman—who has been at the bedside of our four-year-old washer three times this year—to name a really well-built washer, Maytag was the one that occurred most emphatically to him."

But such luminaries have become more the exception than the rule. As a result, beginning in the late 1960s, consumers made clear that they felt their trust had been misplaced. This widespread disillusionment gave birth to the "consumer decade" that led to the enactment of two significant pieces of legislation affecting product quality: the Product Safety Act and the National Highway Safety Act. Under these laws, errors ignored or overlooked on the assembly line now led to a rash of recalls on everything from pacemakers to Pontiacs. These recalls, in turn, confirmed consumers' doubts about the level of quality of many American products.

Subsequently, consumers have turned away from their country's products in droves, even as unions and business groups wrap their mistakes in the flag and make buying substandard American goods and services a patriotic duty. "Sure I would have preferred to buy an American car if I thought the car was worth it, but I didn't think it was," remarked Stephanie Ponamarkenko, a seamstress in a Buffalo apparel plant. Ponamarkenko, whose own job is threatened by foreign competition, told reporter Art Pine, "I really am not sure it's just the fault of imports that these American workers are being laid off." Pine, who in 1983 toured areas of high unemployment, found little protectionist sentiment even in these hard-pressed areas. "If anything," wrote Pine from Buffalo, "interviews here show many Americans seem convinced that the U.S. is part of an international marketplace and must keep its doors open." In other words, Americans want quality and their money's worth, and whether the product or service comes from a U.S. firm no longer matters much.

Recent surveys suggest that such yearnings haven't adequately reached the remote sanctums of the executive suite. One, taken in 1981, found that while three out of five executives of the country's largest thirteen hundred companies believed quality was improving, 49 percent of seven thousand consumers questioned thought it had declined in the past five years; 59 percent expected the decline to continue during the coming five years. A 1984 Harris poll showed most consumers believed service was worse than it had been ten years earlier. Yet another survey, commissioned by the Reagan White House to assess service by U.S. companies, found that fewer than one in six buyers who faced major problems complained to the manufacturer. The reason: They believed their complaints wouldn't be satisfied. And about 90 percent of disgruntled buyers refused to buy that product again.

At least three confluent trends seem responsible for declining quality of American goods and services:

1. *High tolerance of error.* Mass production is the cornerstone of the American industrial success story. That production success, however, exacted a high price—which was quality. Since high-speed assembly lines, once rolling, are costly to close down, manufacturers came to expect and accept imperfection; the damaged goods would be shipped right along with the perfect ones. Better flawed goods than delayed goods.

Tolerance of error was formalized during World War II when the government instituted something called AQL, or acceptable quality level. AQL assumes that a certain small percentage of defective products is inevitable—typically about 2.5 percent of every product batch. "When I was in the electronics industry in the late 50's and early 60's, talk of AQL was all over the place," recalls Roger Wellington, chief executive of Augat in Mansfield, Massachusetts. "It got people into terrible habits."

Four decades after World War II, AQL lives on. A 1983

Harvard Business Review article asserts that "the majority of U.S. manufacturers use an 'acceptable quality level' system." Comparing this approach to that used by the Japanese "who budget for zero defects and measure discrepancies in parts per million," the authors conclude;

> The difficulty with AQL applied to components is that satisfactory performance of an assembly requires that all parts work properly. When building anything as complicated as an automobile (15,000 parts) or a copying machine (1,500 parts), a system that permits any defective parts—even a fraction of one percent—delivers a finished product containing several defective parts. This allowable defects approach puts U.S. manufacturers at a significant competitive disadvantage to their Japanese counterparts, who do not knowingly accept any defective parts.

A recent example of the evils of AQL is Commodore International, which in the fall of 1983 had the only hot-selling home computer on the market, the Commodore 64. The company was pumping out computers to meet orders, yet with the Christmas sales season looming, computers were returned to the company almost as fast as they were being shipped. Retailers found that upward of 30 percent of the 64's were defective. So even as Commodore boasted a 63-percent boost in earnings for the fiscal first quarter, its stock was on a downward spiral. Complained one retailer, "I call the company and get no response. And I've never had a phone call returned." A company spokesman sniffed: "Our manufacturing problems are our internal affairs."

During the 1950s, when U.S. manufacturers were fine-tuning their production line, the Japanese were listening to the gospel of quality control preached by W. Edwards Deming, the noted mathematician and consultant. Having been ignored or rejected in his own country, Deming in the 1950s found an eager audience in Japan for his rigid principles of statistically controlling quality. This translates roughly into, do things right the first time. "Inspection is too late," proclaims one favorite Demingism. "When you make toast, do you want to burn the toast and scrape it?" In Japan there even is a Deming Prize, which is awarded each year to a company that shows innovation in quality control. Which helps explain why when the editor of *Science* magazine toured the Matsushita color TV plant near Osaka, he noticed there were no inspection stations along the way and asked an official why. "He replied that until a few months ago there were such stations, but they never found any defects and so they were scrapped." Returning to this country, the editor says, "I tried to arrange to see a comparable plant here. I was told that none existed."

Recently, Deming's statistical intolerance finally was welcomed to these shores. Ford, among other reform-minded automakers, retained the octogenarian as a consultant, and when we visited the Escort and Lynx assembly plant in Wayne, Michigan, we saw the old man's advice at work. A huge area of the cavernous plant, where not long ago completed cars were inspected for defects, now stood empty of machines and men. In times past, so many mistakes were found that some cars had to be practically rebuilt in the inspection area—a costly, time-consuming process. Under the present system, Ford has adopted Deming's fourteen points for improving quality and productivity, which call for better human relations as well as tough statistical controls at every step in the production process. Other auto manufacturers have similarly revamped their assembly lines— Deming is also a consultant for Pontiac—and the only startling thing about it all is that it didn't happen a long time ago.

Attaining intolerance of error is one thing, maintaining it is something else. While manufacturers of quality goods have been trying for zero defects for a long time, even the best of them find rigorous quality control difficult to sustain against creeping mediocrity. For example, Caterpillar Tractor, ranked number two for quality in the *Fortune* poll, calls its approach "process control," a system for continually monitoring work in process. But as one Caterpillar executive notes, "You could go out on the floor in the sixties and there were process control charts all over the place. You went out in the seventies, and you couldn't find one."

2. The customer's always wrong. For many American companies, customer relations really means "us versus them." The customer is no longer "always right," if he/she ever was.

The typical customer complaints are familiar enough: overcharges, breakage, late delivery, bad design, poor durability, and lousy workmanship. As banks stretch the definition of banking to encompass a broad range of "financial services," old-fashioned services suffer as customers face long lines, poorly trained tellers, and increasing charges for decreasing service.

But business has frequently become inured to the voice of the consumer. In his book, *When Consumers Complain*, Arthur

Best observes that business controls the complaint process, and asserts its power with a variety of anticomplaint mechanisms, such as the "silent treatment," "legal gimmicks," and "intimidation." Legal anthropologist Laura Nader, who has extensively studied how different societies handle consumer complaints, concludes that "delays and confrontation experienced by complainers leads to a sense of powerlessness, and to apathy and uninvolvement."

Indeed, many companies simply apply the old bromide to all consumer complainants: Ignore them and they'll go away. One reason companies stonewall is to avoid publicizing their errors. They recognize that stories about individual consumers challenging giant corporations or banks is a slice of life that fascinates everyone—and may provoke imitators.

Companies don't like such publicity. Says Best, "Perceiving problems is the vital first step in obtaining redress for deficiencies in purchases. Thus businesses are the beneficiaries of the current low levels of problem perception." When the Chevrolet customer relations department accidentally discarded nineteen boxes of microfilmed complaint letters, General Motors bought back the boxes from two scrap dealers who ended up with them. Noting that companies are often paranoid about keeping complaints secret, Laura Nader observes that it "would be overgenerous to presume that GM quickly paid $20,000 out of a desire to better understand the nature of customer dissatisfaction."

As discussed in the first chapter, when companies get big and bureaucratic, concern for customers is often forgotten. But whether anticonsumerism is accidental or intentional, the corporation ultimately loses. When complaints are ignored or handled in a disorganized way, no pattern is discernible and correctable. It stands to reason that complaints taken seriously should lead to better performance by a business. Moreover, complaints become all the more important for management in this age of potentially dangerous products. "Even though companies may tend to believe that people use general complaints as a strategy to solve individual problems," says Laura Nader, "people often complain in order to encourage the company to change its production policy or improve the quality of its product. A company that ignores or misunderstands such complaints may fail to perceive the seriousness of underlying product defects."

3. Safety doesn't sell. When Commissioner R. David Pittle of the Consumer Product Safety Commission (CPSC) sent inquiries to the hundred largest advertising agencies asking if they ever advised clients to promote safety in ad campaigns, the answers he received, he says, were generally something like, "Not on your life! Safety doesn't sell." Many of the executives told Pittle a story to make their point, a Madison Avenue tale invariably recited whenever safety is mentioned. In 1956, when Ford stressed safety in its advertising campaign and its cars didn't sell, safety was blamed. Critics counter that safety became a scapegoat for Ford mismanagement; nevertheless, ever since that year the very mention of the word triggers a Pavlovian response from ad executives: "Remember what happened when Ford sold safety and Chevy sold cars."

Businessmen, in fact, have long been ambivalent toward product safety regulation. They favor it so long as their company is not the target. For example, many industry groups strongly supported the controversial CPSC when Reagan budget-cutters moved to gut the agency. "Industry believes there is a responsibility at the federal level to oversee product safety," explains Jan Amundson, assistant general counsel for the National Association of Manufacturers. "Regulation is the club that keeps everybody in line." On the other hand, companies, and often entire industries, fight furiously against government regulators rather than make fundamental changes in their products to avoid dangerous defects.

Convinced by marketing experts that safety doesn't sell, chief executives are reluctant to spend corporate funds on something that won't grab the attention of Wall Street and the stockholders. There's no bang for the buck from safe products. Also, corporate legal departments caution that if a company emphasizes safety, it might attract the attention of product liability lawyers, whom businessmen view as nothing less than leeches on the corporate body.

Indeed, the whole question of product safety disturbs thoughtful and ethical executives. We asked Peter Pestillo, the Ford vice-president who appears prominently elsewhere in this book, whether the auto industry wouldn't be better off accepting responsibility in some cases rather than automatically saying no to every claim of product defect. "Unfortunately, [saying no] is probably the safer course—a way to contain liability. You ought to do what's right all the time, but the frailty of it is—and I think it is one of the American problems that ultimately we must deal with as a people—we are the most litigious people in the world. And you must make every decision, regrettably, based on its legal implications."

Pressures for higher profit margins on products and fears of litigation cause executives to be suspicious, often cynical, toward consumers who have safety complaints. Indeed, Pittle, who since leaving the CPSC in 1982 has been technical director of Consumers Union of the United States, finds many manufacturers openly contemptuous of the people who buy their products. This is particularly the case among corporate brand and product managers, who are closely involved with the design and manufacture of the product itself. Says Pittle: "The knee-jerk response for many of these mid-level managers, when someone gets hurt using their company's products, is, 'Well, the damned fool, if he had only used it like the instruction book tells him to he wouldn't have been hurt. You can't make products idiot-proof.'"

This attitude leads companies to embrace the simplistic philosophy of gun advocates ("Guns don't harm people, people harm people") in seeking solutions to product defects ("Let's not change the product, let's educate people about how to use the product"). But studies show that educational campaigns fail because, as the Simon and Garfunkel song puts it, "A man hears what he wants to hear and disregards the rest." Reviewing the effects of such campaigns in an article in the *Yale Journal on Regulation,* Pittle and coauthor Robert S. Adler conclude, "A considerable body of research has cast doubt on the notion that mass persuasion techniques work very well in campaigns designed to alter public attitudes and behavior regarding health and safety concerns."

Not long ago, the lawn mower manufacturers blamed stupidity for the seventy-eight thousand injuries a year when operators came in contact with moving blades. And when the CPSC promulgated a ruling that a mower blade must come to a complete stop within three seconds after the operator leaves the controls, the industry fought it first in the courts and then in Congress with a propaganda campaign predicting lost sales and massive layoffs. (Lawn mower manufacturers weren't the only ones to use this tactic. Makers of mattresses, pajamas, and unvented gasoline space heaters, among others, reacted to CPSC safety proposals with similarly dire predictions that never came to pass.) Invoking what might be labeled the "stupid operator argument," the mower makers alleged that many injuries happened when users hoisted up the mowers to trim their hedges. (After hearing this curious claim repeated incessantly over the years, Pittle made a determined effort to find someone injured while using a mower to cut a hedge. He couldn't find a single case.)

Even as big American manufacturers, like Toro and Snapper, were spending huge amounts of time and resources to fight the CPSC and claiming the technology wasn't there to meet the agency's demands, Honda and a small American company, MTD Products, quietly began marketing mowers that met the proposed federal specifications. Finally, in 1983, after nearly a decade of resistance, the others too reluctantly complied.

From this evidence, it's clear that many American companies must alter their attitudes toward quality and customers if they expect to compete in world markets. A good first step in this self-evaluation would be for an executive to read a report in the *Harvard Business Review* about quality standards among manufacturers of air conditioners. Plenty of studies look at individual companies or groups of companies; what makes this investigation unique is that it encompasses an entire industry. While the report happens to concentrate on the mundane business of manufacturing air conditioners, its troubling findings have implications for almost all American industries where quality has given way to waste, mediocrity, and worse.

The author, David Garvin, a Harvard Business School professor, spent "several years studying the quality performance of virtually every competitor, American and Japanese, and every plant in a single but broadly representative manufacturing industry: room air conditioners." In an indictment of quality control in American plants, Garvin learned that the failure rate at the *poorest*-performing Japanese company was less than half that of the *best* U.S. manufacturer. Garvin also found that the failure rate of products from lowest-quality producers (that is, American firms) were between *500 and 1,000 times* greater than those of products from the highest (Japanese firms). "The 'between 500 and 1,000' is not a typographical error but an inescapable fact. There is indeed a competitive problem worth worrying about," asserts Garvin.

Garvin discovered that the differences grew mostly out of the relative care and concern by management for producing quality air conditioners: Japanese quality control managers reported directly to plant managers, Americans reported through go-betweens, if at all; Japanese reviewed defect rates daily, Americans ranged from weekly to ten times monthly; Japanese managers rated quality control as their highest priority, while at nine of eleven U.S. plants Garvin was told "their managers attached far more importance to meeting the production schedule than to any other manufacturing objective"; at the best Japanese companies, vendors were closely monitored to be sure their quality met set standards; the Japanese systematically collected information about the products *after* they left the plant, such as failure rates at the later years of a product's life, information ignored by the Americans. Significantly, Garvin found that two of the three American companies with the highest rate of assembly line defects paid workers on the basis of total output, not defect-free output.

Quality within an industry can be contagious. Professor Garvin, for instance, tells us that a number of the U.S. air conditioner manufacturers have read his report and in response begun working on their quality problems. An American company that has set a standard that an industry follows is L. L. Bean, the famous Maine retailer of sportswear and camping gear. Some 96.7 percent of three thousand customers surveyed by Bean said that quality was the attribute it most liked about the company. For its part, Bean conducts regular customer-satisfaction surveys, tracks customer inquiries and complaints by computer, and guarantees 100 percent satisfaction on sales and provides full cash refunds. As a result, competitors have had to emulate the Freeport, Maine, trend setter, and one that succeeded by matching Bean in price and quality is Kreeger and Sons in New York. Its founder puts his reputation on the line in every advertisement, which promises, "My guarantee: As always if any item purchased through Kreeger and Sons fails to satisfy you, please return it to us for a prompt refund. Doug Kreeger."

What is ironic is that companies often short-cut quality to get quick profit returns, yet study after study shows that corporations which keep quality standards high also enjoy higher profits than those that don't. Harvard professor Garvin proved statistically how quality air conditioners paid off. Japanese firms incurred warranty costs averaging 0.6 percent of sales; at the best American companies, the figure was 1.8 percent, at the worst

5.2 percent. Nor did the cost of maintaining quality compare with not doing it. The total cost of quality incurred by the Japanese producers was less than one half the failure costs incurred by the best U.S. companies. Concluded Garvin, "The reason is clear: failures are much more expensive to fix after a unit has been assembled than before." Another study of costs ties return on investment (ROI) to quality. It shows that, among companies with less than 12 percent of a market, those with poor quality had an ROI averaging 4.5 percent; those with average quality, 10.4 percent; and those with superior product quality, 17.4 percent.

In summary, Philip B. Crosby, business adviser and author of the widely read *Quality Is Free*, believes that the cost of poor quality—engineering mistakes, excess inventory, warranty payments, consumer lawsuits—can total 25 percent of sales at manufacturing companies and up to 40 percent at service companies. The solution, says Crosby, is defect *prevention*, which means the goal of zero defects at the manufacturing level, rather than defect *repair* after the product has left the plant.

Energy Waste: Corporate Conservers and Utility White Elephants

As the energy-led inflation of the 1970s demonstrated, few costs are passed on to the consumers with as little hesitation as energy costs. Yet while the OPEC-fueled oil embargoes and resulting gas station lines made price hikes inevitable, much of the corporate consumption and production of energy was permeated by avoidable waste. Today, while many corporate users of energy are moving rapidly to reduce energy waste, the nation's utilities are sinking into a swamp of insolvency—pulled down by the weight of their failed policy of building ever larger nuclear plants.

Not long ago when energy was a cheap and plentiful resource, American business built large capital projects with little thought to energy usage. But as price rose, oil and electricity took an ever bigger bite from profits, and by the end of the 1970s, companies that were heavy consumers of energy found their utility costs soaring: In 1979, for example, energy costs equaled 10 percent of Allied Chemical's sales and 15 percent of Armco Steel's sales. Worrisome reports questioned whether American corporations could curb their energy addiction. A 1976 report by the University of Southern California Center for Future Research warned, "The costs of adjustment to a less energy-intensive mode are extremely high, especially if adjustment is attempted over a short time. [Corporations] demand for energy, then, tends to be very inelastic."

Now, nearly a decade later, it is clear that some businesses have managed to conserve energy without curtailing production by efforts ranging from such big-ticket items as "cogeneration" to steps as simple as turning off the lights. Although energy prices have been low compared to the 1970s, many businesses seem to be controlling their wasteful ways of the past, mindful of the inevitability of higher energy costs in the future. The highly regarded Energy Group at Harvard Business School, for example, found that "energy conservation is proceeding more rapidly in the industrial sector than in any other part of the economy, and the process has been accelerating since 1973." With industry leading the way, energy conservation saves the United States $100 billion a year, according to the Oak Ridge National Laboratory.

Tapping into this new "conservation energy," in the apt phrasing of the Harvard report, doesn't mean building hulking power stations, stringing miles of wires, or laying miles of pipe. Instead, firms are able to eliminate waste by simple attention to energy consumption at each level of production and by installing efficient parts in existing machinery. Dow Chemical's "War on BTUs [a standard energy measurement]" is instructive. One of the three largest energy users in the country, Dow shrank its energy consumption per pound of product by two fifths in the late 1960s and early 1970s, presciently anticipating the oil shock to come. Throughout the vast chemical empire, top management set targets for the amount of energy each product should require, and monitored the results with daily reporting of energy consumption. An employee's contribution to energy frugality was taken into account in annual job performance reviews and merit raises.

But these efforts dim before the prospects of cogeneration, a process metaphorically described by the Harvard Business School study as "an Alaskan oil strike, a major new source of energy, waiting to be developed." A commonsense revival of technology widespread decades ago before the advent of cheap electricity, cogeneration involves the harnessing of steam and heat from electrical generation within the factory itself (and harnessing the electricity from heat generation, when applicable). Currently cogeneration accounts for only 11,000 Mw of U.S. electricity (2 percent of the total capacity), but the Department of Energy projects this figure will grow to 45,000 Mw by the year 2000. Companies, moreover, can go into the utility business, reaping profits by selling their excess electricity to their local utility. In April 1984, for example, the Dow complex at Freeport, Texas, paid an $18.1-million electricity bill—but sold the utility electricity worth $24.3 million.

Less energy waste by corporations means less energy use, and this, ironically, has helped speed the consequences of another kind of energy waste: the utility monopolies' self-destructive commitment to large-scale power plant construction, especially the expanding herd of nuclear white elephants.

Some examples of the recent sad history of nuclear power:

- The Long Island Lighting Company's (LILCO) Shoreham plant, perched on a beach fifty-five miles east of Manhattan, has cost $4.1 billion to construct—1,000 percent over the original 1965 estimate, and about 160 percent of the utility's total equity. In 1983, LILCO announced that a 56-percent rate increase would result if the costs were passed on to customers once the plant went on line. The project has been plagued by consistent engineering errors; after it was 98-percent complete, for example, hairline cracks were discovered on the reactor's turbine. As local officials questioned whether it would ever be possible to evacuate narrow Long Island in case of emergency, regulators pondered whether it would be cheaper to start or scrap the plant.

- Citing bad welds, missing documents, poor materials, and intimidation of inspectors, the Nuclear Regulatory Commission (NRC) in 1982 halted work on the Zimmer nuclear plant in Moscow, Ohio, built by Cincinnati Gas and Electric (CG&E), Dayton Power and Light, and Southern Ohio Utilities. In its investigation, the NRC found that CG&E's chief executive, William H. Dickhoner, had personally vetoed an urgent request for quality assurance personnel, a management attitude that prompted commissioner Victor Gilinsky to call Dickhoner "the architect of disaster." Then a Bechtel study of the 97-percent completed plant estimated that the remaining 3 percent would cost at least $1.7 billion, the same as the first 97 percent. In 1984, the sponsors announced they would convert the would-be nuclear plant to a coal-burning facility.

- Overlooking the Pacific Ocean are two $2.3-billion Diablo Canyon reactors. In 1969, geologists discovered that the plant straddled the Hosgri fault, a major seismic fissure. By the time the consequences of an earthquake on the site were considered, however, Diablo Canyon already was two-thirds completed. Pacific Gas and Electric officials reinforced the site against possible quakes, paying special attention to the more vulnerable of the two reactors. But in 1981 it was discovered that the blueprints for the two reactors had been accidentally reversed: so the special attention and investment had been lavished on the wrong reactor.

To Nuclear Regulatory Commissioner Victor Stello, the cause of the nuclear power fiasco is obvious. "Ineffective management," he asserts. "There are myriad excuses and reasons why management fails. But management ineffectiveness leads to physical defects that are built into a plant." This view is seconded by securities analyst Roger B. Liddell, who was a lonely voice on Wall Street in 1976 when he warned of the coming crisis in a report, "Problems of Nuclear Power." Says Liddell, "The managements of utilities like LILCO, Consumers Power in Central Michigan, Public Service in both New Hampshire and Indiana, and others mortgaged the future of their companies in an orgy of construction."

Symptomatic of the role of executive egos in the construction binge is that many of the new plants bear the names of the company's top executive. The Alvin Vogtle nuclear plant outside Augusta, Georgia, was named for the chairman of the parent, Southern Company, when construction began, as was Carolina Power and Light's Shearon Harris Nuclear Power Plant outside Raleigh. Then there's the William H. Zimmer Power Station in Moscow, Ohio, which was supposed to be a nuclear operation back in the 1970s when Zimmer was president.

The utility industry's rush to nuclear power in the 1970s and early 1980s is emblematic of its dogged commitment to large-scale, fixed-capacity central power stations. "My fear is that we're committing billions to a technology that's not the newest but the oldest," says New York Public Service Commissioner Rosemary Pooler. "It's like building an awesome horseshoe factory after Henry Ford has his insight into the automobile assembly line."

This bias toward building huge wasteful facilities has roots in the financial and regulatory structure of the industry. Nearly all utilities are privately owned, but they are granted a monopoly with the proviso that government can regulate rates. This artificial market offers perverse incentives for waste. Over the years, indulgent state power authorities accepted the industry's overblown predictions of vast power demands for the 1980s and beyond. They doled out construction permits without carefully weighing either power companies' nuclear plant designs or their own arithmetic. "Many of the plants themselves were being designed by the same engineers who gave these inflated growth forecasts," says Liddell.

More fundamentally, most states offered utilities a "guaranteed rate of return," a codification of the cost-plus system that has worked so poorly in the defense industry. Most states permit the costs of a new plant not to be included in the rate base until it comes on line. Called AFDC (allowance for funds used during construction), this arrangement treats current expenses as future additions to the rate base. This may have made sense in the days when all plants were completed and when regulatory agencies rubber-stamped rates, but no longer. Indeed, when the industry got into trouble in the 1970s and 1980s, AFDC exacerbated the problem. Utility customers, lulled by cheap rates, suddenly got socked with huge increases as costly nuclear plants came on line. Utility investors also got a false picture from these same phantom earnings, which quickly disappeared when the monumental costs of a nuclear power plant was belatedly factored in.

Certainly the best-known disaster growing out of this system was the 1984 bankruptcy of Washington Public Power System. It was done in by a combination of incompetent managers, undemanding regulators, declining energy demand, and public concern for the safety of nuclear energy brought on by the Three Mile Island scare. But the WPPS financial disaster was simply the most obvious example of how the wasteful industry's past has caught up with it. In 1970, eight utilities had AAA bond ratings; ten years later, only one still did. During the 1970s, the number of utilities rated BBB rose from four to twenty-three, and those rated A rose from twenty-five to forty.

Surveying the industry's wreckage, Carl Walske, president of Atomic Industrial Forum, a lobbying group for nuclear vendors and operators, said that many utilities that had been "darned good" at building big coal plants believed that nuclear energy was just another way to heat water. As it became clear that the industry was in over its head, the purchase of new reactors slowed to a halt. Of the thousand nuclear plants once envisioned, today there are only seventy-eight in operation. Since 1978, no new plants have been ordered, and seventy-five projects have been abandoned or scuttled. This industry is failing not because of external critics, but because of internal waste.

Looking back, these combined problems of mismanagement and structural waste all resulted from the utility's status as a regulated monopoly. Whatever the economies of scale that may have spawned this arrangement, they are gone now. "It is inevitable that people come to recognize electricity as a commodity, and back away from the notion that a utility is a natural monopoly," argues Roger W. Sant, chairman of a firm that builds cogeneration plants. Cogeneration and other nontraditional approaches to energy production become feasible with deregulation, says Sant.

One vision of a deregulated electricity market would have municipalities, utilities, and consuming companies bid for power in an "open auction." This is increasingly feasible because new technology and computerized record-keeping makes it possible to move electricity around from state to state as is needed. The Energy Conservation Coalition, a network of environmental groups, has suggested that Congress consider operating the interstate transmission network as a common carrier to assist the auction.

Another challenge to the old attitude toward utilities of waste-as-usual is the smattering of competing utilities, vying with each other for consumers' favor. A study by economist Walter Primeaux found that in those twenty-three cities where utilities compete, the marginal price was 16 to 19 percent lower than where there are monopoly utilities. Lubbock (Texas) Power and Light, for example, and Southwest Public Services share a "duopoly." The two firms compete based on quality of service, since by law they have the same rates.

For those jurisdictions with a monopoly utility, reform of the rate process can cut costs and rationalize rates. The Georgia Public Service Commission denied a routine $150-million bond float because of a badly built nuclear power plant. A more formalized system might penalize utilities for exceeding cost estimates and reward them for falling below. Additionally, strengthened measures for consumer participation in the rate-making process might approximate competition and hold prices down. States including Wisconsin, Illinois, and New York have set up Citizens Utility Boards (CUBs), voluntary rate-payer organizations that seek members through enclosures in utility billing envelopes. In Wisconsin, the five-year-old CUB has 125,000 members and a budget of $810,000, and lobbies the PSC and state legislature for rate relief and reform of the industry structure.

Ultimately, conservation will enable utilities to compete with other energy-producing systems. As Amory Lovins, a physicist and activist who now advises utilities on energy issues, points out, "Something like 80 percent or 90 percent of the electricity now sold is uncompetitive with electricity-saving technologies. Even if you've just finished building a new reactor, it would be cheaper to write it off than to operate it." Thus utilities should promote conservation, he urges.

Health Costs: Passing On the Disease

A vivid example of how corporate inefficiency is passed on to consumers is business's anesthetized approach to health benefits. Many companies exhibit more bargaining savvy purchasing paper clips than health care. Having few cost restraints, it has evolved into a "cost-plus" system with consumers ultimately footing the bill by paying higher prices for products and services. Thus employee health care costs add $500 to the price of every Chrysler car—and $2 to a $57 tire.

By any estimate, the corporate health bill is huge. Business is spending about $120 billion annually—far more than it paid out in dividends. According to a study of 225 companies by Coopers and Lybrand, the share of payroll costs taken by health care has risen from .5 percent two decades ago to 8 percent today. For some companies, health payments take up fully one quarter of payroll costs. And the U.S. Chamber of Commerce estimates that American companies may spend $2,400 a year per employee on insurance premiums and outlays. In all, business firms account for 25 percent of total health care spending in the U.S. through their employee benefit and retirement programs.

Why is the cost of corporate health care rising so much and so rapidly? Primarily it's because medical costs generally are climbing, boosted upward by too many hospitals, duplication of services, proliferation of costly equipment, and growing doctors' fees. Doctors, who pay as much as one quarter of their income for malpractice insurance, practice "defensive medicine" against lawsuits by causing patients to take far more tests than necessary. Insurance pays for all these excesses, which translate into higher insurance premiums for everyone, corporations and individuals alike.

In 1984, for the first time, Americans spent $1 billion *a day* on health care—9.5 percent of the gross national product. During the inflationary spasms of the 1970s, health care costs spurted ahead of other economic sectors—increasing 770 percent from 1965 to 1983 ($41.7 billion to $355 billion), while the consumer price index rose a comparatively modest 242 percent. And while the consumer price index rose only 3.2 percent in 1983, health care costs nostalgically continued to rise 10 percent.

Given their great financial leverage, corporations, if they had the will, could force reductions in health costs. However, corporate treasuries have been as lax as the federal Treasury when it comes time to pay the doctor's bill. For as we have described elsewhere, direction in a company comes from the top, and most chief executives have long considered insurance questions complex and mundane, shifting responsibility to a lowly insurance manager. Not until Chrysler's provocative CEO, Lee Iacocca, began talking about how much health care costs add to the price of each car did the severity of the problem begin to penetrate the thinking of many top executives.

Indeed, the Coopers and Lybrand study found that most of the companies surveyed lacked basic information about what their money bought—statistics as simple as the number of hospital admissions and average length of stay. In 1981, according to the Health Research Institute, only 11.3 percent of 602 major companies it surveyed audited employees' hospital bills. Moreover, many of the firms' health plans had built-in incentives for waste, such as encouraging employees to choose expensive hospital care for procedures that could be done on an outpatient basis. Such lax controls predictably lead to fraud and abuse. The Employee Research Institute estimated in 1984 that phony billing and other health care fraud accounted for 10 percent to 15 percent of the amount spent annually on employee health insurance.

Another reason why health care costs are out of control can be traced to the complex and profitable relationships between the various people involved. According to Samuel X. Kaplan, whose Los Angeles-based U.S. Administrators, Inc., advises corporations on cutting their medical bills, "Insurance companies won't crack down on doctors and dentists because they sell them big malpractice policies. What's more, insurance companies don't want to cut back on premiums that come from selling big policies because that would affect their tens of thousands of insurance agents who sell the policies and work on commission." In addition, insurance companies are big lenders to corporations, and many insurance executives are on the boards of directors of companies that are their insurance clients and also borrowers. Such hand-in-glove relationships make it difficult for any CEO to use his corporation's financial leverage to force lower rates from an insurance company.

Corporations' "it's only money" attitude toward health insurance also flows from the tendency of managers and employees to pile up health benefits as a seemingly low-cost alternative to wage increases. In the words of Joseph Califano, former secretary of Health, Education and Welfare and a member of the Chrysler board of directors, "With each round of bargaining, managers who fought with other suppliers over the price of each nail or screw, and union leaders who fought for each half-cent an hour, kept adding health benefits to contracts without realizing that they were becoming hostage to costs beyond their control—costs that over the long run endangered jobs and hobbled profits."

Some firms have reflexively responded to swelling medical bills by trying to pass them onto employees. Ford, which has seen total health care costs triple in the past ten years despite a 34-percent reduction in the average number of working employees, now requires salaried employees to share the costs. "That's the quickest way to a white collar union," comments one expert. Indeed, employees bristle at attempts to cut back on their health protection, which they rightly regard as their bulwark against potential catastrophe. Thus when Chrysler, Caterpillar, and AT&T tried to wrest health care concessions from unions in the early 1980s, negotiations broke down.

Instead, more and more firms are experimenting with alternatives that cut their medical bills without burdening employees or sacrificing the quality of care. These efforts range from self-insurance by the company, which now accounts for nearly 20 percent of the health insurance market, to "stay-well" plans that reward employees for not incurring unnecessary medical expenses.

Two of the more successful alternative approaches included preferred provider organizations (PPOs) and health maintenance organizations (HMOs). A PPO is a consortium of doctors and hospitals. It contracts with companies to provide medical service at discounted prices (saying, in effect, "We'll give you that appendectomy wholesale"). Firms persuade their employees to join the PPO instead of choosing more traditional plans by offering them broader coverage (for example, covering home care and ambulatory services) or lower rates (at the Ameritrust Bank in Cleveland, employees pay a thirty-five-dollar-a-month premium for a PPO and sixty dollars for Blue Cross). The company gains by being able to monitor costs and hospitalization rates—in some cases signing inspection agreements with the involved hospitals, many of which participate to stem falling occupancy rates and low cash-flow. "Until very recently, [insurance] providers held all the cards," noted Stuart Altman, a health care economist at Brandeis University. "The PPO, for the first time, gives the purchasers some bargaining leverage."

HMOs are more established alternatives in which patients pay a fixed monthly fee in exchange for guaranteed coverage. "HMOs are able to reduce the cost of care by combining the incentives of prepayment with the efficiencies of an organized health care delivery system," explains Congressman Henry Waxman (D., Calif.), a congressional supporter. "The result has been that they substitute ambulatory care for more costly hospital services." Because HMOs involve clinics and a network of doctors, they are most convenient for firms whose employees are bunched in one or a few locations. Some in that category, including Gillette, R. J. Reynolds, and the United Mine Workers, have their own HMOs. Others have encouraged formation of regional HMOs in their areas. The Twin City Health Care Development Project, including companies such as General Mills, Honeywell, Control Data, and Cargill, have provided seed money and assistance to seven HMOs that now enroll a full 25 percent of the Minneapolis-St. Paul population.

Chrysler was one company especially weakened by feverish health cost inflation. Its annual medical cost of $5,700 per employee meant that in 1984, Chrysler had to sell seventy thousand cars just to pay its health care bills. When the company realized that every decrease of a percentage point in health care costs would save more than $400 million over the next ten years, it hired experts to pore over health and hospital records. According to Califano, Chrysler found that "as much as 25 percent of its hospital costs may be due to waste and inefficiency." For example, Chrysler found that *two thirds* of hospital admissions for lower back problems were unjustified.

The auto manfuacturer began a generic drug promotion program, saving $250,000 a year; encouraged outpatient surgery (saving $2 million a year); mandated second opinions before some types of surgery (saving $1 million a year); encouraged individual employees to scrutinize hospital bills by agreeing to share the amount of any overcharges with them; and gave workers financial incentives to join HMOs.

Chrysler is, of course, the paradigmatic example of how the prospect of bankruptcy can break the wasteful habits of even the worst corpocracy. It remains to be seen whether enough other firms will choose preventive medicine or wait for necessary emergency surgery.

The Consumption of Advertising

How much of advertising is wasteful? This is a question that, if not answerable, is at least explorable.

Nobody would dispute the importance of advertising to the American economy, society, and psyche. But the consensus ends there, for the debate over the cost and value of advertising to corporations and consumers can be as intense as the look on the TV housewife's face as she tries to figure out which detergent washes cleaner.

To some, advertising is inseparable from our national purpose, a blending of commerce and culture that can be traced back to the folkways of American business. The original national advertising agents of the late nineteenth century saw themselves as progenitors of a new democracy, one that would make everything available to everyone, according to historian Daniel Pope, author of *The Making of Modern Advertising*. The apostles of advertising have often been quick to overstate the concerns of bona fide critics in order to belittle them. "Critics are not attacking advertising as such, but the capitalist system," asserts Neil Borden, Harvard business professor and author of *The Economics of Advertising.*

If quantity is a measure of success, advertising is a roaring one. According to a 1981 report by business journalist A. Kent MacDougall, all advertising expenditures amounted to 2.1 percent of the gross national product, 3.3 percent of personal consumption spending, and $681 per household. By another measure, some $30 billion is spent annually on advertising, a sum equal to the total amount America spends on education. "Even allowing for inflation, [spending on] advertising has grown faster than the U.S. population since the beginning of the century and faster than the gross national product and personal consumption spending since 1976." The number of network television commercials doubled during the 1970s to an average of 585 each day, with the average American exposed to 1,500 ads a day from all sources.

However, excess apparently has not enamored the public of ads or the people who create them. In one recent study, 70 percent of the public said that "advertising insults the intelligence of the average consumer." Another survey showed that while three quarters of Americans thought ads made products more expensive only 4 percent thought they brought prices down. According to a 1983 Gallup poll to determine what people thought of the honesty and ethical standards of people in various fields, advertising executives ranked near the bottom, just above car salespeople.

Still, advertising keeps hammering away at an increasingly skeptical public. The reason is that the ad race, like the arms race, is driven by fear of the unknown. The superadvertisers, like the superpowers, are locked into an action-reaction cycle. When Wendy's asks, "Where's the beef?" Burger King responds by touting flame-broiling. Pepsi pitches itself as the cola of a generation, so Coke counters that it's the "real thing." As Veblen wrote eighty years ago, "Each concern must advertise because the others do." Like nuclear deterrence, we know when advertising doesn't work, but we can never know for sure when it does. Hence, the tendency toward excess.

Hershey Foods Corporation offers a celebrated example of this phenomenon. For forty-nine years, Hershey refused to advertise, instead following the credo of its founder, Milton S. Hershey, who said, "Give them quality, that's the best kind of advertising." However, other candy makers, particularly Mars, flooded the airwaves to win the allegiance of TV-age children. As it saw its market share dwindling, Hershey in 1970 began advertising and by 1980 was one of the hundred largest advertisers in the country, spending some $42 million annually on ads.

Yet while advertising has helped Hershey ward off rivals, it has not expanded the universe of chocolate-eating people. Per capita candy consumption declined 23 percent during the 1970s, as the population of five- to thirteen-year-olds declined. Using ads to deter rivals may buy short-term security but in the long run it will not create conditions required for sustained business growth.

Beyond this short-term sense of security, it's difficult to prove the value of advertising to the firms that practice it most. Examining the resource allocation of companies such as General Foods and Miles Laboratories, which spend more than twice as much on ads as they make in after-tax profits, two Berkeley business professors conclude that "there are probably a substantial number of advertisers who should experiment with reduced advertising expenditures." However, caution professors David A. Aaker and James M. Carman, "looking for the relationship between advertising and sales is somewhat worse than looking for a needle in a haystack. Like the needle, advertising's effects, even when significant, are likely to be small."

And apparently it's getting smaller all the time. A 1983 survey found that only 7 percent of people watching television could identify the brand touted in the previous commercial. (That's down from 12 percent in 1974 and 18 percent in 1965.) Moreover, shoppers are buying fewer products because of their brand names. In recent years, sales of generic household products have doubled, while brand name product purchasing has dropped slightly.

The debate over the role of advertising usually focuses on two different types of advertising: informational and image. The difference between the two was neatly summarized during an exchange on the David Susskind television program. "What is advertising supposed to do?" asked Susskind of a panel of ad executives, almost all of whom responded that advertising was meant to give information. At which point one other executive blurted out, "You and I are in different businesses. I spray poison gas."

David Ogilvy, one of this generation's most successful admen, offered the following, somewhat stereotypical advice to his brethren: "The consumer is not a moron, she is your wife. Try not to insult her intelligence." Ogilvy's recommendation reflects the usual justification of advertising presented by its defenders: the consumer is smart, needs information, and sees through blue smoke and mirrors in advertisements.

When ads are informational, this thesis has legitimacy. General Motors and Peugeot run very detailed, factual two-page ads in national magazines, nutritional food sales have resulted from advertising and labeling of the products' healthy ingredients and effects, and Apple's advertising inserts in magazines are as informative as some computer owners' manuals.

At its best, advertising fosters competition, drives prices down, and enhances consumer sovereignty. A perfect example was described in a staff study by the Federal Trade Commission comparing eyeglass prices in states that allowed advertising and those that don't. The FTC found that "prohibitions or restrictions on information discourages or prevents individual consumers from price shopping, reduces retailers' incentives to engage in price competition, and results in higher costs to the public." Supreme Court Justice Harry Blackmun, in striking down Virginia's ban on prescription drug advertising, described the proper role of advertising in the consumer market: "It is a matter of public interest that [consumer] decisions be intelligent and well-informed. To this end, the free flow of commercial information is indispensable." And after the 1975 high court decision striking down a ban on advertising by attorneys, a federal study found that personal legal fees were lower in cities where lawyers advertised than where they didn't.

Unfortunately, most national advertisements emphasize image and disregard information. Typically, they tell how "Coke is it," talk about "a company called TRW," show Brooke Shields's hips, air Rodney Dangerfield's demands for "respect" in plugging Miller Light, and reveal Dewar's profiles of Scotch-sipping Yuppies. Two Oregon marketing professors, Alan J. Resnik and Bruce L. Stern, studied nearly four hundred TV commercials and determined that less than half contained *any* of fourteen informational attributes that would assist a rational economic choice.

Many popular image advertisements not only sidestep information, but also push products that are unneeded. "Nonprice advertising often promotes bad values, whether it effectively sells products or not," observes sociologist Michael Schudson in his book, *Advertising, The Uneasy Persuasion.* "It peppers the airwaves with the insouciant promotion of values that, on a personal basis, few advertisers or copywriters or artists would affirm for themselves or their children."

Economist John Kenneth Galbraith argues that the "central function [of advertising] is to create desires—to bring into being wants that did not previously exist." Advertising, says Galbraith, turns the notion of consumer sovereignty on its head: "Is a new breakfast cereal or detergent so much wanted if so much must be spent to compel in the consumer the sense of want?"

As evidence of how advertising often misuses its estimable powers of persuasion, consider the marketing of feminine hygiene products. In 1980, during the toxic shock syndrome crisis, companies like Procter and Gamble moved to capitalize on the scare by promoting the use of sanitary pads instead of advising women how to use tampons safely. The total ad budget for sanitary pads rose from $38.1 million in 1980 to $68.5 million in 1982. These millions sought not only to persuade women to switch to sanitary pads but also to increase sales dramatically. *The Wall Street Journal* reported that "companies are trying to persuade women to use pads more frequently—even every day of the month." One analyst commented, "These marketers have decided to teach women that they aren't clean." Or, applying Galbraith's thesis, if women through the ages had needed to use sanitary pads every day, would they now need $68 million of ads to tell them about that need?

Sometimes misleading image advertising is not only wasteful, it is also lethal: America's most advertised product, cigarettes, is also this country's biggest killer. Page upon page of ads in magazines show attractive young people smoking, and on city streets, young women hand out free cigarettes, while the U.S. Surgeon General attributes three hundred thousand premature deaths a year to smoking-related diseases.

Advertising seeks to reinforce the habits of those smokers already addicted, an effect graphically described by former FTC chairman Michael Pertschuk: "Roughly two-thirds of the heroin addicts in Viet Nam overcame their addiction upon their return to the United States without formal treatment programs. But when an addict is subjected to the same environmental stimuli which were associated with the onset of his addiction, those stimuli provoke what addiction researchers refer to as 'delayed abstinence syndrome.' The researchers fear that the constant pressure of cigarette advertising and promotion tend to reactivate the symptoms of addiction in smokers who are attempting to quit."

But the pitch is meant not only to keep nicotine lovers chained to their habits, it lures others to a life of addiction. Here's how a Brown and Williamson Tobacco Corporation executive described his company's marketing strategy: "Nobody is stupid enough to put it in writing, or even in words, but . . . market expansion in this industry means two things—kids and women. I think that governs the thinking of all the companies."

If tobacco ads implicitly mislead people about the effects of smoking, how often are advertisements blatantly deceptive or fraudulent? Consider, for instance, those familiar claims made by makers of nonprescription analgesic drugs, a $1-billion-a-year industry. The claim that "Bayer works wonders" may not be deceptive because everyone knows aspirin is not a wonder drug. But performance claims such as, "What's better than aspirin? New clinical evidence says Excedrin," troubled the FTC in the late 1970s, and the agency sought supporting evidence for the claims of "hospital studies" and "medical endorsements" intoned in ads by white-coated technicians in laboratory settings. The FTC held an administrative hearing at which numerous analgesic testing experts testified and, according to FTC commissioner David A. Clanton, "the commission could not find that the companies had even one well-controlled clinical test to support their claims." In short, acetylsalicylic acid is acetylsalicylic, no matter what brand it is.

Most Americans, never seeing a bill called "advertising" or what percent of a product's price is traceable to this cost, are generally indifferent when it comes to the question of whether advertising is a waste. And business people often fall back on the old chestnut offered years ago by Philadelphia retailer John Wanamaker, who said, "Half of the money I spend on advertising is wasted, and the trouble is I don't know which half." Consumers are equally ambivalent. "For nearly half a century," Daniel Pope writes, "a variety of surveys have found that approximately half of the public has found advertising to be dishonest." So it would be easy to conclude that judging the wastefulness of advertising ultimately comes down to a cultural preference: It is waste when it promotes things we don't like or don't need (designer jeans, feminine hygiene spray) and effective when it promotes things we do like or need (nutritious food, fuel-efficient cars). But that facile answer ignores the power of advertising to affect competition.

Selling a new laundry soap requires that a firm have an ad budget large enough to compete with the $680 million total media spending of P & G. Consequently, advertising poses a huge barrier to entry in markets dominated by corporate giants. Advertising entrenches the dominance of old-line firms in "mature" markets. "Industries in which products are intensively advertised have shown major increases in concentration since 1947," observes Wharton School professor Edward Herman.

The ad race also corrodes the competitive market system by encouraging "product differentiation"—that is, packaging and styling which add nothing to the value of the product but which are designed to make products that, in reality, are identical or similar appear unique. As one Boston account executive put it, "When it comes down to it, there really is no difference between one kind of flour and another. But I have to convince people that King Arthur [flour] is better."

This approach encourages firms to compete not by higher quality or lower costs but by marginal product differences. Consultants Booz·Allen and Hamilton found that that product differentiation added $1,000 to the cost of an American car over the past two decades. "Marginal differentiation" is what sociologist David Reisman dubbed this wasteful phenomenon.

Such excessive image advertising has important and disturbing consequences for the whole culture. As Marty Solow says in his office of Durfee and Solow Advertising, a half block off Madison Avenue, "Advertising is our primary means of consumer education. Kids spend more time watching TV than they do in school. The ultimate message that comes through is 'buy.' Advertising creates wants, needs, desires which are assuaged by buying." But isn't the real message the celebration of style over substance, form over fact?

Perhaps it's time for businesses to innovate with a truly "new" and "improved" idea by cutting back on wasteful, uninformative, and downright misleading advertising. If business people would tell their ad agencies what editors tell reporters—"stick to the facts"—we would all be better off.

8

The Gross Legal Product: The High Cost of Lawyers' Featherbedding

The ideal client is rich as Croesus and scared as hell.
—Michael Tigar, Esq.

It is the trade of lawyers to question everything, yield nothing and to talk by the hour.

—Thomas Jefferson

It was, for an American Bar Association annual meeting, an unprecedented event. Usually bar meetings involve lawyers telling other lawyers how wonderful their profession is. But at this August 1977 gathering, in the Grand Ballroom of Chicago's aging Drake Hotel, a panel of eight businessmen lectured four hundred attorneys about what annoyed them in their relationship with counsel. One recurrent leitmotif was the high and growing cost of lawyers.

"Corporate people are becoming much more attentive to the legal cost of doing business," said William Johnson, chairman of the board of IC Industries in Chicago. "Years ago, most legal proceedings were rather unusual. Now there's so much legal work and it's become so customary that it's just another operating expense—a very large one."

Lester Pollack, then chairman of the finance committee of the CNA Financial Corporation of Chicago, agreed with Johnson and elaborated on his thesis. "I think lawyers assume a combative posture best likened to gladiators in an arena, a fight to the death, victory at all costs," he told the corporate attorneys, who listened politely, if not with great enthusiasm. Pollack continued, "I think this tends to expand the litigation and certainly increases the cost of the litigation . . . . The lawyers' [fee] interest sometimes clouds the time to assess the risks of the matter."

Seven years after this candid session, Steven Brill, editor of *The American Lawyer,* interviewed ten corporation general counsels about their assessment of their companies' own outside law firms, and found a level of dissatisfaction not unlike that expressed in the earlier ABA session: The general counsels thought outside firms will overcharge if not watched carefully; are often arrogant; have a significant number of partners and associates who could not make it in-house; and have an inflated view of themselves and their role.

For years, average citizens have strained under the weight of ever higher legal fees. Now it is the turn of large companies— watching the leap in lawyers' rates per hour, in overall fees and in overlawyering—to share in the general dismay. And to wonder what to do about it.

In 1983, corporate legal expenses topped $40 billion—quadruple their 1973 outlays of $9.9 billion. Manufacturing companies are now spending upward of one percent of their total revenues on legal services. Today, the value of legal services, most of which are consumed by the corporate community, exceed that of the steel or electric power industries. With an annualized growth rate of 12.1 percent in 1972–83, legal services have outstripped by fourfold the growth of the economy, and, as of 1984, are for the first time included in the Department of Commerce's Annual Industrial Outlook survey.

Part of the problem is the increasingly lucrative nature of corporate lawyering. A Price Waterhouse survey shows partners at large firms across the country earned a median income of $203,610 in 1983. "Summer associates" pull in an average of $900 a week at large New York firms—an annual rate of $46,000. With salaries like these, it's no wonder that over the last twenty years the number of law graduates has more than doubled and the number of U.S. law schools has gone from 136 to 174. Forty thousand new graduates are coming out of law schools each year to join the 612,000 already practicing.

For corporations, all these facts and figures add up to one thing: exorbitant bills. To give an idea of the magnitude of fees we are talking about; In recent years, Chevron pays Pillsbury, Madison and Sutro of San Francisco $20 million annually and Citibank owes Shearman and Sterling of New York City $25 million a year.

Historically, many businesses have been oddly uninterested in, or reluctant to ask their attorneys about, high fees. Timothy

Robinson, editor-in-chief of the *National Law Journal,* recounts how he and an executive in one of Washington's largest companies scanned the company's legal bills for the previous two years: "The names on the letterhead were Washington's biggest law firms. . . . Then there was a lot of white space on the billing sheet until you came to a line that read something like, 'For legal services rendered,' and following that, a figure that would feed a good sized community for a month. . . . He was as surprised as I was."

Inquiring clients at some firms are told that either they were happy with the quality of the work product or they could go elsewhere. As a result, many major corporate law firms in cities like New York and Washington, D.C., are unilaterally able to set the ground rules of the client-lawyer relationship. Comments corporate critic Ralph Nader, "When I met business executives on airplanes, I used to talk about the weather, because that was the one thing we had in common. Now we talk about outside legal fees."

Why Companies Overpay

Business executives agree that legal fees are high. But how did they get that way? Is it due to the cost of quality work—or the nemesis of "avoidable waste"?

First, corporations pay exorbitant legal fees because no one seems to care. In the words of David Boies, a prominent partner at Cravath, Swaine and Moore, "When the consumer fails to keep track of the costs, the costs will go up." According to a 1981 survey done by the *National Law Journal* of the legal departments of the largest corporations, for every large company that said it closely monitored outside counsel, there were as many that seemed to accept without question outside billings. An Arthur Young study shows that most legal departments require outside counsel to submit budgets "at least occasionally" but that they "are not required as a standard procedure."

Although corporations retain law firms, it is consumers (in the form of higher prices), shareholders (in the form of reduced dividends), and taxpayers (who subsidize some one half of legal expenses because of their deductibility) who end up footing the bill. Yet consumers and taxpayers are obviously unable to determine what percent of their purchase price or tax bill is caused by lawyers' fees—and even if they could, there exists no mechanism by which they could do anything about it.

Nor are shareholders alert to the problem. They rarely, if ever, know the level of outside legal outlays—which, though they run in the millions, are still usually a small percentage of a large corporation's costs of doing business. Indeed, most managements, when possible, keep shareholders uninformed about and uninterested in their legal bills. When dissident shareholders proposed that the Exxon Corporation publish a list of its outside law firms and their fees to detect if there were any conflicts of interest or waste, the Exxon management controlling the shareholder proxy machinery refused and prevailed. The company argued that the data would be too costly to accumulate, which leads to the incredible conclusion that Exxon doesn't already have a list of such firms and fees.

A second factor that jacks up corporate legal costs is not unlike the MAD (mutual assured destruction) theory of the arms race: Each corporate entity, unsure of its opponent's prowess, continues to build its own legal stockpile for fear of being caught short by the other side. The net result is that "the average litigant is overdiscovered, overinterrogated, and overdeposed; and as a result he is overcharged, overexpensed and overwrought," writes Judge Ruggero J. Aldisert of the Third Circuit Court of Appeals. And, according to business adviser John Diebold in his 1984 book, *Making Business Work,* "I know from long experience in business dealings that if anyone walks into a room with a lawyer, everyone else suddenly has to have one too." So the costs in litigation are very much a function of opponents' spending. You can try a case with one lawyer for two years or ten lawyers for twelve months. But it won't be considered fair unless both sides do the same things, and that leads to the kind of excesses that characterize the arms race.

This lack of discipline can be seen in redundancy of efforts— which Xerox general counsel Robert Banks says results in lawsuits being conducted "with all the backups of a manned spaceflight." Duplication of work is legend in large firms, with armies of associates producing careful memorandums of law on points already analyzed by associates down the hall in similar cases. Cases are often overstaffed, a habit perhaps derived from the days when lawyers' ancestors were paid by the word for documents they prepared. "Relatively small legal points seem to me to be way overresearched," notes Jay Pritzker, chairman of

Hyatt Corporation. "In the areas of litigation, I find—particularly in New York—lawyers travel like nuns, in pairs or three at a time, and the clock is running and it's very annoying as a client to observe it helplessly."

Third, there is the prevailing ethos that lawyers perform a complex service requiring expensive legal training, and are therefore entitled to a big income. Lawyers are professionals, not bricklayers, and should earn incomes comparable to their medical brethren. "A lawyer cannot be truly independent unless he is economically secure," attorney Cullen Smith wrote in an ABA publication. "Those lawyers who do not produce adequate income may be tempted to cut corners, solicit business, commingle funds of clients, fall behind in their education and do slipshod work." That is, ethics depends on profits.

Such justifications, incanted often enough, can easily create a constant, upward pressure on corporate legal fees and expenses. This self-fulfilling zeitgeist led bar associations to formulate their traditional "minimum fee schedules," which the Supreme Court, in a 1975 decision, ruled was illegal price-fixing. It is this kind of tradition that leads corporate lawyers today to view rates of $250 an hour as fair, without any need for further explanation.

Fourth, general counsels of major corporations are often forced, by professional pressure if not by traditional corporate ties, to retain only high prestige law firms. "Imagine yourself a new general counsel," hypothesized one Washington attorney in an interview. "You could shop around to see who's good but not expensive. But if you lose the case, the company will scream, 'Idiot, why didn't you get the best?' So you get the best." It is like buying a stereo set, said David Shakow of Davis, Polk and Wardwell. "A $500 set is much better than a $200 set, but a $1,000 unit is only slightly better than a $500 one. The difference between 97 percent satisfaction and 99 percent satisfaction can be very expensive."

Martin Lasser, a former in-house counsel at the Ford Motor Company, describes the high costs of losing with the right people.

> In L.A. a few years ago, the case of *Hasson* v. *Ford* was tried and lost by an insurance defense firm; the verdict was over $3 million. This firm appealed the case to the California Court of Appeals and lost, and then appealed to the California Supreme Court and won a retrial. Just as this firm began preparing for retrial, it was fired. Its legal bill for two and a

half years was well under $1 million. A prestige firm was then hired—McCutcheon, Black, Verleger & Shea—which prepared for retrial (using evidence gathered by the insurance defense firm), retried the case and lost. The verdict this time was well over $10 million. The bill for *six months* was *$1.6 million.*

Not only did Ford want to have the right law firm losing its case, it also considered blind acceptance of the legal fees a price for the privilege of being represented by an elite letterhead. When Lasser sought to challenge what he considered excessive charges for such services as legal research, jury instructions, and depositions, he was told by Ford higher-ups to pay the bill and forget it.

A fifth reason why corporate legal bills are so high is that companies often hand over complete decision-making responsibilities to their lawyers, something William McGowan, CEO of MCI Communications Corporation, calls a "horrible mistake . . . a fundamental, crucial mistake." A corporation that wants to get its money's worth for its multimillion-dollar legal bills must always be in control and in touch with its lawyer.

Good lawyers are advocates, not pragmatists, says McGowan. Their carte blanche approach can lead to wasted time, dollars, and effort. Ted Dinsmoor, a partner at the Boston firm of Gaston, Snow, Ely and Bartlett, agrees. "Lawyers without direction can put in a great deal of time not working towards a client's real goals."

In a case involving Lincoln Steel Products, a group of former employees took customer lists to establish a competing firm. Lincoln Steel, a New York-based manufacturer, retained Marshall, Bratter, Greene, Allison and Tucker to stop them. The firm originally estimated a $25,000 fee. Instead it charged $105,000, based on fifteen pretrial motions, 335 hours expended in trial preparation, and a 103-page post-trial memorandum. Lincoln Steel refused to pay anything over $35,250. Marshall, Bratter sued and lost. Judge John P. Donohoe of the Westchester County Supreme Court said that the original estimate did not mean "carte blanche to proceed to work up a bill. . . . [Marshall, Bratter] lost all perspective as to the needs of its client, the client's ability to pay and the most effective way of obtaining a desirable end."

Sixth, big legal fees reflect the big dollars at stake in big business transactions. If the matter involves a $2-billion acquisition and the investment banker is getting $8 million, the lawyers' fees may be an afterthought, especially since they are tax-deductible expenses. And in such cases, recalled former corporate lawyer Victor Kramer, lawyers often think to themselves, "If a client is making so much money, why shouldn't we?"

For example, once a corporate takeover fight begins, all firms charge higher than usual rates. According to its formal billing policy, one firm specializing in takeovers bases its charges in part on "the responsibility assumed and the result achieved." That means not less than 200 percent and sometimes more than 300 percent of base time charges. Rough translation: $400–$600-plus per hour per lawyer. In the Mobil-Marathon-U.S. Steel struggle, of the dozen or so law firms involved—including Donovan Leisure Newton and Irvine; Jones, Day, Reavis and Pogue; and White and Case—lead counsel for the three companies each had fees of more than $10 million.

Seventh, when lawyers sit on the boards of clients, they can't help but compromise their and their boards' objectivity—or as Justice Louis Brandeis wrote in 1932, "Long ago, it was recognized that 'a man who is his own lawyer has a fool for a client.' The reason for this is that soundness of judgment is easily obscured by self interest." Self-interest can irresistibly tempt a lawyer-director to urge a business strategy that requires billable lawyers hours . . . or that stymies a board's ability to consider competing law firms.

Indeed, Paul Cravath, founder of Cravath, Swaine and Moore, made it firm policy that "neither firm partners nor associates should hold securities of any client, or have a financial interest, direct or indirect, in any transaction in which the firm is acting as counsel." Shortly before retiring, Cravath called for a canon of ethics "forbidding a lawyer in substance to become his own client through acting as a director or officer of a client."

Yet in 1983, thirty-two attorneys served as directors of public companies that paid more than $2 million in fees to their respective firms. Although the percentage of companies with lawyer-directors has dropped from 53 percent to 28.8 percent between 1973 and 1981 in response to criticism, the practice continues for obvious reasons. "Competition," writes one partner of a large Wall Street law firm, "prevents any individual firm from establishing such a policy. The fear of turning around some day and finding a lawyer from a competing firm on the board leads you to keep one of your own partners there."

The eighth and final reason for high legal fees is the failure of corporations to act as tough consumers in policing the wasteful behavior of the law firms themselves.

Billing practices appear to be almost random, or have a "seat-of-the-pants" quality, in Washington lawyer Lionel Kestenbaum's phrase. A big New York City firm associate reports that "one guy bothered me on my honeymoon. That cost them an extra $5000. It didn't bother me and it didn't faze them." According to an informal *American Lawyer* survey, few law firms have a formal policy on how to bill for time spent in planes and taxis. Most leave the decision up to the individual lawyer, which for Melvyn Weiss of New York's Milberg Weiss Bershad Specthrie and Lerach means "Business hours or not, it's my time and I bill it." *The American Lawyer* also found that most lawyers bill for time in cabs going to local meetings. In other words, a firm that charges for the twenty minutes it takes to go to a one-hour meeting is billing 30 percent more than the firm that doesn't.

Everett Clary of Los Angeles' O'Melveny and Myers, in explaining his firm's somewhat mysterious billing policies in the Equity Funding scandal case, reasoned that "the guideline is not an hourly rate to be charged as a plumber would charge for his work, with all due respect to that honorable and necessary profession . . . other factors would require a fee that is some multiple of the guideline. Where the project has special time demands as a result of other factors that were projected, we would normally charge a multiple of the guideline." Clary's justification for the increase should further put businesses on the alert: He cited his firm's hard work under pressure on an important matter. But isn't that what lawyers are presumably supposed to do? It is as if a barber charged $15.00, not $7.50, because hair got in the way of his scissors.

Irregular billing policies crop up regularly when law firms aren't properly monitored. In a 1983 New York State inquiry into the outside legal fees paid by the Metropolitan Transit Authority to labor counsel Davis, Polk and Wardwell, over $2 million in billing discrepancies were turned up. Some fees were as high as $341 an hour, nearly triple the maximum $125 an hour rate allowed other state agencies. Bills from Davis, Polk summarized the work by saying meetings were held, research documented, and contracts prepared. But there was no statement of the number of lawyers, for how long or at what rate they worked. Sidney Schwartz, inspector general for the MTA, found in spot checkups about seven instances in which records of lawyers' hours were counted twice.

Such haphazard billing practices result in what can only be characterized as absurd fees. In the now infamous *Corrugated Container* price-fixing action, attorney Stephen Susman and his Houston law firm were awarded $7.4 million for work done over a period of three years. Aggregate fees for all firms involved worked out to $250 an hour, but the records show that Susman's firm collected $300–$1,000 per hour. (Susman has disputed the calculations that show his firm garnering such high hourly fees and protested that the award of fees is "complicated.")

Like the executives who overindulge in little-reported perquisites, whom we met in Chapter 5, "From Pay to Perks to Parachutes," some attorneys similarly pass on the costs of high living in high bills. In one glaring case, Winthrop Munyan, a partner at Curtis, Mallet-Prevost, Colt and Mosle, ran up $1.9 million in fees and disbursements working as a tax lawyer for wealthy Americans living abroad before he was kicked out of the prestigious New York law firm. According to court papers, Munyan and his wife flew the Concorde to Europe, paid on average $75 per person for lunches and dinners, and booked expensive rooms they did not use. On one trip, they kept a suite at the exclusive Connaught Hotel in London, another at the Hotel Regina in Paris, and stayed at neither. While partner Keith Highet charged in a deposition that "they lived like potentates," Curtis, Mallet and its clients will have to pay the $1.9 million unless it wins its pending action against Munyan.

As these eight phenomena indicate, the law firm market is a perversion of the competitive market. "There's nobody standing on our shoulders keeping fees and expenses down," observed Victor Kramer. Those who pay—consumers, taxpayers, shareholders—have no real say. And those who hire—general counsels—often institutionally favor well-known big name firms, in part because they may have spent their early professional years at these firms. Indeed, in a demonstration of Groucho Marx's quip that he would never join a club with standards so low as to accept him, corporate law firms who charge very big fees become per se the most prestigious. Low fees become a sign of low status. To large corporations, a Cravath, Swaine and Moore is Tiffany, and Covington and Burling, Gucci. How else can you explain the client of one New York City law firm who eagerly supported a hike in his law firm's fees, considering it clear evidence the firm was an even higher quality outfit than previously imagined.

Alternatives to Excessive Lawyers

There is a fear among some lawyers that fees have become so high that corporate law firms may eventually price themselves out of the business market. With the average partner billing rate $183 an hour in New York and $168 in Los Angeles, and with fresh law school graduates able to command salaries upward of $47,000, it's no wonder Charles D. Breitel, past chief judge of the New York State Court of Appeals, charged that if lawyers just continue to "grab, grab, grab . . . they may be killing the goose that lays the golden egg."

Until recently, wasteful practices and high fees by law firms have been matched only by the incompetence of corporations in controlling these costs. But as many budget-conscious managers are discovering, the high cost of legal services can be confronted and controlled. From building in-house legal departments to using alternative dispute resolution to becoming good old-fashioned consumers, there are a host of cost-saving models that can meet the objections of both frustrated corporations and dismayed lawyers like Judge Breitel.

In-house Counsel

In-house departments are one of the fastest-growing segments of the legal economy—attorneys working for corporations doubled between 1970 and 1980—and with good reason: It is about one half as expensive to use an in-house lawyer on salary per year as it is to pay an outside lawyer per hour. The average cost per attorney for an in-house staff is $85 an hour (the range is $66–$94) with senior attorneys averaging an annual salary, with bonuses, of $67,581. The reported average billing rate for a New York partner is $183, while the national median income for partners in large firms is, again, $203,610. The arithmetic became all too clear to Standard Oil Company of Ohio when it chose to add another lawyer to its own staff at $50,000 instead of retaining an outside firm for an antitrust case at half a million dollars.

"In-housers" can also do legwork that would otherwise be billed at high outside rates. Mobil Oil Corporation, for example, uses its own staff for some discovery procedures; and at Aetna Life and Casualty Company, no outside paralegals are used without the consent of department chairman Peter Mear—again, not only because Aetna paralegals are billed at less than one half the rate of outside paralegals (about $40 an hour versus an annual Aetna salary of $14,300), but also because they know and understand the company better.

Preventive legal care is probably the single most valuable aspect of a sophisticated in-house staff. When company lawyers and paralegals are familiar with its operations and are involved on a daily basis with the decision-making process, they not only become problem solvers but problem spotters. Luther McKinney, vice-president of law and corporate affairs at Quaker Oats, believes he was hired precisely because the company felt the need for a lawyer knowledgeable about federal procedures and the legislative process *before the fact*. "Even though there are terrific cost pressures . . . I don't think that's the only explanation for the growth of in-house departments," he says. "In the business structure it has become desirable to have someone on staff who is more familiar with the issues and who can provide informed counsel."

Because lawsuits are filed all over the country and are better handled by local counsel, litigation is the one area still performed primarily by outside legal expertise. Still, effective general counsel in companies can put a lid on spiraling litigation costs by utilizing a budget process. Robert Banks, the Xerox Corporation general counsel widely credited with putting litigation budgets on the map, acknowledges lawyers' complaints that budgeting in litigation is an imprecise science. "Recognizing the existence of unknown factors, and estimating their impact is hardly unheard of in financial planning," he says, adding that the budget is a "tremendous management tool. It gives you an insight into strategy and tactics, and it can't help but make you cost-conscious. When I began this [budgeting campaign at Xerox], I had a selling job to do in house. A lot of lawyers think it's too demeaning, it's nonprofessional, but that's because lawyers don't know how to manage."

As Xerox was winding down its massive antitrust action, for example, Banks trimmed outside legal expenses more than $12 million in 1982. In the same period, the law department shrank from 152 lawyers to 70. Of course, litigation had greatly subsided, but at the same time the legal department had assumed responsibility for other areas of the law while Xerox Corporation was doubling in size.

Since Peter Mear has taken over the helm at the litigation department of Connecticut-based Aetna Life and Casualty, he's slashed the budget by 30 percent. For every suit handed to an outside firm, Mear requires a budget and strategy session to lay the ground rules. The session is usually followed up by a written agreement reiterating the points of the meeting, including the objectives of the case, the division of work, and estimate of fees.

Alternative Dispute Resolution

Alternative dispute resolutions (ADRs) offer a less adversarial, nonjudicial approach to disputes. ADRs encourage the negotiation and deal cutting more often associated with executives than with lawyers. They come in three basic versions—minitrials, mediation, and arbitration.

Minitrials. "You can get control back into the hands of businessmen who will bring some common sense to bear," says TRW vice-president James McKee of minitrials, which his company has used to solve some of its disputes. This method gives decision-making power to the corporate executives involved, who tend to focus on business rather than legal concerns.

In a minitrial, each side's lawyers make informal and abbreviated presentations of their cases to a judicial panel consisting of three or more members: a top management executive from each party plus a neutral adviser. The lawyers argue the case to the principals, with the adviser moderating the proceedings and pointing out important facts and issues.

Here's how minitrials work: An ADR consulting firm offers both parties a selection of available advisers, generally retired jurists and eminent trial lawyers, whom participants must approve. (Such advisers have included former Judge Simon Rifkind, former cabinet secretary Elliot Richardson, and Ambassador Sol Linowitz.) The management representatives then meet privately with the adviser to debate the merits of the case and to negotiate a settlement. If a settlement fails to emerge quickly, the adviser may be asked to produce a nonbinding opinion on how a court would probably decide the case. The parties then resume negotiating with a clearer picture of how they might fare in court. Costs are controlled by limiting pretrial preparation and discovery as well as oral arguments and questioning.

Wisconsin Electric Power Company (WEP) and American

Can Company estimate they saved more than a year and untold legal bills when they turned to Endispute, the first ADR group in the country to settle a complicated contract dispute. The conflict arose in late 1982 when WEP canceled its contract to purchase garbage-processed fuel from American Can. Disputed claims totaled $61 million for both parties. After the two sides estimated that a trial would take about seventy-five days and could not get under way for two years, they called in Endispute in January 1983. By September, negotiations and settlement were complete, with the parties agreeing to cancel the original contract and WEP agreeing to help American Can sell off its refuse treatment plant.

Former Judge Harold Tyler, Jr., presided over the minitrial, charging his normal partner rate of his New York law firm, Patterson, Belknap, Webb and Tyler. Endispute was paid on an hourly basis of $150–$250 per principal. Tyler spent a total of sixty–seventy hours on the case. "Compared with the total expenses anticipated for a major case of this sort, the costs associated with the minitrial were very modest," said one American Can attorney. Even if no settlement had been reached, Wisconsin Electric's general counsel Robert Gorske estimated, the parties could "salvage 90 percent [of the minitrial costs] in terms of better, earlier preparation for the trial itself."

The cost-effectiveness of minitrials varies with the size of the claim involved. When billions of dollars are at stake, if not the future of an industry, a corporation may prefer to pull out the stops and ignore thrift. On the other hand, in cases involving small damages that require little discovery, parties may not be best served by an ADR consultation which could result in a stalemate. Minitrials are best suited for cases in between the huge and the small, allowing both lawyers and executives to do what they do best: lawyers championing positions and executives closing deals.

Mediation. Led by an impartial mediator, mediation emphasizes negotiations between the disputants. The mediator is often experienced in the problems at issue and helps guide the parties to a resolution. Unlike courtroom litigation or arbitration, mediation allows the parties themselves to hammer out the settlement from the start. In 1983, for example, Chicago's Jenner and Block formed a dispute resolution group to provide clients with a negotiator to work separately from litigators as a way to resolve complex disputes. Jenner and Block partner William

Snapp who brought a real estate investment client to the ADR group, was able to resolve the dispute without litigation. "What came out of the settlement negotiations were that the parties had compatible interests. . . . It was a matter of bringing in someone who could take a fresh look at it and [who] had not been involved in the litigation."

Arbitration. Arbitration requires participants to present their arguments to an impartial arbitrator, whose judgment is final, binding and virtually nonreviewable (unless the parties opt for nonbinding arbitration). Often contracts specify that differences be settled by arbitration rather than a court of law. Arbitrators are chosen by mutual agreement of the parties or with the aid of the American Arbitration Association or a judge. Discovery, if any, is limited. The arbitrators are not bound by the rules of evidence and do not have to explain their determinations.

Smart shopping

By far the most effective alternative to lawyers' featherbedding and fee hiking is intelligent consumerism. Most people wouldn't buy a house without shopping around, negotiating, determining a price, checking out the structure and foundation. Why shouldn't a business person use the same approach with lawyers?

Shop around and negotiate. There is nothing sacrosanct about outside counsel—just because a corporation has used law firm X for twenty years doesn't mean it must continue to use firm X. Law firms should be forced to be competitive. In looking around for counsel to handle a matter, companies should require law firms to demonstrate what they can offer in terms of competitive rates, experience, and speed.

When the Northeast Solid Waste Committee, a consortium of twenty-two Massachusetts communities, was set up to build garbage-powered energy plants in 1984, one of the first things they did in seeking to float a $200-million bond issue was solicit bids for a law firm. "Corporations are realizing that they can negotiate with the law firms they currently employ and that other equally good firms will put in bids for their business," comments Boston attorney Leonard Kopelman. And in return for steady work, corporations are asking for and getting flat fees. Kopelman also suggests that incentives be included in legal services contracts: "After you get the bill down through negotiation, propose something like this: We want a ten percent discount. At the end of the year, we'll sit down and negotiate whether you get nothing more because of poor service, full payment if you did a good job, or a bonus of twenty-five percent if you were innovative and kept costs down."

At the same time, corporate clients should try to divide up work among firms to provide "yardstick competition." Often a large company's legal problems require many attorneys. To the extent practicable, businesses should give legal work to a couple of law firms in one city. A client can then tell more readily if one firm is overcharging and overlawyering, or if both are roughly comparable. Also, they should compare intercity performance and charges. This approach is consistent with the spirit of the 1975 Supreme Court decision, *Bates* v. *State of Arizona,* in which the Court struck down a ban on the advertising of fee information.

Inquire about rates. Once a law firm is selected, shyness at asking about specific fees at the opening conference is tantamount to surrendering your car to a mechanic with the instruction, "There's a funny noise under the hood." Corporations at this initial stage should always cross-examine the law firm about predicted expenses and their rates—for paralegals, junior associates, senior associates, junior partners, and senior partners.

Companies should be careful that expenses are separated from legal fees and that each is broken down into its major components. Also, hourly rates are not etched in some stone, but vary according to various subjective considerations. It is essential for cost-conscious clients to find out whether they were billed at the usual "guideline" rate or at premium or a discount—and why. "Keeping the communications going is the way we get our money's worth," says MCI Communications general counsel John Worthington, "and we spend millions."

For those skeptics who say final fees are unpredictable, there is an answer: They're wrong. "One of the problems is, on the face of it, that litigation is thought to be unpredictable," observes William Langston of the Homestake Mining Company. "But in the real world it is predictable. When you work on a per-hour basis, and there are only so many hours in a week and so many weeks in a month, and you take a look at the number of people you staff on a project, you get a pretty quick idea of what costs can be cut. . . . Any in-house counsel who doesn't try to call the shots is copping out," he continues. "Law firms are institutions run by rules and to a degree bound by them. But you just have to try and get around them . . . you can't afford to have the outside counsel own you."

He continues with a colorful anecdote. "You ask a doctor how much an operation is going to cost. Most will tell you. Of course if he opens you up and finds a can of worms you can't expect him to stick to it, and you can't on some major antitrust cases. But you can on most matters."

Determine ground rules from the start and use a budget. Says MCI's Worthington, "When a matter comes up and we're hiring outside counsel, we want fees, the time needed and who will be used and how it will be handled all made clear. We put them on a budget and while we must be flexible, we expect that any substantial deviation from the budget will be explained."

Xerox's Robert Banks, who spends over $5 million a year on outside legal fees, demands a budget from all firms that service his law department. Over one hundred firms submit in advance a projection of fees as well as an overall legal strategy. In addition, Banks issues a written billing policy with rules such as "Charges for air travel, except on international trips of ten elapsed hours or more, will be at the coach rate."

Similarly, in 1983 Control Data issued a tough new policy statement to its outside lawyers saying that it will not normally pay for such desirable long-term law firm investments as computerized legal research, word processing, special publications, and attendance at continuing legal education seminars—all items that might have been included in past bills. Out of town travel must be approved in advance by Control Data attorneys, as must the hiring of associate counsel, consultants, or expert witnesses. Controls at Household Finance Corporation are just as stiff. Robert Bourman, the general counsel of Household International Incorporated, the parent company, explains that "outside counsel doesn't do anything without our permission."

Keep inquiring as the matter progresses. The era of quarterly legal bills that simply had a total dollar figure next to the explanation "For services rendered," should be over. Arnold and Porter won a new major client in 1984 because the client was furious that its prior law firm submitted no bill for four months—and then sent a six-figure bill.

Avoid overstaffing. Corporate clients ought to inquire how many attorneys are working on your particular matter, and what their specific responsibilities are. Even lay queries—"Why do we need two senior partners in court rather than one?," "Why do we need three associates at the deposition?" or "Why aren't paralegals doing the statistical work rather than associates?"—can put law firms on notice that you are a careful consumer, and hence discourage legal featherbedding.

What is the internal organization of the firm? Just as a house hunter wants to know about the foundation of a home, a business client, with its substantial managerial skills, may want to observe and comment on the managerial practices of its law firm. Beyond such details as the paralegal-lawyer ratio (one to four is about right), the critical issue is whether or not the law firm has an administrative partner and an overhead budget. If not, a client should not be surprised at law firm waste, big expenses, and, hence, high bills.

Avoiding Lawyers

Preventive law can be practiced by either inside or outside counsel: At some companies, such as Chicago's Household International, for example, lawyers conduct legal "audits" to determine if the company is violating equal credit or environmental laws. Avoiding lawsuits helps avoid lawyers.

Also, corporations should push to settle early and often. The cost of litigation may often be more than 100 percent of the difference between the parties' views. It would be in the corporations' best interests to require a cooling-off period after the initiation of legal action, where no action could take place and a settlement would have to be discussed. As William Langston has said, "Traditional legal proceedings are, at best, wasteful and time consuming. Once legal proceedings begin, you lose some control over your own affairs. Most major legal proceedings are resolved by settlement. It is often easier and less expensive to settle before positions have hardened."

Avoiding Court Delays

The *Federal Rules of Civil Procedure* were written before electronic reproduction, word processing, or even electric typewriters. The rules for document production, depositions, and interrogation were designed to help small litigants find out facts. Now in the 1980s, in the era of modern office systems, those same procedures have the opposite of their intended effect. The rules of civil procedure can encourage lengthy discovery, the costs of which account for up to 90 percent of litigation. If those rules were modified to provide greater judicial supervision in civil cases, the length and costs of court proceedings could be greatly reduced.

"Except in exceptional cases, we should give only two years for a case to be brought to trial and that for an exceptionally large case," says trial lawyer David Boies, who, having tried the IBM-antitrust and CBS-Westmoreland cases, is in a position to know. Such constraints would force lawyers to decide what they need to get done. Currently courts allow so much discovery because there's no time limit. It would vastly improve the situation, continues Boies, "if a corporation and its lawyers, when they get into litigation, could agree to try a case within a certain time frame, to limit their demands and set their own rules."

Some combination, or certainly all, of the five steps described above—in-house counsel, alternate dispute resolution, smart shopping, avoiding lawyers, avoiding court delays—could enable corporations to reduce law firm waste and bills. Companies that perennially complain about their lawyers but do nothing about it are like citizens who bellyache about politicians but never vote. If corporate executives treat law firm bills as leniently as they often do their own pay and perks, then lawyer waste will continue to be another bloated charge passed on to consumers. When it comes to lawyers' fees, as in so many other areas of internal corporate economics, managers should spend *shareholders'* money as if it were *their* money.

9

Corporate Welfare: America's Implicit Industrial Policy

If tomorrow it was announced that all government intervention in business were ended, there would be coronaries in every boardroom.

—Senator Paul Laxalt (R., Nev.)

Here I was, a free enterpriser, coming hat in hand and asking for government involvement and regulation and so forth. . . . Somebody's got to do the damn thing. I couldn't just sit around and be ideological.

—Lee Iacocca, CEO of Chrysler, of his successful effort to obtain a $1.5-billion federal loan guarantee

"It's time to cut back on unwarranted subsidies for business. Let's get rid of corporate welfare." Is this Ralph Nader launching another consumer crusade? No, it is Congressman Jack Kemp, the conservative Republican, speaking about the need to get off the corporate dole.

Government intervention to benefit business can assume many guises—direct and indirect subsidy programs, bailouts, tariffs and quotas, federal tax "incentives," Pentagon procurement policies and state "incentives" for new plants—but they all add up to an increasing corporate dependency on public aid. Call it "corporate welfare," or, in the cheeky formulation of Public Citizen's Congress Watch, Aid for Dependent Corporations (AFDC). Government subsidies and tax preferences to advance particular industries, for example, have grown from $77.1 billion in 1950 (9.2 percent of the GNP) to $303.7 billion in 1980 (13.9 percent of the GNP).

How could this happen in the face of a business ideology so hostile to a larger government role in the economy? As Lee Iacocca's opening comment indicates, the answer is need over creed—and the political power of private, commercial interests to redefine the Constitution's "general welfare" clause as meaning "corporate welfare."

This is a long and well-recounted story. James Madison told the Constitutional Convention that his greatest fear for our new democracy was the power of *private* groups. Around the beginning of the twentieth century, Thorstein Veblen concluded that in a representative government, corporate interests hold sway: "It seldom happens, if at all, that the government of a civilized nation will persist in a course of action detrimental, or not ostensibly subservient, to the interests of the community's businessmen." Two decades later, President Wilson complained that "the government of the United States at present is a foster child of special interests"—and six decades later, scholar Grant McConnell's book *Private Power and American Democracy* explained how organized interests got their way in a democracy. More recently, Mancur Olson's *The Rise and Decline of Nations* developed his theory how, in nations current and past, special interest economic groups used the government as a sort of accounts receivable—preserving their benefits at the cost of economic stagnation.

This cost is actually threefold: *waste to consumers, waste to the economy,* and even *waste internal to the company* that is the apparent beneficiary. Consumers suffer because they pay higher prices for domestic products when trade barriers keep out high-quality and low-priced imports. The economy generally suffers when business tax preferences and loan guarantees create massive dislocations in the allocation of capital. What William Niskanen, a member of President Reagan's Council of Economic Advisors, said in an interview in his White House office about bailouts applies as well to most corporate welfare. "Even if those particular episodes, ex-post, look like they were a success, it doesn't mean they were the right thing to do. Because we gave money to Lockheed and Chrysler means that somebody else didn't get it. Who it was who didn't get the capital is not known. . . . But that's a problem with our political system because it focuses on the particular."

As for waste internal to the corporation, when a business seeks and obtains federal assistance, it must increasingly invest executive time and firm funds in the political marketplace instead of the economic marketplace; it chooses to make safer, short-term investments that exploit the subsidy state rather than make riskier, long-term investment to counter international competition; and when a company or industry persuades the government to shield it from the usual rigors of marketplace competition, the beneficiary can grow lax and inefficient, enjoying what Judge Learned Hand in another context referred to as "the quiet life" of a monopolist. It's especially at this confluence of America's two great bureaucracies—federal and corporate—that the economy falters and waste proliferates.

How Business Regulates Washington

Federal Loans: Back-Door Subsidies

Washington's zeal for subsidizing private activity has produced this fiscal irony: The U.S. government is at the same time the world's biggest debtor and the private sector's biggest creditor.

In 1983, Congress added nearly $200 billion in deficit spending to the national debt, crowding out business borrowing and bidding up of interest rates. But largely hidden from public view and congressional scrutiny, a handful of federal agencies that same year extended or sponsored a total of $286 billion in new credit to corporations and consumers through some 350 different loan programs. Net federal lending alone amounted to 22 percent of the total funds advanced in U.S. credit markets in 1982. Because of this magnitude, federal credit programs have a major influence on who does or does not receive financing and on the cost of capital for all business enterprises.

During 1985, total outstanding federal and federally assisted credit will pass the $1 *trillion* mark. This is like a second national debt—except this one is owed by the private sector to the government.

While the bulk of this $1 trillion in credit is floated to needy individuals who would otherwise be unable to finance a socially desirable purchase—such as students trying to obtain an education or low-income farmers and veterans a home—another large chunk flows to businesses in selected industries. Of the $21 billion in direct loans and $18 billion in loan guarantees extended to businesses in 1984, 98 percent issued from five programs: the Export-Import Bank, the Rural Electrification Administration, the Small Business Administration, the Commodity Credit Corporation, and the Agricultural Credit Insurance Fund. By shouldering all or most of the default risk, these programs secured credit for uses that might otherwise be deemed too risky to qualify for financing or require a risk premium. But since many recipients, such as utilities and foreign buyers of big-ticket export items, could easily borrow at prevailing market rates, they end up paying below-market rates when the government assumes the risk of default.

For example, in 1984 the farm sector harvested the equivalent of 11.5 percent of its annual production value in direct federal subsidy and credit aid, while utilities netted 4.2 percent. The business of agriculture is hugely affected by the Commodity Credit Corporation, which alone accounts for 25 percent of all spending on credit that directly supports private industry.

Other smaller and less visible programs offer low-interest loans to preferred industries. In 1983, the Federal Aviation Administration guaranteed the supposedly deregulated airline industry 90 percent of the principal and 100 percent of the interest on loans up to $100 million per company for the purchase of aircraft and equipment. Under authority of the Merchant Marine Act of 1936, the Maritime Administration guarantees about $900 million in construction mortgage loans each year to help shipping companies build U.S. flag vessels in the United States. The fate of the program is uncertain once it reaches its legal limit of $9.5 *billion* in outstanding loan guarantees during 1985. Direct and guaranteed loans are given to multinational investors by the Overseas Private Investment Corporation (OPIC), which claims to encourage economic development overseas by advancing investment funds and insuring against losses due to political upheaval.

The Congressional Budget Office has also warned that loan subsidies can make a nuclear power plant commercially viable when it should never have been built at all. Since the nation currently has between 10 and 20 percent more electric power capacity than it needs to maintain peak period reserves, the net effect of the credit program is to drain the economy of more capital than is transferred to consumers in the form of lower electric bills.

Credit assistance shares with tax expenditures several generic problems of inefficiency and market distortion. One dollar of government-subsidized capital does not add one dollar in capital resources to the favored activity because many (if not most) business recipients would make the investment regardless—and if they wouldn't, you have to wonder why. The primary effect is to substitute government-subsidized financing for equity capital and private borrowing. Since the government is funneling more than 20 percent of all the capital available on U.S. credit markets to these preferred users, it bids up the costs for other borrowers, which distorts the availability and allocation of investment capital.

Even where credit assistance appears to be set up to encourage any firm pursuing a preferred activity, such as export promotion, the benefits are highly uneven across firms and industries. The Export-Import Bank provided about $11.5 billion in direct and guaranteed loans at below-market interest rates in 1984 to finance foreign purchases of U.S. export goods. Since the mid-1970s, though, more than two thirds of the Ex-Im Bank's credits have gone to subsidize the purchase of aircraft and electric-power-generating equipment, both of which are almost entirely purchased by foreign governments from the largest U.S. multinationals. Unless the Ex-Im Bank is a disguised vehicle for foreign aid, it seems that a smaller firm trying to establish itself abroad with a new product would be a more deserving target. But Ex-Im has a predilection for big over small: 70 percent of its loans enrich just seven large corporations, including General Electric, Westinghouse, and Boeing.

Ironically, the one low-interest loan program for business that is reasonably targeted at enterprises otherwise unable to secure conventional financing is the one most often singled out for elimination—the Small Business Administration. The SBA's business loan and investment fund operates on two tiers. If a small business cannot come up with sufficient collateral to secure a commercial loan, it can qualify for a loan guarantee. If it is still unable to secure the bank loan, the SBA can issue a direct loan (up to its limit of about $1.3 billion each year). Distortions in the capital markets are not as significant in programs like SBA that are at least targeted at new wealth and new job-creating activity, which most certainly would not have happened in its absence.

Federal Handouts: Front-Door Subsidies

Perhaps more than anyone, Matthew Lesko should understand the early 1984 headline in *The Wall Street Journal,* "Soaring Success for Select Businesses." Lesko started his business by grace of a federally guaranteed loan, and, literally, subsidies *are* his business. A self-made millionaire by age thirty-five, Lesko compiles information on some one thousand different grant, subsidy, and credit programs for executives and others who could profit from them. His book, *Getting Yours,* can help you join the ranks of the Golden Door health spa in California, which received $1.75 million in financial and technical assistance from the Small Business Administration. Low-interest loans are fine, Lesko counsels, but from Erica Jong (who got a $6,000 grant from the National Endowment for the Arts to write *Fear of Flying*) to the Shell Oil Company (which repaid nearly $3 million in a single year in agriculture subsidies) cash grants are the least-risk form of Aid for Dependent Corporations.

While direct subsidy programs are probably the least costly version of "lemon socialism," providing nearly $14 billion to business enterprise annually, they are also the most visible. What they lack in magnitude, direct payment programs make up for in sheer charity. Unlike the beneficiaries of tax expenditures, protectionism, and federal credit activities, these recipients rarely bother to explain their largesse as a society-serving incentive intended to stimulate new capital investment or to save American jobs from alien competitors. From sugar, dairy, and tobacco price supports (which together cost consumers and taxpayers about $6 billion each year), to cheap hydroelectric power from Hoover Dam, to the Clinch River Breeder Reactor—direct subsidy programs share the simple virtue of appearing to be exactly what they are: a grab for cash by a few industries or firms with constituencies powerful enough to command access to the public purse.

Agriculture, of course, is the most dependent federal client, receiving $8 billion in direct aid in 1984, and over $20 billion including credit and other federal supports. Fully 8.3 percent of the farming sector's total value added came from direct subsidies and an additional 3.2 percent from low-interest credit assistance. The costliest of the Commodity Credit Corporation's direct payment programs is the Target Price Program, which pays a farmer the difference between a commodity's "target price" and the actual market price, if the latter is lower.

It may well be a legitimate social goal to help keep family farmers in business. But then why are there subsidy programs for cotton, wheat, corn, rice, and feed grains—but not for fruits, vegetables, poultry, and livestock? Why was the traditional $50,000 ceiling on price support payments to any one farmer waived, allowing dozens of agribusiness conglomerates to reap in excess of $1 million each in 1983? And why make the benefits under programs like target pricing and the ill-fated payment in kind (PIK) system proportional to output, which disproportionately benefits the largest, most profitable agribusiness concerns? In 1981, 80 percent of direct farm subsidies went to the most successful 29 percent of grain and cotton firms.

Sometimes "special interest" subsidies pile billions onto the national debt in the name of a more general interest, such as "consumer protection." A good example concerns one of J. Peter Grace's 2,478 ideas to cut wasteful public spending—charging market rates for hydroelectric power generated by the Hoover Dam. In 1984, Congress extended—to the year 2017—a contract written in 1937 that guarantees electric power to parts of Nevada, Arizona, and southern California at Depression-era prices one fifth to one fifteenth those that unsubsidized businesses and residences pay. It's a strange sort of "consumer protection" that provides one region electricity at half a cent per kilowatt because of Senator Barry Goldwater's repeated protestation that otherwise it would cost him $500 to air-condition his four-bedroom home.

Another type of direct subsidy arises when the government decides private investors are too timid, shortsighted, or thinly capitalized to supply what Washington imagines to be a demand for some society-serving product—such as nonrenewable energy. One government-sponsored study, for example, estimated that between 1950 and 1980, taxpayers spent more than $250 *billion* in direct and indirect subsidies to supply energy to corporations and over $20 billion in direct subsidies to the nuclear power industry alone (for reactor development, research, regulation, and uranium enrichment).*

This significant amount notwithstanding, the government prepared to underwrite what was expected to be the largest energy-subsidy ever, the Synthetic Fuels Corporation (SFC), part of President Carter's plan in 1979 to replace 2.5 million barrels of oil per day with synthetic fuel. Congress authorized as much as $88 billion in government-backed loans and price supports over twelve years to develop a private sector synthetic fuels industry. But by the end of 1984, only five synfuel plants had received federal funds, and the SFC was scheduled to be completely

---

*One energy expert, Amory Lovins, founder of the Rocky Mountain Institute, estimates that when the value of tax expenditures, subsidized credit, and hidden subsidies like the Price-Anderson Act—a law passed in 1957 that makes the federal government liable for all damage due to a nuclear accident exceeding $560 million—are included, the total cost of federal subsidies to nuclear power alone is closer to $68 billion.

phased out the following year, after having spent $10 billion. In 1983, the agency spent $19.4 million for administrative expenses versus $820,750 to fund a single project. Of course, that's a far cry from the ambitious goals of lawmakers who claimed in 1980 that by the end of the decade dozens of federally supported synfuels plants would dot the western states and stimulate the production of two million barrels a day of synthetic crude by 1992. But by 1983, a worldwide oil glut, falling energy prices, and slackening demand made the subsidies appear embarrassingly wasteful.

A final subsidy was as traditional as the political pork barrel— the project pushed through by some powerful committee chairman from a state that would most benefit.

Possibly the biggest such boondoggle of all was the Clinch River Breeder Reactor. First authorized by Congress a decade ago, because of the influential voice of Senator Howard Baker (R., Tenn.), the breeder reactor was much ballyhooed as the flagship research project of the nuclear industry—a nuclear power plant that could indefinitely produce more energy than it consumed. Built along the Clinch River in Tennessee, it was originally projected to cost $669 million. But by late 1981, as a study by the House Energy and Commerce Committee reported, the project was a management and financial fiasco. The committee report blamed most problems on the "unbelievably loose" and unenforceable construction contracts the government entered into with Westinghouse, the prime contractor. Cost overruns of 450 percent lifted total estimates to $3.2 billion by early 1982, although the General Accounting Office, the investigatory arm of Congress, warned that final costs could exceed $8 billion. And since the project's private sponsors were limited to a onetime $257 million investment, the government paid the difference—more than $1.6 billion before the project was finally abandoned in 1983.

Bailouts: "All Anyone Wants Is a Fair Advantage"

By 1985, it may seem a bit prudishly principled to question bailing out big banks and corporations. After all, aren't Chrysler and Lockheed securely on their feet and even profitable again? Chrysler not only survived but reported record profits by the first quarter of 1983, leaving the U.S. Treasury a tidy profit on sale of options in the automaker's stock.

Yet however comforting to the collective psyche, bailouts are economic laetrile—they can mask and delay the verdict of the market, but a permanent cure they are not. If bailouts *really* produce a net benefit to society rather than compensation to select workers and stockholders at someone else's expense, how could the government in good conscience let *any* firm fail? With enough federal capital, concessions, and guarantees, couldn't Congress pass a law to assure that *every* company can stay in business forever if it wants to? To imagine hundreds, even thousands of bailouts is to reveal the flaw in the formula. Since bailouts essentially redistribute someone else's job or profits to the failing firm, their extensive use would be at best a costly leveling exercise, redistributing a shrinking pie. They forgive inefficiency, reward failure, and allocate their mercies to those companies and unions powerful enough to obtain political favoritism. Ultimately, bailouts bring to mind former Senator Warren Magnuson's apt aphorism, "All anybody wants is a fair advantage."

As economic commentators like Robert J. Samuelson have pointed out, bailed-out firms must inevitably shed their unprofitable operations or remain forever on the dole. Despite the $1.5-billion loan guarantee it received in 1980, for instance, Chrysler slashed its payroll in half, from 132,000 workers in 1978 to 68,000 workers in 1983.

Thanks to its friends in Nixon White House, Lockheed survived the eye-popping cost overruns it ran up on the C-5A Galaxy military transport plane. In fact, while Lockheed's $250-million federal loan guarantee amounted to a premium-free risk insurance policy that never led to public liability, the bailout was far from cost-free. The Department of Defense also agreed at the time to absorb more than $1 billion in cost overruns on the C-5A that congressional critics argued Lockheed was obliged to pay under the terms of the original contract.

Deputy Secretary of Defense David Packard, now chairman of Hewlett-Packard Company, argued at the time that Lockheed's collapse would jeopardize national security as well as sixty thousand jobs, most in his and the President's home state of California. But after Lockheed's decade of decline as a defense innovator—and its $2.5-billion loss on the L-1011 Tristar commercial aircraft—Packard now doubts the wisdom of such artificial resuscitation. "Looking back on it, I don't think it would have been a disaster if Lockheed had gone under," the billionaire electronics pioneer recently said.

With federal aid, though, Lockheed was able to continue production of the Tristar, and its ill-fated effort to compete in the commercial airliner business. But since the bailout alone couldn't make the Tristar profitable, the company eventually stopped producing jumbo jets. If Lockheed had been forced to spin off its profitable military business, the McDonnell Douglas Corporation's DC-10, or the Boeing Company's 747, it could have reached the break-even point sooner on their risky investments in jumbo jet production. That's why industry insiders are quicker than government bureaucrats to identify the unsung heroes of the Chrysler and Lockheed bailouts—competitors who saw the increased market share they won fair and square in the marketplace snatched away by federal intervention.

In the case of Chrysler, the hidden costs of the bailout were split in some unknown proportion among GM, Ford, American consumers, small businesses, and Japanese automakers whose "voluntary" import restraints after 1979 were probably the single biggest factor in Chrysler's—and Detroit's—comeback by 1983. The Chrysler bailout significantly strengthened Ford's and GM's cases for import quotas. After all, if government intervention was going to keep Ford and GM from capturing Chrysler's share of the U.S. market, then government intervention should at least guarantee that Toyota and Nissan didn't take away their existing shares.

In addition to prolonging inefficiencies by being discriminatory, defensive, and redistributive, the very existence of a government rescue crew on call begins to have distorting effects on business decision-making. It is entirely conceivable that after the 1984 nationalization of Continental Illinois Bank, loan officers at the big New York banks perceive the downside risk of loans to risky energy ventures and developing countries a bit differently. Unspoken assurances of a safety net surround them. The year before the FDIC breathed new life (and $4 billion) into Continental Bank, Congress voted to pump another $8.4 billion into the nearly bankrupt veins of the International Monetary Fund (IMF). The IMF, in turn, will grant that money to the same Third World governments to ensure they don't threaten a collapse of the international financial system by defaulting on their interest payments to big American banks. Thanks to the IMF bailout, loan officers at Chase Manhattan Bank, among others, sleep better after rolling the unpaid principal on those overdue foreign government loans into new, larger loans.

Investors can also be influenced. Savvy stock analysts today study politics. If a corporation or its workers have enough political clout to put the firm on Washington's list of companies "too big to let fail," then a speculator would be wise to gleefully buy in, even as other more traditional investors bail out. One portfolio manager, a top executive at a multibillion-dollar equitable fund in California, told an investment management class at the Stanford Business School recently that his fund made tens of millions of dollars in profit by assuming that after Chrysler, Washington would never let Ford fail. He said the fund eagerly acquired hundreds of thousands of Ford shares during a period when Ford's share price plunged from above 40 to below 20.

Another type of bailout occurs when a company or industry gets in over its head, usually in legal liability due to its own negligence. An example is the $56-million children's sleepwear industry bailout bill passed by Congress in 1983. The bill allowed consumers injured by sleepwear treated with Tris, a toxic chemical flame retardant banned in 1977 because of its asbestos content, to file for compensation with the government. An obvious problem with the Tris bailout is that it insures companies that cut costs by negligently ignoring safety problems, while competitors that market a safer, more expensive product are left with fewer sales and no government aid. Although President Reagan signed that bill, he rejected the recommendation of his own Nuclear Safety Oversight Committee that urged the government to bail out General Public Utilities Corporation for the estimated $1.3-billion cost of cleaning up the damaged Three Mile Island nuclear reactor.*

The Perils of Protectionism
There is probably no more cherished principle in the lexicon of traditional economics than "free trade." Yet the most powerful industry associations, multinational corporations, and labor unions are seeking to escape from such global competition—and from its therapeutic pressure to keep costs down and innovations up. Although they always blame the other guy's government, proponents of protectionism rarely acknowledge that

---

*Chapter 3, "Wasteful Workplace," discussed how in situations of potential bankruptcy, employee buyouts are preferable to federal bailouts. With such private sector self-help, there are none of the discriminating and redistributive effects that occur when the government favors one of many corporations.

trade barriers are little more than governments rigging the marketplace to inefficiently transfer welfare payments from rising to declining sectors and from many consumers to some producers. The result, claims Harold Malmgren, a former U.S. deputy trade representative, is that the economy ends up "led by losers."

Trade barriers, to be sure, don't look like subsidies. Some are like the classic duties and quotas levied on sugar (by the Agriculture and Food Act of 1981) which cost consumers more than $1.5 billion annually. Less obvious are the "Buy American" provisions enforced by the U.S. government and several states; "orderly marketing agreements" negotiated to limit the import of products like color TVs from Japan, Korea and Taiwan; or the "voluntary" import quota of 1981 that limited Japanese auto firms to 1.85 million cars for 1985. Of course, the quotas were about as "voluntary" as that country's military surrender in August 1945—Japanese automakers volunteered to restrict their exports the day before the Reagan administration was scheduled to impose a mandatory quota.

The perils of protectionism are several. First, it isn't the Japanese or Germans who pay most of the costs of this transfer-payment system we call protectionism. Consumers pay because less efficient domestic producers can keep prices high behind a wall of tariffs or quotas. This hidden tariffs' tax has been estimated to cost American consumers more than $46 billion a year—and then there was about another $4 billion annually from car quotas. Because of auto barriers (which concluded at the end of 1985), U.S. car buyers overpaid $1,300 per Japanese car and $660 per American car.

Second, protectionism beggars a neighbor's business most visibly when the protected good, like steel, is used in manufacturing a finished product, like a Buick. Stiffening the "voluntary" quota on European, Brazilian, or Asian steel may be good news for U.S. Steel employees, but it's bad news for GM, Ford, and Chrysler employees. Government intervention in steel pricing causes U.S. automakers to pay about 25 to 30 percent more for steel than their European and Japanese competitors. As a result, some of that cheaper foreign steel will come into the United States anyway, molded and welded onto foreign cars and other products made with steel. And consumers now buy fewer American-made cars, which indirectly further reduces demand for American-made steel. Hence this not untypical irony: NBC began a recent news documentary with the shot of an under-employed steelworker demanding trade barriers to protect his job, before he drove off in his Toyota.

Luckily for Detroit, however, trade barriers feed upon themselves. Protectionist-inflated steel prices ironically bolstered the auto industry's case for quotas. Steel is also a major cost for farmers who invest in heavy equipment like tractors—and for farm machinery makers like International Harvester which watches its export markets erode. That in turn becomes one justification for $1.75 billion in export promotion subsidies granted to farmers—not to mention the $8 billion to $14 billion the farm sector has received each of the past few years in direct and credit program subsidies. Thus does protectionism create a chain reaction of dependency.

Third, protectionism can provoke retaliation. Trade wars produce a domino effect, as each succeeding barrier affects the sales and profits of other firms and nations. But as in other subsidy areas, politics is more relevant than abstract theories about free markets and free trade. The United States, complaining in 1983 of subsidies the Common Market provides its farmers, sold one million tons of flour to Egypt at subsidized prices. That angered the French, who traditionally supplied the Egyptian wheat market. So they offered bargain terms on wheat sales to the Chinese, who were anxious to get back at the United States because of new American quotas on imports of Chinese textiles. Concerning another potential ripple effect, economist Richard Cooper warns that "if we protect our markets against their goods, Latin American countries would have an excuse to repudiate their debts." Mexico and Argentina, for example, are major exporters to the United States *and* owe U.S. banks $35 billion.

Business lost to retaliation can be considerable. Ex-U.S. special trade representative William Brock estimated that "over $200 billion worth of U.S. exports and millions of jobs would be in jeopardy" in a spiraling trade war. Twenty percent of U.S.-manufactured goods are exported, 16 percent of U.S. factory jobs depend on exports, and 40 percent of U.S. agricultural produce is sold abroad. In the long run, import barriers thrown up to help one U.S. firm or industry can boomerang to impoverish other U.S. companies on the export side.

But every new handout by Washington increases the incentive for companies in trouble to reason that the return on lobbying is higher than on research and development. Harley-Davidson, America's last remaining motorcycle manufacturer, taught that lesson when their persuasive lobbying effort led to an increase in the tariff on higher-priced motorcycles from 4 percent to 49.5 percent, just to save that single company.

As a fourth cost of protectionism, even the protected firm may end up being more victim than beneficiary. Protection reduces the incentives to innovate by easing the pressure of international competition. "There's a real possibility that protected industries won't rebuild, regroup and innovate," argues Robert Strauss, associate dean of the School of Urban and Public Affairs at Carnegie-Mellon University. "It's tough out there in the marketplace. If we get into protectionism, we may never get out." This is one of the conclusions reached by Donald F. Barnett and Louis Schorsch in their analysis of the steel industry's decline, *Steel: Upheaval in a Basic Industry.* "[T]he commitment of resources to public relations campaigns and political lobbying has made it more difficult for steel firms to recognize the fundamental economic changes that are eroding both their competitiveness and their political clout."

Virtually nobody advocates a "pure" form of free trade, without exceptions. Adam Smith approved of barriers for national security, arguing its priority over the mere "opulence" of cheap imports. And America's first secretary of the treasury, Alexander Hamilton, added the "infant industry" exception, when a new technology that could give a country a comparative advantage in some line of commerce needs some time to establish a market position in order for economies of scale to operate. (But justifying the extension of quotas to imported clothespins on the grounds of national security, as the Reagan administration did, or slapping high tariffs on motorcycles—certainly no infant industry—demonstrates how plausible exceptions to free trade can be stretched to fit the political needs of the moment.) Third, and most significant, in a world where Korean steelworkers get paid a dollar an hour, totally open trade can have the effect of depressing livable U.S. wages. When unfettered wage competition produced inhumane wages in the early twentieth century, public policy established a floor under workers called a minimum wage, which is now regarded as a necessary exception to the presumption in favor of market competition. Theoretically, a country such as the United States could similarly attempt to create minimal standards which, rather than protect inefficient domestic producers, operate to discourage slave wages abroad from dragging down domestic pay.

Until theory and execution jibe, what's the alternative to cheap imports that produce intolerable levels of unemployment in older towns and cities? Preferable to trade barriers would be a conscious subsidy policy meeting two requirements: Any protection should be *temporary,* not open-ended; and it should be explicitly *conditioned* on the protected industry plowing the value of the subsidies into retraining, restructuring, and modernizing. It is a billion-dollar version of "bait and switch" for steel firms to spend the profits of protectionism on nonsteel mergers or for auto executives to use it to pay lavish bonuses to themselves.

Going further, government should intervene on the *labor side* to cushion the blow of industrial decline for workers and communities. Capital is a mobile commodity and can quickly transform itself from a blast furnace into a computer console, or move itself from Topeka to Tokyo. Attempts to subsidize or shield capital only lead to the sorts of hidden transfers, dependency traps, and retaliation costs described above. But since no single firm has an incentive to retrain or relocate pockets of newly unemployed workers, or to locate in a community with high unemployment, the government should aid not mobile capital but immobile labor—that is, to protect not companies but jobs. "As long as change entails real misery for workers and their communities," writes public policy analyst William Drayton, a former EPA official in the Carter administration, "our remarkably responsive political system will fight it at all levels— usually successfully. The only way to avoid triggering this powerful braking mechanism is to do something about the reasons people fight back."

Drayton goes on to suggest a "Workers' Productivity Incentive" that gives workers laid off because of foreign competition a certificate to make their next employers eligible for either tax credits or subsidies equal to half their wages (for, say, three years). This job voucher system would encourage employers to hire and retrain workers injured by foreign competition; and taxpayers cannot object to a system that subsidizes work rather than welfare. "By assuring [employees and their communities] that change means good new jobs," concludes Drayton, "it would begin to break the connection between change and pain."

A Taxing Code: "Does Anyone Here Believe in Capitalism?"

Nowhere is the government subsidy game played for higher stakes or with greater waste than on the field of corporate taxes. Over the years, Congress has superimposed on the tax system's revenue-raising function the burden of giving business people an "incentive"—called "tax expenditures"*—to make a profit. As a result of years and layers of such "incentives," these preferences now equal 87 percent of all taxes collected (versus 10 percent in Germany, for example). The corporate contribution to government revenues has plunged from about 25 percent to 8.5 percent over three decades. "Everything's gone but the grin," said Van Ooms, chief economist of the House Budget Committee.

Economists agree the ideal tax system would both be neutral with respect to competing investment choices and apply low marginal rates. The current code, instead, is a form of government intervention that causes massive marketplace distortions and picks tax "winners" and tax "losers."

In recent years, the tax code's implicit industrial policy has resulted in a preference for real estate over computers and a substantial bias in favor of short-lived equipment and against longer-term investments. This only reinforces American management's impulse toward short-term thinking which earlier chapters and other books have commented on. "In the long run," said Alan J. Auerbach, associate professor of economics at Harvard, tax-induced distortion "means too much capital in industries with low tax rates and too little in others and ultimately there will be a reduction in the size of the whole pie."

What follows are seven ways the IRS generates waste in specific companies and in the economy generally—what might be called the "seven deadly sins" of a taxing code.

Sin Number 1: Good Investments Look Bad, Bad Investments Look Good

A glance at the statutory tax rates suggests the burden is high and uniform—a flat 46 percent for corporate income exceeding $100,000. In fact, the average effective tax rate dropped to

---

*The Congressional Budget Act of 1974 defined a "tax expenditure" as "revenue losses attributable to provisions of the federal tax laws which allow a special exclusion, exemption, or deduction from gross income or which provide a special credit, a preferential rate of tax, or a deferral of tax liability."

about 16 percent in 1983. Rates vary widely from below zero to almost 40 percent, depending on the industry and type of investment. According to Robert McIntyre of the Citizens for Tax Justice, a tax research group in Washington, D.C., companies *within* the same industry often pay taxes at dramatically different rates. Whirlpool Corporation pays nearly 46 percent of its profits in taxes, while General Electric pays no taxes, and actually received $283 million in tax rebates between 1981 and 1983. IBM and Digital Equipment paid more than 28 percent of their profits in taxes from 1981 to 1983, while Sperry Corporation, Control Data, and Wang Laboratories paid virtually no federal taxes. K mart pays upward of 40 percent, but Sears pays only 4 percent.

At the same time, a study released by the Congressional Joint Committee on Taxation in November 1983 revealed startling differences in the effective tax rates paid by *different* industries in 1982. Of the twenty-nine industries examined, the effective tax rate on U.S. income varied from 39 percent in the rubber industry to minus 17.7 percent in chemicals. Firms in the telecommunications industry paid an average effective rate of 2 percent on profits.

A foreign observer might surmise that such an extraordinary departure from the 46-percent statutory rate reflected a policy decision by Congress to encourage high technology. But assuming this was so, then Congress missed the computer industry, which was taxed at an average rate of 26 percent. The pharmaceutical industry paid U.S. taxes at a 33-percent rate, but the chemical industry's effective rate, again, was minus 17.7 percent. "We couldn't get away with giving direct subsidies to encourage new investment, so we did it through the tax system," says the chief counsel to a congressional committee, who requested anonymity. By distorting the market return on different types of investment, these tax rate differentials put certain firms at a competitive disadvantage, while some others receive outright public subsidies—in other words, some new investments earn more *after* than *before* taxes.

These uneven tax rates produce wasteful results. Since investors and managers allocate capital based on its *after-tax* rate of return, investments that would look good in a tax-neutral system may never be made, while before-tax losers can become after-tax wonders. Capital follows the after-tax rewards, not before-tax productivity. Investment decisions within the firm become similarly distorted, since not all new investment enhances productivity. If a typist already has a satisfactory word processor, but her or his firm decides to buy a new one because the purchase is tax-subsidized, that doesn't add to productivity—it subtracts from it by depriving more productive, but less tax-favored, investments of the capital.

Congress should give greater weight to a major study of capital formation (investment in productive assets) released by the Federal Reserve Board in 1981. It concluded that attempts to boost savings and investment through accelerated depreciation and investment tax credits actually had an adverse affect on the quality of capital formation. The Fed found that in order to maximize their tax benefits, firms increasingly invested in assets of shorter life, which meant more investment to replace obsolete equipment but less for modernization and expansion. From an efficiency standpoint, most firms and the overall economy would profit from replacing across-the-board tax subsidies with marginal rates far lower than the statutory 46 percent.

Sin Number 2: The Me-Too Politics of Taxes

Since a succession of special tax breaks allows some industries to pay little in taxes, those firms left holding the tax burden are learning that investments in political quid pro quos can earn surer returns than investments in R and D. And when the after-tax return on investment becomes substantially a product of political muscle rather than business skills, big declining industries and old technologies will tend to prevail over small- and medium-sized growth companies employing newer technologies.

"If you have high effective tax rates, it's because your assets are not getting very good treatment in the political marketplace," observes Jack Albertine, president of the American Business Conference (ABC), a lobby for some 199 mid-size growth firms. The increasing importance of investing in the proper care and lobbying of Congress was best demonstrated by the temporary achievement of what had previously been unthinkable: the ability to buy and sell tax breaks.

"Safe harbor leasing" (until its repeal in 1983) was the ultimate in tax break me-tooism, ensuring that companies did not miss out on tax incentives merely because they paid no taxes. Since big, unprofitable firms in declining industries did not have enough taxable income to benefit immediately from investment tax credits (ITCs) and faster write-offs, the Basic Industries Coalition persuaded Congress to permit them to sell their tax credits and deductions to more profitable firms. Negative tax rates went into effect for certain preferred types of investments in equipment. In an ironic parody of the socialist credo "from each according to his ability, to each according to his need," corporate profits were effectively redistributed from the most profitable sectors of the economy to the least.

In a 1982 commentary on the Reagan tax reform program, Michael Kinsley, then the editor of *Harper's,* asked: "Does anyone around here believe in capitalism?" He described safe harbor leasing as a "fictional transaction somewhat like a welfare mother selling her children to an affluent childless couple so the tax deduction doesn't go to waste, then leasing them back for her own use and enjoyment." The political appeal of leasing was that the losers got off-budget subsidies, and the winners reduced their taxes, all without requiring the Treasury to take the embarrassing step of writing welfare checks.

A notable example was Ford Motor Company's sale of $1 billion in deductions to IBM. Ford, the troubled automaker that supposedly needed the investment incentives, received $153 million in cash from IBM, while the prosperous computer giant pocketed $600 million in tax savings in return for playing middleman between Ford and the Treasury.

According to ABC's Albertine, a 1983 study by McKinsey and Company showed that the highly successful ABC companies paid effective tax rates that were nearly double those of the largest one hundred corporations. Albertine complained that "in virtually every sector of the economy [the tax system] skews resources away from high-tax industries (often new, rapidly growing sectors) and toward low-tax industries (frequently older, declining sectors)." This was the unconscious "industrial policy" that Congress jerry-rigged through a series of tax changes since 1980.

Younger, smaller industries are learning the tricks of old masters, like the billboard lobby, which used careful targeting of campaign contributions to win one of the most lucrative tax shelter preferences in the code. Chief billboard lobbyist William V. ("Red") Reynolds sent this memorandum to his clients, dunning them to invest more in Congress: "It's that time again! . . . You all know how the game is played in Washington. Need I say more?"

When some firms gain exceptional tax treatment, others feel

the pressure to organize to get their fair share. For example, wholesalers are given "very little tax shelter," protests Bruno Mauer, president of a large Milwaukee machine parts company, and therefore pay an average 36 percent in tax. Mauer's solution? "Why can't the government give inventory and receivables some tax breaks too—maybe credits somewhat like ITCs?"

Such escalating me-tooism forces executives to spend considerable time lobbying for tax breaks rather than producing for profits.

Sin Number 3: "Too Much Falls Around the Edges"

Tax expenditures provoke economic waste because they are generally instituted without restrictions. According to Jerome Kurtz, former commissioner of the IRS and chairman of the American Bar Association's Tax Shelter Committee, "Taxes don't encourage a particular kind of investment, but any kind. Consequently, tax expenditures tend to be vastly wasteful in terms of revenue lost. Too much falls around the edges."

Standard public choice theory dictates that government should subsidize private economic behavior *only* when market imperfections prevent a firm from realizing the total benefit from an investment decision that benefits society as a whole. It would be wasteful and unnecessary to subsidize activity that would and should take place anyway. Adam Smith's "invisible hand" is premised on the belief that society does not have to pay people to act in their own self-interest.

Some short-lived or narrowly targeted tax preferences might efficiently produce desired economic behavior. But most tax-based "incentives" are overly inclusive and become entitlements for uneconomical investments. In 1981, for example, Congress passed the Accelerated Cost Recovery System (ACRS)—popularly dubbed "10-5-3." ACRS permits firms to write off (deduct from gross income) the cost of assets far faster than they actually wear out. The ACRS depreciation schedule arbitrarily treats all assets, from typewriters to blast furnaces, as if they remain productive for either three, five or ten years—thus the moniker, "10-5-3." A machine expected to produce income for ten years, for example, could be fully depreciated in three or five years, providing a "tax shield" that serves to shelter other income.

The investment tax credit (ITC) is among the most over-inclusive of all tax subsidies because it makes Uncle Sam a partner in the purchase of all new industrial equipment. Firms can deduct directly from taxes owed 10 percent of the costs of new assets with useful lives of more than three years. Defenders of the ITC argue that it stimulates new business investment by reducing the cost of an asset, thus increasing its after-tax rate of return. It certainly does. The combined effect of ACRS and a 10-percent ITC is to increase the rate of return on an asset to 13.8 percent, assuming the asset would otherwise yield 10 percent under straight-line depreciation.

"The bulk of the investment tax credit goes to subsidize equipment that would have been purchased anyway," said Bill Raby, senior tax partner at Touche Ross, the Big Eight accounting firm. Meanwhile, the federal deficit grows, exerting upward pressure on real interest rates, in itself a disincentive to investment. A study by Harvard economists Alan Auerbach and Lawrence Summers concluded that over its first sixteen years, the ITC caused severe economic distortions, high interest rates, and a general "undesirable effect on the economy" compared to simply letting market rates of return guide investment decisions. According to an analysis by economist Robert Eisner for the Treasury Department, "10-5-3" depreciation and the ITC netted less than fifty cents in new investments for every dollar in tax revenue lost. "It would be more cost-efficient to have the government buy the new plants and equipment and give them to business," said Eisner.

Even some executives who benefit from ACRS argue that investment incentives should at least be targeted or conditioned on productive reinvestment. Jean Riboud, CEO of Schlumberger, which sells services to OPEC nations, told author Ken Auletta that his firm should have been compelled to show that the $30 million it saved in U.S. taxes in 1982 would be put into new capital investments and enhanced productivity likely to generate new wealth and jobs.

The research and development tax credit is another example of a subsidy that could be more tightly targeted. In 1981, a special 25-percent tax credit was adopted with the intention of subsidizing incremental increases in R and D expenditures in the current year over the average of the three preceding years. (Previously, since 1954, all R and D expenditures could already be fully deducted from taxable income in the current year.) Is this enormous across-the-board subsidy—in particular the 1981 credit—justifiable on a cost-benefit basis? Economist Edwin Mansfield of the University of Pennsylvania surveyed 110 companies and found that firms increased real R and D by only .3 percent in 1981 and 1 percent in 1982, well below expectations. Most of these firms reported higher operating costs as R and D. As Mansfield put it, "When a man is sent down to fix the boiler, and he repairs it, it's maintenance. If he can't repair it, it's R & D."

Sin Number 4: Merging Assets, Not Maximizing Profit

The goal of economic activity in a competitive market economy is the creation of new wealth. Yet certain tax provisions rearrange assets rather than maximize shareholder wealth.

The most powerful incentive for conglomeration and diversification is the so-called double-taxation of corporate profit. Dividend income is taxed once at the corporate level and again as ordinary income (at a maximum rate of 50 percent) when distributed to shareholders. But if earnings are retained, the second-level tax is deferred; shareholders then can later realize any increased value in the form of more lightly taxed capital gains income (at a maximum rate of 20 percent) by selling the stock. So pools of retained earnings build up, tempting ambitious executives to make uneconomical acquisitions lest all that money sit idle or attract "raiders."

Because many business groups cite this double taxation as antibusiness, Touche-Ross, the Big Eight accounting firm, was surprised to discover that a majority of the *Fortune* 500 executives it surveyed *opposed* ending the double-taxation of dividends. Accounting expert Bill Raby explained the apparent paradox of management's self-interest in perpetuating the tax penalty on dividend payouts. "It would in effect take away the rationale for retaining earnings and provide an environment where every time we want to do something we have to go back and make a case to the capital markets or to the shareholders," Raby said, glancing past his collection of Hopi Indian kachina dolls and out over Phoenix to the desert beyond. "Now executives just finance whatever they want to do out of retained earnings."

Given the tax penalty on dividend distributions, it should come as no surprise that while companies paid out about 70 percent of their after-tax income in dividends during the 1920s (when tax rates were much lower), in the 1970s that figure fell as low as 43 percent. By contrast, West Germany, famous for its steady growth with high rates of savings and investment, treats dividends and capital gains with the reverse bias. From 1953 to 1977, the German split rate system taxed dividends at 15 percent and retained earnings at 51 percent. In 1977, they converted to an "imputation system," which effectively taxes distributed profits at 36 percent and retained earnings at 56 percent.

The tax code not only encourages acquisitions with retained earnings, it encourages acquisitions financed by debt. Workers at closing U.S. Steel mills were outraged to learn the company had invested seven times as much acquiring Marathon's energy reserves as in new plant and equipment. In fact, the bulk of the tax savings that fueled the merger resulted from the newly merged company's ability to deduct the interest payments on the $5.4 billion in new debt (used to finance the merger) from Marathon's taxable income. Because U.S. Steel already had a surfeit of tax deductions, the cost of debt-financing the merger proved far cheaper than financing modernization of its steel plant. Allowing firms to fully deduct the interest costs of debt without restrictions rewards the debt-financed purchase of old assets as much as it encourages new investments.

Sin Number 5: The Cost of Uncertainty to Business

A major cost imposed by the tax code is never collected by the IRS: the waste of indecision and delay as corporate planners struggle to anticipate its impact on long-term investment options. Between 1981 and 1984, the corporate tax rules were subjected to a major overhaul no less than three times. The least significant one, the Deficit Reduction Act of 1984, ran to twelve hundred pages. Meanwhile, back at the IRS, the rule makers lag months behind Congress in issuing regulations to clarify the new changes.

When business decisions become dependent on their tax consequences, the capital-budgeting process can be paralyzed and long-term investment may appear artificially risky. Managers fear Congress will turn this year's tax-preferred investment into next year's after-tax catastrophe. At Gould, Inc., the incremental 25 percent R and D tax credit has led the firm to require division managers to submit their budget proposals on an after-tax basis, according to Gould vice-president and treasurer Michael I. Miller. But since it remained uncertain whether Congress would reauthorize the tax credit in 1985, firms were forced to map out their R and D strategies in the dark. Complained Robert Perlman, director of taxes at Intel, "You've got to do something, so you take the deduction and then set aside reserves like hell in case the IRS decides you're wrong."

Perlman recalled how the firm planned for two years to locate a subsidiary in Switzerland because the tax rules made it profitable. But then Congress pulled the plug on that preference in 1984, completely changing the profitability of the deal. "You study, you wait, you finally decide. Then six months or a year later you walk into the boardroom with egg on your face," Perlman said.

Another example of tax code confusion comes from Silicon Valley, where executives at National Semiconductor Corporation planning a $50-million R and D facility have to decide whether to purchase or lease the equipment without knowing the tax consequences. "If I lease the equipment and the R&D credit isn't extended, I'll have a lease that's economical in year one and noneconomical for the rest of its life," explains Gary Arnold, vice-president of finance.

There may indeed be nothing more certain than death and taxes—but there's often nothing *less* certain than how much and on what income your business will be taxed next year.

Sin Number 6: Subsidizing Capital at Labor's Expense
In investments, more is not necessarily better. Although a definition of increased productivity is additional output per hour of labor, some people confuse an increase in the *volume* of investment with an increase in the *productivity* of investment. Yet if across-the-board preferences subsidize one factor of production (capital), it may be inefficiently substituted for another factor (labor). And if government subsidizes the substitution of capital for labor at a rate faster than workers can be retrained, relocated, and given new jobs, unemployment increases, a cost measured in human suffering and unemployment benefits.

Certainly, corporations should invest in labor-saving machinery whenever it boosts real productivity. But when the tax rules are biased in favor of heavily capital-intensive investments, it may be leading to a capital-to-labor investment ratio that makes society pay for unnecessarily idle workers. The 1982 *Economic Report of the President* observed that while companies bore the full burden of taxes on labor-generated profits, they were paying little or no taxes on profits generated by capital investments eligible for superaccelerated depreciation under ACRS. The *Report* went on to warn that "switching from wage and capital taxation to wage taxation alone can reduce economic welfare and efficiency even though this structural change could lead to more capital formation."

Beyond a certain point, subsidizing capital leads to long-term growth only if labor becomes more mobile and learns new skills. Indeed, if managers regard capital investment as a panacea, they are likely to neglect other intangible factors crucial to growth— training, labor-management cooperation, quality control, technology, employee involvement, and morale.

Sin Number 7: Professional Tax Avoidance

Complicated tax rules not only attract management's attention away from wealth creation and toward tax avoidance activity, they also waste billions each year in transaction costs paid to a growing cadre of tax lawyers, leasing agencies, accountants, and investment bankers. "You spend an inordinate amount of time worrying about the tax consequences of doing certain things instead of worrying about the business consequences; it's an enormous waste," said Robert Noyce, president of Intel Corporation. Intel, which already runs a lean administrative staff, "could get rid of perhaps two hundred people who just keep records" if the corporate tax were abolished or greatly simplified, Noyce claimed.

While even the simplest, most neutral tax requires time and money to comply with, less defensible waste results from a swelling tide of tax shelters. Every week thousands of well-off people seeking to shelter ordinary income from the marginal rate invest in mostly unproductive assets that generate immediate deductions and long-term capital gains. Despite tax changes in 1981 designed to reduce incentives for tax shelters by lowering the top tax bracket from 70 to 50 percent, the volume of tax shelter activity quadrupled by 1984. "Literally hundreds of thousands of people are in so-called tax-shelter partnerships with very little, if any, economic justification," said the then Secretary of the Treasury Donald Regan. "I thought it was confined to the so-called smart boys on Wall Street. You find it in Little Rock, Des Moines, all over the country."

As this book went to press, major proposals for tax "simplification" were on the political agenda for 1985–86. The most promising would broaden the tax base and lower marginal rates, make the code more neutral between competing investments, and remove some of the subsidies for nonproductive activity. Under the reform initially urged by Donald Regan, capital-intensive industries would lose their tax advantage over longer-life equipment and structures. Other reforms include denying the full interest cost deduction for debt that finances a contested takeover; eliminating artificial accelerated depreciation; permitting full-expensing for *all* productive assets in year one (the equivalent of a zero rate of tax on new investment), while taxing all nonproductive and speculative investment as ordinary income, which should stop most tax sheltering; and tightly targeting tax subsidies if they must be used at all.

With such reforms, capital would flow to the most productive pretax investments rather than to after-tax incentives. Or in the words of the Treasury Department, "No longer will the nation's scarce economic resources—its land, its labor, and its inventive genius—be allocated by the tax system instead of by market forces."

Still, the corporate tax also violates the "ability to pay" principle that has long been the philosophical cornerstone of the tax system. Although corporations are actually owned by many people with varying abilities to pay, the corporate tax treats all owners alike by levying a sort of flat tax on every owner's share of that year's profits.

Worse, nobody knows who actually pays the corporate tax. Some is passed through to consumers, some pushed back onto workers, and the rest is absorbed by shareholders. The distribution of this burden will vary in proportion to a firm's market power. The more oligopolistic an industry, the greater the firm's ability to pass the tax forward to the consumers as a cost of doing business. In competitive markets, however, the tax must be passed back onto the factors of production—dividends are cut back to the owners of capital, and workers bear part of the burden through lowered pay, fewer hours, and loss of jobs.

Consequently, many economists and commentators have called for repeal of the corporate income tax. Instead of taxing the corporation and then taxing shareholders again at very different rates (depending on whether profits are realized as dividends or capital gains), each shareholder's portion of the profits could be taxed once each year as personal income. Under this plan, whether profits are distributed or retained would make no difference since the capital gains tax would be eliminated; income would be taxed as earned, like wages. The administrative burden would be no greater than when employees file W-2 forms and would be far more routine and less costly than the record keeping and lawyering necessary to meet and beat the law today. "Attributing profits directly to individuals would enormously intensify pressures on managers to pay out dividends," concludes economics columnist Robert Samuelson. "Only firms that achieved above-average profitability could easily rationalize exceptional profits retention."

Are any of these tax changes probable, or possible? Prospects seem dim because the business community's intransigent affection for tax preferences produces this irony: While 95 percent of business respondents to a Harris poll opposed "direct federal subsidies," 61 percent favored "tax incentives and allowances to help industries." The contradiction was too much for Dr. Albert C. Evans, who wrote in *Business Week,* which had reported the Harris results, "Hey, what gives? . . . A tax credit, incentive, or allowance is just another subsidy. And these guys are businessmen?"

Pentagonism

Corporate welfare permeates defense contracting because military contractors reside at the crossroads of *two* massive bureaucratic systems—corporate and government—in which one guarantees the profits of the other. With profits divorced from performance, the discipline of competition is lost, leaving few brakes on accelerating waste.

Consider the illustrative experience of executive Sheldon Weinig.

"The early sixties was the great era of government contracts," recalls Weinig, the founder of Materials Research Corporation whom we met in Chapter 1, "and I was getting contracts from the Atomic Energy Commission and the Navy. During this period I learned the second great truth of my life—which is, when you do research for the United States government it doesn't make any difference whether you do good research or bad research."

One particular episode crystallized Weinig's attitude toward defense work. "I hired a guy who was a retired Army colonel to be my contact with the defense establishment. He comes in one day and says, 'Hey, Doc, I can arrange a program with NASA for two million dollars.' That was an extraordinary amount of

money for this little company, so I said, 'Hey, that's fabulous.'
He said, 'I'll arrange for you to go down and have breakfast
with the appropriate assistant director and you can work out the
scope of this thing. Oh, incidentally, you'll be required to pay a
consulting firm in New Jersey a hundred thousand dollars.'" I
asked, 'Who's the firm?' And he replied, 'Me and this guy in
NASA.'

"I didn't get hysterical and I didn't throw the stealing bastard
out of my office. I just said, 'Let me think on that.' I went home
and put pluses and minuses on a piece of paper. A two-million-
dollar contract was meaningful but on the negative side I'd be
paying for the contract.

"The next morning I called in the colonel and told him, 'I've
considered your proposition and I don't think it's for us.' He
said, 'Okay.' He was an employee. He just cleaned out his desk
and left.

"I decided then not to rely on government contracting. I decided that if you don't want to steal by being in the defense
contract business, then you have to have a product that is
unique, a product that gives you pride and the opportunity to
make money."

Few defense contractors make that kind of ethical decision,
however. Many have become totally dependent on "Uncle
Sugar," and can't afford scruples that would cut them off from
their main or sole revenue source. Like divisions of a corporation, the careers of defense managers and workers are directly
determined by the decisions of central management—in this
case, the government. Yet unlike corporate divisions, defense
firms' rewards are determined not by performance but by politics. And what counts in the politics of defense is less know how
than know-who.

Between 1971 and 1979, 1,942 Department of Defense officials took positions with the eight leading military contractors,
according to a study conducted by the Council on Economic Priorities. Like Weinig's government liaison man, 1,455 of these
had retired at the rank of colonel or above. In the mid-eighties,
this revolving door is spinning faster than ever. More than 2,600
high-ranking military officials went to work for defense contractors in 1982—four times more than in 1975.

The shuttle service between the Pentagon and its contractors
produces one primary result: waste. The Maverick program's
overhead is tremendous; from 1979 to 1983 its costs escalated

$160 million. Pentagon cost-cutter Ernest Fitzgerald quotes a general who told him, "Look Fitzgerald, I'm going to retire in a year or two and I'll become part of some contractor's overhead. If I cut overhead allowances, I'll be cutting my own throat."

According to a Government Accounting Office study, more than 90 percent of defense contracts are awarded without competitive sealed bidding. Contractors have the perverse incentive to maximize not efficiency but costs because of the system of "cost-plus" profits—namely, a contractor's profits are linked to costs; the more costs, the more profits.

Many defense industry executives, like TRW's Simon Ramo, argue that "there can be no free market . . . in weapons systems technology." But the story of the only competitively produced billion-dollar defense item—the GAU-8 shell—belies Ramo's assertion.

The GAU-8 is an eleven-inch-long cannon shell that can pierce the metal of tanks and other armored vehicles. Fired from guns mounted on A-10 Thunderbolt aircraft, the GAU-8 would be a principal tool in our first line of defense in the European theater.

When Pentagon accountants first costed out the GAU-8 in 1973, they estimated that the shells would cost eighty-three dollars a round. But instead of following the usual procedure of farming out the contract to a sole-source supplier, *both* Aerojet-General and Honeywell were given the go-ahead to produce GAU-8's. Major Jack Runkle distributed the Air Force's purchases by giving the low bidder 2 percent more of the order for each percentage point by which their bid came in below the competitor. The low bidder was guaranteed a minimum of 55 percent of each order.

Competition works! Fifty-eight million shells later, Aerojet-General and Honeywell are battling to undercut each other's costs; the production lead switched sides three times between 1976 and 1982. And the cost of the GAU-8 has plunged to less than thirteen dollars in 1973 dollars. Both firms have showed large, steady profits.

This, however, is the rare case. As of September 30, 1982, defense contract cost overruns on major acquisitions in progress totaled $136 billion, an amount that alone could cover most of the average annual federal deficit in the 1980s. Here are some of the reasons why "cost overruns" have become nearly synonymous with the Pentagon and why contractors are so unconcerned with wasteful habits:

• *Buying in and marking up.* Like retailers who tout their "low-low $9.99 price," defense contractors set the price tag for major systems between $20 billion and $30 billion because the Congress and Pentagon, like the undiscerning shopper, have shown they will buy weapons systems in that range. To take one case, the Joint Economic Committee in 1984 charged in a detailed report that not only did General Dynamics submit intentionally undervalued bids to obtain a nuclear submarine contract, but also that Navy officials collaborated in the deception.

Once a company has successfully "bought in," it can strive to cover its true costs plus profits. In his 1980 book *The Defense Industry,* former Pentagon procurement officer Jacques Gansler explains how it works:

> Once the winning development contractor is announced . . . the sole-source supplier is in an increasingly powerful position. As time goes on, the government becomes more and more dependent upon this contractor for a product that is (or is believed to be) badly needed and for which no substitute could be developed in less than seven to ten years. From this point on, the contractor is in a position to go to the government with "explanations" of "government-introduced" problems that are increasing costs, causing delivery delays, and so forth, and to bargain for increased prices.

Once authorized, major military contracts are rarely canceled because of the specific jobs that could be lost. In one none-too-subtle reminder during the 1982 budget battle, Defense Secretary Weinberger said, "We must remember that at least 350,000 jobs are at stake and will be lost if there are drastic cuts [in military spending]"—notwithstanding that independent studies show that equivalent spending on domestic programs creates even more jobs.

• *Spiraling on.* Instead of analyzing how much an item *should* cost, defense contract prices are determined by actual costs—that is, charges made by a company. Those "actual costs" are then used as the base-line standard for estimating the cost of the next similar project. Because of this "historical cost-accounting," waste becomes compounded over and over again, contract after contract. The result is staggering, as Ernest Fitzgerald illustrates by comparing the costs of comparable military and civilian products over time. Ten years ago, Fitzgerald estimated that the Army would have paid $8,000 for a color television set worth $400 on the commercial market if the set had been produced by

the most inefficient military contractor. Now Fitzgerald's calculations lead him to conclude that "the manufacturer would
have to charge about $100,000 for the color television set, which
. . . still costs about $400 in the commercial market."

• *Reaping the benefits.* Such exorbitant costs are boosted by the
payroll expenses of contractors, who simply have no reason to
cut costs. A Pentagon aide described why it happens: "If the
entire effort of a plant is production for government and there is
no credible, ongoing threat of the Government taking its business elsewhere, the only incentive for the contractor is to allow
labor costs to increase . . . permitting increased net profits."
The result, according to an Air Force study of United Technologies, General Dynamics, General Electric, Rockwell, Lockheed, and Boeing, is padded wage bills. In fact, the Air Force
study of these six major contractors revealed that the labor costs
paid by the government were seven to twenty times higher than
the companies' actual labor costs. Predictably, the dollars flow
most liberally to the executive level. Managerial compensation
in the aerospace sector, which is largely defense dependent, is
30 percent higher than in durable goods production generally.
And the defense industry is excessively top-heavy. In production
work, there is a national average of 41 administrative employees
for every 100 production workers; on military jobs, the ratio is
50 managers for every 100 workers. In 1978, Rockwell International's B-1 division had more coaches than players, with 5,000
engineers and 4,000 administrators and managers directing only
5,000 production workers.

• *The bottom line.* In the late 1970s and early 1980s, according to
Senator William Proxmire, it became an article of faith "that
higher profits would lead to greater investment, more efficient
performance, and reduced production costs." In line with this
attitude, Congress eliminated the thirty-seven-year-old Renegotiation Board, the Cost Accounting Standards Board, and
the provisions of the 1934 Vinson-Trammel Act that limited defense contract profits to 10–12 percent. Capital formation became the order of the day, pushing waste-watching off of the
defense agenda.

What was left to reign in excessive defense profits? Nothing,
according to Defense Secretary Caspar Weinberger, who wrote
Proxmire in September 1983 that "[t]here are no statutory standards for realized profits." Consequently and predictably, the
Defense Department's 1982 profit study confirmed that "profits
were higher during 1977–1981."

Who profits? Over 34 percent of defense contract dollars went to the ten largest defense contractors in 1983, making the defense industry an oligopolistic monopsony—that is, when a few corporate giants sell to a sole customer. Or, as Professor Walter Adams phrased it, "The Pentagon creates more monopoly in one day than the Antitrust Division can undo in a year."

Pentagon industrial policy, in the form of research and development and procurement dollars, is nothing new. In fact, ever since Eli Whitney invented interchangeable parts while working on a musket order in 1798, defense spending has helped guide the product evolution and market structure of American business. In the early years of the 1950s, however, the Pentagon concentrated its subsidy monies on a small number of old-line firms. While Western Electric, General Electric, Raytheon, Sylvania, and RCA combined received 78 percent of the Department of Defense's contracts, they had only a 37-percent share of the civilian market.

After Jack Kilby at Texas Instruments built the first integrated circuit, Pentagon subsidies followed the civilian market forward into the 1960s. Upstarts such as Texas Instruments, Transitron Electronic Corporation, and Shockley Semiconductor Laboratories—formed largely by people who fled the stodgy defense-dependent companies—became the leading edge of this "sunrise" industry. And as their military sales grew from $4 million in 1962 to $31 million by 1968, the price of an integrated circuit plunged from $50 to $2.33.

Once the integrated circuit became the dominant design in semiconductors, innovation and productivity increases began to falter. According to an analysis by MIT's James M. Utterback and Albert E. Murray, the Department of Defense's continuing reliance upon a small group of contractors (66 percent of federal electronics R and D funds went to the top four firms in 1977) and its parallel emphasis on standardization resulted in "technical conservatism in design." Japanese innovation, however, surged. By 1982, having produced the first 64K RAM chip, the Japanese controlled 70 percent of the world market and 50 percent of the U.S. market.

Aware of this history, some chip-makers are taking bold action to tailor their products for the market, not the military. Intel has adopted the Weinig approach toward the Pentagon's Very High Speed Integrated Circuit (VHSIC) research and development program. It got out. Explained Chairman Gordon E.

Moore, "VHSIC required the same resources we needed for our commercial programs." Moore thinks the industry can best meet the demand for advanced memory chips through its own efforts, without government subsidies and direction.

Pentagon influence over commercial business is not limited to electronic components. While American industry has focused on costly, complex military technology, other industrial nations have been producing the cheap calculators, radios, and televisions that have taken over the American market. As a result, even Singer—maker of the archetypal American home appliance—now does only defense work in the United States.

Defense-dependence has caused a brain drain in American business. The Japanese are fully aware of their advantage, as indicated by a story that economist Lester Thurow tells:

> The president of MIT recently asked the president of Sony why he was doing so well and the president of Sony gave him a simple answer. He said, look, I can go to the University of Tokyo and hire the brightest engineering people to work on consumer electronics. My competitors in the United States can't do that because the brightest people in the United States go into defense electronics and they sell defense hardware and I sell consumer hardware.

Statistics substantiate Thurow's anecdote. Forty percent of American electronics research and development technicians are paid by the federal government, while only two percent of their Japanese counterparts are publicly funded.

The debilitating effects of defense-dependency become particularly apparent when military-oriented firms start new commercial ventures. Defense business practices were ill suited for General Dynamics' early 1950s attempt to produce dishwashers, United Aircraft's (now United Technologies) 1950s plunge into the turbo train field, Boeing-Vertol's mid-1970s conversion to building light-rail trolley cars, and Texas Instruments' effort to break into consumer products. All of these products became significant embarrassments for their manufacturers.

Other giants of the defense industry have tried to reduce their anesthetizing overreliance on Pentagon contracts by acquiring existing commercial firms. Raytheon, TRW, Aerojet, United Technologies, and others now do less than half of their business with the Pentagon compared to the 1950s and the 1960s when virtually all of their sales were in the defense sector.

But because Pentagonism produces institutional inefficiency, such acquired firms often suffered under new management. The experience of the Grumman Corporation is instructive.

The firm's credo was tidily summarized in 1971 by Lew Evans, chairman of the board of Grumman Aerospace: "We're not mass-consumer-market oriented, and we're not able to function profitably under the different types of contracts and procurement processes that exist in other markets. . . . Grumman is in aerospace—and I mean 'pure' aerospace—to stay." Over the next decade, Grumman would prove Evans right.

Grumman's major project in the early 1970s was the F-14 "Tomcat" fighter plane which the Navy ordered as its principal fighter. Eager to win the sort of contract that can sustain a defense contractor for decades, Grumman "bought in" to the F-14 program in 1969 on a fixed-price basis. When the Navy decided to buy more F-14's a short time later, Grumman sliced $474 million off of its bid to fend off a challenge from McDonnell Douglas.

The true cost of the F-14 buy-in quickly became apparent. In 1972, only three years after winning the contract, Grumman reported to the Navy that the price of *each* plane would be $2.2 million more than the original contract price. (By the end of the decade, F-14's would cost $25 million each, more than double the original price.) Grumman was being pulled under by the weight of its low bid; a Grumman official, E. Clinton Towl, told a congressional committee that the company's losses on the F-14 program were $85 million in 1971 and $106 million in 1972. And Banker's Trust cut off Grumman's short-term credit. Grumman chairman John Bierwirth declared the stakes when he warned, "If we are forced to produce the plane under existing conditions, two months later we will have to close the doors."

So Grumman went scrambling for help. In 1973, Congress was convinced to help pull Grumman back from the brink of bankruptcy by allowing the Navy to break the F-14 contract and buy new planes on a year-to-year basis. "The maneuver was new," *The New Republic* editorialized, but "the result was familiar: a 'bailout.' . . . Grown paunchy on a heavy diet of tax dollars, the Tomcat [F-14] is turning into the fatcat."

Chairman John C. Bierwirth devised a two-pronged strategy for corporate recovery. First, Bierwirth cultivated a new source of corporate welfare, the shah of Iran, by providing the Iranian monarch with custom-made flying suits and arranging private air shows for him. The doomed shah proved to be a willing benefactor not only by buying eighty F-14's but also by arranging a $200-million loan to Grumman from a consortium of Iranian and American banks. For the first time, a foreign government and foreign banks were financing an American defense contractor.

Bierwirth's second strategy was to increase the nondefense share of Grumman's business to 50 percent. But Lew Evans had been right when he declared Grumman unable "to function profitably" in civilian markets.

Most notable was Grumman's 1978 purchase of the bus-making Flxible Company. The long, twisted saga of the Grumman-Flxible buses, which is still being unraveled in court and a congressional investigation, again illustrates the wasteful business habits created by Pentagonism.

The New York City Transit Authority (TA) purchased $89-million worth of Grumman Model 870 "advanced design buses." But after one year on the streets, the first sample bus already had eight major defects. A TA team of engineers studied it and other Grummans in service in New Orleans, Houston, and Los Angeles and reported that "there appears to be no part of the structure of the 870 bus that is immune from problems." The head of Atlanta's transit authority called it "a horse designed by a committee, which came out a dromedary." New York's Transit Authority chief David Gunn calls it "the worst bus ever made." (When years of trouble were capped by a midtown Manhattan bus fire in February, 1984, the Grummans were pulled permanently off New York City's streets.)

Just as military contractors forget to ask soldiers how well their M-16 rifles performed in Vietnam (they often jammed), no one at Grumman thought to ask bus drivers about the design of the bus's dashboard, which didn't even have a fuel gauge. Also, Grumman's designers sought fanciness over reliability. The buses look sleek and their destination signs can wish riders a nice day, but the windows are too dark to see through at night and they don't open.

The major problem with the Grumman buses is that their lightweight frames are unable to stand up to the wear and tear of daily urban use. Grumman blames New York's potholed streets and TA maintenance failures but that is like United Technologies blaming the Ayatollah's sand and U.S. military mechanics for downing their Sikorsky helicopters during the American rescue mission. Closer to the truth was one transit official who told columnist Beth Fallon, "These corporations get fat off government contracts. They build crap for the military and get their cost overruns and no one cares. The federal government doesn't care. So they wind up building crap because that's all they are used to building."

Bidding for Business: Economic War Between the States

Any discussion of America's implicit industrial policy would be incomplete without considering the economic development efforts of the fifty states. Like their federal counterparts, state development policies extend the carrot of tax incentives, capital subsidies, and sometimes direct grants-in-aid. Most states pursue the goal of luring as many new jobs and high-value industries into their states as possible, with the quintessential example being GM's search for a home for its new Saturn division in 1985, which produced the spectacle of seven governors vying for the facility on the *Phil Donahue Show*. Unfortunately, both taxpayers and most businesses are ultimately victimized by this new economic war between the states.

In 1983, the state of Illinois offered $12 million in tax breaks and subsidies to the H. F. Huster Company, a fork-lift manufacturer, if it agreed to locate two thousand jobs in Kewanee and Danville. But when Huster's chairman, William Kilkenny, arrived in Chicago to discuss the deal, he was sporting a bluegrass pin on his lapel and a $15-million tax break bid from Kentucky in his hip pocket. "They [Huster] put their cards right on the table," recalled M. Edward Martin, then assistant director of the Illinois Department of Commerce and Consumer Affairs (DCCA). "Here's what Kentucky's doing, what's Illinois doing?" What Illinois did was up its bid to $15 million.

The year before Illinois anted up $277,000 to help General Electric Company open a new plant in the state. "If we hadn't, Ohio would have," explained Peter Fox, the thirty-year-old businessman who headed the DCAA. Other states are busy marketing their business climates like health spas, often knocking the opposition in the process. During New York's big blizzard of 1978, investors trapped at home by the snow saw television ads showing a hand chopping away a block of ice to reveal the warmer business climate in Texas.

Since it is rare for a corporation to move a plant from one state to another, most of the tax breaks, subsidy programs, and expensive advertising campaigns are aimed at the lucrative market for *new* investment—more than three fourths of the *Fortune* 1,000 have located a new plant between 1978–1983. State and local politicians have discovered that the politics of "beggar thy neighbor" allows them to take credit for concrete examples of job creation while the waste and inequity generated by differential subsidies remain largely hidden.

Local governments attempt to attract new investment primarily by arranging financial incentives, such as tax abatements, grants for retraining labor, or most commonly, cheap capital by issuing tax-exempt bonds. Open *Business Week* or *Forbes* and you are likely to see full-page ads publicizing a menu of "tax breaks" for new investment that includes a 6-percent investment tax credit, a 10-percent R and D credit, a ten-year business property tax exemption, a jobs tax credit, and a long-term capital gains exclusion and deferral.

Although states are becoming increasingly creative (more than forty have set up additional agencies dedicated to snaring emerging high-tech industries), the costliest incentive is still small-issue industrial development bonds (IDBs). Some forty-seven states permit them and the volume issued has soared from $10 billion in 1960 to $20 billion in 1970, to $35 billion by 1982 (in constant 1982 dollars). Tax-exempt bonds are a good deal for both local governments and businesses since the cost of borrowing at below-market rates is paid by the federal Treasury in the form of forgone tax revenue. The Treasury Department figures to lose at least $15 billion a year on tax-exempt bonds, which are mushrooming despite a congressional restriction passed in 1968 limiting tax-exempts to "small issues" of $10 million each.

But business also can lose in this bidding game—losses that go unacknowledged in all the glossy magazine ads. Consider what happened at two recently acquired companies, the 130-year-old Otis Elevator Company, once the largest employer in Yonkers, New York, and the Playskool toy factory in Chicago, owned by Milton Bradley Company.

In 1972, Yonkers invested $14 million in local, state, and federal urban renewal money to acquire and develop a site it sold to Otis for $1.3 million, a fraction of its market value according to Yonkers Mayor Angelo Martinelli. But instead of expanding the work force from thirteen hundred to two thousand, as promised, Otis sold out to United Technologies, which decided to close it entirely. Although a spokesperson for UT called it "a business decision," the expectations raised by accepting public handouts led to lawsuits and bad press.

Playskool benefited from a $1-million industrial development bond. Because such bonds are tax-exempt and issued by the municipality, in this case Chicago, the interest rates are generally 3 to 5 percent below the market rate. Playskool borrowed the money at 8.2 percent, when rates hovered near 14 percent, thereby saving an estimated $500,000 since 1980. But instead of hiring 446 new employees, as promised, the work force shrank. Then in September 1984, Hasbro Industries acquired Milton Bradley and quickly announced the entire plant would soon be shut down. "Their action is an arrogant breach of trust," Chicago Mayor Harold Washington told the media as he announced a lawsuit seeking a permanent injunction to block the closing. "Speaking for [the Playskool workers] and for the taxpayers of Chicago who backed this company, this is a slap in the face."

But when governments compete, the tax revenue base erodes, squeezing funding for public services and education. Also, local and more well-established companies end up at a competitive disadvantage relative to newcomers with the brash and brawn to extort public subsidies before agreeing to carry out a business decision they would probably carry out in any case. William Brown, president of the Council of State Chambers of Commerce, criticizes property tax abatements and similar enticements that distort business decision-making and discriminate against existing businesses. "I don't feel that offering subsidies or special privileges to new business makes for a good business climate," Brown said. "It makes for a bad business climate."

Local officials like Patrick Quinn, one of two commissioners on Illinois's Board of (Tax) Appeals, agree and are urging an end to property tax abatements. Cook County doled out $446 million in 1982, which he claims "hurts business generally since only a few get the breaks." Quinn says the savvy firms send their lawyers in to claim "we won't locate here," or "we're ready to close down and leave a thousand workers unemployed" unless the county springs for a tax break. "Our view is that economic blackmail arguments are irrelevant," Quinn concludes. "Businessmen seem happiest when our tax board is fair and consistent."

Tax expert Robert McIntyre believes that it's up to the local chambers of commerce to "demand that local governments stop this." He notes that IDBs have been dubbed "Burger Bonds" because chains like McDonald's and K mart have been notorious for gaining an advantage over their mom-and-pop competitors through the tax-exempt bonds and property tax abatements they gain by promising to create a couple dozen low-wage jobs. "The greasy spoons are beginning to ask City Hall why they are paying taxes so that McDonald's can come in and take their business away," McIntyre said. (The 1984 Deficit Reduction Act did set federal limits on the IDBs that states and cities can issue to $150 per capita or $200 million, whichever is greater.)

While it is clear that subsidies aimed merely at moving a company from one state to another contribute nothing to the national economy, it remains unclear whether even the most persuasive states benefit in the long run. New York City offers tax abatements of up to nineteen years to new businesses, yet a 1983 report by the city's Department of Investigations concluded that "no reliable estimates to annual exemption commitments are available." Many local governments not only do not know what they're spending—they don't know what they're buying either. "We have no studies to justify the expense, and no standards to administer the programs," admitted Edward V. Regan, the New York State comptroller, in 1980. "Right here in New York State we have several striking examples of how tax concessions were granted, not to keep or lure businesses to the community, but to profit the owners and stockholders." Similarly, Edward J. Martin, executive director of Philadelphia's Board of Revision and Taxes, concluded that his city could not determine whether $100 million in special tax credits prompted any increase in investment or employment of additional workers.

Even businesses that benefit often wonder why cities and states actually send out salesmen to bribe them with special subsidies that play no role in their business judgment—for the decision where to locate a plant depends on variables far more significant than the level of only one of the many costs involved. An analysis of seventeen major surveys by the Council of State Planning Agencies, an affiliate of the National Governors' Association, found that executives of new or recently expanded firms listed business taxes fourteenth on the list of deciding factors.

For instance, officials in Seneca County, Ohio, offered a new bicarbonate plant a twelve-year property tax abatement, yet the company comptroller later admitted, "The tax abatement was a nice kicker on the end, but we chose Ohio mainly because of its strategic location for distribution and market growth." In 1980, the Savin Corporation received a $715,000 credit on its corporate franchise tax after selecting Binghamton, New York, as the location for a new plant. Savin executives, however, later said that they chose Binghamton because of its proximity to feeder plants, not because of the tax breaks offered by the state's Job Incentive Program.

"Taxes are not the primary basis for a location decision," acknowledged William Brown. He noted that surveys show the location criteria that business people report as most important are a good reflection of the elements necessary for long-term economic growth: a skilled work force, adequate public services, access to raw materials, and capital.

If both business and local economies would be better off spending these subsidies to improve the quality of the labor supply and public services, why are governments so eager to offer, and businesses so aggressive in seeking, special breaks? "Businesses take them because they are there," Brown said. "If the company is going to locate some place anyway, and they don't seek the subsidy, what are the shareholders going to say about the management? My criticism is of the local government that offers it."

Some don't. Farsighted states like California and Massachusetts now appreciate that limited public revenues are more wisely invested in excellent schools and services than in preferential tax breaks—which is why these two states have been so successful in attracting new investment in growth sectors. Other states too should realize that bidding for business is a parody of capitalism: *marketplace* competition is one thing, but *location* competition makes Americans pay twice, as consumers and as taxpayers, for the prerogative of a free enterprise economy.

All these loan guarantees, subsidies, bailouts, trade barriers, tax breaks, procurement cost overruns, and IDBs are hard to dislodge because of what Peter Steinfels has called "the veto society"—if the benefits of a policy flow to a small group while the costs are absorbed by a larger group (society), the more motivated small group can veto change and retain their privileges. This is especially true since no overt scandals draw attention to these political preferences. As Robert Reich has observed, "No bureaucrats intrude on corporate discretion. Legislators vote no budgets. Those costs do not appear on any national accounts, and those who bear them are seldom aware of the source or extent of the burdens."

So the subsidy state continues largely unperturbed, as many businessmen who advocate the virtues of marketplace competition seek exemption from their own economic principles.

Epilogue: The $862-Billion Annual Weight—Fault-Lines and Trend-Lines

Great progress has been made during the year in the national movement for elimination of industrial waste.

—Herbert Hoover, Secretary of Commerce, 1925 Annual Report of the Department of Commerce

Despite Mr. Hoover's optimism in 1925, corporate waste and bureaucracy is today a ball-and-chain around the ankle of the economy. And since the performance of our leading corporations has such a huge impact on our economic quality-of-life, the problem of business waste is one of the great unacknowledged tragedies in our country—tragic because it's avoidable.

Government fiscal, monetary, and trade policies—not to mention the international debt crisis and domestic deficits—can, of course, significantly affect the health of the body economic. But beyond macroeconomic concerns (economywide), what about microeconomic failings (firmwide)? What about American management that has been, in the words of Commerce Secretary Malcolm Baldridge, "too fat, dumb and happy in the past ten years? [It's not] labor productivity that's a problem. It's management, and I speak as a former manager."

As we have seen in this book, economic growth can be slowed or stopped by the wasteful practices of American executives— by a corpocracy that doesn't motivate white-collar employees to give a full day's work for a full day's pay . . . by managers who too often demonstrate self-absorption rather than exercise leadership . . . by a focus on asset acquisition instead of product innovation . . . by a system of compensation pegged more to position than performance . . . by an indifference to the cost of low-quality products and high-priced lawyers . . . by fraud and abuse that taxes consumers' wealth and health . . . and by a government-business alliance that too often protects companies from competition. Indeed, is there a better measure of the hidden profits in U.S. corporations, that the costs of mismanagement are unblinkable, than the 1985 study from the Columbia University Graduate School of Business documenting that "Japanese companies [*in the United States*] generally outperformed their American counterparts in terms of quality products, the absenteeism rate, the relationship with workers and their relationship with customers"?

How heavy is this ball-and-chain? Critics of government "waste, fraud, and abuse" have thought it helpful to tally the cost of their grievance. Professor Murray Weidenbaum, for example, estimated that the (direct and compliance) cost of federal regulation came to about $120 billion a year. And in 1983, the Grace Commission concluded that there were $424.4 billion in possible savings over three years from the reduction of very broadly defined government waste (for example, it included all federal legal assistance for the indigent)—for a potential gain of some $141 billion annually. It should, then, be similarly illuminating to estimate the possible "waste dividend" from the reduction of corporate waste and bureaucracy.

To be sure, the methodology here is necessarily primitive and imprecise. There are categories of waste that are impossible to measure ("excessive" compensation; the loss of shareholder confidence due to insider trading) or very difficult to measure (the cost of oligopoly). The table that follows is the best survey of credible expert data that can convey a rough order of magnitude of waste in American business. The total of at least $862 billion annually is more than six times the size of the oft-cited Grace Commission estimate of government waste. Not even in an ideal world could all of this waste be recaptured even by efficient firms. But much of it could be if mismanaged, oversized companies adopted the successful practices of anticorpocracy firms.

THE ANNUAL COST OF CORPORATE WASTE (IN BILLIONS)*

I. Market Constraints
    Oligopoly/monopoly/
        price-fixing $32–$265.2

*Sources for each of these estimates can be found in the book's footnotes. Whenever there were several credible calculations of waste, the authors took the most conservative number.

II.	Corpocracy	
	Bloat (excessive layers of management)	$74–$111
	Lost management productivity	$100
III.	Environmental Abuse	
	Air pollution	$38.5–$79
	Water pollution	$12.3
	Toxic waste dumps	$10 (over each of ten years)
IV.	Employment Discrimination	
	Racial discrimination	$37.6
	Gender discrimination	$81.2
V.	Crimes	
	Bribery and kickbacks	$3.5–$10
	Employee theft	$30–$40
	Insider trading	n/a
	Financial fraud	n/a
VI.	Occupational Hazards	
	Injuries	$23
	Disease	$30–$50
VII.	Product Safety	
	Product-related injuries (CPSC)	$10
	Auto injuries/deaths	$9
VIII.	Product Quality	$68.5
IX.	Innovation	$111–$148
X.	Consumer Waste	
	Auto repair	$20
	Tariff barriers	$46
XI.	Employee Waste	
	Non-participating workers	$85
	Health care	$40
	Unfair firings	n/a
XII.	Lawyers	n/a
XIII.	Compensation	
	Excessive pay without performance	n/a
	Minimum Total	$861.6 billion

This documented magnitude should lead those executives who routinely blame various government policies for business's ills to instead heed the maxim "Physician, heal thyself." Can the corpocracy heal itself? If unchallenged, no. The comfort level of insulated CEOs, middle managers, and workers can be too high to change easily. Or should external threats suddenly arise, some managements stuck in the rut of habit bring to mind what Richard Adams called "tharn" in his allegory, *Watership Down*—rabbits so paralyzed with fear that they just sit inert as enemies kill them.

But if the bad news is this $862-billion fault-line running through American business, the good news is several trend-lines that may shrink its size. Some of these developments are painful medicine, though they may prove to be long-term antidotes to excess bureaucracy.

• *Recession.* The 1982–83 recession was so severe—with unemployment hitting double digits and lost production reaching one trillion dollars annually—that it was the equivalent of a two-by-four to a mule. Lax business and labor leaders accustomed to a pass-along economy suddenly stopped automatic yearly hikes in wages and benefits; corpocracies shrank; many perquisites were eliminated. Businessmen publicly articulated the silver linings, even as laid-off employees quietly suffered the consequences of the prior waste: "It weeded out a lot of fat in the industrial complex"; "We had sloppy habits that had to change"; "It put a dose of reality into our lives—shaped us up." Indeed, as one very rough gauge of the extent of avoidable waste in our economy, 70 percent of businessmen surveyed by *The Wall Street Journal* thought the recession a good thing. Ideally, an economy should be healthy enough not to desire an amputation to make it well.

• *Imports.* The era when American manufacturing monopolized domestic markets because of oceanic insulation is obviously over. The share that imports grabbed of U.S. sales rose by more than half in 1975–83 (from 11 percent to 17 percent), at the same time that the U.S. share of world exports to non-Communist countries fell from 15 percent to 12 percent. Foreign shoes accounted for 2 percent of domestic sales in 1959 and 66 percent in 1983; today foreigners sell us 20 percent of our steel, 25 percent of machinery, 25 percent of cars. And in 1984–85, this process accelerated as the unusually strong dollar (making imports cheaper and exports more expensive) knocked years off the half-life of many older industries by speeding up their exposure to foreign trade.

This tidal wave of imports forced many companies to cut overhead and boost efficiency to survive. Audrey Freedman, chief labor economist for the Conference Board, a business research group, points out that in the past decade managers focused on investment return and deemphasized operational management. Now, after the recessions and import surge of the 1980s, "they're shocked that the Japanese and other competitors have out-Americanized us in production management. And we are rediscovering that it's terribly important how you manage what you produce." That two of the quintessential corpocracies of our business economy—GM and U.S. Steel—were striving in 1985 to condense their layers of managers is a testament to the inspiration of imports.

• *Deregulation.* The drive for deregulation in trucks, trains, planes, telecommunications, banking, and brokerage has caused much dislocation—and cut much waste.

Just as it's hard for a zoo-born tiger to be plopped back into its native habitat, companies previously protected from competition by federal restrictions often do not readily adjust to the rigors of the marketplace. Braniff and Continental went bankrupt, and Eastern nearly so; 40 percent of all unionized trucking firms are in trouble; AT&T and many of its customers are confused in the post-Ma Bell era. Still, there are more new firms than failed firms in deregulated sectors, and regulated companies with middle-management bulge have gone on a corporate diet. Long-distance airline rates, for example, have fallen by half in real dollars since the 1978 deregulation bill, spurring more passengers and fewer empty seats. "Airlines did best if they adjusted well," says Michael Derchin, a transportation analyst at First Boston. "They've had to learn how to become businessmen instead of bureaucrats."

• *The participation solution.* As the economy becomes more computerized and competitive, it is clear that what ultimately gives a nation a comparative advantage is its treatment of people—as expressed by Alfred Marshall's quoted observation that "the most valuable of all capital is that invested in human beings."

By this measure, the trend-line is favorable. We've come from 1911, when Frederick Winslow Taylor told approving managers that "in the past, the man has been first; in the future, the system must be first" to the plaintive question exactly eighty years later asked by an employee at Ford's inefficient assembly plant at Louisville, Kentucky, "Who was the son-of-a-bitch who wrecked this place?" The plant's labor relations manager provided the answer: "We were completely caught up and strangled by a quantitative approach to business, without any thought to the people involved . . . the human element." Indeed, by replacing adversarial relations with cooperation, that plant has turned itself around, one of thousands of examples of firms experimenting successfully with more employee participation programs.

This culture of partnership, even in giant corporations—*especially* in giant corporations—is superior to authoritarian management. Even beyond the benefits of greater employee satisfaction, corpocracies can reduce the number of supervisory personnel when hourly employees engage in more self-management. To take the paradigmatic example of Ford, the company has estimated that its so-called EI program (for employee involvement) saves $5 for every $1 invested. Jerome M. Rosow, president of the Work in America Institute, concluded that the growing involvement of union leaders in business decision-making is a "major breakthrough which has great potential for improving the competitive edge of those companies." Lynn R. Williams, president of the United Steel Workers, enthusiastically concurs. Combining employee participation with the "entrepreneurial urge," says Williams, will "inject a new dynamism and new creativity into our whole society."

• *Computers.* "Today it seems clear that the chip will change the world as decisively as did the telephone and the automobile," concludes T. R. Reid in his 1984 book, *The Chip*. The computer has moved with blinding speed, technologically speaking, from a garage experiment of a few tinkerers to an everyday desktop accessory of millions. This computer revolution, according to Michael Piore and Charles Sabel, is bringing us to what they call "the Second Industrial Divide"—a moment when a new, dominant technology shapes the whole economy's future trajectory. Piore and Sabel contend that, after a century of mass production and mass markets, the industrial economy is evolving toward "flexible specialization." Because of the economy and efficiency of computers—which they only slightly tongue-in-cheek describe as "a machine that meets Marx's definition of an artisan's tool: capacities of the user"—there can be a profusion of products tailored to meet narrow markets. For example, they describe how in Italy textile manufacturing has been reorganized around small shops, high-tech looms, adaptable production techniques and a cooperative network of subcontractors and brokers.

Thus, computers are lowering the economies of scale necessary for efficient production. If both giant GM and little Materials Research Corporation can afford the same high-speed computers, companies needn't conclude that only huge corpocracies can achieve profitability. Indeed, as executives of large companies watch smaller, more flexible and aggressive competitors maneuver in a high-tech business world, they feel the pressure to get smaller.

With the new computer technology, companies that want to fight corpocracy and waste can do both.

These developments, in combination, have the potential to lighten the weight of waste that has been pulling down the U.S. economy—if only our leading companies can institutionalize the ethic of anticorpocracy. During times of creation and crisis—like the brash People Express in 1980 or the venerable Paine Webber in 1983, respectively—companies can win the corporate war on waste. The real challenge is how to keep trim and efficient not only in extraordinary times but day-in and day-out as well.

This book has described dozens of firms that have done it, that have been "wastebusters." The formula seems to pivot on four fundamental assumptions: First, think big and stay small, for an excessive corpocracy puts distance between managers and markets; second, apply the golden rule to employees, at least by giving them more say and more stock, which can yield extraordinary productivity gains; third, look to vigorous marketplace competition to keep companies sleek and profitable—and avoid if possible the allure of corporate welfare programs that steal from Peter to pay Paul; and fourth, find executives who—like Sheldon Weinig—care about the long-term health of their enterprise, rather than those who—like David ("What's in it for me?") Mahoney—care largely about their own short-term wealth.

Ultimately, then, America's much-discussed search for growth and productivity must look more to Wall Street than to Washington, for it's up to business executives themselves whether they want to stay bureaucrats or be entrepreneurs. Those companies that follow the above simple prescriptions can successfully discover the hidden profits in their own boardrooms and workplaces—and provide more jobs, more stable consumer prices, and more dividends as we strain to exit bureaucratic capitalism and enter the new Partnership Economy.

Notes

Introduction: An Inquiry into "Avoidable Waste"
Page
11 First book on waste and bureaucracy: Since 1981, there has been an impressive body of literature on management—and mismanagement. Though none of these works have concentrated solely on business waste and bureaucracy, they have contributed to our effort. These include: *The Art of Japanese Management* by Richard T. Pascale and Anthony G. Athos; *Theory Z: How American Business Can Meet the Japanese Challenge* by William Ouchi; *In Search of Excellence* by Thomas J. Peters and Robert H. Waterman; *Corporate Cultures* by Terrence E. Deal and Allan A. Kennedy; *The Next American Frontier* by Robert B. Reich; *Industrial Renaissance: Producing a Competitive Future for America* by William J. Abernathy, Kim B. Clark, and Alan M. Kantrow; *Beyond the Waste Land* by Samuel Bowles, David M. Gordon, and Thomas E. Weisskopf; *Working Together* by John Simmons and William J. Mares; *Profits Without Production* by Seymour Melman; *The 100 Best Companies to Work for in America* by Robert Levering, Milton Moskowitz, and Michael Katz.

12 1981 article: *The Washington Post,* October 9, 1981, p. B1.

13 Market imperfections: See generally, L. Thurow, *Dangerous Currents: The State of Economics* (1983), and Kuttner, "The Poverty of Economics," *The Atlantic Monthly,* February 1985, p. 74.

14 ". . . always done it that way": This remark was said to Donald Marron, CEO of Paine Webber. Interview with Donald Marron, August 9, 1983.

15 Growth of supervisory personnel: Bureau of Economic Statistics, *Handbook of Basic Economic Statistics* 241 (November 1983).

17 Hays and Abernathy: *Harvard Business Review,* July-August 1980, p. 67.

17 Spending on social services: R. Reich, *The Next American Frontier,* p. 222 (1983).

17 Plant shutdowns and environmental expenditures: See generally, R. Grossman and R. Kazis, *Fear at Work: Job Blackmail, Labor and the Environment* (1982).

18 Baldridge: Appearance on PBS's *Firing Line,* "Is Reaganomics Working," June 2, 1983, p. 18 of published transcript.

18 Samuels: Interview with Howard Samuels, December 9, 1983.

19 Judson: "The Awkward Truth About Productivity," *Harvard Business Review,* September-October 1983, p. 93.

19 Rourke: Interview with Charles Rourke, August 18, 1983.

19 Veblen: *The Theory of Business Enterprise* 28 (1904).

19 McGowan: Interview with William McGowan, October 6, 1983.

20 Iverson: Interview with Ken Iverson, May 20, 1983.

20 Parker Pen bonuses: Nelson-Horchler, "Paying for Productivity," *Industry Week,* April 4, 1983, p. 6.

21 Weinig: Interview with Sheldon Weinig, July 14, 1983.

21 Pestillo: Interview with Peter Pestillo, June 23, 1983.

Chapter 1. Corpocracy: The Rise of the Corporate Bureaucracy

23 Weber on bureaucracy: M. Weber, *From Max Weber: Essays in Sociology,* trans. and ed. H.H. Gerth and C.W. Mills, p. 196 (1946).

23 Government waste: Interview with J.P. Grace, August 5, 1983. Also, *The Washington Post,* December 6, 1981, p. F3; and *The New York Times,* January 13, 1984, p. 1.

23 D.B. Marron: Interview, August 9, 1983.

24 Westerman on bureaucracy: *Fortune,* May 4, 1981, p. 358.

24 Main on bureaucracy: Ibid., p. 357.

24 Weber, *Essays on Sociology,* p. 197.

24 H. Gunders: Interview, July 12, 1983.

25 B. Klein: Interview, October 5, 1983.

25 Westerman, op. cit., p. 358.

26 On forming CIGNA Corp.: Anonymous source in interview. Also, *The Wall Street Journal,* July 29, 1983, p. 36; *Philadelphia Inquirer,* October 31, 1983, p. 1-D.

26 Diminishing control: A. Downs, *Inside Bureaucracy,* p. 143 (1966).

26 ABC study: *The Winning Performances of Midsized Growth Companies,* done by McKinsey & Co. for the American Business Conference.

27 Rise of administrators: S. Bowles, D.M. Gordon, T.E. Weisskopf, *Beyond the Waste Land,* p. 167 (1983).

27 50 percent increase: *Handbook of Basic Economic Statistics,* Bureau of Economic Statistics, November 1983, p. 241.

27 F.M. Scherer: Interview, February 7, 1985; "Economics of Scale and Industrial Concentration," in *Industrial Concentration: The New Learning,* H. Goldschmid (ed.) et al. (1974).

27   J. Rich: Interview, August 17, 1984.

27   Opinion Research Corp., Princeton, N.J., "Research Institute Recommendations," November 25, 1983.

28   A. Briloff: Interview, October 25, 1983.

28   J. Rich: Interview, August 17, 1984.

28   J. Schnapp: Interview, September 7, 1984.

28   W. Abernathy: Interview, April 28, 1983.

29   E. Morris, *The Rise of Theodore Roosevelt* Chapter 19 (1979).

29   Sohma on walking around: *Journal of Japanese Trade and Industry,* September 1982.

29   W.G. McGowan: Interview, October 6, 1983.

30   Lehman Brothers: K. Auletta, "The Fall of Lehman Brothers," *The New York Times Magazine,* February 17 and 24, 1985.

30   Getting ahead at Chemical: Anonymous source.

31   FOCUS at Citibank: Anonymous source.

31   Weber, *Essays on Sociology,* p. 233.

31   J. Bensman: Interview, November 7, 1983.

32   JETRO seminar: *Journal of Japanese Trade and Industry,* September 1982.

32   Coffee on information loss: J. Coffee, Jr., "Beyond the Shut-Eyed Sentry," *Virginia Law Review,* November 1977, p. 1138.

32   FMC Corp.: *Business Week,* October 8, 1984, p. 124.

32   President of Apple Computer on one-page memos: *Fortune,* August 22, 1983, p. 6.

33   A. Krasnoff: Interview, July 21, 1983.

33   T.J. Peters and R.H. Waterman, Jr., *In Search of Excellence,* p. 17 (1982).

34   Folger's coffee decision: "Why Procter & Gamble Is Playing It Even Tougher," *Business Week,* July 18, 1983, p. 178.

34   Getting a raise at Cigna: Anonymous source in interview.

34   T. Levitt, *The Marketing Imagination* (1983).

34   L. Young on CEOs: *The Ward Howell Roundtable,* published by Ward Howell International, February 1981.

35   Warner and Atari: *Fortune,* January 1, 1983, p. 82; *New York,* January 24, 1982, p. 24; *Los Angeles Times,* March 20, 1983, Part V; *The Wall Street Journal,* July 25, 1983, p. 1.

36   Xerox problems: "What Happened to Xerox," *Dun's Business Month,* May 1983, p. 56.

37   R. Jackall, "Moral Mazes: Bureaucracy and Managerial Work," *Harvard Business Review,* September-October 1983, p. 125.

37   *Forbes* on consultants: "Are All These Consultants Really Necessary?" October 10, 1983, p. 136.

37   J. Horn: Interview, June 6, 1983.

38   Jackall, op. cit., p. 127.

38   J.R. Hackman in letter to authors, November 18, 1984.

38   Financial Accounting Standards Board: *Viewpoints,* June 24, 1983.

38 Avis stashes debts: *The Wall Street Journal,* December 13, 1983, p. 1.

39 Continental Illinois: J.L. Rowe, Jr., "How a Bank Lent Itself to Disaster," *The Washington Post,* July 29, 1984, p. A1.

39 S.C. Gwynne, "Adventures in the Loan Trade," *Harper's,* September 1983, pp. 22–26.

40 B. Klein: Interview, October 5, 1983.

40 For more on oligopolistic behavior, see J.M. Blair, *Economic Concentration* (1972); W.G. Shepherd, *Market Power and Economic Welfare* (1970); F.M. Scherer, *Industrial Market Structure and Economic Performance* (2nd ed., 1980).

40 Sparrows Point story: Anonymous source in interview.

41 Resisting radials: J. Fallows, "American Industry: What Ails It. How to Save It," *Atlantic,* September 1980, p. 35.

42 R.A. Charpie: Interview, September 16, 1983; Cabot annual reports.

42 Buehler and AT&T: *The Wall Street Journal,* December 16, 1983, p. 1.

42 Exxon story: Anonymous source in interview.

43 Suchodolski of Michigan Consolidated: A.F. Westin, *Whistle Blowing! Loyalty and Dissent in the Corporation,* p. 83 (1981).

43 Splendid isolation: J.P. Wright, *On a Clear Day You Can See General Motors,* p. 17 (1979).

43 Losing sight of goals: Ibid., p. 7.

43 Fourteenth-floor gossip: Ibid., p. 19.

44 Steel CEO and Austin: Described by Ralph Nader in "Reforming Corporate Governance," *California Management Review,* Summer 1984, p. 131.

44 Blue Cross in Boston: B. Kuttner, "The Declining Middle," *Atlantic,* July 1983, p. 63.

44 J. Heller, *Something Happened,* p. 13 (1974).

45 Iacocca on *Donahue:* Multimedia Entertainment, Transcript No. 12263, p. 3.

45 C.W. Mills, *White Collar: The American Middle Classes* (1951); E. Fromm, *The Sane Society* (1955); W.H. Whyte, Jr., *The Organization Man* (1956); A. Harrington, *Life in the Crystal Palace* (1959).

45 M. Maccoby, *The Gamesman,* p. 44 (1976).

45 E. Shorris, *The Oppressed Middle* (1981); interview with Earl Shorris, December 23, 1983.

46 Jackall, op. cit., p. 119.

46 Management ranks increased: Bureau of Labor Statistics figures cited in *The New York Times,* April 14, 1983.

46 M. Pilot: Interview, January 24, 1984.

46 S. Levitan: Interview, January 23, 1984.

47 The Hay Associates survey reported in *Industry Week,* July 25, 1983, p. 58.

47 Opinion Research Corp., op. cit.

47 A.D. Chandler, Jr., *The Visible Hand,* p. 3 (1977).

47 Founding of business schools: Ibid., p. 467.

47 Jackall: op. cit., p. 119.

48 Reiner on "planner" title: *Business Week,* April 25, 1983, p. 54.

49 Drucker on titles: *The Wall Street Journal,* March 25, 1983.

49 GE's hierarchy: Told to the authors by GE public relations official Art Demaris.

49 J. Rich: Interview, August 17, 1983.

50 C. Argyris, "Interpersonal Barriers to Decision Making," *Harvard Business Review,* March-April 1966, p. 84.

50 Downs, *Inside Bureaucracy,* p. 147.

51 C. Bernard, *The Functions of an Executive,* p. 231 (1958).

51 G. Tullock, *The Politics of Bureaucracy,* pp. 137–141 (1965).

51 J.Q. Wilson on change: In 1963 speech to the American Political Science Association.

51 D.L. Landen on quality circles: *Industry Week,* July 25, 1983, p. 60.

52 Lipp: Interview with former Chemical Bank executive, who requested anonymity.

52 J. Bensman: Interview, November 7, 1983.

53 Downs, *Inside Bureaucracy,* p. 58.

53 Authority on spans: Interview with C.K. Rourke, August 18, 1983.

53 P. McFadden: Interview, September 3, 1983.

54 Smith on staffers: *Business Week,* December 21, 1981, p. 70.

54 On IBM, 3M, and DEC: Peters and Waterman, *In Search of Excellence,* p. 312.

54 Reichert: *Business Week,* April 25, 1983, p. 52.

54 R.E. Wintermantel on layers: *Business Week,* May 23, 1983, letter to the editor.

54 P. Drucker, *The Wall Street Journal,* March 25, 1983, Op-Ed page.

54 Opinion Research Corp.: *Business Week,* April 25, 1983, p. 54.

55 R.N. Noyce: Interview, March 2, 1983.

56 C.K. Rourke: Interview, August 18, 1983.

57 A. Zaleznik, *Human Dilemmas of Leadership* (1966).

57 Weber, *Essays on Sociology,* p. 232.

58 S. Harman: Interview, February 25, 1985.

60 Buffet on bureaucracy: *Fortune,* August 22, 1983, p. 137; the 1981 and 1982 Berkshire Hathaway annual reports.

61 Reich on "paper entrepreneurs": *The Next American Frontier,* p. 140 (1983).

61 Welch on staffing: In a speech before the Edison Electric Institute Annual Convention in Minneapolis, June 8, 1983.

61 F.T. Vincent: Interview, September 21, 1983.

62 J. Bensman: Interview, November 7, 1983.

62 Maccoby, *The Gamesman.*

62 Coffee, op. cit., p. 1103.

62 Hammer: *Facts on File,* June 19, 1976, p. 442.

63 Uhl of Fairchild: "Handing Down the Old Hands' Wisdom," *Fortune,* June 13, 1983, p. 97.

63 SEC on nepotism: *The Wall Street Journal,* July 9, 1982, p. 6, and December 2, 1982, p. 18.

63 *Tavoulareas* v. *Washington Post: The Wall Street Journal,* April 6, 1983, p. 12; *The New York Times,* December 4, 1984, p. D1.

63 Examples of nepotism: *Fortune,* February 6, 1984, p. 143.

64 "Inexorable pressure": January 2, 1969, memo from Ireland to Geneen.

64 "X" folder: From Ireland's personal files.

65 The plot: Memorandum to the file about interview with J. Borkin by L. Hammond, member of the Watergate Special Prosecution Force, January 12, 1974; memorandum to the file about interview with John Tobin, Ireland's personal attorney in New York, with Hammond, April 5, 1974; copy of Ireland's questions, hand-written, for the government to ask Geneen; "Report of the ITT Task Force" to Special Prosecutor H.S. Ruth from R.J. Davis, August 25, 1975.

65 H. Geneen with A. Moscow, *Managing,* p. 252 (1984).

65 Unloading assets: *The Wall Street Journal,* January 17, 1985, p. 3.

66 Ling anecdote: Related by L.H. Young in Ward Howell Roundtable, published in February 1981.

66 Lilco: See Chapter 7.

66 Agee-Cunningham: A. Sloan, *Three Plus One Equals Billions,* pp. 26–27 (1983).

67 T.A. Vanderslice: Interview, August 8, 1983, *The Wall Street Journal,* December 2, 1983, p. 4.

68 Toro's troubles: L. McDonnell, "Trials at Toro," *Pioneer Press Dispatch* (St. Paul), October 11, 1982, p. B1.

68 L. Young: Interview, April 13, 1983.

68 Gencorp: *The Wall Street Journal,* October 23, 1984, p. 1.

69 J. Bensman: Interview, November 7, 1983.

69 K. Bouldir.g, *American Economic Review,* May 1968, p. 5.

69 A. Smith, *The Wealth of Nations,* p. 741 (Glasgow ed., 1976).

69 Board of directors manages: E. Knight, *Corporate Governance in America,* Congressional Research Service, December 31, 1982.

69 For history of state chartering: R. Nader, M. Green, and J. Seligman, *Taming the Giant Corporation,* pp. 33–61 (1976).

70 W.O. Douglas, "Directors Who Do Not Direct," *Harvard Law Review* (1934), p. 1305.

70 M.L. Mace, *Directors: Myth and Reality,* p. 41 (1971).

70 E.S. Herman, *Corporate Control, Corporate Power,* p. 266 (1981).

70 Outside help: C.E. Meyer,. "Small Firms Go Outside for Advice," *The Washington Post,* February 10, 1985, p. 61.

71 E. Faber: "How I Lost the Great Debate about Corporate Ethics," *Fortune,* November 1976, p. 180.

71 W. Niskanen: *The New York Times,* December 23, 1984, p. 1.

72 C.C. Brown: *Putting the Corporate Board to Work,* p. 100 (1976).

72 Brandeis on interlocks: "Breaking the Money Trusts," *Harper's Weekly,* December 6, 1913.

73 On interlocks: F.D. Schoorman, M.H. Bazerm, and R.S. Atkin, "Interlocking Dircctorates: A Strategy for Reducing Environmental Uncertainty," *Academy of Management Review,* Vol. 6, No. 2 (1981); Federal Trade Commission, *Report on Interlocking Directorates* (1952); *Interlocking Directorates Among the Major U.S. Corporations,* staff study of the Committee on Governmental Affairs, January 1978, p. 27.

73 Williams on boards: In speech, "Corporate Accountability," before the fifth annual Securities Regulation Institute, San Diego, January 18, 1978.

73 H.M. Williams: Interview, February 28, 1983.

74 H. Gunders: Interview, July 12, 1983.

76 Written resources on RCA's developing problems: D. Smith, "The Decline and Fall of the RCA Empire," *Channels,* June-July 1982, p. 26; A.F. Ehrbar, "Splitting Up RCA," *Fortune,* March 22, 1982, p. 62; "RCA: Still Another Master," *Business Week,* August 17, 1981, p. 80; RCA annual proxy statements and Form 10K's.

76 Delaware decision: Discussed in "A Landmark Ruling That Puts Board Members in Peril," *Business Week,* March 18, 1985, p. 56.

77 L. Korn: Interview, March 1, 1983.

77 Korn/Ferry International, *Board of Directors Tenth Annual Study,* February 1983.

77 Greenwald: *The New York Times,* February 23, 1983, p. D1.

78 Schwartz on illusion: "Shareholder Democracy: A Reality or Chimera?" *California Management Review,* Spring 1983, p. 54.

78 Project on Corporate Responsibility: Nader, Green, and Seligman, *Taming the Giant,* pp. 82–83.

78 Institutional stock ownership: *Business Week,* August 13, 1984, p. 86.

78 Voting against Penn Central: *Institutional Investor,* October 1983, p. 178.

78 Voting against Superior: *The New York Times,* June 12, 1983, p. F4.

79 Voting against International Paper: *Institutional Investor,* October 1983, p. 188.

79 Voting against Bendix: Affidavit of R.C. Dinerstein (Citibank vice-president) in *Martin Marietta Corporation* v. *The Bendix Corporation,* U.S. District Court, Southern District of New York, September 16, 1982.

79 P. Vermilye: Interview, November 28, 1983; ". . . cause for celebration," *The New York Times,* June 12, 1983, p. F4.

79 Odyssey versus TWC: Interview with Lester Pollack, one of the Odyssey Partners, October 25, 1983.

80 Schwartz, op. cit., p. 60.

81 Hackman on timing: Letter to authors, November 18, 1984.

84 People Express: Interview with J.R. Hackman, August 31, 1983; P. Nulty, "A Champ of Cheap Airlines," *Fortune,* March 22, 1982; "People Express," Case Study No. 9-483-103, Harvard Business School (1983); J.R. Hackman, "The Transition That Hasn't Happened," *New Futures: The Challenge of Managing Corporate Transitions* (1984); L. Rhodes, "That Daring Young Man and His Flying Machines," *Inc.,* January 1984,

p. 42; "Peoples *(sic)* Takes on the Big Boys," *Newsweek,* August 27, 1984, pp. 52–53; *Aviation Daily,* November 14 and 27, 1984.

87 Discussion of David Mahoney is based on the following: T. Redburn, "Mahoney: He Dealt Himself a Hot Hand," *Los Angeles Times,* July 10, 1983, p. 1; "Buying His Own Company," *Newsweek,* June 20, 1983, p. 56; R. Raissman, "The Battling Maverick as Corporate Chieftain," *Advertising Age* magazine, May 23, 1983, p. M-4; L. Bridges, "Trying Harder," *Success!,* March 11, 1983, p. 18; C.J. Loomis, "Incredible Shrinking Norton Simon," *Fortune,* March 7, 1983, p. 86; D.S. Looney, "David Mahoney," *People,* January 31, 1983, p. 31; "The Power of Positive Thinking," *Forbes,* August 20, 1979, p. 123.

88 Weinig profile: Interviews with S. Weinig, April 1 and July 14, 1983; Materials Research Corp. annual report and Form 10K for 1983.

92 D.B. Marron: Interviews, August 9, 1983 and November 26, 1984; C. Welles, *The Last Days of the Club* (1975); "Paine Webber, Back from Brink, Catching Up with Competition," *The Washington Post,* February 13, 1983, p. F1.

92 One in nine jobs . . . : *The Economist,* July 30, 1983, p. 59.

93 Iacocca on arrogance: *Time,* March 21, 1983, p. 50.

93 Ford on quality: *The New York Times,* January 10, 1983.

93 U.S. automakers lose market share: *The New York Times,* September 22, 1983, p. D1.

93 W.J. Abernathy, K.B. Clark, and A.M. Kantrow, *Industrial Renaissance,* pp. 39–40 (1983).

93 Sloan aphorism: Yates, *Decline and Fall,* p. 215.

94 "The Detroit Mind": Yates, *Decline and Fall,* Chapter 2.

95 J.C. Bowling, Interview, July 6, 1983.

95 Outside Supplier: Interview with Pestillo, March 6, 1985.

95 "Era of stunning complacency": S. Flax, "How Detroit Is Reforming the Steelmakers," *Fortune,* May 16, 1983, p. 126.

95 Rylander: Ibid.

95 Bradford: Ibid.

96 DOT's statistics: *The New York Times,* March 28, 1983, p. D12.

96 Harbour: *Business Week,* September 14, 1981, p. 97.

96 Red balance sheet: *Forbes,* April 25, 1983, pp. 98–99.

97 P.J. Pestillo: Interview, June 23, 1983.

97 D. Ephlin: Interview, June 24, 1983.

97 Forty-seven thousand laid off, thirteen offices closed: Ford public relations department.

98 "Deep distrust": *Fortune,* April 18, 1983, p. 63.

98 Profit-sharing figures: Ford public relations department.

98 D.E. Petersen's remark: *Business Week,* December 21, 1981, pp. 69–70; Salary cuts: Ford public relations department.

98 Caldwell warns suppliers: Pestillo interview.

99 Quick results: *Dun's Business Month,* June 1983, p. 75.

99 Wixom plant: Interviews with Ford officials.

99 Louisville: *Fortune,* April 18, 1983, pp. 64 and 70.

100 Wayne assembly plant: Interview with officials and workers at the plant.

100 Caldwell "the Stamper": Ephlin and Pestillo interviews.

101 Quotas: A.B. Fisher, "Can Detroit Live Without Quotas?" *Fortune,* June 25, 1984, pp. 20–25; L. Minard, "Saab, Mercedes, Volvo, BMW, Jaguar, Watch Out!" *Forbes,* September 10, 1984, pp. 41–48.

101 D. McCammon: Interview, June 23, 1983, and Ephlin interview.

Chapter 2. Wasteful Workplace: The Participation Solution

103 Cupples: Interview with Walter Cupples, November 8, 1984.

103 Caldwell and Ephlin: Interview with Donald Ephlin, June 24, 1983.

104 Jobs saved: Cited in Egerton, "Workers Take Over the Store," *New York Times Magazine,* September 11, 1983, p. 164.

104 Keynes: J.M. Keynes, *Essays in Persuasion,* p. 344 (1932).

105 "Human capital" more productive: New York Stock Exchange, *People and Productivity: A Challenge to Corporate America* (1982), p. 5.

105 Pope and Reagan: Quoted in *Congressional Record* by Sen. Russell Long, November 17, 1983, S16629, etc.

105 Hart: Speech delivered in New Brunswick, New Jersey, May 25, 1984.

106 Luce: Quoted in Siegel, "Why Things Don't Work," *Playboy,* September 1982, p. 95.

106 "Time and Motion" studies: For an excellent summary, see J. Simmons and W. Mares, *Working Together,* pp. 17–28 (1982); also, Kovach, Sands, and Brooks, *Advanced Management Journal,* Winter 1981, pp. 4–14.

106 F.W. Taylor, *The Principles of Scientific Management,* pp. 41–47 (1947).

107 Reich: R. Reich, *The Next American Frontier,* p. 67 (1983).

107 Burck: "Working Smarter," *Fortune,* June 15, 1981, p. 70.

107 Bluestone: "Workers Have Brains Too," *Workplace Democracy,* Summer 1982, p. 6.

108 Lordstown: See generally, Garson, "Luddites in Lordstown," *Harper's Magazine,* June 1972, p. 68; Kremen, "Lordstown—Searching for a Better Way of Life," *The New York Times,* September 9, 1973, p. III-1.

108 Grebey: "Labor Costs Get a Working Over," *Time,* December 19, 1983, pp. 48–49.

109 Chernow: "Grey Flannel Goons," *Working Papers,* January/February 1981, p. 19.

109 Hospital workers film: *NBC Nightly News,* February 23, 1984.

109 Patterson: *The New York Times,* September 12, 1984.

110 Williamson: New York *Daily News,* September 23, 1983, p. 5.

110 Coors: R.E. Smith, *Workrights,* p. 67 (1983); also, interview with Robert Ellis Smith, March 14, 1985.

110 AFL-CIO official: Ibid. See generally, Samuels, "What If the Lie Detector Lies?" *The Nation,* December 3, 1983, p. 566.

110 Magnet: Magnet, "Phelps Dodge's Lonely Stand," *Fortune,* August 22, 1983, p. 107.

110 Warlike atmosphere: Ibid.

110 Kuttner: "Can Labor Lead?" *The New Republic,* March 12, 1984, p. 12.

111 Labor grievances: Cited in Simmons and Mares, *Working Together,* p. 283.

111 Lost days to strikes: Reich, "The Profession of Management," *The New Republic,* June 27, 1981, p. 29.

111 NLRB reinstatements: Cited in speech by Tom Donahue, secretary-treasurer of AFL-CIO, "The Future of Work," January 10, 1984.

111 Weiler: Weiler, "Promises to Keep: Securing Workers' Rights to Self-Organization Under the NLRA," *Harvard Law Review,* Vol. 96, June 1983, p. 1769.

111 Kotter: J. Kotter, *The General Managers* (1983).

111 Maccoby: "Trust as a Labor-Management Cost Item," *The New York Times,* March 31, 1978, p. A27.

112 Suggestion box: *Business Week,* August 18, 1980, p. 102.

112 Simmons and Mares: *Working Together,* pp. 28–29.

113 Bluestone and Harman: Bluestone, op. cit.

114 NYSE study: NYSE, op. cit.

114 Gyllenhammar: Simmons and Mares, *Working Together,* pp. 226–227.

115 McKenna: *The Wall Street Journal,* September 20, 1983, p. 39.

115 Trojan horse: D. Olsen, "Labor's Stake in a Democratic Workplace," *Working Papers,* March-April 1981, p. 12; see generally, Compa, "The Dangers of Worker Control," *The Nation,* October 2, 1982, p. 300.

115 Gompers: Quoted in Kaus, "The Trouble with Unions," *Harper's,* June 1983, p. 35.

115 Roehl: Interview with William Roehl, March 15, 1985.

115 Winpisinger: Interview with William Winpisinger, February 1, 1984.

115 Halal and Brown, and Haire: Halal and Brown, "Participative Management: Myth & Reality," *California Management Review,* Summer 1981, p. 20.

116 NYSE study: NYSE, op. cit., p. 5; for an excellent compilation about participation and productivity, see K. Friedan, *Workplace Democracy and Productivity* (1980).

117 Department of Commerce study: Conte and Tannenbaum, "Employee-Owned Companies: Is the Difference Measurable?" *Monthly Labor Review,* July 1978, pp. 23–28.

117 Donahue: Interview with Tom Donahue, February 2, 1984.

117 Gotbaum: Olson, *Working Papers,* March-April 1981, p. 15.

118 Rosow: Guyon, "Life on the Job," *The Wall Street Journal,* April 29, 1981, p. 1.

118 Michigan study: Cited in Yankelovich, "The Work Ethic Is Underemployed," *Psychology Today,* May 1982, p. 5.

118 Simmons: Press release, John Simmons, April 16, 1984.

119 Kelley: *Newsweek,* December 19, 1983, p. 43.

119 Sporck: Interview with Charles Sporck, March 4, 1983.

119 Beiber: Engel, "Labor's New Chieftains," *Industry Week,* July 11, 1983, p. 34.

120   14 percent: NYSE, op. cit., p. 23.

120   750 firms: Cited in Simmons and Mares, *Working Together,* p. 102.

120   Settling early: Ibid., p. 141.

120   57 percent to 86 percent: NYSE, op. cit., p. 281; and J. Simmons, letter to the editor, *Fortune,* May 28, 1984, p. 14.

121   Toyota: Kenichi Ohmae, *The Wall Street Journal,* March 29, 1982, p. 18.

121   Lockheed and General Foods: *Fortune,* July 27, 1981, p. 62; "Stonewalling Plant Democracy," *Business Week,* March 28, 1977, p. 78.

121   Solar Turbines, etc.: W. Werther, "Quality Circles and Corporate Culture," *National Productivity,* Summer 1982, p. 301.

121   McPherson: Simmons and Mares, *Working Together,* pp. 172–173.

121   Oswald: Interview with Rudy Oswald, February 2, 1984.

122   Ford plant in Great Britain: *Business Week,* May 18, 1981, p. 44.

122   Danjin: Simmons and Mares, *Working Together,* p. 71.

122   Burck: "What Happens When Workers Manage Themselves," *Fortune,* July 27, 1981, pp. 65–68.

122   Denver bank: Interview with Walter Cupples, July 26, 1983.

123   Solar Turbines: American Productivity Center, Case Study No. 1 (1980).

123   Camens: American Productivity Center memorandum, "Steel—An Industry at the Crossroads," September 1982.

123   LMPT savings: Ibid.

124   300 LMPTs: "Steel Listens to Workers and Likes What It Hears," *Business Week,* December 19, 1983, p. 92.

124   Circle member on interest cost: Quoted in Sims and Manz, "Conversations Within Self-Managed Work Groups," *National Productivity Review,* Summer 1982, p. 261.

124   Thorsrud: Raskin, "Workable World," *The New York Times,* November 25, 1975, p. 37.

125   University of Michigan: Simmons and Mares, *Working Together,* p. 267.

125   *Journal of Corporation Law:* Marsh and McAllister, "ESOPs Tables: A Survey of Companies with Employee Stock Ownership Plans," *Journal of Corporation Law,* Spring 1981.

125   National Center: *Employee Ownership* newsletter, March 1983, p. 1.

125   Ford in Alabama: Reich, *Frontier,* p. 188.

126   Ward off takeovers: Blumstein, "New Role for Employee Plans," *The New York Times,* January 2, 1985, p. D1; and "ESOPs: Revolution or Ripoff?" *Business Week,* April 15, 1985, p. 94.

126   South Bend Lathe: For a discussion of this firm and this problem generally, see Zwerdling, "Employee Ownership: How Well Is It Working?" *Working Papers,* May-June 1979, p. 15.

126   Whyte: 1977 Report to Department of Labor, *Organizing Strategies for Saving Jobs and Strengthening Local Communities.*

126   Taylor: *The New York Times,* June 17, 1984, p. 6.

126   Rath generally: Gunn, "The Fruits of Rath: A New Model of Self-Management," *Working Papers,* March-April 1981, p. 17; Morris, "Workers at Employee-Run Rath Packing Are Divided, Bitter After Chapter XI

Filing," *The Wall Street Journal,* November 14, 1983, p. 33; "Gripes of Rath," *The Wall Street Journal,* December 2, 1981, p. 1.

127 Eaker's: National Center for Employee Ownership, *Employee Ownership,* March 1983, pp. 7–8.

128 Hyatt-Clark generally: *The New York Times,* August 24, 1984, p. D20; NYSE, op. cit., p. 32; The Conference Board, *Employee Buyouts: An Alternative to Plant Closings,* study (1983), pp. 7–12; Beale, "When the Workers Are in Charge," *Philadelphia Inquirer,* August 15, 1982, p. 28; *The New York Times,* April 27, 1982, p. B1.

128 Weirton generally: Conference Board, op. cit., pp. 24–33; Greenhouse, "Employees Make a Go of Weirton," *The New York Times,* January 6, 1985, p. III-4; *The New York Times,* August 29, 1984, p. D20; Goldstein; "Saving Jobs, But at What Price?" *The Nation,* December 10, 1983, p. 594; Corrigan, "Workers at Weirton Steel See Only One Way to Save Their Failing Plant: Buy It," *National Journal,* August 13, 1983, p. 1672; "Refusing to Say Uncle," *Time,* August 9, 1982, p. 18; Labich, "A Steel Town's Bid to Save Itself," *Fortune,* April 18, 1983, p. 103.

130 Cooperative employee-owners: See generally, D. Ellerman, *Notes on the Cooperative/ESOP Debate,* Industrial Cooperative Association, 1983; Lewin, "Worker-Held Enterprises," *The New York Times,* April 17, 1984, p. D2.

131 WOSC: Miller, "Workers Owned," *Southern Exposure,* Winter 1980.

131 Bernstein: *Democratization of Organization: Theory, Practice and Further Possibilities,* Section 4, Ph.D. Dissertation, Stanford University, 1972.

132 25 percent to 60 percent: M. Carnoy and D. Shearer, *Economic Democracy,* p. 147 (1980).

132 Bennett: "An Interview with Leamon J. Bennett," *Harvard Business Review,* January-February 1979, p. 75.

132 *O'Toole:* J. O'Toole, *Making America Work,* pp. 95–96 (1981).

132 Reuther: Cited by Sen. Russell Long in *Congressional Record,* November 17, 1983, S16629.

132 Smith: *Fortune,* April 16, 1984, p. 132.

133 Metzger: *Business Week,* June 28, 1982, p. 45.

133 Fraser: *The New York Times,* January 9, 1983, p. IV-2.

133 17 million workers in 435,000 firms: Hoerr, "Why Labor and Management Are Both Buying Profit-Sharing," *Business Week,* January 10, 1983, p. 84; *Fortune,* March 5, 1984, p. 7.

133 77 percent: NYSE, op. cit., p. 36; *Fortune,* March 5, 1984, p. 7.

133 D'Amico: *Business Week,* August 8, 1983, p. 20.

133 Majerus: *Fortune,* April 16, 1984, p. 132.

133 1,000 corporations: Nelson-Horchler, "Paying for Productivity," *Industry Week,* April 4, 1983, p. 36.

134 Motorola and TRW: Ibid.

134 Columbus Auto Parts: American Productivity Center, Case Study No. 2, 1980.

135 Thurow on bonus plan: "A Strategy for Revitalizing American Industry," *California Management Review,* Fall 1984, pp. 29–32.

135   GM-UAW: Mills, "A New Cooperation Sweeps Detroit," *The New York Times,* October 7, 1984, p. III-3.

135   Savodnik: Saul, "When Firing's Just Not Fair," *Newsday,* October 7, 1984, p. 88.

136   *Petermann* case: Discussed in *The Wall Street Journal,* June 11, 1984, p. 24.

136   Canned employees: See generally, A. Westin and S. Gillers, *Individual Rights in the Corporation* (1980); D. Ewing, *Do It My Way or You're Fired* (1983); Gould, "Protection from Wrongful Dismissal," *The New York Times,* October 22, 1984, p. A21; Horton, "If Right to Fire Is Abused, Uncle Sam May Step In," *The Wall Street Journal,* June 11, 1984, p. 24; Seligman, "Fire Power," *Fortune,* May 30, 1983, p. 48.

137   Brown: *The Wall Street Journal,* September 13, 1981, p. 1.

137   Five states: Otten, "States Begin to Protect Employees Who Blow Whistle on Their Firms," *The Wall Street Journal,* December 31, 1984, p. 11.

137   Roche: "The Whistleblowers," *Time,* April 17, 1972, p. 85.

137   Drucker: R.E. Smith, *Workrights* (1983).

137   McGraw, Jr.: A. Westin, *Whistleblowing! Loyalty & Dissent in the Corporation,* p. 3 (1981).

138   Stieber: "Curtailing the Freedom to Fire," *Business Week,* March 19, 1984, p. 29.

138   West German situation: *The Wall Street Journal,* June 11, 1984, p. 24.

138   Ewing: *The Wall Street Journal,* January 3, 1983, p. 22.

139   Westin: Interview with Alan Westin, March 14, 1985.

139   United Technologies: Mackin, "Strategies for Local Ownership and Control," Industrial Cooperative Association, January 1983.

140   40 percent still unemployed: Cited in Woodworth, "Workers as Bosses," *Social Policy,* January-February 1981.

140   30 times suicide rate and 70 percent health insurance: Ibid.

141   Atlantic Richfield: Chavez, "Why Arco Left Town," *The New York Times,* July 25, 1982, p. III-1.

141   Brown and Williamson, *The Wall Street Journal,* April 12, 1983, p. 1.

141   Maine and Massachusetts: *The Wall Street Journal,* June 26, 1984, p. 37; "Plant Closing Bills: Labor Takes a Beating," *Business Week,* August 20, 1984, p. 40; "Plant Shutdowns: States Take a New Tack," *Business Week,* October 24, 1983, p. 72.

142   Comparison of U.S.-Japanese firms: NYSE, op. cit., pp. 17–20.

142   Chrysler-Toyo Kogyo: *The New York Times,* March 30, 1983, p. D19.

142   Packard: *Business Week,* December 31, 1984, p. 48.

143   Hewlett-Packard: T. Peters and R. Waterman, Jr., *In Search of Excellence,* p. 244 (1982).

143   "The kind of blunders": *The New York Times,* May 14, 1976, p. D1.

143   Fraser: Raskin, "The Labor Leader as Company Director," *The New York Times,* April 27, 1980, business section, p. 1; Sawyer, "Chrysler-UAW Deal: More Than Just a Peek at the Books," *The Washington Post,* January 19, 1980, p. A5.

144 *Business Week:* "Labor's Voice on Board: Good or Bad?" *Business Week,* May 7, 1984, p. 153.

144 Class collaboration: *The New York Times,* January 5, 1978, p. 37.

144 Fraser on Chrysler board: Simmons and Mares, *Working Together,* p. 249.

144 Fraser on "always reacting": Hoerr, "A Union Seat on the Board: The Test Isn't Over," *Business Week,* November 22, 1982, p. 30.

145 14 corporations: *Business Week,* May 7, 1984, p. 151.

145 Eastern-labor antagonism: Sherman, "Eastern Airlines on the Brink," *Fortune,* October 17, 1983, p. 102.

145 Borman ploy: Discussed by John Simmons in unpublished article, "Eastern Airlines: The Unions and Management Try a New Approach," October 23, 1984 (Participation Associates, Amherst, Mass.).

146 Eastern-union pact: "Eastern's Revolutionary Treaty with Its Unions," *Business Week,* December 26, 1983, p. 22.

146 *Wall Street Journal* headline: October 31, 1984, p. 1.

146 Borman on "only way to manage": Quoted in press release, Participation Associates, January 7, 1985.

146 Mace: *Directors: Myth and Reality* (1971).

147 Blasi: "A Modern ESOP's Fable," *Newsweek,* December 31, 1984, p. 58.

147 Thurow: "A Strategy for Revitalizing American Industry," *California Management Review,* Fall 1984, p. 27.

Chapter 3. Innovation: Corporate Luddites or Pioneers?

150 M. Twain, *A Connecticut Yankee in King Arthur's Court* 5 (Dodd, Mead, 1960 ed.).

150 Adam Priest: Interview with his mother, journalist Alice Priest.

150 Hitachi pleaded guilty to theft on February 8, 1983: *Facts on File,* 1983, p. 112D.

151 Nobel Prize statistics: *Christian Science Monitor,* December 8, 1983.

151 On scientific achievement: *Science Indicators 1982: An Analysis of the State of U.S. Science, Engineering and Technology,* report of the National Science Board (1983), p. 164.

151 America lags developing products: *The Washington Post,* May 1, 1983, p. 1.

151 U.S. losing preeminence: *Science Indicators 1982,* pp. 32–33.

151 Morita on America: L. Weymouth, "Meet Mr. Sony," *Atlantic,* November 1979, p. 33.

152 B. Evans and C. Evans, *Dictionary of Contemporary Usage,* p. 420 (1957).

153 Research defined: E. Mansfield et al., *Research and Innovation in the Modern Corporation* (1971).

153 Mansfield on plant construction: E. Mansfield et al., *Technology Transfer, Productivity, and Economic Policy,* p. 227 (1982).

153 J.A. Schumpeter, *Capitalism, Socialism and Democracy,* p. 88 (1942).

154 Mansfield on R and D patterns: Mansfield, *Technology Transfer.*

154 Civilian R and D spending: *Science Indicators 1982,* p. 2.

154 Worker productivity: *The New York Times,* April 8, 1984, p. 1F.

154 OECD prediction: *Facing the Future: Mastering the Probable and Managing the Unpredictable,* OECD, Paris (1979).

155 L. Mumford: *Technics and Civilization,* pp. 160–162 (1954).

155 J.A. Schumpeter: op. cit., pp. 87–106.

155 J.K. Galbraith: *American Capitalism, the Concept of Countervailing Power,* p. 9 (1952).

155 D.E. Lilienthal *Big Business: A New Era,* p. 69 (1952).

155 J. Jewkes et al., *The Source of Invention* (1958).

155 Examples of how long inventions take to be developed: J.M. Blair, *Economic Concentration,* pp. 230–231 (1972).

156 Xerox: Milton Moscowitz et al., *Everybody's Business: An Almanac,* pp. 415–418 (1980).

156 Goldman on large corporations: *Research and Development: Key Issues for Management,* Conference Board Report No. 842 (1983).

156 A.A. Kennedy on bigness: *Inc.,* April 1984, p. 106.

157 Mansfield on the Pacific: *The New York Times,* August 24, 1982, p. A1.

157 "Some trade specialists . . .": Ibid.

157 Mikuni on Japan as global price-setter: Ibid.

157 Japan, 1950 to 1980: James Abegglen, retired director, Boston Consulting Group, Tokyo, at a symposium sponsored by the Japan-America Society of Washington, October 21, 1981.

158 M. Boretsky, "Trends in U.S. Technology," *American Scientist,* January–February 1975, p. 81; interview with M. Boretsky, June 3, 1983.

158 "Fire sale": Abegglen at the Japan-America Society symposium.

158 Computer graphics: *The Washington Post,* May 1, 1983, p. 1; interview with D. Morgan, May 31, 1983.

159 Light-waves: *The Washington Post,* May 5, 1983, p. 1.

159 Consumer electronics: W.J. Abernathy and R.J. Rosenbloom, "The Institutional Climate for Innovation in Industry: The Role of Management Attitudes and Practices," *The 5-Year Outlook on Science and Technology 1981,* Vol. II, National Science Foundation, pp. 407–419.

160 W.O. Baker: Interview, July 8, 1983.

160 T.A. Vanderslice: Interview, August 8, 1983.

160 M. Boretsky: Interview, June 3, 1983.

161 Two surveys: *The New York Times,* May 7, 1984, p. 1.

161 R. Noyce: Interview, March 2, 1983.

162 W.O. Baker: Interview, July 8, 1983.

162 Two conflicting tales: R.A. Burgelman, *Designs for Corporate Entrepreneurship in Established Firms,* Research Paper Series No. 721, Graduate School of Business, Stanford University (1984), pp. 7–8.

162 J. McManus: Interview, August 16, 1983.

163 A.C. Sigler: Interview, July 13, 1983.

164 Raytheon, Burroughs, 3M, AM International: L.P. Cohen, "Failed Marriages," *The Wall Street Journal,* September 10, 1984, p. 1.

165 Exxon Office Systems: Former top executives who requested anonymity.

165 Ross on the American backwater: *Science,* July 1982, p. 130.

165 Pake on the GI Bill: New York City speech, February 23, 1983.

166 World War II and after: R.B. Reich, *The Next American Frontier,* pp. 100–102 (1983).

166 E. Alterman, *Washington Monthly,* June 1984.

166 Source of R and D funds: *Newsweek,* August 9, 1982, p. 54.

166 $140 million for robots: *The Washington Post,* May 1, 1983, p. 1.

167 C. Johnson in speech before the Foreign Correspondents Club, Tokyo, December 17, 1982.

167 S. Melman, *Profits Without Production,* pp. 173–174 (1983).

168 Footnote: "The Chip," *National Geographic,* October 1982.

169 Description of Silicon Valley: Interview with Regis McKenna of Regis McKenna Public Relations, March 2, 1983; "Silicon Valley, HQ for the 21st Century," *Australian National Times,* February 1981; "Silicon Valley Spirit," *Esquire,* November 1981, pp. 13–14.

169 Japanese chip drive: *Fortune,* June 28, 1982, p. 79; *Business Week,* May 23, 1983, p. 80.

170 SIA goes to Washington: *The Effect of Government Targeting on World Semiconductor Competition: A Case History of Japanese Industrial Strategy and Its Costs for America,* Semiconductor Industry Association (1983).

170 Motorola, TI, IBM, Western Electric: *Fortune,* June 28, 1982, pp. 79–80.

170 Anderson message: T.R. Reid, "Meet Dr. Deming," *APF Reporter,* Summer 1983, p. 14.

171 Osborn memo: Dated June 13, 1983; the memo from the American Embassy, Tokyo, was addressed to the secretary of state, Department of Commerce, and to embassies in Bonn, Geneva, London, Paris, and Seoul.

172 Foster on time: *Research and Development,* Conference Board Report No. 842, pp. 72–75.

173 History of steel: P.R. Lawrence and D. Dyer, *Renewing American Industry,* pp. 55–85 (1983).

173 *Fortune,* March 1936.

173 Consultant describes U.S. Steel: George V. Stocking testifying before the Subcommittee on Study of Monopoly Power, 81st Cong., 2nd sess., pt. 4A, p. 967.

173 W. Adams and H.J. Mueller, *The Structure of American Industry,* p. 118 (1982).

173 W.T. Hogan, S.J.: Interview, April 6, 1983.

174 D.F. Barnett and L.M. Schorsch, *Steel: Upheaval in a Basic Industry.*

174 Industry passes costs to consumer: Interview with H. Mueller, May 8, 1984.

175 Booz•Allen and Hamilton survey: *The New York Times,* December 18, 1983, p. 1F.

175 T.A. Vanderslice: Interview, August 8, 1983.

175 T.V. Learson: Interview, July 25, 1983.

176 Deere, GE, and GM: *The New York Times,* December 18, 1983, p. F1.

176 On FMS: G. Bylinsky "The Race to the Automatic Factory," *Fortune,* February 21, 1983, pp. 52–64.

177 Robot origins and development: P. Hagan, "Once and Future Robots," *Across the Board,* June 1984, p. 23; *The Washington Post,* May 1, 1983, p. 1; *The Wall Street Journal,* September 10, 1984, p. 1.

177 W. Skinner, "Manufacturing—Missing Line in Corporate Strategy," *Harvard Business Review,* May-June 1969, pp. 136–145; interview, June 13, 1984.

178 K. Iverson: Interview, May 20, 1983.

178 Johnson Controls: J. Rowen, "Midwest Survival of the Fittest," *Across the Board,* June 1983, p. 13.

179 Monsanto: *Fortune,* March 5, 1984, pp. 62–68; April 30, 1984, p. 57.

179 Big firms buy a piece of the action: "Acquiring the Expertise But Not the Company," *Business Week,* June 25, 1984. pp. 142B–142F.

179 "Heartening trend": *The New York Times,* December 18, 1983, p. F1.

180 Hackman comments in letter to authors, November 18, 1984.

180 A.A. Kennedy on IBM: *Inc.,* April 1984, p. 106.

180 IBUs AT IBM: *Fortune,* June 13, 1983, p. 78.

180 Estridge on independence: *Business Week,* October 3, 1983, p. 88.

181 Branscomb on software: *Research and Development,* Conference Board Report No. 842, p. 90.

181 Apple gives employees computers: *Fortune,* October 15, 1984, p. 80.

181 IBM's problems with PCjr: "How IBM Made 'Junior' an Under-achiever," *Business Week,* June 25, 1984, pp. 106–107.

181 Scully bets the store: *Business Week,* January 16, 1984, p. 78.

182 *A Nation at Risk: The Imperative for Education Reform,* National Commission on Excellence in Education (1983).

182 *Science Indicators 1982,* p. 77.

182 J.R. Opel in *Science,* pp. 217, 1116 (1982).

183 T.A. Vanderslice: Interview, August 8, 1983; speech on May 16, 1983.

183 Daewoo ad has appeared in numerous U.S. publications, including *Business Week,* August 15, 1983.

183 Ferguson's totem pole: *Washington Monthly,* June 1983, p. 17.

184 S. Weinig: Interview, April 8, 1983.

184 H. Shinto in column by H. Rowen, *The Washington Post,* April 10, 1983.

184 F. Rohatyn, "Time for a Change," *New York Review of Books,* August 18, 1983.

185 J.J. O'Toole on M.B.A.'s: "Declining Innovation: The Failure of Success," Center for Research, University of Southern California, January 1982.

185   J.H. McArthur: *The New York Times Magazine,* January 4, 1981, p. 14.

185   Luddites: *Encyclopaedia Britannica,* p. 468 (1953).

186   M.K. Eickhoff: Interview, May 25, 1984.

186   Blair, *Economic Concentration,* p. 202.

186   E. Mansfield, Department of Economics, University of Pennsylvania, "Public Policy Toward Industrial Innovation: An International Study of Direct Tax Incentives for R and D" (1984).

187   Wyden on survival: *The Washington Post,* May 14, 1983.

Chapter 4. Mergers: The Production Ethic
Versus the Predator Ethic

189   *The New York Times,* August 19, 1984, p. F13.

189   M. Lipton: Interview, February 27, 1984.

189   Merger statistics: *Fortune,* April 2, 1984, p. 18; and interview with Martin Sikora, editor, *Mergers and Acquisitions Magazine,* February 6, 1985.

190   Bigger in size and number: *Fortune,* ibid.

190   Interview with H.M. Williams, February 28, 1983.

190   James River: *The Wall Street Journal,* October 21, 1983, p. 31.

190   Emerson Electric: *Business Week,* April 4, 1983, p. 60.

191   Drucker: *Forbes,* January 11, 1982, p. 34.

191   "Negative sum game": Samuelson, *National Journal,* January 15, 1983, p. 126.

191   On Carborundum/Kennecott/Sohio: In addition to reading press accounts too numerous to mention and corporate memorandums, the authors interviewed J. Olesky, investment counselor, and T.R. Berner, CEO Curtiss-Wright Corp., April 22, 1983; F.J. Ross, former Carborundum chief operating officer, May 16, 1983; K. Feeney, former Kennecott auditor, June 17, 1983; W. Wendel, former Carborundum CEO, June 21, 1983; D.E. Glynn, reporter, *Niagara Gazette,* June 21, 1983; T.V. Learson, former Carborundum/Kennecott board member, July 25, 1983.

193   For more information on the history and development of mergers, see M.S. Salter and W.A. Weinhold, *Merger Trends and Prospects for the 1980s,* Office of Policy, U.S. Department of Commerce, December 1980; D.C. Mueller, "The Effects of Conglomerate Mergers," *Journal of Banking and Finance* 315–347 (1977); F.H. Esterbrook and D.F. Fischel, "Takeover Bids, Defensive Tactics, and Shareholders' Welfare," *The Business Lawyer,* July 1981, pp. 1733–1750; M. Lipton, "Takeover Bids in the Target's Boardroom: A Response to Professors Esterbrook and Fischel," *New York University Law Review,* December 1980, pp. 1231–1236.

194   "Merging for monopoly": Salter, *Merger Trends,* p. 2.

194   "Merging for oligopoly": Ibid.

194   Celler-Kefauver: 81st Congress, Public Law 899, amending Sect. 7 of the Clayton Act.

194   Third wave: Salter, *Merger Trends,* p. 6.

195   Inco-ESB: *New York,* February 22, 1982, p. 12; *The Wall Street Journal,* April 26, 1983, p. 37.

195 Nixon quote: Transcript prepared by the impeachment inquiry staff of the House Judiciary Committee from conversations recorded by President Nixon commencing April 19, 1971.

195 General Dynamics case: *U.S.* v. *General Dynamics Corporation,* 415 U.S. 486 (1974).

196 Baxter-Miller: "Baxter Rejects Call to Curb Mergers," *The New York Times,* June 3, 1983, p. D1; "Rewriting Antitrust Rules," *Newsweek,* August 29, 1983, p. 50; "The Antitrust Revolution, *Fortune,* July 11, 1983, p. 29; "Judging Baxter's Antitrust Record," *The Wall Street Journal,* January 27, 1984, p. 31.

196 TRB: *The New Republic,* July 25, 1981, p. 4.

196 Pertschuk dissent to GM/Toyota joint venture: December 2, 1983.

197 E. Kelly: Interview, April 13, 1984.

198 Pickens's $12 million: J. Nocera, "It's Time to Make a Deal," *Texas Monthly,* October 1982, p. 254.

198 *Fortune* speculated: April 2, 1984, p. 18.

199 Junk securities: J.D. Williams, "How 'Junk Financings' Aid Corporate Raiders," *The Wall Street Journal,* December 6, 1984, p. 1; *Business Week,* March 4, 1985, p. 90.

199 *Business Week* on money managers: A. Priest, August 13, 1984, p. 86.

200 M. Lipton: Interview, February 27, 1984.

200 Davidson in 1980 paper, "Are Mergers Strategic Decisions?" which was adapted for publication in the *Journal of Business Strategy,* Summer 1981, p. 13.

200 H. Simons, *Economic Policy for a Free Society,* pp. 52, 59 (1948).

200 H.M. Williams: Interview, February 28, 1983.

201 Judge Friendly on mergers: "Make Haste Slowly," in *Commentaries on Corporate Structure and Governance,* D. Schwartz, ed. (1979).

201 Baxter on mergers: Testifying June 3, 1983, before the SEC Advisory Committee on Tender Offers.

201 Brozen on growth fears: In 1982 study for the American Enterprise Institute.

201 L. Thurow, *The Zero Sum Society,* p. 47 (1980).

201 Gray: *The Washington Post,* April 19, 1980, p. 1.

201 Riordan: Ibid.

201 L. Lowenstein, "Pruning Deadwood in Hostile Takeovers," *Columbia Law Review,* March 1983, pp. 249–334.

202 D. Birch testifying before the House Subcommittee on Antitrust and Restraint of Trade, February 12, 1980.

202 "The Bottom Line of Ten Big Mergers," *Fortune,* May 3, 1982, p. 89.

202 Wharton study: *The Wharton Magazine,* Summer 1982, p. 19.

202 Hogary: "Profits from Mergers: The Evidence of Fifty Years," *St. John's Law Review,* Spring 1970, pp. 378–391.

202 Mueller: "The Effects of Conglomerate Mergers," *Journal of Banking and Finance* (1977).

203 E. Kelly: Interview, April 13, 1984.

203 On Pickens: *Texas Monthly*, October 1982, p. 142; *The Wall Street Journal*, November 2, 1983, and February 28, 1984, p. 35.

204 Exxon-Reliance: *The New York Times*, March 21, 1981, p. 1; *Fortune*, October 19, 1981, p. 68.

204 AMF annual reports, Form 10K's, and proxy material.

204 Divestitures: Interview with Tomi Simic, director of research, W.T. Grimm Company.

205 Conglomerate trades: *Los Angeles Times*, September 27, 1981; *The New York Times*, July 3, 1983, p. F1; *Business Week*, February 6, 1984, p. 50.

205 Carey on mergers: *The New York Times*, June 23, 1978, p. A25.

205 "Pie-slicers": R. Reich, *Washington Monthly*, September 1980, p. 13.

205 Thorp: *American Economic Review*, March 1931, p. 86.

205 Morgan got $60 million: Salter and Weinhold, *Merger Trends*, p. 2.

205 Rohatyn on fees: *Financial Times*, February 10, 1982, p. 26.

206 "Deals of the Year": *Fortune*, January 21, 1985, p. 126.

206 Morgan Stanley: *The New York Times*, March 7, 1984, pp. D1, D4.

206 Goldman, Sachs, good guy: A. Sloan, *Three Plus One Equals Billions*, p. 41 (1984).

207 First Boston's savior: *Business Week*, pp. 70–72, August 30, 1976; August 7, 1978, p. 74; *The Wall Street Journal*, April 21, 1982, p. 1; *Fortune*, September 6, 1982, p. 55; *Institutional Investor*, April 1984, p. 140; interviews with B. Wasserstein, J. Perella, and W. Lambert of First Boston.

208 Pitofsky on mergers: Testimony before the House Subcommittee on Monopolies and Commercial Law, March 23, 1984.

208 Bendix-Martin Marietta debacle: Sloan, *Three Plus One*, and news accounts too numerous to list.

208 Bass Brothers: *The New York Times*, March 7, 1984, p. D1.

208 Murdoch payment: *The New York Times*, July 3, 1984, p. D6.

208 Steinberg payment: Ibid.

209 Phillips deal: *The New York Times*, March 5, 1985, p. D1.

209 First Boston ad: *The Wall Street Journal*, January 18, 1984, p. 47.

210 SEI and United Technologies defenses: *The Wall Street Journal*, January 6, 1984, p. 1.

210 Cumulative voting and Delaware: R. Nader, M. Green, and J. Seligman, *Taming the Giant Corporation*, pp. 51–61 (1976).

210 LBO statistics: "Luring the Banks Overboard," *Forbes*, April 9, 1984, p. 39; interview with M. Sikora, February 6, 1985.

211 Management LBO profits: *Across the Board*, December 1984, p. 33.

211 Klein: Interview, March 6, 1984.

211 Stokely-Van Camp: Commissioner B. Longstreth in remarks to the International Bar Association, Toronto, Canada, October 6, 1983.

212 Comanor, Smiley: "Monopoly and the Distribution of Wealth," research paper No. 156, Stanford University School of Business, May 1973.

213 Stern on absentee control: Quoted during hearings on "Conglomerate Mergers—Their Effects on Small Businesses in Local Communities," House Committee on Small Businesses, 96th Cong., 2nd sess., 1980.

213   Draper Looms: Ibid.

213   *Fortune,* July 9, 1984, p. 44.

214   Abegglen on Japanese: *Mergers and Acquisitions,* Vol. 17, No. 4, Winter 1983.

215   M.A. Siegel: "How to Foil Greenmail," *Fortune,* January 21, 1985, pp. 157–158.

216   Bronfman: *The New York Times,* September 29, 1982, p. 32.

216   Goldsmith: "The Raiders," *Business Week,* March 4, 1985, p. 83.

Chapter 5. From Pay to Perks to Parachutes: Why Not "Merit Pay"?

218   GAF executives: GAF Shareholders Committee, "Time for the Issues," April 6, 1983; see also GAF proxy statement, 1983.

218   Heyman's salary: Interview with Samuel Heyman, June 29, 1983.

218   Riklis: Seligman, "Believe It or Not, Top-Executive Pay May Make Sense," *Fortune,* June 11, 1984, p. 58.

219   13.7 percent increase in 1983: Patton, "Why Corporations Overpay Their Underachieving Bosses," *The Washington Post,* March 3, 1985, p. C1.

219   Foote: Interview with George H. Foote, October 4, 1983.

219   Albright: Interview with Archie E. Albright, May 9, 1983.

219   *Fortune:* Loomis, "The Madness of Executive Compensation," *Fortune,* July 12, 1982, p. 42.

219   Two Million: *The New York Times,* May 2, 1984, p. D1.

219   Executives' increase four times blue-collar: Sibson & Co., 1985, *Executive Compensation Report;* "The Big Raises Go to the Big Wheels," *Business Week,* October 29, 1984, p. 24.

220    $919,659: Towers, Perrin, Forster, and Crosby, *1984 Executive Total Compensation Study,* February 1985.

220   Commentator on industrial leadership: Jones, "The Rise of a New Profession," *Popular Science Monthly,* September 1914, p. 2.

220   Sloan: A.P. Sloan, Jr., *My Years with General Motors,* p. 407, Chapter 22 (1964).

220   Raskob: *Literary Digest,* May 10, 1930, p. 73.

220   "I hope no one finds out.": Crowther, "How Much Is a Man Worth?" *Saturday Evening Post,* June 13, 1931, p. 6.

220   *Literary Digest:* August 8, 1930, p. 73.

221   American Tobacco Challenge: "Does the Million-a-Year Man Earn It?" *Literary Digest,* March 28, 1931, p. 42.

221   *Rubáiyát:* Quoted in *Fortune,* November 1964, p. 177.

221   12.4 percent: *Business Week,* May 15, 1978, p. 66.

221   Blumenthal: Interview with W. Michael Blumenthal, August 10, 1978.

222   Heyman: Interview with Samuel Heyman, June 19, 1983.

222   GAF spokesman: Interview with William P. Raines, Director of Corporate Relations, GAF.

223 Korn/Ferry surveys: Korn/Ferry International, *Board of Directors Tenth Annual Study,* February 1983.

223 $12,000 to $32,000: Pear, Marwick, Mitchell, & Co., *Directors Fees in the Top 1,000 Industrials* (1983).

223 Conway: Interview with Virgil Conway, May 30, 1983.

224 Crystal: Interview with Graef S. Crystal, June 2, 1983.

224 Laster: Interview with Richard Laster, May 9, 1983.

224 Haines: Interview with Robert Haines, May 26, 1983.

224 Western Pacific difficulties: Western Pacific Industries proxy statement, March 30, 1983; and *Western Pacific Industries Annual Report, 1982.*

225 Whitney: *The New York Times,* June 10, 1984, p. III–14.

225 Silberman: Interview with Samuel J. Silberman, August 9, 1983.

225 Randall: C. Randall, *The Executive in Transition,* p. 130 (1967).

226 Bonuses to *Fortune* CEOs: Hewitt Associates study cited in "Santa's Golden Handcuffs," *Newsweek,* December 24, 1984, p. 28.

226 Conference Board study: *Top Executive Compensation: 1983 Edition.*

227 Iacocca: *The Wall Street Journal,* April 16, 1984, p. 8; see generally, *The Wall Street Journal,* May 16, 1984, p. 23.

227 Smith and Morgan: *The Wall Street Journal,* November 12, 1984, p. 5.

227 McCardell . . . "superb": Loomis, "Archie's McCardell's Absolutism," *Fortune,* December 15, 1980, p. 89; *The New York Times,* Nov. 23, 1982, p. D2.

227 ACF: ACF industries proxy statement, April 8, 1983; and 1982 *Annual Report.*

228 Veale and Lynch: *Business Week,* May 9, 1983, p. 4.

228 Formula plan: M. Walters and P. Chingos, "Executive Compensation," in Seidler and Carmichael, eds., *Accountants' Handbook,* Vol. II (1981).

229 Pace: Wojahn, "The Take at the Top," *Inc.,* September 1984, p. 46.

229 Stock incentives growth: Towers, Perrin, Forster, and Crosby, *1983 Executive Compensation Study;* and *1982 Executive Compensation Study.*

229 SARs: Peat, Marwick, Mitchell, & Co., *Capital Accumulation Trends Among the 1,000 Largest Industrials: 1982 Report.*

230 Acker: *The Wall Street Journal,* June 9, 1983, p. 1.

230 Brindisi: Interview with Louis J. Brindisi, Jr., June 2, 1982.

230 Riegel's success: Incentive share plan agreements sent by Joseph T. Allmon, vice-president, Riegel Textile Corporation.

230 Smith: Interview with R. Lane Smith, June 10, 1983.

231 GE incentive plan: *Business Week,* April 25, 1983, p. 56.

231 Amos: Morrison, "Those Executive Bailout Deals," *Fortune,* December 13, 1932, p. 85.

231 Ward Howell: *Fortune,* November 14, 1983, p. 207.

232 Halkyard: Interview with Edwin M. Halkyard, June 16, 1983.

232 Conoco: Riger, "On Golden Parachutes—Ripcords or Ripoffs?" *Pace Law Review,* Fall 1982, p. 28.

232 Chafee: Written personal statement from Sen. John H. Chafee, June 7, 1983.

233 Kaufman: *Fortune,* December 27, 1982, p. 17.

233 Conoco agenda: Morrison, "Those Executive Bailout Deals," *Fortune,* December 13, 1982, p. 85.

233 Matthews: Interview with Arthur Matthews, May 23, 1983.

233 Gulf Resources and Clore: *Business Week,* January 9, 1984, p. 34; *Business Week,* January 23, 1984, p. 46.

234 Heinz: H.J. Heinz Company proxy statement, August 8, 1983.

235 Knapp: *The Washington Post,* September 19, 1978, p. 1.

235 Tavoulareas: *The Wall Street Journal,* February 1, 1985, p. 25.

235 Lorenz: *The New York Times,* July 10, 1978, p. 1.

236 Amerace: Amerace Corporation proxy statement, March 21, 1983; and *Amerace Corporation 1982 Annual Report.*

236 Foote: Interview with George H. Foote, October 4, 1983.

237 Greenbrier: Interviews with James A. Searle, Jr., Director of Sales and Marketing for the Greenbrier, and Dr. Arnold Brody, Director of the Greenbrier Clinic, September 19, 1983; promotional brochures for the Greenbrier.

237 Two executives at Needham: *The Wall Street Journal,* June 9, 1983, p. 1.

237 "We don't have to.": Interview with Louis A. Tripodi, Sr., vice-president, Needham, Harper and Steers, June 29, 1983.

237 Cars and tickets: American Management Association, *Executive Compensation* (1981).

237 Araskog: *U.S. News and World Report,* May 21, 1984, p. 80.

237 Iacocca on Ford: L. Iacocca with W. Novak, *Iacocca* (1984).

238 "I'll do what I want.": *The Wall Street Journal,* September 20, 1984, p. 20.

238 *Forbes*: Flanagan, "More Sweets to the Suite," *Forbes,* June 8, 1981.

239 Playboy: Playboy Enterprises proxy statement, November 8, 1983.

239 Baehler's friend: J. Baehler, *Book of Perks* (1984).

239 Iverson philosophy: Interview with Kenneth Iverson, May 20, 1983.

240 CBS profits slump: See Bachler, *Book of Perks,* p. 18.

240 Perot: *Omaha World-Herald,* November 18, 1981.

240 Eastern and Borman: *The Washington Post,* April 30, 1978, p. F1.

241 140 companies, Simon and LaMothe: Loomis, "The Madness of Executive Compensation," *Fortune,* July 12, 1982, p. 42.

241 AMA: E. Redling, "Myth vs. Reality: The Relations Between Top Executives' Pay and Corporate Performance," *Compensation Review,* Fourth Quarter 1981, p. 16.

241 148 companies: W.S. Albrecht and P. Jhin, "The Million Dollar Men," *Business Horizons,* August 1978, p. 14.

241 Sibson & Co.: "Executive Pay: The Top Earners," *Business Week,* May 7, 1984, p. 88.

242 Ungson and Steers: "Motivation and Politics in Executive Compensation," Graduate School of Management, University of Oregon, Technical Report No. 12, July 1983.

242 Sears: *Sears, Roebuck & Co. 1982 Annual Report.*

243 Clevepak: Interview with David Hamrick of Clevepak Corp., November 29, 1984; see also Louis, "Business Is Bungling Long-Term Compensation," *Fortune,* July 23, 1984, p. 64.

243 Emhart: "Rewarding Executives for Taking the Long View," *Business Week,* April 2, 1984, p. 99.

245 Patton: "Why So Many Chief Executives Make Too Much," *Business Week,* October 17, 1983, p. 24.

245 Buckley, Jr.: William F. Buckley, speaking at Yankelovich, Skelly, and White conference on "Business and the Media," November 19, 1981.

246 Smith: Quoted in R. Heilbroner, *The Worldly Philosophers,* p. 71 (5th ed., 1980).

246 GM bonus: "GM's Bonus Flap: The Timing Was Wrong," *The Wall Street Journal,* April 30, 1982, p. 30.

247 Greyhound: *The Wall Street Journal,* December 20, 1983, p. 1.

247 Western: *Business Week,* April 18, 1983, p. 44.

247 Smith's two trains: *The Wall Street Journal,* April 30, 1982, p. 30.

247 Defense contractor's engineers: Cited in P. Drucker, "Reform in Executive Pay or Congress Will," *The Wall Street Journal,* April 24, 1984, p. 34.

248 Ephlin: Interview with Don Ephlin, June 21, 1983.

248 Iverson: Interview with Kenneth Iverson, May 20, 1983.

249 Entitlements: For a discussion of this concept, see Williams, "Why Chief Executives' Pay Keeps Rising," *Fortune,* April 1, 1985, p. 66.

249 Salter: Quoted in J.E. Heard, *Executive Compensation 1983,* published by the Investor Responsibility Research Center, June 1983, p. 22.

250 Vincent: Interview with Francis T. Vincent, Jr., August 11, 1983.

251 *Washington Post:* September 26, 1983, p. 1.

251 Chafee: Statement by Sen. Chafee before the U.S. Securities and Exchange Commission, October 7, 1977.

251 Baker: "Are Corporate Executives Overpaid?" *Harvard Business Review,* July-August 1977, p. 53.

252 Drucker: "Is Executive Pay Excessive?" *The Wall Street Journal,* May 23, 1977, p. 20.

252 Pay ratios: *The Wall Street Journal,* April 18, 1984, p. 20.

252 Connecticut survey: *Public Opinion,* June-July 1981, p. 32.

253 43 managements: *The New York Times,* May 8, 1983, p. D5.

253 Cochran and Wartich: "Golden Parachutes: A Closer Look," *California Management Review,* Summer 1984, p. 111.

Chapter 6. The Waste of Fraud and Abuse: When Laissez *Isn't* Fair

255 Drew and robber barons: E. Sutherland, *White Collar Crime: The Uncut Version,* p. 250 (1983). See generally, M. Josephson, *The Robber Barons,* p. 72 (1934).

255 Rockefeller: For classic critical biography of Rockefeller, see I. Tarbell, *The History of the Standard Oil Company* (1925).

255    $50 billion in new stock: *Time,* February 1, 1982, p. 33.

256   J.P. Morgan and Whitney theft: E. Sutherland, *White Collar Crime: The Uncut Version,* p. 254 (1983).

256   White-collar crime more serious: *The Wall Street Journal,* November 11, 1975, p. 22.

256   *Journal's* one day news: "A Day in the Corporate Life," *The Washington Post,* March 10, 1984, p. A18.

257   Defending one's bureaucracy: See, e.g., A. Etzioni, *Modern Organizations,* pp. 15–19 (1964); and C. Perrow, *Complex Organizations: A Critical Essay,* p. 90 (1972).

257   Heinz: *The Wall Street Journal,* November 8, 1979, p. 1.

258   "Differential association": E. Sutherland, *White Collar Crime,* p. 234 (1949, The Dryden Press ed.). See p. 242 for references to studies of delinquency rates, mentioned in text subsequently.

258   *Harvard Business Review:* Baumhart, "How Ethical Are Businessmen?" in G. Geis, *White Collar Criminal,* p. 119 (1968).

258   "It is free enterprise": F. Cook, *The Corrupted Land: The Social Morality of Modern America,* p. 37 (1966).

258   Many companies price-fix?: M. Green et al., *The Closed Enterprise System,* p. 472 (1972).

258   Opinion Research Corporation survey: Cited in Kohlmeier, "The Bribe Busters," *The New York Times Magazine,* September 26, 1976, p. 47.

259   Clinard and Yeager: M. Clinard and P. Yeagar, *Corporate Crime,* p. 274 (1980).

259   *U.S. News:* "Corporate Crime: The Untold Story," *U.S. News and World Report,* September 6, 1982, p. 25.

259   Edelhertz: *The Nature, Impact and Prosecution of White Collar Crime,* published by the National Institute of Law Enforcement and Criminal Justice (1970).

261   Presidential commission: *President's Commission on Law Enforcement and the Administration of Justice,* p. 158 (1968).

261   Levi-Strauss: Blueweiss, "Consumers Win in Levi's Case," *Daily News Record,* July 20, 1982, sect. 1.

261   Contractors' bid-rigging: "The Crackdown on Colluding Road Builders," *Fortune,* October 3, 1983, p. 79.

261   Judge Gray and oil company case: *The Wall Street Journal,* December 16, 1984, p. 1; *The Washington Post,* December 17, 1984, p. E1.

261   Inflates prices by 25 percent or more: Smith, "Antitrust and the Monopoly Problem: Toward a More Relevant Legal Analysis," *Antitrust Law and Economics Review,* Spring 1969, p. 33.

261   Air pollution costs: Crocker, et al., "Methods Development for Assessing Air Pollution Control Benefits," Office of Research and Development, U.S. Environmental Protection Agency, February 1979. See generally, Green and Waitzman, *Business War on the Law: An Analysis of the Benefits of Federal Health/Safety Enforcement,* rev. ed., pp. 114–119, Corporate Accountability Research Group (1982).

262   82 percent failed to comply: *Wastewater Dischargers Are Not Complying with EPA Pollution Control Permits,* report by the Government Account-

ing Office, December 2, 1983. See also Drayton, *America's Toxic Protection Gap,* published by Environmental Safety in Washington, D.C. (1984).

262 Water pollution costs: Freeman III, A. Myrick, "The Benefits of Air and Water Pollution Control: A Review and Synthesis of Recent Estimates," Council on Environmental Quality, December 1979, p. xv; see also J. Lash et al., *A Season of Spoils* (1984).

262 $22 billion to $100 billion: *The New York Times,* March 10, 1985, p. 1.

262 7 to 10 percent: Boffey, *The New York Times,* March 20, 1984, p. C1.

262 Kepone: Stone, "A Slap on the Wrist for the Kepone Mob," *Business and Society Review,* Summer 1977, p. 4.

263 Dow and Dioxin: *The New York Times,* April 19, 1983, p. 1; *The Wall Street Journal,* June 28, 1983, p. 1; *Fortune,* May 30, 1983, p. 83.

263 *Amicus Journal:* Schneider, "Faking It: The Case Against Industrial Bio-Test Laboratories," *Amicus Journal,* Spring 1983, p. 14.

264 Alabama civil suit: *The New York Times,* February 15, 1983, p. A14.

264 Congressional Research Service: "The Cost of Racial Discrimination," hearing before the Joint Economic Committee, 96th Cong., 1st sess., 1979, p. 4.

264 Grant: "Progress Report on the Black Executive: The Top Spots Are Still Elusive," *Business Week,* February 20, 1984, p. 104.

264 Rytina: "Earnings of Men and Women: A Look at Specific Occupations," *Monthly Labor Review,* April 1982, pp. 25–31. See also *Newsweek,* September 1983, p. 80.

264 Willimar 8: Krucoff, "The Willimar 8: Banking on Courage," *The Washington Post,* January 16, 1984, p. B1.

264 Carlson: Interview with Kay Carlson, February 17, 1984.

265 Companies contribute to shortage: *The Wall Street Journal,* February 7, 1984, p. 1; see also "You've Come a Long Way Baby, but Not as Far as You Think," *Business Week,* October 1, 1984, p. 126.

265 Black's story: Tracey, "How United Brands Survived the Banana War," *Fortune,* July 1976, pp. 145–146.

265 $1 billion in payoffs: Clinard and Yeager, *Corporate Crime,* p. 162; *The Wall Street Journal,* June 23, 1978, p. 34.

265 Top management knew in half of cases: *Report of the Securities and Exchange Committee on Questionable and Illegal Corporate Payments and Practices,* printed in Senate Banking, Housing and Urban Affairs Committee, 94th Cong., 2nd sess., 1976.

265 Ball: *The New York Times,* October 20, 1976, p. 39.

266 Odom: *The Wall Street Journal,* June 23, 1978, p. 34.

266 Bechtel in South Korea: Dowie et al., "Bechtel: A Tale of Corruption," *Mother Jones,* May 1984, pp. 10–22; *The Wall Street Journal,* April 23, 1984, p. 2.

266 McKnight: See generally, "Again, Political Slush Funds," *Time,* March 24, 1975.

267 American Airlines kickbacks: Clinard and Yeager, *Corporate Crime,* p. 167.

267 Frigitemp: *The Wall Street Journal,* December 8, 1983; September 20, 1984, p. 1; and October 12, 1984, p. 8.

267 Kroll: *The New York Times,* March 16, 1976, business section.

267 Jeter and *Wall Street Journal* investigation: *The Wall Street Journal,* January 15, 1985, p. 1.

267 AMA estimate: American Management Association, *Crimes Against Business* (1977).

268 100,000 deaths annually . . .: NIOSH, *President's Report on Occupational Safety and Health,* May 22, 1972, p. 111.

268 Injuries cost $23 billion: National Safety Council, *Accident Facts* (1979).

268 60 percent: N. Ashford, *Crisis in the Workplace,* p. 114 (1976).

268 Preventing a quarter of injuries: *Making Regulation Pay,* final report of the Interagency Task Force on Workplace Safety and Health, December 14, 1978, p. II–7.

268 $30 to $50 billion: Green and Waitzman, *Business War,* p. 77.

268 Asbestos workers: *The Washington Post,* July 5, 1983, p. A12.

268 Knew of asbestos hazards: Mintz, "Workers Unwarned of Asbestos Peril, Lawmakers Learn," *The Washington Post,* November 16, 1979, p. B11.

269 Illinois manslaughter: "Job Safety Becomes a Murder Issue," *Business Week,* August 6, 1984, p. 23; see also "Why More Corporations May Be Charged with Manslaughter," *Business Week,* February 27, 1984, p. 62; *The New York Times,* March 5, 1985, p. D2.

269 Sloan: M. Mintz and J. Cohen, *America Inc.,* p. 260 (1971).

269 Metropolitan Edison: *The Washington Post,* November 8, 1983, p. E13.

270 Wyeth and Gore: Interview with Rep. Albert Gore (D., Tenn.), February 21, 1983, See also Claybrook, *Retreat from Safety,* p. 6.

271 De Lorean and Wright: Quoted in "How Moral Men Make Immoral Decisions—A Look Inside GM," in M. Green and R. Massie, *The Big Business Reader: Essays on Corporate America,* p. 43 (1st ed., 1980).

271 Manufacturers knew about defects: See generally, Mintz "Jail Terms Sought for Business Health, Environment Violators," *The Washington Post,* November 25, 1979, p. A1.

271 Ford and Pintos: Dowie, "Pinto Madness," *Mother Jones,* September-October 1977, p. 18.

271 Internal memorandum on Firestone: Quoted in Clinard and Yeager, *Corporate Crime,* p. 11.

271 *Fortune,* Referred to in M. Moscowitz et al., *Everybody's Business,* pp. 285–286 (1980).

271 X-cars: *The Wall Street Journal,* December 9, 1983, p. 21; *The New York Times,* October 21, 1983, p. B16.

271 *National Journal:* Swallow, "Consumer Product Agency Is Battling for Its Independence and Its Life," *National Journal,* June 27, 1981, p. 1164.

272 California computer company: "Stealing from the Boss," *Newsweek,* December 26, 1983, p. 78.

272 Wells Fargo and Central Fidelity banks: "Crackdown on Computer Capers," *Time,* February 8, 1982, p. 60.

272 U.S. Chamber of Commerce: *White Collar Crime: Everybody's Problem, Everyone's Loss,* p. 4 (1974).

272 Price Waterhouse: "The Peter Berlin Report on Shrinkage Control," January 1984.

272 Bequai: Interview with August Bequai, March 11, 1985.

272 Zeitlin: *The New York Times,* November 9, 1975, p. III–16.

273 Insider trading: See "A Talk of the Money World," *Time,* April 16, 1984, pp. 44–45; "Stock Tips Aren't Candy Bars," *The New York Times,* April 14, 1984, p. 24; Longstreth, "Halting Insider Trading," *The New York Times,* April 12, 1984; "Illegal Insider Trading Seems to Be on the Rise," *The Wall Street Journal,* March 2, 1984, p. 1.

273 *Journal of Finance:* Cited in "Insider Trading Prior to Mergers Abounds, Study Says," *The Wall Street Journal,* December 21, 1981, p. 27; see also Bleakley, "Wall Street Worries Over Insider Leaks," *The New York Times,* January 25, 1985, p. D1.

274 Amway: *The Wall Street Journal,* November 11, 1983, p. 56; *The New York Times,* November 11, 1983, p. D1.

274 Illegality and bank failures: *Business Week,* October 8, 1984, p. 209.

274 First National: *The Wall Street Journal,* March 6, 1985, p. 14.

274 Weidenbaum: "On the Causes of Business Corruption," *The New York Times,* May 4, 1975, p. III–14.

274 Shapiro: *The Washington Post,* October 23, 1981, p. C3.

275 Jenner: "Crime in the Suites: On the Rise," *Newsweek,* December 3, 1979, p. 14.

275 Arkin: "Too Many Executives Are Going to Jail," *Fortune,* December 17, 1979, p. 113.

275 Shareholders and Jones: *The New York Times,* May 16, 1976, p. IV–18.

276 Seventy-four and seventy-five companies: Clinard and Yeager, *Corporate Crime,* p. 180.

276 Clinard and Yeager: *Corporate Crime,* p. xi.

277 Allen: *The Washington Post,* January 11, 1976, p. H1.

277 Blumenthal: *The New York Times,* May 25, 1975, p. III–1.

277 Burke speech: "Advertising Council Speech," November 16, 1983, mimeographed text.

277 Johnson credo: Burke speech, November 16, 1983.

278 J&J reaction: Foster, "Handling the Tylenol Story: Good PR," *American Society of Newspaper Editors Bulletin,* March 1983, p. 23; also, interview with Jim Murray, March 14, 1985.

279 Cummins: Moscowitz et al., *Everybody's Business,* pp. 282–284.

280 Jones: Quoted in R. Nader, "In the Public Interest," newspaper column, September 7, 1984.

280 Suwya: "Putting the Disabled to Work: Major Effort at Du Pont," *The New York Times,* April 11, 1984, p. D1.

280 Avon: M. Moscowitz, "Company Performance Roundup," *Business and Society Review,* Summer 1982, p. 65.

281 Rasmussen: Ibid.

281   Arab boycott: Green and Solow, "The Arab Boycott of Israel: How the U.S. and Business Cooperated," *The Nation*, October 17, 1981, p. 1.

282   Jones: Interview with Peter T. Jones, November 11, 1980.

282   Seibert: D.V. Seibert and W. Proctor, *The Ethical Executive*, p. 204 (1984).

283   Relative immunity from prosecution: For an excellent overview, see *White Collar Justice*, a special report published by the Bureau of National Affairs, April 13, 1976.

283   Business's special influence: See generally, C. Lindblom, *Politics and Markets*, Part V (1977).

283   Justice Department 5.5 percent: "White Collar Crime," hearings, Subcommittee on Crime of the House Judiciary Committee, 95th Cong., 2nd sess., 1978, p. 84.

283   President Carter on "big shot crooks": Ibid. p. 79.

283   FBI cuts: *The Wall Street Journal*, February 1, 1984, p. 27.

283   *Business Week:* "The SEC Under Shad: Can a Deregulator Protect the Public?" June 13, 1983, p. 135.

284   Dingell: *The Wall Street Journal*, October 27, 1983, p. 39.

284   SEC lawsuits: *The Wall Street Journal*, January 12, 1984, p. 12.

284   Fedders and Citibank: Gerth, *The New York Times*, February 18, 1982, p. 1.

284   "cases that didn't offend": *Business Week*, March 11, 1985, p. 42.

285   Three cases in Sherman Act's first eighty years: See M. Green, *The Closed Enterprise System*, Chapter 5 (1971).

285   Clean Water Act: *The Wall Street Journal*, June 26, 1978, p. 5.

285   Begelman: See D. McClintock, *Stealing from the Rich* (1977); McClintock, *Indecent Exposure* (1982).

285   Grace and Rowan: Loving, "How Bob Rowan Served His Time," *Fortune*, August 27, 1979, p. 42; Nathan, "Coddling Criminals," *Harper's*, January 1980, p. 29.

285   Consent decrees: See generally, "Those Troubling Consent Orders," *The Wall Street Journal*, May 18, 1978, p. 20; *Newsweek*, October 24, 1977, p. 94.

286   OSHA fine of $240 per citation: OSHA Federal Compliance Activity Reports, October 1983–March 1984.

286   U.S. Senate investigation: *The Washington Post*, September 20, 1983.

286   Stone: C. Stone, *Where the Law Ends*, p. 46 (1975).

286   Fruehauf board: Nathan, op. cit., p. 29.

287   Park: *United States* v. *Park*, 421 U.S. 658 (1975).

288   Rickover: *Hearing on Defense Expenditures*, Joint Economic Committee, January 28, 1982.

288   Bernard: Quoted in M. Maidique, "The New Management Thinkers," *California Management Review*, Fall 1983, p. 152.

289   McCloy: *The Wall Street Journal*, March 16, 1976, p. 1.

289   *Business Week:* October 8, 1984, p. 209.

290 ABA report: "American Bar Association Report on Economic Offenses" (1977).

290 France, Norway, and West Germany: *Corporate Social Reporting in the United States and Western Europe,* report of the Task Force on Corporate Social Performance, U.S. Department of Commerce (1979).

290 Kreps: Interviews with H. Moyer, Jr., General Counsel, Department of Commerce, June-July 1978.

291 Renfrew: See Renfrew, "The Paper Label Sentences: An Evaluation," *Yale Law Journal,* Vol. 86 (1977), p. 590.

292 Critics: Baker and Reeves, "The Paper Label Sentences: Critiques," *Yale Law Journal,* Vol. 86 (1977), p. 619.

292 Richards: Interview with Mark Richards, February 2, 1984.

292 Webster: "Crime in the Suites," op. cit., p. 14.

292 Sethi: *The New York Times,* February 12, 1978, p. 3F.

293 Batavia, New York: Taylor, "Instead of Jail, One County in New York Imposes Sentences of Work, Reparations or 'House Arrest,'" *The Wall Street Journal,* December 23, 1983, p. 28.

293 *Harvard Law Review:* "Developments in the Law—Corporate Crime: Regulating Corporate Behavior Through Criminal Sanctions," *Harvard Law Review,* Vol. 92 (1979), p. 1229.

293 McCloy Report: Quoted in and see generally, J. Coffee, Jr., "Beyond the Shut-Eyed Sentry: Toward a Theoretical View of Corporate Misconduct and an Effective Legal Response," *Virginia Law Review,* Vol. 63, (1977), p. 1099, fn. 2.

294 NAM and Ashbrook: Mintz, "Jail Terms Sought for Business Health, Environment Violators," November 25, 1979, p. A1.

295 *Harvard Law Review:* Vol. 92 (1979), p. 1365.

Chapter 7. Consumer Value: The Pass-Along Economy

296 Miller, *Death of a Salesman,* Act II.

297 Three-Mile Island: C. Perrow, *Normal Accidents,* pp. 4–10 (1984).

297 Conrail: *The World Almanac and Book of Facts,* pp. 914–947 (1980).

297 Oil rig: Ibid.

297 DC-10: Ibid.

297 Kemper Arena: Ibid.

297 General Mullins: April 26, 1984, speech at Hanscom Air Force Base.

297 "Shoddy workmanship": *The New York Times,* November 2, 1984, p. B10; *Facts on File,* August 31, 1984, p. 636.

298 Trident I: *Facts on File,* August 31, 1984, p. 637.

298 Hughes Missile Systems: *The New York Times,* November 2, 1984, p. B10; *Facts on File,* August 31, 1984, p. 636.

298 Navy rejects GE: Announced by the Department of the Navy, Office of Information.

298 Texas Instruments: *The New York Times,* November 2, 1984, p. B10; *Facts on File,* October 19, 1984, p. 773.

298 Garreau buys a car: *The Washington Post,* June 19, 1983, p. B1.

299   Welch on consumers' memory: *Business Week,* March 16, 1981, p. 113.

299   Hood hears complaints: Ibid.

300   Quality defined: Tuchman, "The Decline of Quality," *The New York Times Magazine,* November 2, 1980, p. 38.

300   *Fortune:* January 10, 1983, p. 38.

300   V. Packard: *The Waste Makers,* p. 91 (1963).

301   Pine: *The Wall Street Journal,* September 19, 1983.

301   Three of five executives: *Wall Street Journal*–Gallup survey, in *The Wall Street Journal,* October 12, 1981.

301   Harris poll: *Business Week,* June 11, 1984, p. 170.

301   White House survey: Ibid., p. 165.

301   Wellington: Interview with Roger Wellington, August 16, 1983.

302   AQL: Jack Reddy and Abe Berger, "Three Essentials of Product Quality," *Harvard Business Review,* July-August 1983, pp. 156–157.

302   AQL and Commodore: *The Wall Street Journal,* October 28, 1983, p. 33.

302   Touring in Japan: P.H. Abelson, *Science,* May 12, 1980.

303   Deming: W.E. Deming, "Improvement of Quality and Productivity Through Action Management," *National Productivity Review,* Winter 1981–82; "The Curmudgeon Who Talks Tough on Quality," *Fortune,* June 25, 1984, pp. 118–122.

303   Costly process at Wayne assembly plant: Interviews, June 24, 1983.

303   *Fortune:* January 10, 1983, p. 38.

304   Best: *When Consumers Complain,* pp. 63–83 (1981).

304   L. Nader: "Disputing Without the Force of Law," *Yale Law Journal,* April 1979, p. 1018.

304   Best: *When Consumers Complain,* pp. 33–34.

304   Chevrolet's boxes: *San Francisco Chronicle,* April 29, 1971.

304   L. Nader on GM: L. Nader, op. cit., p. 1003n.

304   Why people complain: Ibid., p. 1002.

305   Pittle: Interview, October 11, 1984.

305   Business supports CPSC: *National Journal,* June 27, 1981, p. 1163.

306   Pestillo: Interview, June 23, 1983.

306   Simon and Garfunkel: "The Boxer," *Simon and Garfunkel's Greatest Hits* (1972).

306   Adler and Pittle: "Cajolery or Command: Are Education Campaigns an Adequate Substitute for Regulation," *Yale Journal on Regulation,* November 2, 1984, p. 162.

307   Lawn mowers: Pittle interview, *National Journal,* June 27, 1981, p. 1165.

308   Garvin: "Quality on the Line," *Harvard Business Review,* September–October 1983, pp. 65–75.

308   L.L. Bean: *Harvard Business Review,* July–August 1983, pp. 140–141.

309   Quality pays: Garvin, op. cit., pp. 65–75.

309   ROI data: Ibid., p. 68.

309   Garvin: Interview, October 15, 1984.

309 Allied Chemical: R. Stobaugh and D. Yergin, ed., *Energy Future: Report of the Energy Project at Harvard Business School*, p. 156 (1979).

310 Energy conservation: Stobaugh and Yergin, *Energy Future*, p. 155.

310 Oak Ridge: *Democratic Fact Book 1984*, p. 280.

310 Dow: Stobaugh and Yergin, *Energy Future*, p. 165.

310 Cogeneration: "Are Utilities Obsolete," *Business Week*, May 21, 1984, pp. 119, 126.

311 Shoreham cost overruns: *The New York Times*, December 8, 1983, p. B8.

312 Zimmer plant: *The Wall Street Journal*, January 18, 1984, p. 31.

312 Bechtel study: *The New York Times*, January 26, 1984, p. D2.

312 Diablo Canyon: The best account is contained in S. Tolchin and M. Tolchin, *Dismantling America: The Rush to Deregulate*, pp. 189–236 (1983).

312 Stello: *The Wall Street Journal*, December 30, 1980, p. 8.

312 Liddell: Interview, December 12, 1984.

312 Naming plants: Information provided by the companies.

313 Pooler: *Business Week*, May 21, 1984, p. 116.

313 Bond ratings: *Bond Guide, Year End Prices* (1/71 and 1/81) September 31, 1984.

314 Walske: *The Wall Street Journal*, January 18, 1984.

314 Reactor orders: The Atomic Industrial Forum, *Historical Profile of U.S. Nuclear Power Development*, 1985, p. 16.

314 Industry failing: "Consumer Follies," February 11, 1985, p. 82.

314 Sant: *Business Week*, May 21, 1984, p. 119.

314 Open auction: Testimony of Alan Miller, hearings on "Least Cost Energy Strategies," Subcommittee on Energy Conservation and Power, House Energy and Commerce Committee, September 30, 1981, p. 136.

314 Competition: Bellamy, "Two Utilities Are Better Than One," *Reason*, January 1981, p. 27.

315 CUB: Green and Waldman, "CUB Comes to New York," *Village Voice*, September 20, 1983, p. 20.

315 Lovins: "The 'Soft Path' Solution for Hard Pressed Utilities," *Business Week*, July 23, 1984.

315 Chrysler: J. Califano testimony before Joint Economic Committee, April 12, 1984.

315 More than dividends: *The Washington Post*, August 21, 1983, p. F1.

315 Coopers & Lybrand: "The Corporate Rx for Medical Costs," *Business Week*, October 15, 1984, p. 130.

315 Payroll share: Coopers & Lybrand, *1983 Group Medical Plan Cost Survey*, p. 1 (1983).

315 Chamber study: Chamber of Commerce of the United States, *Employee Benefits, 1983*, p. 13 (1984).

315 25 percent: E. Davis, Business Roundtable, in testimony before House Republican Research Committee, June 5, 1984.

316 Health inflation: Califano testimony.

316 10 percent: Davis testimony.

316 HRI: *Business Week,* October 15, 1984.

316 Incentives for waste: *Business Week,* October 15, 1984, p. 130.

317 S.X. Kaplan: Interview with Samuel X. Kaplan, October 5, 1983.

317 Califano: Testimony.

317 Ford: *The Wall Street Journal,* August 5, 1983, p. 2.

317 Concessions: *The Wall Street Journal,* October 26, 1983, p. 31.

318 PPOs: *The Wall Street Journal,* November 22, 1983, p. 1.

318 Waxman: Hearing before Subcommittee on Health and the Environment, House Energy and Commerce Committee, March 18, 1981, p. 1.

318 HMOs: P. Samors and S. Sullivan, "Health Care Cost Containment Through Private Sector Initiatives," in J. Meyer, ed., *Market Reforms in Health Care,* p. AE1 (1983).

319 Chrysler efforts: Califano testimony.

319 D. Pope: See generally, *The Making of Modern Advertising* (1984).

320 N. Borden: *The Economics of Advertising,* p. 6 (1944).

320 MacDougall: *Los Angeles Times,* November 26 and 29, 1981; December 6, 13, and 20, 1981.

320 "insults the intelligence": Cited in speech by John O'Toole, Foote, Cone and Belding Communications, November 8, 1984.

320 Gallup poll: *Gallup Report,* July 1983, p. 3.

320 T. Veblen: *The Theory of Business Enterprise,* pp. 32–36 (1904).

321 Hershey: M. Moscowitz et al., *Everybody's Business: An Almanac,* p. 41 (1980); M. Schudson, *Advertising, The Uneasy Persuasion,* pp. 24, 25 (1984).

321 Aaker and Carman: *Journal of Advertising Research,* August-September 1982, p. 57.

321 Brand identification: L. Bogart and C. Lehman, "The Case of the 30-Second Commercial," in Ibid., February-March 1983, p. 11.

321 Generic products: I. Cunningham, A. Hardy, and G. Imperici, "Generic Brands Versus National Brands and Store Brands: A Comparison of Consumers' Preferences and Perceptions," in Ibid., October-November 1982, p. 25.

321 D. Ogilvy: *Blood, Brains and Beer: The Autobiography of David Ogilvy,* p. 149 (1978).

322 Eyeglasses: L. Benham, "The Effect of Advertising on the Price of Eyeglasses," *Journal of Law and Economics,* (1972), p. 337.

322 Blackmun decision: *Virginia State Board of Pharmacy* v. *Virginia Citizens Consumer Council, Inc.,* 425 U.S. 748, 48 L.Ed.2d 346, 96 S.Ct. 1817 (1975).

322 Federal study: Federal Trade Commission, *Improving Consumer Access to Legal Services: The Case for Removing Restrictions on Truthful Advertising* (November 1984).

322 Information on TV ads: MacDougall, *Los Angeles Times,* November 29, 1981.

323 M. Schudson: Schudson, *Advertising,* p. 240.

323 J.K. Galbraith: *The Affluent Society,* pp. 124–126 (rev. ed., 1976).

323 Feminine hygiene products: *The Wall Street Journal,* December 8, 1983, p. 33.

324 M. Pertschuk: Remarks before the Public Relations Society of America, October 26, 1983.

324 Brown & Williamson executive: M. Pertschuk, remarks before Society of Professional Journalists, November 10, 1983.

324 Clanton: Interview with David Clanton, March 15, 1985.

324 Public perceptions: Pope, *Modern Advertising,* p. 277.

325 Herman: *Corporate Control, Corporate Power,* p. 194 (1981).

325 Product differences: *The Wall Street Journal,* December 15, 1983, p. 33.

325 Solow: Interview with Marty Solow, November 16, 1984.

Chapter 8. The Gross Legal Product: The High Cost of Lawyers' Featherbedding

327 Brill interviews: "Jealous Co-Counsel: Inside v. Outside," *The American Lawyer,* June 1984, p. 10.

327 Legal expenses/$40 billion: Heins, "How to Cut Legal Bills," *Forbes,* April 9, 1984, p. 83.

327 Legal expenses/$9.9 billion: "The U.S. May Finally Have Too Many Lawyers," *Business Week,* September 17, 1984, p. 48.

327 Manufacturing companies: Heins, op. cit., p. 83.

327 Legal Services, values, and growth: Nader, "Cutting Legal Costs for Business," *Proceedings on Ralph Nader's Conference on Excessive Corporate Legal Fees,* May 18, 1981.

327 Price Waterhouse: "Legal Affairs: A Special Report," *The Wall Street Journal,* August 30, 1984, p. 1.

327 Law graduates: "The U.S. May Finally Have Too Many Lawyers," *Business Week,* September 17, 1984.

327 Forty-thousand new graduates: *The Wall Street Journal,* October 3, 1983, p. 30.

328 Timothy Robinson: Nader, op. cit.

328 Ralph Nader: "The U.S. May Finally Have Too Many Lawyers," p. 46.

328 Boies: Interview with David Boies, January 14, 1984.

328 *National Law Journal:* Whitehead, "In-House, Outside Counsel," *National Law Journal,* June 7, 1982, p. 16.

328 Arthur Young: E. Murk, A. Lynch, and T. Tilghman, "National Survey of Corporate Law Departments: Compensation and Organizational Practices" (Arthur Young for the Association of the Bar of the City of New York), 1984.

329 Judge Ruggero Aldisert: Taylor, "Justice System Stifled by Its Costs and Complexity, Experts Warn," *The New York Times,* June 1, 1983, p. A17.

329 John Diebold: Diebold, *Making the Future Work,* p. 137 (1984).

330 Shakow: Interview with David Shakow, October 12, 1977.

331 $1.6 million: Nader, op. cit.

331   Ted Dinsmoor: Heins, op. cit., p. 83.

332   Kramer: Interview with Victor Kramer, September 9, 1977.

332   $10 million: "Profit pressures on the big law firms," *Fortune*, April 19, 1982, p. 94.

332   Judge Louis Brandeis: Smyser, "In-House Corporate Counsel: The Erosion of Independence," *Verdicts on Lawyers*, R. Nader and M. Green, p. 213 (1976).

332   Paul Cravath: Smyser, op. cit., p. 213.

332   Directors of public companies: Nelson, op. cit., p. 18.

332   1973–1981: "Some Lawyer-Directors' Firms Getting Hefty Fees," *Legal Times*, August 2, 1982, p. 12.

332   Fear of competition: Smyser, op. cit., p. 214.

333   Kestenbaum: Interview with Lionel Kestenbaum, September 10, 1977.

333   *American Lawyer:* "Travel Time: Is the Meter Running?" *The American Lawyer*, January 1984, p. 35.

334   MTA: Blumenthal, "State Inquiry Faults M.T.A. on $2 Million in Legal Fees," *The New York Times*, September 13, 1983, p. B1.

334   $300–$1,000 an hour: "$1,000 an hour: It's a Living," *The Wall Street Journal*, February 17, 1984, p. 33.

334   Susman response: "Lawyers' Fees in Class Actions," letter to the editor, *The Wall Street Journal*, February 29, 1984, p. 29.

334   Winthrop Munyan: Lewin, "When Law Partners Split Up," *The New York Times*, November 26, 1984, p. D1.

335   In-house departments: "Profit Pressures on Big Law Firms," *Fortune*, April 8, 1984, p. 84.

335   Senior attorneys: Murk, Lynch, and Tilghman, op. cit.

335   New York partners: "The Big Law Business," *Newsweek*, April 16, 1984, p. 87.

335   National median income: "Legal Affairs: A Special Report," *The Wall Street Journal*, August 30, 1984, p. 1.

335   Standard Oil: "U.S. May Finally Have Too Many Lawyers," op. cit., p. 46.

336   Aetna paralegals: Pollock, "Staying Ahead at Aetna," *The American Lawyer*, February 1984, p. 70.

336   McKinney: Interview with Luther McKinney, July 31, 1984.

336   Financial planning: Banks, "Companies Struggle to Control Legal Costs," *Harvard Business Review*, March-April 1983, p. 169.

336   Budgeting is demeaning: Lewin, "Putting Litigation on a Budget," *The New York Times*, April 2, 1982, p. D3.

337   Written agreement: Pollock, op. cit., p. 70.

337   Minitrials generally: Lewin, "New Alternatives to Litigation," *The New York Times*, November 1, 1982, D1.

338   Robert Gorske: Lempert, "Two Companies Find Big Promise in Little Trial," *Legal Times*, October 24, 1983, p. 48.

339   Jenner and Block: "Jenner's Stumbling Block," *The American Lawyer*, January 1984, p. 30.

339 Arbitration: "An Outline of Procedure Under Arbitration Law," April 1984 (Association of the Bar of the City of New York), p. 6.

340 Leonard Kopelman: Heins, op. cit., p. 83.

341 William Langston: Cramer, "How Homestake's General Counsel Pinches Pennies," *The American Lawyer,* December 1980, p. 17.

341 Xerox billing policy: Lewin, *The New York Times,* April 2, 1982, p. D1.

341 Robert Bourman: "U.S. May Finally Have Too Many Lawyers," op. cit., p. 46.

Chapter 9. Corporate Welfare: America's Implicit Industrial Policy

344 Iacocca: *The Washington Post,* July 24, 1983, p. F3.

344 Kemp: Clark, "Attacking Corporate Welfare," *National Journal,* January 28, 1984, p. 177.

344 $303.7 billion in 1980: I. Magaziner and R. Reich, *Minding America's Business,* Chapter 19 (1982).

345 Niskanen: Interview with William Niskanen, October 6, 1983.

346 Corporate subsidies generally: See Public Citizen's Congress Watch, *The Kindest Cuts of All: Cutting Business Subsidies in FY 1982,* Fall 1981; Fossedal, "Corporate Welfare Out of Control," *The New Republic,* February 25, 1985, p. 18.

346 $286 billion in loan programs: Congressional Budget Office (CBO), "An Analysis of the President's Credit Budget for Fiscal Year 1984," staff working paper, March 1983, pp. 14–15.

346 22 percent of all lending: Testimony of Randolph G. Penner, Director of the Congressional Budget Office, before the House Subcommittee of Economic Stabilization, Committee on Banking, Finance and Urban Affairs, September 15, 1983, pp. 4–5.

347 Five programs: CBO, *Federal Support for U.S. Business,* January 1984, pp. 29–31.

347 Farm sector and utilities subsidies: Ibid., pp. xii, 31.

347 FAA guarantees: CBO, Analysis, op. cit., p. 81.

347 Nuclear power plant viability: CBO, *Federal Support,* op. cit., p. 31.

347 10 to 20 percent more electric power; *Financing Rural Electrification,* American Enterprise Institute, January 1984, p. 25.

348 Substitute government-subsidized financing: Penner testimony, p. 9.

348 U.S. multinationals: CBO, *Federal Support,* op. cit., p. 33.

348 70 percent to seven corporations: Fossedal, op. cit., p. 18.

349 Lesko: Barrett, "Government Has Billions It Can't Even Give Away," *The Chicago Tribune,* September 30, 1984.

349 Jong to Shell: Sinclair, "Agribusiness Windfall: Conglomerates to Reap Millions from PIK," *The Washington Post,* July 28, 1983, p. 1.

350 80 percent of subsidies: *The New York Times,* December 9, 1984.

350 Hoover Dam electric prices and Goldwater: Will, "Conservative Cowboys Head 'Em Off at the Hoover Dam," *The Washington Post,* August 9, 1984.

350 $250 billion to energy-supply corporations: Battelle Pacific Northwest Laboratory, *An Analysis of Federal Incentives Used to Stimulate Energy Production,* prepared for the U.S. Department of Energy, February 1980.

350 Lovins on nuclear power subsidies: Testimony before hearings on "Long-Term Electricity Demand," Subcommittee on Energy Conservation and Power, House Energy and Commerce Committee, February 7, 1984.

351 SFC: Stanfield, "Why Won't the Synfuels Corporation Work: The Real Problem May be Technology," *National Journal,* June 9, 1984, pp. 1124–1128; Rothberg, *Oil Shale Development: Outlook, Current Activities and Constraints,* Congressional Reference Service, May 16, 1979.

351 Wasteful synfuels: Pasztor, "U.S.-Based Synfuels Program Is Likely to End in 1984," *The Wall Street Journal,* December 19, 1983, p. 10.

351 Clinch River "fiasco": Hilts, "Panel Calls Breeder Reactor a Management Fiasco," *The Washington Post,* July 20, 1981, p. 1.

352 Samuelson: "The High Cost of Bailouts," *National Journal,* May 5, 1983, p. 1126; see also Behr, "When the Taxpayers Saved Lee Iacocca's Bacon, What Did They Get Out of It?" *The Washington Post,* May 13, 1984, p. C1.

352 Cost of Lockheed bailout: "Lockheed Aid Cost U.S. Nothing, Give or Take $1 Billion," *The Wall Street Journal,* May 12, 1983, p. 16.

352 Packard: Harris, "Back from the Brink, Lockheed Shows Signs of Prospering Again," *The Wall Street Journal,* May 12, 1983, p. 1.

354 Portfolio manager at Stanford Business School: Interview with Michael Calabrese, December 10, 1984.

355 Malmgren: Quoted in Guzzardi, "How to Foil Protectionism," *Fortune,* March 21, 1983, p. 76.

355 Hidden tax of $46 billion: Munger, *The Cost of Protectionism: Estimates of the Hidden Tax of Trade Restraint,* Center for the Study of American Business (1983), pp. 4, 22–23.

355 Car buyers overpaid: Data comes from International Trade Commission, cited in *The Washington Post,* February 15, 1985, p. F1.

356 Chinese textiles: "A Rising Tide of Protectionism," *Newsweek,* May 30, 1983 p. 27.

356 Brock's estimate: "How Import Barriers Would Backfire on U.S.: Interview with William E. Brock, U.S. Trade Representative," *U.S. News and World Report,* April 26, 1982, p. 70.

356 20 percent . . . 40 percent: Bacon, "Protectionism Rising in New Castle, Ind., and Across the Nation," *The Wall Street Journal,* December 2, 1982, p. 1.

357 Strauss: "A Rising Tide of Protectionism," *Newsweek,* May 30, 1983, p. 27.

358 Drayton: Drayton, "Breaking the Link," *The New Republic,* April 2, 1984, p. 7.

359 Preferences equal 87 percent of taxes: R. Kuttner, *The Economic Illusion,* p. 188 (1984).

359 Van Ooms: *The Wall Street Journal,* November 20, 1984, p. 1.

359 Auerbach: Quoted in Wayne, "The Corporate Tax: Uneven, Unfair?" *The New York Times,* March 20, 1983, p. 1F.

360 McIntyre: R. McIntyre, "Corporate Income Taxes in the Reagan Years: A Study of Three Years of Legalized Corporate Tax Avoidance," Citizens for Tax Justice, October 1984.

360 Joint Committee on Taxation: "Study of 1982 Effective Tax Rates of Selected Large U.S. Corporations," prepared by the staff of the Joint Committee on Taxation, November 14, 1983.

361 Fed study: *Public Policy and Capital Formation* (April 1981).

361 Albertine: Brown, "High Tech's Quiet Push for Lower Taxes," *The New York Times,* September 23, 1983.

362 Profits redistributed: "Analysis of Safe Harbor Leasing," Joint Committee on Taxation, U.S. Congress, June 14, 1982, p. 35.

362 Kinsley: "Reagan's Industrial Tonic," *Harper's,* June 1982, p. 8.

362 McKinsey & Co. on ABC: *National Journal,* July 16, 1983, p. 1496; also interview with Jack Albertine, June 29, 1983.

362 Albertine: Albertine, "Let's Get Rid of the Corporate Income Tax," *Inc.,* March 1984, pp. 15–16.

362 Reynolds memorandum: Sinclair, "On the Road with Billboards, Or, the Greening of Congress," *The Washington Post,* November 3, 1979.

363 Mauer's solution: "A Crazy Quilt of Demands for Corporate Tax Reform," *Business Week,* March 15, 1984, p. 84.

363 Kurtz: Interview with Jerome Kurtz, *People and Taxes,* March 1983, p. 5.

364 Raby: Interview with Bill Raby, September 13, 1983.

364 Auerbach and Summers: McIntyre, "Credit Where Credit Isn't Due," *The New Republic,* April 22, 1978, p. 17.

364 Riboud: K. Auletta, *The Art of Corporate Success* (1984).

365 Mansfield: E. Mansfield, *Public Policy Toward Industrial Innovation: An International Study of R & D Credits,* National Science Foundation (1983); "Tax Credits Aren't Doing Much for R & D Spending," *Business Week,* September 12, 1983.

365 Raby: Interview with Bill Raby, November 21, 1984.

365 43 percent: Samuelson, "Creating Wealth," *National Journal,* December 3, 1983, p. 2535.

366 Germany's "imputation system": Kuttner, "Tax and Capital Formation in the U.S. and Europe," *Tax Notes,* April 19, 1982, p. 167.

366 Miller: "Did Supply-Side Incentives Work?" *Fortune,* November 26, 1984, p. 54.

367 Perlman: Quoted in Hector, "Business Planning in a Tax Turmoil," *Fortune,* November 26, 1984, p. 40.

367 Arnold: Ibid., p. 45.

368 Noyce: Interview with Robert Noyce, March 2, 1983.

368 Tax shelter filings: Hamilton, "Growth of Tax Shelters Seen Threat to System," *The Washington Post,* February 18, 1984, p. C1.

368 Regan: Quoted in Reilly, "The Coming Tax Increase: Business Will Bear the Brunt," *Fortune,* November 26, 1984, p. 32.

369 Treasury's words: "Taxation Sensation," *The New Republic,* December 24, 1984, p. 6.

370 Samuelson: Samuelson, "Self-Inflicted Wound," *National Journal,* February 5, 1983, p. 238.

370 Evans letter to the editor: *Business Week,* June 27, 1983, p. 9.

370 Waste in defense contracting: For some of the best material on this subject, see generally, S. Melman, *Profits Without Production* (1983), *Permanent War Economy* (1974), and *Pentagon Capitalism* (1970); A. Ernest Fitzgerald, *The High Priests of Waste* (1972); D. Rasor, ed., *More Bucks, Less Bang: How the Pentagon Buys Ineffective Weapons* (1983); testimony of Admiral Hyman Rickover, House Joint Economic Committee, January 28, 1982; G. Adams, *The Iron Triangle: The Politics of Defense Contracting* (1981).

371 Weinig: Interview with Sheldon Weinig, July 14, 1983.

371 Council on Economic Priorities study: Adams, *Iron Triangle.*

372 ". . . cutting my own throat": Fitzgerald, *High Priests,* p. 69.

372 Ramo: S. Ramo, *America's Technology Slip,* p. 80 (1980).

372 Falling cost of GAU-8: Greve, "A Career Cut Short by a Mission Well Done," in Rasor, *More Bucks, Less Bang,* pp. 284–288.

372 $136 billion in overruns: Center for Defense Information, "Taking Stock: The U.S. Military Build-up," *Defense Monitor,* Vol. 13, No. 4, p. 6.

373 Weinberger: National Press Club, March 8, 1982, as quoted in R. DeGrasse, *Military Expansion, Economic Decline,* p. 7 (1983, Council on Economic Priorities).

374 Fitzgerald: Testimony on "Defense Contracts: Renegotiation and Related Matters," hearing before the Subcommittee on General Oversight and Renegotiation of the House Committee on Banking, Finance and Urban Affairs, September 29, 1983, pp. 139–140.

374 Pentagon aide on labor costs: C.D. Parfitt, "Labor Rates in Production of Aerospace Weapons Systems," July 13, 1982, released as appendix of A.E. Fitzgerald, testimony before the Committee on Governmental Affairs, U.S. Senate, March 1, 1984.

374 Air Force study: Biddle, "New Study Finds Inflated Labor Costs on Weapons," *The New York Times,* October 11, 1984, p. A17.

374 50 managers for 100 workers: Melman, *Profits,* pp. 158–159.

374 Proxmire: "Defense Contracts: Renegotiation," op. cit., p. 7.

374 Weinberger to Proxmire: Ibid., p. 22.

374 Profits higher: Ibid., p. 78.

375 34 percent defense contract dollars: Interview with Center for Defense Information, November 19, 1984.

375 Adams: Conversation with authors, April 1971.

375 Utterback and Murray: "The Influence of Defense Procurement and Sponsorship of Research and Development of the Civilian Electronics Industry," Center for Policy Alternatives, Massachusetts Institute of Technology, June 30, 1977, p. 3.

376 Moore: Quoted in Steinberg, "The Military Boost to Industry," *Fortune,* April 30, 1984, p. 46.

376 Thurow: "The Defense Adjustment Act," hearing before the Subcommittee on Employment Opportunities of the House Committee on Education and Labor, October 12, 1982, p. 116.

376 Forty percent . . . two percent: Cooper, "Will the Pentagon's Ad Hoc 'Industrial Policy' Ultimately Hamper U.S. Industrial Creativity?" *National Journal,* February 26, 1983, p. 432.

376 Raytheon, TRW, etc.: J.S. Gansler, *The Defense Industry,* p. 289n (1980). For Texas Instruments, see *The New York Times,* October 31, 1983, p. D1.

377 Grumman: *Grumman Plane News,* March 12, 1971.

378 F-14: On Grumman's F-14 contract and the financial and political difficulties that ensued, see *Business Week,* March 17, 1973; August 4, 1973; August 24, 1973; January 26, 1976; February 7, 1977; November 14, 1983. See also *Fortune,* February 1976; *The New Republic,* August 11, 1973; *Time,* August 26, 1974.

378 Grumman bus story: *New York City's Action in Permanently Retiring Grumman-Flxible's "Model 870" Transit Buses,* House Public Works and Transportation Committee, Report 98-82, 1984.

378 TA team of engineers: Memorandum written by Hyman Feldman, Executive Officer for Surface Transit, New York City Transit Authority, April 16, 1979.

378 Gunn: New York *Daily News,* February 9, 1984, p. 5.

379 Illinois bid: Lancaster, "Competition by States to Lure Firms Turns into Fierce Struggle," *The Wall Street Journal,* December 28, 1983, p. 1.

380 Three fourths of *Fortune* 1,000: Rosenberg, "States at War," *The New Republic,* October 3, 1983, p. 18.

380 *Business Week* or *Forbes* . . .: See, for example, "New York: The State That Listens to Business," a twenty-six-page special advertising section paid for by the New York State Department of Commerce, *Business Week,* May 4, 1984.

380 $35 billion by 1982: Stanfield, "State, Local Governments Divided Over Limits on Revenue Bonds," *National Journal,* January 7, 1984, p. 21.

381 Otis and Yonkers: Kurtz, "Unusual Questions in Yonkers Touches Off Acrimonious Debate," *The Washington Post,* May 15, 1983, p. A5.

381 Hasbro and Chicago: Moberg, "After Playskool," *In These Times,* December 5–11, 1984, p. 2.

381 Washington: Longworth, "City Sues to Keep Playskool Plant Open," *Chicago Tribune,* December 5, 1984, p. 3.

381 Brown: Interview with William Brown, September 14, 1983.

381 Quinn: Interview with Patrick Quinn, September 15, 1983.

382 McIntyre: Interview with Robert McIntyre, September 7, 1983.

382 Regan: Lieberman, "Business and Breaks: Incentive or Giveaway?" New York *Daily News,* December 7, 1980.

382 Martin: Lowe, "Tax Break: Little Incentive for Small Firms," *Philadelphia Daily News,* April 13, 1981, p. 8.

383 Company comptroller: Jacobs, "Battling for Business," *People and Taxes,* September 1978, p. 9.

383 Brown: Interview with William Brown, September 14, 1983. See also M. Kieschnick, *Taxes and Growth: Business Incentives and Economic Development* (Washington, D.C., 1981), who notes that per $100 in corporate profits, the standard deviation in taxes among the states is $5.60, compared to $48 for wages.

384   Reich: Reich, book review of Mancur Olson's *The Rise and Decline of Nations,* in *The New Republic,* December 19, 1983, p. 29.

Epilogue: The $862 Billion Annual Weight—Fault-Lines and Trend-Lines

385   Baldridge: Quoted in J. Simmons and W. Mares, *Working Together,* p. 273 (1983).

386   Market constraints: Economist F.M. Scherer, a past head of the FTC's Bureau of Economics, places the loss attributable to "monopolistic resource misallocation"—including the "welfare losses" due to monopoly and oligopoly, as well as price-fixing—at between .5 percent and 2 percent of the GNP (see Scherer, *Industrial Market Structure and Economic Performance,* 2nd ed., 1980, pp. 464–465). In his book, Scherer offers a "best guess estimate" of the cost of such market restraints at .86 percent of the GNP, or $32 billion a year, based on the 1984 GNP of $3.7 trillion.

    This estimate is very conservative, judging by at least two other studies. Two FTC economists in 1979 estimated the monopoly loss in the U.S. food industry alone at $15 billion (R. Parker and J. Connor, "Consumer Overcharge in the Food Manufacturing Industry," *Journal of the American Agricultural Economic Association,* Vol. 61, 1979, pp. 628–639). Economist Willard Mueller, in a May 13, 1985, interview, put the food overcharge figure at between $18 billion and $26 billion today— an amount close to Scherer's for *all* industries.

    Finally, in a widely cited study, economists Keith Cowling and Dennis Mueller put the market constraints tally at 4 to 13 percent of gross corporate product ($2.04 trillion for 1983), or $81.6 billion to $265.2 billion annually (Cowling and Mueller, "The Social Costs of Monopoly Power," *Economic Journal,* August 1978, pp. 727–748), a minimum figure that scholarly reviewers Dennis Olson and Donald Bumpass find the most persuasive based on their critique of the existing literature (Olson and Bumpass, "An Intertemporal Analysis of the Welfare Cost of Monopoly Power: U.S. Manufacturing of 1967–1981," in the periodical *Review of Industrial Organization,* Vol. 1, #4, 1984, pp. 308–322).

387   Bloat (excessive layers of management): Economist William G. Shepherd, author of *The Economics of Industrial Organization* (2nd ed., 1985), estimates that "simple slack in companies" leads to excess management that totals 2 to 3 percent of the GNP, or $74 billion to $111 billion a year. This order of magnitude is consistent with a range estimated by F.M. Scherer and Jude Rich in separate interviews: Scherer said that managerial bloat was 10 percent of management costs; Rich, now a management consultant at Sibson and Co., put the figure at 30 to 40 percent.

387   Lost management productivity: A Booz•Allen & Hamilton team, headed by senior vice-president Harvey Poppel, concluded that "productivity leakage" from poor utilization of "knowledge workers, the millions of managers and professionals who populate our [executive] offices," equaled 15 percent of their time, which was the equivalent of $100 billion a year to American industry ("Management/Professional Productivity," *Outlook,* published by Booz•Allen & Hamilton, Fall/Winter 1980).

387   Air pollution: These totals come from the addition of two sources: A 60 percent reduction in sulfates and particulates will yield $33.5 billion to $74 billion in annual health benefits (T.D. Crocker, et al., "Methods

Development for Assessing Air Pollution Control Benefits," Office of Research and Development, U.S. Environmental Protection Agency, February 1979). And Lester Love and Eugene Seskin estimate that control of mobile source pollutants—carbon monoxide, oxidants, nitrogen oxide—would produce $5 billion more in annual benefits (Love and Seskin, *Air Pollution and Human Health,* 1977).

387 Water pollution: A. Myrick Freeman III, "The Benefits of Air and Water Pollution Control: A Review and Synthesis of Recent Estimates," Council on Environmental Quality, December 1979.

387 Toxic waste dumps: A study by the congressional Office of Technology Assessment put the total cost of cleaning up all toxic waste dumps at $100 billion (Joel Hirschman, *Superfund Strategy,* May 2, 1985). For purposes of this table, this total has been spread over ten years.

387 Racial discrimination: "The Cost of Racial Discrimination," hearings before the Joint Economic Committee, 96th Cong., 1st Sess., 1979, p. 4 (study by the Congressional Research Service).

387 Gender discrimination: This total is based on several sources. Rand Corporation researchers James Smith and Michael Ward estimated in an October 1984 study that women made 64 percent as much as their male counterparts in 1983. Author Helen Remick calculates that women would make an additional 20 to 24 percent of male salaries if they had equivalent experience, education, training, etc. ("Comparable Worth and Wage Discrimination," *Public Personnel Management,* Vol. 10, No. 4, pp. 371–383), which leaves an unaccounted-for wage gap of 12 to 16 percent. Recent settlements in Minnesota and Washington have awarded women back pay amounting to at least this wage gap, which many scholars and advocates of comparable worth compensation maintain is due only to wage discrimination. If the 30.9 million full-time working women *(Employment and Earnings,* Bureau of Labor Statistics, January 1984) received the additional 12 percent of the 1983 average male salary of $21,881 (1984 Census Report P-60, #146), they would have earned an additional $81.2 billion.

387 Bribery and kickbacks: American Management Association, "Crimes Against Business," December 1, 1977.

387 Employee theft: American Management Association, "Crimes Against Business," December 1, 1977. See also, U.S. Chamber of Commerce, *White Collar Crime: Everybody's Problem, Everyone's Loss,* 1974, p. 4.

387 Occupational hazards: The $23-billion figure is based on a 1978 estimate by the National Safety Council for the lost wages, medical expenses, insurance claims, productivity delays, and lost time of co-workers for workplace injuries; $30 billion to $50 billion for occupational disease come from a NIOSH study done by the University of Washington (cited in Nicholas Ashford, *Crisis in the Workplace,* note 25, 1976, p. 11). Interview with Robert Copeland, Office of Program Analysis, Department of Labor, 1979.

387 Product safety: The total of $19 billion is based on two figures: Of the $36-billion annual cost of all injuries and deaths caused by automobiles (National Academy of Sciences, "Injury in America: A Continuing Health Problem," May 1985), approximately one quarter—or $9 billion—could be avoided by improved car design: passive restraints, brakes, pedestrian protection (interview with Joan Claybrook, past administrator, National Highway Traffic Safety Administration, May 14,

1985). The $10-billion cost of product-related injuries is based on a May 17, 1985, interview with William Zamulla of the Consumer Product Safety Commission, describing the figure used in the forthcoming *1984 Annual Report of the United States Consumer Product Safety Commission.* The figure includes medical and insurance costs (including overhead), litigation costs and awards, foregone earnings, and transportation costs for victims of product-related accidents.

387 Product quality: Philip Crosby, author of *Quality Is Free* and an adviser to many major American companies on quality problems, said in an interview that he'd looked at the quality problems in some 400 to 500 companies, "and I haven't found anywhere the cost of poor quality was less than twenty percent of all costs" (interview, May 21, 1985).

Others have reported similar orders of magnitude: One Booze•Allen & Hamilton study of the costs of quality failure among military contractors puts it at between 5 and 20 percent of all costs (L.S. Duncan and G.L. Bowen, "Boosting Product Quality for Profit Improvement," *Manufacturing Engineering,* April 1984, pp. 106–108); and Edward Bynam, a quality consultant to IBM, concluded that because Big Blue didn't reduce its cost of quality from 25 percent of revenues to 10 percent, "the difference for IBM in 1983 was over $6 billion and that exceeded our net profit" *Electronic Business,* June 1, 1984, pp. 82–84).

Utilizing 10 percent as a likely low figure for the cost of poor quality in the manufacturing sector—and based on the $685 billion in gross domestic manufacturing product for 1983—we conclude that the waste of poor manufacturing quality is at least $68.5 billion annually. (Since poor quality fundamentally means mistakes in manufacturing, and since the guesstimates of quality breakdowns in the service economy are too unreliable, we exclude entirely from the total an estimate for quality in services.)

387 Innovation: Economist William G. Shepherd of the University of Massachusetts estimates that "retardation of innovation" amounts to 3 to 4 percent of GNP, or between $111 billion and $148 billion annually (interviews with William Shepherd, February 8, 1985, and May 21, 1985; W.G. Shepherd, *The Economics of Industrial Organization,* (2nd ed., 1985).

387 Auto repair: "Evaluation of Diagnostic Analysis and Test Equipment for Small Automotive Repair Establishments," U.S. Department of Transportation, July 1978, p. 6. See also, hearings before Sub-Committee on Interstate and Foreign Commerce, House of Representatives, 95th Cong., September 14, 1978, p 5.

387 Tariff barriers: Michael C. Munger, "The Cost of Protectionism: Estimates of the Hidden Tax of Trade Restraint," July 1983 (published by the Center for the Study of American Business). Dr. Animesk Ghoshal, a professor of economics and trade expert at De Paul University, agrees with the $46-billion estimate, pointing out that there are also non-tariff trade barriers, but the costs of tariffs are most susceptible to calculation.

387 Non-participating employees: A study by the New York Stock Exchange (*People and Productivity: A Challenge to Corporate America,* 1982) calculates that productivity would rise 20 percent in one year if the benefits of employee ownership and participation were widespread. Corey Rosen, head of the National Center for Employee Ownership, estimates that companies engaged in successful ownership and participation programs enjoy a 5 to 15 percent gain in productivity. Assuming only a 5 percent average annual employee productivity gain (since the NYSE's 20 percent wouldn't occur year after year), and multiplying by approximately $1.7

trillion in employee compensation, yields a minimum annual benefit of $85 billion from increased employee ownership and participation.

387 Health care: David Glick, vice-president of Towers, Perrin, Forster and Crosby in charge of national group benefits, said in an interview that based on his twenty-two years' experience in corporate health insurance, "it's inconceivable that one-third of what corporations are spending on health care couldn't be eliminated. That's forty billion dollars a year" (interview, May 15, 1985). Glick's figures are supported by the magnitude of savings enjoyed by Chrysler and other corporations after their attack on excessive medical costs.

388 Businessmen on recession: *The Wall Street Journal,* January 13, 1984, p. 1.

388 Freedman: *The Wall Street Journal,* January 25, 1983, p. 1.

389 Derchin: *Fortune,* June 11, 1984, p. 155.

389 Comments about Ford's Louisville plant: Quoted in "Managing America's Business," *The Economist,* December 22, 1984, p. 96.

390 EI savings: Serrin, "Giving Workers a Voice of Their Own," *The New York Times Magazine,* December 2, 1984, p. 136.

390 Rosow and Williams: "New Unions Are Helping to Run the Business," *Business Week,* December 24, 1984, p. 69.

390 Reid: *The Chip,* p. 196 (1984).

390 Piore and Sabel: *The Second Industrial Divide* (1984). For two reviews that contributed to the subsequent discussion, see Kuttner, "The Shape of Things to Come," *New Republic,* January 7, 1985, p. 29; Heilbroner, "Beyond Mass Production," *The New York Times Book Review,* January 6, 1985, p. 7.

Index

Aaker, David A., 321
A & P, 228
Abegglen, James, 158, 160, 213–214
Abernathy, William J., 28, 93, 159
Accelerated Cost Recovery System
    (ACRS), 363
accidents, industrial, 268
ACF Industries, 228
acid rain, 261–262
Acker, C. Edward, 230
Adams, Walter, 173, 375
Adler, Robert S., 306
advertising, 319–325
    of cigarettes, 323–324
    image, 321–324
    informational, 321–322
    persuasion by, 322–324
Aerojet-General, 372
Aetna Life and Casualty Company,
    336–337
Agee, William, 66, 231
aggregate concentration, 211–212
Agricultural Credit Insurance Fund, 346
agriculture, 349–350
Albertine, Jack, 361–362
Albrecht, William Steve, 241

Albright, Archie E., 219, 223, 238, 246
Alco Standard, 228
Aldisert, Ruggero J., 329
Allen, Fred, 277
Allied Chemical, 262, 309
Allied Corporation, 66, 208, 234
Allied Tube and Conduit, 143
Alterman, Eric, 166
alternative dispute resolutions (ADRs),
    337–339
Altman, Stuart, 318
Amerace, 236
American Airlines, 139, 260, 267, 297
American Arbitration Association, 339
American Bar Association, 290, 326
American Business Conference, 26
American Can Company, 338
American Management Association, 237,
    241, 267, 272
American Motors, 219
American Telephone and Telegraph
    Company (AT&T), 42, 280–281,
    317
American Tobacco, 220–221
AMF, 204
AM International, 164

Amstar, 210
Amundson, Jan, 305
Amway, 273–274
Anderson, Richard, 170
annual reports, 59–60
antitrust laws, 186–187
Apple Computer, 32, 181–182, 322
Araskog, Rand, 237
arbitration, 339
Arendt, Hannah, 45
Argyris, Chris, 49–50
Arkin, Stanley S., 275
Arnold, Gary, 367
Arnold, Thurman, 196
asbestos, 268–269
Ashbrook, John, 294
Association of Executive Search
      Consultants, 265
Atari, 35, 227
Atlantic Richfield, 141
Auerbach, Alan J., 359, 364
Auletta, Ken, 364
·Austin, Paul, 44
automobile industry, 92–101, 353–356
Auto Safety Act (1966), 283
Avco, 235
Avis, 38
Avon, 280

Baehler, James R., 239, 248
Bailey, Ralph, 232
bailouts, federal, 351–354
Baker, Howard, 351
Baker, John, 251
Baker, William, 159, 161
Baldridge, Malcolm, 385
Ball, George, 265–266
Bank of America, 138, 198
banks, banking:
   and employee stock ownership plans,
      126, 129–130
   fees for, 205–207
   mergers and, 198, 205–207, 216
   short-term perspective in, 38–39
Banks, Robert, 329, 336–337, 341
Barnett, Donald F., 173–174, 357
Barrow, Thomas D., 193
Baxter, William, 195–196, 201
Bazemore, Tim, 131
Beatrice Companies, 57, 205, 281
Bechtel Group, 266
Becton Dickinson, 179
Begelman, David, 235, 285
Beiber, Owen, 119, 144, 227

Bell Laboratories, 151–153, 158, 159–160
Bendix, 66, 79, 208, 254
Beneficial Corporation, 231
Bennett, Leamon, 132
Bensman, Joseph, 31, 52, 62, 69
Bequai, August, 272
Berkshire Hathaway, 58–60
Bernard, Chester, 50–51, 288
Berner, T. Roland, 192–193
Bernstein, Lawson, 267
Bernstein, Paul, 131–132
Best, Arthur, 303–304
Bethlehem Steel, 40, 220
B. F. Goodrich, 172, 291
Bierwith, John C., 377–378
Birch, David, 202
Black, Eli M., 265
Blackmun, Harry, 322
Blair, John, 186
Blasi, Joseph, 147
Bludhorn, Charles, 204
Blue Cross, 44
Bluestone, Irving, 107, 113–114
Blumenthal, Michael, 221, 254, 277
boards of directors, 69–77
   CEOs and, 69–71
   choice of, 69–70, 73–74, 77
   compensation committees of, 224–225,
      250
   compensation for, 223
   conflicts of interest and, 72
   election of, 209–210
   executive compensation and, 218,
      222–226
   independence of, 69–73
   information and, 71, 223–224
   interlocking, 72–73
   labor represented on, 77, 143–144
   law compliance committee proposed
      for, 290–291
   lawyers on, 332
   and mergers and acquisitions, 209–210
   nepotism and, 74
   ‚outside directors on, 222–223
   size of, 71
Boeing, 235, 300
Boies, David, 328, 343
bonuses, 135, 220–221, 226–229
Booz • Allen and Hamilton, 175, 241, 325
Borden, Neil, 320
Boretsky, Michael, 157–158, 160
Borg-Warner, 289–290
Borkin, Joseph, 64–65
Borman, Frank, 145–146, 240

Boston Consulting Group, 160–161
Boulding, Kenneth, 69
Bourman, Robert, 341
Bowling, James, 94–95
Bradford, Charles, 95
Brad Ragan, Inc., 266
Bradshaw, Thornton, 75–76
Brandeis, Louis D., 72, 106, 332
Braniff International, 247, 260
Breitel, Charles D., 335
Brengel, Fred, 178
Bressler, Richard, 227
Brill, Steven, 327
Briloff, Abraham J., 28
Brindisi, Louis J., Jr., 230, 237, 242
Bristol-Myers, 230
Brock, William, 227
Bronfman, Edgar M., 216
Broomall, L. M., 281
Brophy, Thomas, 66–67
Brown, Bob S., 115–116
Brown, Courtney, 72
Brown, Frederick, 137
Brown, William, 381, 383
Brown and Williamson Tobacco
    Company, 141, 324
Brozen, Yale, 201, 212
Buchwald, Art, 287
Buckley, William F., Jr., 245
Buehler, William F., 42
Buffett, Warren, 57–60
Burck, Charles G., 107, 122
Burditt, John F., 228
bureaucracy:
    chain of command in, 24–25
    defined, 24
    see also corpocracy
Burke, James, 277–278
Burlington Northern, 227
Burr, Donald C., 81–83
Burroughs, 164
business judgment rule, 234
Business Roundtable, 277
business schools, graduate, 47, 184–185
Bylinsky, Gene, 176
Byran, Charles, 145–146

Cabot Corporation, 41–42
Caldwell, Phil, 96–97, 98–100, 103–104,
    226
Califano, Joseph, 317, 319
Callahan, Robert, 146
Camens, Sam, 123
Carborundum, 191–193

Carey, William, 205
Carlson, Chester, 155
Carlson, Kay, 264–265
Carman, James M., 321
Carpenter, Sherman B., 243
Carter administration, 221, 283
Caterpillar Tractor, 300, 303, 317
Central Bank and Trust of Denver,
    122–123
Central Fidelity Bank, 272
C-5A Galaxy transport plane, 352
Chafee, John, 232, 251
Chamber of Commerce, U.S., 272, 315
Champion International, 163
Chandler, Alfred D., 47
Charpie, Robert, 41–42
Chemical Bank, 30, 51–52
chemical waste, 262
Chernow, Ron, 109
chief executive officers (CEOs), 55–69
    annual reports and, 59–60
    as autocrats, 61–65
    and boards of directors, 69–71
    charitable contributions and, 60
    corporate size and, 25–26
    cost of, 67–68
    as egoists, 65–68
    information and, 56, 68–69
    as isolationists, 68–69, 257
    mergers and, 199–200
    nepotism and, 63
    "paper entrepreneurs" as, 60
    performance vs. pay of, 241–246
    power of, 56–57
    responsibility and, 61–62, 244–245
    restraints on, 61
    short-term thinking by, 56
    stress and, 244
Chrysler, 77, 143–144, 196
    bailout of, 351–353
    employee stock ownership plan at, 124
    health care costs of, 317–319
CIGNA, 25–26, 34
Citibank, 30–31, 39, 78–79, 138, 284
Cities Service, 203
Citizen Utility Boards (CUBs), 315
Civil Rights Act (1964), 137
Clanton, David A., 324
Clary, Everett, 333
Clayton Antitrust Act (1914), 72–73
    Celler-Kefauver Amendment to, 194
Clean Water Act (1972), 285
Clements, W. W., 211
Clevepak, 243

Clinard, Marshall, 259, 276
Clinch River Breeder Reactor, 351
Clore, Alan, 233
Cochran, Philip, 253
Coffee, John C., Jr., 32, 62
Columbia Pictures Industries, 61
Columbia University Graduate School of
    Business, 386
Columbus Auto Parts, 134–135
Comanor, William, 212
Commerce Department, U.S., 166, 327
Commodity Credit Corporation, 346–347,
    349
Commodore International, 227, 302
communication, 31–33
compensation, *see* pay, compensation
competition:
    corpocracy and, 25
    government relief for, 186–187
    innovation and, 163–165, 181–182
    product fixing and, 187
    research and, 187
computers, 390
    chips for, 158, 168*n*, 169–171, 375–376
    isolation and, 44
    personal, 180–181
Conference Board, 31–32, 125*n*, 226
Congress, U.S., 65–66, 104, 187, 274, 283,
    346, 350, 351, 360, 373
Congressional Budget Office, 347
Congressional Research Service, 264
Conoco, 208, 232–233
Conrad, Anthony, 75
Conrail, Sunset Bay derailment of, 297
consultants, 37
Consumer Product Safety Commission
    (CPSC), 271, 305–307
consumers, 296–325
    advertising and, 319–325
    business relations with, 299–300,
        303–304
    complaints by, 303–304
    corporate welfare and, 345
    energy costs passed on to, 309–315
    health costs passed on to, 315–319
    illegality as tax on, 259
    legal costs passed on to, 328–329
Continental Bank, 353
Continental Group, 210
Continental Illinois National Bank, 39,
    353
Control Data, 138, 341
Conway, Virgil, 223
cooperatives, worker, 130–132

Coopers and Lybrand, 315–316
corpocracy, 23–101
    communication stifled by, 31–33
    competition and, 25
    conformity in, 42–43
    cost of, 24, 27
    as habit-forming, 39–42
    and insecurity of middle management,
        25
    insensitivity to employees in, 28–29
    isolation spawned by, 43–44
    law of counter control in, 50
    and law of diminishing control, 26
    "line loss" in, 26
    markets forgotten in, 34–36
    paralysis by paperwork in, 33–34
    politics encouraged by, 29–31
    responsibility diffused by, 36–38
    short-term thinking encouraged by,
        38–39
    size and, 25–26
    solutions to, 80–101
    telltale traits of, 27–44
Cost of Living Council, 221
Council of State Planning Agencies, 382
Council on Economic Priorities, 371
Crandall, Robert, 260
Cravath, Paul, 332
crime, *see* illegality, corporate
Crosby, Philip B., 309
Cross, John, 70
Crystal, Graef, 224
Cummins Engine Company, 133, 279
Cunningham, Mary, 238
Cupples, Walter, 103

D'Amico, Joe, 133
Danjin, Richard, 122
Davidson, Kenneth M., 200, 211
Davis, Martin, 204
Davis, Polk and Wardwell, 333–334
Deal, Terrence, 110
Dealy, John, 62–63
Dean Witter Reynolds, 191
decision-making, 36–37
Deere and Company, 176
defense contracting, 167, 370–379
    bidding in, 372
    "buying in" and, 373
    corporate inefficiency from, 375–379
    cost overruns in, 372–375
    cost-plus contracts in, 167, 372
    historical cost-accounting and, 373–374
    labor costs exaggerated in, 374

profits from, 374–375
  for R and D, 166, 375–376
Defense Department, U.S., 298, 352, 371,
    374–375
Deficit Reduction Act (1984), 240, 366
Delaware, 69, 76, 210, 233
De Lorean, John Z., 43, 270–271
Deming, W. Edwards, 302–303
Dennison, Henry, 289
Depression, Great, 220–221
Derchin, Michael, 389
deregulation, 389
Deutsch, George S., 236
Devol, George, 176
Diablo Canyon nuclear reactors, 312
Diamond Lands, 210
Diamond Shamrock, 210
Dickhoner, William H., 311–312
Diebold, John, 329
Dingell, John, 284
Dinsmoor, Ted, 331
dioxin, 263
discrimination, 263–265, 280–281
disease, occupational, 268–269
Distillers Ltd., 256
Dr. Pepper, 211
Donahue, Tom, 117
Donohue, John P., 331
Douglas, William O., 69–70
Dow Chemical, 139, 263, 310–311
Downs, Anthony, 26, 50, 53
Draco, 287–288
Draper Looms, 213
Drayton, William, 358
Drew, Daniel, 255
Drexel Burnham Lambert, 198
Drucker, Peter, 48–49, 54, 137, 191, 252
Du Pont, 172, 208, 280

Eakers, 127–128
Eastern Airlines, 102, 145–146, 240
Eaton, 191–192
Eberhard Faber, 70–71
Economic Development Administration,
    149
Economic Recovery Act (1981), 186
economies of scale, 154–156
Edelhertz, Herbert, 259
education, 182–185
Eickhoff, Kathryn, 186
Eisner, Robert, 364
E. J. Korvette, 135–136
Electronic Data Systems, 240
electronics, consumer, 159

Ellinghaus, William, 281
Emerson Electric, 190
Emhart Corporation, 243
employee participation, 102–105,
    111–135, 143–149, 389–390
  board of directors and, 143–147
  bonuses and, 135
  fundamental principles for, 119
  government and, 148–149
  increased competition and, 116
  and labor-management participation
      teams, 123–124
  labor unions and, 115, 117
  middle management and, 114–115
  opposition to, 113–116
  productivity and, 105, 116–117
  productivity sharing as, 134–135
  profit sharing and, 132–134
  and quality-of-work-life circles, 120–124
  rise of, 111–118
  worker-management partnership as
      paradigm for, 147–149
  workers' attitudes and, 117–118
Employee Research Institute, 316
employees:
  health care costs and, 317
  insensitivity toward, 28–29
  theft by, 272–273
employee stock ownership, 111–113,
    124–132, 210n
  banks and, 126, 129–130
  buyouts as, 126, 128–130
  problems of, 125–126
  profitability of, 125n
  rationales for, 124–125
  taxes and, 127
  worker cooperatives as, 130–132
Endispute, 338
energy:
  corporate consumption of, 309–311
  federal subsidies for, 350–351
  and power plant construction, 311–315
  utility monopolies and, 314
Energy Conservation Coalition, 314
Energy Department, U.S., 273, 311
Engelberger, Joseph, 176
Environmental Protection Agency (EPA),
    261–263, 284
Ephlin, Donald, 96–101, 103–104, 108,
    248
equal pay, 255, 279–280
Equity Funding, 287
ESB Corporation, 194–195
Esmark, 87, 205

Estridge, Philip D., 180
ethics, corporate, 276–282
see also illegality, corporate
Evans, Albert, 370
Evans, Bergen and Cornelia, 152
Evans, Lew, 377–378
Ewing, David, 138
Export-Import Bank, 346, 348
Exxon, 28, 42, 198, 273
office systems and, 164–165
Reliance Electric acquired by, 204
Exxon Enterprises, 159

Faber, Eberhard, 70–71
Fairchild Industries, 62
Fairchild Semiconductor, 168
Fedders, John, 284
Federal Aviation Administration (FAA),
347
Federal Campaign Act (1974), 266
Federal Communications Commission
(FCC), 68
Federal Corrupt Practices Act (1978), 289
Federal Express, 226, 229
Federal Reserve Board, 361
Federal Trade Commission (FTC), 196,
212, 221, 261, 322, 324
F-18 fighters, 297–298
Ferguson, Eugene, 183
F-14 "Tomcat" fighter, 377
Fidelity Management and Research, 78
Financial Accounting Standards Board, 38
Financial Corporation of America, 235
Firestone Tire and Rubber, 258, 271
First Boston, 206–207, 209
First National Bank of Boston, 274
Fitzgerald, Ernest, 372–374
flexible manufacturing systems (FMS),
175–176
Flom, Joseph, 189
FMC Corporation, 32
Fogel, Isaac, 70
Food and Drug Administration (FDA),
270, 287
Food, Drug and Cosmetic Act (1938), 287
Foote, George H., 219, 236
Ford, Gerald, 259
Ford, Henry, 143
Ford, Henry, II, 93
Ford Motor Company, 93–101, 103–104,
125, 219, 287, 317, 362
employee involvement (EI) at, 99–100
executive compensation at, 226–227,
235, 245–246

labor-management relations at, 96–98
layoff policies at, 142
legal costs at, 330–331
product safety and, 271, 305
quality controls at, 303
Foreign Corrupt Practices Act (1977), 266
Fortune, 24, 85, 95, 107, 110, 173, 198,
202, 204, 213, 219, 233, 241, 271,
300
Foster, Lawrence G., 278
Foster, Richard, 171–172
Fouraker, Lawrence, 75
Fox, Peter, 379
France, 290
Fraser, Douglas, 77, 98, 133, 143–144,
246–247
fraud, financial, 273–274
Freedman, Audrey, 32, 388–389
Freeman, Richard, 108*n*
Friendly, Henry J., 201
Frigitemp, 238
Fromm, Erich, 45
Fruehauf Corporation, 285–286

GAF, 218, 222
Galbraith, John Kenneth, 14, 155, 323
Gallup polls, 118, 258, 320
Gansler, Jacques, 373
Garreau, Joel, 298
Garrett, Ray, Jr., 265
Garvin, David, 307–309
GAU-8 shell, 372
Gelb, Richard, 230
GenCorp, 68
Geneen, Harold, 63–65
General Accounting Office (GAO),
116–117, 351, 372
General American Oil, 203
General Dynamics, 195, 245, 267, 373
General Electric (GE), 49, 138, 176, 231,
258, 289, 298–299, 379
General Motors (GM), 78, 93–94, 135,
176, 269–271, 322
customer complaints and, 304
executive compensation at, 220,
226–227, 246–247
Hyatt plant of, 128
layoffs and, 142
quality-of-work-life circles at, 120, 122
Taylorism at, 108
Toyota venture with, 196
General Public Utilities, 354
*General Theory of Employment, Interest,
and Money* (Keynes), 248

Georgia Public Service Commission, 314
Gilinsky, Victor, 311–312
GK Technologies, 245
Glass, David, 230
golden parachutes, 231–234
Goldman, Jack E., 156
Goldman, Sachs, 206
Goldsmith, Jimmy, 216
Goldwater, Barry, 350
Gompers, Samuel, 115
Gordon, Slade, 234
Gore, Albert, Jr., 270
Gorske, Robert, 338
Gotbaum, Joshua, 130
Gotbaum, Victor, 117
government, U.S.:
    competition and, 186–187
    executive compensation and, 221
    innovation and, 165–168
    private interests and, 344–345
    worker-management partnership and,
        148–149
    see also defense contracting; welfare,
        corporate
Grace, Eugene, 220
Grace, J. Peter, 23, 350
Grace, William, 285, 286
Grace Commission, 386
Grant, Charles, 264
Gray, Harry J., 201
Gray, William P., 261
Great Britain, 111
Grebey, C. Raymond, 108–109
Greenberg, Edward, 66
Greenhill, Robert, 195, 206
greenmail, 208–209, 215
Greenwald, Gerald, 77
Greyhound, 247
Griffiths, Edgar, 75–76
Grumman Corporation, 377–378
GTE, 66–67
Gulf and Western, 204–205, 225, 233n
Gulf Oil, 198, 200, 203, 293, 297
Gulf Resources and Chemical, 233
Gunders, Henry, 24, 74
Gunn, David, 378
Gwynne, S. C., 39
Gyllenhammar, Pehr G., 114

Hackman, J. Richard, 38, 80–82, 84,
    179–180
Hagan, Charles, 270
Haines, Robert H., 224
Haire, Mason, 116

Halaby, Najeeb E., 254
Halal, William E., 115–116
Halifax, Lord, 288
Halkyard, Edwin M., 232
Hammer, Armand, 62, 237
handicapped workers, 137–138, 280
Harbour, James E., 96
Harley-Davidson, 356–357
Harman, Sidney, 57–58, 113–114
Harman International Industries, 57–58,
    114
Harrington, Alan, 45
Harris polls, 301, 370
Hart, Gary, 105
Hartford Fire Insurance Company, 64–65
Harvard Business Review, 45–46, 258,
    302, 307–309
Harvard Business School, 310–311
Hasbro Industries, 381
Hawthorne effect, 112–113
Hay Associates, 46–47, 53, 202, 236–237
hazards, occupational, 268–269
health costs, corporate, 315–319
    alternatives for, 317–319
    and health maintenance organizations,
        318
    increases in, 315–319
    insurance companies and, 317
    and preferred provider organizations,
        318
health maintenance organizations
        (HMOs), 318–319
Health Research Institute, 316
Heilbroner, Robert, 294
Heilman, Dick, 130
Hennesy, Edward L., Jr., 66
Herman, Edward S., 70, 325
Hershey, Milton S., 320
Hershey Foods Corporation, 320–321
Hett, Ross M., 235
Hewlett, William, 162, 168
Hewlett-Packard, 142–143, 162, 168, 170,
    300
Heyman, Samuel, 218, 222
H. F. Huster, 379
Highet, Keith, 334
Hill, George W., 220–221
Hitachi, 150, 158
H. J. Heinz, 234, 257
Hogan, William T., 173
Hogary, T. F., 202
Honda, 307
Honeywell, 48, 372
Hood, Edward E., Jr., 299

Hoover, Herbert, 111
Horn, Jennifer, 37
House of Representatives, U.S., 65–66,
    274, 283, 351
Household International, 342
Hudson and Odom Tire Company, 266
Hughes Aircraft, 297
Hughes Missile Systems Group, 298
human relations school of management,
    112–113
Hutton, E. F., 258, 286
Hyatt Clark Industries, 128–129

Iacocca, Lee, 45, 93, 144, 179, 196, 227,
    237–238, 245, 316, 344
IBM, 138, 152, 362
    innovation at, 180–181
    personal computers of, 180–181
    product technology and, 175
Icahn, Carl, 78, 209, 216
illegality, corporate, 254–295
    codes of conduct and, 277–279, 288–289
    as consumer tax, 259
    deterrence of, 287–295
    differential association and, 258
    economic cost of, 259–274
    executives exonerated for, 286
    fines for, 286, 294–295
    frequency of, 258–259
    history of, 255–256
    information on, 290
    institutional pressures for, 257–258
    jail sentences for, 284–285
    law compliance committees and,
        290–291
    law enforcement and, 283–284
    laws and, 274–275, 283
    prosecutors and, 275, 283–284
    punishment of, 282–287, 291–295
    resistance to, 276–282
    restitution for, 291
    settlements in cases of, 285
    shareholders and, 275–276
    stonewallers and, 274–276
    supervisors as responsible for, 293–294
    trust sabotaged by, 259
    victim notification proposed for, 291
Illinois, 379
imports, 388–389
Improshare, 134–135
Inco, 194–195
incorporation, 69
Industrial Cooperative Association, 131

industrial development bonds (IDBs),
    380–382
Infant Formula Act (1982), 270
information:
    accuracy of, 31–33, 51
    boards of directors and, 71, 223–224
    CEOs and, 56, 68–69
    on corporate illegality, 290
innovation, 150–188
    bigness and, 154–155
    commercial applications and, 151
    competition and, 163–165, 181–182
    computer chips and, 168–171
    and economies of scale, 154–156
    education and, 182–185
    European immigrants and, 165–166
    government and, 165–168
    hesitation toward, 155–156
    human initiative and, 161–163
    importance of, 152–154
    Japan and, 151–152, 157–161
    management and, 171–177, 179–182
    mismanaged manufacturing and,
        175–177
    nurturing of, 162
    progresss in, 177–182
    protectionism and, 357
    as quick fix, 163–165
    resistance to, 171–174
    steel industry and, 172–174
    taxes and, 186–187
    technological chauvinism and, 157–161
    in U.S., 150–152, 157
    see also research and development
Intel, 55, 168, 366–367
Internal Revenue Service (IRS), 198, 238,
    266, 366
International Bio-Test Laboratories, 263
International Brotherhood of Teamsters,
    247
International Conference on Improving
    the Quality of Work Life, 113
International Harvester, 227, 356
International Monetary Fund, 353
International Paper, 79
International Telephone and Telegraph
    (ITT), 63–65, 218–219, 237
investment tax credit (ITC), 363–364
Iran, F-14 fighters for, 377–378
Ireland, Charles T. "Chick," 64–65
Israel, Arab boycott of, 281–282
ITT World Communications, 40–41
Iverson, Ken, 178, 239, 248

Jackall, Robert, 36–38, 46–47
James River Corporation, 190
Japan, 27, 87, 88, 111, 154, 376
    automobile exports limited by, 100–101,
        226, 353, 355
    automobile industry in, 95–96, 100–101
    communication style in, 31–32
    computer chips and, 169–171, 375
    education in, 182–183
    government-supported research in,
        166–167
    innovation and, 151–152, 157–161
    labor-management relations in, 98
    lifetime employment in, 141–142
    mergers and acquisitions in, 213–214
    product quality in, 302–303, 307–309
    technology exported by, 160–161
    technology licensing and, 157–161
Jenner, Albert, Jr., 275
Jenner and Block, 338–339
Jensen, Robert K., 245
Jesup and Lamont Securities Company, 92
Jeter, Billy Jon, 267
JETRO (Japan External Trade
        Organization), 31–32
Jhin, Philip, 241
Jobs, Steve, 181
Johns Manville, 268–269
Johnson, Jack W., 145
Johnson, Robert Wood, 277–278
Johnson, William, 326
Johnson and Johnson, 179, 277–279
Johnson Controls, 178
Jones, Peter T., 254, 279–280, 282
Jones, Thomas V., 275
junk financing, 198–199
Justice Department, U.S., 64–65, 89, 187,
        260, 266, 283, 287

Kaiser Steel, 174
Kant, Immanuel, 288
Kaplan, Samuel X., 317
Kaufman, Louis C., 233
Kay, Andrew F., 63
Kaypro Computer Corporation, 63
Kelley, Paul X., 119
Kellogg, 241
Kelly, Edmund, 197, 203
Kemp, Jack, 344
Kemper Arena roof collapse, 297
Kennecott, 191–193
Kennedy, Allan, 110, 156, 180
Kennedy, Edward, 113

Kennedy, John F., 166, 172
Kennedy, Joseph, 221
Kennedy, Marty, 100
Kepone, 262–263
Kestenbaum, Lionel, 333
Keynes, John Maynard, 104, 247
Kilkenny, William, 379
Kimberly-Clark, 142
Kinsley, Michael, 362
Kirkland, Lane, 288
Klein, Burton, 25, 40
Klein, William, 211
Kleindienst, Richard, 195
Knapp, Charles, 235
Knicely, Howard, 134
Kopelman, Leonard, 339–340
Korn, Lester, 76–77
Korn/Ferry International, 77, 223
Kramer, Victor, 332, 334
Krasnoff, Abraham, 33
Kreeger and Sons, 308
Kreps, Juanita, 290
Kristol, Irving, 244–245
Kroll, Jules, 267
Kurt, Howard, 128
Kurtz, Jerome, 363
Kuttner, Bob, 44, 110

labor, labor unions, 96–98, 103–111
    antiunion actions and, 108–111
    boards of directors and, 77, 143–147
    capital subsidization and, 367–368
    corporate bankruptcy and, 108
    employee participation and, 115, 117
    executive compensation and, 246–247
    grievances of, 111
    management relations with, 96–98,
        105–111
    profit-sharing and, 133–134
    and quality-of-work-life circles, 121–122
Labor Department, U.S., 140
labor-management participation teams,
        123–124
laissez-faire theory, 105–106
LaMothe, William E., 241
Land, Edwin, 188
Landen, D. L., 51
Langston, William, 340–342
lasers, 158–159
Lasser, Martin, 330–331
Laster, Richard, 224
Latkowski, Dough, 122
lawyers:
    on boards, 332

lawyers (*cont'd*)
  redundancy of, 329–330
  salaries of, 327
lawyers' fees, 326–343
  and alternative dispute resolutions
    (ADRs), 337–339
  alternatives to, 335–343
  arbitration and, 339
  avoidance of lawsuits and, 342
  billing practices and, 333–334
  court delays and, 342–343
  decision-making responsibility and, 331
  ground rules for, 341
  in-house counsel and, 335–337
  inquiry about, 340–341
  mediation and, 338–339
  minimum fee schedules and, 330
  minitrials and, 337–338
  monitoring of, 328–329
  negotiation of, 339–340
  opponents matched in, 329–330
  and organization of firm, 342
  overstaffing and, 341–342
  prestige and, 330–331, 334–335
  professionalism and, 330
  shopping around and, 339–340
  takeover fights and, 332
  transaction importance as reason for,
    331–332
  yardstick competition and, 340
Lazarus, Charles, 226, 253
Learson, T. Vincent, 175, 192
Lee, Jerry, 238
Lehman Brothers Kuhn Loeb, 30, 74
Leontif, Wassily, 148
Lesko, Matthew, 348–349
leveraged buyouts (LBOs), 210–211, 216
Levi Strauss, 261
Levitan, Sar, 46
Levitt, Theodore, 34
Lewis, David, 68
Lexitron, 164
Liddell, Roger B., 312–313
Life Sciences, 262
Lilienthal, David, 155
Lincoln Steel Products, 331
Lindblom, Charles, 275
Ling, Jimmy, 65–66
Lipp, Robert I., 51–52
Lipton, Martin, 189–190, 200
Litton Industries, 110–111
L. L. Bean, 308
Lloyd, Henry Demarest, 255
loans, federal, 346–348

  as substitute for private borrowing,
    347–348
Lockheed, bailout of, 352–353
Lohr, Steve, 157
Long, Russell, 113
Long Island Lighting Company (LILCO),
  66, 311
Longstreth, Bevis, 211
Lord, John, 284
Lorenz, Paul, 235
Loughhead, Robert, 130
Love, Howard, 129
Lovins, Amory, 315, 350*n*
Lowenstein, Louis, 201–202
LTV, 65–66
Lubbock Power and Light, 314
Luddites, 149, 185
Lundine, Stanley, 149
Lynch, Charles A., 228

McArthur, John H., 185
McCammon, David, 101
McCardell, Archie, 36, 227
McCloy, John J., 289
Maccoby, Michael, 45, 62
McColough, C. Peter, 36
McConnell, Grant, 345
McDonnell, Linda, 68
MacDougall, A. Kent, 320
Mace, Myles L., 70, 146–147
McFadden, Patrick, 53
McGill, Archie, 42
McGowan, William G., 29, 331
McGrath, Paul, 260
McGraw, Harold, Jr., 137
McGregor, Douglas, 113
McIntyre, Robert, 360, 381–382
McKee, James, 337
McKenna, Thomas, 115
McKesson Corporation, 179
McKinley, John, 208
McKinney, Luther, 336
McKinsey and Company, 362
McKnight, William L., 266
McLaren, Richard, 195
McLaughlin, David, 67–68
McManus, James, 162
McPherson, Rene, 121
Madison, James, 345
Magnet, Myron, 110
Magnuson, Jay C., 269
Magnuson, Warren, 352
Maguire, Kenneth, 135
Mahoney, David, 84–87, 241

Main, Jeremy, 24
Maine, 141
Majerus, Ray, 133–134
Malmgren, Harold, 355
management incentive plans (MIPs),
    230–231
Mansfield, Edwin, 153–154, 186, 364–365
Mansfield, Mike, 157
Marathon, 368
Mares, William, 112
Maritime Administration, 347
market concentration, 211–212
Marketing Corporation of America, 162
markets, 34–36
Markham, Jesse, 193
Marron, Donald B., 23, 89–92
Marshall, Alfred, 389
Marshall, Bratter, Greene, Allison and
    Tucker, 331
Martin, Edward J., 382
Martin, M. Edward, 379
Martin Marietta, 79, 208, 229
Massachusetts, 141–142
Materials Research Corporation, 87–88,
    370–371
Matthews, Arthur, 233 ᐈ
Mauer, Bruno, 363
Maverick missiles, 371–372
Mayo, Elton, 112
MCI Communications, 29
Mear, Peter, 336–337
mediation, 338–339
Medoff, James, 108n
Melman, Seymour, 167
mergers and acquisitions, 25–26, 189–217
  absentee control from, 212–213
  acquired company smothered in,
    203–205
  advocates of, 201
  aggregate concentration from, 211–212
  antitrust laws and, 195–196
  bankers' fees and, 205–207
  banks and, 198, 205–207
  boards of directors and, 209–210
  conglomerate, 194
  corporate secrecy and, 215
  defenses against, 207–211
  as distraction for management, 200
  economic incentives for, 197–199
  efficiency and, 201–203
  ego and, 199–200
  golden parachutes and, 231–234
  greenmail and, 208–209, 215
  growth after, 202

historical overview of, 193–195
  hostile takeovers as, 194–195, 206–211,
    213–214, 231–234
  human cost of, 212–214
  joint ventures and, 196
  junk financing and, 198–199
  legislation suggested for, 214–216
  leveraged buyouts and, 210–211, 216
  for monopoly, 193–194
  for oligopoly, 194
  predator ethic and, 191–193
  predator's advantage in, 214–216
  productive, 190–191
  research preceding, 190–191
  short-term profits from, 199
  taxes and, 198, 216
  tender offers and, 190, 194
  trial and error in, 203–205
  volume of, 189–190
  "white knights" and, 207–208
Merrill Lynch, 75, 92
Metropolitan Edison, 269
Metropolitan Transit Authority (New
    York), 333–334
Metzger, Bert, 133
Meyer, André, 74
Michigan Consolidated Gas, 43
Microelectronic and Computer
    Technology Corporation (MCC),
    187
middle management, 44–55
  ascendancy of, 47–48
  cutbacks in, 45–46
  defined, 45–46
  employee participation and, 114–115
  golden parachutes and, 232–234
  insecurity of, 25
  management spans and, 53
  motivation of, 49–50
  objectives set for, 48
  paternalism and, 52
  policies sabotaged by, 50–51
  politics and, 51–52
  security sought by, 48
  staff jobs and, 53–54
  status symbols and, 54–55
  title inflation in, 54
  top management and, 46–47, 49–52
Mikuni, Akio, 157
Mill, John Stuart, 111
Miller, James, III, 196
Miller, J. Irwin, 279
Miller, Michael I., 366
Mills, C. Wright, 45

minitrials, 337–338
Mitchell Hutchins and Company, 90
Mitsubishi Motors, 196
Mobil Oil, 63, 201, 235, 335–336
Monsanto, 178–179
Montgomery Ward, 254, 279–280
Moore, Gordon E., 168, 375–376
Morgan, Dan, 158–159
Morgan, James, 227
Morgan, Stanley, 192, 195, 206
Morita, Akio, 151
Moskowitz, Milton, 279
Motorola Incorporated, 134
MTD Products, 307
Mueller, Dennis C., 202
Mueller, Hans J., 173
Mullins, James P., 297
Mumford, Lewis, 154–155
Munyon, Winthrop, 334
Murdoch, Rupert K., 208

Nader, Laura, 304
Nader, Ralph, 43–44, 328
National Association of Manufacturers, 294
National Cash Register (NCR), 172
National Center for Employee Ownership, 125*n*
National Commission on Excellence in Education, 183
National Exchange Bank, 272
National Highway Safety Act, 300
National Highway Traffic Safety Administration, 271
National Institute for Occupational Safety and Health (NIOSH), 268
National Labor Relations Board (NLRB), 100–111
National Science Foundation (NSF), 151, 182
National Semiconductor, 367
National Steel, 115, 129–130
Natomas, 210
NBC, 75–76
Needham, Harper and Steers, 237
nepotism, 63, 74
Newman, Howard E., 224
New York, N.Y., tax concessions in, 382
New York Stock Exchange (NYSE), 89, 114, 116, 256
Niskanen, William, 71, 345
Nissan Motors, 246
Nixon, Richard, 195, 266
NL Industries, 205

no-layoff policies, 88
Northeast Solid Waste Committee, 339–340
Northrop, 275
Norton Simon, Inc., 38, 84–87, 205, 241
Norway, 290
Noyce, Robert N., 55, 161, 168, 368
nuclear power plants, 311–315
Nuclear Regulatory Commission, 311
Nucor Steel, 177–178, 239, 248

Oak Ridge National Laboratory, 310
Occidental Petroleum, 203, 237
Occupational Safety and Health Administration (OSHA), 268, 284, 286
Oceana, 229
Odom, William, 266
Odyssey Partners, 79
Ogilvy, David, 321–322
oil industry, mergers and acquisitions in, 203–204
Olin, 276
Olson, Mancur, 345
O'Neil, M. Gerald, 68
Ooms, Van, 359
Opel, John, 182
Opinion Research Corporation, 27, 47, 54, 118, 258
Organization for Economic Cooperation and Development (OECD), 154
Osborn, Jack, 170–171
Oster Corporation, 109
Oswald, Rudy, 121–122
Otis Elevator, 380
O'Toole, James, 132, 184
Overseas Private Investment Corporation (OPIC), 347

Pace, Emmett, 229
Pacific Gas and Electric, 312
Pacific Telesis, 224
Packard, David, 168, 352
Packard, Vance, 300
Paine Webber, 23, 89–92
Pake, George E., 165
Pall Corporation, 33
Pan Am, 230, 254
paperwork, 33–34
Park, John R., 287
Patterson, Carl, 109
Patton, Arch, 245
pay, compensation, 218–253
    alternatives suggested for, 248–253

boards of directors and, 218, 222–226
bonus plans as, 135, 220–221, 226–229
compensation committees and, 224–225, 250
competitive, 247–248
consultants for, 225
determination of, 222–226
for directors, 223
disclosure of, 221, 250–252
golden parachutes as, 231–234
government and, 221
growth of, 219–220
incentive value of, 245–246
for labor, 248
limits on, 252–253
long-term incentives as, 229–231
management control of, 223–226
"merit," 249
"merit-less," 218–219
for performance, 240–243
perquisites as, 236–240
severance pay as, 235–236
shareholders and, 250–253
short-term incentives as, 226–229
in stock, 220–221, 229–231
stock-appreciation rights as, 229–230
stock options and, 220–221, 229
strategic management and, 242–243
payoffs, 254, 258, 265–267
Penn Central, 78
Penn Square National Bank, 39
People Express, 81–84
  hierarchy at, 82–83
  "precepts" of, 82
  profit-sharing at, 83
  self-management at, 83
Perella, Joseph, 207
Perlman, Robert, 366–367
Perot, H. Ross, 240
perquisites ("perks"), 236–240
Pertschuk, Michael, 196, 211, 323–324
Pestillo, Peter J., 96–100, 305–306
Petersen, Donald E., 98, 179
Peterson, Peter G., 30, 74
Peugeot, 322
Phillips Petroleum, 203, 209, 232
Phoenix air-to-air missiles, 297
Pickens, T. Boone, 198, 203, 209, 216
Pillsbury, 211
Pilot, Michael, 46
Pine, Art, 300–301
Piore, Michael, 390
Pitney Bowes, 138, 277
Pitofsky, Robert, 208

Pittle, R. David, 305–307
Playboy Enterprises, 239
Playskool, 381
political action committees (PACs), 266
Pollack, Lester, 326
pollution, 261–263
Polybius, 295
Ponamarkenko, Stephanie, 300
Pooler, Rosemary, 312–313
Pope, Daniel, 319, 324–325
Posner, Victor, 63
power plant construction, 311–315
preferred provider organizations (PPOs), 318
Price, James, 268–269
Price-Anderson Act (1957), 350n
price-fixing, 260–261
Price Waterhouse, 272, 327
Priest, Adam, 150
Primeaux, Walter, 314
Pritzker, Jay, 329–330
Procter and Gamble, 33–34, 323
product defects, 296–299
  in Japan vs. U.S., 307–309
  safety and, 305–307
product fixing, 187
productivity, 104–105
  employee participation and, 105, 116–117
  labor relations and, 111
  and R and D, 154
productivity sharing, 134–135
product quality, 296–304
  and AQL (acceptable quality level), 301–303
  defined, 299–300
  Japanese, 302–303, 307–309
  and return on investment, 309
  tolerance of error in, 301–303
  of U.S. products, 298, 300–303, 307–309
Product Safety Act, 300
profit sharing, 132–134
Project on Corporate Responsibility, 78
protectionism, 354–358
  alternatives to, 358
  innovation and, 357
  perils of, 355–357
  reasons for, 357
  retaliation against, 356–357
Protestant ethic, 47
Proxmire, William, 374
Public Agenda Foundation, 118
Public Citizen's Congress Watch, 344

Putnam, Howard, 260

Quaker Oats, 211
Quaker State Oil, 208
quality-of-work-life (QWL) circles, 51,
120–124
Quinn, Patrick, 381

Raby, Bill, 364–365
Ralston Purina, 286
Ramo, Simon, 372
Randall, Clarence B., 225
Rapid-American, 218
Raskob, John J., 220
Rasmussen, Wallace, 281
Rath Packing, 126
Rawls, John, 245
Raytheon, 164, 218–219
RCA, 74–76, 172, 179
Reagan, Ronald, 101, 105, 166, 354
Reagan administration, 214, 222, 273, 301,
357
recessions, 388
Reed, John, 30–31
Reed, Thomas, 273
Reeves Brothers, 211
Regan, Donald, 368–369
Regan, Edward V., 382
Reich, Robert B., 61, 107, 383–384
Reichert, Jack F., 54
Reid, T. R., 390
Reiner, James J., 48
Reisman, David, 325
Reliance Electric, 204
Renault, 246
Renfrew, Charles, 291–292
research and development (R and D),
152–153
applied, 153
basic, 152–153
competition and, 187
financing of, 155
military, 166, 375–376
tax credits for, 364–367
Resnick, Alan J., 322
Reuther, Walter, 132
Rexham Corporation, 228
Reynolds, William V. "Red," 362
Riboud, Jean, 364
Rich, Jude, 27–28, 49
Richards, Mark, 292
Richardson-Merrill, 256
Rickover, Hyman, 288
Riegel Textile Corporation, 230–231

Riklis, Meshulam, 218
Riordan, James Q., 201
Robertson, David, 130
Robinson, Timothy, 327–328
robots, 166, 175–177
in FMS, 175–176
Roche, James, 137
Rockefeller, John D., 255
Rockwell International, 213, 374
Roehl, William, 115
Rogers, William S., 231
Rohatyn, Felix, 184, 205
Roosevelt, Theodore, 29
Rosen, Corey, 127
Rosenbloom, Richard, 159
Rosow, Jerome, 118, 246, 390
Ross, Frederick J., 192–193
Ross, Ian M., 165
Ross, Steven J., 34–35
Rourke, Charles K., 53, 55–56
Rowan, Robert, 285, 286
Rural Electrification Administration, 346
Ryan, Dwight F., 36
Rylander, Gus W., 95
Rytina, Nancy, 264

Sabel, Charles, 390
safety, 305–307
of products, 269–271, 305–371
Saga Corporation, 228
Salter, Malcolm S., 244–245, 249
Samuelson, Robert J., 191, 352, 370
Sant, Roger W., 314
Sanyo Manufacturing, 29
Sarnoff, David, 74
Sarnoff, Robert, 74–76
Savin Corporation, 383
Savodnik, Morton, 135–136
Scanlon Plan, 134
Scherer, F. M., 27
Schnepp, John, 28
Schorsch, Louis, 357
Schudson, Michael, 323
Schumpeter, Joseph, 153, 155
Schwartz, Donald, 77–78, 80
Schwartz, Sidney, 333
scientific management, 106–107
Scully, John, 181
Sears, Roebuck, 191, 242–243
Securities and Exchange Commission
(SEC), 62–63, 89, 221, 238,
250–251, 284
Sée, Henry, 116
Seibert, Donald V., 282

SEI Corporation, 209
semiconductor industry, 168–171
Semiconductor Industry Association
    (SIA), 169–170
Seneca County, Ohio, 382–383
Sethi, S. Prakashi, 292
severance pay, 235–236
Shad, John, 283–284
Shakow, David, 330
Shapiro, Irving, 274
shareholders, 77–80
    annual meetings of, 79–80
    corporate illegality and, 275–276
    executive compensation and, 250–253
    institutional, 78–79
    legal fees and, 328–329
    leveraged buyouts and, 210–211
    management opposed by, 78–80
    and return on equity (ROE), 228, 241
    "Wall Street rule" and, 78
    see also employee stock ownership
Shearson-American Express, 190–191
Sherman Antitrust Act (1890), 285
Shinn, George L., 206–207
Shinto, Hasashi, 184
Shockley, William, 168
Shorris, Earl, 45
Sibson and Company, 27, 241–242
Siegel, Martin A., 215
Sigler, Andrew C., 163
Signode Industries, 211
Silberman, Samuel J., 225, 233n
Silicon Valley, 168–171
Silk, Leonard, 275
Silverman, Fred, 75–76
Simmons, John, 112, 118
Simon, Norton, 85
Simon, William, 259
Simons, Henry, 200
Simplicity Pattern, 210
Skinner, B. F., 119
Skinner, Wickham, 177
Sloan, Alfred P., Jr., 93–94, 220, 269
Small Business Administration (SBA),
    346, 348
Smiley, Robert, 212
Smiley, Ronald, 76
Smith, Adam, 69, 246, 260, 357
Smith, Cullen, 330
Smith, Frederick, 226, 229
Smith, J. Stanford, 53–54
Smith, Marshall F., 227
Smith, R. Lane, 230–231
Smith, Roger, 132, 226, 246

Snapp, William, 338–339
Socal, 198, 203, 206
Sohio, 193
Sohma, Tanemichi, 29
Solar Turbine International, 123
Solow, Marty, 325
Sony, 75, 151
Southwest Public Services, 314
Sporck, Charles, 119
staff jobs, 53–54
Standard Oil, 255
"Star Wars" program, 166
steel industry, 172–174
    protectionism and, 355–356
Steers, Richard M., 242
Steinberg, Saul, 208
Steinfels, Peter, 383
Stello, Victor, 312
Stern, Bruce L., 322
Stern, Robert, 212–213
Stieber, Jack, 138
Stigler, George, 193–194
Stock, Bernard, 213
stock-appreciation rights (SARs), 229–230
stock fraud, 255
stock options, 220–221
Stokely, William, II, 211
Stokely-Van Camp, 211
strategic management, 242–243
strategic planning, 49
Strauss, Robert, 357
strikes, 106, 108, 111
subsidies, federal, 348–351
    special interests and, 350
Suchodolski, Arthur, 43
Summers, Lawrence, 364
Supreme Court, U.S., 195, 273, 330, 340
Susman, Stephen, 334
Susskind, David, 321
Sutherland, Edwin, 258
Suwya, Mark, 280
Swift, Jonathan, 257
Syntex, 270
Synthetic Fuels, 350–351

Tavoulareas, William, 63, 235
Tax Act (1984), 234
taxes, corporate, 359–370
    and Accelerated Cost Recovery System,
        363
    assets and, 365–366
    corporate legal fees and, 328–329
    credits on, 361–365
    on dividends, 216, 365

taxes, corporate (*cont'd*)
  and employee stock ownership plans, 127
  golden parachutes and, 234
  incentives and, 363–365
  innovation and, 186–187
  on investments, 359–360
  investment tax credit (ITC) and, 363–364
  leveraged buyouts and, 210*n,* 216
  mergers and, 198, 216
  "me-too" politics of, 361–363
  "perks" and, 240
  professional advice on, 368
  protectionism as, 355
  R and D and, 364–367
  rates for, 359–361
  reform of, 368–370
  subsidization of, 381–383
  uncertainty about, 366–367
Taylor, Frederick, and Taylorism, 106–108, 110, 389
  Hawthorne effect and, 112–113
Taylor, Lyle, 126
technology management, 171–177, 179–182
Texaco, 208, 273
Texas International Airline, 81
Thatcher, Margaret, 105
Thayer, Paul, 258, 273
theft, employee, 272–273
Theory X, 113, 116
Theory Y, 113, 116
Thornton, Thomas, 285
Thorp, Willard, 205
Thorsrud, Einar, 124
3M, 164, 266
Three-Mile Island nuclear accident, 297
Thurow, Lester, 135, 147–148, 201, 376
tire industry, 41
Toro Company, 67–68
Touche-Ross, 365
Towers, Perrin, Forster & Crosby, 220
Towl, E. Clinton, 377
Townsend, Robert, 249
Toyo Kogyo, 142
Toyota, 121
  GM venture with, 196
Toys "R" Us, 229, 253
Transportation Department, U.S., 95
Trans Union, 76
Trans World, 79
Treasury Department, U.S., 369, 380
Trident I missiles, 298

Trippet, Robert S., 285
Tris, 354
Truman, Harry S., 172
TRW, 134
Tuchman, Barbara W., 299–300
Tullock, Gordon, 51
Twain, Mark, 125
Tylenol poisonings, 277–279
Tyler, Harold, Jr., 338

Uhl, Edward G., 62
unemployment, 104, 139–143
  "no layoff" programs and, 141–143
  notice of, 141
  as waste, 140
Ungson, Gerardo R., 242
Unimation, 177
Union Carbide, 287
unions, *see* labor, labor unions
United Auto Workers (UAW), 97–98, 135, 246
United Electric Coal Companies, 195
United States Steel, 173, 366
United Steelworkers of America, 123, 174
United Technologies, 102–103, 139, 208–210, 380–381
University of Michigan, 118, 125*n,* 140, 246
University of Southern California Center for Future Research, 310
Usery, W. J., Jr., 145

Vanderslice, Thomas, 66–67, 160, 175, 182
Veale, Tinkham, II, 228
Veblen, Thorstein, 257, 320, 345
Vermilye, Peter, 78–79
Vermont Asbestos Group, 125
Very High Speed Integrated Circuits (VHSIC), 375–376
Vincent, Francis T., 61, 250–251
Vogel, David, 275
Volvo, 114

Wagner Act (1935), 103
Wal-Mart, 230
Walske, Carl, 313–314
Walt Disney Productions, 208
Wanamaker, John, 324
Ward Howell International, 231
Warner Communications, 34–35, 208, 227
Wartich, Steven, 253
Washington, Harold, 381
Washington Public Power System, 313
Wasserstein, Bruce, 207

Waxman, Henry, 318
Weber, Max, 24, 57
Webster, William, 292
Weidenbaum, Murray, 274, 386
Weiler, Paul, 111
Weinberger, Caspar, 166, 373–374
Weinig, Sheldon, 84, 87–89, 183, 223,
    370–371
Weirton Steel, 129–130
Weiss, Leonard, 212
Weiss, Melvyn, 333
Weitzman, Martin, 135
Welch, John F., Jr., 49, 61, 179, 299
welfare, corporate, 344–384
  amount of, 344
  bailouts as, 351–354
  capital subsidization as, 367–368
  consumers and, 345
  defense contracting as, 370–379
  federal loans as, 346–348
  from localities, 380–383
  protectionism as, 354–358
  special interests and, 350
  from states, 379–380, 382–383
  subsidies as, 348–351
  waste from, 345–346
  see also taxes, corporate
Welles, Chris, 89
Wellington, Roger, 301
Wells Fargo Bank, 272
Werner, Jesse, 218, 222
Westerman, Jewell, 24–25
Western Airlines, 247
Western Pacific, 224
Western Union, 281
West Germany, 27, 111, 138, 154, 290,
    365–366
  "codetermination" in, 143–144
  education in, 182–183
Westinghouse, 177
Wharton Econometrics Forecasting
    Associates, 101
whistleblower protection laws, 137–138
white-collar employment, 27
Whitney, Michael, 225
Whitney, Richard, 255–256
Whyte, William Foote, 126
Whyte, William H., Jr., 45
Williams, Harold L., 73–74, 190, 200, 284

Williams, Lynn R., 390
Williamson, Steve, 110
Wilson, James Q., 51, 256
Winpisinger, William, 115
Wintermantel, Richard E., 54
Wisconsin Electric Power Company,
    337–338
Wisscha, Ter, 264
women, discrimination against, 264–265
Wood, Robert E., 109
Woodrum, Bob, 84
workers:
  arbitrary firings and, 135–138
  arbitration panels for, 138
  due process for, 135–139
  handicapped, 137–138, 280
  intimidation of, 109–111
  job as most valuable asset for, 139–140
  morale of, 103
  motivation of, 103
  "no layoff" programs and, 141–143
  notice of plant closings for, 141
  and quality-of-life programs, 113
  Taylorism and, 106–108
  as whistleblowers, 137–138
Workers' Owned Sewing Company, 131
Work in America Institute, 140
Worthington, John, 340
Wright, Patrick, 270–271
Wriston, Walter, 30
Wyden, Ron, 187
Wyeth Laboratories, 270, 279

xerography, 155, 161–162
Xerox, 35–36, 152, 156
  legal counsel at, 336–337

Yates, Brock, 94
Yeager, Peter, 259, 276
Yonkers, N.Y., 380–381
Young, Arthur, 328
Young, Lewis H., 34, 68

Zaleznik, Abraham, 57
Zampano, Robert, 276
Zarcllo, James, 129
Zeitlin, Lawrence, 272–273
Zenith, 281–282
Zimmer nuclear plant, 311–312